A Critical Cinema 5

I am deeply grateful to the National Endowment for the Humanities for its support of the Critical Cinema project, most recently in the form of an NEH Fellowship awarded at the end of 2003. Of course, it should be understood that any views, findings, conclusions, or recommendations expressed in this book do not necessarily reflect those of the National Endowment for the Humanities.

A Critical Cinema 5

Interviews with Independent Filmmakers

Scott MacDonald

University of California Press
Berkeley / Los Angeles / London

University of California Press, one of the most distinguished
university presses in the United States, enriches lives around the
world by advancing scholarship in the humanities, social sciences,
and natural sciences. Its activities are supported by the UC Press
Foundation and by philanthropic contributions from individuals
and institutions. For more information, visit www.ucpress.edu.

University of California Press
Berkeley and Los Angeles, California

University of California Press, Ltd.
London, England

© 2006 by The Regents of the University of California

Library of Congress Cataloging-in-Publication Data

MacDonald, Scott, 1942–.
    A critical cinema : interviews with independent filmmakers /
Scott MacDonald.
    Includes bibliographical references and index.
    ISBN 0-520-05800-3 (v. 1 : cloth)
    ISBN 0-520-05801-1 (v. 1 : paper)
    ISBN 0-520-07917-5 (v. 2 : cloth).
    ISBN 0-520-07918-3 (v. 2 : paper)
    ISBN 0-520-08705-4 (v. 3 : cloth).
    ISBN 0-520-20943-5 (v. 3 : paper)
    ISBN 0-520-24269-6 (v. 4 : cloth).
    ISBN 0-520-24271-8 (v. 4 : paper)
    ISBN 0-520-24594-6 (v. 5 : cloth).
    ISBN 0-520-24595-4 (v. 5 : paper)
    1. Experimental films—United States—History and
criticism. 2. Motion picture producers and directors—United
States—Interviews. I. Title.
PN1995.9.E96M34   1988   87-6004
791.43'75'0973—dc21

Manufactured in the United States of America

15 14 13 12 11 10 09 08 07 06
10 9 8 7 6 5 4 3 2 1

This book is printed on Natures Book, which contains 50%
post-consumer waste and meets the minimum requirements
of ANSI/NISO Z39.48-1992 (R 1997) (*Permanence of Paper*).∞

For *Amos Vogel and Frank Stauffacher, Jonas Mekas, Karen Cooper, Howard Guttenplan, Robert Haller, Steve Anker, Alf Bold, Richard Herskowitz, Ruth Bradley, Kathy Geritz, R. Bruce Jenkins, Mark McElhatten, Chris Gehman, Susan Oxtoby, and the many, many other programmers who have made it possible for me to see the work I need to see.*

Contents

Acknowledgments ix

Introduction 1

Kenneth Anger 16

Tony Conrad
On the Sixties 55

Nathaniel Dorsky (and Jerome Hiler) 77

Peggy Ahwesh 111

Alan Berliner 143

Robb Moss 180

Phil Solomon 199

James Benning
On His Westerns 228

J. Leighton Pierce 255

Matthias Müller 281

Sharon Lockhart 311

Jennifer Todd Reeves
On *Chronic* and *The Time We Killed* 333

Shiho Kano 347

Ernie Gehr 358

Filmography 405

Bibliography 423

Index 431

Acknowledgments

In completing *A Critical Cinema 5*, I have had the support of a number of individuals and several organizations. I am particularly grateful to the filmmakers themselves, who were consistently generous with their time and energy, and with what must often have seemed tedious questions and requests for information; to Dominic Angerame at Canyon Cinema and to M. M. Serra at the New York Film-makers' Cooperative, who made prints of films by many filmmakers available to me, often on short notice, and always at a humane cost; to the National Endowment for the Humanities, which—still once more—supported the Critical Cinema project, this time with a Fellowship for Independent Scholars that I held from January through August 2004; and to Bard College, Hamilton College, and Utica College, for making it possible for me to have a teaching life, with a budget for renting films, as well as a research life.

Particular thanks to Kathleen Randall, William C. Parker, and Joel D. Scherer of the Media Center at Utica College; to Marilyn Huntley, Chip Hadity, Timothy J. Hicks, and Stefany Lewis at Hamilton College Audiovisual Services and Marianita J. Amodio in Photographic Services; to Matt Goddell, Technical Director for the Department of Film and Electronic Media at Bard College, for making their services, equipment, and expertise available to me, again and again; and to Robert Haller and John Mhiripiri at Anthology Film Archives for all manner of assistance.

I am grateful to the following journals for permission to include revised, expanded versions of several interviews: *Film Quarterly,* for "Sacred Speed: An Interview with Nathaniel Dorsky," vol. 54, no. 4 (Summer 2001): 2–11;

"The Old West Meets the New West: An Interview with James Benning," vol. 57, no. 3 (Spring 2005): 2–10; *The Independent,* for "Transcendental Domesticity: An Interview with Leighton Pierce," vol. 22, no. 6 (July 1999): 32–35; and *Millennium Film Journal,* for "Interview with Peggy Ahwesh," nos. 39–40 (Winter 2003): 1–30.

Finally, I am deeply grateful to many colleagues for their practical and moral support of my efforts, especially David E. James, R. Bruce Jenkins, Patricia O'Neill, Mary Beth Haralovich, Stephenson Humphries-Brooks, John Pruitt, Steve Anker, Su Friedrich, Chris Gehman, Joanna Raczynska, Frank Bergmann, P. Adams Sitney, Kim Landon, and my partner and beloved, Patricia Reichgott O'Connor.

Introduction

1

In the introductions to earlier volumes of the Critical Cinema project, I have focused on the "critical" function of the films that instigate my interviewing: their creation of an evolving critique of conventional media and the audience that has developed for it, their potentially "critical" educational function in expanding the awareness of teachers and students about the pedagogical opportunities of cinema. And I have discussed the extensive, varied history of critical cinema as a valuable aesthetic tradition in its own right, now endangered by modern technological developments (see especially the introduction to *A Critical Cinema 4* [2004]). In none of the previous general introductions, however, do I focus on what I have come to believe is a crucial element in virtually all the films and videos I discuss with filmmakers: their attempt to mechanically/chemically/electronically incarnate the spiritual. Indeed, in the general theoretical and critical literature about cinema there is remarkably little attention to the spiritual (I use "spiritual" here in the most conventional sense, to refer to that mysterious dimension of experience beyond the material, or incarnated within the material, that is exhausted by neither the senses nor the intellect and is generally perceived as the foundation for moral reflection and action). This paucity of comment seems increasingly strange to me, since I have come to think of the modern history of cinema, and the considerable history of critical cinema in particular, as an echo of, or at least a parallel to, the way in which the spiritual has been historically understood and how it has evolved within human culture.

There are, of course, good and obvious reasons for cineastes to be suspicious of the spiritual: cinema came of age during a remarkably violent century, and in many instances this violence was overtly or implicitly justified, even instigated, by organized religion—a pattern, of course, that has continued into the new millennium. On a more microcosmic level, my own childhood and adolescence (I was born in 1942) were informed by the frequent use of "God" and "Christianity" as a support for racial, gender, and sexual bigotry—again a tendency that remains powerful. But if the reader can forgive a New Age mantra, "spiritual" and "religious" are two different things: religion is the institutionalization of the spiritual, and the effects of any institution can be either positive or negative and are usually a complicated amalgam of both. In fact, it is often the very complexities of institutionalizing the spiritual that periodically instigate new moves away from the encumbrances of the social surround of religion and back toward a purer sense of spirit. Of course, the personal quest for a tenable relationship with the spiritual, whatever one wants to call it, has informed much of what we have considered the greatest literature and art, and it is, I believe, a formative and pervasive dimension of cinema.

I have read many attempts to understand how it happened that the particular form of the motion picture we call cinema arrived in the world at the conclusion of the nineteenth century. My own conjecture (and I recognize that this is hardly a new idea) is that cinema evolved as a way of replacing, or at least redirecting, certain dimensions of spiritual life that, in earlier eras, had been an automatic part of popular religion. In his short story "Absolution" (1924), F. Scott Fitzgerald depicts a young Roman Catholic boy in the rural Midwest who turns away from the Catholic Church because religion has come to seem drab and depressing. The implication of the story is that in earlier eras religion had power because it was the site of what was most gorgeous in human experience; now that the church can no longer provide the boy with this, his quest to find a place where "things go glimmering" is inevitable—and in fact the best evidence of the vitality of the boy's spirit. Of course, for Fitzgerald's generation the cinema was such a place, and to some degree it has remained so for us.

The film experience, at least the traditional theatrical film experience, shares a number of elements with many traditional forms of worship. We arrive at the theater, most often on a weekend—and with special frequency during holiday periods—where we sit in the semidarkness with others, all of us attracted to what will be revealed by a light from high above us. It is understood—at least in most theaters—that we will maintain a respectful silence during the "service," except in those instances where the text of the presentation specifically calls for our response. In a majority of cases, at least in the popular cinema, the particular text we experience is highly ritualized:

we can predict many dimensions of the stories enacted on the screen; nevertheless, we enjoy experiencing the predictable with fellow devotees. Presumably because of the physical demands of looking at reflected light in a darkened space, we often avail ourselves of particular kinds of food traditionally identified with the ceremony of attending a theatrical film. In fact, in recent years we have come to recognize that in an economic sense our participation in theater concessions is all that keeps the theatrical film experience alive: that is, eating popcorn or Dots or Milk Duds is the cinematic sacrament that maintains our access to the light-from-on-high. As regular moviegoers we understand that not every film experience will be entertaining, much less more than entertaining; but those of us who continue to frequent movie theaters, even in a television culture, do so with the expectation that, sooner or later, what we see and hear in the theater will be magical, miraculous, even transformative in something like a moral sense.

These fairly obvious parallels between the theatrical cinema and traditional religious services have a considerable prehistory in the West. The decoration of medieval churches with events from the lives of Christ and the saints; the "illumination" of the medieval Books of Hours with imagery (not simply images we would recognize as sacred, but often with horrific and/or sensual imagery clearly meant as entertainment for those using those prayer books); the elaborate stained-glass windows of Gothic cathedrals, which, before the modern tendency to create a uniform lighting inside and outside, would gradually change as the sun moved across the sky; the great religious paintings of the Renaissance, many of them equally visual and narrative, that decorated cathedrals and churches and the homes of the wealthy; the Hudson River school of American landscape painting and its quest to reveal the divine within our natural surround, often using elaborate, sometimes theatrical presentational strategies—all these are protocinematic or precinematic.

In earlier eras when communities were comparatively homogeneous, where virtually all members of a community shared a particular set of beliefs and a particular form of worship, there was no need, or no possibility, of a sacramental gathering outside the auspices of the local cathedral/ temple/mosque. But in more recent centuries, as diverse societies were increasingly exposed to one another, and became increasingly diversified as a result of the emigration of individuals and groups from society to society, what had been the comparatively common ground of religion was increasingly shattered into particular, separate religious communities (and/or, especially during recent centuries, as a result of the Enlightenment and the rise of science, into various religious communities and nonreligious groups). These developments culminated during the last century and a half. There are few, and fewer and fewer, places anywhere in the world where virtually all members of particular societies or even local communities share organized spiritual experiences of a single type. Yet, if we can agree that a spiritual community is one of the crucial elements of human experience—and the amazing pervasiveness of religious worship across the globe and throughout history certainly suggests that this *is* a fundamental element of human culture—the maintenance of traditional religions and sects in an increasingly diverse world in effect creates a loss of some of the very things that a spiritual community has traditionally provided: in fact, the continuity of each distinct religious community now creates as much separation and distinction as it does connection within the larger society.

Is it any wonder, then, that cinema evolved into a major entertainment form, at least in this country, at exactly the moment when new waves of immigrants were transforming an already diverse nation? As they made their way into American society, the new immigrants were hoping not simply to maintain their heritage but to be integral components of their new society. They could honor their heritage in their local churches, temples, synagogues, mosques; but they could *also* feel a part of the larger community by participating in that other "spiritual" gathering, together with hundreds of their fellow citizens, in the local movie houses or, on special occasions, in the increasingly grand motion picture cathedrals in city centers (they came to be called "movie palaces," but architecturally they always had more in common with cathedrals and grand churches). Here, in a public yet special space removed from direct church control, they could participate in the formation of a distinct American piety and values.

As the Hollywood film industry expanded during the 1920s, 1930s, and 1940s and into the 1950s, it came to regard itself—and most Americans came to regard it—as the only truly significant producer of cinema and, implicitly, the only major source of this particular aspect of spiritual community. The advent of television during the 1950s and 1960s created a crisis in the industry, from which it gradually recovered; but while television did siphon off a substantial percentage of the film industry's day-to-day business, going to the movies eventually regained its status as a special occasion, a crucial element of weekends and holiday periods, and a continuing focus of modern culture. As of the new millennium the Disney World/Universal Studios complex in Florida and smaller installations in California and elsewhere are primary pilgrimage sites in American culture, at least for families, and a considerable television audience forms every year for the annual rite of the Academy Awards: as a public television ritual, only the Superbowl surpasses the awards show, at least in this country.

The power and influence of Hollywood on American culture during the twentieth century were so pervasive that by midcentury it had begun to instigate various forms of rebellion among a good many filmmakers and would-be filmmakers and in some portions of the moviegoing audience, who had become disenchanted with the general decadence, conservatism, and repressiveness of the commercial cinema—and with its spiritual vacuity. The result was a cinematic reformation that took a variety of forms. Beginning in the mid-1940s the film society movement, which had swept across Europe during the 1920s, finally arrived in the United States. Frank Stauffacher at Art in Cinema in San Francisco and Berkeley and Amos Vogel at Cinema 16 in New York City led the way. Programming types of film that had no chance of being seen on commercial screens (or in some cases had been successful but were now ignored), especially those forms of film we call "avant-garde" "experimental," or "critical," Stauffacher and Vogel became models for a nationwide network of film societies dedicated to the idea that moviegoing could offer more than entertaining communal escapes from reality. As the audiences for alternatives to Hollywood grew, so did the energy of filmmakers committed to the potential of cinema to provide deeper, more fully spiritual experiences than were available commercially. By the 1960s it was not at all uncommon for filmmakers to image themselves as apostles of new spiritual orders, and taken as a group—and a very diverse group they were: among critical filmmakers there have always been many sects—they can be understood as an ongoing protest against the catholic power of the entertainment industry. By the mid-1960s a new cinematic protestantism seemed (at least in the minds of some) poised to challenge the overwhelming domination of the industry.

This cinematic revival drew inspiration from several spiritual traditions. In *Reminiscences of a Journey to Lithuania* (1972), Jonas Mekas returns to his native land for the first time in twenty-eight years, only to realize that during the intervening quarter century he has found a new home within the community of artists, and especially film artists. During the final section of *Reminiscences,* Mekas visits Peter Kubelka and Hermann Nitsch, along with Ken and Flo Jacobs and Annette Michelson, and together this extended artistic family tours an ancient monastery. It is clear—from Mekas's comments, from the Gregorian chants on the sound track—that Mekas sees himself and his colleagues as monks of a new aesthetic order, the Order of Cinema. Much the same idea is suggested during the final reel of Mekas's *Lost Lost Lost* (1976), when he and Ken and Flo Jacobs attempt to invade the Robert Flaherty Film Seminar to screen Jack Smith's *Flaming Creatures* (1963) and Ken Jacobs's *Blonde Cobra* (1963). Rejected by the seminar, Mekas and his colleagues sleep in their truck. When they awake in the cold Vermont morning, they wrap themselves in blankets so that they look like monks—and, again, to the accompaniment of Gregorian chant—do some ritual filming. For Mekas especially, but also for any number of those who saw themselves as part of the New American Cinema, monasticism was an appropriate and valuable metaphor and inspiration for avant-garde filmmaking, which Mekas envisioned as a brotherhood (or brotherhood/sisterhood) dedicated not to material advancement or technological progress but to the search for a more devout way to live in the world.

Equally important for the American cinematic reformation were the spiritual influences arriving from the East—especially from India and Japan—during the 1960s. Many West Coast critical filmmakers saw their work as a way of carrying on one or another Eastern spiritual tradition. Jordan Belson's filmmaking career was devoted to the production of cinematic mandalas, a way of exploring and expressing something of the inner world his study of Buddhism and his practice of hatha yoga had opened to him: "I am essentially an artist of the inner image. . . . I'm involved with the kind of imagery that has been dealt with in Tibetan art and in some Christian art of the Middle Ages . . . [forms of imagery] that have always been associated with the quest for spirituality" (Belson, in *A Critical Cinema 3* [Berkeley and Los Angeles: University of California Press, 1998], 86). Bruce Baillie frequently depicted himself as a wandering mendicant, a cinematic monk something like the Japanese haiku master Matsuo Bashō in the travel sketches now known as *The Narrow Road to the Deep North* (1680s); and his spiritual inclinations were reflected not only in his filmmaking but in Canyon Cinema, the informal community organization he created in the early 1960s that evolved into this nation's most dependable distributor of critical cinema (the announcement of the founding of Canyon Cinema distribution identified the founders as "devotees" of the "magic lantern muse"). Robert Nelson, a very different kind of filmmaker from Baillie (and another of the spiritual fathers of Canyon Cinema) for years has identified himself as a Taoist, and a Taoist sensibility informs much of his work.

Instances of critical filmmakers influenced by medieval Christian worship and monasticism and by Buddhism, Zen Buddhism, and Taoism can be found throughout this history, and some filmmakers have written essays explaining the importance of these influences on their work and lives. James Broughton's *Making Light of It* (San Francisco: City Lights Books, 1977), for example, explores connections between Zen and cinema: "Zen is an art of seeing. It does not follow a script. It is not founded on written words but on direct experience. It is outside the established teachings. Hence Zen is truly avant-garde cinema. . . . Zen is poetry in action. It is the reality one creates out of what already exists. Its big movie is made out of innumerable haiku moments frame by frame" (53). More recently, Nathaniel Dorsky's *Devotional Cinema* (San Francisco: Tuumba Press, 2003; a version of this essay is also available in Mary Lea Bandy and Antonio Monda, eds., *The Hidden God: Film and Faith* [New York: Museum of Modern Art, 2003]) takes as its subject the relation of religion and cinema—"not where religion is the subject of a film, but where the film is the spirit or experience of religion." Dorsky explains, "The word 'devotion,' as I am using it, need not refer to the embodiment of a specific religious form. Rather, it is the opening or the interruption that allows us to experience what is hidden, and to accept with our hearts our given situation. When a film does this, when it subverts our absorption in the temporal and reveals the depth of our own reality, it opens us to a fuller sense of ourselves and the world. It is alive as a devotional form" (15, 16).

There have been two breakthrough surveys/histories of films resonant with spiritual aspiration: Gene Youngblood's *Expanded Cinema* (New York: Dutton, 1970) and P. Adams Sitney's *Visionary Film: The American Avant-Garde* (New York: Oxford University Press, 1974; a revised edition was published in 2003). *Expanded Cinema* is fueled by Youngblood's fascination with the ways in which, during the sixties, an evolution of consciousness was being expressed and instigated by filmmakers, video artists, and the creators of other forms of mixed media. His chapters on Jordan Belson, James and John Whitney, and other "spiritual animators" (not Youngblood's term, but often used for these filmmakers) demonstrate the many connections between this work and Eastern religious teachings. While Youngblood's focus is on conceptually synthesizing the many ways in which mediamakers exemplify "man's ongoing historical drive to manifest his consciousness outside of his mind, in front of his eyes" (41) and move humanity toward a new, more open, more spiritual way of being in the world, Sitney's focus is on a set of filmmakers—especially Maya Deren, Sidney Peterson, Kenneth Anger, Bruce Baillie, Stan Brakhage, James Broughton, Gregory Markopoulos, and Harry Smith—engaged in a lifelong process of cinematically generating new mythologies of the imagination for a spiritually destitute era. Sitney is committed to exegesis; *Visionary Film* demonstrates that the films he analyzes are, like biblical texts and other great literature, informed by complex spiritual visions that analysis can assist us in understanding.

While I admire both Youngblood's passionate faith in the transformational possibilities of media and Sitney's textual explorations and discoveries, my primary fascination has been with the simple *act of viewing* as a form of spiritual engagement. In fact, it was not until I discovered films that seemed to demand the kind of reverent attention that I had sensed around me during my early churchgoing experiences that I was drawn to what was then called "avant-garde" and "experimental" film and, in time, to the idea that my "mission" might be to serve this work. My first interviewee was Larry Gottheim, whose *Fog Line* (1971)—an eleven-minute single-shot film of fog gradually clearing over a green pasture in central New York State—was the pivotal moment in my becoming seriously engaged with the history of critical film; the quiet serenity of Gottheim's lovely cinematic haiku has, as fully as any film experience I have ever had, continued to inform my exploration of this field.

One of the most obvious dimensions of all the spiritual practices that have influenced critical filmmakers, and of the cine-spiritual practices of the filmmakers, is an explicit or implicit vow of poverty. Devotees of the spirit, especially those emulated by critical filmmakers, have traditionally accepted a vow of poverty as an essential ingredient of their spiritual questing. For filmmakers working in the shadow of a wealthy and decadent industry, with generally only the most limited financial resources and little desire to pursue material wealth, the idea that less not only can be more but can be transcendentally more, has been, and has remained, a potent motivation. Indeed, what nearly all avant-garde practices have in common is the desire to accept, and transcend, material limitation and personal poverty.

Of course, in the case of cinema, this hunger for transcendence over the material is deeply paradoxical. Not only do filmmaking and film viewing of all kinds require a complex material apparatus, but film history is the painstaking creation of material objects that are, slowly (and sometimes not all that slowly), but relentlessly destroyed by the mechanical process for which they are produced: the light that projects imagery onto the screen automatically causes the imagery to fade; the friction between filmstrip and projector inevitably creates damage. At best, in other words, even when they are successful, the filmmakers' efforts at embodying the spirit cannot *overcome* the material; they can only honor those brief, transcendent moments when spirit is incarnated within the material so that it can be enjoyed by the senses. I am reminded of Whitman's lines:

> Clear and sweet is my soul, and clear and sweet is all that is not my soul.
> Lack one lacks both, and the unseen is proved by the seen,
> Till that becomes unseen and receives proof in its turn.
>
> ("Song of Myself," no. 3)

Critical filmmakers have struggled to honor the potential of cinema to unite the spiritual and the material so that *both* can be deeply appreciated, each through the context of the other.

The desire for a sense of transcendence has taken various forms in the hands of particular filmmakers, some of them consciously working to participate in a more spiritual life, others with no conscious interest in the spiritual at all. Jordan Belson's cinematic mandalas are produced on homemade equipment in his San Francisco apartment on tiny budgets, but they are at least as interesting and look as high-tech as any industry-produced special effect. Jack Smith and his flaming creatures worked with stolen, outdated film stock, aspiring to the angelic from what appear to have been the depths of poverty. When Tony Conrad made his remarkably powerful *The Flicker* (1966)—more than any other critical film of which I am aware, *The Flicker* evokes charismatic Christian worship—the only film equipment he owned was a two-dollar, 8mm splicer, a role of splicing tape, and a take-up reel. Peggy Ahwesh chose Pixilvision, a cheap child's video camera with crude black-and-white resolution, for *Strange Weather* (1993), her film about drug addicts during a Miami hurricane; and in *Martina's Playhouse* (1989), she transformed the tradition of making inexpensive Super-8mm home movies of children's antics into a sophisticated theoretical enterprise. In *Side/Walk/Shuttle,* Ernie Gehr uses the simplest cinematic means, and his remarkable visual imagination, to create a panorama of San Francisco that turns our usual sense of the film frame on its head. Phil Solomon, Matthias Müller, and Jennifer Reeves have worked like cinematic alchemists to transform personal trauma and the material detritus of modern commercial culture into spiritual gold. Leighton Pierce focuses his films and videos on the mundane particulars of his domestic surround, transforming the simplest everyday moments into mysterious, evocative visual adventures. In *The Same River Twice* (2003), Robb Moss uses relatively inexpensive digital video to explore the adult, domestic lives of the men and women whose Edenic rafting voyage down the Colorado through the Grand Canyon he recorded in 16mm twenty years earlier.

Also related is the formal simplicity of the rigorously framed, long single takes used in neostructuralist work such as Sharon Lockhart's *Goshogaoka* (1997), *Teatro Amazonas* (1999), and *NŌ* (2003); James Benning's California Trilogy: *El Valley Centro* (1999), *Los* (2000), *Sogobi* (2001), and *13 Lakes* (2004); and Shiho Kano's films and videos. For Sitney the emergence of what he named "structural film" posed something of a problem: as undeniably arresting as many of the early structural films seemed, they did not lend themselves to interpretation in the same sense that Markopoulos's or Anger's or even Brakhage's films did. For me, however, the *experiences* of many of the landmark "structural films," and especially those that use what would normally be considered minimal means—Tony Conrad's *The Flicker,* Michael Snow's *Wavelength* (1967), Yoko Ono's *Film No. 5 (Smile)* (1968), Taka Iimura's *1 to 60 Seconds* (1973), Anthony McCall's *Line Describing a Cone* (1973), J. J. Murphy's *Print Generation* (1974), James Benning's *11 × 14* (1976)—were the cinematic equivalents of forms of worship characterized by a commitment to rigorous simplicity and plainness (I am thinking of the Shakers, the Quakers, the Amish) and/or of rigorous yoga or Zen practices. However one interprets these film experiences once they are over, they offer the opportunity for extended moments of silent meditation and communion—moments that can provide invigorating reprieves within the day-to-day frenzy and hysterical consumption of modern life, as well as insight into the material and psychic fundamentals of cinema.

Groups committed to these more rigorous kinds of film experiences have sometimes tended to design screening rooms that are as simple and spare as Quaker meetinghouses: spaces with walls painted black and often with chairs as rigid as pews. The epitome of such a screening space was Peter Kubelka's "Invisible Cinema," which for a time was housed in the Public Theater in New York City. The Invisible Cinema was designed so as to allow no visual distraction from the film image: the walls and the seats were black, and baffles were placed between the seats to isolate individual viewers from one another (this has always seemed to me a strange and counterproductive choice, an attempt to deny the communal nature of the cinematic experience). I designed such a space (sans baffles) when I was first teaching film at Utica College of Syracuse University, as did many of those with the means to provide screenings of critical cinema in the early 1970s; I remember being much impressed with the screening room at the State University of New York at Binghamton. While the rigorous simplicity of these spaces seemed in tune with the seriousness of the films we presented in them—or at least with the seriousness with which we devotees approached these films—what was essentially a rather monastic reaction to conventional movie theaters may have been, in the long run, counterproductive in building audiences for critical cinema. These days, the few institutions that do evidence a commitment to critical cinema rely on theaters that provide first-rate screening conditions along with reasonable comfort: the Walter Reade Theater at Lincoln Center in New York and the screening room at the Pacific Film Archive are particularly good examples.

Recently I was a guest at the Aurora Picture Show in Houston, Texas, a small theater in what once was a small church (on its Web site, the Aurora Picture Show calls the membership that supports its regular screenings and visiting artists "the congregation"). If the screening conditions at the Picture Show cannot compare with the screening conditions I have just described, the atmosphere is inviting: refreshments are available, as are pillows for those uncomfortable on the hard wooden pews; and the audience that attends the screenings sees itself as a community. The Aurora Picture Show is part of what has recently become a network of "microcinemas." These intimate screening venues have developed in reaction to the comparative anonymity of conventional theaters and the general vacuousness of their offerings, as well as to the pretentious formality of so many museum screening rooms (including those just mentioned). They have made it possible for a new generation of critical filmmakers to travel from coast to coast, presenting their work. Like the film societies of the late 1940s and 1950s, these microcinemas are run by women and men with a deep commitment to critical cinema but with no interest in chasing profits; they are evidence of still another attempt to respiritualize the moviegoing experience, to provide tiny congregations of cineastes with fitting chapels for their cinematic devotions.

I am grateful for the network of microcinemas, impressed with the considerable devotion of those who maintain this network, and hopeful that this network of screening spaces will continue to develop. But I must also continue to hope for other tiers of access, including increased opportunities to experience the widest range of critical cinema with considerable public audiences in the best possible circumstances. And I must continue to believe that, sooner or later, this remarkable alternative to commercial film history—this endlessly invigorating testament to the continuing spiritual vitality of cinema—will be appreciated as the major cultural achievement it is and recognized as one of the most underutilized academic resources available to those responsible for liberal arts education.

2

I have approached each Critical Cinema volume as a distinct work *and* as part of a series. Each collection has reflected my sense of what seem to be the most remarkable cinematic contributions of a specific cultural moment and my (inevitably limited) understanding of the particular issues dominating the field during a given period. At the same time, as the Critical Cinema books developed into a series, I could hardly fail to recognize that the several volumes are characterized not only by obvious formal continuities but also by the reappearance and evolution of particular motifs, themes, characters, and controversies.

The seventeen interviews in *A Critical Cinema* (1988)—with Hollis Frampton, Larry Gottheim, Robert Huot, Takahiko Iimura, Carolee Schneemann, Tom Chomont, J. J. Murphy, Vivienne Dick, Beth B and Scott B, John Waters, Bruce Conner, Robert Nelson, Babette Mangolte, George Kuchar, Diana Barrie, Manuel DeLanda, and Morgan Fisher—provided a skeletal sense of independent filmmaking in the United States, from the 1960s to the early 1980s, and from coast to coast, as filmmakers confronted the question of how fully to evoke the commercial cinema in order to critique it. Some makers developed new forms of anti-Hollywood melodrama; others substituted explorations/interpretations of their personal lives for the characters and plots of conventional cinema; and still others defied commercial cinema altogether, finding inspiration in other cultural traditions. The filmmakers interviewed for *A Critical Cinema* debated the possibilities and limitations of "structural film," "diary film," "conceptual film," "new narrative," and "punk film."

The eighteen interviews in *A Critical Cinema 2* (1992)—with Robert Breer, Michael Snow, Jonas Mekas, Bruce Baillie, Yoko Ono, Anthony McCall, Andrew Noren, Anne Charlotte Robertson, James Benning, Lizzie Borden, Ross McElwee, Su Friedrich, Anne Severson, Laura Mulvey, Yvonne Rainer, Trinh T. Minh-ha, Godfrey Reggio, and Peter Watkins—extended the discussion of many of the issues explored in *A Critical Cinema;* expanded the historical, geographic, and theoretical range of the project; and, in particular, reflected the developing interest in and sensitivity to issues of gender and transnationality that had developed during the late 1970s and through the 1980s.

The twenty-one interviews in *A Critical Cinema 3* (1998)—with Amos Vogel, William Greaves, Jordan Belson, Arthur Peleshian, Charles Burnett, Kazuo Hara, Gunvor Nelson, Christine Choy, Rose Lowder, Peter Hutton, Valie Export, Patrick Bokanowski, Yervant Gianikian and Angela Ricci Lucchi, Elias Merhige, Aline Mare, Cauleen Smith, John Porter, Raphael Montañez Ortiz, Martin Arnold, Ken and Flo Jacobs, and Sally Potter—along with five reworked Robert Flaherty Film Seminar discussions (with Peter Watkins, Ken Jacobs, Nick Deocampo, Mani Kaul, and Craig Baldwin)—expanded the project's exploration of aesthetics, gender, and transnationality and reflected a more thorough engagement with the use of cinema to explore ethnic identity and spiritual development, and a greater focus on the institutions that have been crucial for critical cinema.

My belief in the ongoing energy and accomplishment of modern critical cinema led me to structure the first three volumes of the Critical Cinema series so that each volume was more extensive and elaborate than the one that preceded it, a way of suggesting that the field was continuing to grow and expand. This particular choice was a reaction on my part to those who had argued that the avant-garde had peaked in the 1960s and that little of comparable interest had been produced after the mid-1970s, except perhaps by those who had developed their reputations in earlier decades (the two best-known polemics to this effect are Jim Hoberman's "Avant to Live: Fear and Trembling at the Whitney Biennial," *Village Voice,* June 23, 1987, 25–28; and Fred Camper's "The End of Avant-Garde Film," *Millennium Film Journal,* nos. 16–18 [Fall/Winter, 1986–87]: 99–124). Originally I had planned to maintain the metaphor of ongoing expansion, but when what was to become *A Critical Cinema 4* had grown so extensive as to be impractical for the University of California Press to publish, it became *A Critical Cinema 4* and *A Critical Cinema 5.* Hopefully, the fact that two volumes of the series have appeared within a year of each other will help to maintain a sense that this remarkably underappreciated field continues to expand.

A Critical Cinema 4 includes only twelve interviews, but the extensiveness of my interview with the late Stan Brakhage makes it a substantial volume. The eleven other interviews, one with scholar P. Adams Sitney focusing on the late 1950s and early 1960s when Gregory Markopoulos was a crucial figure, the others with film- and videomakers Jill Godmilow (and Harun Farocki), Peter Kubelka, Jim McBride, Abigail Child, Chuck Workman, Chantal Akerman, Lawrence Brose, Peter Forgács, Shirin Neshat, and Ellen Spiro are arranged in a rough chronology and, as in earlier volumes of *A Critical Cinema,* with an eye to demonstrating the considerable contrasts, and the surprising continuities, between juxtaposed filmmakers. Among the "themes" of *A Critical Cinema 4* are the cinema's increasingly complex engagement with its own history, particularly the ever-more-diverse possibilities of recycling all kinds of earlier films—commercial features and shorts, educational films, even earlier critical films—into new work; the increasingly elaborate dissolve between film and video; and the interplay within the careers of individual film and video artists between commercial work and critical work.

The fourteen interviews in *A Critical Cinema 5,* with Kenneth Anger, Tony Conrad, Nathaniel Dorsky (and Jerome Hiler), Peggy Ahwesh, Alan Berliner, Robb Moss, Phil Solomon, James Benning, J. Leighton Pierce, Matthias Müller, Sharon Lockhart, Jennifer Todd Reeves, Shiho Kano, and Ernie Gehr, continue the explorations begun in the earlier volumes and deepen this project's focus on contributions to several overlapping histories within the larger evolution of critical cinema, especially first-person filmmaking and what has become known as Queer cinema. Further, both *A Critical Cinema 4* and *A Critical Cinema 5* confirm that something like a community with a shared history has continued to develop around, and sometimes within, critical cinema. The filmmakers interviewed in these recent volumes often discuss other filmmakers interviewed for the Critical Cinema project, as well as filmmakers I have not interviewed. The recent deaths of Stan Brakhage and Jack Smith, for example, were of particular importance for a number of the interviewees in *A Critical Cinema 5.*

It must also be said that, to some degree, the shape of any particular Critical Cinema volume is determined by factors beyond my control—or perhaps beyond my abilities. I had hoped to interview Ernie Gehr for my first collection of interviews, and for the second, third, and fourth, but the timing was not right for Gehr. I had hoped to include Kenneth Anger in *A Critical Cinema 4* but was not able to interview him in time. And I have wanted to interview other filmmakers, including Todd Haynes, whose journey from *Superstar: The Karen Carpenter Story* (1987) to *Far from Heaven* (2002) is fascinating and thrilling; and Charles Lane, whose early films, *A Place in Time* (1976) and *Sidewalk Stories* (1989), are a remarkably gentle, thoughtful, and accomplished African American evocation of the great silent comedies. Unfortunately, I could not find a way to contact Haynes and was unable to convince Lane to do an interview.

I have also begun interviews that I have not completed. I recorded con-

Charles Lane *(middle, on his back on the sidewalk)* as street artist in Greenwich Village, in Lane's *Sidewalk Stories* (1989). Photograph by Lisa Leavitt. Courtesy Charles Lane.

versations with the Toronto-based film- and videomaker Mike Hoolboom (whose *Inside the Pleasure Dome: Fringe Film in Canada,* now in a second, expanded edition [Toronto: Coach House Books, 2001], is a Canadian version of the Critical Cinema project); and with the Hungarian Béla Tarr, whose grim, elegant narratives are often filmed in extended, carefully composed shots reminiscent of James Benning and Peter Hutton—but, for a variety of reasons, did not turn them into interviews. In other words, each Critical Cinema volume is a compromise between the book I imagine and the book I am able to produce, given my passions and limitations, and the demands of time and the University of California Press.

My interviewing methods have not changed appreciably since the 1980s. My goal in each interview is to provide readers with the most thorough and illuminating experience of the interviewee of which I am capable. In nearly all instances, this involves careful study of as many of each filmmaker's films (and videos, paintings, photographs, sound works) as I am able to find my way to; open-ended recording sessions that allow makers to have as complete a say about their work and their careers as they wish; precise transcriptions of the resulting tapes; extensive editing of these transcriptions, with an eye to fashioning a readable and informative metaconversation; and careful fact checking in collaboration with the interviewee. While I sometimes play fast and loose with the particulars of the transcribed conversations—I see the original recordings and transcriptions as raw material—I never publish an interview until the filmmaker has signed off on the final version. I am not interested in exposé but in providing space and time for the considered thoughts of film artists whose work I admire—and, of course, in the long run, in instigating more interest in and support of their work.

More than any previous volume in this series, *A Critical Cinema 5* feels something like a conclusion. I am not yet convinced that a sixth volume would add appreciably to the effectiveness of the series—though, as I have suggested, there are any number of filmmakers and videomakers I would still like to interview, and I am sure to become aware of others whose work could instigate extended conversations. The question for me now, and this is a question facing all those committed to the history of critical cinema, is how I can best continue to serve this increasingly precarious field. Hopefully, the answers will come with time, and in time.

Kenneth Anger

Unlike most filmmakers identified as avant-garde or experimental, Kenneth Anger never seems to have assumed that his filmmaking would be a marginal enterprise. Growing up in Hollywood, Anger was surrounded by the film industry during one of its most halcyon decades and from time to time was part of the excitement: at the age of four, he played the Changeling Prince in the Max Reinhardt–William Dieterle adaptation of *A Midsummer Night's Dream* (1935). He was making his own films by the age of seven, and ten years later, when it had become clear to Anger that the films he wanted to make would be seen only by American film society audiences, he moved to Europe, where his work seemed more fully appreciated: he was introduced to the French film scene by Henri Langlois and worked as Langlois's assistant at the Cinémathèque Française for years. Even in Europe, funding for his projects was difficult to find. Anger worked when he could and supported himself by writing a legendary history of Hollywood scandal, *Hollywood Babylon* (published first in a French edition in 1959 and subsequently in English editions, in 1975 and 1981), which was followed in 1984 by *Hollywood Babylon 2*.

Anger's first seven films appear to be lost, but *Fireworks* (1947), his earliest extant film, is a landmark in at least two senses. Along with Maya Deren and Alexander Hammid's *Meshes of the Afternoon* (1943) and Sidney Peterson's *The Lead Shoes* (1949), it helped to define what has come to be known as the psychodrama: a film that uses symbolic action and detail to dramatize a disturbed state of mind, usually the filmmaker's own. The particular disturbance dramatized in *Fireworks* is Anger's recognition of his powerful

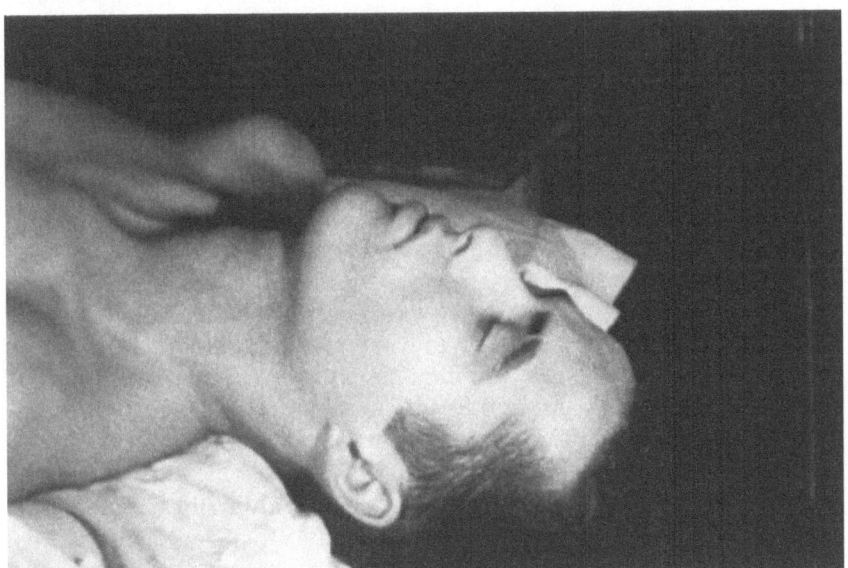

Kenneth Anger in *Fireworks* (1947). Courtesy David E. James.

sexual desire for other men within a thoroughly heterosexist American society. Indeed, one of the film's most memorable images—of Anger lighting a firecracker phallus sticking out of his pants and achieving an orgasm of sparks—is easily read as Anger's declaration of independence from America's repression of homosexuality and of film history's, and especially Hollywood's, complicity in this repression. *Fireworks* is not just a landmark in what has come to be called Queer cinema; it is, so far as I am aware, the first openly gay American movie. In retrospect what seems especially poignant about the film is its good humor: for Anger, being gay—even "coming out" in *Fireworks*—is less a trauma than a psychosexual inevitability that must be faced with the same high spirits, the same whistling-in-the-dark humor, as other aspects of maturation.

During the nearly sixty years since *Fireworks* was finished, Anger's career has been frustrated by frequent financial setbacks—the projects he envisions are remarkably inexpensive by commercial standards but more expensive than most avant-garde films—but the films he has found ways to complete are distinctive and memorable, often gorgeous and thrilling. And they are consistently evocative of Anger's spiritual quest to use cinema as a means of acknowledging, honoring, and participating in those many spiritual traditions that have been suppressed by the evolution of modern society. In the exquisite *Eaux d'artifice* (1953) Anger depicts the gardens of the Villa d'Este, in the Alban Hills east of Rome, particularly the elaborate system of fountains designed by Pirro Ligorio. He not only brings the mythological sculptures spouting water to life but also creates an incarnation of the spirit of the garden: a tiny woman (Carmilla Salvatorelli), who appears from a fountain, inhabits the enchanted space and finally dissolves back into a fountain. In *Rabbit's Moon* (1950), Harlequin uses a magic lantern to create the spirit of Columbine, who as usual frustrates Pierrot, in Anger's homage to the commedia dell'arte.

In *Inauguration of the Pleasure Dome* (1954), still his longest and in some ways most elaborate film, Anger introduces a protagonist, Lord Shiva (Samson De Brier), who reveals within himself a multitude of spiritual entities from various religious traditions—Osiris, Isis, Pan, Astarte, Lilith, the Great Beast, the Scarlet Woman—and even one of the crucial spirits of early film history: Cesare, the Somnabulist, from Robert Wiene's *The Cabinet of Doctor Caligari* (1919). For Anger cinema is, and always has been, a form of ritualized experience that offers the opportunity for entering imaginative worlds and for creating new worlds where entities from diverse geographies and histories can commingle and celebrate their spiritual power.

Like *Inauguration of the Pleasure Dome, Lucifer Rising* (1980) evokes spirits from several mythological traditions—Egyptian, Celtic, biblical—who communicate with each other across time and space, reminding us that underneath the conventional surface of our lives lie forces that inform our experience, even though we may be unaware of them, and that these forces, like the volcano we see in *Lucifer Rising,* can at any moment burst forth and alter whatever world we thought we were living in. Aleister Crowley and his teachings seem to have been crucial for Anger during much of his career. Crowley is invoked literally by means of a superimposed photograph in *Inauguration of the Pleasure Dome* and implicitly in *Inauguration* and *Lucifer Rising,* both of which were at least partially inspired by Crowley's famous rituals in which people assumed the identities of gods and goddesses.

Anger's best-known and most widely influential film, *Scorpio Rising* (1963), is a depiction/interpretation of a motorcycle gang, foregrounding the spiritual dimensions of young men's fascination with their bikes and the biker life, as these are revealed in their preparations for a raucous Halloween party and for the final motorcycle race of the year. Anger's inventive use of pop music in conjunction with, and as an ironic comment on, the activities revealed in his visuals have caused *Scorpio Rising* to be understood as one of the progenitors of the music video (along with Bruce Conner's *Cosmic Ray* [1962], which was completed the year before *Scorpio Rising*). While Anger has never finished a film with dialogue, he has always taken his sound tracks very seriously, working inventively and precisely with a wide range of music:

Vivaldi's *The Four Seasons* in *Eaux d'artifice,* Janácek's *Glagolithic Mass* in *Inauguration of the Pleasure Dome,* American pop songs in *Scorpio Rising* and *Kustom Kar Kommandos* (1965), Mick Jagger's Moog synthesizer track in *Invocation of My Demon Brother* (1969), and, in the case of *Lucifer Rising,* a sound track composed in prison by Anger's friend (and for a brief, unfortunate moment, Charles Manson groupie), Bobby Beausoleil.

Although his work since 1980 has received little attention, Anger remains active, presenting earlier films and working on new projects, including the recent *The Man We Want to Hang* (2002), a documentation of a show of Aleister Crowley's artwork in London in 1995; and *Mouse Heaven* (2004), a brilliant, high-spirited rumination on the early Mickey Mouse, using a collection of pre-*Fantasia* (1940) Mickey Mouse toys and memorabilia. *Mouse Heaven* must be numbered among Anger's finest films.

I spoke with Anger in his apartment in Echo Park, Los Angeles, in March 2004 and subsequently by phone.

MacDonald: What do you remember about the LA independent film scene in the forties, and how did you get involved?

Anger: I got involved after I had made some films that I wanted to show in public. I think the first film I showed publicly was *Escape Episode* in 1946, the year before I made *Fireworks,* and then I showed *Fireworks* at the Coronet Film Society at the Coronet Theater—it was a new theater at the time—on La Cienega here in LA. Later I took *Escape Episode* to San Francisco, where there was already a small group of filmmakers—Frank Stauffacher, James Broughton, Jordan Belson—beginning to show independent work at the Art in Cinema Film Society at the San Francisco Museum of Art.

MacDonald: I understand that at some point you and Curtis Harrington had a small distribution effort.

Anger: Yes, it was called Creative Film Associates. It was basically just Curtis and me, though we involved a few other people, like the Whitney brothers and Jordan Belson, who donated prints. We made these prints available for rental and sent out brochures. Creative Film Associates lasted about a year and a half. The prints were rented by colleges and film societies.

MacDonald: Was there a demand? Did it work as a small business?

Anger: On a very small scale, yes. I gave it up when I moved to Europe in 1950, and Curtis didn't express any interest in continuing it on his own.

MacDonald: I've heard that there was even a phantom secretary.

Anger: Yes. Curtis and I thought her up. Her name was Violet Parks. We didn't do any telephone orders, so she didn't need to speak. We bought some violet ink and Curtis signed for her. She was our phantom lady.

MacDonald: You were making films very young, and by the time of *Es-*

cape Episode you had a body of work. It's surprising to me that you got so much work done so young.

Anger: Well, they were all short films. The longest, *Escape Episode,* was a half hour, but most of them were five or ten minutes. *Fireworks* was fifteen.

MacDonald: You told Robert Haller that it was no great loss that most of those early films no longer exist.

Anger: I don't remember saying that!

MacDonald: How did those films get lost?

Anger: I lived like a gypsy. I've been moving constantly most of my life, and when you're moving constantly, it's very hard to hold on to a lot of things. Sometimes you store things with friends and come back a year later, and they don't know what happened to the stuff. This place [Anger's apartment in the Echo Park area of LA] is basically just where I store my paper archives.

Some things seem to have disappeared even rather recently. I left a box of my material with Anthology Film Archives in New York, including some of my early films, and when I went back, the box had disappeared. They think it may turn up, but the box wasn't kept under lock and key, and I think someone may have appropriated it.

MacDonald: Are your films being preserved?

Anger: At the moment UCLA is graciously allowing me to keep my masters in their cold vault, in the former Technicolor Building.

MacDonald: Fireworks is the earliest of your films still available. I teach it almost every year, and my students are always astonished, as am I, not just at the continuing power of the film, but that, in 1947, as a seventeen-year-old, you had the courage to make it.

Anger: Well, everything just fell into place. I didn't think it was particularly courageous; it was just something I wanted to do, and so I did it.

Of course, later, when I tried to get *Fireworks* printed, it almost got confiscated at Consolidated Film Lab here in Hollywood. At that time there were very few big labs that did negative-positive printing in 16mm. In fact, there are fewer and fewer now; it's almost like 16mm is on the way out. But at that time I went to Consolidated, and it turned out that the head of the lab was a navy veteran, and he looked at the negative and found it had some people in naval uniforms in it. He was considering calling the FBI, as if *Fireworks* were some subversive thing. One of the lab technicians there told me later that he had saved it by telling the head of the lab, "Oh, it's just some little film; it's of no importance—don't bother with it!"

MacDonald: I think what strikes those of us who see it as courageous is that it's the first film, at least the first I'm aware of, where a man openly, clearly expresses a desire for other men. I grew up in that postwar period—I'm a little younger than you are, but I remember the era—and there was so much repression . . .

Anger: As I said, it's just something I wanted to do, and I did it. I suppose in retrospect you can put a badge of courage on it, but I don't necessarily choose to think of it that way—though I suppose it *was* reckless.

MacDonald: It has a great sense of humor, a whistling-in-the-dark kind of humor, which still works wonderfully.

Anger: Yes. Thank you. If you don't catch the humor of the film, you really miss the point.

MacDonald: A general question: You're regularly cited, along with Jack Smith and Jean Genet, as one of the fathers of what's now called Queer Cinema. I wonder how you feel about being thought of that way.

Anger: I consider myself an individual artist, and I don't like being put in a cubbyhole. There's nothing I've ever hidden; I've always been very upfront about myself. I can respect what other filmmakers are doing, but I don't think we need to be put into a category.

I knew Jack Smith and in fact spent a day in Oakland with him, looking for a prop for one of his movies—I think it was called *Normal Love* [1963]. He wanted a little morning-glory gramophone, the kind with the big tin horn, and we finally found a bent-up one in a junk shop, but it was more than he could afford. Jack always liked to get everything for nothing. So finally, just so it wouldn't be a wasted day, I bought him a rusty Buck Rogers ray gun for a dollar. Later I saw the unfinished footage of *Normal Love,* and the ray gun was in it. Jack left a lot of unedited material; he didn't seem to like to finish things.

But I've never identified either with him—I mean in a group way—or with John Waters or anyone else.

MacDonald: Sitney describes an auditory prologue that was on early versions of *Fireworks.* At what point did you remove the introduction?

Anger: I still have a print with it on. It was my voice over a black screen, rather than an introductory main title. It was very short: it says something like, "In *Fireworks* are released all the explosive pyrotechnics of a dream. The inflammable desires ignited at night . . ." and so forth—rather purple language. The last sentence is, "These imaginary displays provide a temporary release." I took the introduction off when my films were being released by Canyon; it seemed more practical to have a copyright title at the beginning.

MacDonald: You made *Fireworks* on a single weekend?

Anger: In seventy-two hours. I had a "window of opportunity," as they say nowadays, to turn my house into a movie studio because my parents were absent, which was rare. They had gone back to Pittsburgh to attend the funeral of an uncle.

MacDonald: What did your parents do? I know very little about your background.

Anger: I was the third child, and there was a lapse of about eight years between me and my older brother and sister. I was the tail end of the family. The member of the family I was closest to was my maternal grandmother, who had worked in costumes in the silent era. She told me a lot of stories about Valentino and Clara Bow and sparked my interest in the silent period.

She bought me my first 16mm camera, as a birthday present. It was a used Bell & Howell. It had seen some war service; those handheld Bell & Howells were used by cameramen during the war.

MacDonald: Was your family supportive of your filmmaking?

Anger: They didn't know too much about it. My grandmother did see *Fireworks*—it was made with the camera she gave me—and she had one word to say: "Terrific!" Considering that she was a lady approaching her eighties, I think that was quite remarkable. But my family wasn't particularly supportive of what I was doing. I had to make my own way.

My father was an engineer at Douglas Aircraft. My older brother went into aviation, and I was expected to. I could have gone to Cal Tech, if I had been so inclined; they would have paid for it, but I declined. I wanted to be an artist, and only my grandmother supported me in this. She had made her money in real estate, back in the twenties, and had retired by the time she was part of my life. She was a landscape painter and the president of Women Painters of the West, a plein air school of landscape painting. I used to go with her to various places that she liked to paint, like when the wildflowers were in bloom in the spring. There used to be magnificent stretches of California that were covered with wildflowers for a brief period, and I would go with her and carry her easel; it was very pleasant.

MacDonald: What do you remember about the early screenings of *Fireworks*?

Anger: That first screening at the Coronet Film Society was at midnight, after the regular screenings. To my surprise, there was an audience, including some rather remarkable celebrities who just happened to show up: James Whale, for example, the director of *Frankenstein* [1931] and other wonderful films. Later, we became friends. And Robert Florey, another very interesting maverick Hollywood director, was there. And Dr. Alfred Kinsey came. He was on the West Coast doing interviews. Dr. Kinsey came up and spoke to me afterward and said he'd like to interview me; he offered to buy a print of *Fireworks* for the Institute for Sex Research at Indiana University in Bloomington. Now it's called the Kinsey Institute.

MacDonald: How did these guys know to be at this screening?

Anger: Kinsey apparently heard on the grapevine, which he was very good at listening into, that this screening was going to happen and that *Fireworks* was an unusual film that he should see. There had been some publicity for the event. I was very pleased to meet Dr. Kinsey, and later I went downtown to the Biltmore Hotel, where he was staying, to do the famous Kinsey interview. My statistics are part of *Sexual Behavior in the Human Male,* which came out in 1948.

MacDonald: Did *Fireworks* have censorship trouble?

Anger: No, because it was shown in so few places, and in a very discreet way. And when it was made available for rental, I had no particular problem: I assumed that the fact that it came back in one piece meant that the showing had gone well, wherever it was shown.

MacDonald: Sitney talks about *Fireworks* as one of the early psychodramas. At what point were you seeing films by other people who were also moving into the mind as an environment to explore?

Anger: Well, Curtis Harrington made a short called *Fragment of Seeking* [1946] at about the same time; it's a kind of psychodrama. Curtis was coming to terms with the homosexual issue in his own way, which was more oblique than mine. And at the same time, Gregory Markopoulos was beginning to make films.

Back in the forties, when there were very few of us working, I was certainly encouraged by the example of Maya Deren: she made her films with very limited means on 16mm, and they were very consciously works of art. I thought it was very daring of her to have her films silent; she wanted them silent. *Meshes of the Afternoon* was conceived as a silent film. Of course, she had a very good collaborator, her husband, Alexander Hammid, who was an excellent photographer, so her films always had a professional polish to them. We never met; we did exchange a couple of letters.

In 1949 I heard there was going to be a festival in Biarritz, called Le Festival du Films Maudit (the Festival of Damned Films)—films that had had trouble with censorship or used subject matter that some people might want to condemn. So I wrapped up a print of *Fireworks* and mailed it airmail to the address I had in Biarritz, not knowing if they'd show it or even if I'd ever get the print back. *Fireworks* was awarded the prize for poetic film. The head of the jury was Cocteau, and he sent me a letter, a handwritten letter, with his signature and a hand-drawn pentagram—his way of saying how much he liked it. I decided at that point that I should go to Europe, where I seemed to be appreciated more than I was in the States, and meet Cocteau. And in 1950 I moved to Paris. Fortunately, I was offered a job by Henri Langlois, the head of the Cinémathèque Française.

MacDonald: How did the job come about?

Anger: Henri had a reception for me in Paris and showed *Fireworks.* He had invited Jean Genet and Cocteau. And he decided to hire me to be his assistant at the Cinémathèque Française. "Hire me" should be in quotes, because I wasn't paid but was housed and fed (of course, Langlois loved eating in the best restaurants, so I ate very well—the beginning of a lifetime of affection for French cuisine). I moved in with Mary Meerson (Lazare

Meerson, her late husband, had been René Clair's set designer in his early films) and Henri; they had a guest room in an apartment overlooking the Parc Monsouris. The apartment had been designed by Lazare Meerson; it was a wonderful Moderne design. I guess you'd call it art deco today. I had a wonderful relationship with Mary Meerson and Henri Langlois that lasted for about twelve years while I was working there. Then I started to travel again.

MacDonald: You mentioned that Genet was at the Parisian screening of *Fireworks.* What was his response?

Anger: Well, I believe I understood him to say that he found it *"fascinante."*

I arrived in France speaking French, and I couldn't have gotten along as well otherwise. I went to Beverly Hills High School and took French. I was motivated and got As. I'm sure I had an American accent, but I knew my basic grammar, and I could speak French and I certainly could hear it. At the time, we had a theater here in LA, called the Esquire, which specialized in foreign films with subtitles. There was always an audience for European film in Hollywood, especially French films. I would go to these French films, which included Cocteau—as I remember, they had *Blood of a Poet* [1930] and films made in France during the occupation and afterward, like *The Eternal Return* [1943, directed by Jean Delannoy] and *Un Carnet de bal* [1937], a beautiful film by Julien Duvuvier, which was very popular.

I would go more than once to these films, or I would stay and see them again and again (in those days you would pay your admission, and you could stay and see a movie twice or three times if you wanted to). The first time, I would watch a film the usual way; the second time, I would just listen to it: so I had some very famous French actors, like Arletty and Jean-Louis Barrault, teaching me French pronunciation. By the time I arrived in France in 1950, I'd already seen things like *Children of Paradise* [1946, directed by Marcel Carné] and all those films, felt familiar with them, and could talk about them.

MacDonald: What kinds of projects did you do at the Cinémathèque?

Anger: Langlois was having a festival in the town of Antibes on the Riviera, and he invited me to take the various films that had been made from Eisenstein's aborted Mexican project, *Que Viva Mexico!,* and recut them more in the order specified in Eisenstein's script. So I reassembled the material in *Thunder over Mexico, Death Day in Mexico,* plus a couple of travelogues that had been made from *Que Viva Mexico!* after Eisenstein was removed from the project by the producer, Upton Sinclair. It was fascinating to work with Eisenstein's material and to see how certain ideas that were in the script were not reflected in any of the films. For example, he had a sequence that began on Death Day starting before dawn; dawn slowly comes, and the scenes get brighter and brighter, and then when it's full light you have this fiesta on the graves, which is a Mexican tradition; they eat candy skulls and things like that. That was a fascinating project.

MacDonald: What filmmaking were you doing?

Anger: It was through the Cinémathèque that I was able to make *Rabbit's Moon*—in French, *La lune des lapins.*

MacDonald: I've never understood the title.

Anger: It refers to a Japanese legend. The Japanese see in the full moon the silhouette of a rabbit. See, the odd thing about the moon is that when you're in the latitude of the Orient, you're seeing the moon at a different angle. We see a kind of face, two vague eyes and a smile—the "Man in the Moon." But the Japanese don't see that; they see the body of a rabbit with two ears sticking up. If you use your imagination, you can see the rabbit by tipping your head to the side. The Japanese have developed a whole mythology about this benign lunar spirit, and every full moon they leave out rice cakes and sake for the Rabbit in the Moon. The next morning the children note that the sake cup is empty and the rice cakes have disappeared, and they think that the spirit came down and helped itself, and is happy with them.

I combined that Japanese mythology of the Rabbit in the Moon with the European commedia dell'arte tradition of mime theater, which involved basically three characters. There's Pierrot, the white clown—a lunar spirit who dates back to the Middle Ages—who is unhappy, but it's OK to make fun of him. He's quite a poetic figure, and he has two passions: he has a longing for the moon—the phrase "reaching for the moon" refers to something you want but can never have—and he's infatuated with Columbine, who's a tease. His rival is Harlequin, who is a devil figure—the devil in his form of the prankster. Just with variations on this simple combination of three characters the Commedia dell'Arte made any number of little plays that were popular across Europe. It started in Italy, then went to France, and was very popular in the seventeenth and eighteenth centuries. The best representation of Pierrot in commercial film is in *The Children of Paradise,* where he's played by Jean-Louis Barrault.

MacDonald: I see *Rabbit's Moon* as a film about you as a filmmaker. You're a combination of both Pierrot and Harlequin: you're always reaching for the moon, longing for the light; and at the same time you're playing tricks on the audience who are also longing for something they hope you can give them.

Anger: The magic lantern I used in the film was a real one, from the eighteenth century. It was part of the Cinémathèque's collection of magic lanterns. They loaned it to me. In the film I show that Columbine is a projection of the magic lantern, which is controlled by Harlequin, who is a Lucifer figure.

I had to work very fast on *Rabbit's Moon;* I had to make the costumes, build the set, and do the filming within four weeks. Pierre Braunberger had lent me his little studio, the Cinema Panthéon, just a single soundstage near the Panthéon on the Left Bank. The idea was that I'd be out of there, and the place would be restored to the way it was, when he came back from vacation. Everyone in France goes on vacation in August.

MacDonald: *Rabbit's Moon* was shot in 35mm. Where did the money come from?

Anger: It wasn't a matter of the money. The 35mm raw stock came from Russian friends of the Cinémathèque who had come to Paris to do a film on UNESCO—the children's division of the United Nations. They had a couple of thousand feet of 35mm, something like six cans of unexposed raw stock, left over. It was the same emulsion, they told me, that Eisenstein used to make *Ivan the Terrible* [part 1, 1943; part 2, 1946]: a very fine-grain, beautiful stock. It wasn't fast; you needed quite a lot of light, compared to modern emulsions. I figured those six cans were just enough, if I just shot one take of everything, to make this little fantasy on the theme of the commedia dell'arte and end up with a short film.

I was also lucky enough to have a professional cameraman working on the film: Tourjansky, the son of the famous Russian émigré silent director in Russia and France.

MacDonald: There have been multiple versions of *Rabbit's Moon*. I don't know if I've seen the longer version.

Anger: The longer version is printed in blue and has cut-ins in rose or pink: shots of woodcuts of the moon. That version is twenty minutes long.

MacDonald: It still exists?

Anger: Yes, it'll be on my DVD, which is due to come out later this year.

Rabbit's Moon uses a lot of repeats and deliberately unmatched shots. Pierrot will make a gesture like reaching up to the moon, and then he'll make the same gesture in another shot, but it isn't like the usual tight cutting on movement you see in most commercial films. I knew all those conventional techniques. I had been absorbing movie techniques since I was a little boy growing up in Hollywood around people who were working in the industry—so I knew when I could break the rules. I wasn't just fooling around. From the beginning I had a film language to work from.

At any rate, I had this unique opportunity to have a professional studio with professional lights. My set was an artificial forest scene. I repainted some cut-down tree branches in black and silver, and they were built in perspective, so they got smaller as they went away from the camera—I didn't have much depth to work with in what was a fairly small room. Doing *Rabbit's Moon,* I was inspired by Méliès, and by his flat depth of field. And I was fortunate to have actors from the Parisian mime school (later it became the

Marcel Marceau School), who were trained in pantomime and were happy to work with me.

MacDonald: You mentioned that you only had stock for a limited number of takes. But the film looks very carefully choreographed. Did you spend a lot of time rehearsing?

Anger: They were professionals, thoroughly schooled in what they were doing. I explained that I wanted an imaginary tightrope walk, imaginary juggling; they had done things like that, so they knew what to do. And, of course, they were familiar with the characters of Pierrot, Harlequin, and Columbine. I was working with people who were in a sense already rehearsed. They were a very nice small cast to work with.

MacDonald: It's easy to think of *Rabbit's Moon* as an expression of your happiness at being in Europe.

Anger: It *was.* That can also be said of *Eaux d'artifice.*

MacDonald: In my book *The Garden in the Machine,* I conjectured about the relationship between *Eaux d'artifice* and *Fireworks. Fireworks* is about the repression of your gay desire in America and how that desire finds ways to express itself, even to explode, when it's repressed. When you got to Europe, you were able to express this desire without the resistance you had experienced here, and, as a result, *Eaux d'artifice* suggests an explosion of pleasure and freedom, and of freedom of expression. Is that a fair reading?

Anger: Well, I wouldn't characterize my American period as repression, because it really wasn't. I was able to make films, short as they were.

I've always had parallel projects going on at any one time, for a very simple reason: I was never able to make anything approaching feature-length because that always involved more money than I could round up. At the time that I was doing the early films, there just wasn't a network of foundations backing films. I had to come up with my own ways of financing things.

I went to Italy and lived in Rome to make *Eaux d'artifice,* which was filmed in Tivoli, a town about thirty miles from Rome, in the Alban Hills. The gardens in the film are part of the estate of the d'Este family. In those days, the eldest son of a wealthy family would go into the military, and the next son would go into the church, whether he was suited for it or not. And that's what happened to the fellow who became the cardinal d'Este when he was only sixteen. He supervised the design of that garden on that hill; it was his place to have a good time. The garden is an amazing use of water as an element of architecture; hydraulics, just natural gravity, makes all the fountains work.

The most surprising thing was that I was given permission by the Department of Antiquities in Italy to make my film. Those gardens are a tourist attraction, and I couldn't just go in there with a camera and start filming. I had to block off certain sections of the garden so that I wouldn't have tour

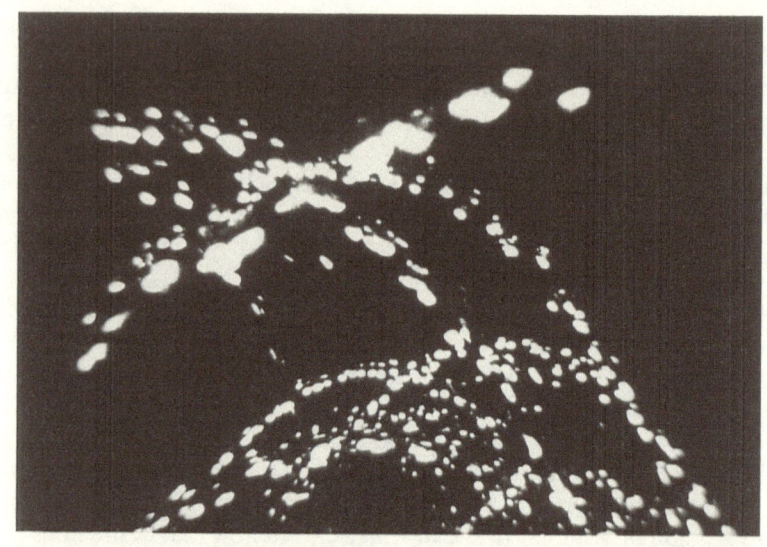

Water from fountains in the gardens of the Villa d'Este in Kenneth Anger's *Eaux d'artifice* (1953). Courtesy Anthology Film Archives.

guides and groups of tourists coming into my picture. I don't know if a young American would be given that privilege today. They told me with good humor, "Don't break any old statuary," which I didn't; I was respectful of everything. Sometimes an American Express guide behind my barrier would be shouting, "Hurry up! We have to get in because we have to go on to see Hadrian's Villa!" But I was able to get the film shot.

MacDonald: How did Carmello Salvatorelli get into the project?

Anger: Ah, yes, she was a little midget I had met socially through Fellini in Rome, and of course . . .

MacDonald: You said "she"; it's a "he," right?

Anger: No, it's a *lady.*

MacDonald: It's not a man in drag?

Anger: Absolutely no. *No, no, no.* Why would you think that?

MacDonald: It's spelled "Carmell*o*" in the program note P. Adams Sitney reproduces in *Visionary Film* [New York: Oxford University Press, 1974, 2002], and in the filmography of *Moonchild,* edited by Jack Hunter [New York: Creation Books, 2002]. I saw the spelling and assumed it was a man.

Anger: No, it's Carmill*a,* as in J. Sheridan LeFanu's short story "Carmilla."

MacDonald: I need to rethink my interpretation of the film! [In *The Garden in the Machine* (Berkeley and Los Angeles: University of California Press, 2002), I use my misreading of Salvatorelli's gender in arguing that in Europe Anger was able to release his feminine side.]

Anger: Carmilla was a wonderful little lady who was patiently willing to work with me through a whole summer. The difficult thing about that project was that not only was I working in a place where I couldn't simply do whatever I wanted, but also I had to work in certain areas of the garden at certain times of day. I was filming on 16mm reversal Ferrania film using a deep red filter for the night effect, which means I was using natural light as if it were artificial light. Because there were a lot of tall cypresses in the garden, the light would sometimes be right in a certain area *only* for ten or fifteen minutes. The light would come through, and then it'd be gone for the rest of the day. So I needed to figure out in advance when the light that I needed, the backlighting particularly, would be coming through the trees, and get specific areas blocked off at just the right moment. Once I figured out where the light would be in a certain place, I had my actor get into position and my two cameramen, Charles and Thad Lovett, go to work.

Charles and Thad were Americans living in Rome—as a matter of fact, I was living *with* them in Rome. They had a camera that I wished *I* could have owned: a 16mm Éclair with a mirrored viewfinder, so you could look through the lens and see what you were shooting. Charles and Thad were very enthusiastic about working with me, so as with *La lune des lapins,* I had skilled cameramen helping me. I was very grateful for that.

Carmilla is a mysterious figure in an eighteenth-century costume, wearing a mask, who you never see in close-up; she's always seen at a distance. I knew I wanted a small person, because when I was first studying the gardens, I compared them to Piranesi's etchings of the same gardens in the eighteenth century. Piranesi also did etchings of the ruins of Rome and other famous old buildings, and when he wanted to give the viewer a sense of scale, he would use very small people, to make the ruins or the fountains or the monuments seem bigger. I decided I would use that same technique. And it worked. When you see the figure in *Eaux d'artifice* come down the winding, curved balustrade, the balustrade is above her head—she has to reach up to it—whereas a normal-sized human would reach down or over to hold onto the balustrade.

MacDonald: Was Vivaldi part of the original conception?

Anger: Yes. I love *The Four Seasons,* and I figured that I would just use one movement, the winter movement, Yes, I always had Vivaldi in mind.

MacDonald: Early on, when you were writing letters to Amos Vogel, looking for financial help to get that film made [see Anger's letters in *Cinema 16: Documents toward a History of the Film Society* (Philadelphia: Temple University Press, 2002)], you refer to the film as "Waterworks."

Anger: That was my working title. But then I realized that "waterworks" often means sewers, so I decided not to use it. "Eaux d'artifice" is a pun I invented. The French have an expression, *feux d'artifice,* their name for "fireworks." So I use e-a-u-x, rather than f-e-u-x: waters of artifice. I wanted to refer back to *Fireworks* and forward to this new project. The French aren't offended by my pun; I've asked various people in France, and they've all said it's okay. I've never seen anyone else use my little pun. I also had an Italian title for the film, "Aqua Barroque," which I thought I would use if there were a chance to open the film in Italy, but that didn't happen.

After *Eaux d'artifice* I did conceive of a couple of other baroque garden films. For example, I visited a garden called Bomarzo; it's located between Florence and Rome. It's quite famous, though it's off the beaten tourist path. It has huge boulders that were carved into monster faces by slaves in the sixteenth century, and you can walk through the mouths into little rooms. It was a folly commissioned by a nobleman. I never got around to filming that garden; if I had, I would have used another movement from *The Four Seasons.* At that time, Bomarzo was an overgrown, wild ruin; I loved it because it was so romantic.

My idea at one point was to do four films about four gardens, one for each of the four seasons, but I wasn't able to find the financing, so I moved on and eventually moved back to the States.

MacDonald: Your career has a lot of beginnings that don't get financed into complete films. I'm thinking particularly of *Puce Moment* [1949], which was originally going to be *Puce Women,* and *Kustom Kar Kommandos.* What was the original plan for *Puce Women?*

Anger: I did have a written script for it; it's filed with Anthology Film Archives, and I also made preproduction drawings for the whole film. Because of my Hollywood background, I picked up on the idea of doing drawings for every shot, and I've done that for several of my projects.

MacDonald: Do the drawings still exist?

Anger: They do for *Puce Women.* But to answer your question: *Puce Women* was to be about forty minutes long. It was to begin early in the morning and go through the day, ending in twilight. Each section would be appropriate to a particular time of day—morning, noon, afternoon, and twilight—and would be represented by a different woman. Each of the women would be based on a Hollywood star of the twenties: the morning woman would evoke Clara Bow, and the noon woman would be like Barbara La Marr, and so forth. They would be dressed in authentic costumes that my grandmother had given me; she had kept costumes, and they were still in excellent condition. I found locations—the houses in Hollywood—I would use, and I'd chosen and blocked in the women I was going to work with, but I was never able to find the money. The only thing I ended up with was basically a test for one woman, who was played by Yvonne Marquis; she had a vivacious quality like Clara Bow.

Puce Moment was one of those projects that I wanted to make so badly that I even tried getting sponsorship from some Hollywood people. I went to see Albert Lewin, who had made *The Picture of Dorian Gray* [1945]. I knew that he had a collection of voodoo art and primitive paintings. I thought he might be interested. I showed *Puce Moment* to him, hoping he might be convinced to provide some sponsorship, and I also showed it to Arthur Freed, while he was a producer of musicals—this was before he did *Singin' in the Rain* [1952]. They politely looked at *Puce Moment,* but then, you know, I never got a check *[laughter].* Later, it seemed to me that I saw some glimpses of the fashion parade I had used in *Puce Moment* in *Singin' in the Rain*—maybe not; maybe it's just coincidence, but it seemed like some moments in *Singin' in the Rain* paralleled my idea pretty closely.

Some grants were becoming available at that time. I applied to the Guggenheim Foundation and was turned down, which was rather annoying because to apply you had to get twelve people to say that you weren't a criminal. I found that very offensive.

MacDonald: I always think of the Guggenheim, especially in those days, as interested in abstract art.

Anger: Probably. I don't know. Later, people told me that you've got to be willing to be turned down about twelve times before they'll give you a grant. That seemed like too much of a waste of time, so I just moved on.

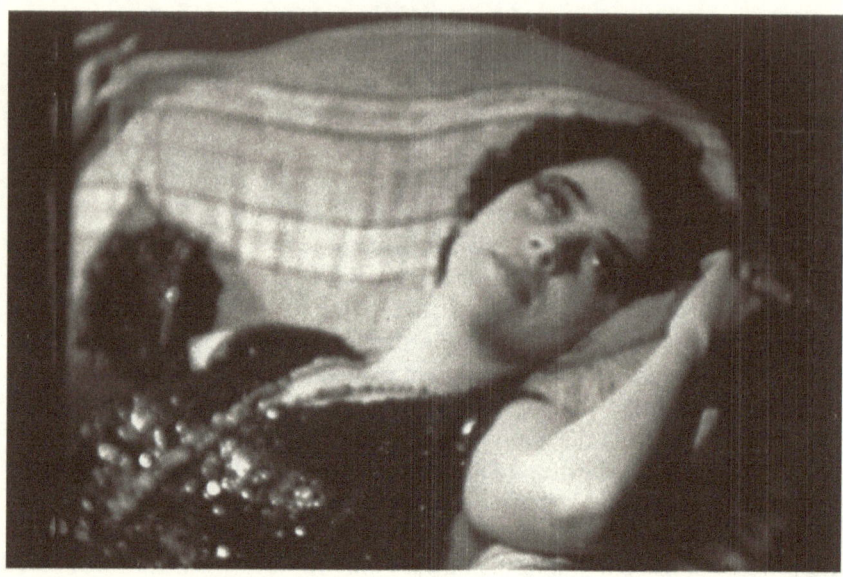

Yvonne Marquis in Kenneth Anger's *Puce Moment* (1949). Courtesy David E. James.

MacDonald: The music on some of your films changes over time, and I'm wondering whether that's because you have a love-hate relationship with pop music; pop music can come to seem out-of-date more quickly than some other forms of music. Is that why the sound tracks change?

Anger: Absolutely not. I consider myself an experimental artist, and even once a film is "done," if I want to try something else, and make a new version of a film, I will. This may annoy critics who are trying to keep track of everything, but this tendency of mine dates back to my earliest films, which were like three-minute or five-minute shorts that had to be run at silent speed because the only camera I had at that time ran at sixteen frames a second. I would just play a record along with a film and see if I liked it, and then I'd try another record. When I'd look at *Who Has Been Rocking My Dream Boat?,* I played the Mills Brothers song "Someone's Rocking My Dreamboat" on my phonograph.

My first sound track for *Puce Moment* was Puccini, the interlude for his first opera, *Le Villi* ["The Willies"]. It has the same plot as *Les Silphides,* the ballet about the phantoms. I liked that piece very much and used it for a while, and then I thought I'd try something else. In the sixties I met the musician who composed what became the second sound track for *Puce Moment.*

MacDonald: What was *The Love That Whirls* [1949]?

Anger: That was my first film in color, in Kodachrome. I had met a remarkable-looking young man, named Ernest Lacy; he had an Irish mother and a Mexican father, so he was an interesting mixture. He had extraordinary eyes. I wanted to make a film with him. The idea for it came from Fraser's *The Golden Bough*. The film was to present a ritual of sacrifice. Many different cultures have had ritual sacrifices, but I was thinking specifically of Aztec rituals. The film involved Lacy climbing to the top of a mountain and sacrificing himself to the sun. During the film he was nude. He had a beautiful body, and I was just using him as a nude figure, which has a long tradition in art, and has *nothing* to do with pornography.

I filmed *The Love That Whirls* on Kodachrome, and at that time, to get 16mm Kodachrome developed, you had to send it to Rochester, New York. When I sent the film to Kodak, they confiscated it because of the nudity, and I never got it back. They had a flat rule about nudity; it didn't matter whether it was a woman or a man or a child. No nudity. Parents couldn't even make home movies of their children in the bathtub or playing in a sprinkler. Looking back, I probably could have gotten a lawyer and at least tried to convince them to send it back. But I didn't do that. So I was shot down by Eastman Kodak. Their monopoly broke up in the sixties, and then there were independent labs that could develop Kodachrome and were willing to print nude imagery.

MacDonald: I think for me *Inauguration of the Pleasure Dome* is your most remarkable film. P. Adams Sitney talks about an early three-screen version of that film. Does that version still exist?

Anger: That version was shown at the Brussels World's Fair in 1958 and at a couple of film festivals. That world's fair in Brussels is where I met Marie Menken; she was there, too, as was Brakhage; they both saw the three-screen *Inauguration*. At that point, the first part of the film used a single screen, but for the last twenty minutes—the party sequence, which begins when the characters start putting on masks—the film split into three images The two side images were mirror images of each other. I varied that a bit, but quite a lot of it had a kind of mirror effect, so that one person might be looking toward the center image from one side and another person from the opposite side.

I knew about Abel Gance and his *Napoléon* [1927], which used a triptych format. I met Abel Gance, and Nellie Kaplan, who was his assistant; they showed some of their films at the Brussels World's Fair too. Gance was fascinated with my film and not at all upset; he was pleased that I had picked up on his three-screen idea and used it.

Of course, the trick with a three-projector piece is that all three projectors have to be in sync, and at that time I had help from the Siemans Company in Germany; they were one of the sponsors of the showings and provided the projectors for the Brussels Exposition. They agreed to supply a coaxial cable linking up the three projectors, which I guess for them was very easy, but would have been impossible for me. I had worked out the three-screen *Inauguration of the Pleasure Dome* only in theory.

And so that version was shown in Brussels and also at the Palais de Challiot in Paris. But a time came when I decided I just couldn't do this version anymore; the logistics were much too complicated. I decided that the three-screen version had been an experiment, that I had completed the experiment; and I made a final, single-screen version. In my final recut of *Inauguration* I use a lot of superimpositions, and to make those, I cannibalized the two twenty-minute reels on the two sides and incorporated them. That's the version that's in distribution now.

MacDonald: When I read about the three-screen version and that it began with one screen and then expanded to three screens, it seemed to work perfectly with the character development in the film. You start with this one character, Lord Shiva, who seems, first, to split into, or to see within himself, two characters—Kali and the Great Beast—and then to keep opening out into more and more figures. I don't think of *Inauguration* as a narrative but as a ritual that allows the complex multiplicity of the central figure's psyche—and, in a sense, everyone's psyche—to be revealed.

Anger: And that's all quite deliberate.

The film is based on a musical form—theme and variation.

MacDonald: Did the three-screen version have the Janáček sound track? When I was first seeing *Inauguration,* it had an Electric Light Orchestra sound track . . .

Anger: For a short while, yes—another experiment.

MacDonald: The different sound tracks tend to create different experiences of the film, with different emphases. Juxtaposed with the ELO sound track, the elegance and extravagance of your imagery moved to the foreground; but with the Janáček, the *humor* of the visuals becomes the foreground—at least for me.

Anger: All along, I was experimenting with various tracks, some of which I never recorded. I had always known about Leo Janáček's *Slavonic Mass,* and I had that in mind even when I was filming the imagery. I found a recording of *The Slavonic Mass* by Raphael Kubelik that I liked, and I used that.

MacDonald: In my book on Cinema 16 I reprinted a number of letters between you and Vogel, written at a time when it looked like the film was going to have a Harry Partch sound track. Does a print with that sound track still exist?

Anger: Well, Harry is not alive anymore, so you can't talk to him, but I'll give you my version. In the early fifties I heard an LP of some of his music performed using his own instruments. He had invented things called "cloud chambers," big glass bells that he had cut the bottoms off and used like gongs, and several stringed instruments. He was quite a unique artist. Looking back, I wish I'd done a documentary on him and his instruments. I liked the music on this LP and told him so, and I asked if it would be okay if I used it on an experimental film I was completing. He said yes. So I went ahead and used his music with my imagery—but his piece was five minutes too long for the picture. I saw a little section that I thought could be trimmed out of the music, so that it would fit exactly with my imagery, and I went ahead and trimmed that section.

When I showed the test print to Harry, he was furious. He said, "You can't cut my music! If you want to use the whole thing, that's okay, but you can't cut my music!" And he asked me to destroy the print, which I did.

Looking at that version of my imagery with Partch's music made for a *very* different experience. In that early version there were no optical effects at all, no dissolves or superimpositions, so every cut was like an abrupt slap; the film had more of a cubist effect, very different from later versions. I'm sorry that what I did offended Harry; I suppose I should have asked him first, but it was a slow little section of the music, and there was no way I could have put additional visuals in to make the imagery fit the sound. After that, I realized that I should commission my own music, so I wouldn't have problems with permissions.

MacDonald: You've obviously spent a lot of time studying world mythologies. When you were making *Inauguration of the Pleasure Dome,* how fully did you assume the audience would make particular identifications? I ask the question on two different levels. Anaïs Nin plays Astarte. I've always assumed that you assumed a substantial portion of the audience would recognize not just the mythological role Nin plays but that it's *her* playing this role. Nin herself was/is something of a mythical figure. To what extent did you think about the audience's awareness, or lack of awareness, about the history of mythologies when you were making the film?

Anger: I've always made my films for myself, and how much of what I put into them is picked up by other people is not my concern. Otherwise I'd have program notes. I *do* sometimes have program notes that identify the cast and the names of the figures they play. But that's about as far as I'll go. My films are enigmas to be figured out. My films are based on my lifelong research, and they add something to that research. If you can pick up on the results, fine; it's all *there* if you want to explore it—but you may have to do some research of your own.

MacDonald: Samson de Brier played a number of roles in *Inauguration of the Pleasure Dome.* Was there a particular reason for that?

Anger: The whole film evolved from a Halloween party at which various friends came dressed as gods and goddesses. Samson had a number of differ-

Anaïs Nin as Astarte in Kenneth Anger's *Inauguration of the Pleasure Dome* (1954). Courtesy David E. James.

ent costumes; he would appear in one costume, then disappear and reappear in another. So I based the film on his personality; he's the main character, sort of the master of ceremonies of this event (which, by the way, was filmed in his house).

MacDonald: In his filmography Haller lists *The Story of O* [1961]. What can you tell me about that project?

Anger: When I was living in France, my publisher was Jean-Jacques Pauvert. He brought out the original edition of *Hollywood Babylon,* which I wrote in French, before it came out in English. At that time Jean-Jacques was the publisher of a rather notorious novel, *Histoire d'O,* by Pauline Reage. It was an erotic novel; I guess you could call it a sadomasochistic fairytale because it's absolutely a fantasy, nothing that could actually happen in real life. I met the author, whose real name is Dominique Aury, and she gave me permission to film the book, and I began work on a black-and-white, silent film. My model for the project was Bresson. I shot about twenty minutes, and then the production came to a halt: it turned out that the father of the young lady who was playing the lead was the French minister of finance. The girl was in her late teens, old enough to make up her own mind about what she wanted to do, but at any rate, the filming had to stop when it became known that she was playing a part in an erotic film. It *wasn't* pornographic, but did involve some nudity and some simulated S&M; most everything takes place off camera. The film was basically an exercise in style. I had a work print of what I had shot, which I left at the Cinémathèque Française. Another unfinished project.

MacDonald: When I think about *Scorpio Rising,* it reminds me a little of *All That Jazz* [1979, directed by Bob Fosse], in the sense that the beginning sequences are the most powerful, and the film seems gradually to fall away from the energy we sense early on. For me, and I'm guessing to some extent for you, the process of getting ready for the big social moment is the most exciting part; and the moment itself can never quite live up . . .

Anger: . . . to the anticipation—yes. Paradoxically, I've always felt that getting dressed up, putting *on* a costume, is more exciting, more fascinating to watch, than striptease. What people choose to put *on*—their clothes, their adornments—is more interesting than the undressing part.

MacDonald: A related thought: as a filmmaker you've had many experiences where you have conceptions, and sometimes far more than conceptions, about what you want to do in a film; and then in the process of trying to get the film produced, you come into contact with a world that really doesn't care about your plans. Once in a while you *are* able to get a film done—and usually it's a remarkable film—but there are so many cases where the actual contact with the realities of money keeps the film from getting made; your professional experience as a filmmaker is often more about the excitement of anticipation than about what results.

Anger: Yes, and some of this has to do with the way I am. I think it took Oliver Stone twenty years to find a producer for his first script, *Platoon* [1986]. But once he'd broken that barrier, he was able to make commercial films; he became "bankable," and large amounts of money were available to him. *I* can't stick with one project for twenty years. I've had some very good projects, but when the money didn't turn up—if I didn't know how to get it, or if I was turned down—I would just move on. I learned not to get tragic about these things, and I'd just move on to something else. I'd think to myself, "Well, okay, that's going to remain a dream project."

MacDonald: In *Scorpio Rising,* you examine, among other things, a very common kind of doublethink, where men get together to enjoy each other sensually, but pretend that the homoerotic element of the experience is not there. Could you talk about the young men you worked with in *Scorpio Rising*?

Anger: All my actors in *Scorpio Rising* were straight. They were working-class guys, Italian Americans mostly, who would have been upset by the way I portray them. *Scorpio Rising* was *me* putting that inference on their society, seeing their society as an outsider, which can be a limitation but also an advantage. In fact, the men had girlfriends, but at the Halloween party they said, "We don't want our girlfriends in the picture; *we* want to be in the picture!" They were showing off a little bit, or maybe a lot, for the camera. This was a case where the camera changed things, but it changed them in a direction that I wanted. So *Scorpio Rising* is my take on their lifestyle, not their lifestyle untouched.

In fact, some of the men that you see getting dressed for the party in the film weren't even at the party. The blonde who puts on a leather jacket when you hear the song "Blue Velvet" wasn't even in New York. When I got back to Los Angeles after filming most of what became *Scorpio* in Brooklyn and was cutting the film, I met this young man, who was a model with the Athletic Model Guild, which was run by a friend of mine named Bob Mizer. Before explicit or hard-core magazines were available, there were these physique magazines, and Mizer had one called *Physique Pictorial* that published some of the early drawings of Tom of Finland, and camp photographs Mizer did of drifters that he'd find around LA, posed either in a leather jacket or blue jeans or a posing strap. I used to go over there to the AMG near MacArthur Park quite often. On one of my visits I met this fellow, and I put him in the film.

Another thing: while I was cutting the film, living in Silverlake, a package was left on my doorstep. Since it was a 16mm film package, I assumed it was for me, and I opened it: it was a Sunday school film rented from the Lutheran Church. I looked at the package more carefully and realized that it was addressed to the same street address, but to a different street. I decided to run the film, and when I saw it, I thought, "Well, I'm just going to keep this and cut it into my film." And that's how I got *Last Journey to Jerusalem* [1948]. I thought of it as the gods acting up, doing a little prank, doing me a favor. The film was perfect for my purposes.

I immediately saw the parallel between the disciples following Jesus and the "disciples" in the motorcycle gang following some idea. And I saw that in both cases, this kind of following could lead into dangerous territory, as it did for the Hell's Angels, who started out just as guys who had been vets in World War II, a little wild, but not dangerous; but later morphed into something else, drifted into drug dealing, and gained quite a negative reputation.

MacDonald: Over the years there's been some debate about the ending of *Scorpio Rising,* whether it's the Scorpio character we're seeing dead in the flashing light.

Anger: No, it's not Scorpio. After the Halloween party, the motorcycle gang went to a place called Walden Pond, in upstate New York. They rode up there on their bikes after staying up all night and on November 1 were part of the last outdoor dirt bike race of the year. Some of them actually rode in the race; the others just went up there to hang out. I rode on the back of one of the riders' bikes with my camera. During the race, there was that accident; one of the bikes flipped over and crashed right in front of my camera. I incorporated that, as the final image. But it's not Scorpio. The man you see in the flashing red light—Jim Powers—was a biker who *was* killed later, but not in front of my camera, though that is the implication I'm making. As a hobby, motorcycle racing is quite dangerous, and I think that's the appeal: the bikers all think they're immortal.

Scorpio is the sign of the Zodiac that rules machines and death and sex. That's the tie-in.

MacDonald: In *Scorpio Rising* the men you're depicting, at least early on in the film, are quite beautiful about getting themselves ready, getting their machines ready; and then as the film moves on, as they gather into a group, at first it's a party but then it turns more toward something creepy. I'm wondering whether one of the things you're suggesting is that very often when you do follow your dreams and find other people who are sharing this dream, there can be great pleasure, but also great danger. I'm trying to understand the Nazi imagery in the film—in your mind is it the *number* of people that makes dreams turn dangerous, or . . .

Anger: Well, *Scorpio Rising* isn't a cautionary tale. I'm not trying to say, "Don't do this because you'll end up a Nazi," but I did find an element of swagger and bullying in this culture. Actually the particular guys I knew weren't threatening, at least to me, and I became quite good friends with some of them—they accepted me as some sort of camera nut, and they saw me accepting them as bike nuts—but there often is a rebellious dimension in biker groups that makes some bikers defiantly enjoy doing things that might scare other people—like sporting swastikas.

I first asked this bunch if I could photograph their bikes when I met them under the Cyclone [a roller coaster] at Coney Island, where they used to meet on Saturdays. Mostly they were from Brooklyn. I was living in Brooklyn myself at the time, with Marie Menken and Willard Maas in Brooklyn Heights.

MacDonald: What was *that* like?

Anger: You may be aware that Marie Menken and Willard Maas, who she was living with, were the couple that inspired Edward Albee to write *Who's Afraid of Virginia Woolf?*—and if you know the play, you can imagine that the experience was unusual. Willard and Marie had a strange symbiotic relationship. Willard was gay, and Marie was not; and there was a son who would show up occasionally. I was with them for about three months in their penthouse in Brooklyn Heights. Marie invited me to live there; I was more Marie's friend than Willard's. Willard was teaching at a college out on

Staten Island; he was a professor of literature. Marie worked at *Time* magazine in the cable room.

They would begin drinking on Friday and would continue to drink all weekend, and then on Monday morning, they'd both go back to work and be on time for their jobs. Each weekend was like a lost weekend—well, a *found* weekend for them, because this was how they could be themselves. Sometimes I was a kind of referee, usually defending Marie—though I never actually had to intervene. Watching their arguments was a little like watching Punch and Judy. If I had been able to film their fights, I would have had quite a film because they did the most extraordinary things. Sometimes when they were both quite drunk, they would get up on this parapet overlooking the skyline of lower Manhattan and the river. It was a fifteen-story drop down to the sidewalk, and they'd be up on the parapet pushing each other; they both knew how to step back and not fall off, but a slight miscalculation and one or both would have gone over that ledge. It was scary, but also entertaining. On those alcoholic weekends I would have a couple of drinks, but I certainly wasn't drinking along *with* them.

Edward Albee was familiar with them from an earlier period. I remember going to the premiere of *Who's Afraid of Virginia Woolf?* with Willard and Marie. They were laughing at it and everything, but they never said, "Oh, that's *us!*" Afterward, Willard was quite critical. He said, "It's too long; Edward should cut out half an hour." He was acting like a professor. They *must have* recognized themselves, but they stayed friends with Edward. The play was a hit, but so far as I know there was never anything like "Give us a cut because you based it on our lives!" They only saw it once.

I was very close with Marie. We traveled in Europe together after the Brussels World's Fair. We went to Paris and then to Spain, and that's where she made her little short called *Arabesque for Kenneth Anger* [1961], in the Alhambra in Granada. I helped her with that film; she was working with this little 16mm camera that used expensive little fifty-foot-load magazines. If she had used a hundred-foot-load, she could have filmed for half price. But she didn't want the bigger, heavier camera. She liked this little thing that she could hold in one hand; so while she was dancing around the columns and the fountains, I would occasionally be behind the camera, guiding her, so that she wouldn't bump into something.

I miss Marie a lot.

MacDonald: In *Scorpio Rising* did you get the rights to use all the music?

Anger: I used about twelve selections, including Elvis Presley's "Devil in Disguise." Since I intended to submit *Scorpio Rising* to film festivals and to show it around, I decided I needed to get the rights. I hired a rights clearance lawyer in New York and turned the whole thing over to him, and he got the clearances, not for a feature film, but for a short. If it had been a feature film it probably would have been more expensive, but the clearance for all the music came to eight thousand dollars. That about doubled my budget.

It was pop music that was playing the summer of 1963, when I was filming; it was just prior to the Kennedy assassination, and just before the Beatles, who came in and messed up American music as far as I'm concerned. They became such a fad and were in the top five for so long that a lot of good American musicians and songwriters got pushed out.

MacDonald: Was the idea of using the individual songs as modules part of the original conception of the film?

Anger: The music was an integral part of what I wanted. I am a pioneer in using music this way, along with Bruce Conner, who began using pop music in a similar way around the same time.

MacDonald: The only film I know of that may be earlier in its use of previously recorded pop music, though it doesn't use rock and doesn't use the music ironically the way you and Bruce do, is *Weegee's New York* [ca. 1952].

Anger: What is *Weegee's New York*?

MacDonald: It's a short city symphony of New York, and especially of Coney Island beach on a crowded summer day, shot by the photographer Weegee.

Anger: Of course, I'm very familiar with Weegee's still photographs, but I've not seen that film.

MacDonald: When Amos Vogel found out that Weegee, who was a member of Cinema 16, made films, he said, "We've got to show this material." According to Vogel, Weegee had no idea how to edit a film and no interest in learning, so Vogel did the editing. The finished film uses pop music of the early fifties, before rock and roll, almost the entire songs, so the structure of the Coney Island section of *Weegee's New York* is somewhat similar to *Scorpio Rising*. Nobody seems to remember who put the sound on the film.

Anger: Weegee had such an eye for the grotesque, like Diane Arbus. I loved his still photography. He was the first one to photograph car accidents and things like that and show that they could be a brutal kind of art.

In *Scorpio Rising,* the songs are an ironic commentary on what's going on in the picture. They're a kind of narration. When I have the fellow from the Athletic Model Guild put on his leather jacket, the music is "Blue Velvet," which specifically says, "*She* wore blue velvet." It's a deliberate gender switch that suggests that he's as vain as any girl would be. Of course, men have a right to be vain about their appearance, to take pains to decorate themselves; that's a human trait, from primitive man or woman on.

MacDonald: In the little monograph by Robert Haller that accompanies *The Magic Lantern Cycle* videos, *Scorpio Rising* is dedicated to "Jack Parsons, Victor Childe, Jim Powers, James Dean, T. E. Lawrence, Hart

Crane, Kurt Mann, The Society of Spartans, The Hell's Angels, and all the overgrown boys who will follow the whistle of Love's brother." Some of these names are familiar to me; others are not. Who, for example, was Jack Parsons?

Anger: He was a famous rocket scientist who invented the fuel that took the *Apollo* to the moon. He was married to Cameron, who plays the Scarlet Woman in *Inauguration of the Pleasure Dome.* Jack was killed in 1952 in an explosion at his home in Pasadena. Apparently he had explosives at home. He and Cameron were supposed to leave for Mexico that morning, and Cameron had gone to a shop close by to get some supplies, and when she got back, the workshop had blown up and her husband was dead.

MacDonald: Who was/is Victor Childe?

Anger: Victor Childe was a friend of mine, a skilled painter in the surrealist tradition. He was working on a large, elaborate painting called *The Bone Garden* for about ten years. He was also a script writer and at one point wrote a script about a mermaid. At that time there were no films about mermaids, and Constance Bennett took an option on Victor's script, and it looked like the film was set for production. Then in England somebody else made a movie about a mermaid, and when Constance heard about this other movie, she said, "Well, I can't do it now because the novelty has been ruined," and decided not to take up the option. Victor was counting on this sale to solve all his financial problems—he had gotten himself in a big hole financially—and he committed suicide by turning on the gas in his apartment, which was above a restaurant in Hollywood. One of the waitresses smelled gas from down below and came up to see what was wrong and knocked on his door; Victor was still conscious and switched off the light, which created a spark that was enough to set off an explosion, and he was killed. *The Bone Garden* was completely burned, covered with blisters—it was a photo-realist painting, an amazing structure of skeletons and bones, totally original. I just wanted to remember him a little bit; that's why I mentioned his name in that dedication.

MacDonald: Jim Powers?

Anger: He was the one who was "killed" at the end of *Scorpio Rising.* It's his head you see in the red flashing police light, and I have a shot of his arm with his tattoo, "Blessed, blessed oblivion." It wasn't long after the filming that he drove his car as fast as he could into a wall in San Francisco and killed himself.

MacDonald: And Kurt Mann?

Anger: Kurt Mann was the son of Thomas Mann. He committed suicide by jumping off a boat to Cuba.

As I wrote in the preface to my friend's book on celebrity suicide [David K. Frasier, *Suicide in the Entertainment Industry: An Encyclopedia*

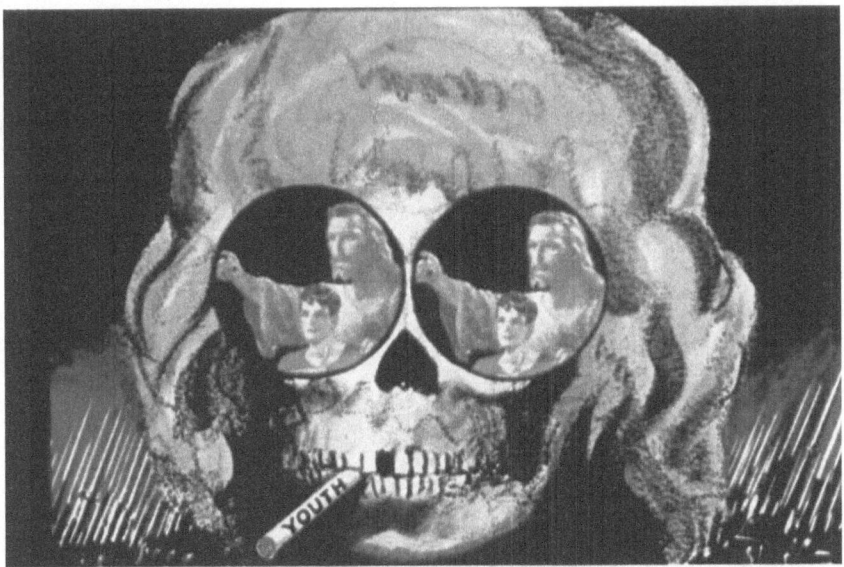

From Kenneth Anger's *Scorpio Rising* (1963). Courtesy David E. James.

of 840 Twentieth Century Cases (Jefferson, N.C.: McFarland, 2002)], there have been quite a few suicides among people I've known. It is odd that I've known so many.

I've recently finished a film tribute—*Elliott's Suicide*—to another friend of mine who committed suicide not long ago. He was a songwriter and singer named Elliott Smith. He's on the Dreamworks label. He killed himself last October. He was thirty-four and had had a fight with his girlfriend and stabbed himself in the chest with a steak knife in his girlfriend's kitchen, which was so *stupid*—but people do stupid things. On the other hand, his lyrics are quite dark; the word "suicide" occurs frequently. He had his own destiny to work out, but I was really upset over his death and the waste of this life, and I did *Elliott's Suicide* as a little tribute to him. I photographed the steak knife and it's in the film. And I use several of his songs, including, "Follow Me to the Rose Parade"; apparently he liked to get stoned on the last night of the year and in the morning go with friends to the Rose Parade in Pasadena. This past January, after he died, I shot part of the Rose Parade, and I've incorporated some of the passing floats in my film. The Rose Parade floats move so slowly that even though they're filmed in actual time, they suggest slow motion, and I use that in an elegiac sense in the film.

MacDonald: Is the film available?

Anger: I haven't printed it up yet; but it's basically assembled. It's eighteen minutes long.

MacDonald: Did you know Spalding Gray's work?

Anger: Yes. He jumped off a ferry—like Kurt Mann. But I understand he had been in a bad car accident in Ireland and was apparently in a lot of pain—he just couldn't deal with it anymore. He was so talented. I'd seen people do monologues before, but he certainly perfected the form. How he could just be there sitting at his table with a glass of water, and maybe a couple of notes, and yet be absolutely riveting—it was remarkable.

MacDonald: I saw him a number of times at the Performing Garage in New York and loved Demme's film of *Swimming to Cambodia* [1987]. Losing him was a blow.

Like *Puce Moment*, *Kustom Kar Kommandos* is a kind of monument to a project that never got financed.

Anger: Yes. Luckily I have at least as much from those projects as I do—two short films. *Kustom Kar Kommandos* is about three minutes long; it was supposed to be forty-five minutes.

I found a whole series of young men who were willing to work with me, by going to the shows where they brought their custom cars. I met them there, and they were very proud of what they call their "babies." What they did was a kind of folk art; they were skilled artisans turning a standard Ford and Chevy into something quite unique. It was to be a study of the whole culture of the remarkable custom car world; it still exists. At that time it was quite new; I discovered it about the same time Tom Wolfe did. The film was to end with a car meet or a race. The project paralleled *Scorpio Rising* to some extent, but wasn't going to end in a death.

MacDonald: The first letters of the title words make up KKK; were you going to do something with the Ku Klux Klan in that film?

Anger: The title has *nothing* to do with the Ku Klux Klan. In the custom car culture, they use Ks instead of Cs.

I had gotten some assistance from the Ford Foundation; they gave a modest amount of money to a dozen filmmakers—only twelve thousand dollars, not enough to make a longer film. I filmed what is now *Kustom Kar Kommandos* with that Ford Foundation money. I filmed in the garage of the young man who's in the film—it was his car, and he did all the work on it—in San Bernadino. The garage was cluttered and full of stuff, and I knew I had to simplify the set, so I brought in a twelve-foot-wide roll of no-seam paper, the sort of thing that's used for fashion model shooting, where you want just a plain background behind the model, and I used that to isolate the car as an art object.

MacDonald: *Lucifer Rising* went through a number of stages, partly because much of the original material was stolen, though some of it ended up in *Invocation of My Demon Brother*.

Anger: Yes, that was when I had a falling-out with Bobby Beausoleil, who I originally cast as Lucifer. I don't really want to go into that whole story again, but when I wasn't home, he came in and took several cans of the unedited footage I had shot of him. All I had left of that material was what I had in my cutting bin, just loose rolled-up bits, but I was determined to do *something* with that material, after all the effort that had gone into filming it. And so those scraps were used in *Invocation of My Demon Brother* and added to that film's rough, disjunctive texture.

MacDonald: Is everything that's not your performance of the ritual in *Invocation* from the earlier film?

Anger: Most of it, yes. For *Invocation* I performed a Crowley ceremony, "The Equinox of the Gods," to commemorate the autumn equinox, at the Straight Theater in the Haight-Ashbury, in 1967. I had someone film it for me, since I was involved in the ritual. I can't remember who it was.

MacDonald: It was Ben Van Meter, I believe.

Anger: It was the only time I worked with him. In the end, *Invocation of My Demon Brother* was something like a first rough sketch for *Lucifer*. Then when I moved to London, I showed that eleven-minute piece to Mick Jagger, and he volunteered to do an improvisation on his Moog synthesizer for the track, which is rhythmic but very disjunctive and dissonant—which is what I wanted. And I recast and re-formed the *Lucifer* project.

MacDonald: When you made *Invocation of My Demon Brother,* was part of the motivation a desire to express your anger at Beausoleil? Were you sending in your "spiritual marines" out of frustration with what had happened to the *Lucifer Rising* project?

Anger: I did have a lot of frustration and rage from working with Bobby. I cut images of soldiers jumping out of a helicopter, which were from a newsreel of Vietnam, into the salvaged footage and my performance of the ritual. I've always considered *Invocation* my War Film; it reflects the feelings of the war—not the actual events but the kind of things that it had unleashed.

MacDonald: Who was the albino boy?

Anger: I met him in the Haight-Ashbury; I met several of the characters who would have been in the first version of *Lucifer Rising* in the Haight-Ashbury, including Bobby: he was the guitarist of an acid rock group called Love, and then he founded his own group called the Magic Powerhouse of Oz; the name is typical of that period—purple prose.

MacDonald: Was there more to choosing to use this albino boy than just his amazing looks?

Anger: Well, it *was* his looks and the fact that he was a light-sensitive person. Albinos have very sensitive eyes. Usually when they're outdoors they wear dark glasses. If you put a bright light on them, it doesn't actually harm them, but their eyes will go into a reflexive spasm, a jerking motion, and I was fascinated by this. I asked him if I could photograph him and if he'd do some gestures with the glass wand, and he said, "Sure." Usually when I meet people, I don't take up much of their time. I don't disrupt their lives. To me this young man was sort of a supernatural entity, and that's why I used him.

MacDonald: I need some help with *Lucifer Rising*. There are dimensions of the film that seem clear to me. The volcano spewing up lava from underground at the beginning of the film is a basic metaphor for thinking about your work: underneath the conventional social surface of things, there are all these other worlds, and art is a means of bringing these worlds to the surface, at least for a limited time. But a number of the mythological figures in the film and even some of the places in the film are mysterious to me. For example, while the Egyptian spaces are very recognizable, there's also the sequence with the two giant natural stone pillars with the bridge across . . .

Anger: Those sandstone pillars are a freak of nature standing in the forest near Externsteine, Germany. It's a beautiful place. The nearest big city is Hannover, an hour or so train ride away. The pillars are considered to be as old as Stonehenge, and of that same Celtic culture. And like Stonehenge they were basically used as a solar temple. The steps leading up to the small temple on top of the one pillar were carved, and the temple itself was carved out of the rock on top. The bridge between the pillars was restored by the Nazis. During their very peculiar pagan revival the Nazis used the site as part of their ceremonies for the Hitler Jugend. That's where the Hitler Youth were presented with their daggers when they were twelve years old.

But it was a solar temple, which is why *I* used it. In the temple room on the top of the one stone pillar there's a round window that's cut into the wall; and on the summer solstice, the longest day and shortest night of the year—and only on that day—the sun comes through that window and illuminates the altar. All we know about that Celtic culture, since they didn't leave any writings, is that they knew about astronomy and they worshiped the sun and natural cycles.

MacDonald: And so, the Celtic gods are communicating with the Egyptian gods.

Anger: Yes, all of them are tied together. I took the main figures in my cast to Luxor, where the opening scene and some other scenes were filmed. Miriam Gibril played Isis, the Egyptian goddess of nature who rises from a fallen granite monolith at the beginning of the film. Donald Cammell—the director of *Performance* [1970] and a friend of mine—played Osiris, the lord of death. In Egyptian mythology Isis and Osiris are a couple, which creates a symmetry: life and death.

Lucifer Rising was sort of a psychodrama because most of the people I cast had something in their personal makeup that was reflected in the roles they were playing. Donald Cammell was always half in love with death, and he eventually shot himself. You can see this tendency in *Performance* (the bullet going into the brain is the last image of *Performance*), and you can see it in his other films, too. I chose Marianne Faithfull to be Lilith. In my mind, Lilith is a complement to Lucifer: she's a female demon, the spirit of discontent—and Lucifer is the original rebel. But *I'm* the one who put them together; you can't find this combination in any mythology. I dressed Lilith all in gray, and Marianne used gray makeup, all of which fits with traditional interpretations of Lilith.

MacDonald: How close was the shape of the final *Lucifer Rising* to the conception that you were working with originally?

Anger: The final version covers the main bases that I'd established. It was always conceived as dreamlike, episodic, and without a narrative line that you could follow in a conventional way.

Originally I did think I would include fragments of dialogue, and as a matter of fact, several people do speak in the film; you see them talking. The dialogue was short and simple. There's a scene where Marianne Faithfull as Lilith repeats, over and over, the word "memory," and anyone who can read lips can see that that's what she's saying. And I had Sir Francis Rose, who played Chaos, saying, "Haven't I seen you somewhere before?" Again, you can read his lips. But when I was finally putting the film together, since Bobby Beausoleil had volunteered to do the music, I decided to use just music and drop the dialogue—but to leave the visuals of the dialogue as a kind of sketchy and mysterious dimension of the film.

Sir Francis is no longer with us. He was a famous character: "mad, bad, and dangerous to know." A friend of Gertrude Stein's. She wrote "A rose is a rose is a rose" for him. He did the illustrations for her books of poems. He was a sketch artist and an oil painter, but also completely mad; and as he got older, he became crazier and crazier. I'm afraid that appearing in my film got him off on a tangent, and he decided he was the devil—soon after the filming he did a shocking crime in Wales: he threw bricks through the stained-glass windows of a church. He was arrested, but because he was a sir, he was let off. I hate to think that I had any indirect responsibility for triggering his madness.

The Lucifer jacket with the letters on the back was made for me by Jann Haworth, the wife of Peter Blake, who was an artist working in cloth. She was with the Fraser Gallery in London. She had made several large dolls of mythological figures, one of which was Lucifer. I saw the Lucifer doll on exhibit, which is the reason I approached her.

MacDonald: It's a great effect near the end with the cone of light revealing the magic circle. As a film person, it's hard for me not to see it as an evocation of the projector beam.

Anger: It's actually a triangle. *Lucifer* is constructed using simple geometric shapes: the circle and the triangle. The triangle is reflected in the Pyramids and in that beam; and there are many circles in the film.

MacDonald: Did you make contact with Bobby Beausoleil, once he was in prison? How did you bring him back into the project?

Anger: Once he was in prison, we exchanged letters. His being in prison was *his* karma. He had stolen my van, and as he was driving from San Francisco toward LA, it broke down in front of the ranch where the Manson group was living, and the girls came out and asked him to move in with them, and that's how he got mixed up with Charlie—a kind of devilish plotting goes into all this. I'm sorry about how it worked out, but he made his own decisions. He was a smart kid, too. But he was taking a lot of acid and just got off on a tangent.

Once he was in prison, we exchanged letters, and then I went to visit him—just a couple of times because I don't like hearing those metal doors slam behind me. Actually, it was easier to be friends with Bobby once he was inside.

Through Bobby I became friends with the chief psychiatrist at the California prison system—Dr. Minerva Bertholt—and Minerva had taken a liking to Bobby, who had expressed an interest in continuing with his music. She arranged for him to do that. He made his own guitar in prison; he knew how to carve it and how to string it—he had made several musical instruments. When he heard I was finishing *Lucifer,* he volunteered to do the music. Through Minerva we were able to record the track in prison. I furnished Bobby with timing sheets, and a workprint that he was able to see on the projector they had there, and I donated a tape recorder, quite a good one, a Nagra, to the prison—because you can't take things in and out. I guess they still have it. The other musicians you hear on the track were in mostly for drug offenses. Several of them had been involved in well-known music groups in San Francisco; they were professional musicians who had made a mistake and ended up behind bars. Bobby, of course, had a murder conviction, so he's still in, but I think some of the others are out now.

MacDonald: I know you have several projects under way. You sent me a video of a very rough version of a film about the Hitler Youth, called *Ich Will*.

Anger: Ich Will is a work in progress. It's already quite changed from what you saw. I've dropped a lot of the marching. I'm trying to get access to the original prints of the Hitler Youth films, some of which are with the Imperial War Museum in London. They're on 35mm. The museum has said that it would be okay for me to do something with that material, but it's the cost that's stopping me.

I'm interested in the kind of bonding that was going on in the Hitler Jugend, and the way the Nazis exploited that bonding by creating rituals out of the boys being presented with their daggers and similar ceremonies. This kind of thing also exists in the Boy Scouts and in many groupings in many different cultures—but Hitler and the Nazis gave it its most sinister twist. The propaganda films that were made about the Nazi Youth are fascinating source material to work from.

MacDonald: The most recent finished film of yours that I've seen is *The Man We Want to Hang* [2002], the film about the show of Aleister Crowley's drawings and paintings. It's not your first film about Crowley.

Anger: That's true: *Thelema Abbey* [1955] was about his villa in Cefalù, Sicily, which he called his "abbey." He had painted murals on the walls of his bedroom and called it *Le chambre de cauchmars,* the Room of Nightmares. I went there and restored the murals, which had been whitewashed after he was kicked out of Sicily by Mussolini's police in the early twenties. The murals were considered obscene, and they *were* deliberately obscene in some cases, like the one he called *The Scarlet Woman Being Mounted by a Goat.* And there were an images of Pan with an erect phallus. It was typical of Crowley to do things like that. I made a documentary on the abbey, which I didn't own because it was paid for by this magazine called *Picture Post.* In the fifties in England, *Picture Post* had a television program, and they paid me to make the film. It was a documentary, a straightforward explanation of what I was doing there. While I was in Cefalù, Dr. Kinsey came to visit me. He knew about Crowley and had already collected his books, and he wanted to see what these erotic murals were.

It was quite an interesting documentary, but by the time I got to England, it had disappeared; the company had gone out of existence. I said, "Well, what did you do with all the television films that were shown on this series?" They said, "We don't know; they were probably thrown out." Nobody thought to save anything.

The Man We Want to Hang is a documentation of an exhibit of Crowley's drawings and paintings, shown at the October Gallery in 1995 in London. I own some of the drawings you see; a large collection of Crowley's work was bought by Jimmy Page of Led Zeppelin, and other paintings and drawings came from Crowley collectors, some as far away as Australia. It was a unique chance to have a good selection of Crowley's work all together because this kind of show had never been done before. I had permission to film it, and I filmed in the gallery. I was showing the work as if you were wandering through the gallery.

MacDonald: How did you decide on the title?

Anger: The title of the show, and of the film, is taken from a headline in the notorious British tabloid *Sunday Express,* which was published in the 1920s by Lord Beaverbrook. Beaverbrook was an enemy of Crowley, and whenever he needed a sensational story, he'd do one about Crowley being a cannibal or something equally absurd. When Crowley was in Cefalù and a student from Oxford died there, from typhoid, the *Sunday Express* story had it that the student was sacrificed. The headline of the editorial in the *Sunday Express,* denouncing Crowley as the wickedest man in the world, was "The Man We Want to Hang." Crowley was amused by it.

My title is an obvious pun: "The Man We Want to Hang" is about hanging pictures: everything in the film is a picture. My film is a "Pictures at an Exhibition."

MacDonald: I assume what drew you to Crowley was that his religion allowed for a spirituality that was nonexclusionary in terms of gods and spirits.

Anger: Basically Crowley created a pagan revival. He blew the dust off figures like Osiris and Isis and Horus, in the Egyptian pantheon. Horus is the solar god with the hawk head that Crowley identified as his personal god. He called the age that we're in right now "The Age of Horus," which replaces "The Age of Osiris," which represented the Christian age. He believed that we go through different cycles, two thousand years each.

I want to tell you about my newest project, about a different sort of art collection. The film will be called *Mouse Heaven.* Last year I applied for a grant from Media Arts, one of the Rockefeller cultural activities, to do a film about an extraordinary collection of Disney toys owned by Eunice and Mel Birnkrant. Their home is like a private museum. In fact, they don't want me to tell exactly where they live because they're afraid the place will be broken into. A few days ago I learned that I got the grant, thirty-five thousand dollars.

Mouse Heaven will have the theme of the iconic Mickey Mouse. It'll be a twenty-minute film. I have to decide whether I'm going to do it on film—and, if so, in 35mm or 16mm—or in digital. Everything seems to be pointing toward digital. You've got to pick up all of the detail of these toys, so I want a medium that will give me absolute razor-sharp clarity.

I want to show *Mouse Heaven* at film festivals, and I've noticed that festivals usually have a hard time with 16mm. When I had a show in Argentina at the Mar del Plata Film Festival last year, they seemed to have only one old classroom 16mm Bell & Howell projector—in all of Argentina! I said, "Is this *all* you've got?!" And they only had a five-hundred-watt bulb. I told them, "It should be twice as bright." But I just had to put up with it; they still seemed to like my films, even dimly projected.

It's too bad about 16mm, but most amateurs who used to have 16mm projectors and cameras to film the baby and so forth have moved on to video. They don't realize that twenty years from now, when they want to look at what they've shot, all they'll have is snow. The magnetic image is fugitive, and it will disappear more quickly than film.

MacDonald: Why Mickey Mouse?

Anger: Well, I'm very fond of Mickey Mouse. He meant a lot to me as a child. I had a Mickey Mouse stuffed doll, and wind-up toys, and got my parents to take me to the movies whenever a Disney Silly Symphony came out. I think Mickey Mouse is one of the most important icons of American pop culture, though the real Mickey has been lost. He was sentimentalized from *Fantasia* [1940] on. The early Mickey Mouse had pie eyes; and they changed the eyes. Basically the Disney people have lost him as a character. He's become the chairman of the board.

MacDonald: He was pretty outrageous at the beginning.

Anger: He was a mischievous little demon—that's why I liked him.

I've talked to a lawyer, and since I'm filming a collection of *antique toys,* I can call it *Mouse Heaven* and have the real Mickey Mouse as my star and main character without a problem. The collection includes everything from six-inch bisque figures to wind-up toys made of tin, made in the thirties in Germany, before Hitler banned Mickey Mouse as a decadent rat. From 1928 to 1933, the Germans were making wonderful tin toys that you could wind up: Mickey plays drums or he marches around. Mel Birnkrant has these toys, and they still work. Of course, he doesn't let anybody touch them, because they're very fragile. He'll wind them up, and I'll film them. I have some tin toys in *Scorpio Rising,* if you remember; this has been an ongoing interest.

MacDonald: The video of *The Mighty Civic* [1992], Peter Wells and Stewart Main's documentary about the Civic Theater in Aukland, New Zealand, has a "Kenneth Anger Presents" on it. What's your connection to that project. It's a very sweet film.

Anger: Isn't it?

I met Peter and Stewart when I was invited to a film festival in Sidney; they showed me the film, and I liked it and asked if I could buy the video rights for America. They agreed, and I paid them a thousand dollars. It's the *only* time I've ever done that.

MacDonald: The style of their film is reminiscent of your work.

Anger: I felt an affinity for it, and they had apparently seen something of mine—I don't know what. They've since made a feature, a costume drama [*Desperate Remedies,* 1993].

I still have a few copies of *The Mighty Civic,* and I'm willing to sell those that I have left, but I don't really want to pursue it further. [Canyon Cinema—see filmography—distributes *The Mighty Civic* in VHS.] I sold copies of the film to members of the Theater Historical Society, an American organization interested in preserving old theaters. Old theaters are one of my hobbies. I'm a member of the Theater Historical Society. We go on what we call "a conclave" each summer in some region and look at surviving old theaters and, when we can, try to figure out ways to save them.

Wind-up toy motorcyclists in Kenneth Anger's *Scorpio Rising* (1963). Courtesy David. E. James.

It's hard to believe that at one point in the seventies there was actually a plan afoot to close Radio City Music Hall and convert it into offices. And we had a petition-signing campaign to save it. In LA some of those grand movie palaces are left, like the Pantages, which was the first art deco theater in LA; it opened in 1930. The Million Dollar is still there on Broadway, and the Los Angeles can be rented to filmmakers; it's been used in quite a few films. And the United Artists has been turned into an Evangelical church, but they didn't paint out the murals, so on one side, instead of the Virgin Mary, they have Mary Pickford. It's nice that they kept the original decor.

At one time I contemplated doing a poetic documentary about old theaters; I had my title: "Temples of Babylon." And I found some great ones. It still could be done, but it's exceedingly difficult to light and photograph those huge spaces. Of course, now with the much faster emulsions and with video and digital you can practically film in the dark.

MacDonald: I might be the last generation to have that big-theater experience, with the organ and sometimes an orchestra, and thousands of people in the theater with you.

Anger: I loved it. I had some great big-theater experiences when I was a kid and appreciated them for what they were. It was like going to a cathedral.

MacDonald: How much experimental film do you see these days?

Anger: Not very much. I don't have much access to it. I do like the fact that living in LA offers the happy option of going to revivals; they've just done a series at the Egyptian on all of the Orson Welles material, including his own unfinished projects and an early film that was incorporated into a stage production. Those retrospectives are valuable, and there are very few places in America where you can see them.

MacDonald: Did you know Brakhage?

Anger: Yes. Stan was quite a good friend of mine. And I admired him for what he accomplished. We knew each other over a twenty-five-year period. He had a collection of prints of my films, including some earlier versions of things, and after he died, his wife wondered what to do with them, and I said, "I'll take them back if you don't know what to do with them." So she sent me a package of prints. I miss Stan.

MacDonald: Every once in a while I hear a rumor that volume 3 of *Hollywood Babylon* is under way . . .

Anger: It's been roughed in, but the recent crop of Hollywood people are kind of a blank to me. I mean I have to *like* the people I write about, even though I can also *hate* them; I have to be emotionally involved at least on some level. The current "stars" just draw a blank, and frankly a lot of them *are* a blank. Anyway, I don't know whether I'll do another book or not.

MacDonald: Have those books been a substantial source of income for you?

Anger: For quite a while. They've been translated into Japanese, German, Italian, and French, and so I still get royalties from those translations. I did the books so I would have an income, and they turned out to provide more of an income than my films ever have. Even though my films are rented quite consistently, I still don't get enough money from them to live on or to make new films.

I've been lucky to have had a sponsor in my life, my friend Sir Paul Getty, who is recently deceased. I was going to do a film on his private cricket ground. The film was to be called *Arrangement in White on Green,* a title taken from Whistler. Sir Paul had approved the project. His cricket ground is the most beautiful in England; it's on the estate of his country house near Oxford. The film would have been forty-five minutes long, and the music was to be Symphony no. 3 by Sir Edward Elgar. I had the great good fortune of having Jack Cardiff agree to be my cameraman (he was the cameraman for Michael Powell's masterpieces, *The Red Shoes* [1948] and *Black Narcissis* [1947], and a director in his own right). Jack is in his late eighties, but still very spry and perfectly lucid, and he agreed to work with me. The whole project was planned very carefully, but Sir Paul died, and since I was doing it *for* him—he was a great cricket fan and had introduced the game to me. I've put the project on hold.

I'm fascinated with cricket because of its Celtic roots and the little mysterious things in the game that go back to pagan rituals. The "white" in the title is the white uniforms, and the green is the grass. Sir Paul had his own cricket team, "Getty's XI," and I recently got an invitation for this season. I have to go to London in September for a show of frame enlargements from *Invocation of My Demon Brother*—at the Modern Art Gallery in London—and I may talk to Sir Paul's widow, Victoria Getty, and see what she feels about my filming some of the matches. Channel 4 has also expressed some interest in the project.

Arrangement in White on Green will probably become another addition to what I call my "graveyard" of films I *wish* I could have made. I'm not a good hustler; I'm not talented at rounding up financing. If I had more of the ruthless fighter in my nature, I suppose I would have gone after these things a little harder—but that's not my character. As I've said, I'm not obsessed with these unrealized projects; if I were, I'd be adding my name to David Frazier's suicide book! Some things work out; some don't. On several occasions I had hopes of making a feature-length film, but I don't have a name that is "bankable": I'm known as an avant-garde artist, which is something quite different—something I'm content to be.

Tony Conrad

On the Sixties

Despite the fact that his *first* film, *The Flicker* (1966), was a major contribution to critical cinema—it remains the most impressive and engaging of all flicker films—Conrad has not been accorded the attention his work in film deserves. In part, this may be a function of the fact that, like Bruce Conner, Conrad has not defined himself solely, or even primarily, as a filmmaker. He has been at least as productive and accomplished in other areas of the arts as he has been in film. Conrad's contributions to American minimalist music, during the 1960s in collaboration with La Monte Young and the Theater of Eternal Music (Young and Marian Zazeela on vocals, Conrad on violin, John Cale on viola, plus hand-drummer Angus MacLise and, at times, Terry Riley on saxophone or singing and Terry Jennings on saxophone) and on his own in such works as *Four Violins* (1964) and, with the German avant-garde group Faust, *Outside the Dream Syndicate* (1972), are as impressive as his film work. In fact (and this is also true of Bruce Conner's drawing and assemblage work in relation to his filmmaking), Conrad's music is an excellent primer for understanding *The Flicker*—and vice versa. While Conrad has continued to perform his music, and in recent years to record it (see the catalogue for Table of the Elements—www.tableoftheelements.com—for a listing of Conrad music available on CD), his investigation of flicker in *The Flicker*—and in *Straight and Narrow* (1970), *Coming Attractions* (1970, co-made with Beverly Grant Conrad), and *Four Square* (1971)—was only the beginning of an exploration of moving-image media that, during the past thirty-five years, has led Conrad into a wide range of conceptual and process-oriented film, video, and digital work, as well as into prolific video production for cable television.

> **WARNING.** The producer, distributor, & exhibitors waive all liability for physical or mental injury possibly caused by the motion picture "The Flicker." Since this film may induce epileptic seizures or produce mild symptoms of shock treatment in certain persons, you are cautioned to remain in the theater only at your own risk. A physician should be in attendance.

The warning to viewers at the beginning of Tony Conrad's *The Flicker* (1966). Courtesy Anthology Film Archives.

These days, *The Flicker* tends to be one of those films that people know about but have never attended. There are a number of reasons for this. First, in the most direct way, Conrad's film confronts the tendency of many contemporary filmgoers to avoid truly challenging cinema. The first image of *The Flicker* is the following text: "WARNING. The producer, distributor, & exhibitors waive all liability for physical or mental injury possibly caused by the motion picture 'The Flicker.' Since this film may induce epileptic seizures or produce mild symptoms of shock treatment in certain persons, you are cautioned to remain in the theater only your own risk. A physician should be in attendance." In our litigation-happy society, few programmers would be willing to take the chance of presenting *The Flicker,* even though, to my knowledge, no one has ever been injured by viewing the film. Conrad's warning to potential viewers foregrounds the fact that *The Flicker* is truly a film *experience;* it is a visceral, engaging, demanding intervention into the smooth continuities of conventional moviegoing.

Awareness of *The Flicker* has also suffered from the recent tendency of many of those who teach film to avoid using 16mm projection: *The Flicker* can only be seen in 16mm, and in fact *should* be seen as a 16mm film projection accompanied by a reel-to-reel stereo tape, feeding through two speakers placed on opposite sides of the theater. Conrad has explored, but has not yet found, a way of transferring the film to an electronic medium. In any case, as fully as any film, *The Flicker* is *about* the experience of adventuring with others into a movie theater and joining with them in an extended motion picture experience (though only twenty-five minutes long, *The Flicker* has at least feature-length impact). The central irony of *The Flicker*, now that it is so rarely shown, is that few films are as much fun to experience or as interesting to think about, and few films provide as clear a demonstration of how fully a critical filmmaker, working with virtually no equipment and no money, can transform the screening space.

My interview with Conrad focuses on one small portion of his career, his involvement with film during the decade of the 1960s when he was a wunderkind musician living in New York City, working, first, with Jack Smith and his flaming creatures on the production and presentation of *Scotch Tape* (various versions 1959–62), *Flaming Creatures* (1963), and *Normal Love* (1963–64), and subsequently, on his own, exploring the idea and potential of cinematic flicker. We recorded our conversation at Conrad's home in Buffalo, New York (where Conrad is on the faculty of the Department of Media Study at the State University of New York at Buffalo), and by phone, during July 2004. The interview was refined by e-mail.

MacDonald: When you arrived on the filmmaking scene in the sixties, you were unusual in that you didn't come from film and didn't really stay in film. You came from music (and to some degree from mathematics and the study of computers).

Conrad: Well, it's true that I wasn't coming to film *from* film, but you have to understand, so far as I knew at that time, there *wasn't* any film to come from. When I was in college, at Harvard, there were no film courses. A few shows of independent film did cross my consciousness, but only vaguely.

Of course, as a kid in the forties, I'd gone to movies compulsively. There wasn't any television. At one point, my little brothers, who were two and a half and six years younger than me, went to a neighbor's house to see *Howdy Doody*, and they told me about TV—but at that point I wasn't into what the little kids were doing. And a little before that, I remember that my mother, who was very alert and interested in all kinds of things, took me down to the Treasury Department, where the Patent Office was (we lived in Virginia, just outside Washington, D.C.), to see the newly promulgated color television system that was being demonstrated for the public. This was a system that was never really implemented, as I understand it, and it was only a little tiny screen—but I remember being struck by it as a marvel of the moment.

But marvel or not, TV didn't mean much to me. In those days going to the movies was *it.* On the other hand, when I got to my adolescent years, Hopalong Cassidy and the other westerns that had been my movie fare earlier on didn't have much connection with the intellectual and emotional explorations that had become important to me or with the exciting challenges of science and mathematics, and subsequently of music and art.

As a young music enthusiast, musician, and fledgling composer, I began to follow a strand of thinking that led me to feel that *changing my mind* and controlling my reactions and emotions was very exciting. I learned a lot, very quickly, from a concert that I went to when I was at Harvard, given by John Cage, who had brought his piano-playing friend, David Tudor, with him. Cage talked about how he composed music by randomly—*randomly!*—picking the notes, instead of selecting the tunes or the chords. What he said flowed together with my finding that I could enjoy things that I had not previously liked, by *focusing* on them and by consciously altering my perspective on them.

When I moved to New York, I found out about Fluxus and the artists around that community, and this helped me continue exploring my own reactions.

MacDonald: What took you to New York?

Conrad: Well, I had met a number of composers and artists and knew there was a scene in New York, and I wanted to find out what was happening and to test the waters, to be *challenged,* to see what kind of challenges there *were:* to *change my mind* some more. My interest was especially focused on the more radical aspects of the Fluxus group. I had become close friends with Henry Flynt, who was involved with the idea that culture *as a whole*—not just music or poetry or art, or whatever—was defective and needed to be tossed out. *[Laughter.]* We went out and picketed against the museums and the cultural icons of the day.

My introduction to the film scene was pretty much accidental. I met Jack Smith through Marian Zazeela, who was La Monte Young's girlfriend. At first I thought very little of what Jack was doing because it seemed to be flowing in the most ordinary direction of human artistic enterprise; it seemed romantic; it seemed like Jack was interested in sexuality and in a certain retro way of constructing images, in making things pretty—everything about what he was doing seemed completely against the grain of my interests. But, on another level, *that very thing* paradoxically made Jack's work quite challenging and interesting to me, once I discovered that I actually *liked* the results.

As I became more exposed to Jack, I found that there was a kind of commitment and investment in his work, and in the scene within which he produced it, that was inviting and challenging at the same time. Of course, the things that were challenging to me in *Jack's* work were *completely* different from the kinds of aesthetic challenges that I had experienced earlier. There were, for example, the *social* aspects of this work: the fact that Jack and the people who surrounded him were, from my perspective, from some other *planet.*

At the time, a lot of us were exploring drugs, and I knew already that there were ways to have challenging experiences, other than by exploring ideas or new music. Smoking pot was particularly interesting to me at that time—partly, I think, because I hadn't grown up smoking pot. For me the experience of smoking pot was a surprise. The kind of high that comes from marijuana is not just a matter of being energized or slowed down; it's a way of entering a very different state of mind, a different condition of being, *and* of being aware of this *as* a different way of being. Ordinarily people don't develop a perspective on their own internal states. If you felt sad because something bad happened to you, for example, it would be unusual that you would think, "Oh, how interesting that I'm feeling *sad!*" And you don't ordinarily think to yourself, "I'd like to learn how to become sad under my own control, and maybe I can even learn how quickly I can become first sad and then happy." But coming out of my background with Cage, I was interested in exactly this kind of experience and in understanding experience in these terms.

Drugs were often part of my explorations in those days. We all explored different drugs. I myself was very vigilant and cautious; I usually did some kind of book research in order to determine to the best of my knowledge that a particular drug would not be deadly or deleterious in some profound way. For example, I smoked opium but was careful not to use it except in isolated instances. And I found that the depression that followed taking amphetamine was a *remarkably* destructive and out-of-control experience—interesting but also disturbing. I learned that there were spaces you could enter where you *lost* control of the emotional set, and I pulled back from those.

MacDonald: Let's go back to Smith.

Conrad: In saying what I've said about drugs, I don't mean to suggest that Jack's work was coming out of a drug culture. I mean only that the experience of Jack's work was, like the various drug experiences, another *way of being,* and offered a number of challenges.

MacDonald: Were particular Smith pieces especially important for you?

Conrad: Well, actually it was *Scotch Tape* that took me around the bend. But to make clear why this was so, I need to say more about my coming to understand Jack's work.

There were several elements of his scene that captivated my interest and attention. One was the sexual explicitness of the group that he was involved with and their fascination with cross-dressing and with sexuality in general.

This was fascinating to me, just because I didn't know anything about it. I was completely naive at the time. I, who had somehow eluded the societal tar pit of getting the job, getting the girl, getting married, getting the baby, getting the promotion, getting the car, getting the house, getting the next baby, and so forth—basically by having gone away to college and studying instead of fucking—was fascinated to find that there were people who had found alternative life patterns *not* through having gone to college, *not* through intellectually hypothesizing their own experiential framework, but through self-definition driven by sexual longings of an unorthodox type. These longings had led them into an alternative space that I *loved;* I *loved* these people, even though I shared very little of their experience.

We found ourselves together, *way* off from where everybody else seemed to be in America at the end of the 1950s. This was in 1962, remember, before there were hippies, before even the Beatles. The Vietnam War hadn't started. What was on the radio was DeeDee Sharp and "Do the Bird" and Paul Anka; we're not talking about "the sixties" in any normal sense of the word. We're still in the fifties, and while everyone else is out there in the little brick house with the baby and the wife and the job, *I* find myself surrounded by people who are interested in things like sucking cocks in a parking lot *[laughter]*—very weird.

Another thing that fascinated me was the fact that Jack personally was such a self-constructed artwork, and so powerful that he exerted the kind of influence that you ordinarily have when you enter a different culture. If you go to Paris—and this was more true then than it is now—you discover that the people in Paris talk differently, they do different things, they eat different food, they look at different things. Jack Smith was *his own country:* he spoke differently; he looked at different things; he liked different things. And everything he did was part of a self-constructed universe built around key features that were largely drawn from his own personal nostalgia. Often it was difficult to tell where these things came from, and it became fascinating to me to try to trace their lineage. As I got to know Jack better, I learned that some of his particular speech af-fec-ta-ti-ons had come from his mentor, Jerry Sims; I learned that some of the tunes that he hummed had come from his mother; I learned that some of his fixations on movie images had come from his boyhood moviegoing experiences.

I guess the way I would describe the problem that Jack Smith and his movies posed for me was: Why would I find myself immediately falling into liking this work and being fascinated with this artist when I was really interested in being *completely under the control of my own aesthetic response? My* program was to find things I *didn't* like and then try to like them. The things that I didn't like included, for example, rock and roll music, so I practiced liking rock and roll music until—somewhat to the astonishment of my friend John Cale—I really *did* like DeeDee Sharp, even went to see DeeDee Sharp in person at the Brooklyn Fox Theater, and had a simply ecstatic experience there. John, of course, was the one who went on to systematically destroy the cultural distance between pop and high-art musical culture . . . but back to Jack. It was the other side of this process of psychic exploration to realize that I *did* like something I *shouldn't* like—that *my liking* was not entirely under my control.

There was a peak moment—an epiphany—the product of a request that Jack made to me. He had a five-minute-long movie that he had shot earlier, his only film at the time—*Scotch Tape*. When I first learned about *Scotch Tape*, I thought to myself, "Phui, what could this pathetic artist possibly do to interest me in his 'movie'?" Jack had been asked to show *Scotch Tape* at the Charles Theater, and he had a 78 rpm record that he wanted to play with the movie, a record that was too short. Knowing that I was a music person, Jack asked me what he could do, and I said—in a voice of authority and presumption, to this fellow who was several years older than me—"Well, it's very simple, Jack, you transfer the record to tape and then make a second copy of the tape and splice the two together." Of course, a more logical solution would have been for Jack to simply play the phonograph record twice; he played his records with his films endlessly up to the end of his life. But I proposed this other solution, and Jack asked if I could actually *do* what I proposed, and I took the bait.

Then I was *so* disheartened by his choice of music, which was nothing very sophisticated at all: Eddy Duchin, the piano player, playing a rumba or a samba. I recorded the disk and cut the tape together and then, when it came time to go to the theater, lugged the tape recorder, actually Marian Zazeela's old tape recorder, which weighed fifty pounds, to the theater.

The tape recorder was placed at the front of the theater under the screen, and when the movie began, I turned on the tape—*and the experience was stunning!* It was *incredible!* And I realized that I needed to understand what had happened to convert such pedestrian sound into something completely magical in the context of the image, *and* what was going on with the *picture* that in the context of that sound it should have become so lambent and affecting.

Later when Jack said that he had been getting ready to make a big movie and was ready to move ahead, I said, "Oh, well, I'd be happy to help if I can." I went along and helped to get the set for *Flaming Creatures* together and participated in a couple of the shooting sessions, and then later, at Jack's direction, made the sound for the film—which led me again into this *place* where picture and sound were conjoined.

One of the reasons that I worked on the *Flaming Creatures* sound track was that Jack had already put me in the titles with a credit for doing the sound. When I asked him about this, he said he had done that because I had made the sound for *Scotch Tape:* I was getting the credit for the sound *I had already done,* in the *new* film. This happened again with *Normal Love* (various versions, 1963–64): I got my name put into the credits for *Normal Love,* even though I hadn't made the sound track for it yet, because I had done the sound for *Flaming Creatures.* In the end the *Normal Love* project was abandoned.

MacDonald: You said you were working under Jack's direction. I assume you also made contributions of your own. Can you talk a little about those?

Conrad: Well, I was alert enough to know that Jack and I were *so* different that I couldn't possibly simulate what he would want; I knew I didn't have the sensibility necessary to even guess what would "work" in his aesthetic language. But Jack *did* know what he had in mind—which, by the way, doesn't seem to have been obvious to *anybody* at the time. In the commentary about Jack that's been published in recent years, people have remarked that while their experience of working with Jack was that he seemed to fumble with everything and was visibly inept in every technological sense, they would subsequently realize that everything he had done had been planned out ahead of time and that in fact Jack knew *exactly* what he was doing at every moment.

So Jack had a pretty darn good idea of what he wanted for *Flaming Creatures.* For example, I remember him saying, "Okay, the sound track's gotta start with this music from *Ali Baba and the Forty Thieves* [1943, directed by Arthur Lubin]." Well, when he says this, my heart sinks because *I* think, "Here's an opportunity to put some real *music* in here and instead, we're going to use this hopelessly derivative, retro music from a really crappy film?!" Well, of course, it turns out that that music is just *wonderful* there.

The questions that tended to arise that I *could* deal with were more technical, questions about recording, like how to record kissing, what kind of sounds to use for the earthquake, and then how to mix things together. I had no equipment, and so for the party sequence at the end of the film, which is a tumultuous mix of different records that were for the most part selected by Jack (I picked one track on one record, the *wrong* track according to Jack's taste, but the mix came out okay nevertheless). That "mix" was made by taking the speaker wires from a whole bunch of phonographs and just twisting them together and running that into the tape recorder. *[Laughter.]* Very, very primitive; we just went for it with what we had.

In the earthquake sequence I decided to use a loop feedback technique that I had developed while I was in college and had used in the only composition that I ever had performed—before turning against musical composition altogether (recently I've pulled back from that symbolic radicalism). I had made "Three Loops for Performers and Tape Recorders" [1961], with the loop delay technique later exploited by Terry Riley in his music

Mock gang-rape scene in Jack Smith's *Flaming Creatures* (1963), for which Tony Conrad did the sound. Courtesy Anthology Film Archives.

and by Steve Reich in his earliest sound pieces; it subsequently, inevitably, gave rise to phasing and other rhythmic forms of minimal music. I decided that in the earthquake sequence I wanted to use that loop feedback mechanism to achieve a density of sound. We had a couple of shrieking sessions and then looped those into a whole dense fabric of bell ringing and laughing and hysteria and noise.

The only *musical* suggestion that I made that carried over into the sound was to use the Bartók unaccompanied violin sonata [*Solo Violin Sonata, Sz117 (1944)*] in the sequence with Judith Malina. I convinced Jack that that would be perfect, and it turned out to be perfectly apropos.

At the earliest screenings of *Flaming Creatures,* I was always present and in charge of the sound, which was running off quarter-inch reel-to-reel tapes. There was a preliminary version of the *Flaming Creatures* sound track, and at a certain point a second version replaced the first and then got wedded to the film. Later on, Jack had a different idea about the film and for a while decided to show it without sound. Jack was notorious for liking to change the sound of a work every time he showed it; he enjoyed working with sound as a direct projection of his own performative personality.

MacDonald: Did you have much to do with Ken Jacobs during that period?

Conrad: No. Jack did introduce me to his friend "Nutty" Jacobs, and I was extremely impressed when I saw *Blonde Cobra* [various versions, 1959–63]. Ken and Flo were very generous in their hospitality, and it was obvious that they had had a really productive relationship with Jack, although they weren't hanging out regularly with Jack at that point. Jack had emerged as a filmmaker to some substantial degree under Nutty's wing. Before he knew Ken, Jack had been a photographer, and in fact still saw himself as a photographer when I first got to know him.

MacDonald: How did your own filmmaking develop?

Conrad: Well, I knew that, as much as I admired it, Jack's scene wasn't an arena I could compete in. I wasn't gay; I wasn't a flaming creature. And I wasn't interested in taking over the turf of the camera. I wasn't even sure how profoundly I wanted to be involved with film. My next-door neighbor, Piero Heliczer, was making films, and I made some sound for him, and Jack had developed a friendship with Ron Rice, and I contributed to Ron's development of sound for *Chumlum* [1964]. I continued to get ideas about the relationship between sound and film.

And then I had a falling-out with Jack.

MacDonald: Over what?

Conrad: Oh, I don't know: probably a girl—after I had gotten involved with Beverly Grant, Jack somehow couldn't be friendly anymore. He found it difficult to be friendly with the guys who were involved with the women he loved. He had been very attached to Marian Zazeela, too, and maybe my involvement with Beverly had resonances with that situation: I was still working with La Monte at that time. In any case, Jack and I had a parting of the ways.

Not long before this falling-out, I had moved into a duplex loft on Grand Street with Jack and Mario Montez in order to form a movie company that Jack had wanted to realize; it was to be called Cinemaroc. I had already had the idea that flickering light might be a fantastically interesting way to work with the magic of film. This idea arose in the context of an event that I happen to have audiotaped.

While I was living on Ludlow Street, from time to time Jack would invite some of the transvestite creatures over for evening dress-up sessions and would mediate fantasy moments that he called "Tangiers fantasies." Of course, these sessions had nothing to do with real Tangiers: each time, *Montezland* was brought to life in some strange version, according to Jack's predisposition at the moment. I would help out by running the phonograph and the tape recorder. I still have tapes of a bunch of these sessions, and because I think they're of great interest, I recently put a number of them together on two CDs [*56 Ludlow Street 1962–1964,* volume 1: *Jack Smith, Les*

Evening Gowns Damnées; volume 2: *Jack Smith, Silent Shadows on Cinemaroc Island,* both available from Table of the Elements]. On one of these pieces, which I call "Mario and the Flickering Jewel," we had used flickering light from an old battered-up lensless projector and discovered that it created an incredibly luminous effect and froze Mario Montez when it was shown onto her. This suggested to me that, used in a special way to create special effects, flickering light might be an arrow in the quiver of Cinemaroc's resources. After the falling-out, I realized that if I were going to do anything with this idea, I would have to do it myself.

As I got to thinking about what frequencies you would have to use in order to get flicker, I remembered that in college I had taken a course in neurophysiology where we talked a lot about flicker. Flickering light affects people in a frequency range which is within the range of cinema, more or less, and since I'd been involved with music and working with harmonic structures and with rhythm, both of which also depend on frequency relationships, it occurred to me that it might be fascinating to develop a whole compositional structure that used flickering light as its medium. As far as I knew, no one had ever done anything like that before. Of course, you could have regular strobe lights or you could simply turn a light on and off, but to actually compose using different frequencies of flicker and to try to relate them in a way that might invoke something like harmonies between the different flickering frequencies—this seemed to me a weird but very interesting challenge, one that held the potential of opening a whole spectrum of experience, much in the way that drugs, and Jack's work, had opened alternative kinds of experience for me.

MacDonald: At what point did you see Peter Kubelka's *Arnulf Rainer* [1960]?

Conrad: After I finished *The Flicker,* it happened that Kubelka came to New York. Jonas [Mekas] introduced us, and I was intrigued that there were other people out there who were working in this area. When I saw *Arnulf Rainer,* I thought, "Oh, well, thank goodness," because it seemed to me immediately that this had *nothing* to do with what *I* was involved with. To other people the films may have seemed similar because both used only black and clear frames, but this didn't seem to be so special at the time, at least to me. Remember, I was also embroiled in Fluxus, and the idea that there would be music with long silences or pictures without images already seemed old hat.

MacDonald: Kubelka seems to have arrived at flicker by thinking about the essences of cinematic language: light and dark, sound and silence. For you flicker was an extension of musical thinking.

Conrad: It *was* an extension of musical thinking, on the one hand; on the other hand, it came out of this experience of the amplification or intensification of the visual response to light that I had already experienced in the flicker session with Jack and Mario. So I had a visual interest, a psychological interest (from my knowing about flicker in relation to perceptual psychology), and an interest related to music. Of course, at that time I knew more about the history of music than I knew about some of these other territories. It's also true that what Kubelka had done in *Arnulf Rainer* had an obvious historical analogue in music, particularly in the Austrian pointillism of Anton Webern.

During the time I was thinking about constructing *The Flicker,* I knew of very little studied information or knowledge that had to do with editing micro-shots together. I did see some films that were edited so that the images simply tumbled onto the retina at an unregisterable velocity . . .

MacDonald: Robert Breer?

Conrad: Perhaps. In any case, no systematization of the micro-shot editing I was seeing was evident to me. It was as though the images were selected randomly, analogous to some kinds of editing that Cage had done with audiotape where he would cut up tapes of radio broadcasts and put the pieces in a barrel, then randomly pull pieces of tape out of the barrel and string them together. I had been fascinated by these possibilities back in the fifties, and in 1959, when I first had access to a tape recorder, I made a tape with four different tones on it, cut it into pieces a sixteenth of an inch long, and spliced them end to end in a random order, to see what would happen. So there were things that I knew about this kind of editing process in audio, but in film it was unclear to me if there *was* anything to be known.

MacDonald: What was the process of physically constructing *The Flicker?*

Conrad: The film began on paper as a diagram. Jonas came to my house one day and brought me several rolls of old negative film—a priceless contribution at that moment!—and he also helped me locate a Bolex, which I borrowed for a few days. I was a rank beginner at that point, but during my time with that borrowed camera, I was able to figure out, with a little guidance, how to load the Bolex with the old film.

The black frames were easy enough; they were made by just covering up the camera lens, but I wasn't too confident about how to expose a frame so that all you would see is projected light. I tried two techniques. One was to take the lens off the camera and expose frames. The other was to shoot a white piece of paper on the wall. Well, it turned out that taking the lens off was a very bad idea; that roll wasted me hours and hours of shooting frame after frame of alternating black and white. But in the end I figured out how to do what I wanted.

I had decided to produce one one-hundred-foot roll of film that would include the forty-seven arrangements of black and white frames that I had in mind. I shot that roll, got it developed, then had the lab make ten prints. I wanted each of the forty-seven variations to be repeated ten times. I cut each of the ten rolls of film apart into forty-seven pieces and then spliced them together in the right order.

I didn't know much about splicing. I'd bought an 8mm splicer for two dollars—the 8mm splicer was fine because 8mm and 16mm essentially have the pins in the same place—and a roll of perforated splicing tape, and I was off to the races. It took a very long time to make these five hundred splices, because in my enthusiasm and inexperience I was almost obsessively careful.

I've always thought of *The Flicker* as a kind of bizarre science fiction movie, as a *space* that you can enter—in the way that you enter the narrative space of a regular Hollywood movie—and go floating off into some weird dimension, and then come back. I constructed the film very carefully so that you're inexorably moved, very deliberately and very systematically, into an experience *completely* out of the ordinary, where perception is dramatically altered. If you look around the theater during *The Flicker,* you find that everything is somehow made strange.

And then, I wanted to move you, relentlessly, back out of that space, back into the normal world. That is, I wanted to exhibit the *power* of the medium by showing that even if you wished to, you couldn't stay in that space, that it was under the control *of the film*—well, under *my* control—and that you had been drawn into and driven by the film, in some very important way. For me the authority of *The Flicker,* its regulative impulse in relation to the audience's experience, was a very crucial element. I wanted people to *lose* themselves *and to understand that they lost themselves* in that world.

MacDonald: For me *The Flicker* has always felt like an adventure film—a little like *King Kong* [1933], which was the formative film of my childhood—in the sense that there's a moment of real fear as the film begins to take you over, when you're not sure whether you're going to be able to handle what's coming. There's a moment where you've got to decide you're going to stay or get out.

As you were planning the film on paper, what was your thinking about organizing the frames?

Conrad: What I wanted to do was to figure out ways of creating the possibility of multiple frequency relationships within the number of frames that I had to work with. Flicker occurs within a range from about six flickers per second, up to about forty. Of course, movies only go to twenty-four frames per second, *barely* enough space to get any harmonic relationships going. Even a slow three flickers per second means that if you've got twenty-four frames per second, you're going to use a mere four frames of black and four frames of white, three times a second. *One* frame of black and one frame of white will give you twelve flickers per second—and that's the fastest you can go! Within these limits I devised a number of different patterns of black

Frame sequence from Tony Conrad's
The Flicker (1966). Courtesy
Anthology Film Archives.

and white frames. In a six-frame sequence, I might have two white frames, then one black, then one white and two more black, or I might make a longer pattern, three white and three black frames, then two white and three black. I just hammered it out; it took a long time.

I did lay down a couple of basic rules for myself. The first rule was to try and balance the black and white frames so that there would be 50 percent black and 50 percent white as often as possible. The experience of the film suggests that *The Flicker* could have been more startling with more black and less white—but there's always next time. *[Laughter.]*

MacDonald: Before you shot the original roll, were you able to do tests and check out each sequence perceptually?

Conrad: No, I had no way to do that. I didn't own a camera. I didn't own a projector. I didn't own *anything*. I had that borrowed camera for only a few days. So I really didn't have any way to actually find out anything ahead of time, though I did have a pretty good idea of what would happen.

Once I had the prints, all I used was the splicer and a piece of lumber with two screws in it. I'd put each little reel from the lab on one side, and on the other side I had a big reel where I wound up all the film. My little splicer was in the middle.

MacDonald: The warning that begins the film is on-screen for a long time, accompanied by this nice old-time music. I've always wondered whether its function is not just to warn epileptics but to create excitement in the audience.

Conrad: Well, a whole mix of thinking went into that warning. I'd contacted the American Epilepsy Association, and the head of the seizure clinic at Columbia Presbyterian Hospital. He told me, "If you put a notice up there, people are going to be having 'seizures' who *aren't* epileptics." His experience was that a lot of the people who came to the clinic for seizure treatments were epileptic wannabes. Well, I didn't think about it that way; I had had a friend—a brilliant African American student at Harvard—who drowned during an epileptic seizure, so I took them very seriously. Of course, this is the reason I had contacted the doctor. In any case, I felt that if the warning were to be for real, then I had to leave time for someone to say, "Oh, well, let's see, actually that's *me* being warned; I'd better leave," and then to explain to his girlfriend or whoever why he was leaving, and still have time to actually get out of the theater.

But, also, I had a sense of timing about the whole film. Remember, in terms of extended-duration art experiences, I probably had had as much experience as anybody in the world at that time—other than the other musicians I was working with. We were doing long-duration music where you had the problem of "nothing happening," a complete novelty at that time. Here was a long-duration *film*. I didn't want people to be in a "Hey, let's get it on!" kind of mood. I wanted them to be compliant, so that the little thing that *was* going to happen would be a surprise, something that they would understand as *going on*—not just passing by, as *Arnulf Rainer* does. In other words, only one thing would be happening, and the audience would notice it, in part because almost *nothing* had been going on before.

I knew from my experiences with long-duration music that once you start the performance, the audience waits to see what's going to happen, and after a couple of minutes, people are thinking, "What *is* this shit?!" and then they get angry or frustrated or whatever, and *then,* after about seven minutes of this, they begin to actually give up or surrender or listen or turn their attention inward; they acquiesce to the situation . . .

MacDonald: Or they leave.

Conrad: Or they leave—fine, if they're going to leave, I want them out of there. I don't want them carping and carrying on through the whole thing. So I wanted *The Flicker* to start off with the warning, followed by the long, slow credits, and then by the opening moment of the film proper, a completely blank section, so that, finally, about seven minutes into the film just a little something would begin to happen.

MacDonald: There's a tease during the credits, isn't there?—a little perceptual trick where you're simultaneously seeing the title credit and the filmmaker credit.

Conrad: That's probably your imagination. I wasn't trying to play any tricks; I was offering minimal stylistic diversion, which is also why I used the Paul Whiteman music, an old-timey sound that's (*perversely*) supposed to create a quiet, complacent mood, so that when the film finally does start, I can let it rip.

MacDonald: It must be afterimage I'm seeing.

What's the sound? Is it some manipulation of the noise sprocket holes make?

Conrad: Not at all. The audio was the product of another line of thinking, very different from what produced the imagery—except for the fact that, like the visuals, the sound was involved with the question of frequency. Since I wanted to explore the spectrum of flicker as an interactive territory for composition, I wanted to have a sound that would inhabit an analogous territory. At the time, I was fascinated by the border between pulsed audio frequencies that are rhythms and pulsed audio frequencies that are pitches. There's this transition point between pitch and rhythm that still fascinates me. One of the earliest things I had done as an audio experiment was to record a metronome and then speed it up into a pitch. For the film I had wanted to develop an unexplored visual spectrum—if I *could;* I'm not sure it ever happened; I'm not even sure it's possible. For the sound track I decided to work in the area between pitch and rhythm at around twenty events per second, and that meant that I had to come up with some kind of gizmo.

At that time I was aware that people were beginning to make electronic musical instruments. I had known about electronic *music* since I first heard Stockhausen's *Gesang der Jünglinge* sometime around 1958, so that wasn't anything new; what was startling was the idea that there would be electronic instruments you could make electronic music with. These instruments were designed by engineers presumably for musicians to use. My whole approach as a musician had been that sound was an area where you *deconstructed* the compositional ideas of the past, rather than assisted musicians in continuing to develop these old ideas with new instruments, so the notion that an engineer would somehow figure out what musicians needed in order to play what they already could play another way struck me as forfeiting a great opportunity. It was clear to me that the big opportunity was for the *musicians* to design instruments that would make whatever new kinds of sound they wanted to make.

For *The Flicker* I felt that the way to go was to build a gizmo to make the sound I wanted, and not to use some premanufactured instrument. So I built a device that would articulate a frequency range of around twenty events per second. And then I made the sound track stereo—and it was *great.* I preferred to have the sound track as a stereo tape that would accompany the print of the film, and later on was *very* reluctant to put the sound on film. Sound fidelity on 16mm film is terrible.

Another reason, a more technical reason, that I wanted that sound in good fidelity stereo had to do with my relationship with Stockhausen's work, which has shifted over the years. The first time I saw Stockhausen, when he visited Boston around 1958, he was a young genius, and I couldn't believe that somebody had accomplished what he had at such a young age. Then I met with him in Europe and was again very impressed by what he had done (I'll come back to this visit in a moment). Then, still later, Stockhausen came to visit a rehearsal of the Dream Syndicate, the group I was involved with at La Monte Young's loft in New York, when we were playing bowed gong and making long-duration improvised music. Well, it turned out that the next thing Stockhausen composed was long-duration improvised music using bowed gong, and I thought to myself, "I guess the game is up. I'm not interested in what he has to offer anymore because it seems like we're out in front of him." It was around this time that Henry Flynt and I, and Jack Smith, picketed the Stockhausen performance event *Originale,* in New York: Henry had concluded that Stockhausen's work represented a culturally imperialist perspective and that it should be denounced. Since then, I've come to understand how fundamentally conservative Stockhausen's larger enterprise has been.

But back in 1961, when I spent a couple of days with Stockhausen at the electronic music studios in Cologne, I found him to be very generous. He gave me copies of his work and, most important, described his relationship with Meyer Eppler and the different things they had been involved with, particularly in relation to *Kontakte* [1960], a fantastic piece of music that is constructed using all pulses—and which therefore has a genealogical relationship to what I was doing in *The Flicker*, which is also made entirely of pulses.

One thing Stockhausen described that I found fascinating was a situation in which you have a series of pulses coming from the two stereo loudspeakers in a room. If you stand in the middle of the room, you hear the pitch that results from those pulses: that is, if there are forty pulses per second, you hear a frequency of forty cycles; but if you stand over to one side and the speakers are far enough apart, the sound from one speaker takes an eightieth of a second longer to get to you than the sound from the other speaker, and *then* you hear the sounds from the far speaker *in between* the sounds from the near speaker, which means that the frequency you'll hear will be *eighty* pulses per second. The idea that the *pitch* depended on the *space* was *so* fascinating to me that I wanted to allow this option to appear in the context of *The Flicker*. But, of course, it only works if the sound is stereo and comes from two separate speakers.

In the end, this aspect of *The Flicker* has turned out to be hopeless. I'm sure it's very rare that anyone uses the reel-to-reel tape and a stereo setup for the film. It's becoming fairly rare that anyone shows the *film!* I never tried to transfer *The Flicker* directly to video, but years ago I did make a computer version of it, on an Amiga, and when I tried to tape that, it just drove all the equipment crazy: video equipment tries to regularize the image, which in this case keeps going up and down. I've got to go back and work this problem through with more contemporary equipment—something I want to do with Woody Vasulka. The transfer of a film, which has a frame-by-frame ratio of twenty-four frames per second, to video is going to result in some real problems, if for no other reason than that NTSC video runs at thirty frames a second. And there's a whole *bunch* of other problems that I don't want to touch on right now; suffice it to say that, even uncompressed, the transfer is going to be a problem, and *compression* just takes the whole problem into outer space. A DVD of *The Flicker* is hard to imagine—but I haven't tried it yet.

MacDonald: Do you have the original diagram you worked with when you shot *The Flicker?*

Conrad: I was first asked about that by Jonas, when he was editing *Film Culture,* number 41. He was interested that I had charted the whole film out and wanted a still of the diagram. I was paranoid. I had never before made a work that was widely seen, so I had no sense of how dangerous it might be to "tell all." Of course, the situation may be very different in film from what it is in painting, but today smart painters don't talk about their work, *if it sells;* it's more likely to continue to engender financial interest if it's mysterious. I must have felt that *The Flicker* should remain mysterious.

So, when Jonas asked for the diagram, I thought, "Okay, I'll provide a diagram, but I'm going to code it in a way that will make it illegible." I made a sculpture, using small tiles to represent the frames; I built the whole pattern of the film with tiles, and photographed *that*. I felt that as an object it would be captivating in a way that would satisfy curiosity, but at the same time would be impenetrable as a score or as a recipe. I still have the sculpture somewhere, though a lot of the tiles have fallen off.

MacDonald: *The Flicker* became well-known as a "structural film," though I'm surprised at how little attention Sitney gave it in *Visionary Film* [New York: Oxford University Press, 1974].

Conrad: George Maciunas, perhaps overly ambitiously, contended that Sitney had been wrong in arguing for the novelty and precedence of the filmmakers that he put forward as the originators of a new "structural" cinema, because the Fluxus artists had done much of what Sitney was claiming as new, earlier on in the Fluxfilms [1966; 16mm prints of a version of the Fluxfilm reel is available from Anthology Film Archives (see the filmography); a videotape version is available from Re-voir (www.revoir.com)]. I remember the Fluxfilms very clearly because I was friends with George at the time when that project came together. One day he told me with a broad laugh that he was going to rent a high-speed camera and that all the Fluxus artists were going to make films in one day, and that it would cost hardly anything. I think George loved being able to *trample* traditions and expectations; here was a way for the Fluxus group to become star filmmakers with virtually no effort or expenditure.

I had no interest in being a Fluxus filmmaker, or a Fluxus film artist. Making art objects or films—*being* an artist—seemed retro to me at the time. So I didn't want to cook up a project just to be included on George's reel. But John Cale had shot a little film, and he gave that to George, and other people made conceptual pieces that they executed using that high-speed camera. Yoko Ono did several, and Chieko Shiomi did the beautiful *Disappearing Music for Face,* a *wonderful* film. George Brecht's *Enter/Exit* is also fabulous, and the Fluxus reel included several great short films by George himself, as well as a piece by Paul Sharits, *Word Movie/Fluxfilm,* and one by George Landow. As it happens, the pieces by the *filmmakers*—that is, Sharits and Landow—are very filmmaker-looking films, whereas the strongest conceptual work was done by the people who had had nothing to do with film and have had nothing to do with it since.

Whether George was right about Sitney's claim, the music I was doing with La Monte and the others at that time *was* at the very edge. Its strong suit, as I saw it at that point, was that it involved the destruction of the function of the composer by allowing the musicians to participate directly in the manufacture of the sound without any imposition of a composer's will. That this position could be seen as a cultural intervention was very important to me at that point, although I think it was less important to the other people in the group, particularly, as it turns out, to La Monte himself, who apparently *did* see himself as the composer of this music, or at least *wished to* see himself that way later on.

MacDonald: After *The Flicker* you continued to play with flicker for a while in *Straight and Narrow* and *Four Square,* and in *Coming Attractions.*

Conrad: Sure. I wanted to find other ways of using the tools I had developed, including in a narrative movie context.

MacDonald: And was *The Eye of Count Flickerstein* [1967, revised 1975] also a flicker film?

Conrad: Well, not really. The basic material of the film is a couple of shots of a TV screen with just snow, made with the camera turned ninety degrees so that the raster lines are vertical, rather than horizontal. All you see is the snow. I shot it around the same time I shot *The Flicker,* and when I first put it together, I included some other junk—cornball titles and some kind of sound. Later, in 1975, when I had more clarity and confidence as a filmmaker, I took off all the junk and just left the basic snow imagery.

MacDonald: Straight and Narrow goes beyond *The Flicker,* in terms of its hypnotic power.

Conrad: Well, *The Flicker* was a very instructive introduction to filmmaking for me. Once I was actually seeing the film projected, several things popped out. One was the way the film turns the audience into a kind of sculptural array. Another thing that's elusive, but nevertheless really there, is the experience of color. During *The Flicker* people see colors, even though all that's actually on the filmstrip is a bunch of black and white frames. It fascinated me that people saw color all the time, and not only colors, but *moving* colors, *whirling* colors.

Of course, I realized all along that dealing with frame-by-frame construction in film is what animation is about, but animation got started and continued in a way which is, at least from a 2004 perspective, functionally mimetic: animation takes single-frame sequences and puts them together in such a way that they don't look like single frames at all; they look like regular shots. I felt that it might be interesting to see what kinds of things in addition to flicker could be done with the potential control that this frame-by-frame way of working offered. And I got a tip by reading an article about somebody who had broadcast on television a black-and-white program which was seen in color, using some kind of sequenced system of presentation. I thought that sounded supercool, so I began seriously looking for information on how you could produce color using black and white. Well, the first thing that came up was a little device called Benham's Top, which is a black-and-white pattern inscribed on a disk that, when you rotate the disk, causes you to see colors.

I was also interested in the idea of animated movement but thought it would be nice to explore the possibility of a kind of movement that would be under the control of the viewer. Let's say, for example, that you have a pattern of black and white stripes on the screen *and* the negative of that pattern and that you keep alternating the positive and negative of the black and white stripes to create maybe the *feeling* of movement, the *possibility* of movement, without the *animation* of movement—in other words, leaving any sense of the *direction* and *experience* of movement completely up to the person who's watching. I decided to arrange a pattern of black and white stripes according to the logic of Benham's Top so that there would be an exploration of movement and color. I worked out a sequence that generally goes from hot to cool colors.

By this time, I was able to print the film myself, and I was doing my own "optical" work. I would take the results to the lab to get the film developed. When *Straight and Narrow* came back from the lab, I was eager to look at it and was getting ready to run the projector when there was a knock at the door. It was John Cale, who would drop by sometimes when he was working at Columbia Records. He had just finished working on a cut from an album that he was doing with Terry Riley, and he wanted to play it for me. I said, "Okay, but I've got this new film: why don't we just play them both at the same time?" So he put on their *Ides of March,* and I put on *Straight and Narrow,* and the two things were immediately married. When you first play some sound with your film, it often seems to be *the* perfect sound, the sound that *must* go with that film forever. It's dangerous because you can be drawn into a false relationship with a poor choice of sound. In this case I feel pretty happy with the outcome.

Straight and Narrow looks especially nice if it's projected small, with a warm bulb. Xenon bulbs aren't very good for that film. Project it small, with a nice tungsten bulb, and it just glows and you see a lot of color.

MacDonald: What was Beverly's part in *Straight and Narrow?* The film is usually listed as hers in the catalogue.

Conrad: That's right. It's listed that way, as is *Coming Attractions,* because we were a collaborative team. I was very conscious of the fact that, given the various ways that we split our jobs, we needed to make sure that she wasn't left out when it was time to give credit—something that happened all too often to women. In the case of *Straight and Narrow,* where most of the production work involved carefully planned stages of bipack contact printing in a little tent at our loft, the credit deserved to be shared: my accomplishing this technical process was supported by the aspects of household life that she was taking care of.

MacDonald: In *Coming Attractions* you and Beverly actually did work together—you as producer, Beverly as director. The film turned out to be a weird revisiting of the Jack Smith experiences.

Conrad: Definitely. And consciously so. A bunch of different threads wove together at that point. One was that Beverly and I had both been cut off from Jack and his scene with unfulfilled ambitions. I was very interested in using the resources of flicker mattes to explore what consequences there might be for the understanding of a narrative sequence if it were composited with purely formal visual devices. That was something I felt was completely unknown, and it seemed to me that the way to explore this unknown would be to try out a range of different formal and narrative intersections in a situation where neither of the two would overwhelm the other; that is, to try to maintain a balance between the formal devices and the narrative/pictorial material. Flicker was the source idea, but then a whole vocabulary of other possibilities suggested themselves.

It seemed that a good way to proceed with the narrative would be to fall back on allegorical settings and simple iconic devices, like walking through the woods or an angel appearing or a gangster murdering somebody. Francis Francine, who is important in *Flaming Creatures,* played the central protagonist. Beverly, who directed, worked with the actors and negotiated the specific roles. I was also interested in seeing how much artistic resourcefulness I could activate (as "producer") if I removed myself to the position of creating these formal devices and oversaw the participation of the various artists in the production. For example, I asked each musician to *bend* in some direction: La Monte Young sang a cowboy song, Terry Riley played barroom music, John Cale played classical music, and so forth.

Coming Attractions was a university education in filmmaking for me. It moved me from a person who had hardly ever shot film to someone who had operated a film lab at home and basically could do everything in-house except manufacture the film, develop it, and put the optical sound on. Each of those—aside from the optical sound aspect, which I never did find interesting enough to learn how to do—was something that I came back to in later years.

MacDonald: So for you, *Coming Attractions* became coming attractions for the next stage of your career.

Conrad: That's right.

Nathaniel Dorsky (and Jerome Hiler)

That cinema can be a meditative practice would come as a surprise to most casual filmgoers and even to a good many contemporary cineastes. For a generation, film critics, scholars, and teachers have honored accomplished auteurs and debated the possibility of authorship; they have explored genre conventions; they have policed cinema in the name of more progressive gender, ethnic, class, and sexual politics; they have used a wide range of approaches developed in other disciplines to expose how cinema functions in modern culture—and they have ignored virtually all forms of cinema that reflect a meditative sensibility on the part of filmmakers and that offer viewers the possibility of a more complex spiritual life. And yet, despite the relentless pop cultural marketing of an accelerated lifestyle, endless accumulation, and increasingly frenzied media overload, some audiences have come to appreciate forms of film experience that offer a respite, that transform the movie theater into something like a sacred space where we can, at least for a moment, ignore the pressures of modern consumer society and more fully apprehend and appreciate the moment-to-moment incarnation of the perceptual world. Among the filmmakers who exemplify this trend are Larry Gottheim, Peter Hutton, Leighton Pierce, and the San Franciscan Nathaniel Dorsky, who has been making a variety of contributions to independent cinema since the mid-1960s.

Dorsky arrived on the New York scene with a trilogy of short films—*Ingreen* (1964), *A Fall Trip Home* (1964), and *Summerwind* (1965)—evocations of his childhood and adolescence in a New Jersey small town (Millburn). Most obviously in *Ingreen*, but to some extent in *A Fall Trip Home,* we see

Dorsky coming to grips with the combined excitement and terror of gay desire, in a cinematic form that recalls the psychodramas of the 1940s and 1950s. Unlike the defiant early landmarks of what we now call Queer cinema—Kenneth Anger's *Fireworks* (1947), Jean Genet's *Un chant d'amour* (1952), Jack Smith's *Flaming Creatures* (1963)—Dorsky's early films reflect what must have been the more usual adolescent experience of confronting gay desire during the 1950s and 1960s: Dorsky seems to make his way through small-town adolescence with a guilty sense that he's different from his family and friends, and full of puzzlement about what to do about this.

By the time he made *Summerwind,* Dorsky had become fascinated with a new form of cinematic perception: an intense looking at the particulars of the physical world that, in the years that followed, would mature into a series of remarkable visual experiences: *Hours for Jerome, Parts 1* and *2* (1982), *Pneuma* (1983), *Alaya* (1987), *Triste* (1996), *Variations* (1998), *Arbor Vitae* (2000), *Love's Refrain* (2001), *The Visitation* (2002), and *Threnody* (2004). The visual sensibility of Dorsky's mature films, all of which are silent (Dorsky asks that they be projected at eighteen frames per second, what he calls "sacred speed"), tends toward the spiritual, the meditative. Implicitly Dorsky asks that viewers consider the successive shots in his films not as parts of a strategy for delivering viewers to a narrative or ideological conclusion, but as an opportunity for becoming more fully aware of the particulars of each image and its interrelationships with the images that precede and follow it. Dorsky's films are a form of visual/conceptual training in apprehending the world, and its representation in cinema, in a deeper, more reverent sense.

Each of the individual images and image clusters of the Lake Owassa area of northern New Jersey and of Manhattan that together constitute *Hours for Jerome* is like a prayer; indeed, Dorsky's title references the Books of Hours that provided medieval Christians with the daily cycle of prayers and relevant illustrations ("illuminations"). "Jerome" is simultaneously a reference to Dorsky's partner since the 1960s, artist Jerome Hiler, and to Saint Jerome, a favorite subject of medieval illuminators. Whereas the Books of Hours focused on the daily prayer cycle, *Hours for Jerome*—like Susan Fenimore Cooper's *Rural Hours* (1850) and Thoreau's *Walden* (1854)—explores the particulars of the seasonal cycle. *Part 1* records spring through summer; *Part 2*, fall through winter. Along with Gottheim's neglected *Horizons* (1973), *Hours for Jerome* is America's most compelling cinematic paean to temperate-zone seasonality.

Both *Pneuma* and *Alaya* (*pneuma* means soul or divine inspiration; *alaya*—as in Him*alaya*—is a Sanskrit word that in Buddhism refers to the primordial individuality that underlies our social selves) focus on particular forms of texture. In *Pneuma,* Dorsky asks viewers to meditate on the film grain of a variety of disappearing film stocks he had collected in the

From Nathaniel Dorsky's *Triste* (1996). Courtesy Nathaniel Dorsky.

1970s; in *Alaya,* he asks them to meditate on sand filmed in a variety of places and in different (and generally stunning) ways. By asking viewers not just to consume endless representations of "reality" but to focus on the essence, the "soul," of cinematic representation, Dorsky transforms the textures of film stock and sand into emblems of the spirit: he breathes life into the "dust" of cinema.

Dorsky's most recent films expand his exploration of what he sometimes calls "polyvalent" montage, a form of editing that means to redirect editing away from the dialectics that energized the Russian films of the 1920s *and* from the narrative demands of pop cinema, toward a refinement of viewers' ability to perceive the subtleties of particular images and the complex webbing of interconnections between them. Dorsky's polyvalence means to place viewers into a cinematic present that cannot be reduced to verbal codes and analysis.

Who knows why contributions to art history strike a cultural nerve at a particular moment? But judging from responses to Dorsky's recent films, I suspect that audiences, and perhaps other filmmakers, are appreciating the openness to perception and the freedom from analytic reductionism that Dorsky offers. Several years ago, Stephen Holden claimed that for *American Beauty* (1999) Sam Mendes had borrowed "an image (and an entire esthetic of beauty) from Nathaniel Dorsky's *Variations,* in which the camera admired a plastic shopping bag being blown about by the wind" (*New York Times,* October 9, 1999). Dorsky remembers receiving a call from someone on the production of *American Beauty,* asking how Mendes might see the film, though he is not convinced that his shot was "borrowed"; there are similar, earlier images elsewhere—in poetry as well as in film—so many, in fact, that Dorsky was originally afraid that his image might be too trite to be included in *Variations.* Nevertheless, some admirers of *Variations* were indignant at what they believe was (still another) unacknowledged industry theft from the avant-garde.

Threnody is the sixth in a series of related films. Each is a silent montage of a wide variety of imagery, constructed so that both the particular shots and the many, subtle interconnections between them grow increasingly clear and rich, as one sees the films over and over. The images themselves are generally of mundane, everyday realities, though Dorsky's skill as a cameraperson and his dexterity as editor allow the experience of these films to remind us of how much beauty and subtlety we tend to miss because of the frenzy of our lives. Dorsky's recent films simultaneously provide considerable sensual pleasure and an ongoing challenge to viewers' attentiveness to the visual world.

Dorsky's early trilogy of films opened the way for him to work on films by others—a job that earned him an Emmy in 1967 for *Gauguin in Tahiti: Search for Paradise* (1967, directed by Martin Carr). Over the years, Dorsky has developed a reputation as a "film doctor" whose advice and editing skills can save ailing film projects. This work makes him just enough money to maintain a life and make his own films.

I spoke with Dorsky in San Francisco in April 1999 and with Dorsky and his partner, Jerome Hiler, in August 1999 (these two conversations are presented separately here). Dorsky's comments should be supplemented with his book, *Devotional Cinema* (Berkeley: Tuumba Press, 2004), now in a second, revised edition (2005).

MacDonald: The earliest films you list in the Canyon Cinema catalogue— *Ingreen, A Fall Trip Home,* and *Summerwind*—can't be your first films.

Dorsky: They were the first films I made after I had taken a big bite out of experimental film in New York, from 1961 to 1964—after seeing things like *Chumlum* [1964, by Ron Rice], *Meshes of the Afternoon* [1943, by Maya Deren], and *Twice a Man* [1963, by Gregory Markopoulos]. I was at a silent, early screening of *Twice a Man* and at one of the famous early showings of Jack Smith's *Flaming Creatures* [1963]. And Stan Brakhage came and premiered *Dog Star Man: Part I* [1962], which I think was the first time I saw one of his films. When I was in Boulder last summer, I saw a great print—I had never seen a great print—of *Window Water Baby Moving* [1959]. I'd always considered *Window Water* a film you showed to students because it has an accessible story line, but that the film was so-so. But when I saw a good print, it was beautiful, and strongly cinematic. I like those early Brakhage films—*Window Water, Sirius Remembered* [1959]—more now than when I was young. At any rate, *Ingreen* is an amalgam of *Chumlum, Meshes of the Afternoon, Dog Star Man,* and *Twice a Man.* I *did* bring what *I* brought to the film, too; but making *Ingreen* came out of my seeing, and being blown away by, those other films.

I met Jerome Hiler, Jerry—my better half—at the premiere of *Ingreen* at the Washington Square Gallery. Jerry was there with Gregory Markopoulos and Ken Kelman. He was Gregory's assistant on *The Illiac Passion* [1967]. He did all the costumes and scouted the locations. Jerry always tells me that when Gregory saw my mother in *Ingreen,* he said, "Is that *the mother?*" Of course, he must have felt his own influence.

So, anyway, back to your question. I had started to make films with an 8mm camera when I was around ten or eleven. I was very influenced by the Disney True-Life Adventures, films like *Beaver Valley* [1950] and *Nature's Half-Acre* [1951—both directed by James Algar]. They were the first time I saw, for instance, flowers growing in time-lapse—very photographic films, held together with music and narration. Both films went through the four seasons, and for some reason I was very taken with that.

As a kid, I was a big fan of John Ford. My parents took me on a trip across the country when I was in fourth or fifth grade. We stopped in Reno, and they went to gamble at Harold's Club. There was a place where parents could leave kids while they gambled; and—I couldn't believe this—not only were they showing free movies with a 16mm projector, but you could have free hamburgers and coke, all you wanted. They showed *Stagecoach* [1935], and I remember being blown away. I loved westerns, and there was so much tenderness in this one, and a pregnant woman. It felt very adult to me. It was both masculine and feminine, like Ford *is.* When my parents came out of the casino, I said, "That was the best movie I ever saw." And I remember telling them the story.

So if someone were to ask who were my main influences, I would have to say Disney, Ford, and Ozu, Antonioni, and Brakhage, and Jerry Hiler maybe most of all—a very visual group. All my films are a little bit Disney-like and Ozu-like, and there are attempts at Fordianism in *Summerwind* and a basic respect for his sense of light and shadow. By the way, recently at PFA [Pacific Film Archive in Berkeley; Edith Kramer is the director] we saw Ford's first feature, *Straight Shooting* [1917]. Ever see it?

MacDonald: No.

Dorsky: It was the first film Ford made beyond a two-reeler. So tactile—dust, light, glistening water. You know the way he shoots toward the sun so that everything is backlit. There's a rainstorm, and cowpokes come up to a porch in the rain, and so much water is coming off the roof that it fills the brims of the hats. Beautiful shots. It had Ford's sense of tension—inside/outside, light/dark—and the humanness of his characters. And the usual Fordian chorus. Jerry and I were saying afterward that the genius of Ford is that every one of his films *is* his state of mind.

Later, during that same childhood trip west, we were visiting some army buddies of my father's in Santa Monica, and my father let me take a shot with his camera. It was of him diving off the diving board and swimming across the pool. I still have it. It's part of a roll of my father's stuff. There are boring pans around Old Faithful and the Grand Canyon, and then all of a sudden there's *my* shot. I guess I was so petrified—I had been warned that I was going to move the camera too fast—that I took this very nicely composed shot that follows him diving in and swimming. It was my first shot. But it was very good!

Later, when I was eleven, I used his 8mm camera to make my first films. One is called *A Bend in the River,* which I realized later in life must have been named after the Anthony Mann film [*A Bend in the River,* 1952]. My *Bend in the River* is a nature film, about the animals in my neighborhood. A turtle, and ducks. It has no formal pretensions, and it isn't a film that says, "You can see a budding genius here." In fact, I showed it to Jytte and Steve when they were looking for films for their 8mm show. [In 1998 Steve Anker and Jytte Jensen curated Big as Life: An American History of 8mm Films, cosponsored by the Museum of Modern Art and the San Francisco Cinematheque; the catalogue, *Big as Life: An American History of 8mm Films,* was edited by Albert Kilchesty.] And they gave it back to me politely. *[Laughter.]* You know what I'm saying. A good friend, Michael August, did half the shooting and cutting. What a great way to spend childhood.

We also blocked out some films that I don't have anymore, based on the silent *Perils of Pauline* [1914, directed by Louis Gasnier and Donald Mackenzie], which was on television at the time. Adventures. People chasing each other. The typical thing kids like. Later on, as a teenager, I didn't make movies, but I was shooting footage, including some rare footage of the Alan Fried rock and roll shows, with groups like the Cleftones, shot when I was in eighth grade.

So by the time I went to Antioch College—I stayed only a year—I had some background and, for whatever reason, was ready to fall in love with film. I saw an older student with a Bolex, and that camera was a magical thing. Everyone feels it when they see a movie camera. It represents some sort of alchemical power.

There was a filmmaker at Antioch who really affected me: Michael Medike—have you heard of him?

MacDonald: No.

Dorsky: I should show you some of his early black and white films. They're beautiful, and almost no one knows about them. He had a primordial sense of film language right from the start. He was an extraordinary person for me to meet at eighteen. I was very fortunate.

During that brief Antioch period, I made three films in black and white. The first one was under a tutorial—a work montage of the new college swimming pool being built. I had been seeing the Russians—Dovzhenko, Eisenstein, Pudovkin—at the cine club at Antioch. On a mundane level, that stuff is easy to emulate. I did two films like that.

Then I did a send-up of *Last Year at Marienbad* [1961], called *Next Year at Marienbad*. I still have it. I saw it lately and was surprised that some of the blocking is beautiful. Some of it is sophomoric. There was a famous publicity image in *Marienbad*—I don't know if it exists in the film—where people had shadows, but the bushes didn't. We did a shot from the roof of a dormitory down on a plaza on a cloudy day. Four or five couples smoking and drinking cocktails. We cut out shadows in black paper, so all the couples *had* shadows, and then the lead couple walks through *without* a shadow. They catch their foot on the last shadow, and it moves. That kind of thing.

At nineteen I made an educational film about my mother's nursery school and won honorable mention in the Kodak Teenage Movie Contest. The "generous" prize was three rolls of regular-8mm Kodachrome. I used them as unslit 16mm to shoot my first color footage for *Ingreen,* which was finished the next summer. I shot it and cut it in four weeks. It just came. I'm not good at many things, but I think I understood cinema very early.

I'm glad you think that early trilogy of films still looks good; they were made very crudely, especially the sound. Recently, the folks here who run Total Mobile Home [Rebecca Baron and David Sherman] said they'd like to show the trilogy, along with *Triste.* I said I'd do it because I hadn't seen the films in twenty years. I thought I'd be embarrassed. But they really look good. Steve Anker was standing in the back with Jerry, who said after *Ingreen,* "Should have quit there." *[Laughter.]*

MacDonald: The early classics of psychodrama are accomplished and interesting, but often visually grim. *Ingreen* seems visually celebratory of the arrival of sensuality, even as it reveals its psychic traumas. There *is* a struggle, but it's not a grim struggle. The color balances the fear of gay desire, the way Anger's humor in *Fireworks* balances his fear.

Dorsky: You know, my actual feeling at the time was the opposite. It was plain old terror. I mean, my being gay was something I had known about since I was seven or eight—or at least you know that you're not entirely like everyone else. I wish I could say that I was a courageous anarchist who didn't believe in any of the surrounding societal values and made my stand. But it's odd enough that I made *the film*. I guess the upside of those painful feelings is that they drive you to make a visually powerful and sensual film. One thing the avant-garde of that time did provide was an openness to gay subject matter.

To my knowledge, no one has ever shown *Ingreen* in a gay festival. Actually, I don't like to show my films in that context.

MacDonald: Well, it certainly *is* a film that should be celebrated as part of the history of Queer cinema.

Dorsky: It's not my cinema orientation to identify myself that way. But the fact is that I did make the film, and the only thing that I can say now is that at that time I was very unhappy because of who I was, and felt that the only way I could depict it was as a problem. Maybe what you see as celebratory is more than I understood myself at that time. The film *isn't* barren and grim; it *is* completely passionate in the terms of the eye, even if it is crude.

MacDonald: I think the only single-layered shot in *Ingreen,* which is full of multiple superimposition, is the boy running across the field and kneeling in front of his father. You can read it as the Boy becoming a Man, giving up the pleasures of boyhood to achieve manhood. You can also read it as a boy being terrified about how his father will feel about the reality of the boy's desire.

Dorsky: I'm almost begging, "Please like me," or "I don't want to hurt you," in the simplest language.

My father died about a year after I made *Ingreen*. Later my mother asked me, "So what did that shot mean?" I was taken aback. I couldn't answer her. I realized then that that film was both extremely conscious *and* extremely unconscious. In a certain way I'm embarrassed by its playing out the early sixties gay psychological stereotype of a close mother and distant father. But in a certain way that was also *true* for me.

It wasn't until much later in life that I relaxed about being gay. Finally you figure you might as well enjoy your life, and you find a place where you can fit into society with some ease, which was not possible in public school.

By *A Fall Trip Home,* I was getting more relaxed as a filmmaker, and then by *Summerwind* I *was* relaxed. I made all three films really fast. During the autumn of 1964 I made *A Fall Trip Home* over a period of three months. I did *Summerwind* the next summer.

If you were a young person in New York at that time, it was cutting edge to go to experimental film screenings. In those days, being interested in experimental film didn't have anything to do with being in school; it had to do with a complete cutting off from the usual, with being renegade. It was genuinely outside the established order.

These days, going to experimental films feels like an obscure remnant of something. I don't know *what* it means anymore, though it often feels somewhat academic. Not long ago the PFA was showing a film by Jeffrey Skoller, where he was attempting to be politically correct and adventurous by depicting a *male* body in an erotic way (Skoller is "straight"). He talked about this afterward, and it all seemed so stuffy. I whispered to Edith Kramer, "We've come a long way since *Flaming Creatures!*" It's that same straitlaced morality all over again. But now left-wing moral fundamentalism has become the canopy under which experimental film is to be judged.

Not that there weren't unfairnesses between the sexes in those days, some of them quite embarrassing. But a certain freedom has disappeared, and a certain energy, and an open spirit willing to reveal the unconscious.

MacDonald: Ingreen seems to be about sensuality, about your personal recognition of how wonderful (and scary) it is to be a sensual being. *A Fall Trip Home* focuses more on your growing awareness that you are also a social being (not that *A Fall Trip Home* is not sensual: the films overlap): football is a major social ritual in many small towns. And *Summerwind* seems about a growing aesthetic consciousness.

Dorsky: There's another thing that happened. In the middle of making *Summerwind,* my oldest friend, Mark Birnbaum, who went on to become a videomaker, opened up his hand, and there was a sugar cube with acid, and he said, "We're going to the woods today." I said, "Okay." That morning I was in New Jersey, but at the end of the day, it was no longer New Jersey. I don't know where I was.

MacDonald: The forest primeval?

Dorsky: The primeval forest, yes! And I was Bambi! In the end, that film was trying to capture my new Bambi consciousness.

On a technical level I knew that I'd made two films based on superimposition, and I was trying to struggle out of that. As soon as I finished *Summerwind,* I started shooting the material that later became *Hours for Jerome,* which I didn't edit for fifteen years. There are sequences in *Hours for Jerome*—the blue snowy trees in the winter, for example—that were shot the winter immediately after *Summerwind.* It was a direct continuation.

MacDonald: How *did* you come to make *Hours for Jerome?*

Dorsky: Just after I moved out to California, I went through the worst psychological period of my life. My father had died (I'm an only child); I had moved in with Jerry, and by doing so, I had distanced myself from my mother. My mother and I had very complex ties, so this declaration of separation, at the same time that *she* was in need, ripped me apart. Nothing was clear. And moving to California was very disorienting for me, because I was like a Native American in a certain sense: the trees, the rocks, the clouds, the air of the East Coast were very much a part of me. All of a sudden, I'm in this place with these weird rubbery trees and strange seasons. The move to San Francisco forced a closure of my filming in the Northeast, where I had been recording imagery since my childhood. So the point is that for the first eight years of the seventies, I was in a very bad state, and was not able to edit. I had so much self-hatred. Just awful.

I began to pull out of it during the late seventies. In 1978 a poet friend from New York, Larry Fagin, came to visit. And I said, "Oh, you've never seen the footage I shot when Jerry and I lived out in Lake Owassa." It was in cans covered with dust: rolls of the original Kodachrome II, which was so beautiful. We took the film out, strung it up, had a toke, and spent the evening looking at it, and I thought, "Oh, my God! There's a *film* there!" Finally, I could *see* what I had shot and realized I could work with it, and wanted to work with it.

MacDonald: At what point did the process of putting this piece together and creating this structure take on a seasonal structure and get connected in your mind with illuminated manuscripts, the Books of Hours?

Dorsky: We were living out in the country when I recorded that imagery, and I felt that the imagery was similar to medieval imagery, in the sense that you were in a place where the natural order, especially the seasons, dominated—along with working-class white contractors. I think I was in the same balance with the landscape as someone who was working on a Book of Hours. I've always loved the Books of Hours and the idea of luminous contemplation. In terms of the number of people in the world, that seems like a nice era, like a certain period of Chinese painting, where you have a sense of human society as a harmonious element in a larger order. Things have become much more grotesque in modern times, if not genuinely strange.

MacDonald: When you were editing *Hours for Jerome,* was the process largely putting things up against each other, trying out connections?

Dorsky: I cut each of the seasons separately. In order to keep myself fresh, I'd work on one season for about a week, put it away; and come upon another season that I hadn't worked on in three weeks. A structure was developed within each season. When I attached the seasons, some work had to be done with the points where the seasons connected. Everyone says, "Oh, that film has such nice color." That's partly Kodachrome II, one of the most precious jewels ever created by Eastman Kodak, plus a very good reversal print stock—neither exists today. But also, the film has nice color because things are very carefully placed in terms of color. Each move had to have visual freshness along with a poetic poignancy. I would put something next to something else, and if it didn't feel additive, adventurous, luminous—and also at the same time poetic—I wouldn't go with it.

Some of the editing in *Hours for Jerome* had been done during the period when I was shooting it. Like those jump cuts of Jerry making coffee at night, with the moon; and the shots of Fourteenth Street in the rain intercut with black-and-white television. I was trying to get at rather aggressive collisions of flint and stone, to create sparks and produce some new kinds of space and luminosity.

That attitude was a reflection of my spirit at that time: I was getting more and more depressed, and as a result I didn't have any tenderness toward the footage. The only way out was through aggression. This isn't unlike many young filmmakers, who are very pained in their twenties. Of course, for the audience, the results may read as beauty. Pain *is* a wonderful fuel for clarity.

Warren Sonbert pushed me to go all the way with my editing. He thought the editing in *Hours for Jerome* was too descriptive. But there was something about that footage that made me feel obligated about its sense of place. When you go into polyvalent editing, as Warren usually did, and as I did in *Triste* and *Variations,* the *place* is the *film.* But in *Hours for Jerome* I had to respect geographic place. And I had to respect the seasons. I still felt I was taking my first steps.

But even though *Hours* is organized into seasons and into clusters or stanzas (whatever you want to call them), I did try to get resonances and polyvalence between those stanzas, and to have synaptic relationships between different parts of the film. *Hours for Jerome* allowed me to discover how to place things so that they would resonate later. Remember the shot taken under the El in Queens? It's preceded by a Ferris wheel in the rain and by a black-and-white cat drinking water. But right before *that* is the sequence of Fourteenth Street pixilated in the rain, intercut with a black-and-white TV. The black-and-white TV has this rippling motion that is echoed by the light coming through the El tracks three stanzas later. I knew that if I took the El and moved it a few sequences further on, nothing would happen; and I knew if I moved it one sequence closer to the TV/Fourteenth Street sequence, it would feel like some corny Russian parallel editing, like when Vertov, in *The Man with a Movie Camera* [1929], cuts between a woman washing her face and someone hosing down a street. I don't like parallel editing. In *Man with a Movie Camera* Vertov was trying every possible syntax, and simple parallel editing is one of the possibilities; but it's usually too one-dimensional for me. I want complex resonances, not simple parallels that can be easily verbalized. Of course, other moments of *Man with a Movie Camera* are the ingenious birthplaces of polyvalence and of true cinematic mysteries rarely seen anywhere.

I was very conscious in using black at the end of each stanza. Many times there is an afterimage, either physical or psychological, during that black, and at times I begin a new stanza with something that resonates tonally with the afterimage resting in the black. An obvious one is that after all the strobes on the autumn trees, your eyes go to blue because there's been so much red-orange on the screen. Afterimage is always the reverse, color-wise. And then into that blue pops that red-and-white rooster. Also, after you see the panoramic autumn landscapes with the pixilated cloud shadows, I fade to black, then come up on Jerry's brown shoe—a huge difference in scale.

17 Reasons Why [1987] also makes use of stanzas. I just saw it recently and was surprised by its beauty. It's almost a piece of folk art, like a quilt. I think to really enjoy it, you have to understand how it was made—the cinematic game that I was playing with unslit double-8mm. (Regular-8mm film was, in fact, 16mm film, one side of which was exposed, then, once the roll had been flipped in the camera, the other; during development the 16mm filmstrip was slit down the middle, into two 8mm strips.)

MacDonald: The more I looked at *Pneuma* and *Alaya,* the more I wondered if they weren't the same film, done in two different ways: with sand, and with film grain. When you made *Alaya,* did you have *Pneuma* in mind? Were they conceived as a pair?

Dorsky: Both came from the desire to express the same kind of thing, but in different ways. *Pneuma* and *Alaya* are about a minute different in length. Both have to do with what is called in painting "allover"—the films articulate through a succession of allovers. And there are other specific parallels: the relationship of close-up, extreme close-up, long shot is one; and about three minutes from the end, each has a cadenza. In *Alaya* it's the time when the sand really starts to collapse; in *Pneuma* it's the long blue section.

MacDonald: That blue is direct painting on film, right?

Dorsky: No, *Pneuma* is entirely made up of film that hasn't been put through a camera or manipulated by paint or hand processing. That blue area was a roll of Ansco 400 that I bought in a camera store for fifty cents when I was working in LA. It was twenty years out of date. It was the last year or so that the Ansco lab would still process their movie film, so I just sent it to them without exposing it and that's what it looked like. I use excerpts from the hundred-foot roll. The modulation you see is the deterioration of the film.

I collected the material for *Pneuma* during the years after shooting the footage for *Hours for Jerome.* I was in LA for a while, working on exploitation features. I was lost and depressed. I had no desire to use fresh beautiful stock. I remember starting an outdated roll that I couldn't get up the interest to finish shooting, so I just ran it out of my camera and sent it to the lab, and the *only* wonderful part was the part I *hadn't* shot.

I said to myself, "All right, I'm not *shooting* anything—I don't like the world enough anymore—so I'll just collect this stuff." And I began to collect *really* outdated film. For whatever reason, working with the grain and color of these film stocks satisfied my needs at that point. What I saw when I developed the film stocks without exposing them felt like an internal world. Somehow, it was therapeutic. Actually, every film I've made has been motivated by a need for self-healing or a rebalancing.

I collected this material and then, after I cut *Hours for Jerome,* I had my energy back and had begun to have a little faith in myself. I examined all the stocks and made *Pneuma.* It was the twilight of all these marvelously individual reversal emulsions: Gevart, Fuji, Ilford, ER, FF, Kodachrome II, Dynachrome—there are about twenty different emulsions in *Pneuma.* Collecting the material *came out of* an experience of vacantness, but then I think the film turned into something not vacant at all. If one touches upon one's greatest vulnerabilities, then there is the material for transmutation.

If you see *Pneuma* projected really well, with the image surrounded by black in a black room, there's a halo around the screen. At times the imagery appears to surround the edge of the screen; at other times the imagery seems out in front of the screen; sometimes it seems right on the surface; and sometimes the screen is a window. After a while, you don't even know where the screen *is* anymore. The pleasure of that film is to relax and enjoy these variations.

MacDonald: *Pneuma* creates such a highly energized frame that it reminds me of Ernie Gehr's *Serene Velocity* [1970].

Dorsky: Yes, it has an atmosphere of the seventies. It was one of my few attempts to make an "avant-garde" film. If someone says *Pneuma* doesn't work, there's nothing I can say. How can I disagree? I was trying something, and whether it's successful or not depends on your willingness to go along with it. I tried various ways to structure these emulsions, and this was the most honest and vulnerable response I could muster.

By the time I made *Alaya,* I had come to actually want to *photograph* something. I was visiting friends on Cape Cod and took a few shots of blowing sand. And here, I live ten minutes from the ocean, where, every spring, there's all this wind blowing the sand. So the subject was right in front of me—a film asking to happen.

When I was editing *Alaya,* I realized I couldn't quite get all the articulations I needed, and that I needed some very dark shots to give the film the muscle it needed to go forward and open out. I started to shoot with very old color and black-and-white stocks, underexposing. There are many times in *Alaya* where a shot is 60 percent film grain and 40 percent sand. And there are times when the grain of the sand and the grain of the film, two graces, or natural *entities,* touch each other in an amazing way. The film, of course, is somewhat "about" this.

Sand in Nathaniel Dorsky's *Alaya* (1987).
Courtesy Nathaniel Dorsky.

MacDonald: Did you sometimes use gels? We'll see a particular texture of grain in black-and-white and then the same texture tinted a color, as if you just put a gel in front of the lens.

Dorsky: It was just the various film stocks. When those sixties film stocks got old, some went blue—like ER. A stock called MS always went a little bit greenish. I worked very hard on the prints so that I had a palette of blue, yellow, green, tan, and black and white. Sometimes you can't tell when it *is* black and white or color. What was thrilling for me is that I knew (as I did when I edited *Hours for Jerome*) that I was working with synapses that went back underneath a few shots and came through. As I placed the shots in *Alaya,* I knew that a shot would work because of the effect of the two or three previous shots. I was thrilled when Stan spoke so clearly of this in a letter to me. It confirmed my own esoterica!

MacDonald: In *Alaya* there are, at times, expansive vistas. Where did you go to shoot those?

Dorsky: It was Death Valley.

MacDonald: Alaya refers to the whole history of the desert as a romantic landscape and as a place where spiritual enlightenment happens—"the word in the desert" [I am referring both to the phrase and to Douglas Burton-Christie's *The Word in the Desert: Scripture and the Quest for Holiness in Early Christian Monasticism* (New York: Oxford University Press, 1993)].

Dorsky: I've never had a better time photographing a movie. To go to these places and be alone on a windy day—you become so high, just standing there! To edit *Alaya* was not fun, but to shoot it was enthralling, and difficult, of course. I almost died of dehydration in Death Valley, but Jerry and a park ranger saved me.

MacDonald: How did you do the microscopic shots?

Dorsky: Well, embarrassingly enough, one of the sequences was shot on a homemade "soundstage." There are three times when I shot very close. The first time—the material that looks like jewels—was shot on a windy day in the dunes on Cape Cod with extension tubes, which allow you to focus closer and closer. The more extension tubes you add, the more the magnification. Then there's an orange sequence that I shot later, here in San Francisco, during a windy sunset. I had to get my camera cleaned about three times. The third time I was in my cellar: I put sand in a baking tray, used my vacuum cleaner (an Electrolux that can blow) to make "wind," set the camera on the tripod, and used two photo floods very close to get depth of field. I needed a great depth of field, because when you use that many extension tubes, you might not be able to keep a single grain of sand in focus from front to back. So I had to use a lot of light to get it up around f-11. The lens was so hot, I couldn't touch it.

MacDonald: It's a stunning film.

Dorsky: I think it's a very *body* film. I believe it was the beginning for me of cinema as a devotional form, cinema as prayer, so to speak.

Alaya is certainly a safer film to show an audience then *Pneuma,* which is quite dicey unless there's great projection, or great love of film itself.

When I sent *Alaya* to Stan [Brakhage], he wrote me a great letter in which he explained that at first he didn't think it *was* a movie, and then he realized that each shot was placed in the light of the previous group of shots, and started to get very excited. That got *me* excited: that you can show someone what you've done and have them write back *exactly* what it is—*that's* extraordinary. I owe Stan so much. His personal instinct, advice, and encouragement were and continue to be very helpful; he was the most excellent of confidence coaches. Sometimes his style of speech was distracting, but then you saw its uncanny truth.

MacDonald: Triste begins with a series of shots that set the stage for a wide range of resonances. The first shot is branches moving. Then there's someone writing a letter in close-up: we see the lines of written text. Then there's a hose which is sort of looped over itself, echoing the overlay of the branches. And then you're in a car, and telephone poles flick by in a way that subtly echoes the motion in the previous shot . . .

Dorsky: Stan seemed intrigued by this cutting. When I'd show a film at his salon,* Stan would say, "The reason the cut from the tree to the hose to the letter works is because the eye is replacing the same *area* of the screen with a rhyming *area* of the next shot." For me they're actually working in a different way, though Stan did add to my consciousness about them.

Stan said something very good about *Triste:* "The shots never have a vanishing point." I had never thought of it in those terms, but it's true. I'm crazy about the period of painting that begins in the 1400s just before the invention of vanishing points. Piero della Francesca, Fra Angelico, Hans Memling, Rogier van der Weyden . . . When I go to Europe, I always make sure to see those paintings because that's a moment in history where depicting the world *as itself* was considered sacred. There was the beginning of perspective, but perspective hadn't become the egotistical thing it became later on. It was expression at a magical point between a negative feeling toward earthly life and an overly worldly sense of things, between a period of antiego and the later era of egotistical intoxification with perspective. That is,

---

For years Brakhage hosted a "salon" in Boulder on Sunday evenings, where he showed films and discussed them with small audiences. At the beginning this formal event was held intermittently in Brakhage's home, but later, Suranjan Ganguly, then chair of the film studies department at the University of Colorado, suggested that the salon be held on campus. From 1993 until Brakhage left Boulder in 2002, the salon was a regular event. Filmmaker Phil Solomon was much involved throughout the salon's existence.

the paintings had perspective as an aspect of human seeing rather than as the totality of reality.

That kind of painting influenced *Triste* and *Variations*. I said to Stan, "I hope every image is both a field of light energy and, at the same time, an icon: you see what it *is.*" But it's neither purely light energy nor purely icon. My cutting is also an attempt to create resonance without taking sides. I don't want to produce mental linkages that can be reduced to language. When Steve Anker saw *Variations* in my apartment, he remarked that to build a montage based purely on the visual and poetic seems so obvious that it's shocking that no one has done it until now, at least not quite in this balance.

Every film I work on to earn money—or 95 percent of them—is using images to *illustrate* language. I do it for money, but it's painful. In my own work, the world itself is the articulation, and film helps us to experience its magic and mystery, its beauty and complexity. I think that's what Ozu does, and Ford, and Antonioni, and Rossellini.

MacDonald: Your talking earlier about your LSD experience in the middle of *Summerwind* is relevant here. Drugs *did* awaken a generation who had learned from the society that looking at non-economically productive aspects of reality is not very important. Especially during those early forays into pot and LSD, suddenly we were really *hearing* sound and really *seeing* texture and *feeling* time. It produced plenty of jokes about being stoned, but for some it opened up a new kind of spiritual sensuality.

During the seventies and early eighties the idea of the spirit was put on the back burner, so that everybody could get their gender and ethnic politics right, and it never got put back on the front burner again. I think we're in a moment when many people are hungry to see in a more spiritual way and in a more perceptually conscious way. As a result, your films and Peter Hutton's are among the most popular films I show students.

Dorsky: Yes, during the early sixties the drugs were there, but the use of them was a bit aristocratic, part of a serious exploration. I hope you're right about the films. Generally my films have been completely out of synch for what's wanted in the larger culture, including the art culture. Usually, so much time goes by between shooting and editing that when I have finished a film, it seems a product of some other moment. I think that in *Variations*, for the first time, I was expressing the now, and I've been able to continue to do this for the past several years. I've caught up with myself, and my filmmaking finally feels "of the moment."

To me there's a real progression from *Pneuma* to *Alaya* to *Triste* to *Variations* (the other films made during that period, like *17 Reasons Why* and *Ariel* [1983], are more ornamental, a form of relief, or play). *Pneuma* is *pre-*image. *Alaya is* image, but it's working with the same principles as *Pneuma*. With both of these, it's always the same basic imagery, and at a certain point you get tired of saying "sand" or "grain," and the film becomes pure energy, or states of mind, and you can enjoy it.

In *Triste,* I'm trying the same thing but with *multiple* subject matter, where the chances of success are greater, but so are the chances of failure. As in life, the more you take on and do successfully, the more full your life is. The downside for me is the danger of falling into language-based meaning. *Triste* is also shot on old film stocks that don't exist anymore; it has this incredible palette of strange colors, a muted burnished quality.

MacDonald: When I first saw *Triste,* I wondered, partly because of the title, whether you had Warren Sonbert in mind when you made it [Sonbert died of AIDS in 1995].

Dorsky: I had been cutting *Triste* for a number of years before Warren died and wanted to show it to him, but it wasn't finished in time. I did bring a projector over to his house and showed him footage while he lay in bed, unable to speak, during the last month of his life. In terms of calling it "Triste," well, the film felt beyond a title. I felt I'd pushed the film beyond any kind of overall label, but I didn't want to call it "Number 3" or "Untitled." I really struggled with the title. Finally, Jerry and I were having tea at the Imperial Tea Court, and I said, "Jerry, I'm going psycho over this title!" Jerry knew it was a film about sadness, and he said, "Why don't you call it 'Triste'?" And I said "Okay," just to get it over with—even though there's *Valse Triste* [1977], which is a very strong film, maybe my favorite Bruce Conner film, along with *Take the 5:10 to Dreamland* [1977] and *A Movie* [1958].

MacDonald: I don't think of *Triste* as a sad film at all.

Dorsky: Poet friends see the title and try to make each image relate meaningfully to it. So in a way, the title is distracting. In fact, people tell me it's the most distracting title I could have given the film, and I agree. It's a terrible title—maybe, therefore, almost good. The only thing I can say is that at least the word is pretty. Maybe it'll help my French sales!

But to come back to Warren, I wasn't consciously referring to him in *Triste.* I can only say that from the early sixties, Jerry, Warren, and I talked of polyvalence, though we didn't use that term, which I first heard in relation to Warren's films fifteen years later. I believe it all began in dialogues between Jerry and myself. Warren, being very bright, picked up on it and went his own way with it.

I believe the origins of this kind of thinking for us began with two simultaneous events (at that time, we were not familiar with *The Man with a Movie Camera*). Around 1966, a poet friend, Michael Brownstein, exposed me to John Ashbery's *The Tennis Court Oath* [1962] and *Rivers and Mountains* [1966]. Of course, there was smoke in the air, and I began to read very slowly, one word at a time, and began to enjoy the resonance of each individual word, each following the next, somewhat like playing single notes on a piano very slowly, one after the other. This kind of mood was in the New York City atmosphere at the time—I'm thinking of La Monte Young and Tony Conrad. I began to wonder if one could make a film, *not* literary of course, but more open to the free-floating journey of Ashbery's poems. I'd ask Jerry, "Do you think a film could change directions with each cut and still hold together?" We hadn't gotten to the more delicate concerns we've talked about, that is, an openness that also accumulates; but we did take film very seriously at that point in time and talked a lot about it. A typical topic might be: Are the qualities in a shot its literal content or the visual texture of that shot? I'd begun to shoot the material that would become *Hours for Jerome,* and Jerry and I often shared our revelations and doubts.

The second "event" was that at this time, Jerry was shooting very beautiful footage and assembling it onto four-hundred-foot rolls. Everyone would come over to see them at Jerry's lovely, cheap apartment at the corner of East Broadway and Essex Street. It was at one of these screenings that I witnessed all that I'd been only speculating about: a roll of film where the purpose of the vision *was* the act of seeing and the montage *was* moving through itself for the very sake of moving through itself—a totally open miracle. The syntax had no obligation to any descriptive agenda, only to its own need to *be* from one moment to the next. This was a true revolution— a progression of visual emblems not unlike Chinese calligraphy.

MacDonald: What do you see as the changes between *Triste* and *Variations?*

Dorsky: By *Variations* I'd really begun to understand how to make a montage that opens up yet accumulates. A shot can't relate conceptually to the previous shot because if it's too similar or too parallel or too literal, or ironic, then a reductive connection manifests. If the shots don't connect at all, then it's nothing. It's easy to do nihilism in film; you just put things together that are so different that the imagery is not solidifying around meaning, like the "eye candy" of TV ads and MTV. At a certain point that kind of filmmaking wears you out. Strangely enough, the way the business world co-opted the avant-garde only emphasizes what in the avant-garde did not have deep roots in some kind of truly wondrous expression.

I want successive images to be disparate *and* connected, *and* I want each shot to link back to earlier shots. The connection can be as simple as the return of a certain red or of a particular pattern. Sometimes it's the iconography. There are various levels where your mind can make connections. They say that grandchildren are actually more like their grandparents than their parents; my method feels something like that. I want each shot to continue to play a role, after the next shot, and the next, have passed. At first I could only do it by chance, but slowly I learned how to make this kind of movie, and by *Variations* I'd begun to understand my method.

Variations is mostly Kodachrome 25 and is much more passionate than

From Nathaniel Dorsky's *Variations* (1998). Courtesy Nathaniel Dorsky.

Triste (Kodachrome II was eliminated around 1974; Kodachrome 25, its replacement, is not nearly as beautiful). Instead of being "monastically" withdrawn, and looking at the world as a quiet loner, the way *Triste* does, *Variations* expresses more involvement in and love for the world.

These changes are not something I consciously tried to do. They just happened as I grew—organically, the way a tree would grow. For me filmmaking has always been that way. I've never been able to turn films out. Making a film has always come from a spiritual or psychological need. With *Variations* I abandoned "the avant-garde" and fell in love.

MacDonald: Are you always collecting footage?

Dorsky: Yes—though *Variations* was the first film since my early trilogy that I made completely in the present tense.

MacDonald: You mean you shot all the material specifically for *Variations*?

Dorsky: Yes. *Hours for Jerome* was made out of existing shards. Nothing was added, except black leader and structure. Even in *Triste,* I used footage that was fifteen years old. For a while, for some strange reason, I couldn't go forward until I had solved all the problems of all the footage I had ever addressed with my camera. I think that was good in the sense that it has made me unsuccessful as a careerist.

Variations was right on the moment, and the films I've worked on since are even more interesting and in the present. These days, I feel quite in synch.

MacDonald: I know you edited several of Ralph Steiner's later films. When I was writing about Steiner for Chris Horak's *Lovers of Cinema* [Madison: University of Wisconsin Press, 1995], I was struck by how the sound tracks ruin his later films—at least for me. It wasn't *his* sound, and it nearly always causes the visual imagery to disappear or move to the background. I guess for his generation the bottom line was that films had to have sound. I think the sound is the weakness in your early trilogy too: the visuals seem so complex, but the sound is simple and obvious. There was a moment in the sixties and early seventies when it became possible, even moral, to choose to make a silent film.

Dorsky: Yes, it was definitely considered more serious. Mark McElhatten told me recently that he projected *A Fall Trip Home* silently at the Robert Beck Theater and that it improved. I've never seen it without sound. Of course, when you're first starting out, you want to try everything and be powerful.

I guess maybe the fact that my sound tracks weren't that sophisticated was an indication of where my interests were. When I first saw silent Brakhage, or Marie Menken, or Ron Rice's *Queen of Sheba Meets the Atom Man* [1963], for instance, I didn't enjoy the silences. I was addicted to picture *and* sound being served up as filmic reality.

Silent film *is* an acquired taste. It requires a certain revelation. Mine came during my third or fourth viewing of *The Passion of Saint Joan* [*La passion de Jeanne d'Arc,* 1929, directed by Carl Theodor Dreyer]. I can always tell if someone has had the same revelation—not necessarily from *The Passion,* of course—if someone actually sees what cinema can achieve with shots and cuts, understands its particular primordial quality. Most people only "read" films, missing the most basic level of the film experience. Yikes!

Of course, there have been remarkable sound films. Within the American avant-garde, Dan Barnett's *White Heart* [1975] has a beautifully worked track. The track is worked as much as the images. That's an amazing, rebellious film that refuses to even *be* a film—like a person not wanting to be a thing. Also, the sound for Jack Chambers's *Hart of London* [1970], which really is only four simple elements, is amazing. I'm always impressed with how much Chambers gets out of so little. In his earlier short film, *Mosaic* [1954], we hear the sounds of being on a fast-moving train, but the black-and-white free-associative montage is of subjects completely other, so that we assume the sound is abstract. Then, suddenly, Chambers cuts to a fast-moving train, where we see passengers in their seats. What has been an abstraction is suddenly surprisingly concrete, humorously so. But then, as the fast-moving-train sounds continue, we cut to a very still shot of people, seated also on chairs, in a waiting room. A series of lovely puns—all understated, poignant, and profound.

And there's Abby Child's recent *Surface Noise* [2000], which also has a very musical sense of sound; sometimes sounds are coincident with picture, then they'll go off on their own. I find this kind of articulation very rewarding. That's a wonderful film.

From an early age, I liked many kinds of music. Like any teenager, I enjoyed rock and roll—but also Mozart operas, and Bach, and Beethoven's quartets. I liked the integrity that music has as a direct articulation of emotion. What I learned to like about silent film articulation is analogous to what I like about classical music. Personally, I feel that many filmmakers in the avant-garde don't know about this type of musical language. Obviously, the combination of sound and picture in a theatrical film can also be fantastic. There has been so much genius in this direction that we can't even begin to talk about that here.

It's interesting that my real insights for a silent syntax come from watching the great dramatic filmmakers who went on to make sound films. It was their sound films that revealed for me the possibilities of a silent language. Antonioni is one of the few visual cinematic geniuses who began as a sound filmmaker. Of course, he made four very photographic shorts before his first (and, I must say, fully accomplished) feature.

It was Jerry who first pointed out to me that in Hitchcock the cuts have a magical snap. Each progressive camera placement is a joy in itself. I remember going with Jerry to *Strangers on a Train* [1951]—I think we'd eaten some hash—and the first third of that film, through the amusement park sequence, had a purity in its shots and cuts that was deeply moving music. Jerry taught me *to be* where each shot was taken from.

Later on, when I fell in love with Ozu, it was his deeply subtle montage, little jolts of space being altered on the cut, that influenced what I've been trying to do with my own work.

From these filmmakers I learned that each camera placement is extraordinarily important to the progressive plasticity of a film. The addition of each additional shot *is* the story: the shot is the encompassing energy, and the cut is the energy that intelligently moves the viewer to the next encompassing energy—the yin and yang of cinema. Cinema has to do with this magical, pith alchemy of shot/cut/shot/cut. It can be used by Stan in a sense that is internal and wild, as in *Anticipation of the Night* [1958], or in a pristine way, as in Ozu.

The point is that when I woke up to that pith alchemy, I started to be able to appreciate it in silent film, and I came to understand that sound was often just in the way. And I realized that silence produced another experience, something more monastic. It's *not* a Saturday night movie; it's not worldly. It's more a Sabbath experience—a chance to be alone and be quiet and come up against what cinema can offer: the screen becoming something, and then becoming something else. When that experience becomes full for you (and, as I said, for me it was an acquired taste), then why *not* use silence? It's cheap. I don't really have any ideas for sound, and I have enough to work with without sound. I'm a very slow maker, and I like to give an audience some time to be alone in this busy, noisy world. If you do become sensitive to silent cinema articulation, you will have the deepest possible of cinematic experiences.

I've always thought that in any film, it's really the music that makes you cry. In Ozu the cinema is gorgeous, to say the least, but it's his bringing in the music *on top of that* that's the last straw—then you break. It doesn't feel exploitive to me; it feels like he *deserves* to break you. I've been trying to see how deeply I can reach with a silent film. Could you make someone cry in a nondramatic situation? I don't think you could make people cry *the same way,* because without dramatic characters you don't create the human empathy with the sadness of our lives that Ozu's or Rossellini's films create. But for me there are things Stan does that are tearful not in their sadness but in their poignancy—some of the *Arabics* [*Arabic 1–19,* 1980–81], and some of the *Egyptian Series* [1983] and *Babylon Series* [1989]. With *Triste* I tried this in my own way. One thing that's very important is that a film must, moment to moment, respect its living presence as an individuated organism. Most avant-garde films and features are shallow in that they're determined externally by the maker, slaves to a declarative mind.

I've been going to see silent, avant-garde films for forty years, and I keep thinking, "Finally, we're at the point where we can accept the idea that under the avant-garde umbrella, some films are silent." But, no, every damn time I show my films, there's always the question: "Why are your films silent?"

I think the trick with that question is to answer it differently each time. Sometimes I say, "I'm an only child, and I like things quiet." Or, "Isn't the world noisy enough?" Another, deeper answer is that when you bring sound and image together, the result is more worldly, more social; but silence (*if* the audience isn't distracted) can go into a more primordial area of the mind. To use silence, of course, really means to *use* it, not just to not have sound.

The last time I showed *Alaya, Variations,* and *Triste,* they accumulated into a real transformation. I was moved because I knew each of those films had taken five years or more of work and a lot of pain, and there they were on the screen, beautifully projected, and I thought, "The silence is palpable and strong. This is almost as gratifying as a good western!"

MacDonald: You're one of the few filmmakers who still asks that the films be shown at eighteen frames a second, what we used to call "silent speed." In the last generation or two of standard 16mm projectors, it's no longer possible to do eighteen frames per second. How do you feel about your films being shown at twenty-four frames per second?

Dorsky: Mark McElhatten so much wanted to show *Triste* at the New York Film Festival [the avant-garde sections of recent New York Film Festivals have been curated by McElhatten and Gavin Smith] that he got them to convert the Walter Reade Theater's 16mm projector so it could show at eighteen frames per second. It cost several thousand dollars. It wasn't just for *my* film: the Walter Reade is a great movie theater, and if they're going to show some silent classic in 16mm, they should be able to show it at silent speed.

Exhibition *is* getting more limited, and I know I'm not being practical about it. But the good places—Yann Beauvais's Light Cone in Paris, the San Francisco Cinematheque—still have the option of silent speed. The PFA can do any increment between twelve and twenty-four frames a second. Recently, Steve Anker and I were looking at *Hours for Jerome;* we both agreed that the film goes a little too fast at twenty-four frames a second. *Part 1* works at eighteen, but for *Part 2,* eighteen is a little too slow. We tried it at twenty frames per second, and it looked fantastic. That's really how *Part 2* should be shown. So that's getting even more esoteric. The films I'm making now are made for eighteen.

Peter Hurwitz and I humorously call eighteen frames per second "sacred speed," as opposed to secular speed. Films that are cut for exhibition at sacred speed *need* that pacing. If you see *The Passion of Saint Joan* at twenty-four frames a second, the heart of it never opens. I mean you'll see something graphic going on there, but if you see it at eighteen, the heart opens. That's because of the way the rhythms were designed. When my films are shown at the wrong speed, their hearts never open. I choose where to cut from one shot to the next according to when each shot has reached the moment of ripeness. If that ripeness doesn't happen (and it's a matter of less than a second), and you go on to the next shot, it's like eating too fast. There's no chance of the *next* moment being profound because the *previous* moment hasn't ripened.

Eighteen frames per second is also closer to the threshold of solidity. Films changed to twenty-four frames a second because of the sound tracks, but twenty-four also made the image more solid. I like working on the *edge* of solidity, and I like that eighteen keeps films closer to the threshold of intermittence. The other and most realistic reason is that when the projector goes at silent speed, it's more calming on my psyche, more ethereal. The noise of twenty-four actually gives me anxiety.

In any case, I might as well do what I want. The audience is so small now that I might as well make *myself* happy. The few places that want to show my films *can* show them well, and my apartment with a projector in the room is my main pleasure.

But, yes, I'm painting myself into a corner because a lot of people may now be seeing the films incorrectly. The first couple of times I saw *The Man with a Movie Camera,* it was shown at twenty-four frames a second, and I thought to myself, "This is pretty good, but a little manic, and it never really has any feeling to it." Then I went to Abby Child's class. She was showing it at twenty-four, and I said, "Abby, could we look at just the first fifteen minutes again at eighteen frames a second?" We did, and *there it was.* All of a sudden it wasn't just rushed cuts; the shots *led* to each other. You digested one thing and moved to the next. I've heard since that Vertov wanted it shown at twenty-four. Oh well—but I do wonder if that's correct for the film, even if Vertov did say at some point that that's what he wanted.

I have a whole bunch of Bell & Howell projectors that have silent speed, but I can't get them repaired anymore because the wiring is so out of date. They're better than the Pageants, which go at silent speed, but have more flicker—something to do with the shutter.

MacDonald: The older Eikis that still have the possibility of eighteen don't have quite enough flicker for some of the early seventies films where the filmmakers used flicker as one of their basic rhythms: Larry Gottheim's *Blues* [1969] is an instance.

Dorsky: I could start to feel sad about all this.

Seeing good prints projected well is, more and more, like going to live music. The prints are vulnerable things; showing them well requires a live-performance kind of energy, and most film people don't have the patience for it. If you run the film department, how much more convenient videotape is. It doesn't even matter if light is coming in the windows. And you don't have the expense of the prints.

In general, things now are like they were in the very early sixties: the corporate mind-set, the whole thing solidified again, including all the alternative cultures. Even the people who are reacting to the status quo spend so much of themselves *reacting* that they've become *part* of it. The atmosphere *is* different than 1951, which was genuinely oppressive, fascist. But now, though modern culture includes a much greater diversity, it feels dead. So to me this feels like a great time to make genuinely libertarian films. I don't mean that the *subject* matter has to be libertarian; I'm talking about the process.

I hope *Variations* expresses this. It's me, a Bolex, maybe a little bit of weed sometimes, a backpack, a sense of the world being sacred. Trying to see if, very tenderly, I can touch that sacredness. There's a great Rossellini quote: "The truth is something very, very small, very, very humble, and that is why

From Nathaniel Dorsky's *Variations* (1998). Courtesy Nathaniel Dorsky.

it's so difficult to discover. If you have no humility, how can you approach the truth?" Working with my Bolex, I feel like someone whittling a stick. I'm not fighting with the larger culture in ways that keep me connected to it. I'm not *trying* to be marginal, just central to myself—and clear-seeing.

MacDonald: When did you begin to do commercial editing?

Dorsky: Around 1963 when I was in New York. I was very lucky: I had a cousin in the film industry. This was a time before there were a lot of filmmakers. Now they're pouring out of the universities, and everyone's looking for a subject to make their film about. I started working as a filmmaker when there was less competition. I didn't have, or need, any formal training.

For a while I had a job as the projectionist for a course at the New School called "Film as Social Comment," taught by Joseph Goldberg. He showed the canon of that period: everything from the Lumières, to Ford, Clair, Hawks, Dreyer, Rossellini. For three years, starting when I was nineteen, I learned a tremendous amount. Goldberg was a wonderful teacher. Adrienne Mancia [formerly at MoMA, now at BAM (Brooklyn Academy of Music)] and Lenny Lipton took that course while I was there.

Anyway, two well-to-do women, twins, wanted to make a film about painters. They asked Goldberg if he could recommend anyone, and he recommended me. I had just made *Ingreen* and *A Fall Trip Home;* they saw them and hired me. I was young and pretty, and I'm sure I was a pleasure to have around; they were maybe forty years old—you know what I'm saying. So we made a film for children about Léger, Chagall, Rousseau, and Gauguin [*Where Time Is a River,* 1966, directed by Gay Mathaei]. We got to go into museums after hours, and into wealthy people's homes, to shoot the paintings.

I did each painter in a different way: Rousseau, I did like *Ingreen*—superimpositions of leaves and tigers. I did Léger in a very cute Eisensteinian way. That was my first job, and after that opportunities just came. Whenever people hired me, I did treat the work seriously.

Soon, I was hired to shoot and cut a series of educational films based on Rudolph Arnheim's writing. One film was on shape, one was on color, and so on. Also, I was hired by Bob Young and Michael Roemer to be a gofer on *Nothing but a Man* [1964]. I won an Emmy for my photography on another film about Gauguin for CBS [*Gauguin in Tahiti: Search for Paradise*], which I felt embarrassed about because the editor, Luke Bennett, just told me what they wanted and I did it. At the ceremony, Imogene Coca gave me a kiss on national television. At home, my mother cried.

I tried to work on features in LA, but the level of anxiety and the struggle for money made me sick. After a year I realized it just wasn't me and came back here to San Francisco. A friend of mine, Richard Lerner, who had shot *The Cheerleaders* [1972, directed by Paul Glickler] and a great Bolex experimental feature called *Stop Motion* [1969], was making a film about Jack Kerouac [*What Happened to Kerouac?,* 1985]. I convinced him to let me shoot the footage to illustrate the audiotapes of Kerouac reading his poems. A thankless chore, because the words are so beautiful that the last thing you want is someone showing images over them. But *some* of the sequences are a little successful. The stuff I shot in Lowell in the winter is still very beautiful. Richard let me edit the film because he had had a falling-out with the editor, Robert Estrand, who had cut *Badlands* [1983] for Terrence Malick.

I've continued to work as an editor, here in the Bay Area, where, because of the Film Arts Foundation, we have a big conclave of documentary filmmakers. I have a reputation—even a little mythology—as a film doctor, because I've come in and "saved" people's films. A lot of films which end up on *P.O.V.* come from here, including three or four I doctored this season. There are films I doctor for two or three months and feel they've got a little bit of my hand in them. But in other cases, I just come in for two weeks or two days and help people when they're stuck. Most of the films I fix wind up on PBS.

The people who make the films I doctor tend to be absorbed in the sincerity of their subject matter, but they don't have a sense of structure. They haven't seen all of Ozu's films three times. They haven't seen every Antonioni, Rossellini, and Ford film that's available, three times. I have this kind of depth. I've seen every Minnelli film in 35mm. I've seen every Sirk film in 35mm (*and* the stuff he made in Germany in 16mm, like *Schlussakkord* [Final Accord, 1936]). I've got it all deep, really deep, in me. Knowing film history gives you a sense of clarity about film structure because you've seen every move that can be made, and you've seen how good those moves can be. Actually, as I'm sure you can tell, I'm a very traditional filmmaker.

During the last ten years Edith Kramer has been showing Borzage's silent films at the PFA. They're extraordinary and not easy to see. They're my favorite films now, in a certain way—my favorite films that until recently I hadn't seen! Borzage's films not only have deep humanity and passion, a male *and* female side, but his stories are expressed *as* the plasticity of cinema. Borzage understood that storytelling, psychology, camera placement, and plasticity of montage *all* have to be in union for a piece of cinema to become alive. And lately we've seen many films by Jacques Becker and Jean Gremillon—fully manifested sound films of amazing genius.

I've also seen avant-garde film for over forty years. As you've said, it was impossible to keep up with Stan, but I'd say I've seen just about everything of his. And so many other films. I love Jack Chambers's *Hart of London,* Rudy Burckhardt's street films, like *The Climate of New York* [1948] and *Eastside Summer* [1959], Stan's *A Child's Garden and the Serious Sea* [1991], and, of course, the free footage of Jerry Hiler.

I make a living. I'll work intensely for maybe three weeks, and then I don't work for six weeks. I stay poor, but I stay me. It does take you a while to untangle your mind from those jobs before you can go back into your own film. You need walks, drugs—because your mind is oriented around a decadent thing, which is using the visual world to illustrate a word-based information system. To me that's hell. I am very good at it, though.

The only way for me to deeply enjoy myself now *is* to live humbly, *be* with the sunlight, *be* with my camera, *using* my senses, confronting the particulars. When I go to sleep at night, I like to feel my being, without language as an interpreter. Getting *close* to something is one of the genuinely human experiences.

You said something earlier that I think is very important: that without the film industry there could be no avant-garde film, since we're dependent on the equipment and film stock that are manufactured for the industry. We avant-garde filmmakers are like poignant weeds growing up in the cracks of the sidewalk. We would not exist if it were not for the ecosystem that supports emulsions and projectors.

MacDonald: Right. You can't be monastic without a world to leave. You can't be pure in comparison to nothing.

Dorsky: Exactly!

MacDonald (to Jerome Hiler): Can we call you an "occasional filmmaker" in the literary sense of "occasional"—that you make films for particular occasions?

Hiler: Definitely. I'm an occasional filmmaker, but with regret—because I love people, and when I meet people who say, "We'd like to see more of your films"—basically telling me that I could make them happy by showing the films—I feel bad. There is a kind of joy that can come into someone's life from seeing something beautiful, and the good-natured part of me sometimes wonders, "Aren't you being a little stingy?"

Perhaps I have an inflated idea of what my films *are*.

MacDonald: How long have you worked with stained glass?

Hiler: Ten years.

MacDonald: Working in glass seems almost the opposite of filmmaking; I assume that once a glass window is finished, you can't not see it.

Hiler: Well, that's not true. I did a program on medieval stained glass at the Cinematheque, using slides: it was called "Cinema before 1300." People do go to the movies mostly at night, exactly when you wouldn't go to see stained glass, but a stained-glass work is changing all the time. As a result of all the things that can happen with the great Projector in the Sky, what a piece looks like at ten in the morning in autumn is *not* what it looks like at six in the evening in summertime. And even on a particular day, clouds drifting in front of the sun, a flock of birds taking off and racing across the sky, can affect the experience of looking at the window. A stained-glass piece never looks the same to me; it's always "a moving picture."

And unlike 16mm film, glass lasts! Which was part of what drew me to it.

MacDonald: Are your pieces in private homes?

Hiler: Yes. So far.

Dorsky: In our youth, there was the fantasy that our kind of filmmaking would make us successful, the way someone can become a successful painter. One was on a wave and would actually find a place in the world and be rewarded. And then at a certain point we understood that that wasn't going to happen. I think Jerry realized that in glass he could create objects that might last *and* get paid for making them.

Actually, I think the first images Jerry ever made with a camera were of stained glass. I remember Ken Kelman saying, "Jerry, film itself must *be* stained glass; you can't just photograph stained glass"—even though Jerry did great pixilated imagery of stained glass.

MacDonald: Nick, talk a little bit about Jerry's influence on you.

Dorsky: I met Jerry at the premiere of *Ingreen* in New York, and we became involved. Sometime later, he gave me a little film, his first—it was a birthday film, no title. What do you want to call it?

Hiler: Fool's Spring! *[Laughter.]*

Dorsky: There it is! A title thirty-three years in the making!

Hiler: Call New York!

Dorsky: We *could* leave a message with Mark and Gavin and see if they could still change the title on their program. Instead of *Personal Gifts,* we'll call it *Fool's Spring.* That's great, Jerry. [*Fool's Spring (Two Personal Gifts)* was shown at the 2001 New York Film Festival; it included Hiler's film and Dorsky's response.]

Anyway, I remember sitting in my apartment, where the second of the two films was shot, looking at Jerry's film with a writer friend, Michael Brownstein, and feeling things *opening* for me. Jerry's film showed a genius in understanding what film could do, perceptually. It was a real alchemical moment for me: film had always been something *not quite that,* and then all of a sudden, it *was* that.

MacDonald: So this helped cause the change in your work from the first two parts of the early trilogy to *Summerwind* and *Hours for Jerome?*

Dorsky: Yes. Jerry's film was the beginning of my using "stanzas," of opening up my structure in the way Jerry had done in the films he would show in his apartment. The openness of the cutting in Jerry's film, its open montage, was transformative. Once I saw it, I knew I couldn't go back; it was like losing some kind of innocence.

Hiler: When I was a youngster, I liked Webern, Stravinsky; and in painting, I liked the abstract expressionists. Back in the days before I was a filmmaker, I was a painter. Whatever my idea of art was, it didn't have to do with descriptiveness; it always had to do with the brushstroke a painter makes, or the sound a clarinet makes.

MacDonald: Was there a spiritual dimension to the idea of open montage, as compared with the intellectual control of so much traditional montage?

Hiler: I think a lot of the spiritual realm for us Westerners is an unconscious realm; we're only starting to become conscious of it now. I think art *was* religion among intelligent Westerners in the twentieth century. Our Western religions—pardon me if I offend anyone—are so corrupt that intelligent people are often not religious people, and yet there is a fundamental spiritual aspect to existence. I think that many Westerners have substituted art for religion.

Of course, in earlier times this substitution wasn't necessary, because the church, being so powerful, could hire the best artists to paint religious subjects. But I do think that we were unconsciously engaging in a religious, or at least spiritual, quest in our explorations of painting and music and film.

I was saying, "I like modern music" but, at the time, wasn't conscious of any spiritual dimension to my preference. Now that seems obvious.

MacDonald: I was in Japan a few years ago and looked at as many gardens as I could fit into the time I was there, and one of the things that struck me as remarkable about the gardens is that on some level they're anonymous; they're made by monks in monasteries. There's no way to put *a* name on a six-hundred-year-old garden. Your reticence about identifying yourself with your films strikes me as a hunger to emulate that—to make work without parading your person around. Even the title of *Gladly Given* [1997] suggests this.

Hiler: It could be. But there are many shades in that stance that make me suspicious—the-egotistical-maniac-disguised-as-a-monk kind of thing. We all constantly play tricks along this line. Am I this feather on the breath of God, or am I Adolf Hitler himself?—you never know which one you are, from one moment to the next. So I can't take one side or the other on that particular issue: maybe I'm the most egotistical person who ever lived, to the degree that I operate the way I do. I can't go along with saying I'm a self-effacing person; the record does not show that to be the case.

MacDonald: Well, the *film* record suggests it.

Hiler (laughter): Maybe. Maybe. Often what you *do* is what your statement is. What you *say* is very weak, compared to what you *do*. But maybe my reticence about letting my films go out is the *most* egotistical stance.

MacDonald: There was a moment, from about 1975 until just recently, when everything had to be "political." It had to have an agenda, often an ethnic agenda. In recent years, many people have been rebelling against this assumption. I read an article the other day about a filmmaker who identified herself as the first Canadian-Japanese lesbian to make a movie. I immediately thought, "Oh, yeah? I'm the first Scottish-British-German-Pennsylvania Dutch American bisexual to write about avant-garde film!" But so what?

Dorsky: All that's just capitalism in another form.

Hiler: It's about finding a marketing niche. Actually, I happen to be a quarter Lakota Sioux, though you would never know it, and I certainly would not desecrate my ancestors by saying that I'm a filmmaker representing the Lakota Sioux. As filmmakers, we're just who we are.

The false idea is that we're *leaders*. We're not leaders; we're just people making movies. And "avant-garde"? *Nobody* is following us except, perhaps, people who make Lexus commercials! So forget "avant-garde": we're not way out in front of anything. To say you're "avant-garde" is so self-aggrandizing and megalomaniacal. The same is true of "political," as if when they see my little film, people are going to take up arms—what vanity!

There was a moment back in the sixties when people not only had trust in mind but *tolerance* of mind, which is to say that you were allowed to, sup-

Jerome Hiler in Nathaniel Dorsky's *Triste* (1996). Courtesy Nathaniel Dorsky.

posed to, bare all of what was really in your mind, and people weren't going to attack you for it. The idea was that we would admit the craziness going on in our heads, let it spill out, and other people would learn from the fact that this really was what we were thinking about. The sad difference between that early generation and the subsequent, seventies generation was that people came in and said, "You can't do this, you can't say that, you can't even *think* this." What a sad development.

MacDonald: What you're "selling" in a film like *Gladly Given* is that anyone can walk out the door and just look around and be exhilarated by the reality of the world—they don't have to *buy* anything, they don't have to be a member of anything. That *is* political—anticapitalist if you want.

Hiler: Well, it's the politics of gentleness. Being gentle opens your heart; you feel your loneliness and your sadness, and then you feel your connection to things in a very simple way, and then nobody can come along and sell you the idea that you should be wearing a brown hat today.

MacDonald: How did *Gladly Given* come about?

Hiler: Accidentally. *Gladly Given* is basically composed of three rolls of film. The rolls were exposed during excursions when I was carrying my camera in my backpack. There was enough of a gap between periods of shooting so that each time I shot, I had no recollection of what was previously on the roll. When I got the rolls back, we looked at them, and a lot of people were saying, "Leave it as it is!" I went along with this because in fact I could see that the film had a nice sense of order that was not based on any manipulation that I had done—everything there was a surprise for me. And that's about all I can say.

I've been coming more and more to the feeling that the more I consciously *think* about something, the less of a good idea it is; my *ideas* for films are always less interesting than what's on the outtake roll. When I look at the outtake roll, there are juxtapositions of shots that make me go, "Wow!" For me outtake rolls are very important because I feel that there's a brilliance *out there*—of course, one should be very suspicious about what is meant by "*out there.*"

MacDonald: I told Nick that recently when I show his work, or work that relates to his in its sense of the world as something to be perceived and savored, students and general audiences are often excited, to a degree that I don't remember happening before. The idea of using film as a way of engaging the world in its moment-to-moment incarnation seems possible now. And so you might look at yourself as having waited for the right moment to release your work.

Dorsky: It would be perfect timing!

Hiler: It's hard for people like us because we're in our midfifties. At a certain point, ten or so years ago, we realized *we* were the old guys, that we were being rebelled against by the young people. But at the same time, I had *no* idea I was getting old. I think that what young people want most is some kind of go-ahead signal to be themselves. If Nathaniel's films say that to them now, that's exactly what Marie Menken and Stan Brakhage said to me when I first laid eyes on their films. That's exactly why Stan Brakhage excited me back in 1960 when I went to a midnight screening at the Bleecker Street Theater. I realized that he was saying, "Go be yourself, do what *you* need to do."

MacDonald: In this era the visual training young people get is primarily on commercial television and via the Internet. Nobody has said to them, "Just look around." You're not allowed to *just look around.* Everything is preparation for consumption.

Hiler: That's true. Sometimes, it looks as if the merchants are going to absolutely take over the universe. The air you breathe is going to be sold to you, breath by breath. It *is* interesting that there is still some kind of hunger among young people to experience basic reality through art.

We always used to call what we were discovering "alternate reality" or "altered states" or what have you—but now we realize that it was *reality itself.* The world of merchandising is the altered state.

Dorsky: I was talking to Steve Anker yesterday, out by the cliffs at Land's End, and I said that when I started making these kinds of films in the sixties and into the seventies, I felt it was a marginal stance. But as I've made my last few films, I've not felt that what I'm doing is marginal. I feel it's the *center*. And I feel that the hypnotized world of commodity is the margin, even if percentage-wise that world is 99.9 percent of what goes on. I said to Steve, "You should have the confidence that *this* is the center now. This *is* sanity."

I think it's become stale and pointless for filmmakers to express their resentment about being marginalized. I don't think I'm doing marginal work anymore. I think things have flipped; *we're* centric.

Peggy Ahwesh

Tom Gunning's "Towards a Minor Cinema: Fonoroff, Herwitz, Ahwesh, Lapore, Klahr and Solomon," the lead-off essay in a memorable issue of *Motion Picture* (vol. 3, nos. 1–2 [Winter 1989–90]), edited by Paul Arthur and Ivone Margulies, was to become a benchmark for a younger generation of filmmakers and the most articulate response to what was seen by some as the pretension of the "International Experimental Film Congress" that had been held in Toronto from May 28 to June 4, 1989. Adapting the term "minor cinema" from "minor literature," coined by Gilles Deleuze and Felix Guatari in their *Kafka: Towards a Minor Literature* ("There is nothing that is major or revolutionary except the minor. To hate all languages of masters"), Gunning argues that the younger filmmakers who most interest him forswear aspiration to mastery and celebrate their marginal identity, "fashioning from it a revolutionary consciousness": "These films assert no vision of conquest, make no claims to hegemony." While an earlier generation of critical filmmakers may have worked at breaking down the "ghetto of avant-garde film," these new filmmakers "proudly wear the badge of the ghetto," in the sense that they "recognize their marginal position outside the major cinematic languages . . . even when—especially when—they make reference to them." Of the six filmmakers mentioned in Gunning's title, Peggy Ahwesh is the least discussed in "Towards a Minor Cinema," though Gunning seems to have planned to write a second essay focusing in part on her *Martina's Playhouse* (1989).

At the time of the publication of Gunning's essay, I was not particularly in sympathy with it. For one thing, I had attended the Toronto event, and

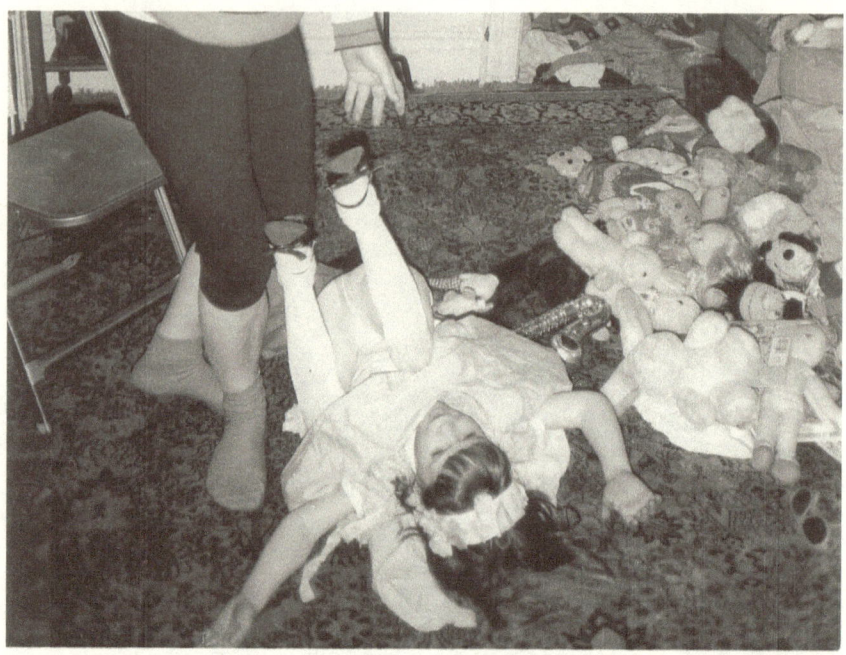

Martina Torr in Peggy Ahwesh's *Martina's Playhouse* (1989). Courtesy Peggy Ahwesh.

while I had reservations about it, I was grateful for the experience and hopeful that it would instigate further gatherings of critical filmmakers, scholars, and exhibitors committed to what was, and of course remains, the most underserved major sector of film history. I had been particularly frustrated with a letter signed by a number of American filmmakers, including all those mentioned in Gunning's essay, that had been circulated at the congress: it protested the "official History" promoted by the International Experimental Film Congress: "the time is long overdue to unwrite the Institutional Canon of Masterworks of the Avant-Garde." That the congress itself would show a very wide variety of work and would host presentations by a considerable range of scholars seemed irrelevant to those who wrote and signed the letter in the days before the Toronto event. I saw the letter as a lazy attempt at moral superiority, which ignored the difficulties of presenting such an event and was useful only in dampening the spirits of those who hosted a long-overdue gathering of those passionately committed to film history and current practice outside the commercial film and television industries. (A useful overview of the Experimental Film Congress and the responses to it, including the text of the protest letter and its signatories, is available in William C. Wees, " 'Let's Set the Record Straight': The International Experimental Film Congress, Toronto, 1989," *Canadian Journal of Film Studies/ Revue Canadienne d'Etudes Cinematographiques,* vol. 9, no. 1 [Spring 2000]: 101–16).

My second objection to Gunning's essay had to do with the assumption that the previous generation of critical filmmakers somehow represented a hegemonic force. That alternative approaches to film had a tenuous hold at a few established institutions hardly represented hegemonic control; indeed, as recent history has shown, whatever purchase the history of avant-garde cinema had achieved by the end of the 1980s did not lead to anything like a secure position for this amazing history, even within cultural spaces that honor a wide range of experimental and innovative work in other areas of the arts. To attack the congress because it was not perfect seemed to me the perfect irony; there were, and are, so many worthier targets! And to honor a group of filmmakers who were rebellious against a generation of makers who had established what little institutional purchase there *was* for alternative cinema, in the name of a "minor cinema," seemed to me the essence of futility. The history of avant-garde film is no more "minor" than the history of poetry, unless one accepts a sense of "minor" that plays into the hands of those who have the resources to nurture the full range of film history but don't want to be bothered with anything but mass-market cinema.

This is all by way of an explanation for why I have resisted certain kinds of work for so long—including the films and videos of Peggy Ahwesh, who may best represent Gunning's idea of minor cinema. As I have become better acquainted with Ahwesh's work, certain characteristics—including those that long obscured my ability or willingness to understand what she has been doing—have become clearer. One of these is the nature of the cultural influences that Ahwesh is willing to admit. A good many, if not most, of the filmmakers I have interviewed have developed art-making procedures and practices that are in overt rebellion against the conventions and cultural surround of Hollywood. But these individuals find sustenance in one or another institutionalized cultural arena: the histories of painting, poetry, and music—especially classical music—most obviously, but also of philosophy, psychology, mathematics, architecture, and the sciences. Ahwesh certainly takes such influences into account—hearing Charles Ives's music when she was a student at Antioch College was pivotal for her; *Martina's Playhouse* is much indebted to Lacan; and *The Deadman* (1990) is an adaptation of Georges Bataille's short story "Le Mort" (1967)—but she also admits to other classes of influence.

The diverse nature of Ahwesh's passions was obvious in a set of programs she assembled at the instigation of John Hanhardt for the Whitney Museum's

New American Film and Video Series in July and August 1997. Ahwesh presented a retrospective of her work within a context of films and videos that were, in one way or another, important for her. For the seventh program of the ten-program series, she showed her own *the vision machine* (1997), a sometimes laugh-out-loud riff on wordplay and jokes, after an auditory tape of the Troggs doing "Wild Thing" and before *Symbiopsychotaxiplasm: Take One* (shot in 1968, finished in 1972), William Greaves's exploration of the filmmaking process. The presentation ended with an audiotape of "I Had Too Much to Dream Last Night" by the Electric Prunes. The final program presented Ahwesh's *The Color of Love* (1994), which recycles and revises a bizarre piece of pornography found in an advanced state of decay, and *Trick Film* (1996), a bit of mock silent-era porn, along with Roger Jacoby's *Dream Sphinx* (1974), a hand-processed film of two lovers; Kurt Kren's *O Tannenbaum* (1964), a documentation of one of Otto Mühl's materialactions, in which a naked man and woman are covered by a variety of art and nonart substances; several trailers for soft-core films by Doris Wishman; and *Bad Girls Go to Hell,* a Doris Wishman soft-core feature from 1965.

These two Whitney Museum programs, like the others in the series, were perfectly coherent thematically but unusual in their combinations of films (and songs) usually seen as instances of quite disparate histories. Further, Ahwesh's tendency to present her work *with* the work of other artists from a variety of artistic traditions is a form of presentational collaboration in which she positions herself within a community of makers—usually rebellious, experimental makers—but without suggesting that this community is in any way exclusive. Classic films by Pier Paolo Pasolini, Walther Ruttmann, and Alberto Cavalcanti are welcome in Ahwesh's world, but so are horror filmmakers George Romero and Dario Argento; and Jean-Marie Straub and Daniele Huillet, and the Fleischer brothers, and Pee Wee Herman, and Jean Painlevé.

This collaborative dimension to Ahwesh's approach to programming is obvious in her own films and videos, many of which have been collaborative projects. *The Deadman* was co-made with Keith Sanborn; *Strange Weather* (1993), with Margie Strosser; and in those instances when Ahwesh is the sole director, her relationship with her performers is often a spontaneous interchange among equals. Further, Ahwesh's finished films and videos often include a wide variety of materials. *Martina's Playhouse,* for example, combines candid home-movie footage Ahwesh recorded of four-year-old Martina Torr and her mother, during which the child and the adult perform their mother-daughter dyad for the camera; home-movie footage of Jennifer Montgomery, who tries to seduce Ahwesh as she films; Martina reading passages Ahwesh selected from Lacan; and some animated flowers into a high-spirited, thoughtful, but open rumination on gender, sexuality, and childhood that is meant to be in dialogue with the television series *Pee Wee's Playhouse.*

Ahwesh's *the vision machine* includes documented scenes during which several adult women dress up as teenagers and enact a wild party: they play old pop music on early toy record players—the 45 rpm records are warped from age, and the music is distorted by the women's rough antics with the record players—and generally horse around until they sit down to a dinner enlivened by their jokes; the party concludes when Jennifer Montgomery assembles the women for a group picture and "photographs" them with "the camera my father gave me," by raising her skirt—an allusion to the climactic dinner scene in Buñuel's *Viridiana* (1961). Scenes of this all-girl party are interspersed with documentary recordings of two students on the Bard campus (where Ahwesh teaches) telling jokes, and with a series of visual texts designed by Keith Sanborn. The fun of both these films is not in their demonstration of an intellectual, or even a tonal, unity but in their very mix of pleasure and seriousness, clarity and mystery; they are a form of open-ended cine-play.

Even when an Ahwesh film seems more uniform, the experience usually includes a dimension that defies decorum—and the high-art pretensions of earlier generations of avant-garde media-makers. For example, *Strange Weather,* an enacted story about crack addicts in Miami, Florida, during a hurricane was recorded with a Pixilvision video camera—a low-resolution camera made for children—with which Ahwesh creates an experience that is gripping not only as melodrama but also theoretically: viewers cannot help but wonder where, along the axis between fiction and documentary, they can position *Strange Weather.* The *subject* is obviously serious, but the means for representing it are not "serious," though Ahwesh finds a way of making Pixilvision seem perfectly, even unusually, appropriate for creating an experience that has less to do with plot than with the nature of our relationship—and Ahwesh's and Strosser's—to what we're experiencing.

Unlike an earlier generation of film- and videomakers, Ahwesh confronts popular commercial culture not by avoiding it and by using methods that cannot be confused with it but by appropriating and recontextualizing it. In this, she has much in common with the two filmmakers to whom she claims particular allegiance: Andy Warhol and Jack Smith. Ahwesh does not struggle for public notoriety as they did—though, in fairness to Warhol and Smith, Ahwesh has found relatively consistent institutional support for her work; and even those of her films that have the power to cause a stir (*The Deadman,* for example, and *The Color of Love*) are usually seen in venues where audiences are predisposed to work that would be considered outrageous elsewhere.

Not surprisingly, Ahwesh works in a variety of media. She continues to make film (early on, she was committed to Super-8mm filmmaking, though in more recent years she has worked in 16mm) but is equally interested in video and digital technologies: *73 Suspect Words* (2000) is a video made up of the words flagged by the spell-check option on her word processor when she typed the Unabomber's "Manifesto"; *She Puppet* (2001) recycles and rethinks the videogame "Tomb Raider," which focuses on the adventures of superhero Lara Croft.

I spoke with Ahwesh at Bard College in February and December 2001, and we refined and expanded portions of the text by e-mail.

MacDonald: You take pride in your Pittsburgh background, in part, I assume, because it's been important in experimental filmmaking, with Pittsburgh Filmmakers, *Field of Vision,* and the scholar Lucy Fischer at the University of Pittsburgh. Also, it's Warhol's hometown. And it's where George Romero made the Dead trilogy [*Night of the Living Dead* (1968), *Dawn of the Dead* (1978), *Day of the Dead* (1985)]. Is it true that you worked for Romero?

Ahwesh: Yeah. I moved back to Pittsburgh after college. I went to Antioch from 1972 until 1978. I studied with Tony Conrad, who I still think of affectionately as a father figure, the elder statesman in the field who bequeathed upon me the esoteric knowledge of initiation that propelled me forward to . . . *[laughter]* whatever. I also studied with Janis Lipzin. And Paul Sharits was there. Cecil Taylor was artist-in-residence. Jud Yalkut had a radio show that I listened to a lot. There was a lot going on.

I particularly remember a show Janis organized: Joyce Wieland, Carolee Schneemann, and Beverly Conrad did presentations. It was a major event for me to meet these women and hear them talk about their work.

I'm from a little coal town downriver from Pittsburgh—Cannonsburg (famous for Perry Como and Bobby Vinton), one of those sad industrial towns. But I loved Pittsburgh and still have a lot of nostalgia for it. I found it very freeing, artistically; I felt like it was *mine.* Everything about it was up for grabs. I liked that it was "nowhere." It was not overdetermined as an art milieu like New York

I got very involved with the punk scene there in the late seventies and made a lot of great friends overnight. We documented the punk bands, and we were all making Super-8 sound films, and there were all these crazy characters to put in your movies.

My first job was at this place called the Mattress Factory, which was just opening in the north side in what was called the Mexican War streets, a rough-and-tumble working-class neighborhood with slight gentrification. I'm sure that neighborhood has changed. The Mattress Factory was this big art warehouse, and I ran a film series there. For my first guest I decided to call George Romero. He told me that no one in Pittsburgh had *ever* invited him to show his work locally. I was the first. I couldn't *believe* it.

He came with his wife, and we showed *The Crazies* [1973] and *Night of the Living Dead* [1968], one program at the Mattress Factory and another in a local high school. It was great. He was so friendly, open, vulnerable, not an egomaniac in any sense. I also knew a lot of people who worked in his movies, including several of the guys who were the redneck bikers in *Dawn of the Dead;* they were George's lighting crew and worked locally.

I worked on *Creepshow* [1982] as a production assistant, but I did all kinds of bizarre jobs—like I was Adrienne Barbeau's assistant at one point, which basically meant going out and buying her specialty foods because she had very particular tastes. And for about a week I was assigned to entertain Stephen King's son; I played Dungeons and Dragons with him. I had a walk-through in a shot where Adrienne Barbeau gets shot in the head at a lawn party. And I worked with the camera crew in the scene where the guy finds this meteor and the green stuff gets all over his place. People had to make the green stuff and dress the set, and I helped the camera people get the right amount of out-of-focus green stuff in the foreground and in the background.

I had a very flamboyant best friend, Natalka Voslakov. She's in some of my movies, and I shot some of her movies. She was one of the staples of my Pittsburgh years, an incredibly striking woman. Of course, *she* got a much better job with Romero than I did *[laughter]*—she was first assistant to the assistant director. My friend Margie Strosser, who I've worked with over the years, was an assistant editor. We all got to know each other.

MacDonald: Were you a fan of the films? *Dawn of the Dead* is a favorite of mine. Romero was so good about gender and race—and class: he gave us the first working-class American horror monsters.

Ahwesh: Oh, yeah. I'd seen all the films: *Martin* [1978], and *The Crazies,* and *Season of the Witch* [1972]. *Night of the Living Dead* is amazing.

At one point when I was working at Pittsburgh Filmmakers, George had given us a bunch of old film to reuse for slug—a whole collection of public service announcements he had done for local television, TV commercials about toilet cleansers, ads for candidates running for office, an antirape PSA, and a film about professional wrestling. I remember looking at this stuff to get inside the enterprise that was George Romero. For me, he's an important model for how to make independent personal films. I liked George's style, and he was such a warm, human person. George's groove was, "Have fun, make a movie, make friends, and mess around." I liked that he was a genre filmmaker and able to penetrate the popular psyche in a really profound way. I liked that he's a populist. There was as little hierarchy as there could be on a feature film. Working with George was really fun.

Ed Harris was very open to hanging out with us local kids. He went out dancing with me, Natalka, and a couple of grips, at one of the local watering holes, and I remember having such a good time. By that time Natalka had been demoted to production assistant, just like me! *[Laughter.]*

MacDonald: Pittsburgh Filmmakers is operating by this time, right?

Ahwesh: Yes. I worked as a programmer there for two years, during the time when Robert Haller was on his way out. I was the next generation. As a programmer I was free to do what I wanted, and I applied for grants and brought in a lot of interesting people and did collaborations with local clubs and the university—a lot of things that couldn't have happened under Haller. In 1980 at Pittsburgh Filmmakers, I did a big group show of local filmmakers. I was hot on the idea of group shows because they got everybody involved.

MacDonald: At what point in this history do you start making films?

Ahwesh: I made Super-8 movies before Pittsburgh, at Antioch and elsewhere, but when I landed in Pittsburgh, everything sort of came together. I was very involved; my boyfriend was a filmmaker—all my friends were filmmakers, musicians, photographers. The punk scene was us and various hangers-on. We would document the bands, and the bands would play at the clubs where we showed movies—we were our own ongoing entertainment.

I did some shows where I'd put people's names in the calendar and make up titles for films they hadn't made yet. For one particular show I announced "Wrapped in American Flags" by one person; "Dreams Congo" by another. But often people *did* make films to go along with these titles. That wasn't a thing you could sustain, but it was fun as a programming concept. We had a good time with it. It was a kind of cinematic matchmaking that went hand in hand with the parties and general flirtations among us.

MacDonald: Tell me about your *Pittsburgh Trilogy—Verite Opera, Paranormal Intelligence, Nostalgia for Paradise* [all 1983].

Ahwesh: It was the summer of 1983, a very hot summer, when I was hanging out with this odd trilogy of people. There was Roger, this very eccentric older guy who lived with his mother, didn't have a phone. I'd write him a postcard and say, "I'd like to come film with you on Sunday," and he would call me back from a pay phone.

His chess partner was a black transvestite, Claudelle, whose boyfriend was in prison. Roger and Claudelle were a dynamic duo. I had gone over to film them playing chess at Claudelle's house, so the scene of *Verite Opera* opens with Claudelle in her trashy apartment, cleaning up to get ready for me to be there. Then she puts on her costume, a blue evening gown and a turban, to play chess with Roger, this disheveled-looking, chubby, middle-aged guy. Roger was a member of MENSA and always involved with these lonely hearts' clubs, looking for an ideal mate with an IQ that corresponded to his. He would write to the women but never meet them. I shot a lot of footage of Roger's attempts to find his high-IQ mate, none of which ever made it into a film.

And finally, there was Margie Strosser, a soul-searching, articulate, concerned, naggy, feminist, aggravated-in-the-world person. Spiky red hair and tons of energy. I spent a summer with these three, and we shot a lot of film together. Basically I made three portrait films.

MacDonald: You titled it, I assume, after Brakhage's Pittsburgh trilogy [*The Act of Seeing with One's Own Eyes, Eyes, Deus Ex* (all 1971)].

Ahwesh: No. *[Laughter.]* No! Hmmm.

MacDonald: If you *were* rebelling against the masters, it might be a logical choice. Your trilogy is about personal friends; the focus of Brakhage's trilogy is social institutions.

Ahwesh: I might have known that and wanted my *own Pittsburgh Trilogy.* I had seen those films, of course, so I probably *did* know that at the time. I love those Brakhage films, but I think it was just that I had three films and they were about three people in Pittsburgh.

That was a great summer for me. The films—what are they *about?* I don't know. They're not diary films, and they're not documentaries, and they're not narratives. "Portraits" seems inadequate, actually, though that's the word I usually use. It was more like me doing conceptual exercises so that I could figure out what kind of relationship I had with the person, and what kind of relationship the camera had with the person, and how do you shoot positive and negative space, and what *is* it about people that makes them interesting? To me these three people were amazing examples of humanity, and I really liked them.

Maybe every maker has a film in which they're trying to work out what they want to convey through filmmaking. In any case, the lessons I learned that summer shooting those films I've carried with me ever since.

When I shot *The Deadman* in 16mm, people said, "Oh, she knows how to shoot! She knows how to use a camera!" But I felt that I was doing the same thing with *The Deadman* that I had done in all the Super-8 films, except that people just couldn't *recognize* it as *style* in Super-8. In *The Deadman* I was just applying all the things I had learned in Super-8 to a different camera. To me, my emotional connection to the action and the sense of three-dimensional space were exactly the same.

MacDonald: Were you a moviegoer as a child or an adolescent?

Ahwesh: I was not a moviegoer. I was horrified by most movies. I thought they had bad gender politics, bad cultural politics, and were a waste of time. I was a hard-core idealist as a youth. My relationship to music was much more profound and organic, which is still the case. Basically, movies came second to music, but I did abhor popular films.

MacDonald: Even early in your life?

Ahwesh: Yes. I only started to be able to watch film in college and only unconventional films. I remember going into Kelly Hall at Antioch to see my first experimental film, Bruce Conner's *Cosmic Ray* [1961], and, the week after that, *Masculine Feminine* [1966, Jean-Luc Godard], but these films I did *not* understand. I was tortured by them and found them completely infuriating—but they stuck in my craw. I couldn't figure them out, but I couldn't forget about them either.

Of course, allowing myself to be turned on to them was a large area of growth for me. I come from a working-class background. My parents were small-town, fairly conservative, churchgoing people who never cared about art.

MacDonald: We're very similar in this. I sat all sullen in a theater in Greencastle, Indiana, making loud comments about how the people in the audience (for Fellini's *8½* [1963]!) were a bunch of phonies for pretending that this gibberish made sense. But that stuck, too.

Ahwesh (laughter): Yeah, you decide at some point that you just have to face it. I entered college as a premed student interested in genetics, but when I started seeing these films, everything just flipped over for me.

I remember so distinctly meeting William Wegman, and the first time I met Tony Conrad, the first time I heard a radio program by Jud Yalkut, the first time I heard Cecil Taylor play the piano live, the first time I heard Charles Ives's music. These things, plus a few drug experiences, have really stayed with me as the peak *moments* of my teen years. I don't know how it works for other people.

MacDonald: Did you have to struggle with all the art experiences?

Ahwesh: No. I had a particularly hard time with the movies. Hearing Ives was a totally familiar, joyful experience. I was seventeen and had never been exposed to anything experimental, but it was almost like I was waiting for this change. My last years in high school had been miserable. I'd spent all my time by myself or with the other discontents, taking acid—we were all miserable people. We'd go to the football games to sit in the corner and yell at our classmates, "You're a bunch of jerks!" We'd go because there was nothing else to do.

The summer I was seventeen, I was in the Antioch College library, and I listened to Ives's *The Unanswered Question*. It changed my life. I understood pastiche from Ives, and homage and dissonance, three elements I value in my own work.

But my adjustment to the movies came later.

Those years, from sixteen to nineteen, having to figure out how language functions, how to be a philosophical person, how to make meaning and communicate it—those things all came together for me with art-making.

MacDonald: When did you go to New York?

Ahwesh: I left Pittsburgh to go to New York in 1982. I had been there the year before, for a one-person show at the Collective for Living Cinema, and I remember thinking, "Oh, I should just move here!" So I went back to Pittsburgh, worked for Romero a little while, then just took off.

MacDonald: No matter how much film I see, every once in a while, I run flat into a wall again. I think I've seen what there *is* to see, that I know what I like, that I understand what I need to understand; and all of a sudden, along comes stuff I just don't *get*. It makes me furious, because all of a sudden I'm stupid again and, at least for a while, don't know what to do about it.

Martina's Playhouse and *The Deadman* are the first of your films I remember seeing; I saw both long after they came out. *Martina* made me feel I was on the *other* side of a generation gap. I couldn't figure out what I was supposed to be doing with this film, what sort of pleasure I was supposed to take from it.

Ahwesh: That's sort of cool.

MacDonald: I also feel that my feelings aren't all that unusual, that lots of people feel the same—even if there are *also* lots of people, including many I respect, who *do* get it. I'm *still* struggling with *Martina's Playhouse*. Of course, sometimes things come along and there's *nothing* there, so you wait for a while until it goes away. But this isn't going away, and I figure it isn't going away for a reason.

So who should I be to get what you mean to give?

Ahwesh: That's not a fair question to ask a maker. Most artists don't make things for a particular audience of people who are going to be "getting it." The process is not that controlled.

But I can tell you what I did to make *Martina's Playhouse*. I was working in complicity with the camera in a space somewhere between the stare of Warhol and the emotional intimacy of home movies. It's a terrain where most of my Super-8 movies are enacted. Formally, they're very slippery movies.

MacDonald: Scary Movie [1993]—I think I do get. And if I get *Scary Movie*, I should get *Martina's Playhouse,* right?

Ahwesh: Well, *Martina's Playhouse* is much more complex. What you're saying is that in that film I'm not playing by the rules of experimental filmmaking you had come to expect. The work is not regulated by the formal devices of modernism—but what better way to address sexuality, girlhood, desire, and mothering than in a provocative home movie?

Formally my work is more like a younger generation's work. Intellectually, I was formed by the seventies. I come out of feminism and the anti-art sensibility of punk. I was in a Lacanian study group when I made *Martina's Playhouse*. Formally, my films are more associative than those of people who rely on structural modes.

Martina Torr in Peggy Ahwesh's *The Scary Movie* (1993). Courtesy Peggy Ahwesh.

MacDonald: When you told me you're the same age as Su Friedrich, I was shocked—I think of you as a generation younger than Su.

Ahwesh: Actually, I'm a little older than Su. In *Hide and Seek* [1996], Su puts young girls in a narrative film where they're playing with records and reproducing a sixties girl party. In my movie *the vision machine,* I have adult women *pretending* to be girls, who smash the records and have a big fight and pour beer on the record player. It's a very similar terrain, except that my imagistic and symbolic relation to experience is inverted. Su and I are friends, and we think very similarly, except that my work shades one way and hers shades another.

MacDonald: Yours shades toward Jack Smith; hers, toward Frampton.

Ahwesh: Totally. I make a pastiche of many things. If I had to pick an experimental filmmaker whose philosophical method I borrow, it would be Jack Smith, although he's one of the most *irritating* performers and filmmakers I've ever known. Just unbelievable. For years I did in Super-8 a lot of the things that he did. I would let people go on for *hours* and *then* turn the camera on, and they'd already be on the floor drunk and not able to function: "I thought we were gonna make a movie!" Or I would shoot a whole bunch of stuff and just use the last roll. Or I'd rearrange the rolls in a way to make what I shot less coherent but more provocative.

Allowing something to erupt out of a nothingness—I love that. And that was already there in those first Pittsburgh films. Nothing was happening in Pittsburgh; we were just hanging around. "What can we do today?" "Let's put on weird costumes and dance around. Let's make a movie." And things would just erupt out of seeming chaos. And films would get shot. Of course, editing is done in an entirely different part of the brain. As an editor, I was always interested in the things that were happening right in front of me that I *didn't* recognize, but that I was involved in on some level.

In my personal relationships, I like people in transition. I'm most comfortable, I think, with people who are going through something—they're having an ecstatic time, or a bad time, or a *lot* of things are happening and they're overflowing with changes. I'm attracted to that.

MacDonald: In the case of *Martina's Playhouse,* the incident that most people talk about is Martina "nursing" her mother. Did that just occur as they were playing? How much do you instigate the "eruptions" in your films?

Ahwesh: This is a question I get a lot, because when you make something that seems sort of unauthorized, or is not authoritarian, it's hard to figure out who's responsible and how, as a viewer, you should take it. In most movies, the plan of the producers is *there,* the directorial position of the filmmaker is *there*. Whereas with experimental film that's the thing people *can't* figure out. But the material I've shot with Martina, and most of what I've shot with kids over the years, I could never have suggested in a million years. I've never had kids, and don't know that much about kids' behavior; I only know about the mother-daughter relationship from the position of the daughter. In *Martina's Playhouse* the things happening in front of the camera were unknown to me, and I filmed them not knowing precisely *what* I was filming. That "nursing" footage sat on my shelf for two years because I had *no* idea what to make of it or how to incorporate it.

MacDonald: I expect it's pretty bizarre even for someone who's had daughters.

Ahwesh: I've gotten a range of responses from people who have children, from "That happens all the time" to "You have destroyed the sacred sanctity of mother-daughter relationships!"

In my Super-8 movies I don't stage things. I have no idea what I'm going to do, but I *like* not knowing.

MacDonald: How do you know you're going to be shooting? Do you say you're coming over to film?

Ahwesh: Yes, I say, "I'm coming over to film." And I usually *do* film, though sometimes it doesn't come out. Also, I have relationships with certain people who turn on when I come over with the camera; or people who call me and say, "I have a story to tell, and I want you to come over with the camera." I say, "I'll be over in twenty minutes." That used to happen a lot.

I guess those days are over for me, because I'm known as a *filmmaker* now; I'm not just Peggy-with-a-camera. And the people I hang out with are photo-aware. They know I'm going to make something and show it at some uptown museum, and that's a turnoff for me. It was different when I made a Super-8 film in Pittsburgh and showed the camera original at a party. The people who are attracted to me now are much more performative, and on the whole I'm much less interested.

MacDonald: In *Martina's Playhouse* the parallel between Martina, who tries to get nude at every possible opportunity, and Jennifer Montgomery, who keeps coming on to you and dropping her pants, brings back my children. The minute I would turn on my little Super-8 camera to make home movies, two of my boys would drop their pants. Did you get a lot of static about Martina's nudity?

Ahwesh: Yeah. The film showed on television, and the TV people wanted me to cut out the shot of the naked girl. It was a show that Steve Anker put together. After *Martina's Playhouse* aired on public TV in San Francisco, there was an investigation by the local DA, but the case was dropped because there was nothing illegal in the film. I find the film explicit but not pornographic.

MacDonald: Any parent sees that kind of nudity all the time.

Ahwesh: Since I don't have children, I don't have a deeply connected physical relationship with children's bodies; and in any case, I've seen so many movies that my world tends to be more about *images* than about the physical reality of people. I'd never bother to make a pornographic movie. I don't even try to make movies that shock people. That might be Nick Zedd's or John Waters's goal—and a perfectly sensible goal for them. But I'm just into a deep analysis, a *looking at* things that are meaningful to me, areas that seem worth investigating. And the childhood sexuality of females is a huge unexplored territory.

Martina's Playhouse is also me trying to figure out what my girlhood was about. In a way all my films are autobiographical. It's still true that there aren't all that many filmmakers who explore these areas.

When I came to make *Martina's Playhouse,* I had all this anecdotal footage about the lives of these friends I'm very close to, and at the same time I was reading *Camera Obscura*—the issue about Pee Wee Herman [No. 17, 1988]. There was also an article about how the baby is portrayed in *Three Men and a Baby* [1987] (which I've never seen), about what the baby symbolizes in that movie in the Freudian sense of baby/penis/feces. When I finally did take the Martina footage off the shelf, I knew exactly what to do with it. "Martina's Playhouse" references both *Pee Wee's Playhouse* and *Three Men and a Baby.*

MacDonald: What exactly was it that you knew you were going to do?

Ahwesh: I knew I had this loaded imagery of Martina, who was my main character, and that I wanted her to recite this Lacan text about the coming-into-being of sexuality for young girls. I also had all this footage of Jennifer, the adult woman playacting the young girl, which resonated in opposition to Martina.

Martina misreads the Lacan text in the movie, and her misreading is fantastic! The text is about the law of the father regarding sexuality, and Lacan is writing about a *boy* and his mother, not a girl. Martina changes the language in a way that's so freeing and enabling; it has so much agency. She rewrites Lacan in her own image.

I arranged the footage thematically, around the Lacan text and Martina's sexuality. The *shape* of the film?—in *Pee Wee's Playhouse,* Pee Wee goes into his house; he's got all his "friends" around him—the chair is a person, there's the genie in the little box; the mailman is a female, a femailman. Then all of a sudden a word drops from the ceiling. Formally I was thinking of that show with its surround-o-vision of symbolic elements and psychological tropes.

MacDonald: That talking flower is certainly reminiscent of *Pee Wee's Playhouse.*

Ahwesh: The flower's text is from Georges Bataille. There's a particular way in which Bataille animates sexuality through the language of flowers.

I put more ingredients into a twenty-minute movie than a lot of people put into much longer works. I don't know if that's *good;* it might *not* be good. My work gets really dense with references to other movies and to philosophical ideas; and there are certain things I won't let go of, like how you give people some control when they're on the screen. Viewers complain, "Your scenes go on too long!" but I want to let the characters finish their thoughts, and I don't want to chop them up into little movie bits.

That makes sense, right? My Super-8 films are like little playgrounds.

MacDonald: When I talked to Ken Jacobs about the Nervous System pieces, I was saying that one of the difficulties with those pieces is that I can't take notes: what's happening is performative and so evanescent that you can't really hold on to it. Now with your films I *can* take notes, but I stay mystified, partly because the films seem so open—though when you talk about *Martina's Playhouse,* it all seems very obvious.

Ahwesh: I think you have resistance to my work—perhaps you simply don't like it. Is it possible that the problem is that it's *so much* from a female point of view—which includes that openness? There are people who don't like the film because there's no explicit authority telling them how to think about the images or structuring the material in a way that reduces it to formality. I *refuse* to do both those things. I just refuse.

I think it's just that you don't *like* my movies—not that you don't get them.

MacDonald: Even when I don't like your films, I still want to understand them.

Ahwesh: Also, my work has an underachiever, self-deprecating quality, and maybe that's deceptive in some sense. You know, working in Super-8 *is* a devotion to the minor, to the low end of technology, to things that are more ephemeral and have less authority in the world. I am on the very edge—another Jack Smith tradition—of a whole enterprise that's on the verge of collapsing.

MacDonald: But on some level you don't really think it's fragile and ephemeral, because you're willing to devote yourself to it.

Ahwesh: It's my own challenge to history. I remember thinking, early on, "Oh, women don't write novels, they keep diaries." And they're minor poets, like Isabelle Eberhart, who had a very fragile, scant production. There's a romance about invisibility. I grew up hearing, "*These* are the *important* filmmakers, and *you're* not one of them. Experimental filmmaking was really important until 1975—you came afterward."

MacDonald: That was always a loony attitude.

Ahwesh: But that *was* what Fred Camper wrote in that famous *Millennium* piece ["The End of Avant-Garde Film," nos. 16–18 (Fall/Winter 1986–87): 99–124], and what J. Hoberman said in "Avant to Live" in the *Voice* [June 23, 1987, 25–28], and that attitude held sway through the early eighties. But now with the Internet, "marginality" has taken on a new cachet.

MacDonald: Last night I looked at *Strange Weather,* and I was struck by a connection with George Kuchar's Weather Diaries. You're inside this house with daily goings-on, and outside there's this major weather event that we hear about mostly through media. Thinking about Kuchar helped me make a distinction. In his melodramas—his fiction films, I mean, not the Weather Diaries—I get the sense that he's *trying* to make "a real movie," but the gap between what he can do and what he wants to do is considerable—and where the energy is. He tries to make the best movie he can, given his limitations. His actors can't really compete with "real" actors, but sometimes this gap makes for interesting un-Hollywood, or anti-Hollywood, work.

In *The Pittsburgh Trilogy* you're not trying to make a melodrama that you're failing to achieve; instead, everybody has decided to perform *themselves,* and you're recording these performances. In his melodramas, Kuchar is trying to do fiction, but the documentary reality that you see in that gap between what he wants to do and what he can do is the surprise, whereas you're actually doing *documentary* with people who are trying to be melodramatic.

Ahwesh: They're willing to fictionalize themselves, and I'm basically getting the documentary of that process. However, I think of it as a Warhol approach more than anything else: that droll documentation of off-beat personalities. Steve Anker [director of the San Francisco Cinematheque until 2002] programmed *Strange Weather* with *The Connection* by Shirley Clarke, and I found that an appropriate way to open up the meaning of the piece as a fake documentary and/or fictionalized real life.

The other big reference for *Strange Weather* was reality TV and *Cops* episodes in particular. Just because you make experimental films, your sources of reference and inspiration aren't necessarily from that world; they can be from anywhere.

I was friends with Roger Jacoby, who did a lot of work with Ondine. I saw Roger's films in San Francisco in the seventies. When I moved back to Pittsburgh, we were buddies for a couple of years. I was really taken with his reason for making work: he was trying to unravel a set of social relations between himself and his partners or his family. He was trying to understand himself as a social being by making films with little clusters of people who constituted some kind of community. I read the Warhol films that way, too: as a dysfunctional, extended family or some strange utopian commune of people, who could only *be* this way because there was film running.

MacDonald: It was interesting for me to go from *The Pittsburgh Trilogy* to *Strange Weather*. In the Pittsburgh films your performers seem entirely conscious of you, though as a filmmaker you're a bit detached, whereas in *Strange Weather*, you're doing this super-in-close camera work with your little Pixilvision camera, and yet *these* people seem oblivious to you.

Ahwesh: Strange Weather is an anomaly in my body of work, because three out of four of those people *are* actors. What was interesting about that film was that I came to it with this long history of making these "documentaries" with people acting in some kind of complicit relation with the camera—knowing the camera is on but agreeing to play themselves. In *Strange Weather*, Margie—who, of course, had been involved with those Pittsburgh films—actually met with the performers for rehearsals.

When we went to Florida to shoot, they ended up abandoning most of the things they had come up with during the rehearsals. That often happens. But we came up with *other* scenes on set and rehearsed and shot *them*. Toward the end the blonde gives this really long speech about the first time she used crack, at this party—it's an eight-minute scene, and a single take. She memorized the speech, and we practiced the scene a lot, and then we shot it once. It's a cliché from cinéma vérité that the longer a shot goes on without a cut, the more believable it is as reality.

It was great working with Pixil because, even though I'd imagined a scene many times, I had to reinvent it when I shot it—so that the results *looked like* I was seeing what I filmed for the first time, like in a documentary.

Initially we wanted the actors to actually smoke crack; we wanted the film to be raw and revealing. We thought we'd shoot it all documentary style—like a journalistic investigative report on drugs. But as we worked on the piece, the conceit of the artificial became this great metaphor, for me, for the artificial paradise described *in* the film, and it seemed best to have the piece be a fiction.

MacDonald: Who initiated this project? I assume it had to do with Margie's sister's stories.

Ahwesh: Margie's sister *was* a crack addict, who lived in Florida and had incredible stories. I think what happened initially was that Terry had decided to get out of that life and had come back north, and she had written up the various episodes of her life, which included living in a house that was a central office for drug sales and shopping at a drive-in drug window. Amazing stories. She got arrested a couple of times. We couldn't use most of her stories because they were way too complicated dramatically. We ended up working with one extended moment when she was hanging out with this cluster of people.

MacDonald: Talk about the collaboration.

Ahwesh: Margie is very political and socially oriented, and she wanted to make more of an exposé about drug use, something that might have fictional elements. For a long time we talked about a piece that would have dramatic elements and documentary elements, maybe interviews—more of an empowering thing for women who had drug problems.

I had all these amazing governmental reports about the drug economy, and I shot a lot of documentary and surveillance footage, including myself scoring drugs on St. Marks Place.

As the piece evolved, it became obvious to both of us that the fictional part was coming to the foreground. I read an interview with Derrida about addiction ["The Rhetoric of Drugs," from *Differences* (September 1993)] that talks about the imagination on drugs as a fictional space, an alternate reality—writing and lying, fiction and drugs, become this activated nexus.

Anyway, we had all these stories—Margie's a storyteller, first and foremost—and the hard journalism drifted away, and we started working with these actors, shaping the piece around the musings of this one girl. A lot of people see the tape and think it's a documentary, and think that the young woman who's telling the stories is lying to herself, because her life is actually much more miserable and screwed up, as we can *see* from our objective vantage point. I think, "This is fantastic!"

I like it when a work involves the viewer in some kind of dilemma about how to read its meaning. I don't do it as a punishment, but it's a very exciting, ethical, and philosophical place for me. My work is not supposed to be comfort food.

MacDonald: I admit I do spend a certain amount of time looking for comfort food. I *love* Sharon Lockhart's *Teatro Amazonas* [1999], but I know that part of what I like is that it feeds into everything I already like. It's a *new* way of doing something I'm familiar with, and it doesn't cause me problems. I could explain it to anybody, and defend it. I'm drawn to being surprised, but there are kinds of reassurance I like, too.

Almost every time I deal with a piece of yours, I either don't know what to do with it, or when I *think* I've got it, as in the case of *Strange Weather,* which I *did* assume was a documentary—duh!—I've got it backward.

So when did the Pixilvision come into the *Strange Weather* project? It's one of the more elaborate Pixil pieces.

Ahwesh: I wasn't sure how *Strange Weather* was going to work out, so I went to Florida with a surveillance camera, a Super-8 camera, and a Pixil camera. The decision to use Pixil had been made in New York before we went. I knew that with the Pixil camera I would be able to make overly dramatic things look *under*dramatic, and things that were nothing to look at, spectacular and tactile—and the drug world look grim and raw. I thought, "Degraded and grainy, Pixil will give me the right texture."

I remember being out on this patio in Florida, knowing I was shooting what would be the first shot in the video, the Pixil palm trees.

MacDonald: A beautiful shot, especially with the sound.

Ahwesh: I remember thinking to myself, this has got to be the first shot of the video, because you can't tell what the fuck it is; you don't know what the *object* is, what the *scale* is; it has odd, unnatural movement—and *then* you realize it's a palm tree and you're in Florida in grainy black-and-white. I made that shot, and thought, "Oh, I know how to make this work!" There was something about the alienation of the shot, the black and white and the semiabstraction, that helped me figure out how the whole video would come together.

MacDonald: How was it working with the actors? The blonde is quite good.

Ahwesh: Really good. She's a working-class girl from Philadelphia. The first time we did auditions for the part, we asked her to do one, and she turned out to be the best. She was having a love affair with Cheryl [Dunye], who plays Crystal, so *that* was sticky. Cheryl was pretty much a bitch the whole time. She *hated* Margie. At one point the two of them took me aside and told me to take over the project and get rid of Margie. Margie can be sort of square about things. She might tell them, "You have to go to bed now, because we have to shoot tomorrow!"—that sort of thing. They didn't respond well to that.

MacDonald: Would Margie agree with you on this?

Ahwesh (laughter): Probably not. Anyway, it's hard to work with other people, and we had a tough time on this one.

MacDonald: How real is the drug use in the film?

Ahwesh: In the drug scenes, they're not actually smoking; it's soap in the pipes.

Audiences often ask, "Did *you* smoke crack?" I never answer directly. I say, "What's interesting is that as a viewer you feel an ethical dilemma: either the director is a crackhead, and that's why she did this piece, or she's making a documentary about these poor people that you're supposed to feel sorry for." That is, only if it's a piece of investigative journalism, where you're trying to root out evil and show these people for who they really are, is it justified; if it's *fiction,* you don't have to feel responsible *and* you don't approve. So I never answer the question, because it's not about me and my drug problem (I don't have one), and it's not about me and my "voyeuristic" relationship to drugs (I don't really have one of those either). But I do like that the film sets up a really ambiguous ethical space.

In reality what happened is that in Florida I found out where to get crack, how they sell it, what it looks like, where to keep it—because you can't have it on your person—and what it's like to smoke it. I felt I needed to know that information for the tape. My two production assistants and a local friend helped find where people deal drugs in Miami.

MacDonald: So what *was* it like to smoke it?

Ahwesh: I have to admit I liked it. I've only done it a couple of times—because it's *incredibly* addictive. It's low grade, oily, *very* oily—like an industrial substance, like a toxic waste dump. If you're at all feeling End of the Industrial Age despair, a despair that's gritty and like the exhaust pipe on a car, you can easily lock into crack. It's a greasy high, almost syrupy. After I did it the first time in New York, I craved it for a week! I thought, "I can see why people get addicted to *this.*" It's a short, fast, up high, really high, heart palpitations, and then you just get completely clouded over. It's not an elegant drug.

I don't do a lot of drugs. I'm too busy. I'm just not the type. But I've tried everything once. The other people in the movie were not interested in taking the drug, because they were *actors* and they wanted to fake it. *Someone* had to figure out how to fake it correctly! And it ended up being me. I did think they were a bit dilettantish about the subject. They clearly weren't actors who were going to gain thirty-five pounds so they could *be* Jake LaMotta.

MacDonald: When you were making *Strange Weather,* had you seen any of the Kuchar Weather Diaries?

Ahwesh: I'd seen *Wild Night in El Reno* [1977]. I love Kuchar, but I wasn't really thinking of him. I don't know the video Weather Diaries. It's more like *Clash by Night* [1952, directed by Fritz Lang] meets *The Connection.*

I would say that with *Strange Weather,* like with everything I've made, I get the footage, and *then* the real work starts. The editing is like putting a puzzle together. I *never* get footage in the can that edits easily. I always have an ornate, complicated pastiche relationship to my editing. I'm always reinventing the work as the process goes along.

MacDonald: I hated *The Deadman* when I first saw it.

Ahwesh: I know, you keep telling me!

MacDonald: It felt like a student film—suburban kids trying to be outrageous. Later I thought that there *is* a student film aspect to it. It's somewhere in between B horror film, porn, and student film.

Ahwesh: I Was a Teenage Biker Deadman Vampire for the FBI?

MacDonald: But the personae in B films are these big adults, whereas in *The Deadman,* they're young adults, almost kids.

Ahwesh: Originally I cast the film with completely different people, who *were* older and gnarlier. Kurt Kren was supposed to play the Count. The people I ended up working with were San Francisco Art Institute grads and had been in Kuchar movies. You might recognize them.

The Deadman was the first film I shot in 16mm. We did have a script, which is unlike my early films, and everybody read the script once, then tossed it away, and we never referred to it again. *The Deadman* was a hybrid of my Super-8 movies and this well-known literary source, the Bataille story, which to me felt very foreign.

I don't think anyone in *The Deadman* was *trying* to be outrageous. These *are* people who would have done anything for fun; they're transgressive people, but if it looks as if they're *trying* to be outrageous, then the film is not working: it's supposed to read as a-day-in-the-life, in some very ironic sense. I was trying to use the woman and sexuality and the body to make a philosophical point.

MacDonald: Talk about the point.

Ahwesh: Yvonne Rainer had made *The Man Who Envied Women* [1985], where at the beginning of the film the woman packs up her bags and leaves the movie. I remember seeing that and thinking, "As a Lacanian response, that's really smart." It's a really knowledgeable, thought-through Lacanian position about women and sexuality in this culture—the woman can't even be *in* the movie because she's *so* misunderstood and misrepresented by language and imagery. I understood that gesture as an end point in a kind of logic about women and sexuality. First, you make the woman into text, and then you remove her from the movie.

Keith [Sanborn—Ahwesh's partner] and I had many discussions about this, and we were interested in somehow reinserting woman as a sexual agent into the movies. A sexed being, female, gendered, who was the *agent* of the action. In a nutshell, that's what we tried to do; that was the game that we were playing. Could you have a woman be the main character and have movie sex, and confront the audience in a material way? The film was basically about that, and about what you can discover in relation to that. So in that way *The Deadman* was a response to *The Man Who Envied Women.*

And also, we thought the original Bataille story was fantastic.

MacDonald: When did you first come in contact with Bataille's story?

Ahwesh: Keith read Bataille in the seventies. The book we published is Keith's translation of "Le Mort." Bataille is part of the canon in France, but here he wasn't known. I knew about Bataille because of Keith.

Bataille is hard to put your finger on, because he wrote anthropology texts, a book on the paintings of Lascaux, fiction, poetry, was into psychoanalysis; he wrote a couple of serious books on economic systems. He wrote on surrealism, on architecture, on eroticism and the history of painting; he was a Nietszche scholar. This is a complex thinker. He doesn't form a cohesive philosophic system, like Lacan does. He's heterogeneous. He's not someone you can make consistent and whole, but the *heterogeneity* of his writings and his interests is fascinating and generative. You have this person who is in touch with all these different fields, has some philosophical relationship to many areas. *The Deadman* is a fiction book that relates to ritual in a tribal culture, to initiation, membership.

MacDonald: Did the original text of *The Deadman* have the summaries of the action at the bottom of the pages?

Ahwest: Yes, the layout of our book mimics the original French and started us thinking about using intertitles in the film.

I like how Bataille does not explain the emotions of the characters in "Le Mort." You're not given reasons why. You're not told that this woman is insane, or has a memory problem, or whatever. Characters don't *feel* in the book. It's a set of actions, a weird outline for something that has to be a stand-in for something else—like how a woman goes through life. She wins and loses. How *does* a woman get agency in a male culture? In a way, the book is a blueprint for that.

MacDonald: I've heard you talk about *The Deadman, The Color of Love,* and *Nocturne* [1998] as a trilogy. Will there be a fourth part; will it be a quartet?

Ahwesh: No, I'm done with that. But it wasn't even planned as a trilogy; it just happened that way, very slowly over a ten-year period. I never thought of it as a trilogy until a programmer—Jonas Mekas, actually—wanted to show the three films together at Anthology and decided they were a trilogy. I thought, "OK, it's a trilogy."

I went out with Abby Child not too long ago, and she said, "All your work is about death, ew." I thought, "I guess that's true." My video piece *She Puppet* has a lot of ecstatic death moments in it. But the protagonist always pops back alive. I think my work is not really about death, definitely not the old death-as-a-punishment-for-sex thing. I like a horror movie you go to to have an experience of hyperviolence and uncanny death. It's like an amusement park ride; you don't really want to *die;* you want to feel some totally hyperreal, bizarre fantasy of near death that allows you to live your normal life in a way that's less stressful and less neurotic. I'm doing the experimental film version of that kind of "death."

Peggy Ahwesh 133

Illustration by Andy Masson from the book *The Deadman* (New York: Ediciones La Calavera, 1989), Keith Sanborn's translation of Georges Bataille's "Le Mort" (1967), published in conjunction with the release of Peggy Ahwesh's film *The Deadman* (1990). Courtesy Peggy Ahwesh.

I *love* violent horror movies; I love the excessiveness of them. I don't want to be violated literally—but I like excessiveness, completely-over-the-top-ness, and all my deadman movies are horror movies. I like the Italian seventies horror movies especially. In terms of my fantasy life, I find horror films very liberating. I'm into preserving the distance between my real life and the movies, both when I go to movies and when I make them. To me horror film is *not* about women having to die.

MacDonald: If you look at the history of the horror genre over the last fifty years, it's about how women need to, and are, getting stronger.

Ahwesh: At the end of *The Texas Chainsaw Massacre* [1974], the only person left is a woman. And the same is true in the Romero films.

MacDonald: By the time you get to the *Nightmare on Elm Street* films, you have the woman getting pissed off and wanting to go back in there and kick Freddy's ass. The woman becomes a battler.

The real premonition of *The Deadman* is probably *Un chien andalou* [1929, Luis Buñuel and Salvador Dali].

Ahwesh: You know, *Un chien andalou* is the only film that Bataille mentions in his writings. We pored over Bataille looking for references to movies.

MacDonald: Thinking about *Un chien andalou* helps me with *The Dead-*

man. I have no problem seeing how funny the Buñuel-Dali film is. If I think about what the people in *Un chien andalou* must have looked like to people in their own moment, it was probably much the same film. Dali and Buñuel are now major figures, and their film has become a classic, so the actors now look very distinguished, and the film feels "important."

Ahwesh: Yes, their shabby clothes have become dignified.

MacDonald: The Deadman did do what a shocking film is supposed to do: it shocked me and pissed me off. I have to give it that.

Ahwesh: I never make movies to shock people. First of all, I don't know how you can predict that that would happen. It seems pretentious.

MacDonald: I can see why you wouldn't see that *Martina's Playhouse* would be shocking, but *The Deadman* is one long transgressive moment. One of the first events is Jennifer squatting down in the woods, in this silly raincoat, and taking a pee.

By the way, I know you're working on a Caldwell project. Did you know that the play *Tobacco Road,* the adaptation of Caldwell's novel, opens with one of the characters walking out onstage and taking a pee?

Ahwesh: I didn't know that, but I think of *The Deadman* as one long female juissance, not a transgression at all.

You don't see a woman spreading her legs and shoving her crotch in someone's face in a way that's provocative, but *not* seductive, and saying, "Look how pretty I am!" The woman in *The Deadman* does incredibly provocative things in an *aggressive* way.

In most movies the women are sexualized in a way that allows them to be incorporated into male fantasy; in *The Deadman* I keep you outside of male fantasy. A woman taking a piss in the woods, or pissing *on* somebody in an unromantic, nonseductive way—there's no category for *that* in the movies. For me these are feminist gestures.

MacDonald: I suppose the only time I've seen comparable activities is in the Mühl-Kren *Materialaktionfilms.*

Ahwesh: Yeah, outside of porn, *Materialaktionfilm* is the one place. In some ways that set of films was an inspiration for ours. We were very involved with Kurt Kren at the time. He was a good friend, and we really wanted him in the movie. In the *Certain Women* project, I would say that the figure who hovers over us is Fassbinder. For *The Deadman* it was definitely Kurt Kren. He was our angel who gave his blessing to the project.

I was also thinking about Iggy Pop quite a bit, making *The Deadman.* Iggy Pop is an American original. You can't really copy Iggy Pop; what he does is so crude and so ridiculously personal, and low end, and scatological, and antisocial—and yet, twenty years of rock music is largely based on him. I was doing Iggy Pop to Yvonne Rainer's David Bowie.

MacDonald: Where did you find the material you use in *The Color of Love?*

Recycled porn imagery in Peggy Ahwesh's *The Color of Love* (1994). Courtesy Peggy Ahwesh.

Ahwesh: A friend of mine dropped off a so-called donation at Bard: six big boxes of cans and reels that had been left out in the rain. In all those boxes there was one reel of Super-8mm. I thought I might as well check it out. I looked at it on the Super-8 viewer and realized it was pretty interesting.

MacDonald: Is *The Color of Love* a ready-made?

Ahwesh: Well, no. I did a lot of editing.

I'm not like Phil Solomon: I'm not an optical printing whiz. And I'm not systematic. Basically, I did an improv on the optical printer with the footage. I treat my machines almost like dance partners. I did two sessions on the printer and messed around, eyeballing it, slowing some sections down and speeding others up a bit, repeating some things, and elongating the cunt shots. And then I recut that material on the flatbed.

MacDonald: And the color and texture?

Ahwesh: I filtered it a bit, made it a little more purple, but basically, the undulations, the emulsion decay, and the color are what was there.

I showed *The Color of Love* footage a couple of times at parties, just the dailies off the printer, and I remember M. M. Serra wagging her finger at me and saying, "Don't make it too long; you'll ruin it!" It's on the verge of being too long.

There are cuts in the music, too. Keith helped me sync it up and be sure the sound was coming in on the right frames.

MacDonald: At Ithaca College, you talked about the assemblage process of doing *Nocturne.*

Ahwesh: Nocturne is a dream space, a return of the repressed in a dream space, and about repetition compulsion. It's not much of a story. The woman kills the guy, and she drags him across the lawn, goes to sleep, and there he is, haunting her. She has restless sleep and senses something, some paranormal presence, and then she has to kill him again. That's it. There's a sensibility, a sense of space and time being collapsed or stopped, protracted, and a struggle between elemental male and female principles. That's how I think of it.

Nocturne is based on a review of a Mario Bava film originally called *The Whip and the Flesh* [1963] and released in the United States as *What!* Bava is one of my favorite Italian seventies horror filmmakers: Dario Argento, Bava, Lucio Fulci. Do you know their work?

MacDonald: No.

Ahwesh: Oh my god! Go see *Suspiria* [1977]; it's fantastic! Argento and Mario Bava—and Barbara Steele, who's the star of a lot of those films—are amazing!

So Steven Shaviro wrote a review of *The Whip and the Flesh* on the Net—eight hundred words—and I never could find the film, so I based *Nocturne* on *the review.* He had already reduced the film down to the relationship between these two people, and I reduced it further.

I finally *did* see the original: Kathy Geritz showed *Nocturne* at Pacific Film Archive along with a 35mm print of *The Whip and the Flesh,* which she borrowed from somebody's archive in LA. My film is black and white; Bava's is in color. His is a whole elaborate Victorian period piece; mine is no-period, basically. His is a drama about a dysfunctional family that lives in a castle by the water, with trick fireplaces—a haunted castle movie with all kinds of gothic cult elements. Mine is a minimal piece, with a little touch of gothic austerity. I like Bava's film, but I don't think he'd be interested in mine.

MacDonald: Did you do any storyboarding? What kind of planning was involved in *Nocturne?*

Ahwesh: I had twenty-five note cards with different scene ideas written on them. We shot all twenty-five in two or three days; and then over the period of a year, I cut it and added cutaways and other kinds of associative material—doing an assemblage not only from the visual material but also from different literary resources that I read *after* the shooting was done. It was totally an assemblage project—like an essay, with narrative elements.

MacDonald: It reminds me a bit of *Damned If You Don't* [1983, Su Friedrich] in its combination of materials.

Ahwesh: Oh, that's interesting. They *are* similar in that way.

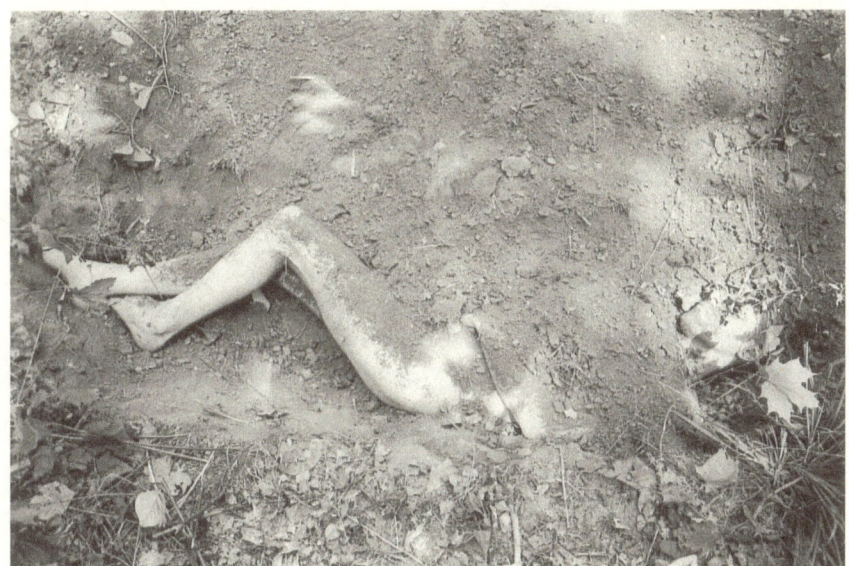

Dead man (Bradley Eros) in Peggy Ahwesh's *Nocturne* (1998). Courtesy Peggy Ahwesh.

You know, we mostly don't know the meaning of what we're doing at any given moment, but after twenty years, you begin to figure your own gestures out.

MacDonald: I'm surprised that *Trick Film,* your little S&M porn film, isn't shown more. It would go well with *The Color of Love,* and in a different way, with *Nocturne.*

Ahwesh: M. M. Serra wanted to do a sex scene with that woman, Beth, because she's so sexy, and we thought the idea of Beth playing the doggie and Serra, the master, would be classic. I built the doghouse and bought the little props and made Serra's outfit. Serra is the dominant type, as you'd never guess from her way of getting through the world; she's always the one with the whip, and would never get down on all fours.

We did another film [*The Lesson,* 1996] in which Serra is the teacher and I'm the bad student who needs to be punished—a funny idea since *I'm* the college professor! I *never* show that one.

MacDonald: How did *the vision machine* evolve?

Ahwesh: I started with the dinner party, a reconstruction of the Buñuel dinner party in *Viridiana* [1961]. I had read in Lacan a reference to "the camera that my daddy gave me," and went back and watched *Viridiana* and decided to make an "essay film" around the psychoanalytic and film-historical idea of joke telling. In Buñuel's dinner scene, the people around the table tell weird jokes that I don't really get (since I'm not part of that culture), and that made me think about Freud's *Wit and Its Relationship to the Unconscious,* and how the jokes in that book aren't funny either!

Freud says that the economy of joke telling happens between men, and that women are psychically so out of the loop of culture that the passage of that kind of cultural meaning doesn't work between them, or even between women and men; and also that jokes are often told at the expense of women. So I decided to play with the gender politics of joke telling. Lucy Smith tells sex jokes at the expense of men, and so on.

MacDonald: Had you heard Lucy Smith's jokes before you recorded her? Her sequences are shot on the Bard campus; was she a Bard student?

Ahwesh: I taught Lucy those jokes, and yes, she was a Bard student at the time.

MacDonald: Is *the vision machine* named after the Paul Virilio book [*The Vision Machine,* 1994]? Why the lowercase title?

Ahwesh: Yeah. The cunt is the "vision machine" of the female. The lowercase is to be humble.

MacDonald: What are the sources of the quotes in the text passages—other than the two pop songs? Keith Sanborn is credited with "text animation"; did he choose the texts?

Ahwesh: The one I remember is "The vapid 'givenness' of the image is at the same time its secret openness to passion and desire"—from Steven Shaviro, a film theorist from Seattle who has written eloquently on personal feeling and subjectivity in experiencing the cinema. Another is from Rosalind Krauss's book on Duchamp.

I chose the texts. Keith animated them, helped me turn them into spirals (some of them reminiscent of the roto-reliefs of Marcel Duchamp, which are full of jokes and sexual innuendo), and so forth.

MacDonald: Recently, you've been working digitally and in video. *She Puppet* has gotten a lot of attention.

Ahwesh: Some people read *She Puppet* as a conceptual work, as an alteration of a cultural product—it's often treated differently from most of my videos or films. It's seen as an *idea* movie. It's entered the art world in a way that my work hasn't before. *I* think of *She Puppet* as another found-footage piece. I collected the material and then reworked it. It's about this female entity, and is a riff off a videogame with this virtual superstar from the popular imagination (Lara Croft).

Over the years, I've usually worked with ordinary people, family members, neighbors, "nobodies." But *She Puppet* is a whole different thing: I worked with a superstar!

MacDonald: It's different in that you collected the material on the basis of your having actually played the videogame—that's a different kind of collecting.

Ahwesh: Right. It's more interactive, and it relates to my interest in improvisation.

MacDonald: Is working with Lara Croft a premonition of your working with well-known actors?

Ahwesh: [Laughter.]

MacDonald: I remember talking with you about Willem Dafoe, who I'd love to see in a Peggy Ahwesh film.

Ahwesh: In some ways I would like to be able to do that, and my *Certain Women* project has made me think that it might be possible. Willem Dafoe burns a hole in the screen, but if you can work with somebody like that so that they actually *fit* within the fabric of the piece—that would be fantastic.

MacDonald: Why did you choose *Certain Women* as the basis for your new film? It's certainly not one of Caldwell's more memorable novels.

Ahwesh: That's true, but it's easier to make a good movie from something that's *not* a great work of literature. The further you get away from great literature, the less demanding the world is on your interpretation, which is liberating.

The earlier Caldwell work, which is definitely better literature, is from the thirties; for us to work with something written in the late fifties seemed more doable. We did update several of the stories. In a way the fifties is the original retro period (it got redrawn in the seventies, and then redrawn again in the nineties). To go back to Caldwell before the fifties would become so regional, and so American populist thirties—it's too far back for me.

Also, the omnibus idea of having various stories that take place in the same town but are presented in these smaller units—a sort of panoply of the ladies, variously shaded aspects of femininity—was very appealing and something we felt we could work with.

MacDonald: How far have you gotten in the film?

Ahwesh: Right now, we're shooting the fifth episode, of five, called "Nannette." It's the saddest and most dour of all the stories; it's *so* pathetic. *[Laughter.]* There's this little mountain girl who loses her parents early on and gets a job at a truck stop where the night manager tries to seduce her, and their sex act gets interrupted by the bitchy wife of the manager, who cuts the girl's face, and she spends the last third of the story, scarred, unable to get a job, rejected by society. A benevolent older lady introduces her to a blind man who hires her.

That's actually the story!

MacDonald: It's good you can blame Caldwell for this plot!

Ahwesh (laughter): Another episode stars Martina, who's in high school now. She plays Louellen, a busty high school senior who can't get a boyfriend and ends up having an affair with an out-of-towner, who dumps her, and all the boys start fighting over her. Martina wore her own clothes. Very contemporary hip-hugger jeans, sneakers, and pink tank tops.

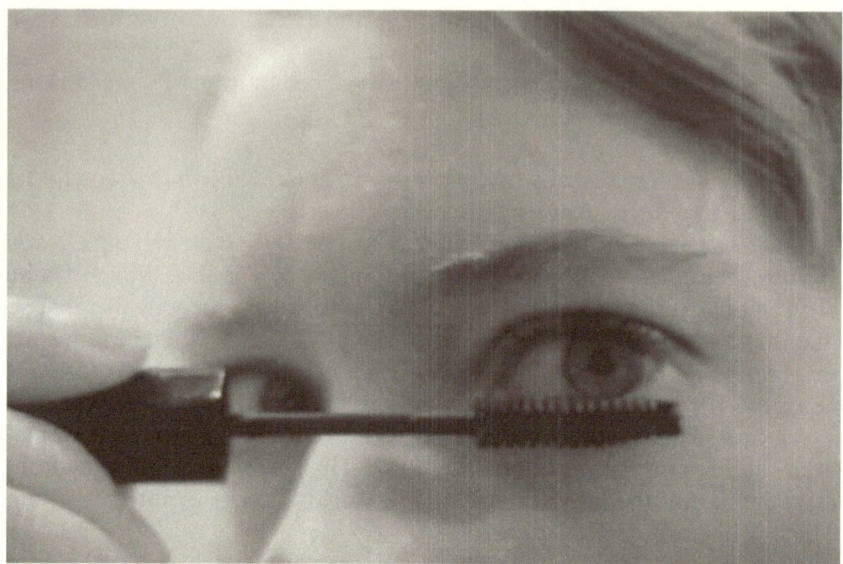

Hilda (Jessica Watson) putting on makeup in Peggy Ahwesh's *Certain Women* (2003). Courtesy Peggy Ahwesh.

Each episode has been different. Basically we try to get the right person for the part, someone who looks right. There are a couple of weak actors, but generally we got the right people.

MacDonald: This sounds like straight melodrama.

Ahwesh: It's closer.

MacDonald: The love-sex trilogy—*The Deadman, The Color of Love, Nocturne*—includes narrative, but ultimately it's like dream narrative. The viewer gives up on figuring out the story. This sounds pretty straightforward.

Ahwesh: The reason I've never liked narrative is because traditionally a narrative film has to have resolution. By the end, you're supposed to be able to figure out why things happened the way they did. And I've always been more into presenting a problem and getting you into an emotional place where you understand the calamity or joy or desire within a person's life. It's like a texture, or a mood, a moment—*not,* "This is the story, and this is how it turns out." Actually, we *are* doing my usual thing again, because none of the stories resolves, and there's no redemption to the women's misery. Our favorite shots are these loving close-ups of faces: the film becomes something like a landscape film of human emotions.

MacDonald: Unlike most of your work, where the action takes place in a conceptual space, *The Star Eaters* is set in an easily identifiable location:

Atlantic City. Atlantic City is a fitting backdrop for the idea of life as a gamble in which winning and losing are both positive/negative options; and it's also a place in perpetual transition.

Ahwesh: Atlantic City is so raggedy and on the skids that I thought it would be a perfect demoralized, loser space for my characters to visit. I guess I think of *The Deadman*'s neighborhood bar in a similar way, but you're right that it's less specific and recognizable.

I went to Atlantic City pretty regularly for a couple of years. I loved it there, though it can be scary. A guy was murdered by a woman—maybe a trick gone bad—in one hotel where we stayed and shot some scenes. The place was condemned a few weeks later. It was a don't ask, don't tell environment, and whenever we got hassled or trespassed, it cost some very small amount of money to make things fine again. The casino people must have been pretty desperate to let an operation like mine shoot for free on their floor.

MacDonald: Are you a fan of Louis Malle's *Atlantic City* [1981]?

Ahwesh: I do like that film, but *The King of Marvin Gardens* [1972, directed by Bob Rafelson] with Jack Nicholson and Bruce Dern as brothers working on some crazy business scheme was more important for me. Rafelson shot the city well. I also like *Cheaters* [*Tricheurs*, 1984] by Barbet Schroeder, about a gambler's superstitions, done in a deadpan acting style. And I had this great instructional tape on how to cheat at cards in which all the players wore bags on their heads so they couldn't be identified. I thought about re-creating it but dropped the idea.

MacDonald: You situate your characters somewhere between adulthood and childhood, in a variety of senses including the sexual. And formally, the film is full of play—I enjoy your use of reverse, in particular—locating your aesthetic somewhere between commercial film ("adult") and the experiments of a beginner ("child").

Ahwesh: You've hit the nail right on the head.

MacDonald: How did you decide to work with Arthur Jafa, and what was his contribution to the film?

Ahwesh: A.J. is a friend and I have an enormous respect for his ideas about behavior, race, camera work, time, and music, among other subjects. He brought to the video a sensuality and visual tension that I wanted, and he helped me explore the possibilities of the video format. He shot most of the action between the main characters; I shot most of the cutaways.

MacDonald: As fully as anything you've made, *The Star Eaters* seems to me a kind of Ahwesh credo. Obviously all the works are *yours* and express your interests and concerns, but *The Star Eaters* helps me understand your approach, in much the same way that Yvonne Rainer's *Privilege* (1990) helped me understand elements of her earlier films that had mystified me.

Do *you* see *The Star Eaters*, more than other works, as an implicit declaration of your aesthetic sensibility?

Ahwesh: I guess each time you make something, you try to do it right, and each time it comes close, but you keep trying! People have told me *The Star Eaters* reminds them of my Super-8mm movies—with its ease of performance and its fun situations and not too much self-importance. And that feels good, although if I had to pick a piece that sums up my aesthetic sensibility, it would have to be *Martina's Playhouse* because it's a film of more depth and consequence. But that was another time and place.

Alan Berliner

Filmmakers interested in presenting critical alternatives to conventional cinema have evinced a variety of attitudes toward audiences. Many filmmakers have assumed that the work they are committed to producing will not appeal to anything like the conventional moviegoing audience and, like Gertrude Stein, have assumed that their audience is themselves and a few friends—though, of course, these "friends" might, in time, number in the thousands, the tens of thousands, or more. Stan Brakhage can serve as a preeminent instance here: Brakhage made his films entirely unconcerned with the conventional moviegoing audience, though he was well aware that some of his films—*Mothlight* (1963), *Window Water Baby Moving* (1959)—were, in the end, seen by a sizable public.

Other filmmakers have assumed that even if the audience for mass media cannot be theirs, something like a mass audience *is* the goal. At her famous Provincetown Playhouse screenings in the 1940s, Maya Deren seems to have assumed that thoroughly experimental cinema can appeal to substantial audiences, and her confidence was an inspiration to Amos Vogel during his development of the New York film society Cinema 16, which sometimes presented programs to audiences of fifteen hundred members, twice a night, and rented films to film societies across the country. Early on, Kenneth Anger seems also to have hoped for audiences comparable at least to those for Bergman, Fellini, Truffaut, Buñuel, Kurosawa—though in the end his quest for something like a mass audience was disappointed.

Alan Berliner has, at various stages of his career, made both assumptions. Trained at the State University of New York at Binghamton during the mid-1970s, when Larry Gottheim and Ken Jacobs had instigated a film department of remarkable energy and influence, and then, as a graduate student at the University of Oklahoma (when John Knecht and James Benning were teaching there), Berliner began by making films—and at Oklahoma paracinematic objects—that had few pretensions to any audience beyond those dedicated to the most experimental forms of visual art. His *Patent Pending* (1975), for example, is a twelve-minute, single-shot film of the feed reel of a 16mm movie projector, during which the increasing pace of the reel's revolutions as a film unwinds from it creates a variety of visual experiences intrinsic to film technology (the title refers to the fact that at the conclusion of *Patent Pending,* the feed reel stops revolving, and we can read "Pat. Pend." on it). *Photo-Film-Strip* (1976) is a seventy-eight-image grid of color photographs at the heads and tails of rolls of film, organized (six images high and thirteen images long) so that a variety of optical effects within and between the individual photographs are evident as one confronts the piece.

As his career has evolved, however, Berliner has been energized by the idea of interacting with audiences well beyond those who might be drawn to his earlier minimalist-conceptualist work. This new energy was evident, first, in a series of relatively short (from ten to fourteen minutes), densely edited, mostly-found-footage montage films Berliner made during the early 1980s—*City Edition* (1980), *Myth in the Electric Age* (1981), *Natural History* (1983), and *Everywhere at Once* (1985)—and subsequently in a series of longer, more elaborate films about family life in general and his own family that have engaged and entertained sizable film and television audiences in this country and abroad: *The Family Album* (1986, 60 minutes), *Intimate Stranger* (1991, 60 minutes), *Nobody's Business* (1996, 60 minutes), and *The Sweetest Sound* (2001, 60 minutes).

Of the four montage films, *Everywhere at Once* is the most memorable. The film does not pretend to make great statements about the world but recycles bits of found image and found sound into an experience that is pleasurable in part because of the precision of Berliner's juxtapositions and the obviously obsessive labor that was necessary to produce the finished film—a form of film pleasure reminiscent of that created by Roméo Bosetti's *The Automatic Moving Company* (*La garde-meuble automatique,* 1910).

If *Everywhere at Once* and the other early found-footage films are a précis of Berliner's commitment to craft and his interest in the possibilities of image-sound relationship, *The Family Album* is a précis of the subject matter that has engaged Berliner since 1985: the nature of family life, especially family life under stress. Berliner's parents divorced after what seems to have been a reasonably turbulent marriage, and like Su Friedrich, whose filmmaking career reveals many parallels to Berliner's, Berliner has used film-

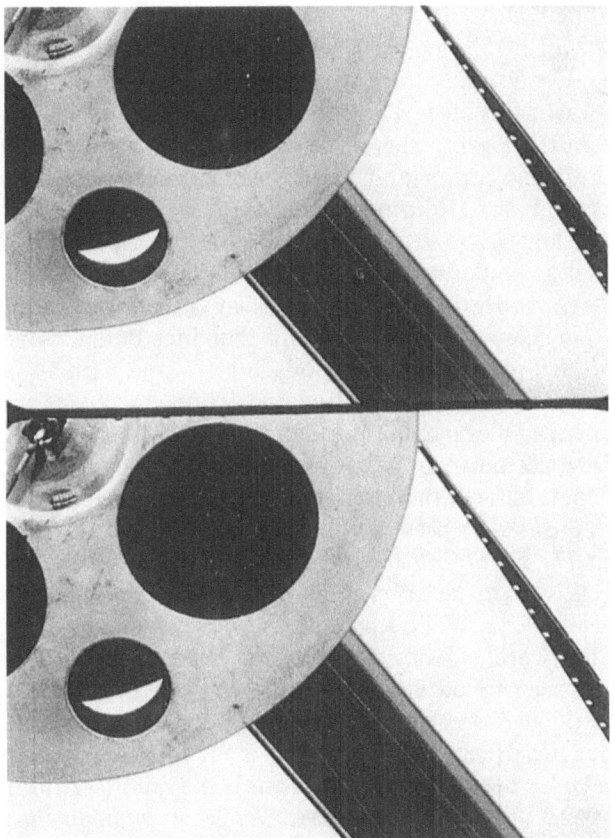

16mm film projector in Alan Berliner's *Patent Pending* (1975). Courtesy Alan Berliner.

making to chronicle his struggle with the divorce and its aftermath. *The Family Album* doesn't focus on Berliner's own family—though the voices of several of his family members are audible on the sound track—but on the home movie as a record that simultaneously reveals and suppresses the realities of family life. Using black-and-white home movies and audiotapes from a variety of sources, Berliner juxtaposes the usually Edenic visual quality of home movies with the voices of families often discussing the kinds of complexities of family life that are not evident in the visuals. *The Family Album* takes the audience through the cycle of life, from childhood through marriage into middle age, then old age.

In *Intimate Stranger* and *Nobody's Business,* Berliner focuses on two dimensions of his own family: the life of his maternal grandfather, Joseph Cassuto, and the life of his own father, Oscar Berliner—two men who, at least on a personal level, could hardly have been more different. Cassuto is remarkable for what his life reveals about the complexity of identity. He grew up in Alexandria, Egypt, where he became a businessman specializing in the sale of Egyptian cotton (and, judging from a photograph, an early Zionist). After World War II(during which he continued to live in Alexandria while his wife and several of his children moved to New York), he worked in Japan, first as a middleman for Egyptian cotton and then in other capacities as well, endearing himself to his Japanese friends and colleagues while distancing himself from his sons and daughter, Berliner's mother. Even when he was living for extended periods in New York with his family, Cassuto maintained his Japanese (and Egyptian) contacts, and his home became a refuge for colleagues passing through New York. In practical fact, Cassuto was a Jew, a Zionist, an Egyptian, and an American—though many of those who knew him felt that he was, essentially, Japanese.

Nobody's Business focuses on Oscar Berliner, whose voice is already loud and clear in *The Family Album* and *Intimate Stranger,* as he wrestles with his son's decision to make a film about him, even *with* him, regardless of his desire to be left alone. While Joseph Cassuto seems to have seen himself as a man of the world, Oscar Berliner sees himself as wholly American. Whereas his father-in-law kept detailed, even obsessive, records of his life as an international businessman, Oscar Berliner has no interest even in talking about his life. His proudest memory is his service in the army during World War II; his deepest disappointment is the failure of his marriage to Regina Cassuto after seventeen years. While in *Intimate Stranger* Alan Berliner came to know his grandfather through an exploration of what he left behind, in *Nobody's Business,* he must confront and engage his father's determined resistance to the idea that he is a worthy subject for a film—he feels his life and especially his divorce, with which his son is deeply involved, are "nobody's business"—and to the idea that the kind of film his son is making is of any value. Along with Ross McElwee's *Time Indefinite* (1993) and *Backyard* (1984), *Nobody's Business* is the most memorable and evocative engagement with the father-son relationship I am aware of, at least within independent cinema.

The final film in Berliner's family saga, at least so far, is *The Sweetest Sound,* in which Berliner focuses on the name Alan Berliner and makes contact with every Alan Berliner he is able to locate, as a way of exploring the idea of naming. *The Sweetest Sound* is less powerful than the earlier family films—largely because it refuses to confront the kinds of family trauma that provide the energy of those films—but it is, like all Berliner's films, resonant with craft and full of information.

Throughout his filmmaking career, Berliner has regularly produced other kinds of work, including a number of installations that relate in various ways to his filmmaking. *Audiofile* (1993), for example, is an installation that makes use of the considerable collection of sounds Berliner began to assemble during the years when he worked part-time for ABC news in New York. It is made up of four file cabinets, each of which contains twenty-seven drawers. When a drawer is pulled out, a particular sound is heard for as long as the drawer is open. Visitors to the installation may open as many drawers as they like, creating a wide range of auditory cacophonies. A closely related installation, *Aviary* (1993), uses a single twenty-seven-drawer file cabinet with twenty-seven different bird sounds.

This interview began in November 1997, when Berliner was visiting Utica, New York. It was continued by phone in June and July 2002 and subsequently by e-mail.

MacDonald: When I think about your career, I can't help but think about that essay Fred Camper wrote for the anniversary issue of *Millennium Film Journal;* he used you as an example of how avant-garde film had fallen into a period of decline. [Camper: "Whereas Kubelka refers to his sync events as 'articulations,' it is tempting to observe that Berliner's sync events are inarticulate in the particular sense that they lack strongly-expressed ideas, ideas that cut into the viewer's consciousness with the force of an edit filled with thought. Although the films themselves look very different from those of the commercial mainstream, in overall effect and ethics they seem to me indeed not very different from the television sit-com: he goes for whatever combination will produce a laugh, with relatively little attention to any overall coherence other than the most obvious sort. In other words, I saw no real values being expressed, no real subject-matter, merely effects for their own sake, or for the sake of manipulating the audience." From "The End of Avant-Garde Film," nos. 16–18 (1986): 99–124.]

In the years since Camper's comments, your career has continued to develop, and you've made a number of impressive films. I wonder if you still think about Camper's piece, and if so, whether you feel your recent successes have proved Camper wrong, or at least premature? It's not that Camper was wrong. I'm sure even you don't consider your early found-footage films comparable to the best of Brakhage or Kubelka.

Berliner: Gee, Scott, what a pleasant way to start an interview. But to answer your last question first, of course not. Those short films were the initial efforts of my poststudent life; in many ways I myself was still very much a work in progress at the time. It was even a bit flattering to have my work measured against the rarefied air of Kubelka. I *want* the bar to be that high. Always.

To tell you the truth, I haven't thought about that article for a long time, but as I remember it, the experience was indeed something of a wake-up call. Before we go on, let me at least slightly defuse Camper's attack by saying that he was also critical of a few other filmmakers in his article, so it wasn't as if I was the only poster boy for what was wrong with avant-garde film at the time.

MacDonald: But your early quartet of found-footage films does reveal a capable young artist, seeing what he can do with certain materials—a perfectly legitimate thing for an artist to do. With the exception, perhaps, of *City Edition,* those films don't pretend to make great statements about the world, and obviously not every worthwhile film has to do that. After all, what makes Brakhage's first ten films, or Frampton's first films, interesting is what came later. Your exploration of found footage in those early films begins to develop into major statements, first, in *The Family Album* and then, even more impressively, in *Intimate Stranger* and *Nobody's Business.*

I'm sorry to go on so long, but I've known you since you were a student at Binghamton, and I guess I have feelings about this.

Berliner: Let me distinguish between the way that I thought about Camper's article then and the way I think about it now. And, by the way, I've never met or spoken to Fred Camper, so I have no idea if he's seen anything I've done since.

Sixteen years later, I can look back with some bemusement at the whole thing. It might very well have been the first time anyone had written *anything* about my work, so naturally I was a bit sensitive about receiving a "negative" review. I mean it's not the kind of thing you want to make copies of and show your friends. Was I disappointed by Camper's treatment? Yes. Was I demoralized? No. Fortunately, in the years that followed, many other critics, including Camper's *Chicago Reader* colleague, Jonathan Rosenbaum, have had some nice things to say about my work, all of which has taught me that while you're never quite as good as your positive reviews, you're also never quite as terrible as your bad ones.

Camper's comments applied primarily to *Everywhere at Once,* a ten-minute collage film of several hundred "found" images, each matched to a uniquely different fragment of "found" music—everything from a single piano note, to a phrase of Gershwin, to a few seconds of the Rolling Stones. Whether image to image, sound to sound, or sound to image, the juxtapositions in the film constitute a compendium of editorial logics—decisions based on color, movement, rhythm, continuity, discontinuity, musicality, irony, and yes, Camper's right, even occasionally on humor—*but most of all,* on the interplay between expectation and surprise.

There are several thematic elements woven throughout the film, for instance, recurring images of orchestra conductors, and traffic cops serving as surrogate orchestra conductors—both of them serving as self-reflexive metaphors for me as filmmaker-editor—all of them/us orchestrating what I intended as a lyrical and playful "mini-cine-symphony." I've often referred to *Everywhere at Once* as my "musical"—the sound track for the film even played on the radio once upon a time.

But, okay, I'll say it: The film is "fun." Or at least it has an energy that many audiences find pleasurable. Even I don't think there's much "depth" in *Everywhere at Once,* especially when compared to the Kubelka paradigm that Camper seems to have in mind. The film wasn't intended to evoke Kubelka. It's closer in spirit to the playfulness of a Conner film; I even included a short fragment of Respighi's *The Pines of Rome* as an homage to Conner.

Still, no one had ever made a film like *Everywhere at Once* before, and my sense was that the community of filmmakers orbiting the Collective for Living Cinema and Millennium at the time, found it—as well as my other films of that period—worthy of their notice.

And while we're talking on the record, despite Camper's decree, *Everywhere at Once* won the Grand Prize at the Ann Arbor Film Festival in 1986. And *City Edition,* the first in that series of found-footage collage films, was regularly rented by P. Adams Sitney for his classes and lectures around that time. Beyond that, these films continue to be rented at universities around the world, particularly for courses about editing. And to this day, I continue to show them alongside my more recent, longer films.

Looking back now, I'd prefer to see those short films the way one might look at the early work of a musician—that is, as etudes or studies, pieces in which I was perfecting my chops, where I was working through my relationship to montage, to bricolage, and, more important, discovering my own filmmaking *process*—my way of working with found and archival images and sounds, with voluminous quantities of them; and of stretching the capacity and flexibility of my associative memory, all of which would serve me well as I moved forward into my next phase of work.

I've used those early films as sources of ideas and images ever since. You don't have to look very hard to recognize shots, sounds, strategies, or sometimes even entire sequences from them in my next generation of films, particularly *Intimate Stranger, Nobody's Business,* and *The Sweetest Sound.* For example, there's a shot in *City Edition* of an anonymous family of four sitting at a kitchen table. It's part of a montage that begins with a short city symphony made up mostly of archival Depression footage, followed by a series of shots that transform into a kind of surreal dream sequence—some scat dancing, a dolphin jumping out of the water, Edison in his laboratory mixing chemicals, a home-movie image of a small boy with a camera, and then this archival shot of the family I'm talking about—father at the head of the table, mother pouring tea, a young boy, and his younger sister. I had thousands of images to choose from for that montage, any one of which would have confirmed the surrealistic sense of shock and dreamlike discontinuity. So why did I use that image of the family?

My best answer is that back in 1980 when I made the film, I wasn't psychologically ready, wasn't emotionally mature enough, wasn't confident enough as a filmmaker, to confront the demons of my childhood. Using a surrogate, almost "neutral" image of the family at that stage of my life was a kind of premonition. Without realizing it, I was planting a seed inside my psyche, telling myself—*reminding myself*—that I had a lot of personal family issues to deal with, and that I would, or could, *or should,* mediate them in a film one day.

Sixteen years later, *Nobody's Business* is the fruit of that seed. Not only was it the inevitable deep dive into my nuclear family suggested by that shot in *City Edition,* but I also use that very same archival image of the family—*which has now become a symbol for my family*—at a critical moment in the film. Maybe fifteen years from now, I'll discover that *Nobody's Business* also contains the seeds of confrontations and ideas, premonitions, not yet understood or acknowledged. I sure hope so.

MacDonald: I think there's another factor. What I remember most about you from your Binghamton years, when you worked as my projectionist when I was first doing research on alternative cinema, is that you seemed almost a kind of "monk." You came out of that generation that made monkishness, in the service of cinema, a noble enterprise—and you took that kind of service very seriously. Watching you, it seemed to me that it just takes some people longer than others to live fully enough to be able to step out of life and say something about their experience. I relate to this because I've always been very slow in developing confidence as a teacher, as a scholar. There are some things I do quickly, but with intellectual things, I always feel I'm behind.

We want to be on the wave, surfing the "big new moment," but I'm always a little too slow to actually hit the wave. I never know what's going on until it's already passed me and I'm standing knee deep in the ocean as the wave spreads up the beach. Being slow used to frustrate me, embarrass me; but I've come to understand—if you can stand this metaphor for another moment—that I love the beach, and that I can get a good view of the beach from many positions.

Berliner: The fullest appreciation for what's going on at any particular "wave" in history always demands multiple perspectives in both space and time. You need reports from people on the shore; testimony from people whose boats were capsized by the wave; the view from people high above the beach, watching on nearby cliffs. What about the vantage point of someone hiding underwater? I don't think there's any proprietary advantage of being "on the wave" per se. In fact, that's the only place from which you can't really *see* the wave, at least not until some *time* has passed.

In any event, I've always thought of you as a great swimmer, Scott—I don't care what anyone says.

MacDonald: Because of the early history of its film department, SUNY-Binghamton was a crucial place for me, and for a lot of people, during the early seventies. While I was mystified by a lot of what I saw there, it *was* clear to me that a wave was certainly breaking.

Berliner: When I arrived in the fall of 1973, it didn't take very long to realize that the cinema department was *the* most dynamic place on campus. It made the art department seem like a Republican Rotary Club. There was an incredible energy all around, an astounding visiting artists program, people coming from all over the world to study or, in some cases, just to hang out and absorb the scene. Imagine: I was taking classes with Peter Kubelka as a freshman! Even though I didn't know exactly who he was or what he represented, I *did know* that something really exciting was going on, and I wanted to be a part of it. It was irresistible.

I had just come from a very difficult high school experience, not to mention a very painful experience at home, culminating in my parents' very ugly divorce. I remember during the summer just prior to entering college, sitting alone for hours in the middle of a stretch of rapids on the Delaware River, making a kind of pact with myself, thinking, "It's time to refocus now. Time to stop getting high all the time. Time to get serious." For many reasons—both good and bad—I was primed for a transformative experience. Between the urgency of my deep psychological unrest and the intensity of my restless creative energies, finding the cinema department at that moment in my life was pure synchronicity.

MacDonald: I've always thought that the Binghamton energy was basically a function of the collision of Larry Gottheim and Ken Jacobs, two very different personalities.

Berliner: Yes, absolutely.

MacDonald: What do you remember about the interaction of Larry and Ken?

Berliner: What do you want to hear, the best or the worst?

MacDonald: Both.

Berliner: At their best, Larry and Ken represented the dialectic of two altogether different modes of temperament and aesthetics. In the collision of their personalities and sensibilities—and we're talking about two *brilliant* people here—was a tension that became fertile, dynamic, and stimulating for everyone. They were both charismatic teachers and both totally—and I mean *totally*—dedicated to the art of cinema.

At their worst it was not unlike a dysfunctional marriage: divisive, destructive, and distracting.

MacDonald: Did you study with both?

Berliner: Yes, although when I first got to Binghamton in 1973, Ken was on a leave of absence. I think the best thing about Ken and Larry and the Binghamton experience was that the focus was always on what it meant to be an artist in the world. They weren't teaching filmmaking so much as they were sensitizing us—*inspiring us* might be a better way of saying it—to make connections with history, with culture, to art, to books, to music, always emphasizing the sacrifices and dedication required of making a lifetime commitment to art-making. Perhaps that's where that "monkish" quality you spoke of earlier comes from. Of course, each of them approached that mission in a different way.

My personal affinity was to Larry, but I strongly felt the impact of each. I bonded with Larry, and I suppose many people might say I also emulated him. When he showed me his methodology for making *Horizons* [1973], with all those index cards [see Scott MacDonald, *The Garden in the Machine* (Berkeley and Los Angeles: University of California Press, 2001), 30–37, for a discussion of the process that resulted in *Horizons*], I remember thinking to myself how Larry's extraordinary attention to subtlety and detail, combined with his incredible obsessive energy, was something I could totally relate to. Something I aspired to. I always felt that I was a perfect audience for Larry's films, and I loved talking about them with him. In many ways, Larry taught me how to look at images. How to savor details and nuances. How the ways in which we describe and notate images while we work with them play a critical role in what we end up doing with them.

Larry also introduced me to the idea of "paracinema," and I was part of a small group of students who presented a performance at the Collective for Living Cinema in 1976, called *The Perils of Space*. The idea that you could work with cinematic ideas and concepts without actually making films was something that excited me, and in many ways helped inspire the installation work I continue to produce to this day. I think I owe that to Larry. I remember hearing that Ken had been doing shadow-play performances in the early seventies, but I never had a chance to see them. Of course these days he's doing these "nervous system" performances, which not only are breathtaking, but somehow still push the boundaries of cinema.

Eventually Larry and I also made the transition from mentor and student—and I say this with all humility—to friends and colleagues. Over the years we shared intimacies about our personal lives, as well as the struggles we were experiencing with our work. Larry and I had a special relationship. I even babysat for his children. Even though I don't see him very much these days, he has a permanent warm spot in my heart.

Now Ken was also a brilliant teacher, no question, but he took no prisoners. In the vernacular of the era, if Larry was *mellow,* Ken was *intense*.

Ken exerted a tremendously powerful hold over students. He was incredibly demanding, both as a person and as a teacher. Some students idolized him to such an extent that sometimes, when they didn't get the follow-through of his encouragement, it seemed as though their spirits were broken. In many ways Ken's personality always reminded me of the late theater director and teacher Lee Strasberg, whose teaching methods were also based on a kind of "tough love"—a sink-or-swim, trial-by-fire pedagogy.

But the truth is, if you had the strength to handle it, Ken's demanding approach could bring out the very best in you. It's just that not everyone is ready—or even able—to be challenged so completely that early in their lives or in their artistic development. From what I've heard recently, though, Ken has mellowed somewhat over the years.

I should remind you that there were other teachers at Binghamton who were important influences on all of us. Saul Levine and Dan Barnett, both of whom were extremely popular and inspiring presences, offered alternative approaches to the poetics and politics of filmmaking. Ralph Hocking was pioneering the development of video art. Ernie Gehr brought his mysteries and his magic. Alfons Schilling came from Switzerland and gave classes on art and visual perception. Peter Kubelka taught for one semester every two years. Visiting filmmakers and artists were passing through all the time. It was an incredibly dynamic place.

By my senior year, I was a teaching assistant for both Larry and Ken. In fact, when Ken became ill early in the semester and wasn't able to continue teaching, instead of hiring an outside professor to take over his film production class, the department asked me to teach the course in his absence. They even paid me! That's when I found out how much I enjoyed teaching.

I was also active on other fronts. I was president of the film co-op. I was coprogrammer of the film society. I was a projectionist for classes. I designed publicity posters for the visiting artists program. I was a work-study student assigned to a man named Bruce Holman, who repaired all of the camera and editing equipment. And, of course, I was also feverishly making films and paracinematically inspired photographs, collages, and sculptures.

To show you how supportive the program was, the department allowed me to convert a room in the basement of the lecture hall into my own private art gallery, where I had a one-person exhibition of my paracinema work as part of my senior thesis. I can't say it enough. Binghamton was a powerful experience for me. For all of us.

MacDonald: You weren't there when Frampton made *Critical Mass* [1971]. Was he a presence in Binghamton?

Berliner: You know, it's always been a curious thing to me: in all the time I was in Binghamton, I never saw a Frampton film, except for *Lemon* [1969]

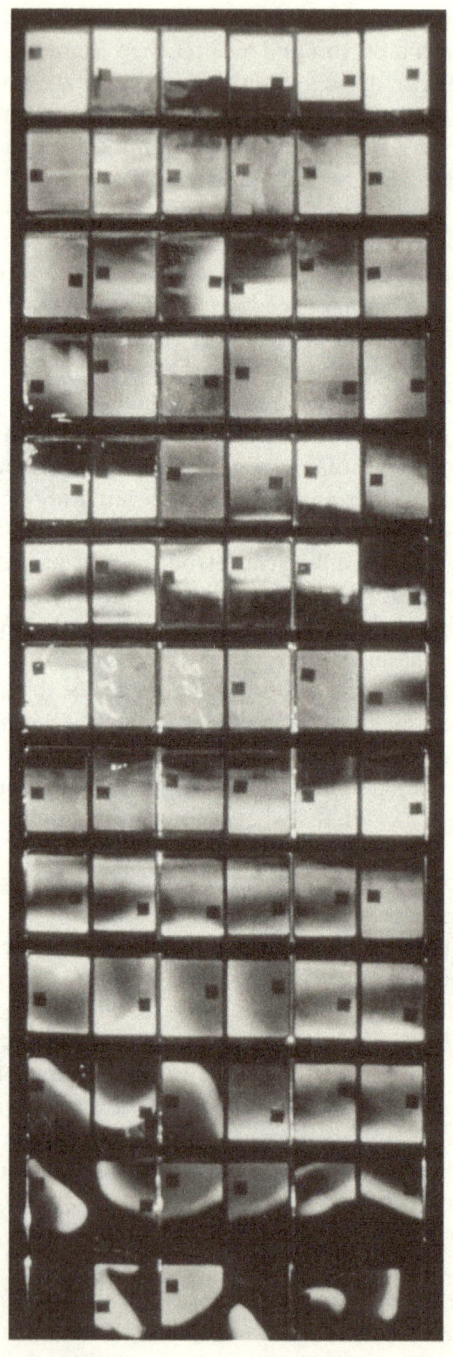

Alan Berliner's *Photo-Film-Strip* (1976). Courtesy Alan Berliner.

and *Works and Days* [1969], both of which were part of the cinema department's film library. For whatever reasons, Frampton was never hailed or discussed very much during the years I was a student. Of course, I stand partly to blame for that as well, because as a programmer of the Harpur Film Society the last year I was there, I didn't show Frampton's work either.

I remember going to Anthology Film Archives in 1976 to see *Zorns Lemma* [1970]. I was blown away. Watching the playful logics, the masterful intelligence running through *Zorns Lemma,* was an epiphany to me. It was as profound and compelling a "first viewing" of a film as I've ever had.

MacDonald: One dimension of you that I see in Ken, though I didn't know this until I interviewed him in his apartment, is his love of accumulating books, devices, whatever, relating to film history. You're a collector also.

Berliner: That's true. We both savor and tinker with the odds and ends, the detritus, of culture. We both like surrounding ourselves with lots of *stuff.* I remember visiting Ken's loft when I was a student and being amazed at all the fascinating things there were to look at, touch, and read. There was very little separation between life and art, which is true of my own home and studio as well. I can't say that I emulated him on this front, because I've always been a bit of a pack rat, but it definitely made a strong impression on me way back then.

And there's something else I got from Ken. A few years ago, when I was presenting my work in Sheffield, England, my film came onto the screen *without sound* for about thirty seconds because of some technical problem. As soon as I saw what was happening, I shouted across the room, "No, no, no! We only do this once, so please, let's do it right!" I made them stop the projector, and we started the film over again, this time with sound, from the beginning.

MacDonald: That's pure Binghamton.

Berliner: The audience applauded me! After the show many people remarked that my having the audacity to actually stop the show and start over again made them appreciate how the intensity and dedication involved in filmmaking doesn't end when the work is completed but carries over into *protecting* the integrity of the film viewing experience—and also includes the responsibility for engaging in meaningful postscreening discussions with the audience. All of that is certainly a carryover from Binghamton.

I'm not sure what happened at Binghamton later on—at some point things seem to have drifted away from the intensity of the mid-1970s. I know there was talk about starting a graduate cinema program there, which for a variety of reasons, including budget problems within the state university system, never came to be. That's a real shame.

Another disappointment—and this isn't just limited to Binghamton—is that they never turned out enough people who could write critically about cinema, in particular about the avant-garde. I assume most people know that J. Hoberman, film critic of the *Voice,* is a Binghamton graduate. We needed more people like him who could articulate and champion radical cinema—not only to the "true believers" but also to more mainstream audiences all over the country. That never really happened on the scale everyone initially hoped for.

Can I mention one more very important thing about going to school at Binghamton?

MacDonald: Please do.

Berliner: The founders of the Collective for Living Cinema had been graduates of the cinema department, and there was always a deep spirit of connection and continuity. The idea of making films worthy of showing at the Collective was a motivation for many students. It certainly was an important goal for me personally. Knowing the Collective was there gave a tangible "real-world" dimension to the highly aestheticized environment we were immersed in at Binghamton. Not only that, but it was also a compelling reason to move to New York City after graduation. In many ways, with all due respect to Anthology Film Archives and Millennium, the Collective was *the* center of the avant-garde film universe in New York—at least in the late seventies and early eighties.

MacDonald: I agree with you.

But you didn't move back to New York City after Binghamton.

Berliner: No. At least not right away. In fact I was talking to John Knecht the other night about how my experience of going to the University of Oklahoma after graduating from Binghamton affected my artistic destiny in a very profound way.

MacDonald: When were you at Oklahoma?

Berliner: From 1977 through 1979.

MacDonald: You got an MFA?

Berliner: Yes. I was the recipient of a special graduate fellowship from the School of Art that included free tuition, a fellowship stipend, the chance to teach filmmaking classes, a private studio, and my own faculty office. It was a fantastic opportunity.

Carmen Vigil, who used to be the programmer at the Cinematheque in San Francisco, came to Binghamton to present a series of avant-garde films from the Bay Area, and I was asked to pick him up at the bus station and show him around town before the screening. The way I understand it, at some point during his return trip back to the West Coast, Carmen stopped in Norman, Oklahoma, and recommended me to John Knecht, who was in the process of creating a dynamic film-video graduate program at the University of Oklahoma. Robert Nelson had had something to do with setting up this program, though I'm not clear on the details. [Nelson: "I would describe it as giving-the-gas to an already existing modest idling contraption. Joe Hobbs (Art Department Chair) and John Hadley brought me there, attracted by my anti-intellectualism. I think it was 1970. The bicycle-fall and the tongue-choir images from *Bleu Shut* were shot there, and that title was from something Joe Hobbs said about a door that blew shut; his Oklahoma twang made those words stand out, and I knew *instantly* that I had the title for the film I was working on"—Nelson, in letter to author, July 2003.]

When I was first contemplating whether to accept the Oklahoma fellowship offer, I remember Larry Gottheim telling me, "In the arts, it doesn't matter where you go; it's what you *do.*" The next thing I know, I'm living in Norman, Oklahoma.

MacDonald: Who was teaching there besides Knecht?

Berliner: James Benning, who I admired and learned a lot from. Ernie Gehr also taught there for a semester. They had a really good visiting artists program, too, bringing in painters, sculptors, photographers, filmmakers, even critics and curators, from all over the world. All in all, it was a very fertile and creative environment.

Had the Oklahoma opportunity not come up, the most logical places for me to have gone to graduate school to maintain my avant-garde cinema "pedigree" after Binghamton would have been the Art Institute of Chicago or the San Francisco Art Institute. In those days, there were very few places where you could get an MFA in avant-garde cinema. Students have many more options these days. Had I gone to Chicago or San Francisco, I would have been one among many other young avant-garde filmmakers from all over the world. Instead, for the first six months at Oklahoma, I was *the only* film graduate student! And in all the time I was there, there were only two others.

The faculty at Oklahoma was also very generous and understanding with me. They brought me in as a filmmaker—and I taught film with all my heart and passion—but during the two years I was there *I did not make any films.* Continuing the paracinema-inspired work I had begun in Binghamton, I concentrated mostly on sculptures, video installations, time-based photo-collages, and paper films. I even studied music theory a little bit. Most of my fellow graduate students were painters, sculptors, and photographers, and I gravitated to their materials and tools and to their discussions and dialogues. I even exhibited my master's thesis, *Workprint*—a seventy-five-foot-long "spliced" photographic scroll (I called it a "paper film")—in the campus art museum [Fred Jones Jr. Museum of Art]. But all the while, I never stopped thinking of myself as a filmmaker! And, looking back, I still believe that *not* making films in Oklahoma ultimately made me a better filmmaker.

Had I gone to either of those other schools for my MFA, I'm sure I would have felt compelled (by peer pressure if nothing else) to make *traditional* avant-garde films—that is to say, "projectable" 16mm films. In the relative isolation of Oklahoma, I was free to grow—or mutate—any way I wanted.

Now remember, I was young, only sixteen years old when I arrived at Binghamton; and only twenty-two when I received my MFA from Oklahoma. Even so, I had every intention of getting a job teaching film somewhere. I loved teaching. At the time, there were only three avant-garde-related job openings in the country, and I applied for each of them. The only problem was that I didn't send out any films with my application; I sent *slides* of the paracinematic work I'd been making in Oklahoma. In the end, no one was willing to take that kind of a chance on me, and in retrospect, I guess I don't blame them.

MacDonald: Sending slides of paracinematic work, conceptual work, was a way of saying, "I don't do the technical stuff." The paradox is that actually you do the technical stuff particularly well.

Berliner: As far as I was concerned, I was just sending out the signal that I was a free spirit who was capable of approaching cinema from different perspectives. Someone who was interested in opening up new frontiers. Someone who was taking cinema apart and putting it back together again in new and unexpected ways. I remember seeing the exhibition Michael Snow: Artist as Filmmaker at the Museum of Modern Art in 1976 and being amazed by his incredible genre-busting dexterity in approach, conception, and range of media. Not to mention the profound impact of his films; I've probably seen *Wavelength* [1967] twenty-five or thirty times. Snow was a paradigm for the creative freedom I aspired to.

One of the most important works I made in Oklahoma—which I also exhibited on the walls of the Collective for Living Cinema when I had my first one-person show there in December 1977—was *Cine-Matrix,* which is, on many levels, the "Lucy," that is to say, the progenitor, of all the work I've done since. *Cine-Matrix* is a cinematically inspired wall-mounted grid of 156 three-inch by four-inch rectangles [twenty-six across by six down]—I thought of them as *frames*—cut out from found corrugated cardboard boxes. I went around to every dumpster in town looking for interesting pieces of cardboard containing words, colors, textures, graphic elements, random markings, photographic images, you name it—an entire language unto itself—and ended up cutting out close to five thousand small rectangles. I think of *Cine-Matrix* as my first successful translation of cinematic logic—in particular, a lot of my ideas about editing—into two-dimensional form.

At a certain point I realized I wasn't going to get a teaching job after graduating from Oklahoma—at least not by sending slides of works like *Cine-Matrix* to represent me—so instead of becoming a professor of cinema, I came home and got thrust into the gauntlet of real life in New York City, which also changed my destiny in all sorts of ways.

MacDonald: How did you find work?

Berliner: My friend Ross Levinson, a violin teacher, gave me the name of one of his students, a woman named Emma Morris, who was working as an assistant film editor in New York. Ironically, had I been in a position to choose a part of the film industry in which to make a living, I wouldn't have chosen editing; I wanted to *shoot* film, to be a maker of images. But after meeting with Emma, I took her list of possible job opportunities— places she'd worked in the past—and arranged them in alphabetical order, which is how ABC Sports, specifically a television program called *The American Sportsman,* became the target of my very first New York City job-search telephone call. To my utter surprise, the guy on the other end of the line said, "Come on in and we'll talk."

I didn't know shit about the film industry. Here I was, having just graduated from art school . . . I hadn't made a film in two years! I had no idea there was such a thing as industry protocol, an official way of doing things. I knew none of the lingo, the code words, the way people talked in real editing rooms. To be perfectly honest, I was applying for an assistant editing job without even knowing what an assistant editor *did.* I didn't even know enough to put together a phony résumé.

But I got lucky. For reasons that I still don't quite understand, Ted Winterburn, the supervising editor, called me two days later and told me that he had *created* a job for me. Not as an assistant editor but as a sound-effects librarian. At that time, *The American Sportsman* had what must have been one of the largest and most authentic collections of sounds from nature ever assembled: winds, rivers, oceans, jungles, forests—any and every kind of animal you could imagine—gathered from all over the world.

My job, or, as I thought of it, "my assignment," for the first nine months was to sit alone in a room every day, put on headphones, and listen. After I gave each sound its own identification number, I then had to annotate its distinctive qualities: in effect, use words to make "aural images," so that other people could make intelligent use of the library in the future.

I remember coming home from work, and friends would ask me, "What did you do today?" "I listened to winds all day: high winds, low winds, warm winds, cold winds, buffeting winds, wind through trees." "What did you do today?" "Today I listened to rivers: the Ganges River, the Yangtze River, the Tigris River, and other assorted brooks, streams, and creeks from around the world." "What did you do today?" "Well, this entire *week* I've been listening to footsteps: footsteps through grass, through leaves, on sand, snow, gravel, metal, wood, on linoleum, on carpet; people wearing high heels, sneakers, shoes, barefoot; one person, two people, five people, crowds of people. . . ." It was an incredible education in close listening and the ability to recognize nuances of difference between sounds that were often only slightly dissimilar, not to mention the ways that sound—and especially the layering of sound—can change the way we look at images. It was the perfect job for me. And, best of all, many of those sounds eventually became part of my own personal sound library.

While all of that was going on, quietly, secretly, without blowing my cover, I got to observe and eventually learn what an assistant editor actually did, so that by the time they came and offered me an assistant editing job—after the sound library project was finished—I knew just what to do and how to do it. Within a year I became a full-fledged sound editor. To this day, no one has a clue that I knew nothing when I first walked in the door.

In the five or six years that I worked for ABC, I was always a freelance employee, never working for more than six or seven months a year. I was very fortunate that the person in charge of scheduling respected the fact that I was also a film artist and was sympathetic to my situation. In December, I'd walk into his office, and he'd ask me, "How long do you want to take off this time?" I'd say, "Can I call you in April or May?" And his response was always, "Just call me the week before you want to come back." He was my guardian angel.

In the professional film-editing world, everyone aspires to be a picture editor, but my instinct at the time was to stay away from the lure of picture editing and earn money exclusively as a sound editor. Sound editing allowed me to work quietly and at my own pace; no head trips, no mind games, no office politics—just give me your film when you're done with it, and let me create an interesting sound track for you. My basic strategy was to work extremely hard—by that I mean many late nights and weekends—for a few months at a time, so that I could make enough money to take five or six months off and concentrate on my own work. I always suspected that some people at ABC thought there must have been something wrong with me, because I was never interested in climbing the career ladder. But I was only protecting my relationship to my work. And my sanity. That world can be very seductive: a steady paycheck, the feeling of accomplishment, access to equipment and supplies. Esteem. If people like what you do, they pull you in to do more of it for them.

Speaking of sanity, I've also been lucky enough to be able to continue teaching since I've been in New York. I taught filmmaking classes at the Collective for Living Cinema for eight years, and still teach editing classes at the Millennium Film Workshop—but a lot of my cinematic thinking gets processed and incubated in a class I've been teaching at the New School for Social Research since 1988, called "Experiments in Time, Light and Motion." It's part avant-garde cinema, part "expanded cinema," part aesthetics, part visual perception, and part whatever else I'm in the mood for at the time.

MacDonald: You won several Emmys for your television work.

Berliner: Yes, ABC submitted some of the work I did to the National Academy for Television Arts and Sciences, and they deemed some of my sound-editing work worthy of Emmy Awards. In the end, I've been nominated for six and won three.

MacDonald: What were the projects?

Berliner: I worked on the sound track for a three-hour documentary on FDR [*FDR: A Biography* (1982, ABC News, Emmy)]. And there was *The Berlin Wall* [1983, ABC News, Emmy nomination], and *To Swim with the Whales* [1985, ABC News, Emmy nomination], and a film about slave labor in the Philippines [*Slave Ships of the Sulu Sea* (1986, ABC News, Emmy)]. Ironically, the most sophisticated sound track I ever created for ABC was back in 1981, on a film about the twentieth anniversary of the Berlin Wall, which wasn't nominated for an Emmy.

My own film *Intimate Stranger* was also nominated for an Emmy (for editing) in 1991, and *Nobody's Business* won an Emmy in 1997. In that professional film milieu, Emmys are a kind of currency—chips I never wanted to cash in. They did help solidify my freelance status, though, so that the man in charge at ABC who let me come and go as I needed could always say, "Well, Alan's obviously worth keeping around." In that sense, indirectly at least, they helped me continue making my own films.

I remember being terrified now that I was out of school and had a real job to go to every day, afraid that giving up my *time* in order to make *money* would distract me from the discipline of making my own work. One of my earliest solutions for coping with that fear was *Natural History: A Photo Journal,* which premiered at the Collective in 1982. Starting January 1, 1981, I gave myself the task of cutting out every single photograph that appeared in the *New York Times* every day for the entire year. Something between a free-form obsession and a daily meditation, it was also an exercise that helped keep me grounded in the process of art-making. By year's end, I had amassed more than ten thousand photographs! I also cut out the daily "quote of the day," and every week I cut out the question and answer section from Tuesday's "Science Times." Above and beyond all of that, I was also cutting out news articles that interested me each day.

Natural History: A Photo Journal was a performance slide work consisting of 365 newspaper photographs, one from each day of the year. Each day's image was projected for six full seconds before dissolving into the next. There was also a very dense and carefully orchestrated sound track composed of four live voices. One person read quotes of the day in relation to certain images, but they bled over, obviously, because some of the quotes took longer than six seconds to read. Another person read questions from the "Science Times," also in specific relationship to certain images. When I say "questions," I mean evocative conundrums like, "Why aren't meadows invaded by surrounding trees?" or "Why don't spiders get caught in their own webs?" Questions that were almost philosophical in their implications, like koan. Two people read passages from articles culled from news events (both large and small) of the year. Sometimes one person was speaking over the forty-minute flow of images, sometimes two together, sometimes three, and there were times when all four voices combined to create a kind of information cacophony. All the stops and starts, the layering of voices and the sound-image relationships were carefully choreographed and scored. We performed it only once, and to this day, I curse myself for not documenting it. Of course, those were the days before digital video cameras.

That piece was one of my first attempts to work with mass media and information overload—seeds of ideas and processes that have woven themselves through some of the films and a good deal of the sculptural and installation work I've made over the years.

MacDonald: How did you get started on *The Family Album?* I'm wondering what you remember about the transition from those earlier montage works to this longer project that then leads you into an ongoing family saga.

Berliner: One evening as I arrived to teach my class at the Collective, I saw an index card on the bulletin board—I still have it somewhere—announcing, "Home Movies for Sale." It contained a list of subjects that were typical of the home-movie genre: parades, weddings, birthday parties, the beach, pets, travelogues, et cetera. I took down the phone number and the next day discovered I was the first person to respond.

MacDonald: You weren't the last; Abby Child also responded.

Berliner: That's right; she got there a bit after me. He sold her a small amount, and then after that, sold me some additional African American home movies from the thirties. I think the two of us cleaned him out.

The home movies were assembled on very large reels, and I spent almost an entire year slowly sorting through and studying them, all the while thinking about how I might make a film out of them one day.

MacDonald: You didn't use any of your own family's home movies in *The Family Album.*

Berliner: There's not one image from my family in the film.

MacDonald: Did you consider using them?

Berliner: Well, my father's films were all shot in 8mm, which, at the very least, presented a technical problem for me. Early on, someone else had offered me some rather old 8mm home movies to consider for the film, and I did a test blowup to 16mm but didn't like the way it looked—it had an enlarged grain structure quite different from the beautiful 16mm material I had purchased, and I wanted *The Family Album* to have a consistent palette. To be honest, I never really considered using my own family footage. This was always conceived as a project made with found or, as I often call them, "orphaned" home-movie images.

The primary reason *The Family Album* took so long to make (I worked on it from 1981 until 1986) is not only that there was a lot of footage to look through, take notes on, and absorb but also because each time I decided to use a particular group of home-movie images, I had to send them to John E. Allen—perhaps the preeminent archival film laboratory in the country—for printing. Sometimes I would send him something in early June and not get it back until August or September.

MacDonald: And what exactly were you having him do?

Berliner: The home movies I bought were all black-and-white reversal original. He was making black-and-white, liquid-gate optical negative masters for me.

MacDonald: Was all the stuff you collected black-and-white?

Berliner: A fair amount of the footage I bought was shot on Kodachrome in the fifties—beautiful stuff—but I made a decision early on to locate the film's time frame from the midtwenties through the late forties and didn't want to use material that looked or felt "contemporary."

The whole process became further complicated when I began to spread the word that I was interested in looking at as much 16mm home-movie footage as I could find. Suddenly I started hearing about other archives and other family collections in Connecticut, Vermont, New Jersey, and upstate New York. I even went to visit Alan Kattelle (the guru of home-movie history and amateur motion picture equipment) in Hudson, Massachusetts, where he very generously allowed me to borrow footage from his impressive home-movie collection for my film.

At some point along the way, my intense engagement with all the anonymous home-movie imagery suggested the idea of creating a "found" sound track for the film, and so I started going to flea markets and garage sales, buying any and every sound element I could find: beat-up old cassettes, all sorts of quarter-inch tapes, microcassettes. I also bought any tape recorder I could find, in any state of disrepair, as long as it still had a roll of audiotape on it. When I took these things home, I invariably discovered the sounds of children playing with microphones, fooling around, singing songs, families recording birthday parties, holidays, music lessons, elementary school teachers recording their classes, garage bands playing—all sorts of stuff. At least half of the sound track of *The Family Album* is composed of found sources gathered this way.

I also started mentioning to people that I was interested in oral histories, which I was just learning about, and it wasn't long before friends and col-

From Alan Berliner's *The Family Album* (1986). Courtesy Alan Berliner.

leagues started offering me access to oral histories (or in some cases just casual conversations) they'd recorded or inherited. One friend of mine loaned me a whole stack of reel-to-reel tape recordings made by her parents, who used to invite their friends over on Saturday nights, go down into their basement, get really drunk, and record the festivities as if it were some kind of perverse radio show!

MacDonald: In *The Family Album* the way you "sync" very particular sounds and very particular movements in the imagery seems most like *Everywhere at Once*.

Berliner: It's funny that you should say that because I was working on *Everywhere at Once* simultaneously with *The Family Album*. At some point, when I was forced to wait four or five months to get some material back from the lab, I decided to focus entirely on *Everywhere at Once* and finally finish it. As different as they are, in some strange way, *Everywhere at Once* and *The Family Album* are cousins. I was immersed in a very particular mode of working with sound and image relationships around that time, which both films share.

MacDonald: When did you decide to put voice recordings of your own family into the film?

Berliner: Well, once I started thinking about oral histories, it was only natural for me to conduct one of my own. I interviewed my mother and my father, asked them your basic boilerplate, personal family history sorts of questions—and it eventually occurred to me that I might want to give myself a more personal stake in the film by hiding a few personal references of my own. At that time, of course, no one knew the sounds of my parents' voices.

MacDonald: When Su Friedrich edited *The Ties That Bind* [1984], she used a network of connections between sound and image as a metaphor, as a way of "binding" herself together with her mother. I don't sense the same feeling in your film. The relationship between image and sound is intricate, but it's not *that* one. Most home-movie imagery, including most of what you use, is celebratory, and what gets shot and what gets kept tends to sing the pleasures of family life. But on the *sound track,* especially as we move further into the film, you reveal this other world that doesn't get represented visually, though it *is* the kind of conversation that takes place at family gatherings.

Berliner: The sound track is a subversion of *the implicit lie* of home movies—that life is all leisure and no struggle. If you came from another planet and only knew human beings from home movies, you'd think that every day was a Sunday, every season was summer, and that human beings only sing, dance, laugh, swim, and make babies.

One of my aspirations for the film was to embody both the light *and* the shadow of life. To use the sound track as a way of contradicting the imagery and somehow, symbolically at least, wipe the smiles off people's faces. I wanted to reveal alternate realities hidden behind the camera and beneath the surface fiction of home movies, by introducing issues like alcoholism, family arguments, divorce, death, and suicide.

At the same time, the entire opening section of the film is grounded in the innocence of childhood, partly because home movies *are* primarily about children. Home-movie cans are usually labeled "Jack, age 1," "Jack, age 2," "Jack, age 3," and so on; but then when Jack reaches the age of say, twelve, thirteen, fourteen, it all stops. Jack goes through puberty and adolescence, and he's not cute anymore; he's starting to rebel; maybe his parents' marriage is going downhill. At this point, if Jack is at the family gatherings at all, he's getting stoned (or, in those days, drunk) in the backyard. There's a huge gap in time before the home-movie camera is brought out again—this time most likely to shoot Jack's wedding.

The flow of images in *The Family Album* is structured from birth to death, from the innocence of children at the beginning to evocations of death and mortality at the end. As the anonymous characters grow older, the issues the film introduces grow more complicated.

MacDonald: The process of making *The Family Album* unleashes your obsession with your own family. By the end of *The Family Album,* you certainly have a technique, and you've explored a longer structure. How did you get started on *Intimate Stranger?*

Berliner: When my grandfather died, in 1974, I was a young student at Binghamton. *I* was the one getting stoned in the backyard.

My grandfather, Joseph Cassuto, had been in the middle of writing his autobiography when he died, and all his papers—thousands of photographs, letters, and an incredible array of other documentary detritus from his life— were put in fifteen large boxes and stored in the back of my uncle's office here in New York City. Fifteen years later, in 1989, I came to the realization that if those boxes were waiting for anyone, they were waiting for me.

MacDonald: Both *Intimate Stranger* and *Nobody's Business* are, at least indirectly, about you and your parents' divorce. Even when you're present to introduce the films, you talk about *Intimate Stranger* being about your maternal family heritage, and *Nobody's Business* as an exploration of your paternal family heritage. Theoretically, one film could be about both parents, but the pair of films reflects the split between your mother and father. And yet, through your filmmaking, you keep your parents together: both play a crucial role in both films.

Berliner: Yes, there is a deep psychological hunger—in both films, but particularly in *Nobody's Business*—to bring my parents back together, to try and facilitate a healing. I was keenly aware of the doomed prospects of my parents' marriage at a very young age, way before a child should have to know about such things.

MacDonald: I remember knowing that my parents didn't love each other by the time I was eight or nine years old.

Berliner: So you certainly know the kind of pain I'm talking about. Sometimes, after all the shouting and fighting subsided, I used to hide in secret spaces around the house and listen to their private heart-wrenching conversations. As I grew older, I became fascinated with the theater of their phony intimacy, and the various ways they pretended to be happily married in public. They had no idea how obsessed I was. Or how wounded.

But let me go back to *Intimate Stranger.* The fact that *The Family Album* was made possible because I had discovered this large treasure trove of anonymous home movies was really exciting to me. I felt extremely lucky to have stumbled upon the gift of that material. But now, the idea that there were fifteen boxes of raw biographical material relating to *my own* grandfather's life, sitting and waiting in the back of my uncle's office, began to feel like another potential treasure beckoning.

MacDonald: Your grandfather becomes fascinating because he's not just a family figure but also an international figure. There's a nice moment early on where your father says, "I defy anybody to show me something interesting about him," and the next voice we hear is a Japanese voice saying what an amazing man he was. How much of your grandfather's internationality had you known about?

Berliner: That's the one thing I *had* known. When I was a kid, he used to bring me stamps from all over the world. In fact, I think stamp collecting as a child had a lot to do with initiating whatever visual literacy I've developed over the years. Also, my grandparents' home was a veritable museum, filled with all kinds of interesting "things" from Egypt, Japan, and many other places around the world. In elementary school I always gave very exotic "show-and-tell" presentations in class. My mother's side of the family was incredibly multicultured and "colorful," which was an aspect of my life that made me feel different from many other kids my age at the time.

When I began working on *Intimate Stranger,* I had no idea why my grandfather was writing an autobiography. I didn't know the details of what he did in Egypt or how he got involved with the Japanese, both before and after World War II. I never knew that his two youngest children resented him, and I had no idea about the so-called cultural warfare that took place between American and Egyptian siblings once they reunited in New York. I walked into all of that rather blindly and only learned about it by carefully reading thousands of letters and documents, and by interviewing my mother and her three brothers.

MacDonald: How far had your grandfather gotten with the autobiography?

Berliner: He was close to finishing two chapters. I think he imagined there would be a book one day, but the Japanese company he worked for had a monthly newsletter, and he was writing installments for that. I know that chapter 1 had been translated into Japanese and was published. Of course, some of his own children thought the whole thing was rather silly and delusional—that his life story, though it may have been "interesting," was hardly worthy of the word "autobiography."

MacDonald: Why so much emphasis on the typewriter in the film?

Berliner: Back in 1981, my film *Myth in the Electric Age* made use of the sounds of a manual typewriter—the rat-tat-tat of the keys, the carriage return, and the small bell that always goes off when you reach the end of a line—to structure several rapid sequences of abstract imagery. Ten years later I brought back those same typewriter sounds as motifs in *Intimate Stranger,* this time to orchestrate and organize the voluminous documentary paper trail of my grandfather's life—all the letters, documents, stamps, envelopes, and photographs that he was so obsessed with.

It felt like an appropriate metaphor. After all, the typewriter was the tool of my grandfather's autobiography and the primary tool of business during his lifetime. I wanted to transform it into a kind of musical instrument

Photograph of Joseph Cassuto in Japan in Alan Berliner's *Intimate Stranger* (1991). Courtesy Alan Berliner.

that would also function as a unifying editorial strategy, a way of allowing my unseen hand to "type" images on and off the screen with a kind of visceral immediacy. The sounds of the typewriter allowed me to "sculpt in time"—if I can borrow that phrase from Tarkovsky—and invigorate the film with *rhythm*.

The typewriter sounds also allowed me to create a set of visual "codes" that appear throughout the film. For instance, before you see any passage of home-movie imagery in the film, a typewriter bell rings over a short fragment of film stock identification circles. Before historical documents come on-screen, a typewriter bell rings over a short image fragment of arrows that shake and tremble. Before any archival footage comes on screen, a typewriter bell rings over a short swish-pan. Still photographs are always preceded by a quick, abstract scissorlike animation, accompanied by the sound of a camera click. These sound-image identification markers are used consistently throughout the film. Eventually the viewer learns to associate each of them with a particular kind of visual and stylistic representation.

MacDonald: Intimate Stranger makes a contribution to a different tradition from the one you came out of: what has become a sizable tradition of personal documentary. Especially during the seventies and eighties it seemed like everybody was making autobiographical pieces about their grandmothers, their home life—how much of that work had you seen? I'm thinking particularly of Ed Pincus, Amalie Rothschild, Alfred Guzzetti, Martha Coolidge, Ross McElwee—filmmakers with connections to Boston in many cases.

Berliner: Of the names you've mentioned, I'd only seen Ross McElwee's *Sherman's March* [1984], which I liked a great deal, but wasn't thinking about at the time. Only in retrospect does it seem a little clearer to me that I might have been weaving together elements from two film traditions—avant-garde and personal documentary. At the time I was just making my next film, following my evolution as an experimental film artist who—in this case—needed to look back into the past for inspiration and healing.

When I was making *Intimate Stranger,* I didn't know where it would fit in. *The Family Album* was the first film I'd ever shown at international film festivals, but it also premiered at the Collective for Living Cinema and was included in the 1987 Whitney Biennial, so I was still getting positive feedback from the avant-garde film community. And although it was embraced by the documentary film world, I never really thought of *Intimate Stranger* as a "documentary film." My primary focus was on pushing the boundaries of storytelling, making what I had to say as interesting as the way I said it.

MacDonald: When I saw *Intimate Stranger* for the first time, it seemed like you had moved away from an assumption that the audience for avant-garde film is a small circle of aficionados. *Intimate Stranger* and, later, *Nobody's Business* are clearly aimed at a broad audience. Were you in conscious rebellion against the limitations of the avant-garde audience?

Berliner: I rarely do things simply to be antithetical. It's just that I've always spoken (and even written) with the intention of being understood. It's just my nature. That part of my character was probably most informed by having to deal with a no-nonsense man like my father all my life; I always had to be clear and concise with him. Or else.

I would even say that I was trying to find a kind of clarity in my very earliest films like *Line* [1976], *Perimeter* [1976], and *Color Wheel* [1977]. Even *Patent Pending,* my first sound film, is a clear and lucid, albeit conceptual, statement. When I think about its almost suprematist composition and the simplicity of its self-reflexive gesture, it reminds me that my relationship to abstraction has always been hard-edged and geometric rather than free-form and expressionistic. I'm more Mondrian than Pollock, more Malevich than de Kooning. It's just the way I'm wired.

MacDonald: It's lucid, yes, but both *Intimate Stranger* and *Nobody's Business* are *entertaining* in close to a conventional sense.

Berliner: I guess I started to realize that I was really interested in storytelling—in finding ways to express intense emotional and psychological states like pathos and irony, while at the same time also allowing my sense of humor to come out of hiding. I'd like to think the films are entertaining because they're engaging, playful, and unpredictable, as well as lucid.

MacDonald: Of course, one could argue that in the history of avant-garde film, the best films usually are lucid: *Unsere Afrikareise, Window Water Baby Moving, Critical Mass . . .*

Berliner: And *Wavelength, Fog Line* [1970], *Zorns Lemma.* Most of Ernie Gehr's work. When I was a student trying to reckon with the lessons of those films, I used to walk around telling myself, "Keep it simple. Simple and elegant. The best ideas are usually right in front of your eyes."

Ironically, I'm someone who likes working with mountains of raw material and a multiplicity of ideas. I like being overwhelmed with possibilities. That's part of my obsessive nature. But at the same time, I'm always trying to simplify and be accessible in my films, regardless of the complexity of the subject and the mix of materials I have to work with.

MacDonald: The idea of making mini-montages within the larger montage of the film is consistent in all your longer films. I'm often reminded of Slavko Vorkapich's pieces in narrative movies. The montage of neon lights in Japan near the end of *Intimate Stranger,* for example, is a lovely contribution to a form that many others have explored: Marie Menken did neon sign films, and there's *Jazz of Lights* [1954], the Ian Hugo film, and a wonderful passage in *Weegee's New York* [ca. 1952]. It's as if you're giving the audience the pleasure of these other forms inside the larger storytelling process.

Berliner: Totally. Listen, there's a part of me that would like nothing better than to make a ten-minute, mind-blowing montage of all those incredible neon lights—and I shot enough of them in Japan to do just that—but the short interlude you mention takes *Intimate Stranger* exactly where I wanted it to go; it links the past to the present and leads my mother to say, "If my father could see Japan today, he would be elated." In this case, abstraction functions as metaphor, as a storytelling bridge. It's part of an ongoing flow of thought.

MacDonald: I came to know your films and Su Friedrich's around the same time, and there are lots of connections between them: you both did a "mother" and a "father" film; you both worked with films of a similar length; you both rebelled against the idea that avant-garde film needs to be opaque to a larger audience. I don't know how much you interacted during the making of the films—I assume some—but I know you were friends at one point. Could you talk about your relationship?

Berliner: In the eighties, Su and I were always one step removed from one another, even though we had several close friends in common. I was even invited backstage after *Sink or Swim* [1989] premiered at the New York Film Festival, where I remember telling Su how the film evoked some of the best qualities of *Zorns Lemma* but managed to transform them within her own personal vocabulary. What an impressive film!

While I knew of Su's earlier work, and had been to some of her screenings at Millennium and the Collective in the eighties, I only got to meet her personally at the press screening of *Intimate Stranger* at the New York Film Festival in 1991. After the film, we had a brief but warm conversation and agreed to get together soon afterward. We became close friends almost immediately.

Su had impeccable avant-garde credentials. *Gently Down the Stream* [1981] is a classic. But she was also someone who was making films that were outside the boundaries of what "traditional" avant-garde films were supposed to look like. And, yes, she had already tackled "the family"—having made films about both her mother and her father. I was drawn to her strength and courage, as well as to her emotional vulnerability. Having just finished *Intimate Stranger,* and finding myself on a collision course with my father just prior to making *Nobody's Business,* I guess I was confronting a lot of those same issues in myself. In any event, we had a strong but unspoken bond. We went to all sorts of avant-garde films and events—even Hollywood films—together, and would often take long walks home while discussing them. We were buddies and comrades, and I took deep solace in my relationship with her. In the late nineties we seemed to drift apart, and so I don't see her very much these days, but I always look forward to seeing her new work, and I remain a big fan.

MacDonald: I think it's safe to say that your father became a Dietrich to your von Sternberg. And, looking back, we can see that begin to happen in *The Family Album.* There's something about his voice, and his defiance, that's memorable and compelling. By the end of *Intimate Stranger* you must have known he had to be your next subject.

Berliner: Yes, once *Intimate Stranger* was over—and of course in that film, my father was the release valve, the naysayer, the Greek chorus, the always-reliable source of snide put-downs of my grandfather—I knew there was something potent in his voice *and* his attitude. But even if we forget about the drama, about the Laurel and Hardy aspect of our relationship, the fact is that my father was easily the most compelling person in my life. I found it almost impossible to accept the overwhelming *sadness* of this man. For more than twenty-five years, Scott, my father's way of saying hello was, "I have a terrible headache." "My eyes hurt." "I didn't sleep at all last night." To be honest, I couldn't get on with *my own* life until I somehow dealt with the story of this wounded man who also happened to be my father. I *had to* make a film about him.

Of course, the guy was also a salesman at one time, and a well-liked salesman at that; you can't *be* a salesman if you don't have good people skills. In his own peculiar way he was not only charming but also sensitive, intelligent, and articulate. But he was also the most stubborn son of a bitch you ever met. And while his resistance in *Nobody's Business* might be described as cynical or stoical, it also has a strong degree of integrity.

I was going to make the film despite—though sometimes I think it might have been because of—his intense resistance. To his credit, he allowed me to make the film the way I needed to make it. It's raw, but it's honest, and as a result, *Nobody's Business* is the film of mine that most people connect with. It's been shown on television all over North America, Europe, in Asia, even in the People's Republic of China!

There are so many ironies. It's a film *about* him, *despite* him. He's a "hero" because he *refuses* to be a hero. He reveals as much about himself through his resistance to telling his life story as anything *I* could ever say about him. What's sad can be funny, but often what's funny *is* funny because it's also so sad. In the end, it's really the strength of his character that allows people to admire him *and* feel sorry for him, to laugh with him *and* at him, to judge him and feel compassion for him—all at the same time.

I knew he'd be resistant. I knew he hated my grandfather, who in *Intimate Stranger* he calls "a nothing and a nobody." So, naturally, when I began *Nobody's Business,* I came back at him and asked, "If *he's* a nothing and a nobody, then what are you?" And he would humbly say, "I'm just an ordinary person who lived an ordinary life." My father liked to hide in that proverbial big crowd. At various points during *Nobody's Business* he claims to be "one of millions, or billions or even 'skijillions' of people." I knew he'd be dismissive of my approach before I started the film, but I *didn't* know that I would not be able to convince him of *anything.* I do not convince him of one thing in the film. Not one.

MacDonald: That's partly the difference between two particular generations: the generation that came of age before the Second World War and the generation that came of age in the sixties and seventies. My father and I had problems that seem quite related.

Berliner: It's a kind of verbal sparring. Part hostility, part love.

MacDonald: Your films are as well shot as they are well edited. The shots of the Jewish cemetery in Poland in *Nobody's Business* and the shots in Japan in *Intimate Stranger* are gorgeous.

Berliner: Thanks. I love making images. Ironically, because my work has taken me on this journey through the lens of the past—using a lot of home movies and other historical and archival footage—I don't get to work with new imagery as much as I'd like to. The focus of my work has been on storytelling and the *montage* of images, much more than the elegance or photographic qualities of the images themselves. Perhaps that will change as my work evolves. I'd like it to. But I've always tried to make images and compositions that are strong, clear, beautiful, and evocative. I keep thinking of that word "lucid" again. I want my images to show that someone has really *looked* at what you're seeing.

This goes back to something I learned in Binghamton. We used to examine films on the analytic projector, shot by shot, frame by frame; we'd look and listen, going back and forth, back and forth, over and over again, making all sorts of discoveries that you might ordinarily miss in normal twenty-four-frames-per-second projection. And then we'd begin to understand, this is why Welles cuts on *that* frame in *Citizen Kane,* and that's how he composes images with light in *Touch of Evil*—the same way we might talk about why Cézanne uses a particular color or brushstroke in one of his paintings.

I want my films to be able to withstand that kind of scrutiny and analysis, and I make them with that in mind. The more you see, hear, and feel "intentionality"—compositional choices, editorial rhythms, or the architecture of a film's structure—the more you understand about the film, and/ but also, the more you trust the filmmaker. I want people who see my films to feel that everything has been carefully considered and calibrated. I want them to appreciate the synergy between my intentions and what they're experiencing. Having said that, I also want to leave room for the mysterious and the miraculous. To leave lots of space for things that can't necessarily be "understood."

MacDonald: The best of all your mini-montages may be the day in the life of your father in *Nobody's Business.*

Berliner: To me that's one of the most profound moments in the film. At one point he's sitting by himself in a restaurant, and I'm shooting him through the glass window from outside, and I juxtapose his words, "I can't go to restaurants alone by myself every night," at the precise moment that you see the reflection of two people walking by, holding hands. It makes his isolation and loneliness feel so very tangible. I want to cry every time I see it.

MacDonald: You regularly include imagery from one film in another film . . .

Berliner: All the time. *Nobody's Business* borrows at least seven minutes of footage from *Intimate Stranger. The Sweetest Sound* borrows images from almost all of my films, especially *City Edition.* Sounds also get repeated and recycled.

MacDonald: A particularly obvious instance is the Statue of Liberty shot we see in *Intimate Stranger, Nobody's Business,* and *The Sweetest Sound.*

Berliner: I love it when people notice those kinds of vertical connections—the way the various films footnote and reference one another. It's always a big thrill when somebody watching *Nobody's Business* hears my father talk about how "Those sons of bitches [the Japanese] bombed Pearl Harbor" and then says to me, "Of course, *that's* why he hated your grandfather so much!" referring to *Intimate Stranger.* "Your father fought the Japanese during the war, and when he returns home, his wife's father not only works with them but considers them his best friends." I'm always trying to weave themes and connections throughout my work as it evolves over time.

MacDonald: When you were doing the early montage films, ten to fifteen minutes seemed the right length. In the family films an hour seems like the right length. At what point does the length decision get made?

Berliner: I get asked that a lot. And, by the way, there are distributors, particularly in Europe, who are very frustrated with me about this. *Nobody's Business* was blown up to 35mm and shown theatrically throughout Europe and Japan—even though it was only an hour long. But exhibitors tell me they've got to give people their money's worth, and so they had to find a short film to play in front of it—a different short film in a different language for each country!

Making one-hour films started rather arbitrarily with *The Family Album.* I don't know why, but that time frame always seems to fit the amount of material I have to work with. In fact, *The Family Album* never wandered more than a few minutes above or below one hour throughout its making. That's mostly true of *Intimate Stranger* and *Nobody's Business* as well. It's hard to say what that represents internally in terms of my process, but it's always felt right, so I've stuck with it.

MacDonald: Many of the major avant-garde works are around an hour long, some exactly an hour. Many are by people born after the arrival of popular television; I wonder how much influence TV has had on this aspect of timing.

The only theatrical film I remember that got released by itself as a shorter-than-one-hour film is Peter Watkins's *The War Game* [1965], and that was made for TV. Of course, *The War Game* felt like a feature, and I think that's true of your films, too. They're so dense, it's hard to believe they're just an hour long.

Berliner: The only guiding principle I have is that they be as dramatically rich and editorially tight as possible. That's a lesson I got from Kubelka once upon a long time ago. Nothing wasted. Every frame matters.

I see lots of films that are eighty or ninety minutes long, especially documentaries, and even if they're interesting, I can feel the jive, the padding that was added just to make the film long enough to satisfy the demands of theatrical distribution. Something about that offends me.

MacDonald: A critique that's sometimes leveled at *Intimate Stranger* and *Nobody's Business* is that the first film is about your grandfather, and the second is about your father: how come there's no film about your mother?

Berliner: You could ask the same question about my grandmother. Why not make a film about her? But it was only through the sheer quantity of personal material saved by my grandfather—and the many, many questions and issues that it raised—that I was able to learn so much about the intense emotional and psychological dilemmas faced by my grandmother, Rose. My grandfather may be the central character in the film—after all, he's the source of all the documentation—but in the end, he's a kind of "Trojan horse," a way *into* understanding the lives of those who surrounded him.

To put that another way, I've learned that when you investigate the lives of the dead, what you're really doing is attempting to better understand the lives of the living. *Intimate Stranger* is very much about my mother and her three brothers and how they still deal with the legacy of their father. And, of course, much of my grandfather's story overlaps with the trajectory of my mother's personal history.

As far as my mother goes, she was and still is a "performer," albeit a frustrated one. That is to say, she never attained the status she'd hoped for, or that she may have been capable of in her prime. But here I am now, traveling all the time, not unlike a performer, showing my work in front of hundreds of people all over the world. For better or worse, my mother has often acknowledged that I'm living out the kinds of aspirations that she at one time had for herself. The ultimate irony, of course, is that while my parents got divorced ostensibly because of my mother's dream of becoming a "leading lady" in the theater—which kept her from being a "good" and "supportive" wife to my father—in *Nobody's Business,* it's my father who is the

Snapshot of Oscar Berliner and Regina Cassuto (Berliner), Berliner's father and mother, in *Nobody's Business* (1996). Courtesy Alan Berliner.

"leading man," and my mother who is somehow relegated to the role of supporting actor.

MacDonald: Tell me about the work you did with Joanne Woodward and Paul Newman.

Berliner: Back in 1989, I edited a film that Joanne Woodward codirected: *Broadway's Dreamers: The Legacy of the Group Theater.* During the course of that project I got to know her a little bit, and we kept in touch. Then, in 1991, when *Intimate Stranger* premiered at the New York Film Festival, I was thrilled to learn that she'd been in the audience. The next day, a messenger delivered a letter from her that started out by saying, "Bravo and congratulations," and ended with a rather startling question: "Do you think if I gave you my home movies, you could make something equally as magical for me?" The next thing I know, a few weeks later, her office calls me up to say, "We're bringing over the home movies"—eight or nine hours of beautiful 16mm Kodachrome color footage that she and Paul had taken, beginning with their wedding and honeymoon and moving through the charmed childhoods of their children.

My first step was to sort through, repair, and organize the footage, before having it all transferred to videotape. Then, over the course of several afternoons, Joanne and I got together and watched it. I remember asking her whether she wanted something for public consumption or a more personal film created specifically for her family. She talked it over with Paul, and they decided that since they're really quite private people—that's partially how they've kept their sanity all these years—it would be made for family members only. And I gladly agreed to do it.

In the end, I hope I've made a film that's both emotionally rich *and* formally interesting for them. I even gave it a title: *A Film for Seven Voices.* I might also add that their home movies are no more fascinating than yours or mine: lots of shots of children running around, playing in the backyard, swimming at the beach, in the pool, horseback riding, and generally frolicking their way through childhood. On the other hand, whenever Joanne or Paul enters the frame, I guess they do become something more than just ordinary home movies.

MacDonald: How did you feel about their decision to have it be private? Did your heart sink?

Berliner: To be perfectly honest, I find it more compelling that it remains a private family film, and to this day I've never been even remotely tempted to show it to anyone. Besides, I would never do anything to betray their trust or confidence. I have my own work to show publicly. That's enough for me. This was a job, a commission. It was fun to do, but it was also a lot of hard work. As long as they're pleased with what I did, I'm happy.

MacDonald: I understand, but as a fan of *yours,* as well as an admirer of Woodward and Newman, I'd be interested to see what you did with their material.

Berliner: As my father would say, "Tough!"

MacDonald: Of your recent films, I like *The Sweetest Sound* the least; it's a capably made film, but . . .

Berliner: The Sweetest Sound was the most difficult film I've ever attempted to make.

MacDonald: Did that have to do with the fact that you made it while going through a painful divorce, but didn't make it *about* the divorce? The reality of your difficult struggle with your father is the heart of *Nobody's Business.* Here, you substituted your "personal" exploration of your name for the truly *personal* grappling with life we see in the previous two films. *The Sweetest Sound* verges on the solipsistic.

Berliner: I know. I didn't even mention the divorce in the film—though at one point I did write, shoot, and edit a section about meeting Anya and

Alan Berliner in his New York studio. Photograph by Cori Wells Braun. Courtesy Alan Berliner.

how I was seduced by her unusual name (actually a nickname; Anya's real name is Evangeline), which naturally would have concluded with an acknowledgment of our divorce. When I brought her in to look at it, she claimed it was too painful for her and asked me not to use it in the film. And so I didn't.

Not only that, but I had to put my father into a nursing home in the middle of making the film. He was losing his mind and could no longer take care of himself. Those were tough days. It was difficult to concentrate amid all the sadness. I was barely sleeping . . .

MacDonald: Also, I feel that the premise that you're annoyed that other people have your name is . . .

Berliner: . . . obviously a conceit. The viewer has to be willing to play along or it doesn't work.

At the time, I thought I needed to get outside the "box" of the family explorations I'd been so caught up with in my previous films. I knew that there was no portrait film I could make that was going to be as intense as the father-son dynamic represented in *Nobody's Business,* and so I chose a subject that was still intrinsic to the "identity" investigations of my earlier work but without the intense personal drama.

Along the way, I tried many things that didn't end up in the film. I spent a full day in Chinatown, asking questions about the history of Chinese names; I spent a day in Harlem, talking to people about African American names. I must have spoken to seventy-five different women about the issue of maiden names: Do you keep them or do you take your husband's name, and if so, what are the "identity" implications of changing one's name? I wanted to make a film that was inclusive of the broadest possible range of naming traditions, rituals, superstitions, and cultures. In the end, most of that material was cut out, despite the fact that a lot of it was both interesting and compelling.

My first fledgling attempts at writing the personal essay voice-over were somewhat timid. I was feeling more than a little bit embarrassed at the thought of spending so much time in a film examining my own name. I remember bringing in Phillip Lopate to look at an early rough cut, and he stopped the film at one point and said, "Alan, stop apologizing. Making a film about your own name is one of the most narcissistic things you can do. You need to *embrace* it, not run away from it. In fact, not only do you have to accept the inherent narcissism at the heart of your project, but you should try and write from within it"—from a place he called "an *ebullient* narcissism." He challenged me to create a persona that the audience could sense was *smiling* as he spoke, someone who *knows* that names live in the narcissistic space of ego, that everyone yearns to be unique, and that most people *are* invested in the propriety of their individual names.

MacDonald: If I say, "I got the *Blue Moses* [1962, Stan Brakhage] joke..."

Berliner: That's an easy one!

MacDonald: "and the Joseph Cassuto photograph joke..."

Berliner: My position in the middle of that first photograph? Good work, Scott.

MacDonald: So what are you working on now?

Berliner: I'm going to take a rest from the personal family stuff for a while. I still have some "unfinished business" with the language of constructing sound-image relationships and some percolating ideas about new approaches to montage. Surprisingly enough, I'm still driven by a yearning to reenter the fray of found-footage filmmaking after all these years. In many ways you could say I'm going back to my filmmaking roots. It's a time for reinvention.

Robb Moss

For the better part of a century, critical cinema seemed to be made up of two major cinematic histories: what has usually been called "avant-garde" or "experimental" filmmaking, and documentary. Each of these histories has offered a varied set of critiques of conventional, commercial moviemaking and the audience that has developed for it, and each has developed a set of recognized traditions, landmarks, and pivotal moments. Nevertheless, the distinction between "avant-garde" and "documentary" has always been conceptually troubled: Robert Flaherty's perfection of a new form of storytelling in *Nanook of the North* (1921) was as "avant-garde" as any other cinematic accomplishment of that moment, and Dziga Vertov's *Man with a Movie Camera* (1929) has long been recognized as a seminal documentary *and* a canonized avant-garde film (indeed, it may have had more influence on avant-garde filmmakers than on documentarians); the distinction seems to grow more troubling every year. Recently film scholars have been merging the two traditions: for example, in their anthology, *Documenting the Documentary: Close Readings of Documentary Film and Video* (Detroit: Wayne State University Press, 1998), Barry Keith Grant and Jeannette Sloniowski include discussions of Stan Brakhage's *Act of Seeing with One's Own Eyes* (1971) and Bill Viola's *I Do Not Know What It Is I Am Like* (1986), works that have usually been identified, respectively, as an avant-garde film and a work of video art. In her *Experimental Ethnography: The Work of Film in the Age of Video* (Durham, N.C.: Duke University Press, 1999), Catherine Russell discusses films and videos by Jean Rouch, Margaret Mead, and others usually considered ethnographic documentarians *and* by Maya

Deren, Peter Kubelka, Su Friedrich, and George Kuchar, major avant-garde figures.

It should come as no surprise, then, that in at least one important instance during recent decades, these two histories have merged. The modern history of avant-garde film has witnessed, among many other trends, a tendency toward the exploration of filmmakers' relationships with family and friends. Stan Brakhage's frequent focus on his (first) family produced a remarkable body of work, including such landmarks as *Window Water Baby Moving* (1959) and *Scenes from under Childhood* (1967–70). And there is Jonas Mekas's chronicling of his attempts to find an artistic family to replace the family he was forced to leave behind when he escaped from Lithuania as the Nazis arrived, in *Walden* (1969), *Reminiscences of a Journey to Lithuania* (1972), and *Lost Lost Lost* (1976). In the 1980s and 1990s, Su Friedrich and Alan Berliner created new forms of personal engagement with family that included exposing particular tensions haunting their own relationships with family members in such landmark works as *The Ties That Bind* and *Sink or Swim* (Friedrich, 1984, 1990), *Intimate Stranger* and *Nobody's Business* (Berliner, 1991, 1996). During the same period, the modern history of documentary has witnessed the development of the "personal documentary," in the films of Ed Pincus (*Diaries,* 1971–76), Amalie R. Rothschild (*Nana, Mom and Me,* 1974), Alfred Guzzetti (*Family Portrait Sittings,* 1975; *Scenes from Childhood,* 1979); and, more recently, in the films of Ross McElwee (*Backyard,* 1984; *Sherman's March,* 1986; *Time Indefinite,* 1993; *Six O'Clock News,* 1997; and *Bright Leaves,* 2004), Camille Billops and James Hatch (*Finding Christa,* 1991), and Robb Moss. These two sets of personal films do carry with them elements characteristic of the histories they represent—the personal documentaries rely primarily on sync sound, real-time recording; the personal avant-garde films use a carefully constructed pastiche of various elements: visual text, still photographs, dense montage moments—but the two sets of films beg to be considered together.

Robb Moss is one of the lesser-known important contributors to this personal cinema, or at least was until the recent success of *The Same River Twice* (2003), his feature about the ways in which the lives of several of his close friends have evolved during the twenty years since they were together on a river-rafting trip through the Grand Canyon in 1978—an experience documented in Moss's lovely *Riverdogs* (1982). *The Same River Twice* is the most recent film in a set of three personal documentaries: the others are *Absence* (1981), a thirty-minute meditation on the idea of absence, filmed during a trip home to California soon after he became a filmmaker; and *The Tourist* (1991), Moss's feature-length rumination "on fertility, futility, and documentary filmmaking." *The Tourist,* which was shot in Belize, Ethiopia, Japan, Hungary, Liberia, Nicaragua, St. Martin, and several American locations, focuses on Moss's experiences as a freelance cameraman and on his and his wife Jean's struggle to conceive a child—two aspects of his life during which Moss often felt himself a "tourist." Moss's personal documentaries, and the two features especially, demonstrate that the mundane experiences of real, middle-class people can compete, in terms of entertainment and poignancy of insight, with the best of the commercial cinema. And like many of the personal filmmakers mentioned in this skeletal overview, Moss uses his personal experiences as a way of thinking about larger issues: in the case of *The Same River Twice,* the transition from youth to middle age, and the ways in which we can define a meaningful life.

Moss's personal filmmaking is the central artistic thread in the weave of a life that has frequently included work as a director and cameraman for film and video projects meant for PBS and, since 1986, regular teaching at Harvard with colleagues Ross McElwee and Alfred Guzzetti. We spoke when Moss was in Tucson in April 2004 to present *The Same River Twice* at the Loft Theater, and subsequently by phone.

MacDonald: You grew up in LA?

Moss: I was born in Texas—Houston. Then my father got work selling real estate in Southern California, and we moved there when I was three. As far as I can tell, my father was the only Jewish man who got into real estate in Southern California in the fifties and *lost* money.

MacDonald: Were you always filmically inclined?

Moss: I loved movies, and I lived in a movie town, but as a kid I had no ambitions to be a filmmaker. I never even thought about what I wanted to be and never knew how to answer that question when I was asked. When I got to college in the sixties, it seemed to me that my job as a college student was *not* to know, and *not* to be ambitious in the traditional way.

MacDonald: You went to Berkeley for undergraduate school?

Moss: Yes, from 1968 to 1972. These were highly political times, and while I wasn't trained very well as a student, I had an amazing undergraduate experience.

I did start to think I might want to do film. I took all the film classes they had. I saw everything I could. I'd go to five films a day sometimes, and I'd often see the same film over and over again. Film encompassed many of my interests: world politics and culture and aesthetics.

MacDonald: Do you remember particular places where you saw film?

Moss: There was the Telegraph Repertory, on Telegraph Avenue, the kind of small, black-box theater—walls painted black, everything black except the screen—that I adored. I saw all of Keaton there, and Godard. It seemed a special kind of space and a special kind of experience, one I never got over.

Also, there were film societies on campus. And the Pacific Film Archive was created while I was a student, so suddenly there was this new building in which you could see films in this beautiful screening environment.

MacDonald: Did you see much avant-garde film?

Moss: Some. There was a fair amount being shown in the sixties, and it certainly affected me. Around 1970 I got hold of a 16mm copy of *The Man with a Movie Camera,* which was just being rediscovered in the West, and I spent a good part of a day watching it over and over in a classroom; I was so astonished by it. And I saw a fair amount of Brakhage.

MacDonald: Were particular teachers important for your film education?

Moss: Bertrand Augst. I think he was in comparative literature. This is before film was approved as a topic in the academy, or right at the transition, so people with an interest in film had to find ways of working that interest into other kinds of courses. I made my very first film as a replacement for writing a paper, in a philosophy course called "Existentialism in Literature."

MacDonald: What kind of film was it?

Moss: I still have it; it's a film that loves film and knows nothing about story. It's silent, black and white, and has all kinds of magical flourishes. A guy is in a room, and he hears something and comes downstairs; as he comes downstairs, he turns into somebody else, and this person sees that there's a refrigerator in the living room and opens the refrigerator: out comes the first of three different stories. At the end of each story, the man returns to his room, then comes downstairs again, and turns into somebody else, opens the refrigerator, and another story comes out. At the end, after the third story, a sex fantasy, he gets into the refrigerator. Much later, I condensed that third story, put a sound track on it, and used it as my sample film when I applied to graduate school [*The Snack,* 1975].

I did what I could to find my way into film at Berkeley, but when I graduated, I didn't go to grad school to learn how to make film. At the time, that seemed silly, a kind of cop-out: one should *make* movies, not *study* how to make movies. I spent the next five years not paying rent. I ran rivers. I studied Spanish in Mexico. I had a great job where I traveled with foreign visitors throughout the United States—I'd had that job during the summers when I was at Berkeley.

MacDonald: How did you come to do that work? It seems to have led to a lot of traveling, including several extended visits to Africa.

Moss: For a long time, my mother was the director of the International Student Center at UCLA, and foreign visitors, including many Africans, came to our house a lot. My mother heard about a program called Crossroads Africa, which sent Americans to Africa to do the kind of programs I later made *Africa Revisited* about [1983; co-made with Claude Chelli: the film documents a group of American students helping to build a grain storage shed in a West African village, and the interracial tensions between the African American and European American students], and brought Africans to America to travel for six weeks during the summers. I was also interested in Africa because it wasn't primarily defined by superpower self-interest.

In 1970 I'd gone to the State Department in DC for an interview to see whether I could be an escort, as it was called. I had to borrow clothes—I didn't have clothes I could wear to the State Department!—and I decided I wasn't going to cut my hair. I had hair to my shoulders and didn't know whether to put it in a ponytail or to leave it down: that is, I had to decide whether I would be more offensive to the State Department if I were a hippie or a homosexual—I ended up deciding that I'd have a better chance as a hippie and left the hair down. They asked me all kinds of questions about how the federal government worked and why should the federal government be interested in California redwoods, and then somewhere in the middle of the interview, they said, "So, how would you describe the Vietnam War to a person from another country?" It was the Columbo moment. I said, "Well, the government would say this; the radical students would say that; the issue is hotly contested in the United States." I didn't tell them what *I* thought. They hired me.

I traveled with groups of Africans in the summers, and then in 1973 I went to Africa as a group leader for Crossroads Africa and lived in Ghana for three months. It was the summer when my college friend Barry, who's a central character in *The Same River Twice,* and I had planned to go to white-water school. Barry did go to white-water school, and afterward he met me in Ouagadougou (in what was then called Upper Volta; now it's Burkina Faso), and we spent the next three months traveling in West Africa and then across the Sahara and into France. Then I came back and ran rivers.

I've always loved traveling. I took a year off between high school and college, worked for six months, and traveled for six months. In Gibraltar I bought a Land Rover (Land Rovers were going cheap because Franco had closed the border between Spain and Gibraltar); and with a friend and an English guy who had fixed Land Rovers in England traveled, first in North Africa and then back into Europe. We were in the south of France in May 1968, and because of the strike, had to fill up with petrol in Spain and carry enough with us to get us to Italy. We continued east and got as far as Afghanistan, which seemed much more hospitable than Iran.

Anyway, in those five years after I left Berkeley, I didn't make any movies (except for a little experimental film I shot in Paris with a Bolex [*13 Decembre,* 1973]), and at some point I thought, "I have to rethink this notion of mine about not going to school." As part of my escort job, I started traveling with foreign filmmakers, midlevel professionals. In one of the film groups there was a Filipino film critic who was interested in film schools, and in 1976 I went with him to MIT and saw what they were doing there. I had already heard about Ricky Leacock and cinéma vérité. Though I had fallen in love with film mainly by watching fiction movies, I hadn't yet committed myself to fiction or nonfiction. There was something about the work being made at MIT—and something about the atmosphere of the place—that I could relate to.

I already knew I didn't want to learn how to make films in Los Angeles; I didn't think I'd be strong enough to resist the siren call of Hollywood, and I didn't want to be tempted. This program seemed an extension of the close-to-the-ground, experiential, observational life I'd been living. The program seemed camera-centric. So I applied and got in and went to MIT.

MacDonald: What do you mean by "camera-centric"?

Moss: I couldn't have articulated this at the time, but there are films that begin with the act of seeing the world through the camera, and there are films that start with a piece of writing. MIT was committed to the kind of filmmaking where you go out into the world with the camera and try to make sense of what you see and what the camera sees.

MacDonald: Who was at MIT besides Leacock?

Moss: Ed Pincus. It was primarily those two.

MacDonald: Pincus did a number of early first-person films. They seem underrecognized now. They could be harrowing.

Moss: That's right. Young people now think first-person filmmaking started with Ross [McElwee]! And in some popular sense maybe it did, but there were a lot of people doing sync sound personal explorations before Ross, and as a teacher and practitioner, Ed was at the beginning of this particular impulse toward autobiography. Ed isn't well known, I think, because he made absolutely no concession to the audience. He didn't try to make himself a character, which is what Ross does so well. Ed was a philosophy student turned filmmaker, and I think he had confidence that he could imagine the world, and the world would see what he imagined.

And then he just stopped making films.

MacDonald: Absence was your first film after going to MIT?

Moss: Yes. I had shot *Riverdogs* on the Colorado in 1978, and I finished it in 1982. I haven't seen *Absence* for probably twenty years.

MacDonald: Were your parents recently divorced when you made it?

Moss: The filming was not so soon after their divorce, but when I would go back home, I would be overcome by their distance, and by what the divorce had done to our little family.

MacDonald: The film has a touch of the surreal about it; as the title suggests, there are strange spaces between people—at the high school reunion, when you're talking with friends, when you're with your father . . .

Moss: That's right. It was a particular moment for me. I was twenty-seven; I was just moving into filmmaking, and it was as if I could hear all these psychic popping sounds as I detached from the things that had at one time been so important to me. I didn't quite know how to film that process, but it's what I was trying to film.

And, of course, as a young filmmaker, committed to *seeing* and *hearing* the world with my camera and tape recorder, I doggedly refused to explain anything in the film. So there's a lot of ambiguity—more than necessary, probably. And a hair in the gate at one point. *[Laughter.]*

MacDonald: I saw *The Same River Twice* before I saw *Riverdogs* and, as a result, had a skewed idea of what the earlier film would be like. *Riverdogs* is a skillfully edited film about the general experience of traveling down the Colorado on a rafting trip. Almost the only talking section is the one that ends up being the focus in *The Same River Twice*.

Moss: At the time, I didn't really know yet what I was interested in *as a filmmaker.* I did know that there was this period in my life that was drawing to a close, partly because I had become a filmmaker, and like the cave painters in southern France fifteen thousand years ago, who seem to have drawn animals on cave walls to memorialize something that had happened to them, I was memorializing the experience of being on rivers. I think of *Riverdogs* as a kind of mural; it has a mural kind of narrative. They get on the river, they go down the river, and that's it.

At the time, I had a young filmmaker's belief in the power of the camera to observe and reveal the world, a belief that if you could just see the world well enough with a camera, something about it would reveal itself to you. When I shot *Riverdogs,* I didn't want to rely on words: I didn't want to interview people; I didn't want to do voice-over. I wanted to evoke the *experience* of a river trip, which was what we went back for again and again and again, and what our small community of river guides had fallen in love with. We were like a small tribal group. The film was a bit like salvage anthropology: this way of life was passing, at least for me, and I was trying to get hold of it with a camera.

MacDonald: It's a seventies film but it feels more like a sixties film.

Moss: It was an homage to the sixties, a seventies film that grew out of sixties values. But I often think of *Riverdogs* in a generalized sense, not as a period film: even if you've never been naked on a river trip, you *were* young once, and the film is an evocation of that.

MacDonald: Was *Riverdogs* filmed on a single trip?

Moss: Yes. One thirty-five-day trip. Actually, it was a miserable trip for me; my girlfriend and I were fighting the whole time.

MacDonald: You're invisible in the film.

Moss: True. I could have been in *Riverdogs,* and I do think of it as an au-

River rafters in Robb Moss's *Riverdogs* (1982) and *The Same River Twice* (2003). Courtesy Robb Moss.

tobiographical piece, just not as explicitly as *The Tourist*. Of course, even in *The Tourist* it's not like you see me on camera all that much. I do turn myself into a character through photographs at one point. But I didn't want to be in *Riverdogs*. It's funny, because even when I was shooting, there were people around me saying, "Why don't you make it about fighting with your girlfriend?" And that might have been kind of interesting, but it wasn't what I was after.

MacDonald: So you finish *Riverdogs* in 1982, and the next film, *The Tourist,* is not finished until 1991. I know you've done a lot of freelance work. Is that what you were doing during the eighties?

Moss: In 1979 I went to West Africa and lived in a village for the summer with a group of American students and made *Africa Revisited*. Then I went back to Africa and in 1981 lived in a village in Liberia, just after the coups. Liberia is the strangest place. It was created as a nation by freed American slaves who went back to Liberia—in 1849 a constitution was written by a Harvard professor, "We the people of Liberia were once slaves . . ."—and then these ex-slaves enslaved the indigenous people and ran the country from the mid-1800s until April 1980, when they were overthrown by the indigenous Africans. We arrived in Liberia the following December. During those months I shot a film that was to accompany a traveling exhibition of African art. My recollection is that the art exhibition lost its funding—this was the beginning of the Reagan years and the assault on the National Endowments for the Arts and Humanities—so the footage still sits . . .

Then I started doing a lot of freelance shooting. Shooting was a piece of filmmaking that I loved, and because I had made several films, I had something to show people so they could consider hiring me. Of course, I was, and still am, a terrible freelancer; I'm so disinterested in selling myself that in those days my strategy for getting into the marketplace was that if I was home when the phone rang, I'd answer it. Amazingly, I got enough work to make a modest living for a few years.

MacDonald: What kinds of projects did you work on?

Moss: I shot a film about the famine in Ethiopia [*Faces in a Famine,* 1985, produced by Robert H. Lieberman]. I shot material for a film about Carl Yastrzemski, during his final season in 1983; I can't remember the name, but it was directed by Bill Cosel. That was fantastic: I was in Fenway Park on opening day! I worked on a series of films about child care [*Baby Basics,* 1986, produced by Lisa McElaney and Adrienne Miesmer], which involved shooting a lot of births and filming families during the first three months of the babies' lives. This was around the time that Jean and I were infertile, so it was like job training for me—it was also a little horrifying to watch everybody else's successful birthing experiences. I worked for the Science Media Group—people making films for public television about learning and teaching science [*Lessons from Thin Air,* 1997, produced by Matt Schneps and Ara Sahiner for the Smithsonian Institution]. I did some shooting for PBS, for *Nova*—things like that.

But I didn't really like freelance work. I didn't like how straitjacketed I felt. Spontaneous, camera-on-the-shoulder, one-chance-at-things shooting is what I'm good at and what I enjoy. If you give me a lot of time and make me set up a shot and light it, I feel like all I can do is screw up. And often when I was shooting for PBS, I'd just be sitting there beside the camera while somebody talked; it just wasn't interesting for me as a cameraperson. It was also unsatisfying because while you can make a lot of money shooting those films, the films are never yours.

Also, I began to notice that I was starting to use the same language for my freelance work as I used for my own work. I'd say things like, "That's great; I love that! That's wonderful!" And I didn't mean it—well, I *did* mean it, but only in that context. I could feel myself losing my ability to distinguish between what I *loved* and what was "great" for these other films.

MacDonald: During the years when you were freelancing, were you also filming your own stuff?

Moss: Yes. I would squirrel some film away for myself and, during times off, go out and shoot for an hour or two.

I started teaching at Harvard, half-time, in 1983, and teaching gave me the ability to say no to freelancing when I wanted to. When I started to have a family, I found myself in a dilemma: I had the ability to make my own films, I could teach, I was part of a family, and I had opportunities to freelance—but I only had time do three of those four. The freelancing fell out. People still call me to do freelance work, but I almost always direct them to other filmmakers.

At around the same time, I started using my freelance experiences as a resource and began what became *The Tourist.*

MacDonald: Did *The Tourist* begin as a personal film?

Moss: I thought I was making a critique of White Boy Filmmaker in the third world. The idea for the film had come out of my getting a lot of jobs that were taking me to the third world and my growing discomfort with this work: I wanted to understand what that discomfort was about. I tried to make a film for several years with what I had shot, but found that I was unable to do it in a way that made sense to me. Gradually I realized that I was simply replicating the original problem in the making, which is to say that originally I had been observing people with my movie camera and now I was observing their *images* on the editing table (and making little pithy comments about the imagery). It seemed to me that for the film to work, I had to be more engaged, at risk on some level, in a not too dissimilar way from the way the people I was filming were at risk. I knew it couldn't be the same, but I had to share, at least to some degree, in the discomfort.

MacDonald: The Liberian children chanting "Sardines and pork and beans" begins the film and is used as a motif. It seems a way of suggesting something about the surreality of the world.

Moss: Yes. We're interrelated through commerce with people and images from all around the world, and we're constantly bombarded with the reality of our relative position: how much some people have and how little others have. In endless ways we traverse this strange, modern, international landscape, and as a cameraman my job was often an attempt to try and make sense of the bizarre juxtapositions and contradictions around me.

MacDonald: Early in the film we hear you say, "It is often the case that the worse things get for the people you are filming, the better it is for the film you are making." In *The Tourist* you try to deal with the uncomfortable reality of this by working, on one hand, to find the light moments, the humor, in this complexity and, on the other hand, by working with the often painful struggle you and Jean had conceiving a child.

Moss: One of my fears in *The Tourist* was and is that people might feel I was suggesting a kind of equivalency: the Ethiopians are starving to death, and *we're* infertile, so we all have pain and we're all equal under the skin! I *don't* think that. There are many registers of pain.

The film is organized so that there is a kind of circular movement between grief and comedy; as the wheel of the film moves forward, grief and comedy seem to invoke each other. The film does mimic my own process of trying to handle how complicated and unforgiving the world is, but I'm always terribly conscious of the various levels of my privilege. People used to go into places like West Africa and bring out ivory and slaves, and now we bring out images and stories. These exotic people interest us; they entertain us; they edify us—and people are willing to pay for images of them. There's no denying that I traffic in that.

I am drawn to humor, as you suggest. When you laugh, your whole body is involved in what is to some extent an involuntary response: on some level you become undefended and suddenly open to new things. I think my life oscillates back and forth between melancholy and amusement. And I think that my films move between those two poles, too.

MacDonald: That's obvious in the sequence where you're at Death Valley at Christmas, just after Jean's miscarriage, with your mother: it's "a low point," but when Jean and your mother start giggling and can't stop, their laughter is infectious.

Moss: One of the dangers with autobiography is to become so self-involved that you inflict your unhappiness on other people. Who wants that? There has to be a way to make even painful events experienceable. I don't mean to diminish such events, or to sugarcoat them, but I do mean to make it possible for people to let the grief in the films into themselves, so they can experience it without thinking, "Why are you *bothering* me with this?"

Making *The Tourist* was a real struggle in a number of ways. During my earlier filmmaking experiences, I could look at the mass of rushes that I had shot and to some extent see the film *in* the rushes; it might be unmade and full of endless possibilities, but you could see *something* and have a sense of where to go next. I felt like a sculptor shaping raw material into the thing it wants to be. But if you look at the mass of material that *The Tourist* came from, none of it would suggest the film that I was trying to make, which was additive rather than subtractive—more like a piece of sculpture that you might weld together from different materials. The experience was one of trying to build something and having it collapse and building something else and having *it* collapse. Finally the autobiographical thread created something sturdy enough to build on.

I also struggled with the voice-over. There's a way in which the film is controlled by the voice to an extent that I don't like. On the other hand, I did work very hard to be sure that the scenes would be built from observational insights so they wouldn't be just illustration of the texts, so that they would have their own life that the voice would have to respond to. Even if the film's superstructure wasn't a vérité superstructure, I wanted the material to be vérité; I wanted *The Tourist* to have vérité innards.

MacDonald: When and why did you decide that *The Same River Twice* was a project you needed to do?

Moss: I actually have an answer for this question! There was a particular moment before which I *didn't* think I would make the film and after which I *did* think so. I'm on the main fork of the Salmon River in Idaho; it's July 1992. My mom died in 1991, and I've been in a reflective mood for a whole year. It's been a while since I've been on a river, and being on the Salmon, fifteen years or so after I had shot *Riverdogs,* seems to be putting a bracket around the time that has passed in the interim. I can see that I've made all these choices and that my life has changed; I can see what the elements of my so-called grown-up life are—I've fallen in love and started a family; I've found work that sustains me; and I'm part of a community—and in that moment for the first time I'm wondering whether I can make a film about this kind of change, a film about the enactment of our grown-up lives, using the old *Riverdogs* footage and finding those people today.

So I had the idea in 1992 but didn't start shooting until 1996: Jean became pregnant with twins, and we bought an old house that needed fixing up; I was teaching a lot more—I just couldn't get to it. I did shoot one scene of another river trip in 1995 but put it aside; it's not in the film.

MacDonald: When you began *The Same River Twice,* did you already have a structure in mind?

Moss: There were seventeen people on the original trip, and I knew seventeen was way too many to make a film about. I also thought that it shouldn't be just one or two; that would be too particular. I was just guessing at that point, but I started by filming six people, five of whom I ended up using. I chose those six because they were people I felt close to, and who I thought were representative of the group as a whole. Also, I wanted a mixture of men and women, and some diversity of geographic locations. And I wanted people who I thought would be good film characters. I did wonder at times whether I should be more exhaustive, and visit all seventeen people to see what they were doing and *then* make the choice. But my instinct was that the people I had chosen, the people I felt close to, would give me an intimate access to real lives that would have its own value.

In the end I couldn't tell six stories. It made the wheel of the film just too big: the individual stories were too far apart to make the cutting dynamic enough.

MacDonald: Who was the sixth character?

Moss: His name was Rick. What I thought was interesting about Rick's life is that he has exactly the same values as everybody else in the film, the same values he had back then—he was thoughtful and communal and not very materialistic—but he's made a lot of money in real estate in Santa Fe. The juxtaposition of his values and his material success—especially compared with Barry's staunch political stance against growth in his small town

River rafters in Robb Moss's *Riverdogs* (1982) and *The Same River Twice* (2003). Courtesy Robb Moss.

of Placerville—struck me as an interesting and fruitful collision. It was the kind of thing you can write about in a grant proposal, but it didn't really play in the movie. In any case, I had one too many people. I'm not sure that Rick isn't thrilled about that now. I felt bad about telling him when I first realized I'd have to eliminate him—but he was fine.

MacDonald: When you looked back at the original *Riverdogs* material, did it strike you that the nakedness, both as a reality—it was an aspect of the way all of you lived for a period of time—and as a metaphor, was providing you with a takeoff point for a film? Without those people being naked, you might have a much less compelling film.

Moss: This is a thought I've had since making the film, but when I was making *The Same River Twice,* it never occurred to me. I knew that I had to deal with the fact that they were naked. I knew that the nakedness was going to be part of the film, and I worried a lot about how to keep the images of naked men and women from becoming the stuff of commerce and pornography: once people are naked on the screen, they're made use of by audiences in ways that you can't really control. But I certainly didn't think that the nakedness was going to *make* the movie, as some people have told me it does.

When I wrote about *The Same River Twice* in grant proposals, I had to discuss the nakedness, and I tried to spin it; I remember writing that not only do the people reflect on their nakedness in the film but that their nakedness serves to suggest that these are their lives before the rest of their lives happened. Their unmarked, healthy, young bodies are a kind of clean slate— and as the rest of their lives happen to them, their bodies bear the marks of those experiences, as all of our bodies do. Seeing them naked suggests the time *just* before this is all about to happen. There's something poignant in that.

MacDonald: Have you had any censorship trouble?

Moss: Not censorship exactly, but perhaps the censorship of commerce in that *The Same River Twice* was too naked for PBS and not naked enough for HBO. Actually PBS is so embattled that I wouldn't want them to take a chance of going under because of *this* film.

I did understand as I was making *The Same River Twice* that, with regard to the nudity, certain things had to be achieved right away. Sometimes when I was first showing *Riverdogs,* the nakedness was so overwhelming to people that it would be ringing in their heads throughout the entire film and would be all they could remember when the film was over. Having seen that happen, I knew I needed to find a way to help people get over the nudity in *The Same River Twice* as soon as possible.

I thought that one of the ways of achieving this was to have the characters themselves respond to their own nudity. When Danny laughs while looking at a videotape of *Riverdogs* and says, "My breast: I recognized it!" we can see that she *is* abashed, but that she's fine with it; and her being abashed *and* okay says to an audience, "This may be a little embarrassing, but it's okay to look." After that there's the scene with Danny's boyfriend, Jim, and "the big oar" . . . so the film acknowledges not only that there is male and female frontal nudity but that the characters know there is as well. So, yes, there is nakedness, but the people in the film *know* that they're naked, and they authorize your looking and your thinking about it by responding themselves.

MacDonald: You couldn't have imagined that this film would do as well as it's done.

Moss: Correct.

MacDonald: How *do* you understand its success?

Moss: Somehow the film intersected the zeitgeist. I made *The Same River Twice* exactly like I've made all my films: slowly and without *any* sense of the marketplace. Barry likes to talk about how, when things go wrong on the river and disasters happen, they always happen as a result of three bad decisions. A high-water trip will be scheduled in Idaho. The water is very cold; the water is very big; the guides have to decide whether to put on or not put on, and they decide, "Let's do it." Bad decision number one. Once on the river, there will be a moment when they should pull over and warm everybody up, but they want to get to camp, so they keep on going—bad decision number two. A sixty-five-year-old man gets knocked out of the boat, and he's in the water for too long because there's nobody in front of him to pick him up (they haven't done a good enough job of having a staggered group of boats—bad decision three), and the man dies of hypothermia.

I think good things probably work that way also. The first thing that happened to *The Same River Twice* was that it got into Sundance, a festival I'd never been in and had never been to. In fact, I turned down some other festivals to submit to Sundance, and I've always hated when people do that. Sundance is usually a vain hope; they accept into competition less than 3 percent of what they get. I certainly didn't assume *The Same River Twice* was going to get in, and then it *did*. It's not like it did incredibly well at Sundance—whatever exactly that would mean—but Sundance is a bit like being shot out of a cannon; I started getting lots of calls.

The film built very slowly; it didn't have the sort of meteoric rise that, say, *Capturing the Friedmans* [2003, Andrew Jarecki] had. *Capturing the Friedmans* came out of Sundance with lots of money behind it and lots of people writing about it, and it did very well—much better than *The Same River Twice,* which is a smaller, word-of-mouth film. But as more and more people saw *The Same River Twice,* it got talked about and written about. That slow build in interest was perfect for the film—the second good thing.

And then Karen Cooper wanted to show it at Film Forum, and the doors opened to the film theatrically.

MacDonald: The parallels between you and Ross McElwee—the fact that you're both at Harvard, that you make closely related kinds of films—are remarkable.

Moss: People who don't know anything about us sometimes write to me as Ross. They don't even mean to reference Ross; they're just conflating *Robb* and *Moss.* And we're not only colleagues, we're close friends, who look enough alike that we could be brothers. And we were in Africa about the same time in the early seventies. Our families often vacation together. Our wives are very good friends. It's bizarre.

MacDonald: So how much has this relationship affected your filmmaking? *The Tourist* is the closest of your films to a Ross film—he even appears in the final shot.

Moss: Ross was a year or so ahead of me at MIT. The fact that our films seem related to each other probably has less to do with each other's films as such, and more to do with whatever originally drew us to MIT, and our initial influences there—the people that we knew and the autobiographical films that were the dominant trope of the place.

I love Ross's films, and he's done something that few people can do in their careers, which is to become associated with an entire approach to filmmaking: whenever people hear autobiographical voice-over in films these days, they often trace it back to *Sherman's March*. Of course, they often miss the essential ingredient of what makes Ross's voice-over particularly wonderful; it's not just that it's in the *first person;* there's a whole complicated set of things that allow him to become the full-blooded, self-conscious character he turns himself into. He's a storyteller in a southern mode.

MacDonald: He has a lot in common with Spalding Gray.

Moss: Yes, absolutely.

MacDonald: Especially in *The Same River Twice* you find a way to be a character without being in front of the camera, and without voice-over. We're conscious of you because of our awareness of the camera and because of the awareness of other people *of* you, but only by virtue of that. We see you only twice, in mirrors, when you're with Barry at the beginning, when he's providing a tour of the medicine cabinets, and later on, when he's recovering from his last radiation treatment.

Moss: I'm more comfortable in my relations with people than in generating a Robb Moss character.

Of course, another reason I'm not in *The Same River Twice* is that I'm not in *Riverdogs. The Same River Twice* is about how we live by our choices, but the choice that I made in 1978 was *not* to include myself in that footage, and that choice shows up again in the new film. I realized early on that if I were to be in the new film, I would have to invent some way to be present in the *Riverdogs* material, or my appearance wouldn't grow out of that original material; it would be something imposed. I think if you're making an autobiographical piece—and I do like a lot of autobiographical pieces—there needs to be something deeply organic about the autobiographical-ness for the film to work.

Actually I am in one shot in *Riverdogs,* running a rapid badly, and at one point I did try to use that bad rapid-running scene with a bit of voice-over right in the middle of *The Same River Twice,* but in the end I decided it was too cute and didn't add anything.

You've wondered if it embarrasses me to put myself in my movies, and I guess it does, but in this case, it wasn't embarrassment; it just didn't seem to make sense. The five people in the film were doing a perfectly good job telling the story.

MacDonald: Indirectly, you are present in the textual indications of where we are and what's happening and who is who.

Moss: Correct. The first text in the film is explicitly a collective first person: "*We* used to be river guides." But it's forgettable because it's not insisted upon later in the film. But that beginning does help gather the film together.

MacDonald: How long were you shooting the new material for *The Same River Twice?*

Moss: From 1996 to 2000. The editing took two years. The shooting was the one thing I thought I understood about the film before I started. I knew that there were going to be two time frames: a *now* and a *then*. The *then* was just a moment, a singularity that then explodes into everybody's future.

I remember trying to track the momentum of people's lives and what the trajectories of their lives looked like over time. I knew that if I employed an interview technique, or if I filmed just a snapshot of their lives, there would be no temporal dimension to the *now*. The now had to generate its own past, so that when you come back into people's lives, you know them and you can refer to the things that have been happening to them; you have enough dots along that trajectory so that you can graph it emotionally. This happens, that happens; people are getting married, are finding out they have cancer, are being treated, are having children. That's how our lives are. And that becomes the past *of the film*. Otherwise, it would be *The Same Stagnant Pond Twice*.

Documentaries often can't work in time because it *takes* too much time. Who has the patience for it? And who can afford it? Of course, one of the nice things about digital video is that while it costs me time and energy, it doesn't cost a lot of dollars. It allowed me to go off and shoot, year after year.

MacDonald: Karen Schmeer was the editor for *The Same River Twice*. What was the nature of your collaboration with her?

Moss: I'd never worked with an editor before. In this case I decided I needed an editor, for practical reasons: my life is so incomprehensibly busy now that I don't have time to do everything the way that I used to, and used to feel I *ought* to. In addition, I felt that *The Same River Twice* would run a great danger of being overly infatuated with its middle-age-ness, and I wanted a younger person to tell me when something just *wasn't* interesting. And finally (and this is maybe a distant third reason for hiring Karen), I thought that I could use a woman to balance whatever male ideas I had about the nakedness.

It turned out that the most important thing was that Karen is just an incredible editor and a wonderful person. I enjoyed coming to work every single day, and thinking about the film out loud with somebody was tremendously pleasurable. It was a genuine collaboration; Karen had lots of ideas.

The thing about Karen, and I imagine this is a characteristic of good editors, is that when she cuts Errol Morris's films [Schmeer was the editor for *Fast, Cheap and Out of Control* (1997), *Mr. Death: The Rise and Fall of Fred A. Leuchter* (1999), and *The Fog of War* (2003)], they look like Errol's films; and when she cuts Martha Swetzoff's film [*Theme: Murder* (1998)], it looks like Martha's; likewise Lucia Small's *My Father the Genius* [2002]; and when she cut *The Same River Twice,* it looked like my film. And yet, she does that without giving up any bit of her own strongly held ideas and her strong visual sense.

What I feared about working with an editor, and what I'd loved about doing my own editing, is discovering the relationships that hold a film together and give it energy. Those discoveries are one of the things that make me feel like a filmmaker. But for the greater good of the making of *this* film, I was willing to give that up, and I was grateful that I was giving it up, and the film is probably better for our having collaborated on it. I should be Karen's publicist!

I've been friends with editors in the business, and often the editor is the *filmmaker,* while the producer is a really smart person who knows how to write. They get into the editing room, and the producer doesn't know quite what he wants, much less how to achieve it, and the editor builds the movie. Then when it's time to show the finished piece to the executive producers, the producer walks into the room—slamming the door in the editor's face—and takes credit for being a genius. Editors don't get the credit they deserve.

MacDonald: The overall structure of *The Same River Twice* is similar to the structure of *The Tourist*. The material that you'd collected as a freelancer has no way to develop in *The Tourist;* it's a part of *your* past that's not developing now. For that film to work, you had to find a story—the story of the "subfertility" and the adoption—that actually did evolve over time, and that the earlier material helped to create a context for.

Moss: I hadn't thought of that. It *is* similar in that sense.

MacDonald: You end *The Same River Twice* with Barry and then Jim giving their overviews of life. Jim's is seasonal; he focuses on the yearly cycle. Barry's focus is the stages of life: youth, middle age, and old age. Those two statements distinguish those two guys and conclude their earlier debate, recycled from *Riverdogs,* about whether to leave the river or to stay one more day.

Moss: Yes, there's the movement from youth to middle age, and there's seasonal time; and there are also other forms of time. There's event time, for example: Barry runs for mayor and deals with the aftermath. I'd hoped to do something with a larger kind of time, with geologic time, which being on rivers puts you in touch with. I don't think I got that into the film, though if you're inclined to think that way, you might be able to dig out an inkling of it.

At one point I even thought of having a whole section on glaciers—glaciers are so beautiful, these giant scouring pads that move incrementally but irrevocably across the earth—but decided in the end that it was a terrible idea. You get a lot of unworkable ideas when you make a movie.

There's even a form of media time in *The Same River Twice.* Of course, every time you see the film in a different environment—in 35mm, or on DVD on your TV screen, or in video projection—the differences themselves between the original 16mm from *Riverdogs* and the later digital video look different. But the fact that the *then* is in film and the *now* is in digital video was my way of attaching the past to film and the present to digital. Whether that comes through is for other people to decide, but it's what I would go to sleep thinking I was trying to do.

MacDonald: Did I understand you to say that you were thinking about a third river film?

Moss: I would go back in ten or fifteen years and film people's lives over a five-year period. I'd love to do that if the people in the film will allow it; it may be a little scarier because of the kinds of things that may be happening. When I joke to Barry that I'll call the third film, "The Naked and the Dead," he cringes; he *doesn't* think it's funny and tells me that *none* of them will think it's funny in ten or fifteen years. I hope I'll be able to find out.

Phil Solomon

Like so many filmmakers of his generation (like Alan Berliner, he studied filmmaking at the State University of New York at Binghamton in the early 1970s), Phil Solomon has been most interested in recycling films made by others into new works that are distinctly his own. While many filmmakers use recycled cinema as a means for satirizing dimensions of American culture or of modern life in general, Solomon's approach was, from the beginning, simultaneously lyrical and elegiac. As a student at SUNY-Binghamton, he studied with Ken Jacobs, whose *Tom, Tom, the Piper's Son* (1969, revised in 1971), which uses rephotography to recycle the 1905 Biograph one-reeler of the same name into a complex and remarkable feature, became an inspiration. Solomon's films are usually evocations of loss—of love, of time, of security, of life—that sing the beauty of what is gone by means of rhythmic and textural evocations closer to music and poetry than to most film.

Since leaving the Massachusetts College of Art in 1980 with an MFA, Solomon has explored the literal substance of film imagery with the optical printer, learning to tease emotional resonance frame by frame from the found materials he works on by means of a wide variety of optical and chemical manipulations. The resulting films can easily be read as elegies for the lives originally encoded on the celluloid, and for cinema itself. *Remains to Be Seen* (Super-8mm version, 1989; 16mm version, 1994) and *The Exquisite Hour* (Super-8mm version, 1989; 16mm version, 1994) are particularly good examples. Both films present a series of visually ambiguous but texturally astonishing sequences in which imagery is just barely identifiable. Often, we know basically what we're looking at—a person riding a bicycle, a landscape, a merry-go-round—but can no longer identify its original context. By means of suggestive sound and editing, however, Solomon invests this disparate imagery with a particular emotional tonality.

In *Remains to Be Seen,* the most pervasive metaphor is of a person in an operating room: the sights and sounds of the operating room are motifs that suggest the precariousness both of the person being operated on and, by implication, of the film image and Cinema itself: it "remains to be seen" how long "the patient" will survive. In *The Exquisite Hour,* the statement on the sound track by an old man struggling to come to terms with the loss of his partner ("I'll never get over it, never") serves as the (broken) heart of the film, which evokes a variety of forms of cinema—early cinema, home movies, depictions of nature—all of which, like the medium itself, seem to be slipping away, despite what the loss means to us.

Solomon's films are unusually open to interpretation; they are less about creating particular meanings than about providing evocative experiences that reward the eye and invite emotional engagement. They are aimed not so much at audiences as at the solitary viewer in an audience who can feel the filmmaker's commitment to the slow, solitary process that produces these films. At times, Solomon has collaborated with other filmmakers—with Stan Brakhage on *Elementary Phrases* (1994), *Concrescence* (1996), *Alternating Currents* (1999), and *Seasons* (2002); with Ken Jacobs on *Bi-temporal Vision: The Sea* (1995)—but his most impressive and memorable films are solitary enterprises, especially *The Secret Garden* (1988), *Remains to Be Seen, The Exquisite Hour, Clepsydra* (1992), and the series of "Twilight Psalms" he has made since 1999: *Walking Distance* (1999), *Night of the Meek* (2002), and *The Lateness of the Hour* (2003).

I spoke with Solomon by phone during the fall of 2000. We added a short addendum in May 2003.

MacDonald: Let's start with your experience as a student at the State University of New York at Binghamton. By the early seventies, Larry Gottheim and Ken Jacobs had put together an academic film program with remarkable energy.

Solomon: Yes, I was there at a fortuitous time, from 1971 to 1975, right at the end of the initial huge endowment of SUNY Rockefeller money—so there was a lot going on.

In addition to Larry and Ken, many filmmakers were there while I was a student: Ernie Gehr (as you know, *Serene Velocity* was made in a SUNY-Binghamton hallway), and Klaus Wyborny, Tony Conrad, Taka Iimura, Alfons Schilling, Saul Levine, Dan Barnett (a key figure for several of us: Mark McElhatten, Mark LaPore, Dan Eisenberg), and Peter Kubelka (I studied

Kubelka's work for an entire semester, with Kubelka, which was very important for me, especially in learning to think about formal economy). Larry, Ken, Saul, and Dan were on the faculty; Kubelka and the rest were visiting artists. It was a very heady time.

Binghamton is one of the major stories of the last few decades of experimental film, both in terms of its legacy of teachers (Dan Barnett, Saul Levine, and Mark LaPore at Massachusetts College of Art, Dan Eisenberg at the School of the Art Institute of Chicago, Steve Anker and Ernie Gehr at the San Francisco Art Institute); of film programmers (Anker, Richard Herskowitz, and Mark McElhatten); and of exhibition venues and workshops: the Collective for Living Cinema, Cornell Cinema, the Boston Film and Video Foundation, Views from the Avant-Garde at the New York Film Festival, and the San Francisco Cinematheque.

But I should tell you how I got to Binghamton in the first place. I grew up in Monsey, New York, just across the Tappan Zee Bridge, in Rockland County. Partly because I'm a New York Jew, my father had the usual doctor expectations for me. I never thought I could be a doctor, but I always loved animals, so I thought maybe I'd be a veterinarian. But I also loved the movies. In my high school yearbook people wrote, "Good luck with directing animal films, or *Lassie.*"

When it came time to look for a college, I was searching for a place with a premed *and* a cinema program—I was covering my bets—and at that time, Harpur, as SUNY-Binghamton was called then, was, so far as I knew, the only SUNY school that offered both (the SUNY schools were the only ones my parents could afford). I expressed an interest in the cinema department in my application, and I received a reply from Ken and Larry explaining that their department featured "cinema as art." I thought, "Right, Bergman, Fellini, European art cinema." I was a semi-hip suburban high school kid; I'd often go to New York to the Thalia and the Bleecker and the Paris—the repertory cinemas showing European art films. I was also interested in the American "art films" of the late sixties and early seventies—Altman, Rafelson, George Roy Hill, Cassavetes. So I thought, "art cinema"—that sounds fine to me.

My first semester I took calculus, chemistry—and Cinema 101 with Ken Jacobs. The first day of class—I think Ken wasn't there—they shut the lights off in this big lecture room and showed Tony Conrad's *The Flicker* [1966]. Now, I had no background in the aesthetics of modern art—I had mostly grown up with pop culture, and rock and roll—and when the lights came back on, I thought, "What the hell was *that!*" I was very suspicious. I thought it must be a put-on. Later, when I began teaching, I discovered that a lot of my students felt similarly, though pop culture has clearly absorbed much of what for us was the modernist shock of the new.

I continued to be kind of suspicious and upset, and about two weeks into the course, I screwed up my nerve—there were probably a hundred or a hundred fifty people in this class—raised my hand, and asked Ken, "When are we going to see some major motion pictures in this course?" Long silence. Ken took the question seriously without getting offended and very calmly explained the nature of what he was trying to do; in fact, during that semester, he *did* show several "major motion pictures" and had *fantastic* takes on the movies.

By the end of the first semester I was opening up to avant-garde jazz, and I began to discover the educational uses of marijuana and acid—and then I saw Brakhage's *Blue Moses* [1962] and had what I felt was a revelation: I began to understand the simple but important notion of modernist reflexivity, that, yes, this film is about Cinema, and narrative cinema was this false front where "behind every camera there's a cameraman" and so on. In the excitement of my breakthrough, I remember going up to Ken and saying something like, "Do you think one can really *learn* this kind of cinema?" And, with one eyebrow raised, he said, "Well, what do you think I'm *doing* here?"

Little by little, as I was becoming disenchanted with premed science and math, I found that I was—much to my parents' dismay—becoming completely committed to this exciting and weird little scene of poetic filmmaking, mostly because of the passion and intelligence of the teachers I had the good fortune to study with. I'm definitely a film artist *because* of the academy, not despite it.

MacDonald: I used to go to Binghamton fairly often to see presentations by visiting filmmakers. The first time I went was transformative for me: a weekend symposium, when a single Saturday afternoon screening premiered Brakhage's *The Act of Seeing with One's Own Eyes* [1971], Gottheim's *Barn Rushes* [1971], and Gehr's *Serene Velocity* [1970]. I think Ken also showed *Soft Rain* [1968], though that wasn't a premiere.

If I remember correctly, another part of the same symposium was a Nicholas Ray film, made with students.

Solomon: What a great period of filmmaking! The Nick Ray film you're referring to was initially called *The Gun under My Pillow,* and later, *You Can't Go Home Again* [1973]—a multiple image film using all different film gauges. Sometimes Nick dreamed he was still in Hollywood, and sometimes he thought he was at Woodstock. You can find out a bit about that period from watching Wim Wenders *Lightning over Water* [1980], which deals with Nick's Binghamton adventures. If you ask *Ken,* you'll learn that Nick nearly ran the department into the ground. He was very used to being indulged. His being at Binghamton didn't quite work out—let's put it that way—but for a lot of people, like Richard Bock, who later went to Hollywood, and

Steve Anker, this was a very memorable project. I don't know what ultimately happened to the film, but at the time it was something of a mess.

MacDonald: Tell me about your becoming a filmmaker.

Solomon: Recently, I was reading an article about Robert Wilson and the idea of the Major Work. I think that my generation of filmmakers turned away from that idea, for many reasons. Tom Gunning's "Towards a Minor Cinema" is exactly right in delineating the changes in attitude and aesthetics that took place for us. Looking at five filmmakers—myself, Nina Fonoroff, Peter Herwitz, Louis Klahr, and Mark LaPore —Gunning talks about the difference between our generation of filmmakers and the generation before us, in terms of our filmmaking aspirations. Our generation *didn't* think about working on a grand scale as aesthetic pioneers; our cinema seemed more hermetic and private, in terms of both subject matter and exhibition strategy (I think it's no coincidence that four of those filmmakers studied with Saul Levine). We didn't feel comfortable with the whole tradition of the Cedar Bar macho artist that some of the American experimental filmmakers of the day still seemed to be playing out.

I felt alienated from the whole avant-garde filmmaker rock-star road show scene and was put off by a lot of the behavior that I saw at public screenings. I thought that many filmmakers seemed aggressively defensive, hostile, and in some cases pretentious, boorish, or just plain crazy. At the time, Frampton and Sharits, among many others, had rather notorious reputations, at least within the student grapevine. Everyone had Jack Smith, Bruce Conner, and Kenneth Anger stories. Even Stan [Brakhage] could be defensive and somewhat haughty back in those days, expecting—and often getting—hostile questions from the audience.

Of course, I knew Ken Jacobs could, on occasion, become quite indignant, and even outrageous, but I was his student and respected his integrity and passion.

MacDonald: One thing I've heard about Binghamton in those years is that students had to make a choice between Jacobs and Gottheim, who, after a certain point, didn't get along.

Solomon: Well, that wasn't really an issue when I was there because there were so many faculty to choose from, and you could navigate those waters fairly easily. I think it became more of an issue when the department was scaled back to the original founding fathers (Larry, Ken, and Ralph Hocking) later on. I studied critical analysis with Ken, and his courses and syllabi were imaginative and inspiring. He turned out to be a great model for my teaching. His classes were very present tense; he didn't do packaged lectures. He thought and reacted on his feet. He legitimized these difficult films for me through his enthusiasm and passion and his peculiar and uncanny nonacademic intelligence and wit.

Larry was a very sensitive thinker—I think I learned a great deal from Larry by just watching him think and work out aesthetic problems. He had what I would call an inward, chamber sensibility—I think of him playing Brahms's clarinet quintet for me.

I had the best of both Larry and Ken in a way, but I studied *filmmaking* primarily with Saul Levine, a different sensibility completely—much more of a freak. Saul had just arrived when I took production. What I learned from Saul, especially as a beginning filmmaker, was to appreciate the mundane. Saul was into a certain kind of funky, raw, regular-8mm, nonglorious, from-the-soul filmmaking. When I think of Saul, I think of the kind of phonograph you had when you were a kid, playing a warped and scratched Champion Jack Dupree blues record—this being part of the sound track of his greatest work, *Notes of an Early Fall* [1976].

When I was starting out, I would bring in loose, off-the-cuff stuff, and Saul had an ability, rare in a teacher, to find good things to say about almost anything. Like many others, I was going through my imitation-Brakhage phase and showed Saul a little out-of-focus roll that I'd shot of my girlfriend, extremely close-up. Saul said it reminded him of Brakhage's *Loving* [1957]—only this was better. *[Laughter.]* I don't know whether that was a put-on or the way he really felt, but I walked out of that class thinking, "I can do this!" I think Saul had a wider range of appreciation and tolerance from a beginning film*making* perspective than some of the other faculty, and he was very good for me at that moment in my development.

MacDonald: I don't know whether *The Passage of the Bride* [1978] is an homage to Jacobs, but it's certainly reminiscent of *Tom, Tom, the Piper's Son*.

Solomon: Oh, absolutely. When I acknowledged my absorption of *Tom, Tom* into my film, Ken countered that my film was clearly its own piece, but more like a Chippendale, finely wrought. And there *is* the difference that *Tom, Tom* is one of those Big Films, a symphonic work—one that *did* hugely influence film aesthetics—whereas mine is a very obsessive, personal, "minor" film with a very limited scope of events and ambition. But the similarities are also obvious. *Tom, Tom* opened the door for the JK optical printing and rephotography aesthetic that would follow in its wake and that has become a major part of experimental film since the sixties.

MacDonald: *The Passage of the Bride* is dated 1978; I assume there are earlier films.

Solomon: I have some early Super-8 films and a couple of 16mm films from 1975 to 1980 that I don't distribute, for a variety of reasons. They were immature in form and derivative, particularly of Brakhage. The first fully realized film I made was my senior thesis, *Night Light* [1975].

You know, I'm one of those filmmakers who doesn't have a problem with the term "experimental filmmaking," because that really does describe part of my process, *part* of it, which is to say that I experiment, and oftentimes films will arise from a specific technique I'm experimenting with. This was true even early on.

When I first got hold of a Bolex, I said, "What's this little notch with a T?" It was for time exposures. I had a roll of film, and I kept the shutter open for a few seconds on some frames, and when I got the footage back, I was so thrilled by this two seconds of stuff that doing time exposures became an obsession for years. *Night Light* was basically an investigation of time exposures, influenced by Brakhage's *Fire of Waters* [1965]. I'm not sure if Brakhage did time exposures for that film, but I discovered affinities between the time-exposure effect I had begun to work with, the dynamics of lightning storms on film, and the rhythms of some nighttime war footage that I think I saw in Frank Capra's *Prelude to War* [1942]. All this eventually led to *Nocturne* [1980, revised 1989].

Before the JK optical printers became widely available, rephotography was an important process. Of course *Tom, Tom* established that method and a sensibility that informed a lot of the work that went on in Binghamton, including my own. I started rephotographing things off the wall, using a Bolex projector that could slow the film down to five frames per second—a proto-optical printer. I also refilmed off Super-8 viewers and whatnot.

Everybody seemed to love *Night Light,* and I snuck out of Binghamton with honors. In fact, after I left school, that film was my very first rental—from Ken. I still have the invoice.

Actually, for a long time I didn't distribute my films. A lot of us were very private about our making. It wasn't until I finished graduate school, in 1980, that I started to feel the need to distribute my work. I spent my graduate school years mostly working on *The Bride*.

After I graduated from Binghamton, I lived a couple of years in Rochester, New York, and continued to make films, and then chose Massachusetts College of Art in Boston for graduate school—because Dan Barnett was there, and later, Saul. The first thing I did was jump on their new JK printer—I've never jumped off! All my films have been made on the optical printer.

From early on, I knew I couldn't do what Stan ["Stan," from here on, refers to Stan Brakhage] did: I couldn't film my life and make it available for distribution. I was much more private and felt embarrassed about the act of shooting film in the world. I don't really feel comfortable shooting people, or even filming *around* people. I've taken lots of Super-8 and video home movies but have always kept them *as* home movies.

For me the optical printer is a way of reseeing the world two-dimensionally, with another layer of aesthetic distance. There's something about the process of rephotography at the frame level that's in tune with my personality; it has to do with a kind of artistic introversion, and with the idea of working with a secret magic machine.

When I was a child, I was drawn to the idea of making tiny worlds. I played with superhero models and created little movie sets in the landscapes of my bed. Also, in his push for my "doctorhood," my father bought me microscopes and chemistry sets. I think looking through those microscopes at the movement of tiny organisms on slide after slide led to, or at least fed, my love of peering down the "corridor" of the optical printer and to my frame-by-frame aesthetic.

MacDonald: The chemistry sets probably fed your interest in making chemical transformations of imagery.

Solomon: That's right! *[Laughter.]* Instead of doing organic chemistry to help mankind, I decided to use weird science to help *myself.*

I remember Saul Levine saying, *half* in jest, "Optical printing is for people who couldn't get it together the first time." In some ways that's absolutely true for me. I have a primary phase where I shoot in the world, and a secondary phase where I resee and transform what I've shot.

With *Passage of the Bride,* someone had given me a single roll of a 16mm home movie made in the 1920s or 1930s. It was a wedding film that apparently included imagery from the honeymoon.

MacDonald: The dock and the swimmers?

Solomon: That's right. I became utterly fascinated with the moment when the woman runs across the lawn, and I kept watching the roll over and over and finally put it on the printer and started to work with it. I spent a year generating material out of this one-hundred-foot roll and ended up with something like two thousand feet of material. I did everything I could to it: I bipacked it with a variety of elemental images; I slowed it down; I sped it up; I went in close; I rephotographed several generations like J. J. Murphy's *Print Generation* [1974]—a film I've never actually seen.

MacDonald: There are a number of moments in your films that remind me of *Print Generation.*

Solomon: Right. I'm kind of glad I've never seen the film, because it continues to live in my imagination.

Now, whenever I followed a strategy like generational rephotography, I wasn't pursuing a formal or structural idea; I was trying to create more metaphorical resonance in the material by using the idea of existential recurrence and cycles, theme and variation. I went to school during the heyday of the "Structural Film Wars"—my (unreleased) in-joke film, *Rocket Boy vs. Brakhage* [1980], is a parody of the academic nature of that debate and the intellectual jousting that went on: Brakhage versus Snow, and so forth. I remember seeing all these structural films in school, and I had notebooks full of structural film ideas—but I'm glad I never actually made those films.

Very few structural films have retained their resonance for me, but some—*Wavelength* [1967] and *Serene Velocity,* for example—are amazing and survive beyond their use as models for film theorists.

MacDonald: Actually, *Print Generation* is as amazing as any of them.

Solomon: I must see it.

Anyway, after the purely experimental joy of wringing out variations from the material, I became obsessed with this wedding imagery as its metaphorical possibilities slowly opened up. In the editing I gradually found a hidden story that related to my own life. In a sense, story *is* important in all of my work. I came to experimental film from a real love of Hollywood film narrative. I was, and still am, emotionally involved with the experience of narrative film. But I find that its emotional resonance often doesn't cut too deeply and quickly wears off as the hypnosis of identification dissolves.

I also found a lot of experimental film too heady, or *only* heady; it didn't reach below the neck. I wanted to make films that you could take home with you and that would continue to resonate as they lived on in the memory; I wanted something of the emotional experience we all have with narrative film, but *without* the shame and the posthypnotic letdown. Of course, the great narrative films, like those by Ozu or Bresson or Dreyer, create genuine, *earned* tears, without shame, because they're meditations on transcendental form as well as content.

In the movies I feel I often lose myself in the identification mechanism, which is very different from the aesthetic contemplation of form that we experience with the other arts. Not that it isn't enjoyable—it can be a great experience; but it's fundamentally different from what I want to do. There is dramatic truth that comes out of great performances—in fact, as I've gotten older, I've become more interested in great acting than in conventional film technique. I could care less about camera movement. When I see a great performance in the movies, I'm often very moved. But I've always known that I had no interest in directing actors and contriving narratives—so much of that process seems only about execution.

My films come out of a longing for the emotional depths that I experience in the great narrative films, but sifted into an economical, poetic form, using allegorical imagery and audio/visual metaphors. So I began to look toward found footage to help me retain some sense of narrative—because I knew immediately that I could not direct people and tell them what to do and say, and then believe the material myself. As a filmmaker, I've always identified much more with the experience of the single artist painting or writing a poem or composing music out of some private personal necessity rather than with the collaborative nature of the industrial filmmaking process.

Ken was instrumental for me in using found footage, because he could look at material from garbage cans and pawn shops, hospital films: *anything* was up for grabs in his search for uncanny and often unintentional truths. This is perfectly realized in his *Perfect Film* [1985], where all he had to do with that piece of found footage was put on his Jacobsian glasses to discover and reveal the real story behind the story. Of course, what makes Ken different from a lot of other found-footage filmmakers is that he genuinely loves and respects the original material and is not speaking ironically about it, from a smug postmodern stance.

I try to approach found footage sincerely, to discover hidden truths in the people and events recorded in the material. Narrative truths. In *The Passage of the Bride,* I was looking at what that woman was doing and at all the men with their hands on her shoulders, forcing her into the car. It became my Zapruder film.

I *did* want to work biographically, but in a "repressed" way. I try to submerge the latent personal meanings and references through a variety of optical printing and chemistry techniques, but it's absolutely essential to me that my work comes out of my life. For example, my high school and college sweetheart and I finally broke up when it came to the issue of getting married or not—and that informed the making of *Passage of the Bride.* At the beginning and end of the film, the male swimmer is alone, swimming in the film grain. I saw that figure as myself, in a kind of dialectical montage with the marriage narrative of the Bride.

On the other hand, while that kind of hidden autobiographical narrative was utterly important for me in *making* the film, it's not necessary for an *appreciation* of the film. At least I hope not. The premise of all my work is that there *is* a private meaning, but *also,* I hope, enough emotional truth so that the meaning will get out even if you don't know the specific biographical data.

Finally, in *The Passage of the Bride* there is also a metaphorical undercurrent of Duchamp's *Large Glass* [*The Bride Stripped Bare by Her Bachelors, Even (The Large Glass),* 1923] and his Bride and Bachelor mythos, which I was very taken with at the time.

MacDonald: What's Out Tonight Is Lost [1983] is a bizarre combination of imagery.

Solomon: The title comes from a line in a poem by Edna St. Vincent Millay, but the poet John Ashbery—particularly his middle period: *A Wave* and *Houseboat Days,* really great books—was a major influence on the style and feel of that film. Ashbery has this calm, sensible, conversational tone that seems so everyday and matter-of-fact, but he continually takes these left turns, and you don't quite know where he's going or why or how to account for the odd juxtapositions. But at the poem's end they seem *absolutely right.* That's where I wanted to go with this film.

I had also become interested in moving away from using montage in the traditional sense. Hard cuts had come to seem brutal to me. When I was in school, I was quite taken by the kinetic excitement of Soviet montage, but I had gradually come to feel that montage was a dead end, especially given the irony of Eisenstein's nightmare: that his dialectical Marxist method has become the ultimate tool of late capitalism, particularly in television commercials and music videos. Radical montage, which had been the exclusive province of the avant-garde and a source of great invention and riches, had become clichéd and brutal, too close to the guillotine—off with everyone's heads.

I wanted to soften the juxtapositions of images and became very intrigued by dissolves; almost all my work has been involved with trying to find new ways to place one image meaningfully next to another. I've learned a great deal from some wonderful narrative film moments that use very powerful dissolves, not just as a time-space displacement but as graphic metaphor. *A Place in the Sun* [1951, George Stevens] and *Dr. Jekyll and Mr. Hyde* [1932, Rouben Mamoulian], for example, have fantastic metaphorical dissolves.

So when I was making *What's Out Tonight Is Lost,* I got very interested in dissolves as segues and in working with texture in general as a kind of emotional weather, so that as the textures change, the mood changes, too. That film, like so many of mine, is ultimately about impending loss.

MacDonald: I've had longer experience with *The Secret Garden* than with any of your other films. For a long time, all I could see in the film was the results of the technique, which are stunning. I'd sit there and think, "Wow, *look* at this imagery!" But by the time I'd get to the second half of the film, I'd have had enough of that, and my mind would wander, and I'd decide that the problem with the film is that all it is is pure technique.

I continued to come back to *The Secret Garden* and got engaged on two other levels. One involved the original materials you were working with: at one point we see the title "The Wizard of Oz" and realize, even if we don't know what all the sources are, that they could be and probably are identifiable pop films. So I came to wonder if I should be making these identifications and how you might be using them. The third level—and this has *finally* been hitting me—is that it's a Fall from Eden story. Clearly, there's an apple being offered halfway through the film after which you move from a world of light to a world of darkness. The time it took me to get to that simple mythic story!—duh.

Solomon: But that revelation *is* the kind of delight and awareness that comes from working with creative and meaningful ambiguities, in both form and content. Hopefully, each viewing *will* reveal something new, on the macro or micro level. The same holds true for the best poetry, painting, and music. Revelations and rewards come with repeated encounters and deeper study. Even the simplest Bach piece seems so utterly complex to me.

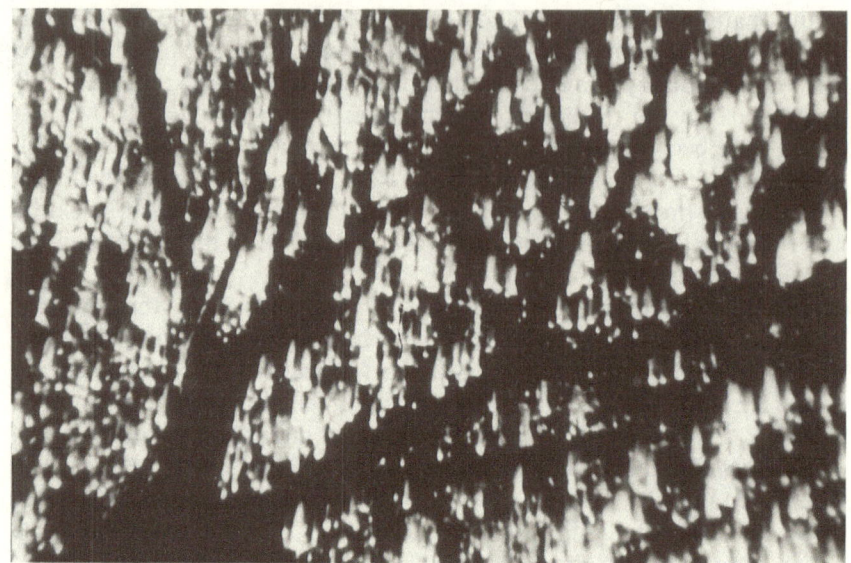

Magical light and tree in Phil Solomon's *The Secret Garden* (1988). Courtesy Phil Solomon.

I watch my films over and over, so I try to build them to last. We experimental filmmakers have this strange gig where we go around with our work and show it and say, "Any questions?" Imagine painters doing that! Actually, I like the experience a lot—again, perhaps unlike a previous generation of filmmakers who were often defensive and contemptuous of the audience's questions. Of course, I understand why: they had to fight the good fight and make a space for this kind of film. They cleared the trees. But my generation had a different take on presentation: we didn't have to see ourselves as defenders of Art or as missionaries. Anyway, I know I'm going to watch my films every time I travel with them, which is *a lot,* so I make them in a way that can keep *me* interested, time after time.

It seems that there are two parts to being an artist: the responsibility to the work in the act of making it; and the social aspect of showing and hosting the work, which is secondary. Like everybody else, I want to be loved, and I want to be understood, and I want my films to be loved and understood. But at the same time, the kind of work I've always been drawn to is precisely the kind of work you *don't* get the first time, but where, in spite of your *not* getting it, you sense real authorship and intent.

John Ashbery is the perfect example. I read his poems and reread them—but I *never* feel like I can close the door on many of them. Robert Frost's "The Road Not Taken" is a lovely poem, a perfect poem in a way, but I think

I *get* it—and I don't really need to go back to it again, except for an occasional visit to a particular place. I like the feeling that even if *I* don't know what a work is doing, *it* feels like *it* does. When you see a Brakhage film, you feel a sense of authority, a will, the guiding light of intent, and you have to trust that *he* knows what he's doing even if you can't decode the film shot for shot or even get a clear sense of its overall form.

Watching films is like being in the passenger's seat of a car. At a certain point during *The Secret Garden,* you decided to get out of the car—but if you've felt that there's something in the film that keeps you getting back in, and if that has slowly led to some revelations about the film, I'm delighted.

Most movies are made to be finished after the first viewing. I was a movie projectionist for almost ten years—I ran an eleven-plex in Boston for a living—and I could watch *anything* once, but *very* rarely could I look out the projection booth window at that same film again. Most of the movies I showed evaporated after the initial consumption.

MacDonald: So what was the technique that drove *The Secret Garden?* Did you do chemical experiments on the material?

Solomon: There's no chemical manipulation of the footage at all.

I didn't have a preconceived idea that I wanted to do something about the Fall. I had a peculiar lens; when you opened it up to a certain f-stop, a certain kind of "unwanted" diffusion would happen. I experimented with that lens on a variety of imagery, and then modified the lens itself in various ways. All of that prismatic imagery early in the film comes from my manipulating the light with a variety of optical techniques. Looking through the Bolex, down the hallway of the optical printer, I started to see interesting things happen, and like a scientist, I would experiment with different materials. I found that certain high-contrast compositions worked best to produce effects that interested me.

And then I discovered that a friend of mine had a beautiful 16mm reduction print of *The Wizard of Oz* [1939], and he was willing to lend it to me. *The Wizard* was a primal film for me as a kid, as it is for so many people. It gave me nightmares, but I loved it. Every year I watched it in black-and-white and was shocked when I finally saw it in color.

So I started fooling around with *that* imagery with this technique, and the footage came back with a diffused, glowing quality, and, along with some imagery of light on water and light through trees, I found myself in the Garden of Eden; *then* I started to think about *The Wizard of Oz* as a classic version of the expulsion from the Garden and the search for God.

The next step was that someone gave me some slug—material you use for spacers when you're cutting sound, usually footage that people throw out—from one of the commercial versions of *The Secret Garden* (though it had English subtitles, I think it's the version from 1949 with Dean Stockwell and Margaret O'Brien). I started to experiment with *that* and made up my own version of what it was about (I've never read the book and have not seen the contemporary film). In my film most of that *Secret Garden* imagery is seen during the second half—and also right at the beginning: the "once upon a time" and "tell me a story" subtitles.

At the end of the paradisiacal section of my film, you see Jack and Jill rolling down the hill—imagery taken from my father's home movies of someplace in upstate New York. My dad took home movies, and his making them and projecting them always seemed magical to me. It wasn't like today, when kids can pop videocassettes into the VCR. My father had to set up the whole apparatus; it was a rare and exciting event. Ah, the musky smell of that 8mm Bell & Howell projector! A particularly formative experience was when he'd show footage of my little puppy crapping on the lawn and then run it backward. My sister and I thought this was endlessly wonderful. In a sense optical printing is just my version of my father running the projector in reverse and having the shit go back into my dog's ass.

So the story started to come to me *after* the material came back. When I was making *The Secret Garden,* my mother was very ill, and there's a whole theme about the absent mother in the film. When my film gets to *The Secret Garden* section—where it starts to flicker—all of the material is bipacked with variations of water, another biblical allusion: first, the Garden, then the Fall, and at the end, the Flood. What looks like cities on fire at the end was just a tiny stream in upstate New York that I filmed and then magnified with my technique until it looked like the end of the world.

You hit on something that's a potential problem with my work. A lot of the time when I have a show, the first question is usually, "So how did you *do* that?" I always hope that my technique has an expressive purpose and is not just a way of saying, "Look, ma, no hands!" Filmmakers in the audience (and most of my audiences *are* filmmakers, it seems) are often distracted by the technique. I do think that goes away on repeated viewings.

MacDonald: I'm not sure it completely goes away. Often your effects are so unusual that the viewer can't *not* ask how they're done.

Solomon: People ask me for chemical formulas and whatnot, but I would rather not emphasize tech when it comes to the meaning and importance of my work. My friend Mark LaPore once said to me, after seeing an image of mine, "Don't ever tell me how you did that!" I think I prefer that kind of response. But basically, I just experiment with different formulas and different chemical variations. I have a way of making multiple copies of the material I work on, so I can try something, and if it doesn't work, I can try something else. I do love the experimental part of generating imagery. Sometimes I'll get something completely unexpected, and then, based on what just happened, I'll try another variation—let it dry differently or throw something else into the mix.

MacDonald: The optical printer allows you to refilm part of a frame or a whole frame?

Solomon: Right. In fact, when I'm shooting out in the world, I often think about how I'll reframe the image when I print it.

The optical printer has been my way around Brakhage. I was talking to Nick Dorsky the other night about Harold Bloom's concept of the anxiety of influence. When I was starting out, Brakhage (and many others from the canon, such as it is) seemed to have covered so much territory. Optical printing provided an avenue that seemed wide open.

Many filmmakers use optical printing for analysis: they break something down and slow it and freeze-frame it—optically *point* to it. I'm using the optical printer mostly as a means of transforming light or amplifying light, controlling color, and reframing reality. The photography blowup sequence in Antonioni's *Blow-Up* [1966] was a primal scene for me: I keep exploring imagery hoping I'll eventually find the body!

MacDonald: That's a particularly good metaphor for your work, because in *Blow-Up,* what we get to is the fact that we *don't* know precisely what we're seeing.

Solomon: That's it exactly.

MacDonald: On one level *The Secret Garden* implies a mythic story of a loss of innocence, but you're also discovering in decaying artifacts from the culture, this new experience—so in a sense the film is reaccessing a kind of Garden within the "Fall" of decay. On that level the film is a modernist parable about creativity being the answer: you reaccess heaven through filmmaking, once you've fallen and know that there is a heaven to fall from.

Solomon: That's beautifully put, and reminds me of the opening paragraphs of Brakhage's *Metaphors on Vision.* Yes, I think my film expresses a *longing* for ecstasy. In *The Secret Garden* I imagined that God (and there *is* a God character, at least for me: the man in an overcoat who walks away at the end) would actually be too beautiful, too luminous, to see. I wanted to create a film where the light would be so strong that it would come off the screen, along the z-axis, into the room and back toward the projector. This reflects my deep yearning to have, and to create, a spiritual and ecstatic experience with film. For me, film *is* a surrogate for the religious experience. I do have informed opinions on social issues, but I'm not much interested in dealing with them in my films; but a longing for a transcendental experience, for Mystery, is absolutely at the heart of filmmaking for me. And I mean this in the grand American–New England tradition, as absolutely unfashionable as that may be, in these postmodern times of ours.

MacDonald: Remains to Be Seen and *The Exquisite Hour* seem closely related.

Solomon: They were made at almost the same time. The original Super-

8s are still in distribution. They're the chamber versions of those two films. The 16mm versions do interesting things, but you lose a sense of detail and intimacy. And, of course, the sound in Super-8 is magnetic, which has a certain quality.

I was invited to show the Super-8 original of *The Exquisite Hour* at the opening night of the Big As Life show at MoMA [see p. 82]. It turned out to be the classic Super-8 experience. There was a house full of the most important experimental film people in New York, including all my friends and fellow filmmakers—one of the best houses I've ever played to. My film was scheduled as the last film of the evening. All evening, everything had gone perfectly—even with the union projectionists on their knees, running the 8mm projectors—until *The Exquisite Hour,* when, suddenly, there was no sound. I ran back to the booth, and there was Steve Anker, drenched with the sweat of thousands of these kinds of shows, frantically trying to figure out the connections. As Steve struggled, I went out to the crowd and said, "Every time I want out of Super-8—they pull me back in!"

But in the end, the film looked amazing. The sound in the Super-8 version of *The Exquisite Hour* was mixed very crudely, during a marathon mixing session with a friend. When the film went to 16mm (those 16mm prints were the first time I was able to use digital sound and digital mixing), I decided to go back to what I remembered of the sound, without actually checking the Super-8 version, and I remixed it from scratch. Some things were lost and some gained.

MacDonald: Did you see *The Exquisite Hour* and *Remains to Be Seen* as companion pieces? They both center on a figure who seems to be dying, and in both cases there's a mix of what seems to be flashback, fantasy, and stream-of-consciousness.

Solomon: Yes. *Remains to Be Seen* was a long, painstaking process, because of all the chemical treatments and whatnot. Then I made *The Exquisite Hour* almost as a release—one of the most magical creative experiences of my life—in a couple of days (all the dissolves were done in-camera). Ordinarily my films are very worked in terms of the editing, but that one was almost completely an in-camera film, and very intuitive.

Both films were made in response to my mother's death after a long illness (about five years). I went to Florida several times to see her and shot a lot of very documentary-like material: wide-angle lens, sharp focus, black-and-white, no chemical interference. I felt *terrible* shooting her—she *hated* being filmed—but I had this primal need to preserve her in some way. I've never been able to do anything with that footage, which is very telling.

I think of *Remains* as burnt orange and burnt yellow, and *The Exquisite Hour* as Cornell blue, so they were complementary in terms of color.

MacDonald: So none of the footage in those two films is actually of your parents?

Solomon: Every time I looked at the Florida footage, the ostensible referent was so strong—it was so much *my mother* and not *film*—that I couldn't work with it. Aesthetics were beside the point. This is when I knew, once and for all, that I couldn't film my life the way Stan and others have done.

My mother died on the operating table, so a lot of *Remains to Be Seen* is about going under. From the very beginning you hear the sound of the breath machine, which "rhymes" with the windshield wipers. During those shots of driving through the Midwest, you see haystacks, which look to me like coffins—again, I really had no fixed idea what I intended by that imagery when I made the film, but I've come to have all kinds of interpretations of it.

Remains to Be Seen began with the bicycle rider footage: the camera follows the rider across the landscape—outtakes of a Vietnamese peasant from a documentary on Vietnam that I was very taken with. That became the central image that everything else spun around.

As may already be clear, I usually begin as a kind of hunter-gatherer. Then I go to the optical printer. My grandfather was the classic Jewish tailor and worked hunched over a sewing machine his whole life. When I work on the optical printer (then on the editing table, and finally, for the sound, on the computer), I feel like I invoke that ancient Jewish vocation of sewing!

Actually, my mother does appear in *Remains to Be Seen,* but it's very obscure. In an overhead shot from my dad's home movies you see people crossing a footbridge over water—the Ausable Chasm in upstate New York. I'm holding my mother's hand. In my mind the water is the river Styx, a bridge to the "Other Side."

I always get choked up at that point when I watch the film.

MacDonald: When you're assembling the various parts of a film, what exactly holds the film together? Is it mood?

Solomon: Mood, atmosphere, air, emotional weather—a feeling. Intuition. Responding to what the images are telling me on a nonverbal level. "No ideas but in things" [William Carlos Williams]. Even though I think of myself as an intellectual and am somewhat well-read and sophisticated about film, when I'm working, I try very hard not to overintellectualize; I try to work from the heart and soul and *respond directly* to the image, and not invest it with too much a priori baggage. After a film is done, I start to see it as an entire piece, and, like anybody else, I begin to interpret it and think about what it *means.*

MacDonald: My original experience with your films is musical. It's like you're a musician of texture.

Solomon: That's certainly part of what I'm trying to do. When you hear a piece of music, what comes through first usually goes directly to the *body,* and to the heart and soul. At least for an amateur listener like me. *Then* you might study further or read the score, and you might pick up on themes

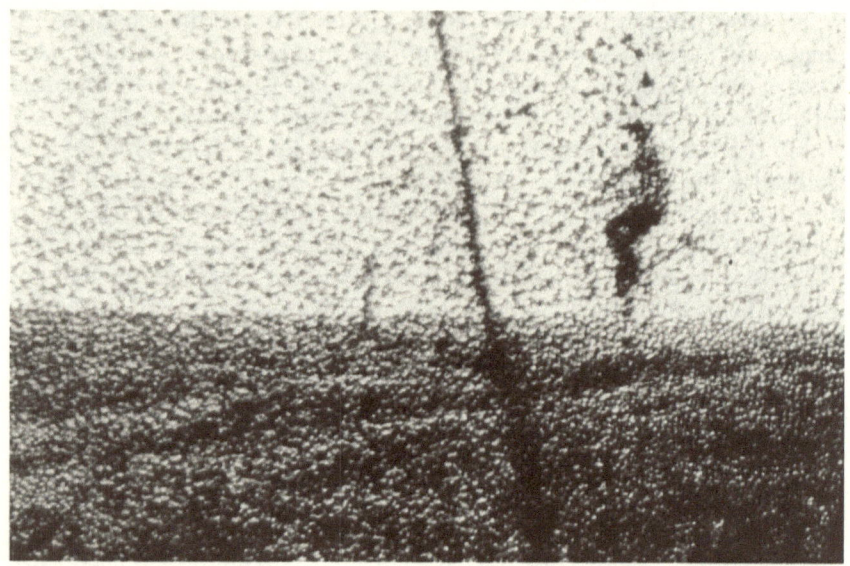

Bicycle rider in Phil Solomon's *Remains to Be Seen* (1989, 1994). Courtesy Phil Solomon.

and eventually find your way to overall form, deep structure, and tonal architecture.

Film is often simply too transparent for me, too denotative. In a conventional movie, the first shot always has this fantastic potential, but then by the second shot, 50 percent of that potential is gone; by the third shot, 75 percent. And five minutes into the film, I know where the whole thing is going. Michael Snow had it right in *Wavelength,* in terms of the dominant, reductive shape of narrative and time: that inverted cone as we move toward the wall and leave things behind us. I want to keep moving, to the white light of illumination. Even though things in my films are ambiguous, visually and thematically, and you might not be able to decode what's going on from shot to shot, there should be a feeling, a mood, an overriding consciousness that feels inevitable and *right,* so that in the long run you stay with it.

I felt this profoundly with Jack Chambers's *Hart of London* [1970], which was a big influence on my work, especially on *Remains to Be Seen.* In fact, at the end of *Hart of London* you hear Jack Chambers's wife say, "You have to be very careful," which he loops; and in my film, you hear, just at the edge of consciousness, a woman say, "It's going to be all right"—my nod to *Hart of London.*

MacDonald: Both *Remains to Be Seen* and *The Exquisite Hour* use very big, machinery-of-the-universe sound—so that there's no question that the imagery we're seeing is, while beautiful, also on some level foreboding.

Solomon: Yes, beautiful and foreboding. That seems to sum up much of my work. I would say all the sounds are *elemental.* Fire and water in *Remains,* wind in *Exquisite Hour.* With *Remains to Be Seen,* the structure is also seasonal: it starts in the summer—you see a swimmer—and then it moves into this fall section with the glittering golden leaves, and it ends with the bare trees in winter blue.

The Snowman [1995] really surprised me. I thought, as I started to work on it, that it was going to be in the elegiac form of *The Exquisite Hour,* and it ended up being something of a *Tempest.* While I was working on it, the imagery called up a kind of "rage against the dying of the light" [Dylan Thomas], perhaps a repressed rage against my father for leaving me an orphan in the storm—hence the sequence where you see the father and son on a diving board, and the little boy jumps into the black and then is seen out in the middle of the storm by himself. A lot of *The Snowman* is about the inevitable separation from one's parents.

MacDonald: How much of what we see in *Remains to Be Seen* and *The Snowman* is decay of original material? How much of it is *your* manipulation of the material?

Solomon: Remains to Be Seen is completely my manipulation of both original material (the trees, waterfalls) and found footage (home movies, outtakes from documentaries).

The Snowman came from the home movies of one of my students; there was already decay, probably from mold, which I amplified on the printer. The way the lines surround figures—I just couldn't believe what I was seeing! Like a field of electricity in the negative spaces between people and landscapes. I'd like to tell everybody that I scratched every individual line, but it's not true. Of course, I did do some things to help it along *[laughter]—*I'll leave it at that.

One thing that perhaps makes my work unique, as far as I can tell, is the attempt at a seamless integration of original and found footage, so that it's very difficult to know which is which. I often think of my "original" material as found, and I use found footage as if I photographed it. I don't want any ironic difference between them. Mostly the films use my invoked decay, *purposeful* decay, but some of it is a result of natural processes—footage that got water-soaked, and so on.

You talked about poetry and music. I think the *form* is akin to music, in that it has lyricism and texture and color and timbre, but the images and ideas that are evoked are like the images and ideas in imagist poetry: metaphors, but hopefully not simple, one-thing-suggests-another metaphors.

MacDonald: The motif structure is very musical. Whatever we see will flow by again later, in a new context.

Solomon: That's exactly right. But the repetition is not *narrative* information, and it's not for structural purposes only, but to allow you to travel back and forth: the contexts change as the film moves through time. Walter Pater suggested that all the arts aspire to the condition of music, and in my case that seems to be true, in that music can create a semblance of human feeling primarily through significant, meaningful, and analogous form. And almost all music makes formal sense by using repetition, with theme and variation. That's how I view the repetition of motifs and images in all of my work.

By the way, we do need to mention Bruce Conner here. A lot of people who work with found footage have taken as their model Conner's earlier films, like *A Movie* [1958] and *Report* [1967], emulating their sharp ironies about modern culture. *I* take as *my* models the later work, especially *Take the 5:10 to Dreamland* [1977] and *Valse Triste* [1979]—very personal films that come from Conner's biography but are full of ambiguous inevitabilities: even though you can't say why shot B comes after shot A, there's an inevitability in the flow that feels just right, that has a perfect cadence. I feel that *The Exquisite Hour* also has that.

MacDonald: It is an exquisite piece.

Solomon: It's the one film of mine that feels absolutely right to me from beginning to end.

The Exquisite Hour has an opening prologue of silent movies dissolving into each other, something which I had been experimenting with, years earlier. Originally, the experiment had no rhyme or reason; I was just interested in sewing the pieces together, almost by chance. Later, the results seemed to fit perfectly with *The Exquisite Hour,* which is an elegy for the dying and for cinema itself. All the images of devouring death are video, by the way—though that was not my intent when I shot that material.

MacDonald: There's an arresting image of a man or a woman looking at something in flames . . . what *is* that?

Solomon: It's from an early film of a magician and his assistant in flames. I didn't even see the original film I took that image from. I was looking through material and thought, "Oh, that's a great image." What does it mean? Many things, including something about otherness, a woman in flames, and cinema as a conjuring and disappearing act.

In the middle, the film goes black, and the sound we hear is a recording of my grandfather lying in a hospital bed—made surreptitiously with one of the first Walkmans. He was in his nineties and had just lost his wife. He would talk in these aphorisms—"It's a hard, high hill to climb," "I'll never get over it, never," "She was an angel." Using his voice that way felt very risky, but I wanted those words evoked in the film, and I couldn't bear to put them over any of the images.

MacDonald: Your use of the old movies seems to take us back to the cultural transformation that took place at the turn of the last century with the arrival of cinema. Then there's a nature section that has a very different relationship to whoever the dying person is. Then, after the vocal passage, we go to home movies, and finally back to nature again. Each of these sections is an evocation of a different part of our development.

Old movies—my life has pivoted on seeing movies, often more than it's pivoted on things actually happening! Going to see *King Kong* [1933] as a kid, without my parents, and not running screaming out of the theater when I got frightened, was an absolutely crucial growth experience for me, and it created a lifelong desire to go into movie theaters and have something scare me, on one level or another. My mother's dying is part of the texture of my life, but—amazingly—I don't look back on it as a pivotal moment. To an amazing degree we *are* our media experiences.

In *The Exquisite Hour* two fundamental histories that everyone is part of—our early media history and our intersections with what we call "nature"—*precede* what we normally consider our most important history: the history of our domestic life.

Solomon: That's an interesting way of looking at it and very appropriate to the work.

MacDonald: Who is that lying in the bed? Is that your imagery?

Solomon: I filmed that man with a long zoom lens through the window of a nursing home down the block from my house in Boston. I'm a little embarrassed to admit I went back every night for I don't know how long—but I was utterly compelled to do it, and felt great empathy for the man. I feel like perhaps I've given him a meaningful resting place in my film.

MacDonald: Ironically it sort of reverses a typical movie gesture: normally we're peeping in at romance or violence; here we're peeping in at the Inevitable.

Solomon: And he's so *alone*. In the middle of the film he gets fed by a nurse (and what you hear on the sound track at that point is a little girl singing, as if she's singing outside his window—actually, a Hasidic girl singing outside my parents' house at night, who I recorded long ago). Later, the man holds up his arm, something like Keir Dullea in *2001: A Space Odyssey* [1968] pointing at the monolith, and you hear, very subtly, the sound of a creaking boat. He kept lifting up his arm, dying this way behind bars, always pointing. One night I went back, and the room was empty.

Something else about found footage: lens manufacturers, Kodak, the entire industry, have worked toward making the cinematic reproduction of life more and more real, in a surface sense. Dolby surround sound is part of this (though actually Dolby makes the whole film experience more plas-

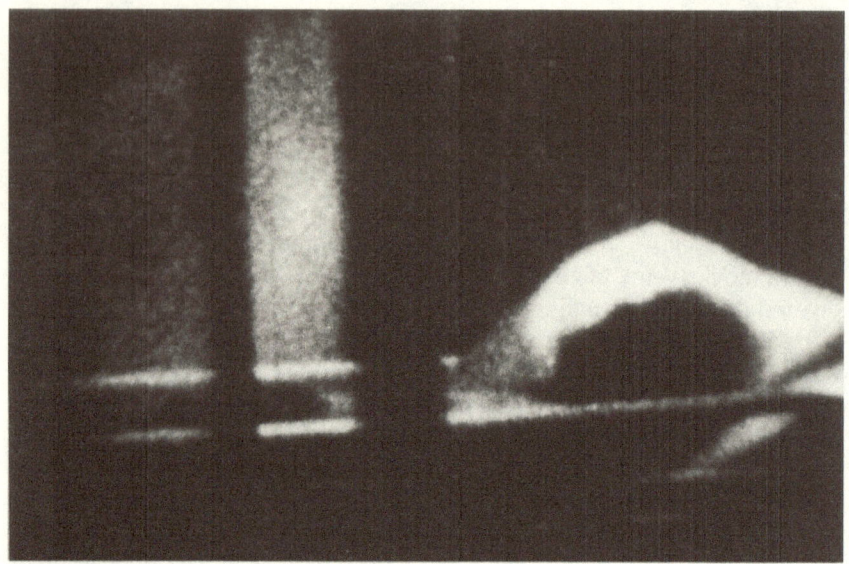

Dying man (head on pillow) in Phil Solomon's *The Exquisite Hour* (1989, 1994). Courtesy Phil Solomon.

tic, less realistic for me). I'm something of an archaeologist in reverse: I try to discover truths in these artifacts by throwing the dirt back on them. I *bury* things rather than excavate them. For me found footage has been a way to unearth lost truths.

In *Clepsydra* a lot of the material came from an educational film, *How to Tell Time.*

MacDonald: I wondered! There are so many clocks—even the merry-go-round becomes a clock!

Solomon: Exactly! Thank you very much. And the door knobs. When I looked at the original film, I couldn't believe how utterly strange it was, especially in its idea of scale—the little girl and this big clock. So I'm playing with a pack of Freudian cards in that film. For me the inside of the house is fraught with horrors, and when she leaves the house at the end, it's like leaving the House of Usher. What the film is hinting at is an incest trauma; it's not direct, but it's in there.

MacDonald: Is there a waterfall in *Clepsydra?* I have trouble identifying some of the imagery.

Solomon: Yes. Boulder Falls. Most of the imagery in that film is bipacked, sandwiched, with water imagery of some kind. Photographically, I would put the waterfall over the imagery and then treat it.

MacDonald: Sometimes it looks like spray-painting.

Solomon: Some of it *is* that. Different sprays.

MacDonald: Did you use the same waterfall in *Remains to Be Seen?*

Solomon: No, that one is Yosemite Falls. In *Remains to Be Seen* I always envision the waterfall existing between the surgeon and the patient—a veil of tears.

MacDonald: There's another particular image I can't quite see. The first image is the girl sleeping, then you pan up and there are these women walking; it's the third image I can't read.

Solomon: The first image is actually a young boy sleeping—the boy who gets on the bus at the end of the film. The image you're referring to is a personal one; it's the person to whom the film is addressed. Actually, I've wondered whether that image might have been an artistic error in the work. It also reappears in reverse as the penultimate image. The camera zooms in at the beginning and zooms out at the end. We're looking at someone I had a relationship with at the time, an incest victim. She's sleeping, and there are venetian blind shadows on her face. It does seem different from the rest of the material in that film, and it has always felt a bit outside the main body of the film and too specifically referential.

MacDonald: Walking Distance strikes me as a kind of nightmare piece, maybe even a Holocaust piece, a visualization of hell.

Solomon: Absolutely, but let me go back a bit and talk about the "Twilight Psalms" in general.

First of all, the apocalyptic theme seems to run throughout my work—from the end of *Nocturne* to the last shot in *Remains to Be Seen* to the dust storm in *The Exquisite Hour.* In *Remains* there's the cosmic flare wiping out the two characters on the beach. *The Secret Garden* sometimes looks like a deluge or cities on fire—the end of the world is how I thought of it. I don't know exactly where this tendency in me and in my work comes from, except that I used to have recurring tidal wave dreams where I would be on the beach and would see the wave coming and I'd be running from it.

MacDonald: I had my version of that dream.

Solomon: To this day I've never seen it rendered on film, except, I must say, in *The Perfect Storm* [2000], which had flaws, though that digital wave came very close to my dream wave. I know the dream comes from when I was a kid at Asbury Park, and a neighbor kid pushed me into the ocean as a joke. I thought I was going to drown.

But I've always been drawn to apocalyptic visions in general: the paintings of Bosch, certain kinds of horror film. So when I got to optical printing, it was a natural impulse to move toward the fantastic, the horrific. When my parents became ill and died three years apart, that became a dominant subject in my work for a long time. I think cinema is particularly adept at invoking loss. Cinema is like a séance: you can conjure up spirits, reawaken the dead.

MacDonald: Walking Distance feels a bit like Pieter Brueghel the Elder's *Triumph of Death* [1562].

Solomon: Yes, and also Francis Bacon and Albert Pinkham Ryder. Edith Kramer [director of the Pacific Film Archive in Berkeley] turned me on to Ryder, and I was overwhelmed at the evocativeness of his paintings and their eternally melting and cracking textures. I've always been intrigued by the dark, by the night.

I reached a certain point in my filmmaking where I felt I needed to take on larger issues than my repressed biography. Also, I wanted to work on a bigger project, a millennial project, though I didn't want to deal with the weight of a single long film, especially since I work frame by frame. At 1,440 frames per minute, *five minutes* is a long film!

I was intrigued by Stan's and other artists' use of series. So I thought I would do a series of films, and I came up with a general title, the "Twilight Psalms." Usually I work the opposite way: I start the film, and the title comes along at some point during the process. *The Twilight Zone* was formative for me; as a child, I was scared and thrilled by the show. And I appreciated its moral quality—every show was about a moral issue.

I started collecting *Twilight Zone* episodes on laser disc and rewatching them. I loved some of the titles, so I started with those. *Walking Distance* comes from an episode with Gig Young, a person in his late fifties, gray-flannel-suit, midlife crisis time. His car breaks down within walking distance of his childhood home, so he goes to visit his home and goes back in time—sees himself as a kid and runs into his father. He tries to talk to himself as a child; he wants to warn the kid to enjoy his childhood now because life gets too tough. The father finally confronts him and says he has to leave: this is *his* time, not *yours*. I found that very moving, and it's the underlying theme of my *Walking Distance*. There's a point in the film where my father appears, and I feel like I'm swimming toward him.

Do you know Robert Wilson's work?

MacDonald: Some of it, yes.

Solomon: I like the way Wilson works with historical characters: Einstein, Poe, whoever. The historical person is a jumping-off place for his theatrical dreaming. That's basically what I had in mind. I thought *Walking Distance* would be *Twilight Psalm I* and that it would focus on Harry Houdini, as an emblem of the twentieth century. In 1999 many people were thinking back through the past century, and I had been reading about Houdini and remembering the Tony Curtis movie, which was powerful for me when I was a kid. Early in my film you see the real Houdini strapped in a chair, struggling to get out, and later on he's taking off a straitjacket. You also see the Tony Curtis Houdini.

At some point during the making, I was diagnosed with a serious lung condition, and the film shifted from my thinking about the twentieth century to the personal issue at hand. I began to identify with the images of Houdini, which is to say that I started to think more seriously about my own death and how I might not escape this illness. One story about Houdini that intrigued me—it might be a mythical story—was when they dropped him, inside a safe, into a hole in the ice, and he couldn't find his way back to the surface. The story is that he breathed through these little pockets of air under the ice, and then heard his mother's voice, which guided him back to the hole—and his mother died that night.

Now, I don't remember how much truth there was in that story, but I do know that later on, Houdini became obsessed with the afterlife, and with exposing fakers who claimed they could speak with the dead. In *Walking Distance* I felt as if I were trying to be in touch with *my* mother and father. In a way, the film was a prayer to them, asking for guidance and help. They are both in there, as I am as a child. So that was my subject, like the latent content of a dream, which no one would know about just from seeing the film. But the feeling is all there.

The film begins with a character suspended upside down on a rope, like a cocoon of some kind, and the last image is a tightrope walker on some kind of journey, like Orpheus ascending. So the rope moves from the vertical to the horizontal over the course of the film, from a tether to a trembling ground. What lies between the ropes is up to you.

Technically, in *Walking Distance* I was, again, trying to get away from the tyranny of the cut. I imagined the emulsion creating the film as you were watching it, as if it were loosened up and molten and flowing down the filmstrip in the projector, and sometimes coagulating into images that then dissolve back into the soup. Like the ocean of reposited memories in *Solaris* [1972, Andrei Tarkovsky]. I think that's the way consciousness works.

MacDonald: In recent years you've worked on a number of films with Brakhage. How did you and he begin to collaborate?

Solomon: In 1991 I applied for a job that had opened up in Boulder. I'd never actually met Stan, though of course I'd seen him present films many times. As part of my interview, we were to have lunch. I was very nervous. I didn't know what to expect, and I especially didn't know what to expect from him in relation to my work. I think the most beautiful surprise of my artistic life was Stan's response to me when I met him: he had his arms wide open for a hug.

Our collaboration began like two guys in a small town with nothing else to do. Initially, I was just trying to help him through some financial problems he was having because of all the optical printing he was doing at Western Cine. I had an optical printer in my house, so he came over and worked there. Initially, I thought I was just helping him with printing this hand-painted work

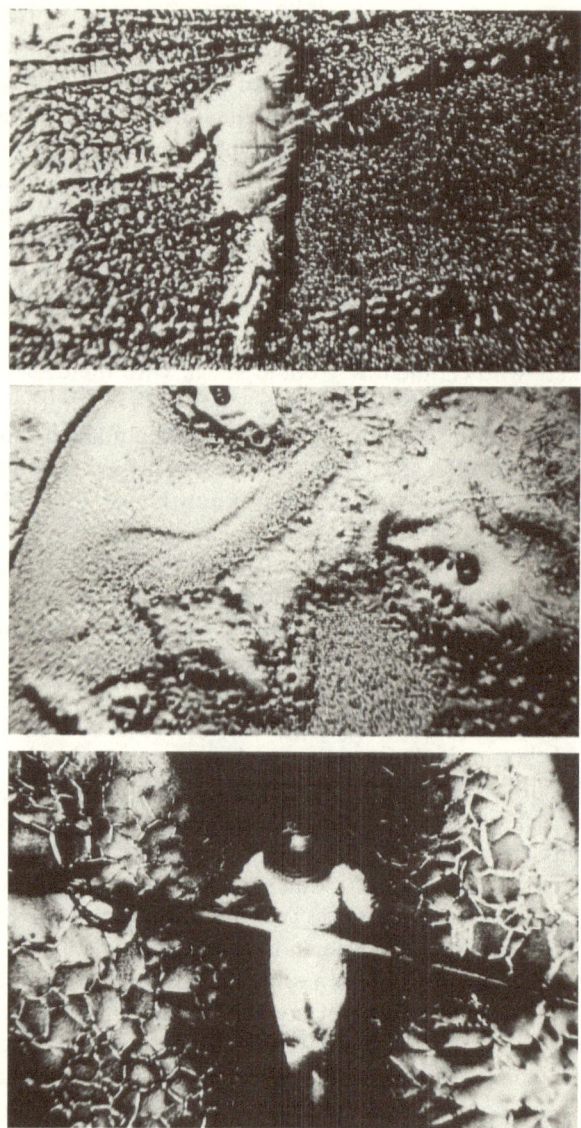

From Phil Solomon's *Twilight Psalm II: Walking Distance* (1999). Courtesy Phil Solomon.

he was doing, but suddenly we were working together like two musicians. What was amazing was how in sync we were about which "phrases" of moving paint were articulate and which weren't. Stan usually works in what he calls a trance, and I have my own version of that—but this was a social kind of making, a duet, and a great deal of the joy and creative energy between us went into that work. *Elementary Phrases* is something of a primer of optical printing and painting techniques.

Since then we've collaborated a number of times, most importantly on *The Seasons,* which was tough for me, but interesting. What happened was that Stan came down with cancer and came to believe, on the basis of the medical information he'd gotten, that the coal-tar dyes in the markers he'd been using may have been a cause. He stopped painting with the markers and began to etch and scratch, carve into film, with dental tools. It was amazing to see him move into this very primal form with so much invention.

At one point, I asked Stan if I could have a bit of the material he was scratching, to see if I could edit it. Typical of his generosity, he gave me all of it, and I went to work. Once I was under way, I showed a roll of the film at our Sunday evening salon [see note on p. 92 for information on the salon], and someone said that a section of it "looks like fall," and I thought, yes, that's what it *is;* it's a season. That sparked my editing, and one day I mentioned to Stan, "I need some summer," and within two days, a loop showed up in an envelope in my mailbox at school, labeled "Summer, for Phil." Classic Stan.

MacDonald: It must seem very strange in Boulder with Stan gone.

Solomon: It's amazing how flat this place feels without him. He did not have a good death, I'm afraid. He was in pain almost to the end.

MacDonald: But, amazingly, he was talking to people and working, even in his last days. He battled through the pain to a remarkable degree.

Solomon: He was heroic. Truly heroic. And a wonderful friend. I have an unfinished project I was making with Stan.

MacDonald: What's the project?

Solomon: We had always wanted to do a musical; we used to call it "Fred and Ginger," because one of our colleagues, who hated experimental film, loved musicals. Stan thought doing an abstract musical would be a fitting revenge. I think I'll use his outtakes from *Elementary Phrases* and finish the film, in memoriam.

We also have Stan's last two films, *Stan's Window* [2003], very simple, very spare—Mary Beth Reed put it together according to Stan's instructions— and *The Chinese Series* [2003], which Stan was scratching into 35mm film stock with his fingernails during his final days—it's only a few seconds, but symbolically it should be out in the world.

MacDonald: Your most recent film, *Night of the Meek,* strikes me as something like a post-9/11 apocalyptic nightmare, though its allusions go way back: I recognize images from *M* [1931] and from *The Golem* [1920], and there is imagery of Nazi storm troopers.

Solomon: Right, *The Golem* and *Frankenstein* [1931] are the prime sources.

MacDonald: So, *was* the film, in your mind, connected with recent events?

Solomon: I'm sure it was influenced by 9/11, but remember, the whole "Twilight Psalms" project was planned as a millennial project, as a summing up of some thoughts about the last century. When I mapped out the various *Psalms* in my head, I knew that *Night of the Meek* would be about World War II and the Holocaust. I couldn't do the twentieth century without dealing with that.

Anne Frank was also a big part of this project (the film is dedicated to her), and one of the things that sparked it was seeing a wonderful documentary, *Anne Frank Remembered* [1995, John Blair], which includes, at the end, the only moving-picture image of her that exists. It was found in a home movie of a wedding outside of her building; the camera pans up from the wedding to the window where she lived, and there she is—this is before she was in hiding—with her head out the window; and she *moves.* Seeing her move was astounding. I thought I would include that image, and I did film it, but in the end, I couldn't work with it—I had to leave it out.

Thinking about her, and then doing some research on the golem—reading different variations of that story—and rereading Mary Shelley's *Frankenstein,* I started to think about monsters and about these little girls: Anne Frank; Elsie, the little girl who gets murdered in *M;* and, of course, the little girl in *Frankenstein* who befriends the monster and then gets inadvertently killed. And in the movie *The Golem,* a little girl saves everybody by pulling the star off the golem, and he collapses. In the golem story, this rabbi creates a creature out of clay in order to save the Jews from a pogrom, and it backfires on him. A lot of people have seen the golem as metaphor for technology that backfires; it's also about the rabbi's hubris: his assumption that he could be a god, that he could control the world, that he could create life from nothing. So these references are all there, mixed up in a historical soup.

The film begins with the world—the opening shot is the Earth—and at times it looks as if the Earth is coming apart during the film, and at the end after the girl pulls the star from the golem and he collapses, there's a shot of the Earth, still there, taken from NASA footage. That's as positive as I can allow myself to be. The world keeps turning; and the children are still here.

I didn't really know what I was doing with this film. It's the first of my films that's not about me. I thought *Walking Distance* would not be about me, but then I got sick, and it ended up being about my sickness. But *Night of the Meek* is not directly about me at all. As a result, it's the film of mine I'm most confused about, most uncertain about.

MacDonald: What's the sound? There are multiple layers of sound, but at the beginning there's this very powerful roar . . .

Solomon: I'm playing that on a keyboard; it's made from winds and variations on lava flow. Essentially, it's white noise that I'm modulating on a keyboard. Deep in the background you can sometimes hear a children's lullaby, and also at the end of the film you hear a person singing, a cantor from the turn of the last century that I electronically treated. It's a similar sound strategy to the one in *Walking Distance:* a kind of primeval wind with ghosts and echoes underneath it

MacDonald: Like a stream of consciousness with things welling up from below.

Solomon: Exactly.

I was very nervous about the piece. After the New York Film Festival screening, I saw Ken and Flo [Jacobs] leave the discussion early, and I wondered if they had had a bad reaction to the piece.

MacDonald: I can't imagine they wouldn't admire the film.

Solomon: Well, you know, Ken and Stan didn't talk for two years because of Stan's *23rd Psalm Branch* [1966/1978].

MacDonald: I didn't know that.

Solomon: Ken said to him, "What have you done to my Jews!" Stan had painted over Holocaust imagery, and they had a real difference about that.

It turned out that Ken and Flo are very fond of *Night of the Meek.*

James Benning

On His Westerns

James Benning made his reputation as a major contributor to independent cinema in the 1970s in *11 x 14* (1976) and *One Way Boogie Woogie* (1977) with his depiction of the Midwest and his inventive uses of composition and sound-image relationship, but he has continued to surprise those of us who have followed his career by confirming the accomplishments of his youth with decade after decade of interesting work. When I interviewed Benning for *A Critical Cinema 2* in 1986, *American Dreams* (1984) and *Landscape Suicide* (1986) had made the 1980s nearly as memorable a decade for his work as the 1970s. But I could not have imagined that Benning's fiftieth birthday (he was born in 1942) would signal not just further accomplishment but the beginning of the most remarkable era in his creative life. Soon after Benning moved to California to teach at the California Institute of the Arts in Valencia, just north of LA, in 1988, he began to explore the American West with the same energy and inventiveness that had made his 1970s explorations of the Midwest so memorable. His *North on Evers* (1991), made in part as a way of coming to terms with his own—and America's—aging, now seems a précis of the remarkable series of films he has finished during the past dozen years. With the exception of Luis Buñuel and Alfred Hitchcock, I can think of no filmmaker who has blossomed so impressively so late in his career.

North on Evers is Benning's *Easy Rider* (1969). It chronicles two motorcycle trips across the United States—each from his home in the small town of Val Verde to New York City across the southern route, then back west by the northern route—during two successive summers. The first trip is presented as a handwritten text that scrolls from right to left across the bottom of the screen; the second is documented in image and sound recorded a year later, as Benning revisited the places and people he had seen on the original trip. By the time he returns to Val Verde, he and we have not only seen something of American place at the conclusion of the twentieth century, we have also considered dimensions of our shared history. On both trips Benning visits old friends and a variety of sites and memorials of events that were crucial during the 1960s, for Benning a particularly formative decade: the Texas Schoolbook Depository in Dallas, the place where civil rights activist Medgar Evers (the "Evers" of Benning's title) was murdered, the Vietnam War Memorial in Washington, D.C. Benning's revisiting of history provides a context for an ongoing consideration of where America is now; and if on some level Benning imagines his journey ending in the decaying spiral of Robert Smithson's *Spiral Jetty* (1970) in the Great Salt Lake, in fact the experience of making *North on Evers* seems to have reenergized him and reconnected him to American geography and history.

In 1995, Benning completed *Deseret,* an exploration of the history and geography of Utah, just in time for the centennial of Utah's statehood in 1996. Using a series of edited *New York Times* stories relating to Utah, narrated by Fred Gardner, Benning tracks the changes in the way Utah has been perceived by America's eastern Establishment. Each story is accompanied by the imagery and sounds of a different location in Utah, so that as we become more familiar with the history of the region the original Mormons called "Deseret," we become more fully aware of the geographic diversity of Utah—and, by the conclusion of *Deseret,* of a variety of ongoing dangers to the state's environment and ecology.

Benning's fascination with Utah led him to the Four Corners area—where Utah, Colorado, New Mexico, and Arizona meet—and to his next project, *Four Corners* (1997). *Four Corners* focuses on the meeting of the north-south and east-west borders of four states as an implicit grid against which Benning can chart the movements through time and space of the various peoples that have created the history of the Four Corners region: the Native Americans—especially the Anasazi, the Navajo, and the Zuni—and the European Americans who settled, and often plundered, the region. *Four Corners* is rigorously organized into four identical sections, each made up of three different forms of information: first, we read eighty seconds of visual text, white on black, that reviews the life of a particular artist—Claude Monet; Alabama folk painter Moses Tolliver; an imaginary Native American painter; and Jasper Johns—leading up to the creation of a particular artwork, which is then presented in a single, continuous shot, accompanied by a voice-over that outlines a particular dimension of history relevant to the Four Corners area. In the first section, we hear the story of Richard

Wetherell, who "discovered" the cliff dwellings at Mesa Verde and sold Indian artifacts to museums until he was murdered by a Navajo; in the second, the history of Milwaukee and Benning's youth there; in the third, the history of Native Americans in the Four Corners region; and in the fourth, the story of Herman Dodge Benally, a Navajo who was killed by high school students in Farmington, New Mexico, in 1974. The third part of each section is a series of thirteen fifty-second shots of a particular location related to the previous history: Chaco Canyon, Milwaukee's South Side, Mesa Verde, Farmington.

Four Corners was followed by *Utopia* (1998), in which Benning recycled the sound track from *Ernesto Che Guevara, the Bolivian Journal* (1997) by Richard Dindo, accompanying Dindo's track with imagery recorded along and near the border of California and Sonora, Mexico. *Utopia* relates Guevara's quest for a more equitable world in South America to the history and current struggles along the U.S./Mexico border, and provides still another rumination on the paradox of the beauty of western geography and the troubled history of this region.

In 1999, Benning completed *El Valley Centro,* what was to become the first section of a trilogy of films about California. Each part of the trilogy—*Los* (2000) and *Sogobi* (2001) are the others—is made up of thirty-five $2\frac{1}{2}$-minute shots. *El Valley Centro* focuses on California's Central Valley, between the Sierra Nevadas and the Coastal Range, where a considerable percentage of America's food is produced; *Los,* on the Los Angeles area; and *Sogobi* (the title is Shoshone for "earth"), on what remains of original California after centuries of still ongoing agricultural and industrial development. At least as of the writing of this introduction, Benning asks that the California Trilogy be screened in its entirety, as a mega-event (each ninety-minute film is separated from the next by a fifteen-minute break)—a way of subtly modeling the reorganization of time necessary for coming to grips with the environmental challenges that face us not only in California but across the nation and around the world. The unusually patient form of the California Trilogy has instigated a further film, *13 Lakes* (2004), a series of eleven-minute shots of thirteen American lakes.

In recent decades Benning's most responsive audience seems to be in Europe, where his films are seen regularly at festivals and by television audiences. In fact, Benning is the subject of an elegant recent documentary, *James Benning: Circling the Image* (2003), by Reinhard Wulf: Wulf films Benning in the process of making *13 Lakes.* While Benning continues to tour the United States with his films, as he has since the 1970s, there seems surprisingly little awareness of the accomplishments of his "westerns." Even a high-profile event like the "Views from the Avant-Garde" screenings, held annually as a sidebar to the New York Film Festival, has never acknowledged

Moosehead Lake, Maine, from James Benning's *13 Lakes* (2004). Courtesy James Benning.

these films, nor has the festival itself. Benning's commitment to feature-length films that are not narrative melodramas seems to have located his work in a no-man's-land exhibition-wise, at least in his native land—despite the fact that these films are remarkably accessible and engaging. Their value for students in academic fields such as American studies, environmental studies, and cultural studies could be considerable, if only those who teach in these fields were aware of Benning's work. One can only hope that, in time, Benning will have the American audience his films deserve.

An interview with Benning, about his films up through *Used Innocence* (1988), is included in *A Critical Cinema 2* (pp. 220–48). This interview began in March 1996 in Utica, New York, when Benning and I talked about his 1990s films up through *Deseret*. We talked again in April 2002, when the Tucson Film Festival presented the California Trilogy. I have frequently e-mailed questions to Benning, which he has been kind enough to answer.

MacDonald: In *North on Evers* and *Deseret,* landscape and cityscape are your focus again, the way they were early in your career in *11 × 14* and *One Way Boogie Woogie.* Where does this come from with you? Except for Peter

Hutton, I don't know any other experimental filmmaker who's been so consistently interested in landscape and cityscape.

Benning: Well, I like to be outside. It may be as simple as that.

But in these two recent films I see landscape in two different ways. In *North on Evers,* I'm using landscape to reveal my movement across the country and to document how the landscape *changes,* geographically and historically. I use landscape as a way of moving through and looking at particular histories that are part of my past. In *Deseret,* I'm showing an unspoiled, virgin kind of landscape that history is written against or on top of, and that human behavior is destroying. *North on Evers* is more personal; *Deseret* is more political.

But I enjoy being outside, and I like looking. I like walking, and I like the way you feel when you're in a landscape, the way you can measure yourself against landscape, the way landscape puts you into a proper perspective.

MacDonald: For someone in our generation, the obvious reference in *North on Evers* is *Easy Rider.* Maybe the connection is only the fact that you travel by motorcycle, and that, like the *Easy Rider* characters, you start in the West and move east, at least at first—but I'm wondering what led to the *North on Evers* project.

Benning: Well, I was making that film for a year, without even *knowing* I was making it, which sounds strange.

MacDonald: You were recording imagery?

Benning: No, no. In 1989 I was feeling somewhat uncomfortable in California and decided to leave for a while. I got on my motorcycle and started to ride east. I didn't have a plan, but during the next three months I went down through Texas and through the Deep South and up to New York State and then back to my hometown in Wisconsin, and back to California by the northern route. I felt better after the trip. And then during the next winter, I wrote a long letter to a friend, describing the trip, and when I finished that letter, I thought, "Maybe I should make a film about this." The letter was very narrative, and I thought it could be an interesting text for a film.

So the next June, I decided to do that same trip again, only this time I'd take a camera. *North on Evers* is handheld because I couldn't get a tripod onto the bike. Well, I suppose I could have if I had tried, but I thought maybe this film should be more diaristic, more home-movie-like. Anyway, I followed that same path I drove the year before, which wasn't really a *path* the year before, but was now.

The one trip was the antithesis of the other: the first was all play, and the second was all work. The text you read in the film is about the first trip; the pictures are from the second trip.

When you do read the text, you realize there are two kinds of displacement between text and image. One is physical, on the film, and the other is temporal. The image and text are off by a few feet on the film—that is, at least at first, you read about a place before you see that same place—but they're really off by a whole year in time. I wanted to create two visual tracks: one you see, and one you create in your mind as you read. It's the space between text and image that I'm interested in.

MacDonald: The title, "North on Evers," obviously refers to Medgar Evers, who is discussed in the text; but there are many incidents in the film; why focus on this one?

Benning: The reason I focus on Medgar Evers is because his death was something of a turning point in my life. That first trip across the country turned out to be a trip into my past; I was seeing old friends and experiencing old events, or trying to find things that would remind me of old events. I grew up in Milwaukee, in a lower-middle-class neighborhood on the edge of a black ghetto, a place that was perpetuating blind prejudice. At eighteen or nineteen years old I was starting to question what I had been taught—not taught in a systematic way, but those border-town neighborhoods have prejudice built into them—and when Evers was murdered, it made an impact on me.

On this trip, I thought it was important for me to see where Evers died. And I discovered that while there was no marker there, nothing that indicated it was an important spot, Jackson, Mississippi, did have a main street named after Evers. All of those things were important to me.

But the title doesn't mean that that particular event is the most important in the film; what's important is the idea of driving through history.

MacDonald: The early section of *North on Evers* is almost a seed for *Deseret,* in the sense of your becoming aware of environmental damage as a topic.

Benning: Absolutely. Driving across the country and seeing all this industry, some of it obvious, some of it hidden away in the middle of nowhere—you can't help wondering what's going on, and what they're doing to the environment.

MacDonald: Was Easy Rider important for you?

Benning: Well, when it first came out, I thought it was kind of heroic, and it made me proud to be a hippy. Then, when I saw it about ten years later, I decided those guys might have gotten what they deserved. *[Laughter.]* Just because of their selfishness. I had the same kind of experience rereading *On the Road.* It's a brilliant book, but I thought it exposed the selfishness of these guys trying to discover themselves, their lack of regard for the people around them.

I saw *Easy Rider* again recently, and I thought, "No it's quite a good movie." But I don't know if it's affected me, or *North on Evers,* at all. It is fun to listen to all that old music.

The motorcycle and text, from James Benning's *North on Evers* (1991). Courtesy James Benning.

MacDonald: One way of thinking about the development of landscape painting in this country, especially on the part of the people writing about it recently, is that it was exactly at the moment when the original American landscape seemed in danger of totally disappearing that it was recognized as something worth holding on to. In *Deseret* you're playing with that theme, too, as you made clear when you were talking about the structure of the film at the screening tonight, and its relationship to Smithson's *Spiral Jetty* and the concept of entropy.

Benning: Absolutely.

MacDonald: The film begins with a beautiful image of a butte, but by the end, we've moved into a sensibility where we're no longer sure whether we're looking at a beautiful landscape or an environmental disaster.

Benning: People living in southern Utah, in one of the most beautiful places in the world, are still dying of cancer from nuclear testing in Nevada decades ago. They became the "down-winders." A piece of landscape that looks beautiful can become the opposite of beauty.

But there's something more marvelous about those landscapes than all of that, something very mysterious. Out in the middle of a western landscape, where nobody's around, there seems to be some answer, a feeling of getting back to something that's much more real than what we generally experience. I think Robert Frank expresses it really well in his video *Home Improvements* [1985], when he points the camera out his window in Nova Scotia and says, "The answer's out there, but every time I look out, it's different; it's always changing." I think maybe that's what it is: a search for an answer *out there,* where every moment is different from the moment before. Landscape is always changing in very subtle ways and sometimes in very dramatic ways, but it has to be *experienced.*

It's quite remarkable to get up at five o'clock in the morning, when it's already eighty degrees, and walk eight or ten miles through the canyonlands to where the Colorado and Green rivers meet, to be out there all by yourself, and it's very hot, and you're wet with sweat, and you hear the wind blow down those rivers and you look down and see one red river and one green river mixing together—there's something special about that moment. But basically the experience is indescribable—you have to *do* it.

And then there's also the feeling of being out of water and hurrying back eight or ten miles; it puts you on the edge of life in a way, and you start to think about the struggles of life in the past, when people were trying to live out there without the conveniences we have today. Those are the same conveniences that seem to be destroying Utah now: the roads and cars and the dumping of nuclear waste from power plants.

MacDonald: Deseret is unlike some of your early films, where the structure is absolutely clear.

Benning: When I started to make *Deseret,* it was going to be an hour long; the first half was going to be thirty one-minute shots, of thirty different landscapes, and the last half was going to be thirty different people, each talking for one minute: they would represent the variety of things that I thought were happening in Utah. But in the making of the film, the plans completely changed, and it seemed more practical to use newspaper articles to talk about the issues I was interested in.

MacDonald: Could you describe the structure of the finished film?

Benning: The film uses ninety-four different *New York Times* stories about Utah, written between 1852 and 1992. Actually, I found many more stories than the ones I used. Knowing something about Utah history, I was able to look for *Times* stories about particular events, but eventually I'm sure I xeroxed at least 90 percent of all the *Times* stories that dealt with Utah.

I reduced the stories I had collected down to a manageable ninety-four and then edited each story down to eight to ten sentences, all the while trying to be true to the language of the time, so that you would have a feel for the journalese of each story. Because of the evolution of journalism, the lengths of sentences tended to get shorter over time.

The visual structure was based on using one shot for each sentence in each story that you hear read by the narrator, plus one shot *between* each pair of stories, which is presented without narration. Those spaces between the stories get shorter and shorter as the film goes along: the shot between the first two stories is fifteen feet long, and the shot between the last two stories is only three feet long.

The shortening of the sentences in the stories and the shorter and shorter shots between narrated stories cause the whole film to speed up, which corresponds to the historical realities of journalism. In the early days, stories from Utah wouldn't reach New York for three or four months. If you pay attention to the dates of the stories (the date of each is superimposed over the first shot), you'll see that, early on, the writers will be talking about something that happened in January in a story dated May: it took that long for the story to get back East. Of course, later the gap becomes a day or two days, and right now it's less than a day.

MacDonald: How did you decide which stories you'd use?

Benning: I found many stories from early on when Utah was still a territory, because the United States government was preoccupied with trying to wrestle control of the territory away from the Mormons. In 1857, troops were sent to Utah, and there are many stories about the war against the Mormons. If you study the structure of the film, you'll see that there are lots of stories during the 1850s, and lots of stories at the end, from more recent years. I purposely did that so you could compare the differences, and the history lent itself to that: the more interesting stories really did happen in the 1850s and in the 1980s and 1990s.

MacDonald: Anything else you want to say about the structure of *Deseret?*

Benning: Well, one shot in each story actually shows where the particular story you're hearing took place.

I also decided *not* to develop any sequence of juxtapositions that would suggest a theme—seasonal change or moving toward the mountains or whatever. I wanted the images themselves to *completely* keep changing.

I *was* very careful when I arranged the film. I mounted one frame from each shot onto a slide and used the slide projector as a poor man's Avid, projecting the slides to decide which images should go next to each other. I was able to study each slide juxtaposed with each sentence, and could be very careful about the way each image would code each bit of language, and how each bit of language would reinterpret the way you looked at that landscape. I wanted the texts and the images to talk to each other.

The whole point of the structure was to create a space between those two aspects of the film that *you* have to complete. When you watch the film, especially the first time, it tends to wash over you, so that you don't really notice all that much about the juxtapositions between image and text, but I do hope I've created something like a narrative space between the two and that some people will see the film often enough to be able to explore the dimensions of that space.

MacDonald: In one sense, the imagery and the narration are analogous. The camera is mounted on a tripod, and the shots are very formally arranged—a correlative to the formal delivery of Fred Gardner's monotone narration. Was that your thinking in choosing Gardner as narrator?

Benning: I've used narrators before, both in *Used Innocence* [1988] and in *Landscape Suicide,* but more sparsely, to give information. Here the narration is more consistent and more important. Yes, Fred Gardner does a monotone delivery. That's because I wanted the *language* to carry the drama, rather than the *voice,* and Fred was very good at doing exactly what I asked for.

Also, to some extent, I wanted to evoke the voice of authority from the early grade school films I saw in the fifties *and* to suggest the authoritative voice of the eastern Establishment and the *New York Times*—another version of that voice from those grade school films. But I didn't want it to *become* that; I didn't want *Deseret* to feel like an educational film. I wanted something that would suggest that, but would be *off,* at an *angle* to that voice, so that a viewer might think at first, "Gee, am I watching an educational film?" but would quickly realize that the film is much more bizarre than that.

The history the film traces is a frightening one for me. It's a history about a Manifest Destiny that's just completely gone crazy. But, of course, that idea was crazy in itself—to think that you should just take a land away from people because God wants you to have this empire.

MacDonald: The settling of Utah by the Mormons and the establishment of the *New York Times* are the two very disparate events with which the film begins: the *Times* is the newspaper of record for the country, the Word on what's set down about the nation; and Mormons were a people trying to escape the establishment that the *New York Times* represents.

Benning: Yes, the *Times* is very close to the federal government ideologically; and Utah was the Wild West.

MacDonald: The history charted by the film becomes a kind of labyrinth: you're watching and listening to try to figure out what the actual relations were between the Mormons and the various native peoples and the Americans.

Benning: And I'm not sure I know, or that anybody knows, exactly what they were. It seems like the Mormons had two relationships with Indians: one was, well, it's cheaper to feed them than to fight them, so let's be their friends; let's teach them how to farm and try to get along with them. The other was, we seem to be having a power struggle with other peoples; let's get the local Indians on our side and use them to do the devious things we don't want to do; let the blood be on *their* hands.

The Mountain Meadows massacre is a very curious part of this history. It's clear that the Mormons participated in it and helped kill something like one hundred twenty-five people crossing the country from Arkansas—and then blamed it on the Indians. What isn't clear is whether Brigham Young had a role in the massacre. The *Times* concludes he knew completely. I'm not sure if that's true or not. Juanita Brooks, probably one of the best Mormon historians, concluded in her book on Mountain Meadows [*The Mountain Meadows Massacre* (Norman: University of Oklahoma Press, 1991)] that nothing could happen in Utah without Brigham Young knowing about it, but still she wouldn't come out and say he knew about *this*.

MacDonald: The petroglyphs by the native peoples are a motif in the film. And then late in the film you start to show modern graffiti, sometimes superimposed over the native imagery. Were the petroglyphs, for you, an image of the world before corruption?

Benning: No. The Anasazi culture was nonviolent, but certainly there must have been corruption even in that society. When people live together, corruption happens, though I suspect corruption was at a minimum there.

To me, the petroglyphs represent a kind of spirituality that's lacking in our society today. They reveal a society that treasured art. People had to go out every day and look for food, but some people spent time drawing on the sides of cliffs, and I'm sure they ate that day because the people around them thought that their drawings were valuable. Some of those petroglyphs are a thousand years old now; they're quite moving, because they have a feel of the gesture of the artist.

There are later petroglyphs, done by more modern Indians—probably Utes—that express things besides spirituality. In one shot, there's a drawing of a cowboy as the devil, probably done in the 1850s, a comment on what that particular Indian thought about the white people who were ranching nearby. Native political art.

MacDonald: You mentioned that when you were putting the various sequences of imagery together to match the sentences of the *Times* stories that at least one shot in each sequence directly connects to the story we hear. Is it sometimes a metaphoric connection?

Benning: Many times it's literal, the exact location that's being talked about. But sometimes it is metaphoric. For a story about a speech that Brigham Young gave, I could give a literal image of one of the churches where he spoke, or I could do something a little less direct: show his summer home or something even less tangible than that.

MacDonald: Were you recording sound at the same time you were making imagery? In your earlier films, you often constructed the illusion of sync sound.

Benning: I do like to post-sync, just so that I can control the sound more. In this case, most of the sound was recorded in Utah; I wanted to represent the *sound* of Utah, too. I cheated a little; I needed something like eighty different sounds of wind, so rather than drive all the way back to Utah, I went out to the Mojave Desert to get relatively the same sounds.

MacDonald: *North on Evers* is full of portraits. As you visit people, you often do family portrait images. You mentioned that originally the plan for *Deseret* was to have a lot of people speaking to the camera, but as it turned out, very few people made it into that film.

Benning: Well, in *Deseret* that's because I wanted people to be represented by the newspaper stories. I thought it would be more dramatic to feature the landscapes as places that history is written upon. Actually, there are three or four shots with people, and two portrait shots. One, in black and white, is a polygamous farm family, shot in the style of Walker Evans. Later in the film, there's a shot of two young Mormon girls who reminded me of the Diane Arbus twins, though they're not twins. That image is used in connection with a *Times* story about how the down-winders and the children of down-winders are having problems with cancer.

MacDonald: You seem very photographically aware in this film. Is photography something you spend a lot of time looking at and thinking about?

Benning: Not really. I spend a lot of time looking, but I don't take many pictures, and I don't look at many photographs. But I like photography.

MacDonald: As a film artist, you're concerned about the damage to original landscape and culture, but on the other hand, you're working in a chemically based medium.

Benning: Yes, I'm demanding a service that's polluting the Earth. Filmmaking isn't a clean industry. So, one can certainly question whatever righteous view *I* might be taking in this film. Also, I drove to Utah nine times during the shooting. We're all the enemy in this story.

MacDonald: Were you filming both black and white and color on the same trips?

Benning: I carried two cameras with me so I could always shoot either in black and white or in color. I knew the film was going to start in black and white and end in color. Of course, that's something nobody should know before they see the film—and most people don't. I like the drama of the switch.

MacDonald: How long did you collect imagery for *Deseret*? How long did you edit?

Benning: First, I spent almost six months collecting the newspaper articles, and another three months editing them down into the text that's used in the film. Of course, all the sound was recorded before the imagery was edited, since the film was going to be edited to the text. The recording of the text took a couple of months; we worked two days a week generally.

I spent about one hundred twenty days shooting in Utah, over a period of fourteen months. After the shooting, the editing took about nine months.

I took my time because I wanted to sequence the film properly and, of course, the post-synching for over six hundred shots took a long time. The film came together slowly.

MacDonald: Four Corners came quickly after *Deseret* and has a particularly rigorous formal structure. I remember your saying at a screening that you were even careful about the number of words you used in the rolling visual texts and in the stories the narrators tell.

Benning: I wanted to be entirely democratic, so each section is exactly the same as the others, down to the number of letters in the text biographies of artists [1,214] and the number of words [1,186] in the voice-over stories.

MacDonald: The film is about the Four Corners region of the Southwest. What led to the "ringers"—the shot of the Monet painting and the history of Milwaukee you narrate?

Benning: The American history I studied in school always started in Europe and gave little attention to Native American history, where it *should* have started. I wanted to refer to our Eurocentric view of the world. Of course, Milwaukee *was* at one time the frontier, and went through many of the same developments that the Four Corner area has—battles with Native Americans, for example—so I felt that it did relate to the topic, the West.

MacDonald: How did you choose the four narrators?

Benning: Hartmut Bitomski, who did the voice-over for the Monet painting, is European, and his German accent relates to both the Wetherell story and the Milwaukee story. Hartmut is a good friend and a fellow filmmaker [Bitomski is a film theorist and a documentarian whose films include *Highway 40 West—Reise in Amerika* (Travels in America, 1981) and *B-52* (2000)]; he was dean of the CalArts film school at the time when I made the film.

My own voice was necessary for telling my own history, which I hoped the rest of the film would put into a much larger context.

Yeasup Song's voice is used for the Native American history because Yesup is Korean—Asian. The Native Americans originally came from Asia across the Bering Strait.

And I used Billy Woodberry's voice for the modern story about Farmington; since Billy is black, his voice would connect the blind prejudice of the Farmington Navajos and poor whites to the blind prejudices referred to in the Milwaukee story of blacks and poor whites. Billy is a friend and fellow filmmaker [Woodberry directed *Bless Their Little Hearts,* 1984].

MacDonald: In the Milwaukee sequence, one of the shots shows a bunch of kids playing basketball outdoors. A car drives into the shot, and someone shoots a gun. Did you set that up?

Benning: No, it just happened. I don't even know if it was a real drive-by, or if the guy across the street just wanted to create some drama for the film. Either way, it kept the guys in the car away from me long enough so that I could finish the shot and run off before they could steal my camera.

MacDonald: The Native American artist whose life is described in one of the artist biographies is a woman. Is this you being politically correct? Is there evidence of Native American artists being women?

MacDonald: This is me being in defiance of the way that historians work. In all accounts it's assumed that men did this work, but I don't see how anyone can come to this conclusion, especially since many of the same designs first appeared on pottery that those same historians claim was made only by women.

Plus, I wanted some romance in the film, and Yukuwa became a romantic figure for me.

MacDonald: What gave you the idea of stealing Richard Dindo's sound track for *Utopia?*

Benning: I wanted to bring revolution to Southern California, where a kind of reversed imperialism exists. Here, cheap labor is brought in so that it can be exploited; what Che saw on his motorcycle travels at nineteen was traditional imperialism: nations moving into other nations to exploit cheap labor. That's what politicized him.

I got the idea for the film and just went ahead and did it, without contacting Dindo. When I met him a few years later, he seemed somewhat flattered by what I had done, and later, when permission was needed for German television, gave me permission to use his track. I don't know if he's seen the film.

MacDonald: Like *North on Evers, Utopia* sets up a situation where the viewer is "seeing" two films simultaneously: the one you've shot and are presenting, and the one we imagine on the basis of the sound track we're listening to. Is your decision to use just Dindo's sound a way of critiquing conventional documentary and the kinds of information it normally presents?

Benning: No, I just wanted to liberate the notion of revolution and bring it home.

MacDonald: Sometimes the images seem closely related to what we hear on the track, and sometimes we're particularly aware of the differences between Bolivian geography and the particular landscapes of Southern California and northern Mexico. I assume you wanted to create a constantly shifting relationship between the story Dindo tells and the one you tell visually.

Benning: Yes, I did. My images move you south from Death Valley down to and across the Mexican border. Occasionally, I cut images so that they relate to the sound in literal ways, but they aren't really literal because the images are from the wrong country—actually the *right* country.

MacDonald: You mean you see Che's activities as equally relevant in the Southwest?

Benning: More so. The United States is where a revolution is really necessary.

MacDonald: How much time did you spend in Mexico?

Benning: Just enough to be scared shitless. Less than an hour. Mexicali is a very poor town. I'm not a rich filmmaker, but I look a lot richer than the Mexicalis, and I was alone and fair game. I made it out before the police and the crooks could get to me.

MacDonald: I've come to see your films in two different ways. I look at each new film for itself, but I'm also seeing you as a person who's developed over several decades and whose development seems to be in very clear stages that have to do with the places you're in. I'm wondering whether, when you're making a film, you're thinking about it as part of an ongoing exploration, or whether you're just thinking about the project at hand.

Benning: When I'm asked who my influences are, I always tend to say, "Well, there are certain filmic influences from the seventies, but basically what influences me most is the film that I made just before the film that I'm working on now." For example, before the California Trilogy, I had worked on a number of films that dealt with text-image relationship. *North on Evers* used a diary written the year before I filmed, and *Deseret* used the texts from the *New York Times;* in *Four Corners,* I wrote four little biographies and four little histories to try to place my life in a larger historical context; and for *Utopia,* I stole the text from Dindo's film. Each film used text and image in a different way from the film before. After *Utopia,* I felt like I had exhausted my interest in text and image, and when I started the California Trilogy, I knew I wanted to completely discard text and work with just image and ambient sound.

If we talk about locations, a different kind of influence is evident. When I made *North on Evers,* I drove through Utah and was interested in what I saw there, so the next film, *Deseret,* was made *in* Utah, and then, because of what I learned and saw while making *Deseret,* I became interested in the Four Corners area, which is partly in Utah, and made *Four Corners. Utopia,* too, was about the West, but it was a California film. *El Valley Centro* grew directly out of *Utopia.* And when I finished *El Valley Centro,* I thought I needed an urban companion to the rural, and made *Los.* So the films just keep growing out of one another. You can trace my films from *11 × 14* all the way up through the trilogy. In fact, the trilogy references *11 × 14,* where I also used many shots with just image and ambient sound.

MacDonald: Those shots in *El Valley Centro* of tractors coming toward the camera and then moving offscreen to one side, then coming back into the image from the opposite side and moving back across the field, are very like shots in *11 × 14* and *$8^1/_2 × 11$.*

Benning: In *$8^1/_2 × 11$*, a friend who was a farmer did the shot for me; I choreographed that tractor. In *El Valley Centro,* I was looking to *find* choreographed movement. I'd see movement in the landscape and then place the camera so that it would create visual drama. I rarely set anything up in the trilogy.

MacDonald: If I read your history in terms of what you seem to be doing at different times, in *11 × 14* and *8½ × 11* and also in the other, shorter, seventies films, there's a kind of youthful, look-what-I can-do excitement about your tricks with composition. Now, you use the filmmaking process to get yourself out into the world rather than to perform a set of tricks.

Benning: When I look at *8½ × 11* or *11 × 14* or *One Way Boogie Woogie,* those tricks, and the little narratives I develop, are the least interesting parts of those films. What's become more interesting to me in all three films is how they matter-of-factly documented a particular social space; *behind* all my play with off-screen space, there is actually a documentation of that time and place, which has grown more interesting as those places have changed, even disappeared.

But when I show *One Way Boogie Woogie* at retrospectives, and say, "I'm a little embarrassed by the little jokes," I'm surprised at how much interest there is in that youthful play. I guess it's part of those films, and maybe it makes the reading of the social spaces and that time period a little more interesting.

MacDonald: You and I are the same age; our parents weathered the Depression, so industry was seen as this very positive thing; and we grew up in an era when we were finding out about pollution and rivers catching fire. For me the most exciting space in the world, when I was a kid, was the industrial area of New Jersey between Newark and New York City. In *El Valley Centro* you reveal, again, your fascination with industry, along with a fear of what it can do.

Benning: Well, as I said, *El Valley Centro* came out of *Utopia.* I became interested in irrigated farming and in the issue of who does the work and who makes the profit. But I was also taken with the fantastic space that's developed in those large farming areas, where the fields go on forever, and with the way machinery moves through that space. I didn't want to make a dogmatic political film about injustice, but I did want to make a film where if you looked at a space that I was enamored with, those other issues would slowly surface, and you would feel my criticism of the control of that space.

In *El Valley Centro,* I wanted to make images that mapped the whole valley onto the film, and to represent the different kinds of activities that happen there: the majority of it is farming, but there are also eleven prisons in the valley; there are large oil deposits in the southern part; and every year, fertile farmland is being taken over by urbanization.

MacDonald: I've heard you talk about the idea of filmmaking as performance, not so much for the audience as for yourself, and about how the

Irrigated field in James Benning's *El Valley Centro* (1999). Courtesy James Benning.

shots in the trilogy are sometimes records, or emblems, of the "adventures" you went through to get the shots.

Benning: That's a part of some of my early work, also. In *Grand Opera* [1978], I documented what I thought of as two one-person performances. For the first, I went to the same spot on the Canadian River outside of Norman, Oklahoma, every day for a whole year and made one shot each day. In the film you see a series of those shots that reference my performance and measure my mental state against the constant of that place, though that "constant" changed every day, because of weather conditions or whatever.

For the second performance, I visited every house I'd ever lived in within a two-month period and made a 360-degree pan of each place.

But it is true that when I made the trilogy, it was really one hundred and five performances: me going to one hundred and five places and recording how I felt at those places at those moments. The trilogy is an accumulation of performance.

MacDonald: The performances you do in *Grand Opera* declare themselves as performances, whereas in the California films, the performance necessary to make the shot is rarely evident: the drive you took from Reno to LA to get your camera, then back to Reno to get the shot of the forest fire doesn't declare itself within the shot.

Benning: But that's true with a lot of filmmakers. When *they* watch their films, it's always a completely different experience, because every shot has a story that for the audience is not part of the film. It's kind of nice to be an audience and *not* know all those stories, so you can watch the film purely.

However, I do think that unconsciously all the work that goes into making an image somehow ends up in that image. That might be a bold statement, and I *don't* think an audience could tell you the exact facts; it's a subtle feeling. For instance, when you see the sand blowing in Death Valley with such intensity, you don't know the story of how difficult it was to make that shot and how I was almost delirious from the one-hundred-thirty-degree heat and the forty-five-mile-an-hour winds that were dehydrating me, but I think the shot itself has such intensity that you almost feel that that could be the story. I'm hoping that's true.

MacDonald: Hemingway said that when a writer knows what he's talking about, he can leave things out and retain their impact; the reader will sense in what's left all that the writer knows.

Benning: Yes, that's exactly what I'm talking about.

MacDonald: Sogobi is full of gorgeous images. But I wonder if you had mixed feelings about what you're looking at in the first two parts of the trilogy. One of the challenges you must have felt is how to make an image of some relatively humdrum event in LA work as part of the film. If you're going to make a complete portrait of a city, there are going to be spectacular

Housing development in James Benning's *Los* (2000). Courtesy James Benning.

things and dull things. I guess what I'm asking is whether you felt that making the first two films gave you the "right" to make *Sogobi*. You've made clear that you mean to show all three films together, which tells me that you see *Sogobi* as a kind of response to *El Valley Centro* and *Los*.

Benning: I think I've always tried to make images that are beautiful, though maybe not always in the classical sense of "beautiful." I think every shot in *El Valley Centro* and *Los* is beautiful—but in a different way than is true in *Sogobi*. In *Los,* the freeway shot is unbelievably beautiful, and the shot of the cows is beautiful, and Dodger Stadium is beautiful, and even the shot of Sixth Street, where the homeless walk by, is beautiful in a subtle way—in the light and shadow. But in *Sogobi,* I did want to have the classic beauty of wilderness, so that when you have the interruptions by human process, they happen within that classical sense of beauty.

But in *Los* I certainly didn't purposely make any ugly images. The shot of the Korean strip mall may seem very mundane, but I find it quite stunning—the blue sky and the palm trees sticking out from behind and the flags that are hanging into the top of the frame, and the arrow on the parking structure. As part of my visual mapping of Los Angeles, I wanted to show activities that weren't spectacular, but I did want each image to be constructed in such a way that it had some interest to it, and a clear sense of design.

The same is true of *El Valley Centro*. I think a lot of the farming shots are just gorgeous. The shot of the crop duster is amazingly beautiful . . .

MacDonald: That's a shot where we're very conscious of you as a kind of filmmaker-adventurer. When the plane goes over the top of you, we wonder what you're wearing, whether you're protected.

Benning: Actually, I didn't have to protect myself. I tried to film crop dusters, and it was impossible; I was in their way, and they wouldn't spray me. I wouldn't have been sprayed anyway; I would have run away before the dust hit the ground. But as soon as I'd set the camera up, they'd fly over and shake their fists at me and yell, "Get out of there!" So I went to a crop-dusting place and hired the plane, and they sprayed water over me instead of insecticide. That's one of the few places in the trilogy where I actually choreographed the movement. I did copy the exact movement that the crop dusters use.

MacDonald: How much do you consciously allude? The shot in *Sogobi* of Yosemite Valley is the classic photographic view that Muybridge and Carleton Watkins and Ansel Adams have recorded. The shot of the ship going under the Golden Gate Bridge is almost identical to shots in Peter Hutton's *Study of a River* [1997]. And, of course, whenever I see a crop duster, I think of *North by Northwest* [1959].

Benning: That is the classic Yosemite image, but in *Sogobi* the waterfall actually changes shape. At first the shot looks like a still photograph, but

Redwoods in James Benning's *Sogobi* (2001). Courtesy James Benning.

once you start searching the image, you see that the waterfall is moving; and then a few bugs fly through the frame—there's a different sense than a photograph can give. I like that particular shot because it references those classic photographs, but I think it has its own presence because it's time based. And you also have the sound track.

You can't make a crop duster shot without thinking of Hitchcock. But I wasn't making the shot as an allusion, but because most of the valley is sprayed with chemicals. You see crop dusters there year round. There are lots of little crop-dusting businesses. And sometimes the crop dusting is quite spectacular; they might spray a bright yellow chemical powder. I *was* very aware that as soon as you'd see the image, you'd think of *North by Northwest*. That doesn't bother me.

Peter Hutton, of course, is a great friend, and I admire his work. But I think it's coincidental that we happened to make the same shot. There's a ship in *El Valley Centro* and one in *Los;* the shot in *Sogobi* is there to echo the earlier two. I shot from the Golden Gate Bridge because I wanted to portray the water as wilderness. It turns out to be very reminiscent of shots in *Study of River,* which I saw after I made my shot. It was coincidental, but I'm delighted to be in Peter's company.

At this point, after a hundred years of filmmaking, a lot of images have been made, and my films are more involved with referencing the beginning of filmmaking, when people put a full roll in the camera and locked it down and let the camera run continuously, recording a train coming into the station for however long their roll of film was.

My rolls are bigger than the ones the Lumières used, but the idea is the same. A standard one-hundred-foot roll of 16mm film is two minutes and forty-seven seconds, so I cut each shot to two and a half minutes so I could have enough leeway, once I cut the heads and tails off, to be able to adjust the timing of the shot. I also wanted to use two and a half minutes—rather than, say, two minutes and forty seconds—because two-and-a-half times thirty-five shots equals eighty-seven-and-a-half minutes, plus two-and-a-half minutes of credits makes exactly ninety minutes. Ninety minutes is a manageable duration, money-wise and audience-wise, for the kinds of films I do. Of course, the trilogy is now five hours if you include a couple of fifteen-minute breaks. But I think that's manageable, too.

MacDonald: I find the trilogy, and especially *Sogobi,* very dramatic. In *The Bear,* Faulkner sets up this one-hundred-mile-square space that's what's left of the northern Mississippi wilderness; and the edges of even this space are being chewed away by farmers and lumber companies. The structure of your three films works the same way; we see the totally developed areas of California in the first two films; then we go to what's not developed—but every once in a while, there will be a "chew" into the "square" of what's left, and it hurts. The trilogy is also a little like *Deseret:* by the end, we're frightened for this beautiful place.

Benning: The whole trilogy is basically about the politics of water. In the Central Valley, corporate farms take advantage of two irrigation systems that were built with public money, one with federal money, one with state money. The corporations paid for none of the construction, but they take full advantage of it: 85 percent of the water in California is used for farming; only 15 percent is used for manufacturing and public consumption. And, of course, Los Angeles was expanded by stealing water from the Owens Valley.

When I made *El Valley Centro,* I was very aware of the water politics, and I thought, "Well, when I make this urban companion, I'll have to make a reference to how those politics continue from one place to another." So *Los* begins with water flowing into LA in the original aqueduct from the Owens Valley. And then, in *Sogobi,* I tried to show where the water comes from.

MacDonald: And that last image of the pipe in the reservoir is almost a punch line; it takes you back to the first image in the trilogy.

Benning: Yes, the very last image explains the mystery of the first. Also, the last image of *El Valley Centro* relates to the first image of *Los;* and the last image of *Los* relates to the first image of *Sogobi.* The trilogy could play continuously, and you could enter anywhere.

Originally, I was going to edit *Sogobi* the way I edited *El Valley Centro* and *Los.* In both those cases I shot forty-eight rolls of film but developed only thirty-eight of them, so I had thirty-eight shots that I edited using slides. With *Sogobi* I shot a lot more—a hundred and twenty or thirty rolls of film—and I assumed the editing was going to be a lot more difficult. I put individual frames from all the shots on slides and was going to choose thirty-five. I was teaching in Korea last year and planned to edit the film in Korea with a slide projector. But I forgot to take the slides with me and didn't realize it until I was on the plane. So I took the in-flight magazine and tore thirty-five little squares out of it, corners of pages that were blank, and wrote down the first thirty-five shots I could remember. I "edited" on the plane by shuffling those pieces of paper. When I got back from Korea, I did decide to change a few things. But almost all the shots I remembered got into the film. So that accident made the process much easier: I didn't have to deal with one hundred and thirty shots.

MacDonald: Do you look back and think some of your films are better than others?

Benning: Well, I don't want to talk about films I don't like, but I'm glad to tell you which ones I do like. Of course, when you have a career, you can't be completely consistent. You need to have some failures; if you never fail, you're not pushing your limits. And when you do push your limits, you can go in the wrong direction and make things that will embarrass you later.

I like the majority of the films I've made. I tend to dismiss my early short films, although I still like them. I think the first film that I made that's *important* is *11 × 14*. And *One Way Boogie Woogie* is almost as important as *11 × 14*. The next film that's important for me is *American Dreams,* one of my favorites. And I love to show *Landscape Suicide,* though I think it has flaws—I'm much more subtle now.

I don't think I'd change anything in *American Dreams,* though. And all the films from *North on Evers* on, I really like.

MacDonald: Is California Trilogy your first sync sound project?

Benning: I've used some sync in almost every film—like the El shot in *11 × 14*. In *Landscape Suicide* the monologues are shot in sync. But I shot the most sync I've ever shot for the trilogy.

MacDonald: Are you always looking for imagery when you move around? For years, Jonas Mekas seemed to have his camera with him all the time.

Benning: I've never been like that. I am always looking, though. I went for a walk this morning through the beautiful desert landscape here in Arizona, and I was constantly thinking of how it would look on film, how light was falling on the back of cacti in a spectacular way. If I come back down here, I might make a shot using what I saw today.

MacDonald: So you think in terms of shots, like a photographer.

Benning: Yeah. But I always think of an image as it changes over time. When we were out earlier this evening, a breeze came up and, of course, you can't show a breeze in a still photograph. The cacti were moving in a particular way because of the breeze, and that could be caught on film.

There are shots in *Sogobi* where nothing happens, and you can't show nothing happening in a photograph: you need to see an image over time to know that absolutely nothing is visibly happening. Remember that shot of the beautiful tree in the fog? Maybe the tree moves a little, but I'm not sure; I've watched it so many times, and I've tried to see some movement and I can't find any. But I wouldn't know that if the image were a photograph.

Things in *Sogobi,* in the whole trilogy, need to be studied; a lot of what's in the trilogy can't really be perceived unless it is studied. This is true for individual shots, and because there are so many cross-references between the three films. Even the first time through, you might notice that there are cows in all three films, and billboards—you might not remember that they're all from the same company, Outdoor Systems—and aircraft, and trains (a freight train, a commuter train, then a freight train again), and oceangoing ships. There's wilderness in all three.

MacDonald: The structure is the most obvious cross-reference. The same number of images, of the same length, the same kind of credits, and so on.

Benning: Even the film stock for all three was bought by the Austin Film Society.

MacDonald: How is it that the Austin Film Society funded a film on California?

Benning: I've been showing in Austin for many years, so they're interested in my work, and when I was making *El Valley Centro,* I needed money to buy film stock. They said, "We'll get you some money," and then when I made *Los,* I happened to be in Austin showing *El Valley Centro,* and they said, "Well, let us give you some more money for film stock." That happened all three times.

MacDonald: You mentioned the other day that these films have actually made money, which is almost illegal in the avant-garde! Since when do they make money, and is the California Trilogy the most successful of your films financially?

Benning: Well, if they more than pay for themselves, I consider them successful because most films don't pay for themselves. *11 × 14* paid for itself. I made *One Way Boogie Woogie* on a Wisconsin Arts Council grant that paid for the film, and made a little profit from the rentals. *American Dreams* had many, many rentals, and it was made so cheaply that it probably paid for itself, too. A number of the films were made with Guggenheim and Rockefeller grants, and I was always careful to make them for less than the grants, so they paid for themselves. *Him and Me* [1982] was made with German television money, so I made money on that film, too.

Recently I sold five films all at once to European television: *Utopia, Four Corners,* and the trilogy.

MacDonald: May I ask how much you got?

Benning: Altogether it was a little over a hundred thousand dollars, which is pretty good. By the time I make my films, I have them paid for, so if money comes in from European television, all of a sudden I have a windfall that allows me to make more films and do other things.

MacDonald: The last time you were in Tucson, you talked about doing a film that would involve your traveling around the border of the United States during all four seasons. Is that still something you're thinking about?

Benning: I'm thinking about it, but I'd need a rather substantial grant to do it. I'd need a year off from teaching, and I'd need to buy a very good vehicle. I'd probably need a couple hundred thousand.

MacDonald: Does your teaching affect your filmmaking?

Benning: Well, it affects the work by taking up my time. *[Laughter.]* But I love teaching, because I get such good students. I make them think on their feet, so they make me think on my feet, too. I think it's real positive. My biggest concern now comes out of the teaching, ironically because at California Institute of the Arts we've had an incredible run of successful recruiting. We've done such a good job at helping them that while they do refine and push the limits of the models we've provided them, I'm afraid we've also *contained* filmmaking in a way that may make for good films, but not for something that's going to change the way that films are made.

When I was younger, I experienced the excitement of seeing entirely new kinds of films arriving on the scene, and I want to experience that again before film is dead. I think to make film *explode,* one has to deny everything that's been done and find something else. I'm not talking about technology at all; I'm looking for an answer within the mind. *Wavelength* [1967] was completely upsetting, and at the same time thrilling, and it questioned narrative and the way light hits the screen. That film was an explosion, and I want some more explosions.

MacDonald: I always wonder whether the explosion was for a limited number of people then, and *always* is for a limited number of people. Once you've had a certain number of explosions, you've had the explosion experience, and it may not be possible to get it again in quite the same way. I'd guess that some of the people who saw your trilogy yesterday found it transformative in the same way you found *Wavelength* transformative.

Benning: The trilogy can confront viewers who are naive. But I want to go beyond that. Maybe it is impossible. But I don't like the idea of just making more good films.

MacDonald: Do a lot of your students go into the industry?

Benning: A few. There's a real moral issue in teaching at an art school: going to CalArts puts people in huge debt, and if you make them serious about their work, they don't have a way to make that money back. I joke with the students, "If I'm successful, I'll make you unemployable"—because if I am successful, I'll be creating students who want to develop new vocabularies and, by definition, that will produce difficult work, which means they won't make any money.

Of course, we take technical expertise very seriously at CalArts, and that's always marketable. But good ideas aren't marketable; they're confusing.

MacDonald: How much have you worked for other people? I know you did sound on Hartmut Bitomski's *B-52.*

Benning: That's about it. I did enjoy just doing sound.

MacDonald: Twenty years ago or so you did a digital piece, the installation *Pascal's Lemma* [1985]. How digital are you these days?

Benning: Not at all. But I'm getting interested in DVD as a way to preserve 16mm film. As DVDs get better and better, and more people own the equipment and set up viewing rooms in their homes that are more like theaters than television rooms—under those conditions I think one can preserve the film experience in a way impossible for the filmstrip, where eventually the emulsion disappears. *Everything* is going to disappear, of course, but on digital you can keep making clones and recopying before the disk deteriorates and hopefully keep things alive that way.

Plus, it would be a lot easier to carry the trilogy on three DVDs!

MacDonald: Do you think of yourself as a Californian now?

Benning: I spent a lot of time growing up in the Midwest, and of course that informs the way you act in later life; and living in New York for eight years certainly affected me. I live in a small town in California, and I do feel like I'm part of the small town, but Val Verde is so different from the rest of California. Of course, once you start to drive, you realize you're definitely in California.

LA doesn't keep anything; there's no sense of history, except for a few old buildings here and there. Pretty much everything looks like it was built after 1960. I was in Chicago and New York recently, and both places seemed so *old.*

There's a good chance that I'll live the rest of my life in California, but I'll *never* be a Californian! I don't know where I belong.

J. Leighton Pierce

During the 1970s, feminists called for a reorganization of domestic politics, questioning the assumption that child care is biologically determined "women's work" and demanding that men learn to function as true domestic *partners* in the quest for economic stability and personal fulfillment, rather than exclusively as "breadwinners." That the domestic round was the new frontier in cultural development was clear in the landmark film by Laura Mulvey and Peter Wollen, *Riddles of the Sphinx* (1977), which argued that who takes care of young children is *the* issue on which the organization of society turns.

While domestic partnership has evolved, at least in some sectors of some societies, during the decades since *Riddles of the Sphinx* was so widely discussed, cinematic attention—or, really, inattention—to the domestic has changed little. The realities of domestic work, and especially child care, have remained virtually invisible. This continued invisibility is one reason why Leighton Pierce's 1990s films and videos seem so remarkable. In Pierce's work the domestic arena becomes the site of visual-auditory dramas that have the potential to undermine conventional ideas about the domestic. Indeed, Pierce's understanding of how mediamaking fits into daily life is nearly the inversion of the conventional assumption shared, it would seem, by both commercial mediamakers and most of those who provide critiques of the commercial. The general assumption, of course, is that the domestic world and the art-making world must remain separate (Stan Brakhage and Jonas Mekas are exceptions that prove the rule). One may create a life that includes both, but such a life requires us to "intercut" between the two spheres.

While Pierce earns his living outside his home (since 1985 he has taught media production at the University of Iowa), he built his reputation as a major contributor to independent film and video history within his home, as *part* of his day-to-day domestic experience. *Thursday* (1991), for instance, is a visual-auditory evocation of his kitchen, shot during the quiet moments during his infant son's naptime on Thursdays: images and sounds of Pierce pouring coffee, washing dishes, of a tree blowing in the breeze outside the window, the sound of a distant train, of a rainstorm . . . are combined into what Peter Hutton might call a "reprieve" from the tendency of modern life and most cinema to project us relentlessly forward (see my interview with Hutton in *A Critical Cinema 3*). Similarly, the video *If with Those Eyes and Ears,* the first section of *Principles of Harmonic Motion* (1991), was made soon after Mackenzie Pierce was born. Pierce spent time in the baby's room, exploring visual and auditory details of the space and combining them into a lovely, haunting experience that simultaneously evokes the baby's fascination with his new world and the father's excitement at sharing life with this mysterious new being.

Pierce's output, in both film and video, has been considerable since the early 1990s, and of consistently high quality. His most impressive work to date, however, is his domestic "epic," *50 Feet of String* (1995; remade in a shorter version in 1998), and the videos he's made since 2000. *50 Feet of String* discovers/creates a gorgeous, somewhat surreal world in and around Pierce's home in Iowa City by combining imagery and sounds collected from midsummer to fall and organizing them into an intricate montage, broken into a series of discrete segments introduced by textual titles—"E," "corner of the eye," "12:30," "lawn care," "white chair," in each of which Pierce engages with particular visual-auditory dimensions of his domestic surround.

What makes *50 Feet of String* and Pierce's other films of the 1990s distinctive are the particulars of his reinvention of the domestic. His use of subtle dimensions of lens technology and camera placement transforms the places he records. Often only one narrow plane of the space within the frame is in clear focus at any moment; the remaining aspects of the space are in varying degrees of blur. In addition to causing his imagery to combine spaces of great clarity with impressionistic renderings of color and shape, Pierce's technique determines the nature of the developments that can occur within any given image, in at least two ways. First, the narrow breadth of the space revealed by the film frame allows for the sudden transformation of the image by the movement of a human or a vehicle into or out of the frame. In the "two maples" section of *50 Feet of String,* for example, movement into and out of the frame is the central visual motif. This brief section (it lasts a bit more than a minute) includes eight shots, each separated from the next by a moment of darkness. The first shot is taken from a moving hammock;

Compass in Leighton Pierce's *50 Feet of String* (1995). Courtesy Leighton Pierce.

in the second, Mackenzie Pierce runs into the distance, apparently having left the hammock; and in the following five shots, we see the boy on a distant swing, as he swings, right and left, into and out of the frame, within three different compositions, each of which provides a tiny visual surprise. The final shot of "two maples" reveals a yard beyond which a blurred car moves left to right, confirming and concluding the swinging movements of the previous seven shots.

The second result of Pierce's combination of techniques has to do with the drama he achieves by manipulating the layers of focus. In "pickup truck," for example, he creates an astonishing moment by extending a single shot for more than two minutes. The shot begins with extended images of several distant trees with yellowing leaves, blowing in the wind, as seen through a blurry "curtain" of plants in the foreground. Because this particular focus plane is maintained for a minute and a half, the subsequent refocusing onto the curtain of weeds comes as something of a surprise (made more dramatic by being timed so as to coincide with the auditory passing of a truck we never actually see that has moved closer and closer during the previous minute). This refocusing continues, as weeds nearer and nearer to us come into focus, and culminates with the sudden coming-into-pristine-focus of first one stalk, then two even closer, and finally, at the conclusion of the shot, a single, thin stem. Each of these final changes in the image has the impact of magic: because our training as filmgoers is to notice what is in focus and ignore what is not, each new visual revelation seems to come out of nowhere.

Each of the two general figures of style evident in the passages discussed here can be read as an aesthetic manifesto. The first of these has to do with the interplay between the space defined by the film frame and Pierce's evocation of what lies beyond the frame. We are always seeing a very particular image *and* seeing and hearing a variety of events that are occurring at the edge of the frame or entirely outside the frame, either nearby or, sometimes, at what seems to be a considerable distance. This particular dynamic is a visualization of the idea that the limited frame of the domestic is, in fact, a more energetic space than it may seem: it is a nexus of those human-environmental comings and goings that provide the fundamental rhythms of experience. The other figure of style, Pierce's layering of space and sound within a particular composition, suggests that the excitement of life is not simply a function of accessing new places but can lie in recognizing the astonishing complexity of the spaces nearby. The long, continuous shot in "pickup truck" is a visualization of the idea that the most crucial drama of experience can be our discovery of what has been in front of us all along.

For Pierce, sound has always been as crucial a dimension of the experience of a film or a video as the visual imagery. Indeed, Pierce was a composer of musique concrète before he became a filmmaker and learned to work with film and video in large measure so that he might offer his listeners something to look at as they experienced his sound compositions. Pierce soon discovered that the combination of visuals and sounds offered virtually infinite possibilities, and he has become one of those few mediamakers who have been able to effectively integrate the two tracks in complex and interesting ways (Peter Kubelka, Abigail Child, and James Benning are others).

During recent years, Pierce has moved more fully in the direction of video and has developed a range of techniques in the newer medium that allow him to take full advantage of digital sound without giving up the kinds of visual subtlety he has developed in his filmmaking. This gradual transition from filmmaker who also makes videos to videomaker who has made remarkable films has been occurring more or less simultaneously with a fundamental change in Pierce's domestic life. As this introduction is written, Pierce's divorce from his marriage of twenty-plus years, and the resulting painful transition, is subtly evident in several of his recent videos.

In *Fall* (2002), *37th & Lex* (2002), and *Evaporation* (2002), Pierce creates a strange and powerful emotional amalgam. On one hand, these three videos are spectacular to look at and listen to; Pierce's dexterity in transforming the visual and auditory particulars of his surround into experiences that are both gorgeous and strange has never been more obvious. But within the technical tour de force of these videos—both hidden by and evoked by their stylistic virtuosity—is a narrative of marital dissolution and a reorienting of Pierce's loyalties. In *Fall,* Pierce's isolation from his family seems clear, and in *37th & Lex,* we read a love letter to someone with whom Pierce is forging a new relationship. Of these recent videos, however, *Evaporation* is, at least for me, the most evocative and the most powerful; it charts the evaporation of the domestic security that has seemed at the heart of so many of Pierce's films and videos.

At first glance, *Evaporation* can seem still another of Pierce's remarkably beautiful evocations of place—in this instance of Niagara Falls and the coast of Maine. But this is a beauty that hides, or at least exists with, a good deal of pain. Periodically during *Evaporation* we see Mackenzie Pierce, first looking at the awesome drop of Niagara from the Canadian side, then staring out a window at the ocean, and still later, walking through a marsh looking down into tiny pools of water. These literal spaces resonate on a metaphoric level. Niagara, one of the world's foremost metaphors for romance and the beginning of marital bliss, in this instance suggests the beginning of the end, the drop away from the domestic security represented by marriage—for a child a fearsome fall into insecurity. Mackenzie Pierce's staring out the window and finding his way through the marsh suggest the shock of these new developments for him, and Pierce's continual return to his son in the video suggests his own empathy for his young child (Pierce himself still has his art-making to stabilize his experience, and in this instance, the beauty of the work suggests that for *him* this moment of transformation is exciting, liberating). Of course, neither father nor son knows how the future or the past will play out in their lives. Is the ghostly image of a man, a woman, and a child, walking through a field, which we seem to see as *Evaporation* concludes, a premonition of the future? An evocation of the past? Both?

I spoke with Pierce in October 1998, and we have remained in contact primarily by e-mail, periodically adding to the interview.

MacDonald: Some avant-garde filmmakers' first films, or early films, are amazing: Kenneth Anger's *Fireworks* [1947], for example; or Deren's *Meshes of the Afternoon* [1943]. But as I got to know your earlier work, it struck me that you're more like Harold Lloyd, who made dozens of films before figuring out precisely what his artistic persona should be, and *then* got started on the films we remember him for. Your early work is certainly capable young work, but it's not blow-away great work, in my view. Then, all of a sudden, right around the time you began having children, you began to make remarkable, and quite distinctive, movies and videos.

Pierce: When I was a graduate student at Syracuse University, John Orntlicher (one of my teachers) said of my early work—like *He Likes to Chop Down Trees* [1980], one of the more aggressive of those early films—"Those are wise-guy films."

That comment stuck with me for quite a while. I started to realize that what I really wanted to do was not just make clever, "wise-guy" structural films but to find a way to integrate my filmmaking into my home life. I had already started to make films about my family—my grandfather and my father—but when we had our first kid, Mackenzie, the stress of teaching *and* having a family *and* trying to make films made me realize I couldn't continue to separate them and get anything done.

Teaching—I *had* to be away from home to do that. But I started to try and integrate my home life with my filmmaking as much as possible. I started shooting in the house, and to make films and videos about my domestic surround. They weren't really *about* the kids (at that time just one); they just allowed me to parent and make films at the same time. So that's when it all started coming together.

MacDonald: Was the video *If with Those Eyes and Ears* the first of the works made at home?

Pierce: Yeah. I ordered my camcorder two weeks after Mackenzie was born. I'd done video all along but not with my own little camcorder. *If with Those Eyes and Ears* was a new beginning for me. I started just being with the newborn and shooting. It wasn't one of these trying-to-see-the-way-the-baby-sees projects. It was just trying to be *with* Mackenzie, as he was staring at the lightbulb or at the fan going around. It was like a form of parallel play. Video was perfect for that because it's cheap, and I could shoot a lot of it.

MacDonald: Had you always explored sound?

Pierce: That's very important. I did sound before I did film or video. I was in art school in Boston (the School of the Museum of Fine Arts), where I studied painting and ceramics—and electronic music. Before that, I'd done more conventional music—ever since I was little. In Boston I did musique concrète, building sounds on tape.

When I finished school in Boston, I hung out for a while, then went back to school in Iowa and continued working with electronic music there. Actually, I *thought* I went to Iowa to be a music major, but I discovered a problem with musique concrète: What do you do at a concert? It seemed very awkward to me, to be sitting in an auditorium "watching" an audiotape! So my first impulse was, "Well, I'm kind of interested in taking pictures; I'll take a film course, and that'll give me something to put the music *to;* it'll be something to look at while you're listening."

MacDonald: Of course, that's how cinema got invented in the first place. Edison had developed the phonograph and decided it needed visual accompaniment.

Pierce: Well, I'm following in his footsteps. I've never taken someone's music and made a film to accompany it, but there are similarities.

I think my films look the way they do because I didn't come to filmmaking *from* film. I never wanted to be a filmmaker—until I actually started working with the material. Then I thought, "This is pretty rich stuff! Images *and* sound, phew!"

I shoot now, and have for years, with the goal of getting to the part where I can do sound. I make images saying, "This'll be fun to do sound to." Sound is still the part I like the most.

MacDonald: When I was first getting involved in avant-garde film, one of the big debates was how to integrate sound into what most people considered a primarily visual art. Few came up with adequate solutions to the problem. There are exceptional works, like Frampton's *Critical Mass* [1971], Snow's *Wavelength* [1967], Kubelka's *Unsere Afrikareise (Our Trip to Africa)* [1965], Larry Gottheim's *Mouches Volantes* [1976], where the sound is really an integral, sometimes even an equal, part of the piece. But even in *Wavelength,* and in J. J. Murphy's *Print Generation* [1974], the sound is *analogous* to what's happening in the imagery, but the complexity of the sound isn't really equal to the complexity of the imagery, at least as most people experience those works.

When I first saw *50 Feet of String,* what struck me was that the motif of the string is a metaphor for both image and sound: the string suggests a spatial measure, *and* it's a string you pluck. Clearly, *50 Feet* was an attempt to make an integral sound-image work, not a *visual* piece *accompanied by* sound.

Pierce: I edit all my visuals silent, and the sound is always the last thing I do. But when I'm editing the visuals, there's a strong rhythmic component and a strong anticipation of what's going to happen on the sound track in conjunction with these visuals. Some of the sounds are sync—I *make* them in sync—when a car goes by, you hear a car go by; others aren't. In one instance I have this long rack focus that goes on for more than two minutes. As I was editing the visuals, I designed *in my head* a series of sound events that would make it OK for the viewer to sit for so long with that one shot.

It's hard to balance between image and sound. One of these days I'm going to make a silent film, just to find out how to make a film that does whatever I want it to do in terms of rhythm and movement, *without* sound. I have done the opposite: pictureless "movies"—sound pieces.

MacDonald: When I think back to *If with These Eyes and Ears,* I *hear* it first. It's as if the fans going around are a *visual* accompaniment to the sound.

Pierce: Maybe in that case you remember the sound first because the sound is more overdetermined than the images are. You can tell what all the imagery *is:* that's a fan, that's a tree . . . But the sound makes the piece hyperreal. For one thing, normally you never hear a fan, *really* hear it, every little hum. I try to make sound that seems to fit with the imagery but still is not entirely "real" in the more conventional senses. Hopefully, it causes you to go to another part of your brain—because it's not *just* a fan sound, it's also something more.

And there's some musical intent as well—in the rhythm of those sounds.

MacDonald: Once you had established yourself as family man *and* a film- and videomaker, *and* as a full-time faculty person at the University of Iowa, you had a serious heart attack. To what extent do you think your heart attack is a result of trying to do and be all this? Is your commitment to making, especially to being a prolific maker, dangerous? It certainly costs money, and it must create stress.

Pierce: I think the heart attack was just genetics. I've got screwy genes. My dad died young. I didn't—though I would have, had I not had the attack just a few miles from one of the few hospitals that can deal with my particular problem.

It's hard for me to talk about the financial cost of my work because for years—ever since I was in graduate school in the mideighties—I've never imagined a film and then tried to figure out how to get enough money to make it. It's always the other way around: What are my resources, and what film can I make within them? It's the same with time: because I'm a father and a teacher, I have little bits of time, and I work at home because I *can* do something in fifteen minutes in the kitchen.

MacDonald: So what are your resources? Are you dependent on grants?

Pierce: I was married; we had the family account and the film account, which got money from tours and grants and awards and so on. It allowed me to buy my tools without guilt. My career was financed by Film in the Cities, which is now defunct. For a while, I was getting grants from Film in the Cities every two years.

And the University of Iowa has given me support. For *50 Feet of String* I had both temporal and financial support. I got a very rare deal from Iowa: a three-year half-time teaching load; I taught one semester each year for three years, plus they gave me money to buy film stock and a computer.

My costs for making a film are just the cost of the film stock, the cost of work-printing, and the cost of the prints. Everything else, the mixing and all that other stuff, I do myself. It's a relatively cheap way to make films.

And video—I can make a video for thirty dollars. I have all the hardware.

MacDonald: You were saying the other day that you read J. B. Jackson [John Brinckerhoff Jackson is the author of *Discovering the Vernacular Landscape* (New Haven, Conn.: Yale University Press, 1984), *A Sense of Time, a Sense of Place* (Yale, 1994), and *Landscape in Sight: Looking at America* (Yale, 1997)]. I thought, "Well, that makes sense: Leighton makes an epic out of his front porch—a totally vernacular space."

Pierce: It *does* relate to my work. Jackson's books are about how we perceive space. It's not like I'm interested in how to represent my front porch, but I am very interested in the mental space that cinema creates, something we generally take for granted in Hollywood narrative work, and in how we can start to bend that mental space in other kinds of films. I'm interested in perception, and how we as people think we understand space. I'm always trying learn more about *that,* and how to make mental spaces in film—because, after all, there is no space in film really; we just think there is.

I read books on perception, cognitive psychology.

MacDonald: Like who?

Pierce: Antonio Damasio's *Descartes' Error: Emotion, Reason, and the Human Brain* [New York: Avon, 1994]—a good read. He's a neurologist. It's a big thing for a neurologist to say, "Maybe there isn't this mind-body split; maybe it really *is* all the same thing."

I was reading Jackson right after that Flaherty Seminar that was supposed to be on landscape [Pierce showed *50 Feet of String* at the 1996 Robert Flaherty Seminar, "Landscapes and Place," curated by Ruth Bradley, Kathy High, and Loretta Todd], but really didn't seem to be, when I was preparing a course for graduate students on the sense of space. I read a lot of stuff for that—much of it had an ecological concern.

MacDonald: I've always had a nagging frustration with the frequent tendency among academics to pooh-pooh the idea of the beauty of landscape and townscape (I'm not talking about Jackson here), to take a position that keeps them from feeling any responsibility for the beauty that surrounds them on so many campuses. What most people have to struggle for, academics get for free—and often ignore it! I think it's more than a question of what we're trained to see as beautiful. Some places *are* more amazing than others—though there are interesting, and perhaps amazing, dimensions to most places.

Pierce: Actually, I've always found it very difficult to shoot when I'm in really spectacular places—like the mountains. When I go to the mountains, I end up filming little sticks on the ground, *not* the overwhelming grandeur. One of the reasons I made *50 Feet of String* at home—and made the "rule" that I had to stay within a hundred yards of my kitchen—was to avoid a way of seeing that is forced on us when we're surrounded by obvious beauty, that takes us over in a beautiful spot. In Yosemite you don't have to learn to look at the beauty, or the grandeur, whatever you want to call it: *it tells you* what to look at.

But if you're sitting in the kitchen you've lived in for years, you might *not* really look at it. It's not that I'm avoiding beauty. I like to go to spectacular places, but not for my work.

MacDonald: Do you read a lot of nature writing?

Pierce: Not a lot. Well, since my heart problems, I've been rereading *Walden* [1854]. Thoreau's grouchy!

MacDonald: The reason I ask is that nature writing usually involves a tremendously disciplined and precise observation of the environment. American nature writing is an elegy to American nature, a way of resisting the seemingly inevitable disappearance of a wide range of increasingly endangered places. By making us more alert to what's left, nature writers attempt to engage us more fully in both vernacular and sublime landscapes, and often in efforts to save them for future generations.

I see a close relationship between nature writing and what you do. By making a "rule" that you're going to stay within the confines of your space in Iowa City, and creating what for some people is a long, slow film in which you create a new awareness of the details of a very limited environment, you're doing an activity analogous to what Mary Austin did in *Land of Little Rain* [1903], when she wrote about the Owens Valley, which has since been drained to feed the first LA aqueduct (both *Chinatown* [1974, Roman Polanski] and Pat O'Neill's *Water and Power* [1989] are about that process) and what, even earlier, Susan Fenimore Cooper did in *Rural Hours* [1850], and that Thoreau did in so much of his work.

Pierce: I think you're right: there *is* a relationship between that kind of work and mine. I have read Terry Tempest Williams's *Refuge* [1992; Williams is an essayist-novelist, and naturalist-in-residence at the Utah Museum of Natural History in Salt Lake City]. I've heard that when Terry Tempest Williams does nature walks, she'll go out her back door, and sometimes that'll be it: she won't move any further. She'll do her whole talk by just looking down, *really* looking—it's a deep looking—at what's right there in front of her. I've only heard this, but I like that idea.

I do have goals for my films and videos. I hesitate to say what they are, because once you admit a goal, then everyone can say, "Well, *that* didn't happen to *me.*" But I *would* like to be able to change people's perception, if only briefly, as a result of these films. I'd like you to walk out of the film and suddenly *notice* this sidewalk you've seen hundreds of times, that tree you've stopped noticing. Just the fact of your being more fully aware of where you are—there's value in that. Once you see exactly where you *are,* then you can make more capable decisions about what you're going to do about what you see.

Riding mower in Leighton Pierce's *50 Feet of String* (1995). Courtesy Leighton Pierce.

MacDonald: Thoreau's line "I have traveled a good bit in Concord" is perfect for your films.

Pierce (laughter): It is.

MacDonald: I think this strand of avant-garde film—the tradition of using cinema to *look* more carefully at the places that surround us, especially to see the sublime *in* the vernacular, has been undervalued. I'm thinking of Peter Hutton's work, Andrew Noren's, Larry Gottheim's, Rose Lowder's, Nick Dorsky's . . . But it's certainly one of the kinds of work that originally attracted me to the field of independent film.

Pierce: I'm aware of occupying an old school of filmmaking—though I'm younger than the people you've mentioned. My work is not overtly political—although I could argue that it *is* political. That Flaherty experience got me thinking about this again. Politics—overt politics—is where a lot of filmmaking *is* now, or has been for a while.

I've often felt the need to apologize for liking to make beautiful things. Some of my students say, "You know, really, you should never admit that you're trying to make a beautiful film, because beauty robs you of thought." And *I* say, "Well, actually, that's the whole idea! I want you to blank out thought, at least until you really look and listen." A film *can* seem apoliti-

Toy tractor in grass in Leighton Pierce's *50 Feet of String* (1995). Courtesy Leighton Pierce.

cal because it's beautiful, to be just about wallowing in "Beauty" and escaping real life, but hopefully there's a lingering effect that's not just escapism and that in the long run has a political impact.

MacDonald: When I was in Japan last January, I was able to visit a number of famous gardens when there were few tourists. My son, Ian, was teaching in Okayama, where one of the "three greatest gardens in Japan" is. Given what I had read about it, I expected the Korakuen Garden to be the size of Central Park. But compared with our city parks, this was a modest-sized garden, but one that included a considerable range of experiences; it modeled, as so many Japanese gardens do, making the most of a small space. In fact, in the case of Zen gardens, making a tiny space remarkable for centuries is a spiritual practice.

Do you see your filmmaking as a spiritual practice?

Pierce: I hesitate to talk about this, but yes, I do think of it as a kind of Zen practice. Shooting the films certainly is. I *embrace* Zen—I would say that. I'm not sure it's correct to say that shooting the films is like a Zen practice, but shooting with this device that changes the way I see, forces me to concentrate, *is* something like meditation.

Then, later, making the films—shooting isn't making the films; it's just gathering the materials—*is* something like making a garden. I hate to be so presumptuous as to say I'm making a beautiful Zen garden, but that is kind of what it's like. And I'm trying to invite people into that "garden."

MacDonald: How often do you shoot?

Pierce: It depends. For *50 Feet of String,* I shot four hundred feet every two weeks during the fall. It was like going to a normal job. I do have that attitude about making films: I "punch in"—"I didn't shoot my four hundred feet this week; I gotta go do it."

So, then, not waiting for the right light or the right moment, I decide *now* is the time to shoot. I think there's value in that. My film *Thursday*—my first really serious rule-bound film—was made according to a schedule that had nothing intrinsically to do with filmmaking. This relates back to what I was saying about the kids. When Mackenzie was one year old, I was home all day every Thursday with him. I wanted to make a film and didn't know what I was going to make a film about. I had eight one-hundred-foot rolls in my freezer and decided to establish a "rule": every Thursday, for the next two months, when Mackenzie took his nap, which was from eleven o'clock to one o'clock—he was a very dependable sleeper—I would shoot a hundred feet. And I made a film out of it, along with fragments of other films if I ever get back to that material.

The point is, I didn't know *what* the film was going to be, but having that two-hour period where I couldn't leave the house forced me to sit down and work even when the sun wasn't out. I found that a very valuable discipline.

And when I'm editing, I just go down to my basement—if I had a time clock, I'd set it up so I could punch in and punch out.

Actually, it's a little embarrassing to suggest that when I go down to edit, I'm on some spiritual journey.

MacDonald: Are you embarrassed because you don't think it's true, or because in certain highly intellectual academic situations you're embarrassed to *admit* it?

Pierce: When I go down the basement, I'm not really approaching a Zen state—but I think I was seeking that, especially in *50 Feet of String,* and in *Glass* [1998], and in *Memories of Water* (*#21, 6, 27;* all 1997). Those films are about trying to get into a meditative state myself and invite people into that state. Some people have no interest in that kind of experience; others do, at least on occasion. So that *is* what I like to do, and that's the kind of work that I'm drawn to.

But you're right: if I were showing these films at the university, I would never bring up this dimension of my work.

MacDonald: I spent much of my life teaching at a place where there was little academic pretension, so I could say whatever I wanted; but the more prestigious the place you're teaching in, in much of current academe, the more de rigueur it is *not* to admit the spiritual component of your experience. And that has a huge effect on film history.

I want to come back to your focus on place. I'm never sure in some of your films—I'm thinking of *Red Shovel* [1992] at the moment—*where* I am. I know you have connections with central New York, and that you spend time in Iowa and in Maine. *Red Shovel* could be the Midwest or Maine, yet the sound tells me it's Maine.

Pierce: Yeah, there aren't a lot of foghorns in the Midwest! *[Laughter.]* Well, maybe on the Mississippi.

MacDonald: I read the sound as Maine, but the imagery could be Iowa, or Maine—or many other places, though in cliché-land, it seems more like Iowa to me than it does Maine.

Do you have rules about place? Do you combine spaces?

Pierce: I mix them up. In the case of *Red Shovel,* both the sound and the image happen to be Maine. But there are plenty of times when I use a combination. When I'm editing, where I got sound or imagery is pretty much irrelevant to me.

In *50 Feet of String,* even though I told you I had this rule to shoot only within a hundred yards of my kitchen, there are two shots that break the rule: one from Maine and one from the Adirondacks. The foghorns are heard several times, so I'm also using sounds that are not Iowa and are not claiming to be Iowa.

In an earlier film, *You Can Drive the Big Rigs* [1989]—the café film—I figured that I was going to make this documentary about cafés and people talking in them. I interviewed lots of people. Then, when I started editing, I decided I hated all the interviews and lopped them all out and made one composite café from about twelve different cafés—though all the cafés *were* in Iowa. I felt a little guilty about that because I knew the people in the cafés were going to say, "Wait, this shot is not from *our* café!" But in the end I decided to make a film about café-ness. I don't really care about the truth of the actual space. These aren't documentaries.

MacDonald: What's the shot that was made in the Adirondacks?

Pierce: It's just a shot of lapping water.

And then there's also a third shot, the long rack-focus shot that moves from trees in the distance to the grass in the foreground: that was done in either upstate New York or in Iowa—I can't remember!—but I know it wasn't near my house.

MacDonald: Especially in the recent films, you do a lot with visual text, as a kind of punctuation device; some of it is to give titles, but it's more than that—it's like a third rhythmic entity. Often the "title" is not exactly a conventional title but something related in a deflected sense to what we see and hear.

Pierce: At one point, *50 Feet of String* was all strung together into one long, continuous sequence, but I realized that in that form, you couldn't *see* certain things because they would be overlapped in your mind by whatever came next. I decided to break the film into segments to allow you to digest what just happened before the next thing came along. That's the function of the black in a lot of the other films, as well. As for the text, I've had my own questions about the text in *50 Feet of String*. I put it in there to emphasize the separateness of segments, even though there are motifs that continue across the segments, and to pose a further question in the viewer's mind. When you see a title that says, "12:30," you may wonder, "What does that have to do with anything?"—because you never see a clock. In fact, the mailman always came around twelve thirty; he was part of the rhythm of the day.

I do worry about the use of text. In *50 Feet of String* and all my recent stuff, I'm trying to move people toward a nonverbal state. There's no talk—maybe tiny little bits of talk in the background, but certainly no dialogue. I'm trying to put people in that other part of their minds, where they're *not* thinking about words, where they're *not* analyzing things. And I'm worried that I eroded that in *50 Feet of String* by using text at all, other than at the beginning for a title and at the end for credits. Those bits of text suggest, and reveal, a thought process that I'm not sure I should be revealing during the experience of the work.

MacDonald: This is an interesting debate that begins in the silent era, when there was a question of how visual text *was.* Murnau, in *The Last Laugh* [1924], tried to avoid intertitles altogether but was forced to come in for a close-up of a crucial letter. There are certain parts of life that are *only* evident in text, and it's very difficult to avoid them.

Keaton, who is equally visual, accepts the text—doesn't overuse it, but accepts it—and often energizes it in one way or another: some of his intertitles have a poetic energy of their own ("hopelessly lost, helplessly wet, and horribly hungry" from *The General* [1926], for example). His intertitles keep the movie moving forward.

I think the texts in *50 Feet of String* work that way: there's a certain point, after four or five of them, where you realize that they aren't building toward an explanation of anything; they're just another visual and rhythmic element to be aware of. There's always at least a tenuous connection to the visuals, and the particular graphic quality of the short texts has its own impact. I don't think the text in *50 Feet of String* takes anything away from its visualness. You use the text to let us know there *isn't* a verbal explanation.

Pierce: That makes me worry less about it.

MacDonald: In his films, Peter Hutton is doing something that's particularly his own—I can't imagine confusing a Hutton film with a film by anyone else: his films not only evoke earlier film practice (the Lumières, in particular); they suggest his awareness of a whole history of painting and photography. That is, he sees his films as resonant of the history of art and assumes that some viewers will see these resonances. I'm wondering to what extent you mean to call on viewers' awareness of earlier art history.

Pierce: I connect mostly to painting. But I wouldn't really put my connection with earlier art the way you do. When I get a film started, and this was true with *50 Feet of String,* part of my work is to go and look at paintings, or at books of illustrations of paintings. I do it very consciously. Hopper is big for me. And Helen Frankenthaler. Rothko's color-field paintings. And Turner. Kandinsky—not that his work relates to mine so much. And Renoir—especially in terms of texture. Monet.

I fill myself up with these kinds of images, and I read what the artists have written. Then I just continue to shoot without thinking too much about what I've looked at and read. But I know that it has an influence. *You Can Drive the Big Rigs* is pretty Hopper-esque. *Red Shovel* is Renoir-esque. I mean, I never try to mimic a Hopper painting, nor am I trying to get people to think, "Oh, Hopper!" necessarily. But I do like it when people say, like someone at Cornell just did, "I just saw a show of Bonnard paintings, and your film reminded me of them." That's good for me.

MacDonald: Did you ever paint? Did you study painting at the School of the Museum of Fine Arts?

Pierce: It was one of the things I did. I entered as a ceramist. I had apprenticed with a potter in upstate New York. That's how I got into art school. In Boston I was doing ceramic sculpture, and then I got into what now would be called intermedia—then it was called multimedia—and worked on electronic music and video.

I *am* certainly interested in the possibilities of techniques that have evolved in the hands of the artists, and the scientists and technicians, who have come before me. And sometimes I organize a project so as to review certain technical dimensions of filmmaking. But usually I'm just gathering stuff and later figure out what's there and what I can do with it. *50 Feet of String* and *Glass* were preplanned films.

My films are all comedies, you know: *50 Feet of String, Glass*—not big guffaws, obviously, but the films are full of little jokes. We shouldn't lose sight of that.

MacDonald: The plucking of that string in *50 Feet of String* can seem funny . . .

Pierce: Actually, I don't think that's funny anymore. In fact, I just finished a shorter version of that film. I've kept the fifty-minute version, but I also have a shorter version where I've cut some segments out—mostly because I'm so sick of that plucking. It's so overstated. I think if I'd have continued to edit *50 Feet* for another few months, I would have taken most of that plucking, or all of it, out—and not just that. The result would have been something more like this new version.

The reason I made the shorter version is to get into the Oberhausen Film Festival, which has a forty-minute cap. But I like the new version better than the original.

MacDonald: Is the shorter version *35 Feet of String?*

Pierce (laughter): Yeah, I rent them by the foot.

MacDonald: The string is plucked like a musical instrument and also suggests a surveyor's device—it's an axis along which the film is arranged.

Pierce: This goes back to painting. I used the string for painterly reasons. I thought to myself, I can do these beautiful soft compositions with lots of grass, with diffraction as well as soft focus, but the string will be a marker, a way to say that this *is* a composition—because string is not normally found in those spaces, so it must be there for something else.

The string demonstrates the other rule I had, which was to always use the shallowest depth of field possible. The string reveals the depth of field in its shape, which is either conelike or triangle-like.

MacDonald: Could you talk further about the particular techniques you explore in *50 Feet of String* and in other films—especially the techniques that allow you to create the unusual visual look of the films?

Pierce: I'm afraid it will be pretty boring. There are several things I work with. One is depth of field and flatness. I want to get a very shallow depth of field (the shortest length of z-axis in sharp focus). To do this I open up the iris all the way (shooting usually at f-2 or f-2.8). Since I'm usually out in bright sun, I need to cut the light with neutral-density filters and usually a polarizing filter, as well. Shooting at a high frame rate also cuts the light down significantly.

To reduce depth of field even more, I also use the telephoto end of the 10–100mm zoom lens (usually a Seiss 10–100, but sometimes a 50 or 75mm prime lens—*Red Shovel* was shot with a Bolex with a 150mm lens). This also has the effect of reducing the perceived depth of the image—flattening it somewhat. Interestingly, since the frame seems flatter from the telephoto effect, lateral movement in different planes creates surprising and interesting figure-ground relationships.

Can you stand this? Do you want more?

MacDonald: Sure. What else is involved?

Pierce: There's diffraction—light getting bent around solid objects. In a lot of shots in *50 Feet*—for example, the shot of the toy tractor moving toward the camera in a field of shimmery grass—and also in *Red Shovel* and *Glass,* I use diffraction to color the depth of the image. Edges of solid objects close to the lens are out of focus, but they bend the light coming into the lens from more distant objects. You can see this yourself by looking at something far away and bringing some edge into your visual field close to your eye. With a telephoto lens and a shallow depth of field, that effect can be concentrated. If there are many objects, all out of focus and waving around (like grass or weeds), you can really start messing with those distant light rays.

Finally, there's camera position. This is obvious, I suppose, but small changes in camera position create extremely different perceptions of the activity in the frame. The toy tractor shots in *50 Feet of String* (and many others too, but I'll keep to this example) took most of a morning to set up and shoot. I changed elevation, tilt angle, location, and so forth—in very small increments. Since I was on the ground, a few inches in elevation drastically changed the horizon and the effect of the out-of-focus but diffracting grass.

MacDonald: From what you said earlier, I assume that you spend an equal amount of time dealing with sound. One place in *50 Feet of String* where this is particularly obvious is in that long, refocusing shot you mentioned earlier.

Pierce: That's right. Actually, while the visuals in *50 Feet* are mostly from my neighborhood here in Iowa City, the sounds in that film are from all over—the East, the Midwest, the West, France—and thinking about those sounds vividly evokes my memories of those places. In fact, I often listen to my raw tapes the way people look at photo albums—to remember. Sound seems to bring me more deeply into memory than photographs do. The thing about sound, though, is that what are geographic markers for me, in most cases, seem to remain ambiguous to others.

In that two-plus-minute shot from *50 Feet,* the truck and the frogs were recorded along County Road 33 in Ontario County, New York, one valley west of Canandaigua Lake (the recording was made at eleven o'clock on a June night in 1988, a warm and quiet night with a crescent moon, strangely few mosquitoes, and I had my recently deceased father in mind). The chainsaw was recorded in Iowa. The foghorns in Lubec, Maine, were recorded on a morning in June 1991, from Campobello Island, Canada, just across the strait; it was foggy and windless. The water sloshing was recorded on the west shore of Seneca Lake in New York State, at night. I think what sounds like a train coupling is actually the sound of a car door, which was also near Seneca Lake.

MacDonald: You're so into the subtleties of sound that I guess your not liking the plucking of the string in *50 Feet* makes sense.

Pierce: I spent a long time trying to make the perfect "clong!"—combining sounds.

MacDonald: In the end, what did you use?

Pierce: A toy piano, the kind with rods—some have bars, some have rods. I'm actually plucking a rod and that's combined with plucking a string on a zither that's tuned too low and is kind of rattly. There's some other stuff, which I can't remember, but those are the main components. I combined them and pitched them down, and did equalization—a variety of things. I can't remember exactly. But I spent a lot of time and finally felt that I had it. But I let it get out of hand.

MacDonald: How time-consuming was it to set up *Glass?* Could you elaborate on the setting-up part of your process?

Pierce: Glass is exceptional among my recent pieces, since it *was* set up. All the other recent work was made from images "shot in the moment": each was discovered and teased out during the editing. But *Glass* was a Rube Goldberg–like arrangement.

I spent a night and a morning setting up and testing a scheme I had planned over many days. Then with four hundred feet of film in the camera, I shot at one hundred twenty frames per second and performed the film. It was all over in two minutes. I did shoot a few more shots on the following day to enrich what I got on the main shoot. Hence, editing was very fast on that film, though sound took the usual fairly long time.

At one point, I was going to do a series, "Science for Filmmakers"—kind of tongue-in-cheek. *Glass* was going to be the optics piece. I was going to have titles in that, too: "diffraction," "diffusion," "absorption," "reflection," "refraction." But it didn't work, and *Glass* ended up having a form that had nothing to do with those plans, and became a film of emotional resonance—I hope—through the added shots and the sound.

MacDonald: When I looked at *Red Shovel* and *Glass* recently, I realized that while your rhythms have remained relatively consistent, over the years you've moved toward longer and longer single shots, or maybe it's just more complex single shots. Do you feel challenged to see how much you can make happen in fewer shots?

Pierce: That was exactly the challenge of *Glass.* I was trying to make it happen in a single ten-minute shot—a two-minute performance documented at one hundred twenty frames per second. The continuous-take performance failed, which led to the additional shots and the (perhaps) greater effect of that film.

MacDonald: The complete title of *Glass* is *Glass (Memories of Water #29).* Why "#29"?

Pierce: "29" implies that there are twenty-eight previous memories. I felt that that was about right. I counted all the "memories of water" that I felt were in my films and videos, and figured this "memory" would be about number twenty-nine. Only three of those other memories were made into pieces. The rest are either ideas, or fragments of other pieces (the rain in *50 Feet,* the drips in *50 Feet,* anything with a foghorn on the sound track).

MacDonald: Could you talk about your sense of the degree to which the mysteries of your process *should be* or *shouldn't be* part of the experience of these works?

Pierce: Hmmm. The question, "How did he do that?" is one I like people having when they look at these pieces. However, I have a very particular preference for the *that* referred to. If *that* has to do *only* with technique, and if the question comes up in a screening, I readily explain the technology and the procedure for attaining a particular "effect."

But the technology is only interesting to me since I cannot separate my tools from my art. I have no interest in maintaining a sense of mystery by holding on to a technical secret (back when I was a potter, I never kept glaze formulas secret, as was the mode at the time). If the value of the piece rests in the technical magic alone, then the piece is just an artless display of virtuosity. I'm impatient with the work I see that is like that, and I don't accept technique as something other than a starting point in my own work.

At a recent screening, several people tried to get me to talk about the "amazing" sound in my pieces by asking me which microphone I used. I kept telling them directly that it was the wrong question—but I did try to answer by explaining the technique (all postconstructed sound, each sound *carefully* miked, regardless of the particular microphone used).

Still, the real question, one that is difficult to ask, since sound is generally considered as *belonging* to the image in some sort of existential way, *should be,* "How did he choose those particular sounds to go with those images—were there other, rejected possibilities—and how do the choices create meaning and affect feeling?" That question is more interesting to me because in most cases I only know part of the answer, and I enjoy exploring it in dialogue; it helps keep me moving forward. In other words, I'd rather struggle with, "How did he do that?" when it's a question of effect or meaning. But that's a harder question for a first-time viewer to ask, so I rarely get it.

MacDonald: You've worked in both film and video. How different is your process, or your thinking, when you work in these different media?

In *The Back Steps* [2001] and *Water Seeking Its Level* [2002], it seems as if digital video allows you to be more painterly, to imitate painting with something like "brushstrokes." Also, in the digital videos, transitions that, in your 16mm films, are done by refocusing seem accomplished in a different, more painterly way.

Pierce: There's much that's the same in my film and DV work. However, the tools of shooting and editing are very different. I've been engaging the possibilities of the new DV tools. I couldn't do the same things in DV that I do with 16mm, even if I wanted to, because the tools are not the same.

DV has the possibility of creating very beautiful imagery with a very small camcorder. Its portability is a big deal. However, with the small camera you get these lenses with very funky focus mechanisms: no footage markings, no absolute position of the focus ring to any particular distance. In fact, focus position is determined not only by the position of the ring but by the speed with which you turn it; it's velocity-sensitive the way a mouse on a computer is. That drives me crazy. It also removes the focus shift technique from my palette (I *could* use a camera with a "real" lens for more dynamic focus control in DV, but then I'd lose portability).

I've been thinking about the film-video question for about twenty years now. Issues of resolution and color and contrast are all still relevant, even though the poles are narrowing. I've always been caught by the fact that while 16mm clearly has more of all of the above, video always seems more *real*. 16mm is veiled compared with video. The veil comes from the way each renders time. 16mm always gives you a discrete one-forty-eighth of a second image presented almost instantaneously, followed by an equal moment of black. Video is continually being drawn on the screen, a half-interlaced image every one-sixtieth of a second; there is no perceived "black" moment. So, video gives much more temporal information, making it more present, more *real*. But I am still attracted to the more veiled nature of 16mm.

With my particular DV camera I can play with the way each frame renders a moment in time. This might be what you refer to as "brushstrokes." Here's how it works: in DV I can shoot at "shutter speeds" down to a quarter second. As is true in still photography, movement has greater blur at slower shutter speeds. So the girls in *Back Steps,* the water in *Water Seeking Its Level* [2002], the cabs and the Empire State Building in *37th & Lex,* the world in the marble in *Fall,* et cetera all are streaked as a result of my shooting at a slow shutter speed (probably one-eighth or one-fifteenth of a second).

An added benefit of those slow shutter speeds is that I can shoot in the dark, as I did in *Back Steps* and *37th & Lex.*

However, since time must march on and the DV tape still records and plays back at about thirty frames per second, when I'm shooting at slow shutter speeds, the image gets a very "steppy" look. For example, shooting at one-fourth of a second, you end up with an effective frame rate of four frames per second. So, in my editing software (Media 100 CineStream), I make layers of identical images and put them out of sync by one frame each. Then I adjust transparency levels so that each layer is more or less equal in brightness, and what results is the swishy look of *Water Seeking Its Own Level,* or *Pink Socks* [2002], or *37th & Lex.*

The "steppiness" is also factor I can play with. On very close viewings, I mean really, really close viewings, one might be able to notice a dynamic change in the steppiness of the image in certain sections. I manipulate the transparency levels over time to make the result smoother and more smooshed

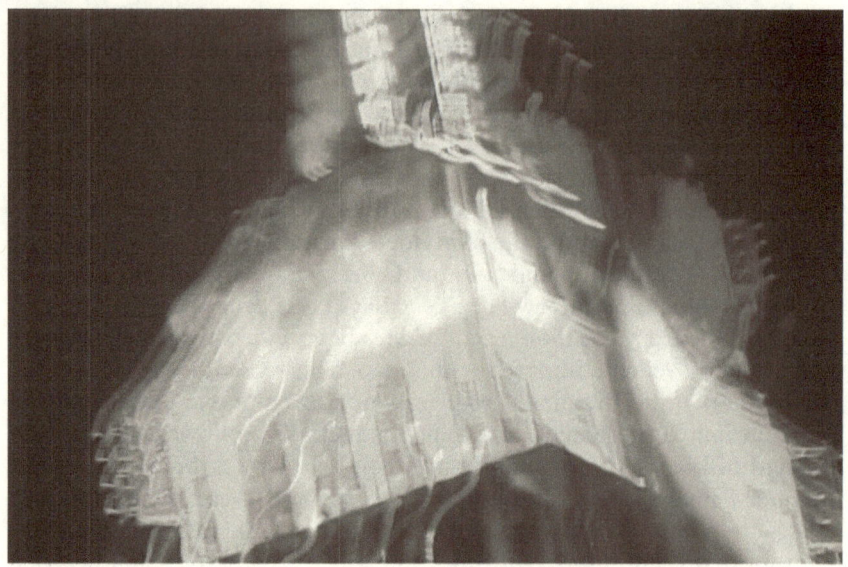

Empire State Building in Leighton Pierce's *37th & Lex* (2002). Courtesy Leighton Pierce.

together, or steppier and slightly sharper. It's a manipulation of microrhythms in the image.

By the way, in those videos I was imitating a process I first used on *Red Shovel* in 16mm film back in 1992. The effect *is* painterly, but I never set out to imitate painting.

One more thing about 16mm versus DV. In DV I have the potential for a very rich stereo sound track. That matters a lot to me. I remember hearing the optical track to *Glass,* with some disappointment. I could solve that by shooting in 35mm, but then I'd give up portability and lose financially in a big way.

MacDonald: Are your digital videos available on DVD? Will they be? They certainly look good on VHS, but wouldn't they look better on DVD?

Pierce: I will need to invest in burning some DVDs, even though I have some serious problems with the compression. I'm concerned about the quantization effects and how that might really screw up a piece like *The Back Steps.* Still, it obviously needs to happen.

MacDonald: Are you as well known in the video art world as you are in the avant-garde film world (I'm still playing catch-up with video)? I assume you don't make a distinction between these two worlds, but distribution-wise, and in some other ways as well, the two worlds remain separate.

Pierce: I would say no, but I'm trying to remedy that. Mostly, I've gotten my work known through festivals. I'm much more interested now in installation using video, and I'm starting to explore that option in New York. I'm tired of having my short pieces subsumed in a program of other works. The recent Whitney Biennial was a good example. *The Back Steps* was seriously eroded by its context in the program it was presented with, and by sharing space with other pieces in the gallery. *The Back Steps* and many of the other recent pieces need to exist in a black room on their own.

MacDonald: In *The Back Steps* and *Pink Socks,* how much is done in-camera, and how much is done after you've shot?

Pierce: Both use the basic process I described earlier, with the addition of a certain loopiness. In each of those pieces (and in the center section of *Fall*—my favorite section of that piece), I loop certain segments of the image with dissolves between the loops. Each piece started with the slow-frame-rate effect from the camera. Then I played with the many layers of image to paint the image in time. Usually, most of the work happens after I've shot. This was especially true for *Back Steps,* which was the first piece to use this process and involved weeks of tedious trial and error. *Pink Socks* was much quicker.

Here's a poem I wrote (one of the only two poems I ever wrote) that talks about the process in *Pink Socks:* it was written with the "Would I have shot this if I had had a Bolex instead of a DV camera with me?" question in mind. It's my catalogue entry for the film. It's called "San Marco":

Now,
I will claim that I was
belly down (in public) because
it sounds like work,
not just messing around,
a kind of sacrifice for art,

>—and you should have seen my shirt
>and on my lips those little downy feathers
>and the wings flapping against my ears
>and the smell, and the dust—

when in fact I appreciated,
I put to good use,
the flip out, tiltable, 3.5 inch (diagonal), color LCD screen
keeping me belly up while
my Sony whined
belly down
on the stone
in the midst of all
the pigeon-ness.

MacDonald: As you're planning videos or films, and as you're shooting them, how much do you consider the potential metaphoric dimensions of the work?

Pierce: Hmmm. This is hard. I can say that I don't think metaphorically at all when I'm planning or shooting—especially because I rarely plan.

I'm even struggling with whether I ever *think* metaphorically. Things are not always just what they are, but they are rarely a specific something else. But let me think.

I guess *Wood* [2000] functions metaphorically to some extent. Those water bubbles at the end are clearly heartbeats, and they stop in black, and the swing is empty. I would resist saying anything about it other than that the whole piece is supposed to represent something of my feelings about my brush with death. With the heartbeat/bubble near the end (the sound stops suddenly in black) and the perhaps too-heavy-handed empty swing at the end, the film moves back to my thoughts of my potential absence from my kids' lives. Is that related to metaphor? The feelings we get from music are unrelated to metaphor, so I don't know. I've really never verbally expressed myself about these things; that's why I'm a film- and videomaker—so that I do have a way to express myself.

In any case, by the time I was editing *Wood* and building that sound track, I knew what I was doing, what it was "about." But when I shot the visual material, I knew nothing about that. I was just documenting moments in the backyard. I was drawn to the parallel activities that my kids were doing in proximity to each other: my son was cutting wood and making a fire; my daughter was playing with water and bowls.

Wood, like all of my pieces, is a little handle on my subconscious. When I construct these pieces, I'm sculpting evocations into something that seems to resonate on the subconscious level.

Back Steps was a home video that became a piece with metaphoric resonance, but only near the end of the postproduction process. For me, it's another piece about the fleetingness of life and of lives and of moments. As is *Water Seeking Its Level.* As is *Fall.* As is *Pink Socks.* As is *Evaporation.*

MacDonald: About *Fall:* this piece seems new, in that the section titles, all of which use "Danger," seem unusual for you. Is the newspaper we see a reference to 9/11?

Pierce: Actually, I just eliminated all the "Danger" intertitles and replaced them with numbers (1, 2, 3). *Fall* is about being out of the country after 9/11 and my feelings of isolation and paranoia. I eliminated the titles because I thought they were too glib, and described too specifically an intent that I would rather render without words.

But more specifically, Part 1 (which was "Danger of Falling Behind") had to do with a certain isolation I was feeling from my family, as well as

Niagara Falls in Leighton Pierce's *Evaporation* (2002). Courtesy Leighton Pierce.

with the general paranoia of the time. Part 2 ("Danger of Falling") is more free and playful and leaks a little bit of passion and fun. Part 3 ("Danger") is more specifically about 9/11 and my fears for the safety of my kids.

MacDonald: Are the three sections in *Fall* filmed in different locations? Part 1 looks as if it could be Venice; part 2 is clearly Cassis (I recognize it from Jonas Mekas's *Walden* [1967] and *Cassis* [1967]); and then there's the newspaper section.

Also, you're visible in *Fall* (and in *37th & Lex*) in a way I don't remember in earlier films.

Pierce: Part 1 of *Fall* is mostly Bandol, down the coast from Cassis; part 2 is purely Cassis; part 3 is mostly Sanary (near Bandol) and Cassis. The locations are all mixed up in each part. I am visible in the second section of *Fall,* which is an oblique self-portrait. I indulge myself in that section. I'm visible also, by the way, in *Glass* (I'm the person who sits down in the chair at the end) and in *50 Feet of String* (I walk out and cut the string at the end), and even in *Thursday* (washing the cup, also at the end)—I end a lot of my movies, I guess.

What *is* different about *37th & Lex* is that my *voice* is visible—and the text, while not very direct, is a lot more direct than any of my other films. I think that's what reveals me in that piece.

MacDonald: You mentioned earlier that the poem you quoted to me is one of two poems you've written. Is the other the one we read in *37th & Lex?*

Pierce: No, I hadn't thought of *37th & Lex* as a poem—more as a letter. But now that you mention it . . .

MacDonald: It's difficult to escape from autobiography. Despite the general abstraction in your films and the lack of the particulars of family interrelationship, the fact that so much of your work develops out of domestic experiences (a Halloween party in *The Back Steps,* a camping trip in *Memories of Water,* a trip to Venice in *Pink Socks,* an outing in St. Pons [St. Pons is an abandoned monastery near the town of Gemenos, just inland from Cassis] in *Water Seeking Its Level*) allows for some deductions about your particular domestic experience.

This seems especially true, now, since I've seen *37th & Lex,* which represents a basic change in your method, and which suggests to me that, not only your media art but your personal life is in a period of transition. Let me detail this a bit.

I see the trajectory of your recent work as having three phases: first, in the long series of films and videos beginning with *Thursday* and continuing past *50 Feet of String,* you're *inside* a domestic life with kids and spouse, wanting to engage parenthood but also to maintain a space within it for your art; then, in *Fall* you seem almost isolated within this family situation, in a *separate* world from the world of domesticity, where you see domesticity as in danger, in crisis; and finally, *37th & Lex* is, or appears to be, a love poem—outside the domestic space altogether.

Am I reading this evolution correctly?

Pierce: Alas, you are, Scott. In fact, I think you hit it right on the head in this analysis of my recent life through my work.

And you're right that *37th & Lex* represents more than just a change in what I point my camera at. It has to do with whom I share my attention, too. Things *are* changing in my work; I do feel a bit like it's opening up— that I'm in the midst of a coming-out of sorts. I'm excited about this, while at the same time, I carry a pretty heavy load of remorse—those two kids. But, yes, things are changing in my life. From here on, there will be a very different take on the whole domestic scene—that's for sure.

Matthias Müller

During the early decades of film history, European and American filmmakers attempted to give their new medium economic and aesthetic legitimacy by incorporating elements of the more established arts, particularly photography, magic, theater, and literature. During the past few decades, as some traditional forms of cinema have seemed increasingly endangered by new technologies, filmmakers have often worked to maintain the legitimacy of cinematic art by celebrating film's own history: by reviving and rethinking genres, by remaking earlier films, and—this is especially true of critical filmmakers—by recycling various dimensions of cinema's now extensive archive. Critical filmmakers have found a remarkably wide range of approaches to this recycling, approaches distinguished by their choices of films to recycle and particular recycling procedures. Bruce Conner has created a distinguished career by transforming film-cultural detritus—moments from old educational films and from commercial films and advertisements—into complexly suggestive montages. Raphael Montañez Ortiz has used a computer, and Martin Arnold a homemade optical printer, to interrupt, investigate, expose, and transform the implications of moments from popular cinema. Chuck Workman continues to invigorate the annual Academy Awards shows by combining memorable moments from popular movies in amusing, evocative, and sometimes penetrating ways. And Phil Solomon uses the optical printer and a variety of procedures to alter moments from various kinds of films—popular movies, family home movies, educational films—and recycles the results into mysterious evocations of psychic disturbance.

Recycling strategies have depended to a considerable degree on what has usually been seen, at least in the United States, as the divide between commercial moviemaking and avant-garde cinema. Chuck Workman can achieve access to the films he lovingly and/or ironically samples for his Academy Awards pieces only because he is a Hollywood insider, while Raphael Ortiz's contempt for Hollywood, especially its ways of encoding ethnic and gender bigotry within its products, has often resulted in aggressive videos, which, however, are kept out of general circulation because of Ortiz's fear of Hollywood retribution. At least one major contributor to "recycled cinema," however—the German Matthias Müller—has been able to create a substantial and diverse body of work by working across this divide—or at least by working far enough from both Hollywood and the centers of American avant-garde filmmaking to be able to maintain a healthy, detached awareness of the accomplishments and limitations of both. One of the contributions of David James's *Allegories of Cinema* (Princeton, N.J.: Princeton University Press, 1988) was to recognize that experiment and innovation are not the province of any particular school or class of filmmaking, but that, during any given cultural moment, filmmaking at all levels can speak to the same issues, reveal the same cultural narratives. Müller's films reflect the same thinking.

From early in his career Müller's work has been in conversation with a broad range of cinema. Sometimes his films and videos are purposely reminiscent of earlier films. *Sleepy Haven* (1993), for example, evokes several landmarks of Queer cinema—particularly Kenneth Anger's *Fireworks* (1947) and Jean Genet's *Un chant d'amour* (1952)—as a context for a cinematic meditation on ocean voyaging, the body as romantic continent, and the filmstrip as psychic flesh. *Home Stories* (1990) recycles imagery of women in Hollywood films, recorded off a television screen, to create a revealing and amusing moment of meta–film noir. *Alpsee* (1994) is Müller's depiction of the childhood of a creative young boy, living alone with his mother—and an homage to Douglas Sirk's American films and their imaging of the gorgeous repression of bourgeois life. The series of six videos called *Phoenix Tapes* (1999), co-made with Christoph Girardet, provides an interpretive tour through the work of Alfred Hitchcock; each video focuses on a different dimension of Hitchcock's films. And the recent *Mirror* (2003, co-made with Christoph Girardet) recalls Michelangelo Antonioni's films (the earlier *Vacancy* [1998], Müller's surreal depiction of the city of Brasília, uses sound from early Antonioni films).

Müller's conversation with cinema has been much involved with the materiality of the media he works in. Early on, Müller worked with Super-8mm, exploring the possibilities of hand processing his own material in a series of films culminating in *Aus der Ferne—The Memo Book* (1989), his psychodrama of coming to grips with the death of a former lover from AIDS. By the 1990s he was also working in 16mm. Indeed, *Alpsee* and *Pensão Globo* (1997), his depiction of a young man with AIDS torn between memory and

Lana Turner in Matthias Müller's *Home Stories* (1991). Courtesy Matthias Müller.

mortality, number among the most gorgeous 16mm films of which I am aware. By the late 1990s, Müller was exploring video and 35mm film. The *Phoenix Tapes* are Betacam videos, as is *Beacon* (2002), an evocation of life after trauma; and as are *Manual* (2002) and *Play* (2003), inventive found-footage pieces, one focusing on cinematic relics of earlier technologies, the other, on audiences for plays and films, as depicted in films (all these videos were co-made with Christoph Girardet). The film *nebel* (2000), Müller's stunning homage to Ernst Jandl's poetry—along with Rick Hancox's *Waterworx (A Clear Day and No Memories)* (1982), it's the most impressive translation of a poet's work to film that I know—is in 35mm, though it includes imagery from other gauges. And *Mirror* was shot in digital video but can be presented as a Cinemascope projection. Müller has also made DVDs for exhibition as installations in art galleries and still photographs.

Paradoxically, Müller's ability to recycle earlier cinema history in works that remain quite his own is, to some extent, a function of his careful choice of collaborators. Dirk Schaefer's sound tracks for *Continental Breakfast* (1985), *Epilogue* (1987), *Sleepy Haven, Home Stories, Alpsee, Pensão Globo,*

Vacancy, Scattering Stars (1994), *Bedroom* (part 5 of *Phoenix Tapes*), and *Album* (2004) are a major addition to these works, reminiscent in their level of impact of Tibor Szemző's sound for Peter Forgács's "video operas." Equally important are Canadian filmmaker Michael Hoolboom's narrations for *Vacancy* and *Beacon*. Hoolboom is a master of the short personal essay, as is clear from his own video *Panic Bodies* (1998), from his book *Plague Years* (edited by Steve Reinke [Toronto: YYZ Books, 1998]), and from his narrations for Müller's films. And most of Müller's recent works were co-made with Christoph Girardet.

This interview was conducted entirely by e-mail, with the assistance of translator Allison Plath-Moseley, beginning in April 2004. I sent questions to Müller; he sent answers in German to Plath-Moseley, and she sent me translations, which I edited and returned to Müller for corrections.

MacDonald: Were movies important for you as a child? And, if so, which movies and movie experiences are most memorable for you?

Müller: Although I'm part of the first generation that was socialized through media from kindergarten on, I really did not grow up with movies and television. In the Protestant pastor's family in which I grew up, images were basically mistrusted, and television was taboo. And it wasn't until the mid-1980s that I accidentally discovered the regular-8 films made by my father, who died at a fairly young age. I used this material for the first time in *Final Cut* [1986], but it is also in *Alpsee, Pensão Globo,* and *nebel*.

I remember seeing a few of Andy Warhol's films on television when I was fourteen or fifteen—something that is hardly imaginable today, given the current commercialization of public television in Germany. The vivaciousness and eccentricity of these films had a hugely inspiring, liberating effect on a small-town boy like me. They also made me realize that I didn't have to be afraid of the technical aspects of production. As a teenager, I familiarized myself with Super-8, and in the late 1970s, I began to make short experimental films.

From the early to mid-1980s, I found myself in a booming experimental Super-8 scene, which developed the very unorthodox notion of filmmaking as a way of life, not as a profession. We went from festival to festival, showing our films in lots of places, often way outside the established cinematic culture. During this time, I developed friendships with other filmmakers: with Martin Arnold, the Schmelzdahin group (a small collective of performance and film artists, including Jürgen Reble) . . . Of these, the one with Mike Hoolboom is the closest and has been the most artistically fertile.

MacDonald: You studied art and German literature at Bielefeld University and art at the Braunschweig Kunsthochschule. Was film part of the curriculum at these institutions?

Müller: When I was studying at Bielefeld, I elected to take film courses—seminars on theory and analysis, classes on directors such as Hitchcock and Ophüls. In the 1980s, the Braunschweig Kunsthochschule was an epicenter of experimental production in Germany. There, the wonderful Birgit Hein had gathered a number of students around her, all of whom had a background like mine: we understood film both as a tool for personal artistic expression and as a subversive art.

Aus der Ferne—The Memo Book and *Home Stories* were made during those years. These films can be understood as responses to the avant-garde works I saw as a student—American psychodrama, for instance, and found-footage films. It was Alf Bold who brought the idea of found footage to Germany; on various occasions he lectured in my classes. He introduced us to works by Bruce Conner, Joseph Cornell, Morgan Fisher, Will Hindle, George Kuchar, and others. I still recall his passionate, committed way of presenting these artists, and this influenced me strongly later, when I was a curator. I also met Christoph Girardet at the school in Braunschweig, and we've been working together ever since *Phoenix Tapes.*

MacDonald: *Final Cut* and *Epilogue,* the earliest of your films I've seen, are impressive in their own right, and they reveal many relationships to later work. How much work had you made before these films?

Müller: I made my first films in 1979. During the 1980s, I made something like sixteen short experimental films in Super-8, which were distributed by the Alte Kinder (1980–85), an artist-run film collective devoted to the distribution and exhibition of experimental Super-8 film. These films were shown many times. Most of them are out of distribution now

MacDonald: In your filmography for the catalogue *Album,* you begin with *Aus der Ferne—The Memo Book,* rather than with the earlier Super-8mm films. Is that because there is now so little Super-8mm exhibition, or because you see the films before *Aus der Ferne—The Memo Book* as apprentice works?

Müller: After years spent exploring my medium, carefully developing and shaping my own themes, *The Memo Book* presented an entirely new challenge. Making *The Memo Book* had to do with using artistic means to work through a crisis. In my eyes, the intensity of this experience made my earlier works seem like practice jumps.

MacDonald: I understand that *Aus der Ferne—The Memo Book* began as a portrait of a lover who had died.

Müller: Yes, it was a response to the traumatic experience of the death of my former lover Mike, who had been suffering from AIDS. It's based on a short home movie, where you see my friend standing under a chandelier that he bought shortly before his death. I shot and collected other visual material that would go with this home movie. At the beginning, I had an actor play my role in this private drama, mainly because I was too cowardly to expose myself. This decision quickly proved to be a mistake. I feel very uncomfortable in front of the camera, and my inhibition is very obvious in my performance; nonetheless, it was important to me that I appear in person in this film.

Through its diaristic intimacy the film attempts to overcome the distance that death creates between the dead and the living. The film was an open-ended project, spontaneous and intuitive, made with a handheld Super-8 camera, without the help of a team. During filming, there was no self-censorship and very little analytical reflection on my part. Everything that seemed to be even slightly connected with this experience of death was filmed. Including interruptions and new beginnings, the process of shooting the material lasted many months.

It was during the editing process that I first began to deliberately reconstruct my experiences of the past, as if it all belonged to a diary—a memo book—that had never been written. So the film combines the immediacy of a diary with the analytical distance that comes from reflecting upon an autobiographical project. Originally, I focused on remembering Mike, but over time the film turned into a confrontation of myself. In one sequence featuring the imaginary resurrection of my dead friend, inspired by a photograph by Duane Michaels, I visit myself in the hospital—I am the patient *and* the visitor, which reflects my fear that I, too, might have been infected. Ultimately, the film follows a journey: my retreat from the world and eventual return to it.

The Memo Book had lasting influence on my later films. I have often used modifications of its combination of original and appropriated material. Eight years later, I worked again on the theme of suffering from a lethal disease, in *Pensão Globo*—this time from the perspective of a man preparing for his own death. I revisited sites where *The Memo Book* had been filmed, including the artificial paradise of the old botanical garden in Lisbon.

MacDonald: The hand processing in *Aus der Ferne—The Memo Book* creates a variety of effects, including kinds of damage to the "skin" of the film that seem to function as a metaphor for the body undergoing the ravages of AIDS, and simultaneously, for the spirit suffering the loss of the loved one.

In the United States, hand processing has become, for some filmmakers, an act of defiance, a resistance to industrial cinema.

Müller: Even the apparently liberated avant-garde cinema reveals repetitive drives and orthodoxies, a petrified code. These days, hand processing is often denigrated to the status of worn-out trademark, a kind of experimental habit (filmmakers such as Phil Solomon and Jürgen Reble, and their admirable, autonomous work, are exceptions). I think that the individualistic, personal video work of older artists such as Robert Frank or George

Kuchar shows a greater sense of modernity than much of the work by younger filmmakers, whose materialist films strain to maintain the obsolete hierarchy between high and low art.

In my work, it often seems to me as if particular themes suggest their own stylistic means. In films like *Aus der Ferne—The Memo Book* and *Sleepy Haven,* which are about decay and the metamorphosis of the physical, it made sense to emphasize the film material. *The Memo Book* was created with the full participation of my entire body. A large part of the film material literally went through my hands, frame by frame, as I processed the footage. Moreover, even the material that I appropriated often refers to my body: for instance, when my legs move like a wipe in front of the TV monitor.

In one shot, Kathryn Grayson moves across a background projection, an orgy of flaming, Technicolor-red evening skies. Her catchy message, "There's beauty everywhere for everyone to share," written in German subtitles across the picture, was an express invitation to me to borrow her film. The process of accumulating borrowed images, as well as one's own, produces alternating currents. Films oppose each other, look at each other, interact with each other. Simply placing the appropriated images next to my own images recodes them: in the context of my project, Fred Astaire and Gene Kelly dance across the sky like a pair of homosexual lovers lost to the world.

In *The Memo Book,* the found footage integrates my introspection into a collective world of images. Creating a hybrid form allows you to recognize yourself in the stranger—and the stranger in what is supposedly yourself, as well. The appropriated material forces my own images to show what lies latent in them: drama, hysteria, pathos, sentiment. Another approach might have been to contrast the opulent production values and elegant style of the borrowed films with the bare-bones conditions I worked with. Instead, I level the obvious difference between the glossy style of the appropriated material and my rough-grained Super-8 aesthetics by embedding the citations within my own imagery. Although most of the found footage was produced by a film industry remote from my own reality, working on this film made it clear to me how strongly my own emotional world is affected by these media-transmitted products, no matter how toxic they might be. And the long period of time it took to produce *Aus der Ferne,* which included a process of distancing myself from the material, made it possible to see my own creations as if they were found footage.

MacDonald: About the title: it is half German (*Aus der Ferne*/from far away) and half English.

Müller: Many of my films feature voice-overs in different languages. I think this corresponds to the heterogeneous, multilayered textures of the images. Just as it is impossible to have *one* valid image, it is also impossible to use only *one* language. That also means that the audience will not be able to understand some of what is said or read. *Aus der Ferne—The Memo Book* is intended to overwhelm the audience's ability to receive. What remains is a territory full of notions, suppositions, as well as a prelingual, subconscious comprehension that avoids being swallowed by the intellect.

MacDonald: I see *Sleepy Haven* as a paean to the idea of severing ties with the conventional and moving toward the romantic and exotic. Now that homosexuality is increasingly normalized, or at least has ceased to be shocking for many people, the risk and excitement of following one's hunger for other men that characterized the coming of age of gay men of earlier generations is disappearing—going the way of those old ocean liners (or so I would assume).

Müller: Sleepy Haven developed from my readings of various late nineteenth-century "sea novels"—texts by Herman Melville and Joseph Conrad, for example. Descriptions of the ocean, its boundlessness and dark depths, as well as the lives of the men on board, fascinated me. There's a cornucopia of interesting subtexts in these novels: many metaphors for the body, many sexual connotations. The sea is described with a mixture of fear and desire; even its dangers have something seductive about them, although they might cost you your life. The all-male society of sailors replaces the laws of the bourgeois world with its own code. I draw references between this world of motifs and a type of physicality and sexuality that, I hope, avoids being clearly defined and generates something new, something not yet named.

MacDonald: It's striking how full of film history your work is. Obviously, *Home Stories* is a riff on certain revealing gestures within commercial Hollywood cinema, but *Sleepy Haven,* too, seems full of earlier films. Sometimes it's as if characters from both Genet's *Un chant d'amour* and Anger's *Fireworks* have gotten together to collaborate with you! Also, I'm reminded of Tom Chomont's *Oblivion* [1969].

Müller: Here, I myself am just a dwarf sitting on the shoulders of giants. Anger's *Fireworks* and Genet's *Un chant d'amour were* influential. The exhaled smoke and the bare chest torn apart are direct references to these films, which have maintained a subversive energy that one can seek in vain in today's gay cinema. And Chomont's *Jabbok* [1967] was important, too. It's amazing that, even nowadays, in a time when homosexuality has supposedly been "normalized," a filmmaker like Tom Chomont is completely marginalized, an outcast: even the gay festivals don't show his films.

Today's gay culture is no longer about the heady freedom of "coming out," but about the normative power of "coming in," of joining the mainstream of consumerism and patterned models of identity. Lots of gay film festivals serve this market, adapting the lies of Hollywood for a homosexual public. Without the massive support of gay audiences, Hollywood would have gone into a massive crisis a long time ago—which is astonishing and upsetting, especially when you read Vito Russo's account of how Hollywood (with the help of many gays) in a brutal, ultrareactionary way, negated, caricatured, and discriminated against homosexuality for decades [see Russo's *The Celluloid Closet* (New York: Harper, 1991)].

For me, *Sleepy Haven* was a chance to work with the common clichés of gay iconography, and at the same time to give some space to the desire for something else, a physicality and sexual identity that rejects the norm and even avoids being named. Inspired by a Foucault quote about the ability of film to let the body bloom, to bud, to celebrate the smallest possibilities of its tiniest fragments in close-ups, the bodies in *Sleepy Haven* have an ambivalent, hybrid quality. This is also expressed through the use of solarization, the simultaneity of positive and negative, which creates a sense of a feverish, transitory condition. The physical armor breaks up, just like the emulsion on hand-processed material always breaks up; the tattoo of a phallus is scraped off, as if someone were shedding his skin; when arms uncross, female breasts are revealed. The way that the men in *Sleepy Haven* touch their bodies has something autoerotic about it, and something autoaggressive, too. The bodies and the ships, anchored in the harbor, slumber—yet it is a restless sleep.

This is interrupted by moments of self-discipline, of suppressing and overcoming the subconscious, as expressed in the image of the tightrope walker balancing above the tumultuous waters of Niagara Falls.

MacDonald: Could you tell me something about the texts we hear (or almost hear) and see?

Müller: The literary texts mentioned earlier are cited in the voice-over. However, they are atomized into tiny units and reassembled to form new units—like the book in the film, which disintegrates underwater. As its pages dissolve, they briefly generate new texts. The vocal texts are mixed so that the voice takes on an intangible quality; they fade in and out—like the wave-shaped, visual fade-ins and fade-outs—existing on the edge of incomprehensibility. In *Sleepy Haven,* as in many of my films, the texts are treated similarly to the ways the images are handled. Basically, I favor using language in a nonauthoritarian manner, which does not ascribe one particular meaning to the ambiguous image.

MacDonald: Is all the imagery of ships found footage?

Müller: I wanted to take my own material and the found footage and associate them as closely as possible, in order to blur the distinction between them. I had access to a large pool of maritime motifs from very different sources. And many of my own images reconstruct motifs from other films. My material and that of others are densely woven together; the image of cloth tearing appears as one of the film's visual motifs.

Dissolving book in Matthias Müller's *Sleepy Haven* (1993). Courtesy Matthias Müller.

MacDonald: According to your vita, you began teaching in 1994, but *Home Stories* seems a film that might come out of teaching film history; it offers a way of seeing the typical gestures of industrial cinema and understanding their gender implications.

Müller: My original idea for the film was to feature only Lana Turner, in a number of different roles. I was primarily interested in the mechanical style of her acting, which always seemed to make the hidden machinery behind the Hollywood melodrama obvious. Even her performances of nervous breakdowns seem to be controlled to an extreme. These kinds of mannerisms lead to a kind of ironic distancing, at least on the part of today's audiences. This doesn't put a stop to my pleasure or admiration. I see Lana Turner as the prototype of the Hollywood star without an identity of her own.

Years ago, I discovered a collection of old movie magazine covers in a memorabilia shop in Hollywood. They showed Lana at various stages of her career and revealed her chameleon-like ability to transform. Depending on the taste of the times, she was transformed to resemble Veronica Lake, Rita Hayworth, or Ava Gardner, all of whom were "ladies with an attitude." Ultimately, Lana Turner's "attitude" was always cleverly borrowed from others.

In researching materials for *Home Stories,* I realized that Turner's exaggerated style mirrors the acting styles of other Hollywood actresses, and at that moment the door opened for the rest of the cast. The central idea was to meld different characters into one role. Because American genre films made during the first two postwar decades were produced under rigid production conditions, with strict codes of representation and rigorous censorship, the material turned out to be astoundingly compatible, some of it almost congruent. That made my job as editor very easy.

MacDonald: Am I correct that the entire film was recorded off television? Would you rather have used film excerpts, or is the television-ness of the imagery one of the "home stories"?

Müller: The film uses shots that were elaborately produced for the big screen. However, I'm only familiar with them from television: that is, incredibly shrunken. The shabby aesthetics of my film, which are far from the original glamour, are supposed to say something about the path that brought these images to me. At the same time, I wanted to bring them back to the screen but in an altered, damaged form—as if it's not insolent enough to degrade the leading ladies by making them my puppets!

MacDonald: Some of the excerpts you use are generic, unrecognizable, and others are very familiar (the shots from *The Birds* and other Hitchcock films). Were you choosing specific films that were interesting for you, or simply looking for particular gestures wherever you found them?

Müller: Unlike my later found-footage films, *Home Stories* was the result of almost amazingly careless research. I worked with the material that I knew, with what I had in my own archive. Today, I have a much larger collection of genre films and am thinking about an expanded, more nervous, almost flickering *Home Stories Revisited.*

The *Bedroom* segment of *Phoenix Tapes* was a second chance to formulate the theme of *Home Stories* in a different, and more precise, way.

MacDonald: I assume you see industrial cinema—at least the industrial cinema of a certain period—as a form of propaganda that confirms women's entrapment within strictly defined social and class roles by making entertainment out of their fear and vulnerability, and by implicitly teaching women that being afraid *is* their birthright.

And yet, there is also considerable humor in *Home Stories*—an implicit satire of how seriously film audiences took these films and how seriously these films took themselves.

Müller: I *am* able to enjoy the films that I reduce to an arsenal of clichéd moments—and I'm not talking about a shameful, stubborn, guilty pleasure. In his great films, Douglas Sirk showed us that the American home is a claustrophobic place, a women's prison. As a homosexual, I have a special relationship to the suffering of his female protagonists in a restrictive, normative society, but I also envy these female characters their privilege of being able to live out their emotions uninhibitedly on the domestic stage, through their large, expansive gestures. In this sense, even though their fates are distant from my own reality, these figures still invite me to identify with them. To quote the last line of Frank O'Hara's wonderful "Poem" ["Poem (Lana Turner has collapsed!)," 1962]: "oh Lana Turner we love you get up."

MacDonald: *Final Cut* includes a number of images that reappear in *Alpsee:* the blue curtain, the milk that overflows, and the woman in the lake. These images seem particularly memorable for you—emblems of your childhood and youth.

Were you an only child?

Müller: Yes, I'm an only child. My father died when I was as old as the boy in *Alpsee.* His home movies were a way to get to know him later, from a distance of many years.

MacDonald: Alpsee is very powerful for me, partly because I feel as if this is *my* childhood: I was born in 1942 and during the early fifties was about the same age as your protagonist, so the period feel of the piece, even the period feel of the mother-son relationship, seems very familiar.

How fully *is Alpsee* autobiographical? My guess is that, as in Hemingway's Nick Adams stories, there are many autobiographical elements, but that the piece is a fiction—a fiction focusing on the general issue of mother and son in a certain time and place, and on the sources of creativity.

Müller: That is completely correct: the film contains particular autobiographical aspects, yet its perspective is expanded into an extremely stylized "period piece" that reflects the spirit and atmosphere of a particular time that had a great deal of influence on me personally. The props typical to the period and the found-footage sequences serve to embed the individual in the collective memory of a certain generation.

MacDonald: Brakhage talks about the boredom of childhood and how it leads, at times, to intense perception [see *A Critical Cinema 4,* 86]. In *Alpsee,* the boy's boredom, the way he hangs around the house, seems to produce not only fantasies—like the milk that doesn't stop pouring and the spaceman imagery—but a kind of creative sensibility: those images of the milk flowing over the table and along the floor become abstract paintings that play perspectival tricks on the viewer's eye. To what extent are you meaning to track the origins of an artistic sensibility?

Müller: I remember that, as a child, I spent hours making film sets with paper dolls for films that were never shot. Imagination and creativity are ways of escaping from a reality marred by a lack of fantasy. His specific perception allows the boy in *Alpsee* to leave his hermetic, claustrophobic home situation. It opens doors, connects him with organic growth, with the expanse of the sky, even with the boundlessness of the universe. Real

Boy and mother in Matthias Müller's *Alpsee* (1994). Courtesy Matthias Müller.

proportions are inverted: a glass of milk floods the house, time expands or contracts, a potted plant mutates into a mammoth tree. Many of the motifs, however, represent the boy's dependency on the life-support system that we call "mother": the astronaut floating weightless in space is connected to the "mother ship" with a tether resembling an umbilical cord; mother's milk is the substance that ensures the survival of the infant.

MacDonald: I have never seen an avant-garde film with a more impressive sense of visual and sound design. *Alpsee* would be powerful for most any audience, including much more conventional audiences than most avant-garde filmmakers aim for. Do you storyboard your films?

Müller: Alpsee is different from all of my other films because it *is* based on a carefully detailed concept and a storyboard. The film tells of a kind of social control that is meant to be expressed in an aesthetic form that must be as controlled as possible, almost like a paralysis. The film was conceived as a stringent, strange ritual.

MacDonald: As you are conceptualizing a project, do you think about color?

Müller: Sometimes the color scheme is one of the last things to materialize; but in *Alpsee,* everything was planned early. Here, the idea of reducing the colors to a barely varied palette of primary hues was an attempt to make the world of the film even smaller. At the beginning, the boy appears from behind a bright blue curtain, and when I blend this curtain into the bright blue dress of the mother, it is as if the boy is born onstage, from the folds of this dress. Recurring colors bring things closer together. The images in *Alpsee* are supposed to have something emblematic about them. They portray a world unto itself, and the color was a means of achieving this. Fundamentally speaking, concentrated color design helps a short film—by nature a fragile thing—achieve a more solid structure.

MacDonald: Are the wedding images at the beginning of *Alpsee,* and the image of the woman in the lake at the end, from your family home movies?

Müller: Both scenes were taken from 8mm home movies that my father filmed in the early sixties. The final image shows my mother in a vacation movie, which already had the title "Alpsee" in 1964. On the one hand, the title refers to the place where the film was made, a lake in the Alps. On the other hand, you can hear the word *Alptraum* in it—the German word for "nightmare."

MacDonald: Of course, *Alpsee* does have a surreal feel, but for me the overall impression of the film is of a kind of lovely nostalgia, very similar to Bruce Conner's *Valse Triste* [1977].

Müller: I like this comparison; in fact, *Valse Triste* and *Take the 5:10 to Dreamland* [1976] really inspired me as I was working on *Alpsee.* Of all avant-garde filmmakers, there is no one whose work I am more familiar with than Bruce Conner's, which has had lasting influence on me. I intended to capture the melancholy, dreamy atmosphere of those Conner films in *Alpsee*.

I also see funny moments in *Alpsee*: for instance, in a cascade of found footage that depicts mothers and sons hugging and kissing each other in an almost libidinous manner. This drastic exaggeration is continued in *Why Don't You Love Me?*, the mother-son segment of *Phoenix Tapes*.

MacDonald: The closing of the drawers, the shutting off of the TV showing the open-heart surgery, and other details confirm the consistent, thorough repression of so much bourgeois life. I would guess that *Alpsee* is also a nod to Douglas Sirk.

Müller: Imitation of Life [1959] has been my favorite film for a long time; its title song was even briefly quoted in the voice-over of *Aus der Ferne*. I really admire the lush production values of Sirk's American films, their sick beauty: everything rises urgently to the surface, where it seems about to collapse. I also like these movies' emotional power—which always stops short of going over the top—as well as the decisive criticism of America that is packed into Sirk's ur-American products.

MacDonald: Do you think of yourself as an "avant-garde filmmaker"? And how do you, or *do* you, conceive of the audiences for your work?

Müller: Many of my works test avant-garde procedures for their usefulness, and they attempt to simultaneously quote and renew these procedures. However, my work is far from the radical impetus of previous generations. There is also no aesthetic program, no dogma in my "impure" films. Their hybrid forms help my films and videos find their audience, and this audience does not have to have an academic background in order to access the work. The brevity and complexity of my films and videos have contributed to the fact that they have become quite visible outside of the closed circuit of the usual festivals: as cinema shorts, in art exhibitions, even on television. Currently, their distribution and sales are in the hands of five distributors and five galleries, so that my work is seen in the art world as well as in the cinema world.

MacDonald: Pensão Globo, like *Alpsee*, is a narrative with moments of fantasy. In fact, since the one film has a fantasy montage of milk pouring and pouring, and the other includes a fantasy montage of blood dripping, then flowing from a shaving accident, I wonder if you conceived *Pensão Globo* as a kind of companion piece to *Alpsee*.

Müller: I like the idea of passing certain motifs from one film to another, and sometimes actively pursue the idea. Often this is not planned, though, and happens on a subconscious, intuitive level, as is the case of the sequences from *Alpsee* and *Pensão Globo* you mention. This allows different works to practically become one, shows my fundamental interest in connective links and, at the same time, how my projects are generated one after the other in a practically organic way: one gives birth to the next. Some projects are preceded by preliminary studies—for instance, *Breeze* [2000] is a sketch for *Phantom* [2001]; others are "afterbirths," like *Scattering Stars,* which is an echo, a paraphrasing, of *Sleepy Haven.*

Scattering Stars takes the structure of the pornographic film, which works like mad to get to the salvation of the cum shot, and turns it upside down. The film starts with a metaphor for orgasm, which is followed by the bodies in afterglow. Like *Sleepy Haven,* from which it borrows a few images, *Scattering Stars* was filmed on Russian Super-8 material, whose emulsion disintegrated during the developing process; it came off completely from the film in some places. I liked the unpredictability, the risk, of working with it.

MacDonald: The sound track of *Pensão Globo* is particularly strong—though the sound tracks Dirk Schaefer does for you are consistently impressive. Could you talk a bit about the nature of your collaboration?

Müller: I worked continuously with Dirk between 1985 and 1998, and most recently we worked together on *Album.* We got to know each other in the early 1980s, when he was producing home recordings with low-tech equipment, using a lot of sampling. I thought this corresponded to my work with Super-8 and found footage.

Dirk first becomes directly involved with the film when it's in final cut. Up to that point, sound is practically irrelevant for me—though when I'm editing, I do try to give the images a musical quality. During the relatively long period of time that I spend working on a concept, and filming and editing, I usually develop a clear idea of what the sound track should be like. I collect sounds and make recordings.

For *Pensão Globo,* I made sound recordings in Lisbon and bought an old fado by Amalia Rodriguez. Dirk sampled a tiny fragment of it and turned it into the musical leitmotif of the sound track. Everything else occurs as Dirk and I are working together, generally over a period of many weeks. He knows how to develop very sensitive and creative sound strategies, which correspond to the aesthetic methods I work with to produce my images.

MacDonald: The decision to superimpose two, and sometimes more, images of the events of *Pensão Globo* creates a number of effects: it suggests the protagonist's difficulty in dealing with his disease, the struggle to keep himself together; it suggests his engagement with past and present at the same time; and it suggests that this trip to Lisbon is one of a series of such trips.

Müller: At the end of the film, the protagonist says to himself, "Sometimes it's like you're already gone, become a ghost of yourself." The thing that makes AIDS different from many other fatal diseases is the completely unpredictable path it takes. That is why the images in *Pensão Globo* are not static but undergo feverish metamorphoses. There is no arrival on this journey, just an endless series of transitions.

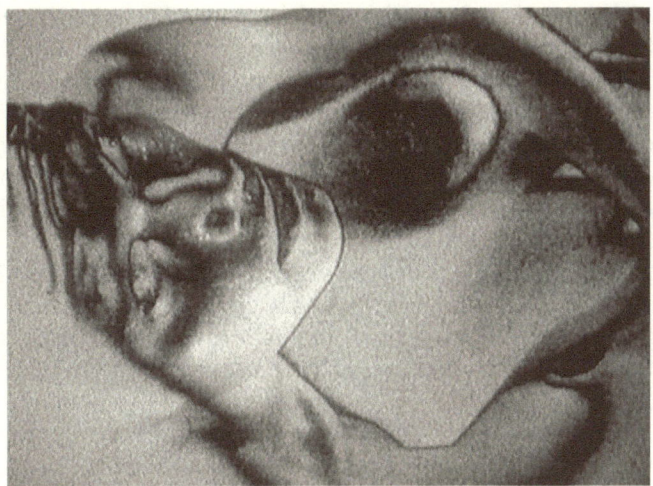

From Matthias Müller's *Scattering Stars* (1994). Courtesy Matthias Müller.

That is also why we filmed in Lisbon, which is a city that has had to continually reinvent itself after surviving many catastrophes. It's also a place where many have begun their journeys toward an uncertain future; it's like a harbor of exiles.

MacDonald: The young man followed by the protagonist looks enough like him to create a sense that he is not just fantasizing or remembering earlier moments of pursuit, but that he is chasing something of his own former self, something of the freedom he experienced before AIDS became his reality.

Müller: I wanted to keep this character as ambiguous as possible. He is clothed in gleaming white, almost like a figure of light, an angel. What starts out as cruising (and recalls Aschenbach's pursuit of the young Tadzio in *Death in Venice*) is ultimately nothing more than another passage: a regression, perhaps, into an earlier condition, a transition into the paradisiacal botanical garden, where the protagonist finds himself alone, surrounded by plants.

MacDonald: The montage near the end, where the protagonist's fondling his body is interspersed with the cacti and other plants, is erotic but also ambiguous.

Müller: Since I myself am not infected, I read some AIDS diaries as part of my research, including those by Wolfgang Max Faust, Hervé Guibert, and Derek Jarman. The imagery in *Pensão Globo* developed from some of the astonishingly similar things in these texts. For instance, facing death, all of the authors mentioned the wish to be surrounded by vegetable growth—a desire for an almost symbiotic melding with the plant, which will survive. The names engraved in the agave leaves, which I found in the Jardim Bôtanico, are a wonderful expression of this.

At the same time, these plants are extremely hardy; agave can survive under the worst conditions, since they can retain fluid over a long period of time. Seen this way, the motif is a counterpart to the flowing bodily fluids that we see in the razor scene.

MacDonald: Cinema has usually worked from the novel. *Pensão Globo* reminds me of a great short story; it's a pleasure to see so much condensed into a short space. Fifteen minutes seems to be a particularly congenial length for you. Do you determine approximate length as you're conceiving a project?

Müller: The German film bureaucracy makes some of the decisions for you. Since many of my films from the 1990s were made with state financing, I had to stick to the rules and not let the films go over the official demarcation line of fifteen minutes. There are no sensible reasons for this, but I've learned to accept this obligatory framework as something appropriate for my work, and to understand this forced condensation as an opportunity to really get to the point.

MacDonald: Vacancy is a kind of conceptual sci-fi film, very evocative of Chris Marker's *La jetée.*

Müller: In 1997, I had a showing in the Teatro Nacional, an Oscar Niemeyer building in the historical center of Brasília, the *plano piloto.* I was totally fascinated by the artificial character of this place, by its monumentality, and by the presumption of this totalized work of urban art. When I realized that the city, which is preserved in its original state, is just a bit older than I am—a place planned for my generation—I became interested in using Brasília as a location. From the start, I was not interested in an orthodox, documentary-style portrait of a city but, instead, in a subjective point of view that would express the fascinating and disconcerting quality of the place.

The stagnation and sobriety articulated in the Brasília of 1997 seemed to be simultaneous with a personal creative crisis I was undergoing, a kind of filmmaker's block. I didn't want to ignore this crisis but was determined to turn it into a theme and connect it with the story of the extinguished vision of Brasília. During the research prior to my returning to Brazil, a year later, to make my film, I stumbled across an unedited 16mm amateur travelogue documenting the inaugural ceremonies in Brasília in April 1960. The filmmaker, by then an old lady of eighty-five, allowed me to integrate sections of her material into my project, so that *Vacancy* features two periods of time, separated by four decades, which seem to blend almost seamlessly.

My interest in modernist projects of the early 1960s also extended to literature, music, and dramatic films. In the sound track, we quote, among other things, short fragments of a New Music work for orchestra and urban sounds taken from an early Antonioni film.

MacDonald: You've used Mike Hoolboom as a narrator more than once. I've always found his monologues quite remarkable—and his voice adds a great deal to your films. Mike also appears as one of the young sailors in *Sleepy Haven.*

Müller: Mike's contributions to *Pensão Globo* and *Beacon* are incredibly important for the films. Since Mike is HIV positive, he was a close consultant on *Pensão Globo.* He allowed me to use parts of his private journals for the voice-over. At the time, he was being treated at the Rosedale Clinic in Toronto, whose business cards are in the suitcase of my protagonist in *Pensão Globo*—a small, hidden tribute to the admirable courage and energy with which Mike faces his illness, as well as to the completely selfless support that he gives to many other filmmakers.

MacDonald: Phoenix Tapes was made for a show at the Oxford Museum of Modern Art [this show, Notorious—Alfred Hitchcock and Contemporary Art, developed by the Museum of Modern Art, Oxford, toured the world in 1999]. Of commercial filmmakers, Hitchcock seems especially important to you.

Müller: Both Christoph and I have always been strongly impressed by Hitchcock's visual intelligence, and the economy as well as the extravagance of his means. Even in his most modest films, there are moments of an especially *visual* pleasure, and sometimes boldly experimental ideas. His influence and authority are challenging; you can either accept him as a sort of überfather or rebel against him—but you cannot ignore him.

As a well-established brand, "Hitchcock" has often been misused in order to sell products of mediocre decadence. Having grown up with an enormous number of shallow genre movies that allegedly follow in Hitchcock's footsteps, working with the originals was as much of a challenge for us as it was a privilege. In retrospect, we can say that our appreciation of and respect for the vitality, complexity, and abundance of Hitchcock's work have considerably increased as a result of our "collaboration" with him.

MacDonald: Each individual section of *Phoenix Tapes* focuses on a different set of particular Hitchcock gestures, and the series of pieces offers a tour through distinctive elements of Hitchcock's films. How fully did you and Christoph think of *Phoenix Tapes* as a single work?

Müller: At the beginning of the project, we established themes that we wanted to treat in individual segments. With these themes in mind, we watched the forty films and recorded a detailed protocol of them. The six chapters were always planned as autonomous segments, which would be shown in the exhibition as individual works; and we always considered what the context of these works in the larger Notorious show would be.

In *Rutland,* for example, we wanted to move into Hitchcock through his location shots, in a sort of geographic way; logically, this work was positioned at the beginning of *Phoenix Tapes* and corresponded to *Scottie's Bedroom,* David Reed's contribution to Notorious. Then we wanted to jump from the total picture to the close-up: *Burden of Proof* ran as an installation, next to photographs by John Baldessari, which also monumentalized objects. *Bedroom* was part of a chamber of horrors, along with staged photographs of rape victims by Cindy Sherman.

It was only later, when festival invitations started arriving, that we thought about *Phoenix Tapes* as a linear, single-channel presentation.

MacDonald: *Why Don't You Love Me?* is the most powerful section for me. It brings up the issue of the Mother, which has been a motif in your filmmaking. How do you relate to Hitchcock's often troubling depiction of mothers?

Müller: At the beginning *Why Don't You Love Me?* was planned as a freak show in which we would display Hitchcock's villains and psychopaths—like a cabinet of curios. As we watched the films, we got the idea of treating the complicity of the mothers. *Why Don't You Love Me?* gave us the chance to work with Hitchcock's puns, his sarcasm, his sharp exaggeration. Our interventions into the original material are rude; the editing is naughty, and the jokes drastic. We didn't want to blame Mommy for all the evil in the world, but rather, to ironically undermine Hitchcock's sometimes one-sided, predictable accusations of blame. The psychiatrist's line in *Psycho* [1960], "Matricide is a crime that is most unbearable for the son who commits it," desperately needs correcting: Mother's murder is demonstrably *most* unbearable for *mother herself!*

MacDonald: I'm not sure I understand the title of *Necrologue.*

Müller: Necrologue shows Ingrid Bergman in *Under Capricorn* [1949]. By the way, Jack Cardiff, the cinematographer, saw *Necrologue* and was pleased with our late interest in this largely ignored film. In *Under Capricorn,* Bergman is being poisoned slowly (as she is in *Notorious* as well); in *Necrologue,* it seems as if she is in a trance, in a state between apathy and agony. On one hand, this motif is typical for Hitchcock's presentation of dazed, weakened, and defenseless women, but this version, with its slightly melodramatic lighting, has a strange ambiguity and unexpected tenderness: the gaze is full of compassion. After *Bedroom,* which ends with a dramatic exclamation point, showing a brutal rape and strangulation, the frozen moment of *Necrologue* shows that there is no salvation: the images of death continue on into eternity.

MacDonald: My seeing *nebel* at the New York Film Festival a couple of years ago ["Views from the Avant-Garde," programmed in recent years by Mark McElhattan and Gavin Smith, is shown as a sidebar to the New York Film Festival each fall] triggered my interest in interviewing you. I found the film stunning, and a rare instance where a filmmaker has communicated something of a poet's work so that *both* the poetry *and* the film are memorable.

Müller: In *nebel,* I appropriated, for the first time, a complete work by another artist and was aware of the problems involved in this decision.

What became *nebel* was originally supposed to be a contribution to an episodic film about Jandl's work, containing different filmmakers' contributions. Unfortunately, the project fell through, and my film was the only one that got made. It was shown for the first time at the opening program of the Vienna Film Festival shortly after Jandl's death. By the way, Jandl was all for the project.

Like *Phoenix Tapes,* my Jandl film allowed me to dive into the extensive oeuvre of another artist and then react to it in my own way. I read Jandl's work with great curiosity and growing excitement. I quickly realized that even considering a "film version" of some of the poems was forbidding. All the problems involved in making film versions of literature are very evident in the case of Jandl. His way of structuring texts is generally far too unique to adequately translate into cinematic language.

But this was not the case with his lesser-known 1977 cycle, *gedichte an die kindheit (poems to childhood)*. As I read these poems, my own images were immediately released, and I hoped to use a collage of images taken from disparate sources to create a correspondence with the heterogeneous structure of his texts. Jandl's poems stand very well on their own: they do not need to be transferred to another medium; and my respect for Jandl prevented me from manipulating his texts—I even used the original chapter structure of this cycle of poems.

In cinema, the moving picture is more seductive, more suggestive, and ultimately stronger than the spoken word. In the case of *nebel,* this led to various decisions. I tried to hold back the collector and producer of images in me, in order to draw attention to the words through just a few repeated motifs. Considering the voluptuous world of images in my previous films, this was an exciting challenge. I never intended to defy the words, to take flight from them. On the contrary, I was concerned with creating a close relationship with them, without devoting myself to mere illustration. Jandl's language is not preoccupied with the description of things; it is simultaneously plain and highly synthetic, full of contradictions and enigmatic ambiguities. Only a few other poets have demonstrated the problems, the limits, and the presumptuousness of language as Jandl has.

The *gedichte an die kindheit* are full of breaks in style; erudite speech and "childlike" language not only encounter each other but dovetail. This creates comic moments. I reacted to the heterogeneity of the text with a visual patchwork made up of very different genres. Because I wanted to prevent the images from being a carbon copy of the words, I maintain words and images on different levels in *nebel*. The editing creates an association: image and sound touch gently and fleetingly yet maintain their independence. When Jandl talks about the immortality of the soul, I show a banal scene from a vacation movie. I react to Jandl's lament on loneliness with the image of an old dog digging a hole in the sand, thus referring to other texts by Jandl in which he portrays himself as a poor dog.

Originally, Jandl himself was supposed to narrate, but because he was in bad health, I had to find someone else to do the voice-over, an experienced actor about the same age as Jandl. Of course, this ultimately liberated me from the "authorizing" voice of the poet.

Aside from the license I took, it's possible to see stylistic similarities between Jandl's process and mine. In using rhymes at the ends of lines, Jandl picks up on elements of traditional poetry, and this in turn reminds me of the editing in *Home Stories*, which features endless cascades of similar, rhyming motifs. In addition, the way he plays through all kinds of linguistic possibilities, all the way to the limits of incomprehensibility, also corresponds to images in my work, which often go through several generations of material until they reach the threshold of abstraction. Jandl's evocation of a childlike way of experiencing things from the perspective of a grown, aging man also has its correspondences in my work. All of it is strongly marked, on one hand, by the desire to hold on to something, but on the other, by the understanding that it is impossible to keep things, situations, moments.

MacDonald: Your imagery relates to the poems and to Ernst-August Schepmann's narration in a wide variety of ways, which gives the film its own complexity. Seeing the film as a non-German speaker, I *hear* Schepmann's tonality—which is wonderful—*and* I read the poems as texts in space (something a German wouldn't experience in quite the same way).

Müller: I had an English translation of the poems done by Peter Waugh, a poet and translator based in Vienna who is very familiar with Jandl's work. He succeeded in producing a congenial English adaptation of the text (even including rhymes when there are rhymes in the German original). The film exists in two versions: a subtitled one for international audiences and a version without subtitles for German-speaking audiences.

MacDonald: nebel offers another sense of childhood from the one offered in *Alpsee.*

Müller: Although we have all been through it, we really know almost nothing about childhood, even though our memories of it mark our present existence. For Jandl, childhood counts as one of the "distant things" covered by a veil of mist. Because it is over, and we can no longer see it, we can allow the cinema to show it to us, continue it for us; its happiness and fears are once again present. Jandl's words and my images are fed by the nocturnal shadows on the child's bedroom ceiling.

Jandl uses the word "Leben" (life) as a palindrome: read backward, it says "nebel" (fog). "I dearly hoped this was true," says Jandl to the notion that things can be reversed, that time and gravitation can be set aside. The promise of the cinema also comes from the magic of the zoetrope, which can turn in both directions. The ball in *nebel,* which my mother throws from an old home movie into the image, like the tears running upward in *Necrologue,* are pure images of yearning—but *cinematic* images of yearning, and therefore as synthetic as they are full of emotion.

MacDonald: Do you see the Jandl lines, "For every age of life he has / a certain way in which / he writes" as relating to your work? You began with Super-8mm, moved to 16mm, then to 35mm and Beta and digital.

Müller: nebel unites analog and digital video, regular 8 and Super-8, my own images and those appropriated from different contexts—from Hollywood to home movies—and translates all this material to 35mm. However, from my standpoint, cumbersome 35mm is *not* more "mature" than Super-8 or digital video. After all, my works have long consisted of a heterogeneous patchwork of various formats and systems. As I said earlier, the themes themselves suggest different media and technology; I gratefully take the recommendations and carry them out. There is no master plan for my choice of certain media or formats, though it generally amounts to "low-tech equals high fidelity."

Yesterday, I showed my students Robert Frank's video *The Present* [1996], a tape that proves that the overconcern of many artists with technique often stands in the way of their discovering more truthful, more moving images.

MacDonald: Were *Phantom, Container* [2001], *Pictures* [2002], and *Promises* [2003] made for art gallery exhibition? All four ask for a somewhat different kind of engagement from a theatrical film.

Müller: My breakthrough in the art world occurred over the period of about a year, starting in 1999, at the "Notorious" exhibition in Oxford, and continuing at the "European Biennial of Contemporary Art, Manifesta 3" in Ljubljana in 2000, to which Francesco Bonami had invited me. Immediately afterward, galleries offered to represent me, and I had my first solo shows.

Of course, a much larger audience can be reached over a weeks-long exhibition than at a single film festival showing. Furthermore, art critics acknowledge film and video in the context of art, whereas film critics generally ignore short film and media art festivals. More important to me, though, than wider visibility for my work is that in a gallery, other works whose content and form relate to my work surround it. This is only occasionally the case at a festival, where in the worst case, films collide with each other, since the only thing they have in common is the year of production. The gallery also allows my work to expand to include other media. In reusing motifs and techniques in various works, I can transform the individual works—particular films, videos, photographs—into a larger whole, something that is hindered when a single film or video is presented at a festival.

On the other hand, you can't make a gallery into a theater just by darkening the windows. The art world's increased interest in the moving picture cannot be seen as merely a liberation from the theater and its limited receptive conditions. Rather, each situation presents specific challenges. For example, the extremely slow series of stills in *Container* aims to capture the disrupted gaze of the viewer in a gallery, instead of (as in the cinema) demanding his continual attention. The calculated gaps in the viewer's concentration become part of the work.

When, through the laws of the art market, a moving picture is transformed into an object—a work of art issued in a limited edition—this transformation can seem an expression of bourgeois possessiveness. After twenty years of making "experimental films," though, I know they will never produce enough profit to secure my existence. Thus, there is no alternative *but* a gallery, which demands that works be sold as limited editions, at prices that correspond to comparable works in other artistic disciplines. According to my experience so far, when a collector buys one of my works, it is not so much an expression of "bourgeois possessiveness" as of a personal liking for a work.

MacDonald: You've worked as a curator. What particular works, or kinds of work, have been most interesting for you?

Müller: The festivals and touring programs I curated in the 1990s were closely connected to the interests I pursue in my own artistic work. Among other things, I've organized two found footage festivals and an autobiographical film festival. These kinds of events not only draw attention to and increase the value of marginalized sectors but also—and this is very self-serving!—help one's own position as a filmmaker, and, of course, they add to one's own pleasure.

In the past few years, I've concentrated on holding workshops in places where knowledge of experimental work is relatively limited. My intense encounters with filmmakers in China, Brazil, and India, for instance, and their refreshing treatment of my work, have often been more enriching than showing my work at the established avant-garde places like the Anthology Film Archives.

MacDonald: Christoph Girardet was your editor on *nebel,* but by *Man-*

ual you and he had begun an ongoing collaboration. Are you both involved in all facets of the work you do together?

Müller: Our collaboration on *Phoenix Tapes* in 1999 proved that we are able to work very well together in all stages of production. We share an interest in researching found footage, but we take thoroughly different stands toward it. Christoph, a video artist in his own right, usually works with more reduced material than I do. He had been working almost exclusively with digital technology, and so his technical abilities really enriched my work.

We work closely together in all phases, and on the same footing—we don't divide tasks according to skill. Basically, cooperative projects are less intuitive than individual projects: every idea, every decision is discussed, and this works very well for us.

MacDonald: In *Play,* you and Girardet continue the fascination with recycled cinema so obvious in your own earlier work. You seem particularly drawn to clusters of similar images—a way of considering the ritualistic dimension of all kinds of cinema?

Müller: Both *Home Stories* and *Play* reduce the system of cause and effect—stimulus and reaction—to representations of behavior whose origins remain unseen, hidden in the offscreen space. *Play* takes us out of the private world of the home to the public site of the cinema or theater auditorium. Whatever is happening onstage is reflected only in a chain of emotional reactions on the faces and in the gestures of the audience members. A series of analogous edits makes a collective event out of individual behavior, which undergoes various emotional stages. The narrative is moved from the stage to the auditorium, and the audience members become the actors in an unpredictable drama. When it's presented publicly, *Play* turns the screen into a mirror: a real audience sees itself in the staged audience on the screen.

MacDonald: In its original incarnation, much, if not all, of the imagery we see in *Manual* was meant to signify the arrival of miraculous new technologies that would save us from ourselves. But your film is a kind of dump, a media dump, like the old airplane graveyard outside of Tucson, where for years all the World War II and cold war planes were lined up, useless, mile after mile.

Müller: Even though *Manual* was commissioned by the Foundation for Art and Creative Technology in Liverpool, which is completely devoted to state-of-the-art media technology, we worked only with images of obsolete, out-of-date, dysfunctional technology—with *images* of machines whose sham quality seems almost amusing. The original material offered visions of a better life in the future; these are condensed, through repetition, to form a collage of unfulfilled promises. In this, the work is comparable to *Vacancy.*

The visual material for *Manual* comes from American sci-fi films and TV

Detail of audience in Christoph Girardet and Matthias Müller's *Play* (2003). Courtesy Matthias Müller.

series from the early 1960s—a specifically male genre, where men are reduced to their hands, which powerfully and decisively get things done by pushing buttons, operating controls, pulling levers, flicking switches. The results of these actions remain unseen. The world today faces its increasing complexity with a flood of instruction manuals, but our comprehension of what is launched by the press of a button remains very limited.

In *Manual,* the body becomes part of the machine; the machine expands into the body. The desire for complete control of the body is shown, through the images of medical equipment that seem to take over the body's functions. The mechanisms of these human machines are reflected in the forced, mechanical rhythm of the editing. This distanced portrayal of a masculine world is counteracted by Ava Gardner's highly emotional voice, taken from a melodrama, which speaks of boundless feeling and the readiness to sacrifice at all costs.

MacDonald: *Beacon* expresses and captures a state of mind, a kind of numbness that strikes me as, possibly, an aftershock of traumatic loss and, in a more general sense, of the passing of youth.

Müller: The tossing ocean and the mysterious phantom sea of *Sleepy Haven* have in fact turned into a quiet, almost leaden surface here. The slow-motion images of *Beacon* are marked by a kind of succinctness, and that *is*—I agree—an expression of getting older. Here, the wonderfully calm Cape Cod paintings by Edward Hopper were an inspiration, and so were the meditative seascapes of Hiroshi Sugimoto.

Most of the images are taken from both Christoph's and my personal archives—filmed during our travels, without any intent behind them. All the sites are close to the ocean, but various oceans are shown: the Irish Sea, the Baltic, the South China Sea, the Pacific. The way they are edited creates a new, imaginary place.

In order to avoid an illustrative text, we gave Mike Hoolboom a catalogue of key words and asked him to simply react with free associations.

MacDonald: *Mirror* is a stunning piece; I wish I could see it full-size! How did you get the opportunity to do a 35mm Cinemascope film?

Müller: Actually, the Cinemascope image of *Mirror* is constructed from two seamlessly edited digital video images. We filmed with two carefully positioned cameras, and their recordings, put together, resulted in a continuous image—Cinemascope for those who don't have the budget. The barely perceptible line in the middle of the image separates and unites the two halves at the same time.

This formal system seemed to us to be appropriate for the representation of an atmospheric image of an "in-between" place, the nameless sphere between belonging and isolation. We filmed in the small auditorium of an old concert hall in the city where I live, which we liked for its unique mixture of art deco elegance and a certain poverty and emptiness. Only the changing lights animate the frozen tableaux of *Mirror:* they alternately isolate and connect the characters. Each motif was filmed under many different kinds of lighting and then digitally processed in complicated postproduction work.

During the last six minutes of *L'eclisse* [*Eclipse,* 1962], Antonioni leaves his actors and allows the mysterious tension of the events to live through objects, spaces, and structures; in so doing, he sheds the narrow corset of the narrative. This sequence is pure experimental film and was, along with other moments in his work, very inspiring for *Mirror.*

MacDonald: The obvious allusion of the film is to Antonioni (the music and dialogue are taken from early Antonioni films), but when I thought of where else I had seen a film in which the flickering of light revealed stationary figures in different positions, I remembered Ernie Gehr's *Wait* [1967]. And—forgive me if this is a ridiculous stretch!—*then* I saw, or maybe wanted to see, the "mirror" referred to in your title not simply as the mirror *in* the imagery, *and* the off-kilter mirroring effect created by the division in your Cinemascope image, *but also* the way in which, in your film and video work through the years, commercial cinema and avant-garde cinema have functioned as off-kilter "mirrors" of one another.

Müller: That's a good thought. It's true that in my work, narrative cinema and experimental film do not have an antagonistic relationship; they are not enemy camps. Rather, they determine each other, comment upon each other, and influence each other. Perhaps one could refer to them as two hemispheres of one world. Fundamentally, my work is marked by an impulse to emphasize associations and commonalties, rather than to increase distance.

MacDonald: Angelika Richter suggests in her essay [in the catalogue *Album*] that in *Mirror* the motion picture has come to a standstill. Certainly Cinemascope was a technology devised to revive interest in an industry threatened by the arrival of television, and it worked for a time. Are you suggesting that you as a filmmaker, or theatrical media itself, is coming to a stop—as a result of the arrival of digital technologies and the increasing domestication and privatization of the experience of media?

Müller: No. In fact, I think *Mirror* proves the exact opposite. It's a film made with semiprofessional digital equipment, but it alludes to the classic format, the aesthetics, and the atmosphere of Antonioni's films. Ironically, this experiment could not have been carried out on film. We show *Mirror* in 35mm Cinemascope format in cinemas, as well as in double DVD projection in galleries. This dissolution of outdated limitations, supported by the keen interest of the art world in cinema, as well as by the destruction of the old hierarchies between film and video, point toward a future that I find very exciting.

I am far from cultural pessimism. The change from film to digital video was a necessary new impulse for my work, and also an important step in the direction of greater independence from bureaucratic financial backers and toward more artistic autonomy: with digital video, complete control over my work lies in my own hands. For a collector of images such as myself, the medium is optimal. Compared with the cost-intensive, highly complex medium of film, video is a democratic means of expression open to all. For me, it's a continuation of my work in Super-8 under better conditions, and anything but a termination of my love for cinema. The "standstill" of the moving picture in *Mirror* is simply a rejection of plot-oriented industrial cinema, which often attempts to hide its emptiness with superficial, purposeless activity.

MacDonald: Album seems a journey along your stream of consciousness; memories and impressions float by. Did you write the texts?

Müller: I did write the texts, but from time to time, I refer to and reformulate ideas by other authors; just as the visual motifs come from the archive of my own images, the words can be traced back to a file card box, in which I collect my own and appropriated texts. Some of them remind me of the situation in which the images were filmed; some of them create connections to moments I personally experienced last year. They circle around the process of remembering, of repeating and preserving, and the aftereffects of things past; they sketch moments, stimulate stories, but remain fragments, like individual lines from a journal.

MacDonald: The image of the plastic bag being blown by the wind recalls a controversy a few years ago—I don't know if it got beyond New York and the American avant-garde scene—about the "theft" of a similar image in a Nathaniel Dorsky film by the makers of *American Beauty* [1999]. Are you aware of this incident?

Müller: I was immediately aware of it during the moment of filming (which, by the way, was completely coincidental), and that shows how very much our perception is already influenced by media. However, this knowledge did not harm the magic of the moment. Maybe the plastic sheet that flew over the Bowery that night was playing a trick on me by reenacting a scene that it saw in the movies. Am I not allowed to film the sky because Brakhage already did? No roses because Baillie already used them in *All My Life* [1966]? What I see with my own eyes cannot be copyrighted. What would be left to film if everything in the public space were turned into private property? *Album* deals with imitation and difference, including the temporary charging of a moment or a visual phenomenon in the public space by a determinedly subjective meaning, and it is this personal reference that distinguishes me from both Dorsky and Sam Mendes. To use Cézanne's words, "Nothing is ever the same." In *Album,* the act of possessing a moment remains a fleeting one: ultimately, the images remain open and autonomous.

Of course, unscrupulous plagiarism exists everywhere. When Madonna misuses a Paradjanov motif in her "Bedtime Stories" video, she is stealing from an artist whose work has survived despite censorship, persecution, and arrest. Every act of appropriation gives rise to a moral question: Is this about exploration or exploitation? I avoid falling into the litany of those who call the mainstream's adaptation of avant-garde ideas fundamentally parasitical; the relationships are much more complex than they're normally considered. Critical work with found footage taken from industrial cinema is ultimately a more effective, lasting act of empowerment than clichéd complaints about greedy Big Brother. And, by the way, my work, like Dorsky's, has also been copied and exploited many times. I've learned to view this with composure, because I know that the true value of the work, its artistic integrity, can neither be stolen nor sold.

MacDonald: Near the end of *Album* your text refers to a scene in *Un chant d'amour*. Do you see the man's blowing smoke into the next cell as a metaphor for your filmmaking?

Müller: I didn't see it like that, but I like the idea. Basically, making motion pictures is about communication, a dialogue with oneself and others, sharing and talking about experiences, ultimately about creating community. If my work has the poetic, sensual quality of that wonderful scene in *Un chant d'amour,* then I can be happy.

Sharon Lockhart

Sharon Lockhart's films function within two different worlds. First, they are contributions to the history of critical cinema—inheritors, in particular, of the formalist-conceptualist tendency instigated during the 1960s and 1970s by such filmmakers as Michael Snow, Yoko Ono, Hollis Frampton, Ernie Gehr, Taka Iimura, J. J. Murphy, Morgan Fisher, and James Benning. Indeed, Lockhart counts Fisher and Benning among her mentors.

Like Benning, Lockhart engages place with a formalist rigor and with considerable wit. In *Teatro Amazonas* (1999), we are presented with a thirty-minute, 35mm shot of the opera house in Manaus, Brazil, made famous by Werner Herzog's *Fitzcarraldo* (1982), filmed from center stage. The opera house is full of people looking at the camera and listening to a chorus, invisible to us, singing a single, continuous chord that gradually, consistently lessens in volume as voices drop away, one by one. As the chorus grows more and more quiet, the sounds of the audience in the opera house and the sounds of the audience for Lockhart's film grow increasingly audible, until we have the sense that we are all in the same auditory space. Immediately following the shot of the audience, Lockhart provides rolling credits that appear to provide the name of each and every person visible in the preceding shot, as well as of every member of the chorus. *Teatro Amazonas* is a meditation on audience that creates an evocative intercultural space somewhere between Manaus and wherever the film is screened, and somewhere between history and film history.

Goshogaoka (1997) and *NŌ* (2003) are also engaged with place. *Goshogaoka* was shot in a school gymnasium in Japan, where a girls' basketball

Opera house and audience in Manaus, Brazil, in Sharon Lockhart's *Teatro Amazonas* (1999). Courtesy Blum and Poe Gallery.

team is doing drills; *NŌ* creates the illusion of a single, thirty-five-minute shot of two Japanese farmers spreading hay on a field. Like *Teatro Amazonas,* both films provide unusual conceptual experiences. As the girls perform their drills, we gradually realize that *these* drills are not their usual workout but something in between sport and dance, a form of choreography related to athletics but clearly designed specifically with this film in mind. Our sense of what these young girls are actually doing and their relationship to the filmmaking process gradually evolves, indeed, does not stop evolving until the credits, which indicate that the "costumes" were designed by Arai Miho, have finished rolling.

NŌ creates a similar experience. At first, the film seems a simple document of Japanese farmers at work as the mist in the lovely landscape behind them slowly clears. But gradually we notice, first, that they seem to be arranging the small piles of hay they are making, specifically in relation to the focal range of the 16mm camera; and later, that they are carefully using the hay to cover *only* that portion of the field revealed by the camera. The early sense of the camera's objective detachment from what is recorded is gradually transformed into a recognition that Lockhart and the farmers are col-

laborating on a work of art. On another level, *NŌ* is a landscape film that echoes dimensions of the history of landscape painting, though in this case, the painting paints itself: the rakes of the farmers are the brushes that transform the image. *NŌ* is particularly reminiscent of James Benning's films in its use of what may seem to be a single, unedited shot (actually there are two shots, though the subtle transition between them will be invisible to most viewers), and in the subtle complexity and mystery of the offscreen sounds.

Lockhart's films also function in a second aesthetic arena, one that offers a new perspective on the economic history of critical cinema. Lockhart is both filmmaker and photographer; and her work is managed by two galleries: Blum and Poe, in Santa Monica, and Barbara Gladstone, in New York City. As a gallery artist, Lockhart holds different assumptions about how her films will exist in the world than most of the critical filmmakers I have interviewed.

At a recent show at Barbara Gladstone (March 22 to April 26, 2003), *NŌ* was one of seven separate Lockhart works on view and on sale. The other six works were sets of large photographs, two of them engagements with Duane Hanson sculptures, in which Lockhart photographs real people along with the superrealistic Hanson figures so that her photographs are documents, in one instance, of two workers installing a sculpture of three workers on a lunch break (*Lunch Break* installation Duane Hanson: Sculptures of Life, 14 December 2002–23 February 2003, Scottish National Gallery of Modern Art [2003]), and in the other instance, of the intervention of a performer within a sculptural scene, so that a sculptured child seems to be gesturing to the performer. The other photographic works were instances of NŌ-no ikebana arrangements (see Lockhart's explanation in the interview) by Haruko Takeichi: four series of several individual images of a Brussels sprout plant in the early stages of decay.

At Barbara Gladstone *NŌ* was presented not simply as a movie but as a work of photographic art of equal value with the other works on display. An edition of six prints of *NŌ* was listed on sale at $30,000 per print. The idea of paying $30,000 for a print of a thirty-five-minute, 16mm film is rife with irony, even paradox. Of course, to strike a print of *NŌ* at a lab would cost a pittance compared with the sale price (though for most critical filmmakers, even established figures like Ernie Gehr or Peter Hutton, the cost of making prints causes considerable stress); and a half-hour 16mm print would rent for $50 to $100. But by refusing to strike more than a few prints, Barbara Gladstone has defied film's heritage as a mechanically reproducible medium and has synthetically limited its distribution as a film in order to maximize its value as an artifact.

The final irony of all this is that, as absurd as this process can seem, there is no question (at least in my mind) that *as a work of art, NŌ* is the equal of the photographs in the show, or of any comparable creative artifact one might find in an art gallery. That is, by any sane *aesthetic* standard, *NŌ* is *worth* $30,000, or at least as much as any other first-rate photograph or painting; and the vast discrepancy between what a screening of the film would net in the world of alternative cinema and what sale of a print might net in the world of prestigious art galleries is an obvious, even embarrassing, measure of how fully the community that has formed around critical cinema has failed to convince the larger culture that the films we admire are major contributions to mainstream art history as well as to alternative film history. I must hasten to add the obvious: that Lockhart does not receive anything like the full purchase price of the film, though selling prints of films, like selling photographs, does allow her to support herself and keep making work.

I spoke with Sharon Lockhart in Ithaca, New York, in April 2001. We refined the interview by phone and on-line.

MacDonald: You come from photography, where you have a solid reputation—I assume you were a photographer before you were a filmmaker.

Lockhart: I did learn photography first, but as an artist, I see myself as always having worked in both media. I started my first film project halfway through graduate school and included it in my thesis show. This was the first time I thought of using a photographic project as a way of commenting on the relation between still photography and film. And later, in both *Goshogaoka* and *NŌ*, I made a series of photographs that are seen in relation to the films, though conceptually, the photographic projects and the film projects are opposites.

I saw *Goshogaoka* as accomplishing certain things in relation to the space of the cinema and to the cinema audience that had to do with duration, while in the photographic project I was interested in the still photograph's way of taking a slice out of time. I deliberately set up pictures that looked like the action pictures you might see in a sports magazine, but then slowly and laboriously re-created them so that there was some disjunction between the fluidity of movement in an action picture and the composed look of my own pictures.

In *NŌ*, the film, you witness the act of mulching in real time from a fixed camera. This relates to landscape painting and the duration of looking in real time. But in the "NŌ-no Ikebana" photographs you see a single arrangement of a Brussels sprout plant, photographed in a studio setting over a one-month period. The photographs are edited down into four series of several images each that mark a particular gesture or movement in time, and that gesture or movement is then extracted from the whole. The photos are also not installed in a linear progression of time. Disrupting the linear progression of time makes a viewer consider time as an element of the work and as a tool for looking at a set of photographs.

MacDonald: For those of us coming to your work from avant-garde film, you seem to be a child of American structural filmmaking. In *Goshogaoka*, your use of a series of shots of equal length, with the same framing, is reminiscent of James Benning's work, and *Wavelength* [1967, Michael Snow] seems an obvious predecessor of *Teatro Amazonas.*

Lockhart: In graduate school (at Art Center College of Design in Pasadena), I took a class with Stephen Prina on the films of Hollis Frampton. This was my first experience with structuralist film, and I must say it changed my life and influenced my practice in both my photography and my films. Artists like Morgan Fisher, James Benning, and Jack Goldstein came to Art Center to show work, which also had a major influence. I feel very fortunate to have studied at Art Center because I was always encouraged to further my investigations in film. Many times I was allowed to rent films for my own research, a luxury that not many schools would offer. I was able to see Warhol, Snow, Chantal Akerman, and Yvonne Rainer, among others. I think all this work really resonated with me because of my photographic background. That work was successful in the way it negotiated the stasis of the photographic image with the narrative flow of cinema. My photographic work at that point was caught up in the way narrative surrounded the photograph and constantly filled in its meaning, so structuralist film seemed like a natural fit for me.

MacDonald: Where did you study before Art Center?

Lockhart: First, I studied photography at the New England School of Photography in Boston for two years, from 1984 to 1986. Instead of starting students with 35mm cameras, they trained us to use a 4 × 5 camera. The process of slowing down in order to make an image has really stayed with me. I can't imagine not having the level of concentration and attention to the frame that you have when working with the 4 × 5. After that, I went on to the San Francisco Art Institute to complete my BFA. There, I pretty much concentrated on performance and the history of video art, but it wasn't until graduate school that I really began to study avant-garde film.

I still haven't taken a film production class, though. I didn't really make a decision about this—it had to do with bureaucratic issues between Art Center's film department and the fine art department. In the end I think my not learning film in a classroom has allowed me a lot of freedom. It's probably why I thought I could make a film. If I had known how hard it is and all the traditional guidelines, I might have shied away from it. For my first film I somewhat naively shot on 16mm and learned the postproduction process over the phone from Morgan Fisher.

MacDonald: This was your thesis film, *Khalil, Shaun, a Woman under the Influence* [1994]?

Lockhart: Yes.

MacDonald: How did you make the connection with Morgan Fisher?

Lockhart: It was incredible. I hadn't even *met* Morgan; I had only seen him speak when he came to show his films. And you know Morgan: he's a bit intimidating at first. Plus, he's such a great filmmaker. Looking back, I think it took a lot of courage to call him up out of the blue, but one of my teachers had suggested it, and I needed the information, so I gave it a go. It was very sweet of Morgan to talk me through each stage: telling me where to do the editing, who should cut the film, where I could find a title house, and get sound transfers done—all of it.

MacDonald: Khalil, Shaun, a Woman under the Influence is a very strange film, because as a viewer, you have no idea how you're supposed to be feeling about what you're seeing. It's somewhere in between emotions.

Lockhart: At the time, I had been researching what I initially thought were two opposing strategies: the theatrical and the clinical. I had become particularly interested in the way pop culture borrowed the look of the objective or the scientific, and the way the clinical borrowed theatrical narrative empathetic strategies.

Anyway, while researching, I came across Dick Smith's makeup tests for *The Exorcist* [1973]. It was some of the best research material I had ever seen. He made over twenty-four hours of film tests of Linda Blair, not in character, with several variations of makeup on her face. It was in some of these tests that I saw what I wanted for my film: a child, covered with the appearance of some horrible disease, behaving as children behave when they're sitting in front of a camera—somewhat self-conscious, somewhat playful. For the first two parts of the film I hired two different special-effects makeup artists and gave them identical packages that included images from various sources. They were given no direction at all; they could create whatever they wanted on the kids. In the end, one made something very real, and the other, something very fictional.

I was really pleased with what happens to the viewer from part 1 to part 2 of the film. You slowly become aware of the fiction and have to rethink the feelings of empathy you initially had with Khalil.

MacDonald: Recently I looked at the Cassavetes film you borrow the scene and part of the title from and realized that the scenes are actually very different. Were you working from memory?

Lockhart: I rewrote the bedroom scene from *A Woman under the Influence* [1974] by adding dialogue and extending a moment from the original. I see my use of Cassavetes's film as a quoting of him as a director, the way I quote Truffaut in my photo series "Auditions." Both filmmakers were influential on me because of their unique styles, their processes of making work, and the way they work with nonactors and, in particular, children.

A lot of the enjoyment I get when making work happens in the process, in my exchanges with my subjects and with the people I work with. For *Khalil, Shaun, a Woman under the Influence,* I worked with people who surrounded me in my daily life: Khalil was the kid next door, Shaun was the nephew of my best friend; Khalil's dad [Abu Harper] operated the boom, and my husband [Alex Slade] did the sound. Khalil worked the clapboard for Shaun's shoot, and so on. Some people think that I figure everything out ahead of time, and that the production of the work is a smooth, almost machinelike process, but it's never seamless like that, and actually I like the unpredictable aspects of making work. In most of my work there is a formal structure, but within that there is a lot of space where chance is encouraged. It's a learning process for all of us, and the subtle level of chaos adds to the outcome. In the final section of *Khalil, Shaun, a Woman under the Influence,* something very tender and real happens within the fiction. I think this had a lot to do with the duration of the shoot and the fact that the people working on it had become quite intimate.

MacDonald: How did *Goshogaoka* come about? Do you have a particular connection with Japanese culture?

Lockhart: In 1996 I was nominated for and awarded a three-month residency in Japan. This was the first time I had ever made an extensive body of work in another culture, completely disconnected from my support group in Los Angeles. When I work in LA, I work with the same camera people, use the same labs, do research at the same libraries and bookstores. This was the first time I was totally on my own, and it was an incredible experience.

MacDonald: When you first arrived in Japan, how much did you know about what you were going to do there?

Lockhart: I was well aware of the problems of filming in another culture and had begun to think about the way ethnographic film works within an art context. It was a real challenge for me, but something I wanted to take on, especially because I was already working with notions of fact and fiction. I did know that I wanted my subject matter to be something very routine and ordinary. Originally, I thought farming might be the perfect subject, but the residency turned out to be in suburbia, so I had to shift gears when I arrived.

I had my eyes open for a subject matter one day when I was riding my bike past a school and heard sounds coming from the gymnasium. I went in to look, and there it was: a gym with a stage with a red curtain at one end, and girls playing basketball. I thought, "Theater and documentary, an American sport in Japan—this is perfect." It just clicked. I immediately realized the potential of the raised stage and how it mirrored the cinema space, and how it would be a constant reminder of staging and fiction.

I was also thinking a lot about postmodern dance because of its focus on everyday movement and how it took dance out of the traditional theatrical/auditorium-type space and moved the performances to rooftops and gymnasiums—spaces not traditionally identified with art.

MacDonald: The final section reminds me of Yvonne Rainer's performances—at least those I've seen in her films.

Lockhart: I love her work and hope that in *Goshogaoka* I'm successful in both acknowledging that history and reintroducing it to the theatrical space of the cinema.

MacDonald: You worked with a choreographer on *Goshogaoka?*

Lockhart: Yes, Stephen Galloway, who is a dancer from the Frankfurt Ballet. He's credited as "movement advisor"—he liked that better. Working with Stephen was one of the best experiences of my life. He is incredibly talented and generous; and, most important, he has a great sense of humor, which he used brilliantly to break the ice with the girls, who were usually very shy.

I had been researching and videotaping the girls for almost two months by the time Stephen came to Japan, so that when he got there I knew the structure I wanted, where the camera would be, that there would be three costume changes, that each section would define a different aspect of the

Girls' basketball team in gym in Sharon Lockhart's *Goshogaoka* (1997). Courtesy Blum and Poe Gallery.

film frame, that each act would be one ten-minute take, and that the film would be shot in one day. We rehearsed with the girls for ten days straight, five hours a day, and shot on the last day. This might make you think it's all choreographed, but it really isn't. There's a lot of chance (and directed chance) involved, too.

We purposely changed exercises at the last minute, or gave the girls an outline with no direction. We also edited the routines and stretched and reorganized them for the camera. The most obvious case of chance seeping in is in the third shot, when the girls do the ball trick for the camera. Just before shooting, we deliberately changed the trick they had rehearsed all week, to bring in something of the individual personalities of the girls. I love that section; it's so sweet. This was also one of the few times we specifically asked the girls to have some eye contact with the camera. During the rest of the film we let them look where they wanted (most chose to look at the floor).

MacDonald: The moments that seem most "Japanese"—at least within the typical American clichés about Japan—are the moments when the girls all run so that their feet hit the floor at the same time: was that them or you?

Lockhart: We never directed them to sync up (although, of course, there

Chihiro Nishijima in chromogenic print (37" × 31"), by Sharon Lockhart. Courtesy Blum and Poe Gallery.

were some exercises they normally do in sync as a team). There is one part in the fourth shot where they are throwing the balls back and forth to each other really slowly, and all of a sudden the balls sync up. That was amazing and unanticipated. I don't think we could have planned it to work so perfectly.

MacDonald: Did the girls and their parents see the film?

Lockhart: A year and a half after I shot the film, I went back to Japan for a show in Tokyo, and went to Moriya to show the film to the girls in a real theater. I think it's really important to bring a film back to where it was made, to the people who are in it, and especially in this case, since the girls worked so hard and the parents and town were so involved. The mothers of the girls actually lent me sewing machines and helped make the costumes. A lot of things like that happened on this project. In a lot of ways, it was a real group effort.

It was great to watch the girls seeing themselves *huge* on the screen, and with their parents, friends, and the people from the town reacting to the film. For the first time I think they fully understood what I was doing. Initially, they all thought Stephen (being a big shot from the Frankfurt Ballet) was going to teach them to moonwalk or something, and so they were surprised when we focused on their normal exercises. Anyway, there they were in the audience, seeing their everyday routines recontextualized and reinterpreted as dance. At first there was a lot of giggling, but eventually they calmed down and watched the film closely.

MacDonald: How have other audiences reacted?

Lockhart: For the most part, audiences think they are looking at a straight documentary of a basketball team in Japan, but slowly they realize that the film is choreographed. The film is a lot about one culture looking at another and interpreting another, and about the baggage we bring to the film experience. Especially at the beginning, it was interesting to study how each different audience reacted. I think that's how I got the idea for *Teatro*. Like my other films, *Teatro Amazonas* is also a very formal film about space—both on-camera and off-camera space—and about the film frame, about staging, and about looking and listening.

MacDonald: The idea that a filmmaker would make a forty-minute film of the type *Teatro Amazonas* is, *in 35mm,* is very unusual, at least in this country. Almost all experimental filmmakers seem to have accepted the idea that since they have so few resources, so little access to money, even *imagining* a film in 35mm is pointless. So how is it that you, a young filmmaker-photographer, were able to make a forty-minute film in 35mm?

Lockhart: I think the reason *Teatro* got made the way it did was that I was never trained within the rubric of experimental film, though I was exposed to it. As an artist I learned that you have to commit to making work based on what you want it to say and then solve the problems of production as best you can. When I first conceived of *Teatro,* I thought about the viewer and realized that it would not be the same experience if you could not clearly see all the little details that mark the reactions and interactions of the audience, and if you could not hear everything in stereo. Even though I usually like the aspect ratio of 16mm better than the wider 35mm image, *Teatro* had to be 35mm and could not have been the same film in 16mm. Maybe I was naive to think the project was possible, but after all, it was a pretty simple shoot in terms of filmmaking: one shot, one reel, flat lighting, sync sound.

I had hoped that after *Goshogaoka* I would be able to get a grant for *Teatro*. I applied for almost two years but never got one. I finally realized that the only way to make *Teatro* would be to pay for it, which I was able to do because of the art world. I made a series of photographs that my gallery, Blum and Poe, sold to raise money for the film, and no one made a profit. We put all the money into the film project.

MacDonald: And the gallery did this because. . . ?

Lockhart: I guess they did it because they were a young gallery and were willing to take a chance, and because they understood that my film work is an essential part of my art practice. I feel lucky that there was a simultaneous recognition of my film and photo work. Because of this, I'm able to continue making films. I think they probably also hoped the *next* film would get funding, and it did. I know *Teatro* seems extravagant, but we were able to get a lot donated: postsound work, film, a camera.

MacDonald: I've often thought *Teatro* would make a perfect double feature with Morgan Fisher's *Standard Gauge* [1987]. *Standard Gauge* begins with a rolling text explaining the history of the development of 35mm as "standard gauge" by W. K. L. Dickson, and then there's a thirty-five-minute shot where he shows and tells us about his collection of 35mm filmstrips. *Teatro* is actually in 35mm, though it's hardly a normal 35mm kind of film, and your thirty-minute shot of the audience is followed by a long, rolling credit sequence—this one making clear that putting this project together was a relatively complicated, time-consuming process, since you know, or at least seem to know, the name of everybody in the opera house.

How did you deal with the language issue?

Lockhart: I had a great translator, Bia Gayotto, a friend and an artist who uses structuralist strategies in her own work. It was important to me to work with an artist who understood my work, rather than a straight translator.

We interviewed over six hundred people from all the neighborhoods in Manaus (I think there were fifty-seven barrios). In the beginning I understood very little Portuguese, but by the end Bia didn't need to translate nearly as much for me.

MacDonald: What did you talk to them about? What did you tell them you were doing?

Lockhart: We started off pretty scientific, because six months earlier I had done a large series of photographic works where I accompanied anthropologists in the field, and I was used to their line of questioning. I *thought* I knew exactly what information I wanted: how they got to Manaus, their family structure, their economic situation, and so on. But by the second day, the questions had changed completely, becoming much more subjective. It was more of a dialogue and less of an interview. We talked about love, food, music, the political situation in Manaus, the opera house, everything and anything.

MacDonald: What drew you to anthropologists?

Lockhart: I've always been interested in science, especially in scientific documentation, from medical photography to ethnography. After I made *Goshogaoka,* I became even more fascinated with ethnographic film, especially Jean Rouch. He took ethnographic film to a whole new level. His ideas of collaboration and being a catalyst are especially interesting to me, like the way he lets his subjects choose fictional characters or roles, through which something very real comes out. I spent a lot of time researching anthropology and anthropological photography. When I did the photographic part of the *Teatro* project, I spent a lot of time watching anthropologists work. I think this came through later on, in my own process of making the film.

MacDonald: What exactly did you tell the interviewees about your project?

Lockhart: I explained that I was casting and that I wanted a literal representation of the city of Manaus to be in the opera house. I told them that the film would be shot in one day, that buses would pick people up and bring them to and from the opera house, and that Becky Allen (a minimalist composer from Los Angeles) had composed a piece that would be presented as a live performance by the Choral do Amazonas on the day of the shoot.

MacDonald: How did you choose Manaus?

Lockhart: The opera house.

MacDonald: And you knew about the opera house because of Herzog's *Fitzcarraldo?*

Lockhart: Well, I had just come out of making *Goshogaoka* when I got the idea for the film. I really see *Teatro* as an extension of *Goshogaoka.* It pushes the ethnographic part of the *Goshogaoka* project to a much more literal level: audience to audience, one culture literally looking at another. Plus *Teatro* also reverses the proscenium perspective of *Goshogaoka.* I wanted a kind of displaced location, the way *Goshogaoka* used an *American* sport; and when I started thinking about European models of culture in the New World, Fitzcarraldo came to mind as the ultimate example. The theater in Manaus was a European intervention at the height of the rubber boom. Many of the raw materials used in the opera house were Brazilian; they were shipped to Europe to be worked by the finest craftsmen and then sent back to Manaus to be installed in the opera house. The clash of cultures becomes really apparent in this building.

MacDonald: Did the people of Manaus know *Fitzcarraldo?*

Lockhart: Some people I interviewed had worked on Herzog's film, which was really interesting for me to hear about. I also found out that a lot of people had never been in the opera house.

MacDonald: How long were you in Brazil working on *Teatro Amazonas?*

Lockhart: A month and a half. We shot the last day.

MacDonald: How many people were in the film?

Lockhart: Three hundred and eight, which is the number of seats the camera saw in full.

MacDonald: Why was all the interviewing necessary? You could have just asked people to sit in the theater.

Lockhart: I did ask them, I invited them. But I didn't want to pick people off the streets and plop them in the seats, and I didn't want to pay people to be in a film the way it is normally done. I thought there would be a certain sense of ease if I knew each person, even if it was only a little. And I hope this can be seen in the film. A lot of the pleasure I get out of making work comes from the people I meet.

I knew what the structure and the idea of the film were, and I knew I wanted to invite people into the process, but until I got to Manaus, even I didn't know I would cast so intensely. At first I expected to travel around and that I would invite the people I would meet in my daily life. But once I got there and started doing research, I got the idea of this literal mapping of the city, which is so spread out. New barrios crop up every month. The city hadn't had a new statistical map made since the seventies, so we had a lot to figure out. We worked with a student anthropologist from Belem, Gercilene Teixeira.

MacDonald: How exactly did you find the interviewees? As you're doing these interviews, I'm assuming you got a certain amount of local press coverage.

Lockhart: From the credits, the film may look as if it was a big organized production, but really it was a funky two-woman show: Bia and I, with a couple of assistants. We started by hanging flyers, and we got a few interviews that way, but not nearly enough. Then one of the people we interviewed suggested radio. Everyone in Manaus listens to the radio. Music is a big part of Brazilian culture. As soon as we went on the air and announced the project, we had no problem.

The exchanges with the people we interviewed were extraordinary.

MacDonald: And the interviewees knew they wouldn't be paid?

Lockhart: Out of the six hundred people that we interviewed, not one person ever brought up the subject of money. Whenever I show the film at a festival, there is always at least one person in the audience who gets upset that I didn't pay the people in the opera house. Some people have actually become a bit outraged.

Money was definitely not part of my exchange. I had thought a lot about this because of the situation in Manaus, which is a poor city; but, in the end, I felt that the introduction of money as a central element of the project would fundamentally change it. The film was about a cultural exchange, and so I wanted to work with people who were interested in taking part in that experience. I felt money would replace my original sense of a personal exchange, of collaboration, with a monetary exchange.

MacDonald: Did you actually shoot just one take?

Lockhart: I shot two takes because the cinematographer from São Paulo, Rudolfo Sanchez, was concerned about the possibility of something terrible happening to the film in transportation or during developing. We shot the first take and broke for a big lunch on-site; then everyone came back, and we did another take. I never even developed the second take, though. Nothing terrible happened to the film on its way home, and I wasn't interested in choosing the better of two takes. I wanted the novelty of the audience's initial reactions to come through in the film.

MacDonald: How big was the choir?

Lockhart: Sixty people. The composition begins with everyone singing at once, and slowly, over twenty-four minutes, voices drop out so that during the last six minutes of the film, you hear only the sounds of the audience in the opera. It was very difficult to perform and could only be done twice in a day (tops). It took a lot of energy for the choir and months of practice.

Because the singers were in the orchestra pit, only the camera and the cameraman onstage were visible to the audience. It was quite theatrical in that way! We gave no direction: we only told the people in the audience to enjoy the concert and that the cameraman would tell them when the film ran out.

MacDonald: As the music dies down, you're left with both the sound inside the opera house and outside the opera house, *and* the sound inside and outside the screening space of the cinema—when I saw the film at Anthology Film Archives, I wasn't immediately able to tell which was which.

Lockhart: I especially like when the picture ends and the ten minutes of credits roll. For the first time, there is dead silence on-screen, and the audience in the cinema literally becomes the sound track, and every sound in the cinema space is amplified. I think *Teatro* works best when the cinema audience is the same size as the audience in the film. It creates this great doubling effect.

MacDonald: The audience in the opera house is acting out what the film-going audience is *feeling,* but may not be acting out, or at least not *visibly* acting out. We're trained to shut up and sit still in the movies, and so it's hard for many Americans—especially movie-wise, college-educated types—to actually interact with the screen. But after a certain point, we can see people in the image laughing and making gestures, a projection, at least part, of our own reaction to the film.

After the shoot, you left?

Lockhart: After we shot the film, the audience was invited up onstage for a talent show. It was incredible, like a happening. Since so many of the interviews revolved around music, I had asked people to bring instruments (if they wanted to) on the day of the shoot. People sang, danced capoeira in groups and alone. The crew even joined in. One of the most touching experiences was when one woman read her own poetry. The party went on for some time. I wish we'd had a video camera to document it.

We left Manaus a couple days later.

MacDonald: Teatro and *Goshogaoka* are quintessential films of their gauge: *Teatro* is a big film; *Goshogaoka* is more tribal.

Lockhart: Goshogaoka used the longest take you can normally make in 16mm: eleven minutes (I used ten-minute shots so I could trim the ends). For *Teatro* I wanted at least a thirty-minute shot, and would have liked a forty-minute shot, but the choir couldn't hold a piece like that for more than thirty minutes, and the longest shot you can make in 35mm is, I think, twenty-two minutes—so we had to shoot three perf, and got a twenty-nine minute shot out of it.

MacDonald: What exactly does "shoot in three perf" mean?

Lockhart (laughter): I don't know—very technical, too high-tech to go into . . .

MacDonald: I'm interested.

Lockhart: Normally 35mm film uses four perforations per frame. I used a camera that used only three perforations per frame. With a four-perf camera the intermittent movement advances the film four perforations at a time. With a three-perf camera it advances the film only three perforations at a time. The actual size of the frame is the same in both systems, since each uses the same size camera aperture. The only difference is that the black frame line in four-perf is wider. Using the three-perf method enabled me to get one-third more frames per load of film. For example, with the normal four-perf system, twenty-four perforations will yield six frames of film. With the three-perf system, I was able to get eight frames within the same space.

Then when making prints, I optically printed the three-perf system back to a four-perf system because all theatrical projection is four-perf. This didn't introduce a problem since print stock rolls are longer than camera stock rolls. In the four-perf system, a camera roll of film gives approximately twenty-two minutes of footage. But with the three-perf system, I was able to go over twenty-nine minutes, which was necessary because the musical composition was longer than twenty-two minutes, and I wanted one continuous take.

Three-perf cameras are hard to come by. Even more difficult to find is a three-perf projector for viewing dailies. Very few labs have them. While doing research on Victorio Storaro, the cinematographer, I found he used the three-perf system to get longer takes. He uses the Technicolor Lab in Burbank because they can do three-perf, and that's where I went for *Teatro Amazonas.*

MacDonald: Shooting in 35mm is a gesture full of hope. The traditional space of the 35mm cinema is so rarely available for a film like this one.

Lockhart: Yes, but, ironically, even though it is "standard gauge," *Teatro* is hard to show in some of the few experimental venues that do show 35mm film. That's because the film is forty minutes long and needs to be shown without a reel change or a cut: the theater that shows the film has to have a large platter system that is usually available only in commercial cinema spaces.

MacDonald: Your route to being a successful filmmaker may seem usual to you, coming out of art school, but it's very unusual for an experimental filmmaker. It's rare that an avant-garde filmmaker has a gallery.

Lockhart: When I was in school, I didn't see myself on a path to becoming an experimental filmmaker. I just saw myself as an artist using film as a tool, a medium. I had some success with my first film, but I was more successful with my photographs. When *Goshogaoka* began showing in film festivals, I finally started to think of myself as a filmmaker. I think it had a lot to do with the whole atmosphere of festivals—seeing lots of great and inspiring films and hearing filmmakers speak about their work.

Because of my photographic work, there was a lot of pressure at first to show the film in a museum or gallery space, but I was insistent that it be shown in cinemas. I had made *Goshogaoka,* like *Teatro,* with the cinema space in mind, and really couldn't see them functioning outside of that space. In the art world, video installation was becoming *really* popular in museum shows, and I think a lot of people didn't understand why I wouldn't want my work shown that way. But I was really pleased that there was another venue and another kind of audience that I could work in tandem with.

I think there has been a slow shift during the late eighties and the nineties in both the film and art worlds. Over time I think the art world has had to take a new look at experimental film, especially because of the importance of videos and video installations. Filmmakers have also seen that there is an audience in the art world for their work and have started to bring their filmmaking there. Chantal Akerman, Eija-Liisa Ahtila, Agnes Varda, Isaac Julien, and Deborah Stratman are some of the filmmakers who have had their work shown within an art context.

There has always been dialogue between the art world and the film world, but different institutional structures have developed to facilitate each practice separately. There are film schools as opposed to art schools, festivals as opposed to museum screenings, and different grant-giving organizations. But historically, Snow, Warhol, Richard Serra, and Bruce Conner have always existed in both worlds. And Frampton wrote in an art context. I feel very fortunate that people in the experimental film world appreciate my work. I really value having an audience that knows the history I'm referencing and can relate to my work. It is very important that it's seen in relation to structuralist film history—at least for me. I do know how hard it is to make experimental films and, worse, how difficult it is to see them.

MacDonald: I've recently seen *NŌ* in your show at Barbara Gladstone Gallery. Was *NŌ* designed for presentation in a gallery or, like *Goshogaoka* and *Teatro,* for theatrical presentation?

Lockhart: When I conceived of *NŌ,* I thought of it as a bit different from my earlier films. As the process of working on it progressed, I thought of it almost like a landscape painting, and because of this, a gallery setting seemed to make sense. *Goshogaoka* and *Teatro* were much more about the social space of the cinema, about having an audience, and assumed an awareness of the theatrical space. Watching *NŌ* is a more personal experience, so it can be viewed in a more intimate setting like the small theater we constructed in the gallery. But I do plan to show it in cinemas at festivals, even though I really did like sitting in that small room with only a couple of people watching the light slowly fade.

MacDonald: What differences did you notice working in a landscape, as opposed to working in the architectural spaces that are so important in *Goshogaoka* and *Teatro Amazonas?*

Lockhart: For me the main difference was the amount of attention that has to be paid to nature when you are working in a landscape. Naturally, I already knew this from my photographic work, but living in a farming community for two months I developed a heightened awareness of all the changes and rhythms that take place in nature. I became aware of the growing and harvesting cycles of different plants, the length of the days, the quality of light at different times of day, and lots of other little things that you don't have to worry about when you are working inside and, especially, with artificial lights. Inside, most things are stable. Outside, there are many more variables, and you are much more dependent on your awareness of them than on your ability to alter them. I think this affected the final result in *NŌ*. The natural process disrupts the clinical gaze.

In other respects, though, the landscape functions much like architecture. It provides a limitation that somehow defines the space of the picture plane. In *NŌ* I worked with the field in many of the same ways I worked with the basketball court in *Goshogaoka* or the theater in *Teatro.*

I organized *NŌ* around the optics of seeing. The film starts just after

Farmers mulching field in
Sharon Lockhart's *NŌ* (2003).
Courtesy Blum and Poe Gallery.

sunset, and as it progresses, the light slowly fades. The mulching that the farmers (Masa and Yoko Ito) do is organized around the camera as well. I had the farmers make piles of hay in the reverse perspective of the camera, following the camera's field of vision. That is, they drop five rows of three piles of hay. Each pile in the row furthest from the camera is made of five armfuls of hay; each pile in the next row is made of four armfuls; in the third row from the back, each pile is made of three armfuls; each pile in the fourth row from the back, two armfuls; and in the fifth row, the one closest to the camera, each of the three piles is made up of a single armful of hay. From the camera's perspective all the piles look the same size and are in a line radiating out from the lens, re-creating a trapezoidal field. After working from background to foreground to make the piles, the farmers come back in and slowly spread the hay over just that portion of the field revealed by the camera, from foreground to background, as if they are covering a canvas.

MacDonald: "Ikebana" means "flower arrangement." What *is* "NŌ-no ikebana"?

Lockhart: Ikebana is the Japanese art of flower arranging and has been around for over five hundred years. In the early twentieth century there was an uprising among a group of freestyle ikebana revolutionaries. They actually issued a manifesto, called "Declaration of the Newly Risen Style of Flower Arrangement." Because of it, a new form was born in opposition to the traditional symmetrical triangle form.

More recently, thirty or forty years ago, an amazing woman named Toshie Yokoi founded a new form of arranging called "NŌ-no ikebana." The character word, "NŌ," means agriculture as applied to all plant life in the countryside. My use of it in the film is a bit of a play on words, since "Noh" is also the name of a form of theater popular in Japan. I think if you saw "NŌ" separate from the image of farming, the meaning would not be clear, but in the context of my image it's clear that my primary reference is to agriculture. I think I was also drawn to the recent, radical history of ikebana because of my interest in structuralist filmmaking.

As I mentioned earlier, the project that became *NŌ* started before *Goshogaoka,* when I first went to Japan with the intention of making a film on farming. It didn't work out then, but many of the ideas from that first trip stayed with me. When I was in postproduction on *Teatro,* I wrote a grant application for *NŌ.* It underwent a lot of changes until it ended up as a short film of the farmers mulching and a set of photographs that take one NŌ-no ikebana arrangement and detail its decay.

Originally, I had planned on filming a whole growing season: an arrangement being made and that same arrangement dying. But after I spent a couple of months in Japan researching farming and NŌ-no ikebana, I decided that for the film I would focus on the process of mulching, which I had seen a lot of during my research. And I decided to represent the NŌ-no ikebana in still photography.

MacDonald: Were there specific reasons you chose those two particular farmers?

Lockhart: I went to Japan with the project fully conceptualized and a film crew organized to shoot. I just had to find a landscape I was interested in and a set of farmers to participate. I chose Masa and Yoko because they were interested in art and in this particular project—and I really liked the landscape where they live. Plus, they were a very sweet and loving couple.

MacDonald: Did Masa and Yoko Ito collaborate on the shape of the final film, and if so, how?

MacDonald: They were definitely collaborators on its final shape. I worked with them and a movement coordinator to figure out the timing, the rhythm of their work, and what their activity looked like. Since the film is really about their work, I wanted them to have a lot of input as to how long an activity takes and what the natural order of activities is. During the research I educated myself on the timing of all their daily routines, and then we tailored the film to fit their schedule.

MacDonald: What are you working on now?

Lockhart: I shouldn't go into it too much at this point because this project will change, as all my work does, in the process. But I am really excited about it. I just started shooting, after researching a small village in Northern California for the last two years. I'm working with the kids in the village. The interesting thing is that, this time, I'm doing all the work myself—all the 16mm shooting (Becky Allen is doing the sound recording). I was able to buy an Aaton camera with the Guggenheim [Lockhart was awarded a Guggenheim Fellowship in 2002]. It's such a great camera! It's pretty easy to operate, but I still made tons of mistakes in the beginning. The experience has been so different. For the first time I'm making a film that isn't shot in one day—a whole new experience! It's so good to be able to return to the village on a regular basis, to shoot more, to see the seasons change, to show people the work in progress, and to get to *really* know the kids over time. I think working so closely with Yoko and Masa on *NŌ*, and with such a small-scale crew, made me want to return to a more intimate relationship with my subjects.

MacDonald: Could you talk about yourself a bit? How did you get to be who you are as an artist?

Lockhart: I wasn't born into an artistic family in the traditional sense—not at all. I come from a working-class background, from small-town New England (a lot like the village I am filming in now). I didn't go to an art museum until I was in my twenties.

But I think my family has had a lot of effect on what I do and why I do it. For sure there were some less than pleasant times, but we usually found a way to turn a bad situation into a comedy. It was a bit like vaudeville, with a large extended family as the cast. There was a lot of dressing up, singing, acting, and practical jokes, and outsiders were often roped in to the act. My family had a knack for talking anyone into participating. The importance of an audience and a director behind the show was very clear to me at a young age. So, I guess you could say my family has given me an ability to bring lightness to a project and, I guess, to get people to be part of things. This relates to my practice, obviously. It's funny to realize it.

Jennifer Todd Reeves

On *Chronic* and *The Time We Killed*

In 1995–96 Jennifer Reeves achieved recognition as a talented young filmmaker (she was born in 1971) for two films: *The Girl's Nervy* (1995), a contribution to the tradition of painting directly on the filmstrip (Len Lye, Harry Smith, Stan Brakhage, and Carolee Schneemann are among the important contributors to this tradition), and her first longer film, *Chronic* (1996), a thirty-eight-minute narrative about a troubled adolescent, based roughly on Reeves's own experiences. What seemed particularly accomplished about *Chronic* was its effective combination of formal experiment and compelling storytelling. Her protagonist, a rural Ohio teen named Gretchen (played by Reeves herself) is gang-raped at a college fraternity party, an experience that exacerbates her tendency to mutilate herself by cutting her skin with razor blades. In time Gretchen enters a mental hospital, where she stays for two years, becoming part of a small community and achieving a greater degree of control over her obsessive behavior. Not long after her release, Gretchen moves to New York City and begins making her way, though when she learns that one of her friends from the hospital has killed herself, the narrator (also Reeves herself) tells us, "The news was too much for Gretchen to handle," and we see her in a bathtub, possibly returning to self-mutilation or even committing suicide.

While the ending of *Chronic* is at best ambiguous, viewers need not leave the film assuming that Gretchen's attempts to recover have been a failure. Reeves's presentation of Gretchen's story involves a subtle narrative strategy that implicitly recontextualizes the events dramatized in the film. At the beginning of *Chronic* the narrator seems to be one of Gretchen's siblings or a close friend ("We grew up in rural Ohio"), but as the story unfolds, it is obvious that this narrator is neither friend nor family member, despite the fact that she identifies herself in the first person: a sister or friend could not know all that this narrator knows. The narrative perspective of *Chronic* is reminiscent of several Ernest Hemingway stories about recovery from physical and psychic wounds—especially "Now I Lay Me" and "The Gambler, the Nun, and the Radio"—where the narrator is subtly revealed to be the protagonist at a point further along in his recovery. While the particulars of Gretchen's life differ from the particulars of Reeves's own experience, Reeves does make clear that Gretchen is a *version* of herself (not only does Reeves play Gretchen and narrate her story, but "Gretchen's" home movies and childhood photographs are Reeves's own). We can read the formal accomplishment of *Chronic*—both the general fact that the film was completed, and its specifics: the impressive montage and inventive composition, the sensuous textures, the deft handling of both spoken and printed narration—as implicit evidence that, while "Gretchen" will continue to struggle with her personal demons, she will learn to use her struggles as a way of fueling her creative self.

Several years after completing *Chronic,* Reeves decided to continue the semiautobiographical story she had begun, using a different but related strategy. The result was her first feature, *The Time We Killed* (2004), starring the poet Lisa Jarnot, who plays Robyn, a novelist and poet who has become a recluse within her Brooklyn apartment. Over a period of six months, Robyn sees almost no one, except in rare instances a neighbor or a handyman, and from time to time her "sister," June (not her real sister but someone she became close to during her stay at a mental hospital— June is played by Reeves). Months go by as Robyn writes a romance novel, listens to events going on in nearby apartments, looks out her windows, and drifts from memory to memory and fantasy to fantasy. Robyn, who narrates, tells us, "Fifteen years ago I jumped off a bridge in Ohio." She lost her memory of her first seventeen years, but this seems to some extent a fantasy that assists her in forgetting things that are too painful to remember. Robyn's depression has been exacerbated by the aftermath of the 9/11 terrorist attack: "Terrorism got me out of the house ['People seemed as frightened as *I* normally do, and I felt closer to them'], but the War on Terror drove me back in."

The Time We Killed covers the period from November 2002 until April 2003, during which Robyn finishes her novel and recovers fully enough to finally leave her apartment, adopt a dog from a local animal shelter, and begin finding her way back into the world. Like Gretchen in *Chronic,* Robyn is certainly not cured of depression, but what has at times seemed like stasis is revealed to have been gradual recovery. And as is true in *Chronic,*

Reeves's own tendency toward depression is dramatized by her protagonist's (much of what Robyn experiences has happened, either literally or figuratively, to Reeves; the imagery of Robyn's childhood is from home movies shot by Reeves's father; Robyn's apartment is Reeves's own), but the fact of *The Time We Killed* recontextualizes what is dramatized in the film. *As filmmaker,* Reeves provides a clear visual counterpoint to Robyn's depression, with her consistently exquisite, high-contrast, black-and-white cinematography and her dexterity in editing visuals and sounds. Robyn may not leave her apartment, but Reeves's imagery and montage reveal a woman exploring both the world and cinema.

During the past quarter century or so, we have seen a particular cinematic tradition emerge from Russia and Eastern Europe. Directors such as Andrei Tarkovsky (in *Stalker,* 1979; *Nostalgia,* 1983; and other films); Alexander Sokurov (in *The Second Circle,* 1990; *Mother and Son,* 1997); Sarunas Bartas (in *Musu nedaug/Few of Us,* 1996); and Béla Tarr (in *Kárhozat/ Damnation,* 1987; *Sátántangó/Satantango,* 1994; *Werckmeister harmóniák/ Werckmeister Harmonies,* 2000) have depicted worlds which for their protagonists are abjectly miserable—indeed, I have heard these filmmakers described as "miserablists"—but they depict this misery in a style so distinctive, so elegant, often so spectacularly beautiful, that the viewer is more enthralled than depressed. *The Time We Killed* is an American blues version of this approach. It was produced with far more humble means—the "miserablist" films reflect the paradox of their makers' access to the highest-quality film equipment within a thoroughly repressive state (or, at least, within psyches conditioned by decades of state repression)—but reflects something of the same feelings of powerlessness, combined with a passionate refusal to accept these feelings as psychically or aesthetically definitive.

Reeves and I spoke about *Chronic* and *The Time We Killed* by phone in July 2004 and refined our conversations by e-mail.

MacDonald: I see from your bio that you were born in Ceylon but grew up in Ohio. Could you tell me a little about your family background?

Reeves: My father was in the foreign service, stationed in Ceylon, when I was born. He was known there as the "musical diplomat" for his trumpet playing in jazz clubs and in the Colombo symphony orchestra. When my folks (James and Nancy) decided to leave the foreign service, they settled the family in Illinois, where my older brother and I went to elementary school. About ten years later we moved to Akron, Ohio.

MacDonald: Before I ask you about *The Time We Killed,* I want to talk about *Chronic*—because the two films seem closely related. In fact, a couple of shots from the earlier film are included in *The Time We Killed.*

Reeves: I did a show in Boston this past March, and I left feeling, "Oh, I'm so glad I'm not going to have to talk about my older work anymore; finally I have something new to talk about!" But I guess there's no escaping the earlier work.

MacDonald: Because *Chronic* seems so personal, so open, questions about how fully autobiographical it actually is seem almost inevitable. So, forgive me if I ask, how much of Gretchen is you?

Reeves: People often ask me this, and I wonder if it has to do with the form of the film, the difficult content, or viewers feeling their own personal connection to Gretchen's experiences. *Chronic* is more fiction than nonfiction, but the themes are autobiographical, and a few anecdotes are true.

I was working with a split of the self. Gretchen has an inherent conflict between self-destruction and recovery, and that is just one of many splits in her character that I can certainly identify with. It *is* an autobiographical *conflict*—but most of Gretchen's specific experiences are not autobiographical. Basically, for any dramatic event that takes place in the film, there's a comparable but different event in my life. For example, Gretchen is gang-raped and left on her lawn unconscious. Pictures are taken of her and circulated. Well, that never happened to me, though I did have traumatic experiences of being sexually assaulted and humiliated by young men. So the fictional sequences do channel pieces of real knowledge, like how a victim of violence (in effect a hate crime against women) can turn on herself when there is little support and no proper outlet for the anger.

MacDonald: Were you ever in a pattern of self-mutilation?

Reeves: Yes. Self-injury might better describe it. Self-injury is a sort of defense mechanism, if you will, and it's a hard one for many people to understand, because it seems to work against the survival instinct. But self-injury serves a function in a similar way that alcohol is often used by people to avoid facing conflicts that seem beyond their control; it's not healthy, but it's not just some crazy, random behavior. Self-injury involves pain, one of the most attention-getting sensations and, so, one of the most effective distractions.

I first cut myself at a very young age, at a time when I had no reference to it as something other people did. And, like Gretchen, I *was* hospitalized as a teenager, but more briefly, and it was my great discovery in the hospital that people from different backgrounds and cultural milieus—preppy jocks, Goth kids, hippies, kids from religious families, a Vietnam vet—were also cutting themselves. It's fairly common.

One thing driving me to make *Chronic* was a desire to more fully resolve what that experience was about for me, and to let go of it. Of course, after I finished the film, I still had related concerns that I wanted to explore, and these carried over to *The Time We Killed.* Another motivation in making

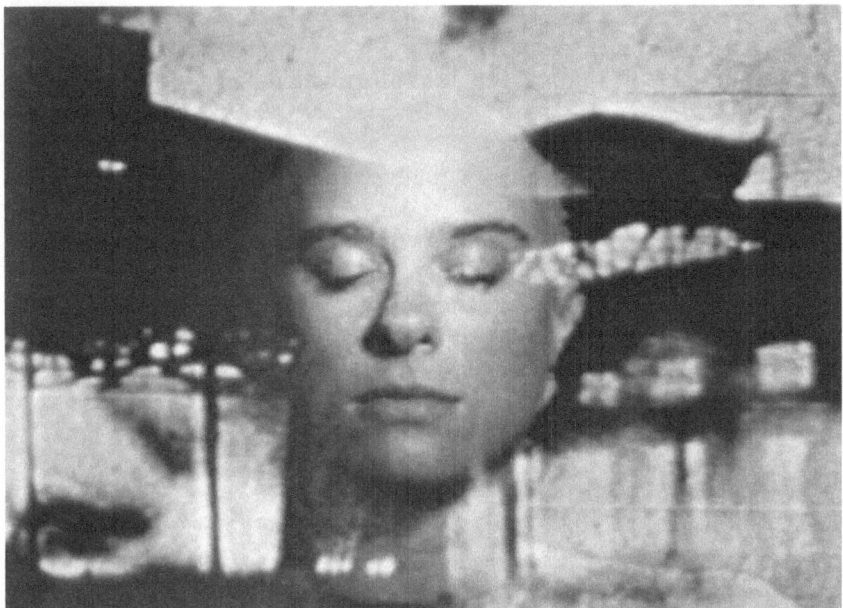

Jennifer Todd Reeves as Gretchen, in *Chronic* (1996). Courtesy Jennifer Todd Reeves.

both these films was the goal to create more subjective cinematic representations of the experience of living with mental illness. Many films dramatizing mental illness portray mysterious characters who "act crazy" and who the viewer can never understand (*Pollock* [2000, Ed Harris], for example, and *The Suicide Diaries* [2004]). And films dealing with recovery often do so in such a simplistic way. For example, *Ordinary People* [1980, Robert Redford], which moved me deeply, is about a family dealing with the suicide attempt of a young man whose brother died in a sailboat accident. There's that moment toward the end of the movie where he has the great realization during therapy that he feels guilty for surviving while his brother died, and so it's happily ever after—because the traumatic memory has been uncovered, the problem resolved. If only recovery in real life were so quick!

I resist this reassuring but reductive form of narrative; it over-simplifies life. In fact, human experience *needs* to be simplified to *work* as a dramatic narrative. Novels have the room, the flexibility, and the exposition to get at more of life's complexities; but traditional film narrative tends to reduce life to myth, because *nothing* in life can be so clear (in terms of cause and effect) as the stories in the movies.

I attempt to make films a little more true to the contradictions of real life experience, and so in *Chronic,* even though I include a traumatic event that had a profound effect on Gretchen (the gang rape), I try to show, from the beginning of the film, that she was already in a dangerous cycle before she went to the fraternity party; she desperately "wanted to be liked," as it says in the voice-over. Of course, she didn't ask for what happened to her, but something inside her, early on, made her vulnerable to that kind of experience. This is more complicated and it's a harder story to hear.

Also, at the end, when Gretchen seems to be improving, the final scenes make her recovery very ambiguous.

MacDonald: Yes, at the end you go back to the bathtub sequence with which the film begins, and we realize that the whole film can be read as a flashback explaining how Gretchen got into the tub. At the same time, since we don't actually see the razor blade during your re-edit of the sequence at the end, we can also read the imagery as suggesting that while she *may* be doing much the same thing, she may now be doing less damage, or no damage, to herself.

Reeves: At the beginning of this sequence there is a fairly abstract close-up of blood magically appearing and streaming down her thigh. It was pixilated so you don't see the razor blade, only the effect of cutting (as if it's caused by a force beyond Gretchen's control), and when she enters the bathtub, the water turns dark. But yes, people can have very different conclusions about what the last sequence implies about Gretchen's fate. For me it's symbolic; I've killed off a part of myself.

MacDonald: Did you write the fraternity boys' conversation?

Reeves: No. There, I'm bringing in a documentary element (I do the same thing in *The Time We Killed*). All the audio from that scene is taken from a real frat house gathering. I obtained the audio from a friend who videotaped a graduation dinner when he was a member of that fraternity (he later became enlightened). The seniors are at the front of this big room, getting drunk, and each guy is stands up and tells his "best" stories of his adventures in the frat to an audience of undergraduate fraternity brothers and new recruits.

The guys are not talking about "Gretchen"; they recount many different stories of sexual conquest, and it's all the more sinister because you hear aggression without intelligence and you know someone has been scarred by the stupid actions these young men find so amusing. For instance, one guy describes having intercourse with an unconscious woman: "I slapped the helmet on, and took care of business. And when the girl woke up in the morning, she looks at her underwear around her ankles, looks at the situation, and says, '*Oh no, not again!*'" which is followed by applause and laughter from the frat-house audience. I place this documentary audio together with the dramatized scene of the unconscious Gretchen being dropped off on her lawn by two guys. This gives the film a quality of being real, even though it's a fiction; and it takes you out of the particular narrative and onto a more universal plane where the experience of many individual women lies. Seeing the victim while hearing the perspective of a victimizer creates a painful irony.

MacDonald: Was all the imagery we see in *Chronic* shot specifically for that film? It uses a number of different processes and there are all these little montages within the film that could be separate films.

Reeves: Most of what you see in the finished film was shot with *Chronic* in mind, though some of the original footage was shot up to six years earlier as a kind of diary. This includes some of the mutilation footage; at the time I didn't know why I was shooting it, but just felt that I had to document what I was doing to myself. This certainly adds to the sense that the film is a personal documentary, though I'm using my visual diary to serve the fictional story of Gretchen.

Chronic was the second film I made after college (*The Girl's Nervy* was the first). At the time, I was living in New York City, working part-time at a video store and part-time at Millennium Film Workshop, as a monitor at the desk. I printed and edited *Chronic* at Millennium, and a Jerome Foundation grant covered the production costs.

MacDonald: You optically printed it so you could control the texture, the chiaroscuro, the moment-to-moment look of the film?

Reeves: Yes. The entire film is optically printed—except for maybe five or six shots.

I wanted the more objective scenes to be in regular black and white. Subjective scenes depicting extreme emotional states or Gretchen's disassociation and numbness had to be high-contrast (one of the traits of borderline personality disorder, which we learn is Gretchen's diagnosis, is "black and white thinking"); and scenes representing vivid feelings (both positive and negative) were often double exposed or bipacked, combining color with black and white. So there's a structure that highlights the intense shifts in Gretchen's perspective and psychological state.

I often attempt to create a form, an aesthetic, that reflects the content in my films. In *Chronic* I set up a parallel between the surface and texture of the film and Gretchen's "surface," her shell, her skin. And the layering I do with bipacking and double exposures juxtaposes the present with the past, and fantasy and obsession with reality. Gretchen's experience or interpretation of her present life is framed and conditioned by previous events in her life.

MacDonald: When you were working on *The Time We Killed,* were you thinking about it as a continuation of *Chronic?* Early on, there's a shot of you drinking Ovaltine, from the hospitalization section of the earlier film.

Reeves: I was aware of many connections between the two films, so using footage from *Chronic* as a flashback for Robyn in *The Time We Killed* made this link complete for me. *The Time We Killed* continues the themes of being locked up and observed, the tension between recovery and self-destructiveness, and the interplay of fiction and autobiography. There's something compelling to me in this kind of personal project, but I needed some distance from it before resuming.

After I finished *Chronic,* I had a full program of films that I could tour with—and it got me in touch with an audience in a way I had never experienced before. After screenings there were often in-depth Q & As, and people who had been very affected by the film were writing to me. I've always been quite shy, so this threw me into the world in an unfamiliar way. I felt a wonderful elation that the film was being received on a deep level by people who were thankful for it and that I was connecting with some of these individuals. But by the end of the touring, I felt very vulnerable and exposed, as well as rewarded for making such a naked work.

My films right after *Chronic* were mostly abstract and nonverbal, and any personal disclosure was very coded. But eventually I was compelled to go back to the unfinished business of *Chronic.* I wanted to explore a character in a later stage of recovery, being in the almost more-difficult period where there weren't intense crises, but more common problems and a lingering struggle to find some sort of balance between being part of the world in that strange time after 9/11 and allowing the inner life to take its course. And Robyn's more developed and free-associative internal monologue references another form of treatment: the talking cure, psychoanalysis.

I should say that I don't think it's necessary that the viewer know my personal reasons for doing what I do, though I think a filmmaker's motivations have to be honest and deeply felt, because that's what communicates the strength of emotion and the unique perspective you have to offer. If the content of the film *is* honestly felt and communicated, even if it's ambiguous, it invites viewers to make their own relationship to what they're seeing. Talking about themes that are personal to me does not feel as risky as the fact that I often bare ugly, difficult, painful emotions that are tied up with shame.

MacDonald: This has more to do with *The Time We Killed* than *Chronic* because we can understand the reasons, or some of the reasons, why Gretchen might do what she does, whereas in *The Time We Killed,* the source of what's keeping Robyn in the apartment is less clear and so maybe more shameful.

Reeves: It's more complicated for Robyn, who's in her thirties, because she has more of a history. Perhaps she's ashamed to show herself until she has resolved her problems and questions (in a sense re-creating her adolescent hospitalization)? Is being a recluse a new form of her earlier self-destructive tendencies? Are there early shameful experiences lost in her amnesia? There is no single answer.

MacDonald: You mentioned at the Flaherty [Reeves presented *The Time We Killed* at the 2004 Flaherty Film Seminar, curated by Susan Oxtoby] how the imagery used in the film accumulated over a period of time.

Reeves: I started what became *The Time We Killed* when I was in graduate school at UCSD [University of California, San Diego] in 1999. Leaving the plurality of New York culture, I felt that San Diego was uninspiring. It's a military town, a vacationer's "paradise," and is very unwelcoming to strangers. Mexico is just to the south and is cut off by a highly fortified border, an armed and patrolled no-man's-land. So I was confronted with some ugly truths and saw our country on the decline, politically.

I also became concerned about "the death of film" (my true love)—because many veteran filmmakers were switching to video, most students were working in video, and labs were closing. With the exception of a few professors (including Babette Mangolte and Thomas Allen Harris), I felt cut off from the community of filmmakers that loved experimental film or film as an artistic medium.

In December of 1998, looking for inspiration, I decided to go off to New Zealand for three weeks to visit friends, and took my Bolex with me. I knew I had to start a thesis film for my graduate degree, and I thought I could make a beginning of some sort. In New Zealand I shot portraits of people I knew and a lot of nature and animals, which all felt alive, unspoiled, and unfettered, aspects of life I was feeling disconnected from in San Diego. A lot of the New Zealand material found its way into *The Time We Killed* in fantasy and flashback sequences: the swimming hole imagery, people on horses, exotic plants, lambs, the pond . . . I was focusing on things that I feared were not going to be around anymore, including the high-contrast black-and-white film stock I was using. (Actually, by the time I finished shooting, certain of the stocks I had used were no longer being made.) I wanted to capture aspects of disappearing beauty while I still had the chance. And when I returned to San Diego, I was seeing the world differently and began shooting the environment and my life there as well. I became involved in a kind of nostalgia-in-the-present.

As *The Time We Killed* began to form in my mind, I realized I wanted to make the entire film in high-con black and white (which I'd used sparsely in *Chronic* and *Configuration 20* [1994]). I wanted to explore, while I still could, how high-con abstracts its subjects and the incomparable way it captures light and shadow. Its stark, shadowy, "incomplete" forms seemed an effective way to evoke the selective nature of memory and to create continuity between disparate places, people, and times.

I was inspired by Warren Sonbert's films, where each shot is a complete unit, a specific space at a particular time, while the larger whole of the film brings this variety of places and times together into one vibrant world. I wanted to bring together all the different elements I observed on random trips to New Zealand, California, Utah, Berlin, and the Midwest over the five years of production. Of course, that's what memory does, too; it combines disparate elements into a continuous flow.

I was also accumulating words, phrases, commentary, and observations about life in a notebook, much the way I was collecting images. Loss, death, and solitude were connecting themes for much of the writing, which no doubt was influenced by my father's death. Much of the time that I was working on *The Time We Killed,* my father's health was deteriorating due to radiation he received for a brain tumor. He became more and more distant and died in January 2001—and some months later what was to have been a montage film evolved into a narrative about a character dealing specifically with death. Robyn has sequestered herself away, partly as a way of dealing with the death of her close friend, Valeska, someone she was in love with and lost to cancer.

MacDonald: One of the things that people at the Flaherty seemed to find helpful during the discussion of the film was your saying that you found Robyn a somewhat unattractive character.

Reeves: Robyn's listlessness is very frustrating. Depression is like being inexplicably caught in a tunnel, trapped in negativity and self-absorption. People on the outside are saying, "Snap out of it! You're smart; we like you; you're beautiful, talented, funny—can't you see that and join us in the world?" In my own periods of depression I find myself quite unbearable. I know how trapped you can feel, *and* also how irritating, even repulsive, you can seem to others—until you're willing to make the tremendous effort and take the risk of coming back out of that tunnel.

MacDonald: Which Robyn does at the end by getting the dog.

Reeves: Yes, for a change, she's trying to do something that's nurturing to somebody, or something, other than herself.

The character of Robyn is a lot of different things to me. She's dealing not just with the loss of someone she loved, and with her feeling of powerlessness to get out of her rut, but also with being an individual in the world right now, when a sense of powerlessness and a fear of other people is part of American political and social life. Robyn's means of dealing with her mental state is to use her imagination, because *that* is totally vast. Her occupation, writing novels, fits her emotional needs; it allows her to *imagine* real intimacy and passionate love and risk taking: *her* protagonist, Tony, is having sex with strangers and has multiple lovers—the opposite of Robyn's solitary existence.

I film the characters Robyn imagines and the people she remembers, making eye contact with the camera: that eye contact expresses the intimacy and the connection that she's lacking and really wanting.

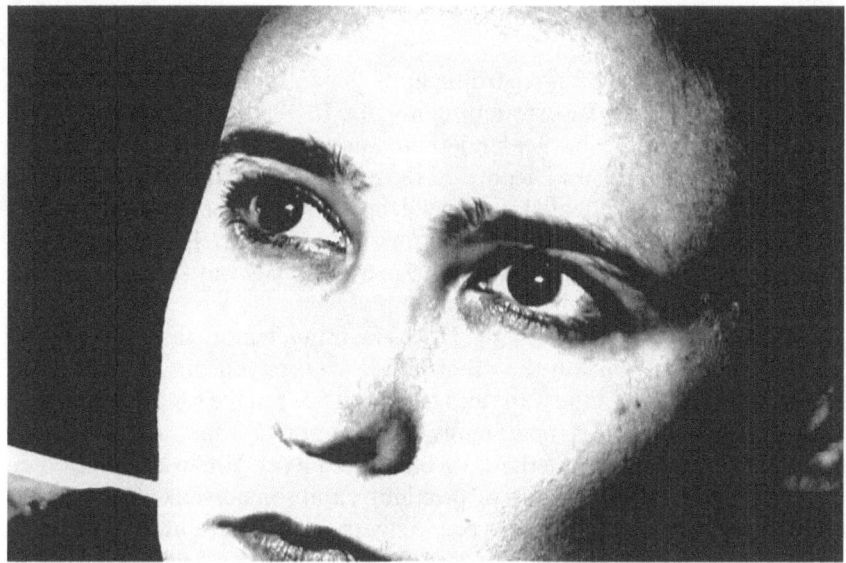

Lisa Jarnot as Robyn in Jennifer Todd Reeves's *The Time We Killed* (2004). Courtesy Jennifer Todd Reeves.

MacDonald: How did you decide on the title?

Reeves: The title is a maybe silly double entendre: Robyn is "killing time" in her apartment, partly because it's "killing time" in Iraq.

For me, the title evokes a number of things, including the strange experience of being an American while our government involves us in a senseless cycle of violence, being one of millions of people who, at least indirectly, have given this country the power to act this way.

Early in the film Robyn is detached. She says, "Sometimes I get the feeling that I'm totally evil," but then she speaks of her *father* doing animal testing for the military, not what *she* has done; she highlights but then sidesteps any notion of her own responsibility. Later in the film Robyn is taken out of a daydream about the "good old days" in New York before 9/11 when the catastrophic "shock and awe" bombing of Iraq appears on her television. Robyn's personal struggles, and most of the arguments of her neighbors, seem absurd against this backdrop. She observes, "There are some bad vibes going around in my building. I think it's the war. Some kind of bad karma for people who just sit by." She is basically saying she feels at fault for not being out there actively opposing the invasion, acknowledging collective responsibility.

MacDonald: You mentioned that there are documentary elements in *The*

Time We Killed. Are the arguments that we're hearing from nearby apartments some of those?

Reeves: Yeah. I've been recording audio since 1995 or 1996, documenting some of the sounds surrounding my life. In 1999, a couple of months after I got back from New Zealand, there was a murder-suicide in the apartment next to mine in San Diego; and the experience of hearing the discovery of those bodies affected me very deeply. Even something that you're an accidental witness to can hit you on a profound level. The audio you hear about the murder-suicide in *The Time We Killed* was recorded during that incident.

As is typical in tenement living, I often hear much more than I'd like, and it's very invasive—but on the other hand, it takes you out of la-la land. Sound travels through the walls and boundaries we make for ourselves, and it provokes associations, imaginings, and memories (especially since sentences are in fragments and there are blanks to fill in). You're aware of other people's struggles just because of proximity, and someone like Robyn can't resist the humanity that she was originally trying to shut out.

MacDonald: Did you ask Lisa Jarnot to write the poetry we hear her recite?

Reeves: No, not specifically. Lisa is a poet and a very good friend of mine. In 2000, Stan Brakhage introduced us, having seen a connection between our work. We have since had a truly inspiring friendship.

I shot all the present-day scenes of Robyn in the apartment with video, on a tripod. With no film crew the material could be more intimate, and the carefully composed video gave the interior scenes a quality of control and claustrophobia (as opposed to the free-form memory and fantasy sequences shot on high-con). So it was just the two of us most of the time. Lisa would come over for a six- or seven-hour day; I would shoot an afternoon scene in the living room when the sun was coming in and then an evening scene. As we were preparing Robyn's scenes, I'd tell Lisa what I was getting at in the film and who her character was. Several times while I was setting up the camera, microphone, and lights, Lisa would be sitting at the typewriter or the computer, getting into character for a particular shot, and she would start writing a poem. The five poems she wrote this way reflected various things we had been talking about, the concerns of the film, the environment of the apartment, or the scene that we had just shot.

Both Lisa and I have been in psychoanalysis; her poetry and my montage work are very free-associative. Either there's a quality we share that makes each of us suited for psychoanalysis, or maybe psychoanalysis has fed into our art. At any rate, when I first read those poems, I immediately responded, "This is perfect!" I was especially excited because the poems give an additional dimension to Robyn. On one hand, she writes these schlocky novels; and, secondly, she's the inward-looking recluse, consumed with past events and what they mean for her presently. Lisa's poetry gave Robyn a third facet: a gift for poetry and a much more complex way of making connections between her thoughts and experiences. Any person's internal life has many different facets, so "Robyn's" poetry makes for a more complete rendition of her consciousness.

MacDonald: Brakhage's admiration of your work, and especially *Chronic*, is well-known.

Reeves: Stan took a liking to *Chronic, The Girl's Nervy,* and *Configuration 20*. In 1998 he curated a show at Anthology Film Archives, three or four programs, and he put those three films in that show. I was so honored. He also told me he liked *We Are Going Home* [1998] and *Darling International* [1998] (which I codirected with M. M. Serra), and I know that he showed *Fear of Blushing* [2001] at his last Sunday salon [see note on p. 92 for information about Brakhage's salon]. He called me to tell me how much he liked it.

I didn't get to know Stan very well. We had some long talks at Bard College in 2000 and met just a few other times. I wish I could've gotten to know him better.

MacDonald: One last question: the final line of *The Time We Killed* is "I left the cave today and there you were; you've changed since I went away." Who's the "you"?

Reeves: The world, New York City, and also the river that she's looking at in the final shots. There's also a flashback to Valeska during her walk to the river; in a way she's also talking to her.

I would say that my films are made up of both instinctive decisions and very conscious strategies of meaning. That final line was one of my more instinctive choices, and it underscores a very simple thing. Of course, if you've been hiding away, things are going to be different when you go out again, but such an obvious fact can still be surprising to discover. What has kept this person from facing the world for so long is a fearful perception of what she might find.

There's a roundabout trajectory to that final sequence when Robyn reenters public space, similar to the way she goes to the roof on her way to the street, rather than using the front door. Robyn is finally outside, and for the first time, we see her in the high-contrast film stock used to shoot her memories and fantasies. It feels a bit unreal. We see views of the street and Robyn walking the dog, which *is* a real activity, but she goes from being aware of the surroundings and the dog to getting caught up in her head again—which is clear from the poem we hear. But when she gets to the river, she's overwhelmed by the place, by the light and the water. The city is providing many of the things that were in her memories and fantasies: there are the trees and the animal she's walking; there's the bridge (like the one she jumped from as an adolescent) and the sun piercing it; and the lapping of the waves provides a sense of calm. At this point I feel the film comes together, and there's a melding of Robyn's interior and exterior spaces.

Of course, in the last shot she's walking back toward the door of her building. She's still primarily alone, and she's going back to the apartment—but hopefully not for another six months.

Shiho Kano

In 1980 the American Federation of Arts asked the film scholar Donald Richie to create a traveling show focusing on the history of experimental film in Japan. Richie worked with Katsue Tomiyama, then the director of Image Forum in Tokyo, to produce "Japanese Experimental Film 1960–1980," two programs of short films that toured the United States in the early 1980s. My memory of these programs has faded, but I do remember that the most pleasant surprise was *Kiri* (*Mist,* 1972) by Sakumi Hagiwara, an eight-minute, single-shot film during which a misty landscape slowly clears, revealing a bit of a distant mountain. *Mist* was a particular pleasure for me, since I had recently begun to write about Larry Gottheim's *Fog Line* (1970), during which a foggy landscape begins to clear, revealing trees, bushes, and other details of a pasture. Certainly, there are differences between the two films—*Mist* is black and white, *Fog Line,* in color; the landscape in *Fog Line* is more fully mediated by technology—and yet, I found it interesting, even poignant, that on opposite sides of the globe two filmmakers had had virtually the same idea at the same time and had produced two lovely, serene films.

I experienced something of the same pleasure at the 2003 Images Festival in Toronto, when I saw three films by Shiho Kano—*Landscape* (1998), *Still* (1999), and *Rocking Chair* (2000)—in a program of Japanese experimental film curated by Chris Gehman. I was particularly taken with *Rocking Chair,* a thirteen-minute, color, sound film that reminded me of some of the recent films and videos of Leighton Pierce. As was true of my experi-

Interview translated by Melek Su Ortabasi.

Foggy mountain landscape in Sakumi Hagiwara's *Kiri* (1972). Courtesy American Federation of the Arts.

ence with *Mist* and *Fog Line,* I could see obvious differences between Pierce's work and *Rocking Chair,* but I was moved that these two artists, working in quite different circumstances, should be motivated to make beautiful work so obviously consonant in spirit and impact.

In her recent work—*White Tablecloth* (2000, which exists as a single-channel video and as a multimonitor installation piece), *Rocking Chair, Incense* (2002), and *Rosecolored Flower* (2002)—Kano has explored minimal indoor spaces by using subtle changes in lighting and camera position, carefully choreographed with environmental sounds. All these works combine a meditative sensibility and a fascination with the magical possibilities of film and video. In *White Tablecloth,* for example, the focus is a small, clear-glass cruet of water, sitting on a white tablecloth, a watermark just barely visible surrounding the cruet. During just over seven minutes, the watermark subtly changes shape and size, ebbs and flows, not simply as a result of the process of evaporation but, we slowly realize, because of Kano's invisible manipulation of the image so that we see it nonchronologically.

Rocking Chair creates a powerful sense of domestic space, or really *artistic* space, as a refuge from the outside world represented by the sounds of automobile and train traffic. During thirteen minutes, Kano reveals several views of a room, as a young woman comes into the space and sits quietly in the rocking chair near the window. In *Incense* we focus on a stick of burning incense in a glass incense holder, as Kano choreographs changes in light and bits of movement (a woman walks through the room, opening and closing a door . . .) in the surrounding room. At one point, the smoke from the incense stick reveals that the action is now moving in reverse, but no sooner do we notice this than we see that the motion is forward again. And in *Rosecolored Flower,* Kano's focus is a small vase on a windowsill, recorded as the video camera gradually, for a while almost invisibly, zooms in on the vase.

Shiho Kano's films and videos—like Leighton Pierce she works equally well, and similarly, in both media—embody a quiet, thoughtful sensibility that functions as a tonic in a high-tech, rapid-fire world. One can only hope that her work becomes increasingly available in North America, and that this young career continues to blossom.

The following conversation was conducted via e-mail through a translator, Melek Su Ortabasi, my colleague at Hamilton College, during the winter of 2003. (In Japan, of course, the surname comes first, then the given name. I've Americanized Kano's name in my text; but in the interview itself, I've used the Japanese form of her name and of the other Japanese filmmakers and exhibitors she mentions, so as to reflect her way of speaking.)

MacDonald: I spoke to Taka Iimura recently, and he mentioned that he knew you, and that got me to wondering what the avant-garde or experimental film scene is like in Japan. Do you even call it "avant-garde" or "experimental" film?

Kano: The labels "avant-garde film" and "experimental film" are fraught with problems. When I want to describe my own works, I end up using these labels for the sake of convenience but have often been confounded when people ask me, "So what *is* experimental film?" Actually, this is an issue that has been debated throughout the years, and each generation has probably come to a different conclusion. Presently, however, the fact that there isn't even a debate about what this kind of filmmaking is has created all sorts of ignorance and misunderstanding, and has affected viewers and filmmakers alike. The common idea about "avant-garde film" and "experimental film" is that it's "obscure," "strange," "nonsense," or—even though new films are being created every day—"something from the sixties." Nobody seems to be trying to define what these terms really mean.

I first came into contact with so-called experimental film and avant-garde film around 1990. As you probably know, there is a small theater in Tokyo, called Image Forum; in Japan, it's the only established venue for showing experimental film. Dropping by frequently, I was able to see all sorts of work. At the annual Image Forum Festival, I would see many domestic and foreign films. I doubt whether I really understood it at the time, but the power of Ito Takashi's *Spacy* [1981], the serenity of Hagiwara Sakumi's *Time* [1971], the stoic beauty of Matsumoto Toshio's *Shiki Soku Ze Kū* [All Is Vanity, 1975]—all these diverse experiences deeply influenced and dazzled my high school student self. I had never seen films so free from convention.

MacDonald: How did you happen to become a filmmaker and videomaker? And what drew you to the kind of work you do?

Kano: After high school, with the aim of becoming a photographer, I entered the Department of Imaging Arts and Sciences at Musashino Art University. I studied photography for three out of those four years. Though I did take some courses on film and studied the works of such directors as Sergei Eisenstein, Andrei Tarkovsky, Mizoguchi Kenji, and Ozu Yasujiro, my weekends were spent producing photographic work. Going out into the city, I would shoot monochrome landscapes, apply photographic emulsions to diverse media—drawing paper, cloth, plastic—and experiment with printing on them. However, I gradually became bored with pursuing the same motifs every day, camera in hand, and I got tired of trying to create new images from photographs, which had me straying ever further from the essence of the photographic medium.

My method for escaping my boredom was to take up animation. In my last year of university, I created two 16mm animation projects, using photographs and watercolors, under the direction of animator Kurosaka Keita. This new experience liberated me; at the same time, I became interested in the relationship of image with time and space. Soon after, as a commemoration of my farewell to photography, I made prints of only the last frames from the vast number of negatives I had shot. Because the last frame on a roll is usually overexposed, it's normally ignored and left unprinted. The inexpressible beauty of that faded image, almost washed out by light, suddenly made me notice the temporality of photography, and it helped confirm my decision to enter the world of the moving image.

MacDonald: For me, your work hovers between magic and meditation. Are there particular filmmakers or videomakers, or painters or artists in other fields, who have been important in the evolution of your approach?

Kano: After I graduated from university, I studied at the Image Forum Institute of the Moving Image for two years, where I had the opportunity to make 8mm films and see a great number of experimental and avant-garde films. That's when I encountered Michael Snow's *Wavelength* [1967] and was deeply influenced by Maya Deren's *Meshes of the Afternoon* [1943] and Oki Hiroyuki's works. Oki Hiroyuki won the Rotterdam Film Festival's NETPACK Award when quite young and was considered a promising filmmaker early on. His recent works are not limited to film; he's quite active in the contemporary art world these days, too.

Being at the institute was a great experience, since I saw so many films, but also because I had the chance to meet the many directors who came to visit. Hearing that the pioneer of Japanese avant-garde film, Matsumoto Toshio, was coming for a lecture, I pressed one of my videotapes on him, asking him to watch it. Despite the fact that we were not at all acquainted, Matsumoto wasn't put out at this nameless student's outrageous request, but even sent me some brief comments a few days later.

Also around that time, I joined the film discussion group Kino Balazs, which was made up mainly of filmmakers and critics in their thirties. At the monthly gatherings, we listened to talks on Hitchcock and Eisenstein, and "expanded cinema" (I believe Tony Conrad visited at some point), and used the group as a forum for exchanging information among ourselves. Once, when we decided on Martin Arnold as a topic for discussion, we used a translation of your interview with him as our text.

It was at this discussion group that I came to know Iimura. Iimura's works and his personality remain a strong stimulus for me.

MacDonald: Landscape [Joukei] seems to be what we would call in the United States your "thesis film"—a film in which you show your adeptness with a variety of techniques. Already your interest in slowing time down, in a more meditative film experience, is evident in the two long images of the woman, but you also seem to be working directly on the filmstrip in some instances, and I assume you are hand processing some of the film.

Could you talk about the process of doing *Landscape?*

Kano: Filmmaker Sueoka Ichiro once showed me a piece called *Vase* [1997] that he had done by hand processing. It was a fantastic, highly conceptual three-minute film that simply showed a vase with flowers in it. That's how I became interested in this technique. I learned it from him as soon as I could, and after a number of experiments, I created those scenes with the woman.

What gave me the most difficulty was how well I could bring the technique into harmony with the concept of a film, and not use it simply as a special effect. In the end, I felt that the accidental scratches and other exposure irregularities that can be achieved with hand processing could draw attention not only to the materiality of film itself but also to the slippage in time between the film-as-material and the filmed image. When we watch a film, the scratches and colors on the surface of the film give evidence that we are watching *film*. With hand processing, I rediscovered the difference between the leisurely speed of the recorded image and the speed of projection itself. I could transform "watching" the image into "experiencing" the image.

Once I had discovered the many layers of time that could be experienced simultaneously with the hand-processing technique, I had the idea of doing multiple exposures while shooting. However, because I did too many exposures, the frames were out of sync during filming, causing the image to become unexpectedly dynamic. It was a bit of an accident, but the subtle movement of the multiexposed image had the surprising result of making it look like the actual frame itself was trembling. I'm very satisfied with the result. It forms the core of the film and gave birth to all the images in *Landscape*. That's why those scenes of the woman reading are so important to the film.

There's also the very last scene, of the woman standing by the window, which forms something of a contrast to the reading woman. That's a photograph I took with slide film. I projected the image from behind a curtainlike fabric with a slide projector, and shot it on 8mm film with multiple exposures. I adjusted it so that the light from the projector would be coming from the same angle as sunlight from a window would have. I also made the fabric sway, as though blown gently by a breeze.

MacDonald: You mention in your program notes that the woman in the film "is not the heroine, and is equated with the landscape." I'm not sure I understand.

Kano: Joukei is a Japanese word that means "landscape as seen through a human sensibility." Even when two people are looking at the same scenery, they often get completely different impressions of it. One could also say that they have completely different experiences in time, while being in the same place. As for the woman, she is a metaphor for the viewer him- or herself. As it is none other than the viewer who is watching the metaphor/woman, one could say that object and observer are in a mirror image relationship to each other.

MacDonald: In *Still* you work "against the grain" of our normal assumptions about still and moving picture photography, in that you film a series of black-and-white (or really sepia-toned) still photographs to indicate that various kinds of motion occur, but you shoot extended color shots in which there is very little motion. The "motion pictures" are comparatively still, and the "stills" suggest motion. You mentioned earlier that you studied photography before you studied film. Is *Still* a way of exploring the different potentials of these two media? Or was it a way of incorporating your interest in photography into what had become your primary interest.

Kano: *Still* was my final project at the Image Forum Institute of the Moving Image. I wanted to assemble the black-and-white photos I had accumulated, into a film. As you point out, in this work, the moving picture is largely still, while movement is expressed with still photographs. I wanted to explore the possibilities of these two different media in a form where they would complement each other.

During the making of the film, I made an unexpected discovery. Surprisingly, when I shot the still photographs with Super-8mm film and saw them as moving pictures, they seemed to leave their material limitations behind and become pure "image."

MacDonald: While I like and admire a good many things in *Landscape* and *Still*, it's not until *Rocking Chair* that you achieve a style and form that seem fully mature. The film's eleven shots are beautifully organized in terms of both image and sound. You seem fascinated with the opportunity film offers for working with the "choreography" of natural light coming through the curtains and your own "choreography" of the aperture.

Kano: For *Rocking Chair* I manipulated the aperture of the camera in accordance with the movements of the woman and the curtain. It's completely different from effects created after shooting. Making the aperture react to unpredictable moments and movements really *is* like "choreography." Furthermore, I didn't move the camera; it was the light alone creating the movement. And since I couldn't check the state of the aperture while I was working, shooting while imagining my "choreography" was very thrilling.

MacDonald: At some point during your accumulation of imagery did you design a storyboard for *Rocking Chair?* What went into the final organization of that film? What led to your separating the specific images from one another with moments of darkness?

Kano: The only things I had decided on were that there would be a woman and a rocking chair in a white room and that I would focus on the manipulation of light. Instead of slavishly reproducing images from a storyboard, I wanted to rely on the light and the air as they actually appeared through the camera's viewfinder. Before shooting, what's important is to decide on the concept, the composition, and the other parts that make up the skeleton of a piece. Actually, I made a storyboard *after* I shot the film—well, not exactly a storyboard, but I separated the shots from each other using cards and thought about how I was going to edit by trying them in different orders. Shooting and editing is a lot like arranging photographs. Thinking about a storyboard as a bunch of interchangeable cards is like thinking about choosing which photos to put in what order on a wall. That's how I decided on the structure of the film: I pretended that all the shots were lined up on a wall. I also imagined how the timing of the particular shots would combine to make up the flow of the whole.

The moments of darkness are like picture frames. In *Rocking Chair* I rejected editing as an investment of meaning in the connections between shots. Instead, I let each shot stand on its own in order to create a larger, overall flow. I once presented *Rocking Chair* as an installation where I ran three differently edited versions of the film simultaneously on three monitors. While each monitor was independent, I set the installation up so that one could watch all three at the same time. I inserted the darkness into the film in order to give equal value to each shot, in the way that the installation gave equal value to each monitor.

MacDonald: Did you shoot all the material in your apartment? Or do you find spaces outside of your personal spaces that you like to record?

Kano: The shooting location was the house where I lived for over twenty years. My parents, sister, and grandmother live there now. For *Rocking Chair,* I wanted a plain, white room. The house was perfect, and there was no time limit on how long I could use the room.

MacDonald: Like your earlier films, but even more clearly, *Rocking Chair* seems to defy the normal expectations of modern film and television, which I assume are not so different in Japan from what they are here. Could you talk about the kind of viewer you hope to appeal to and the nature of the experience you mean to create in *Rocking Chair* and in the other films?

Kano: Personally, I think that all film stems from the primitive images that pioneers like Méliès and the Lumière brothers left us. After film became somewhat established, avant-garde and experimental filmmakers self-consciously took on that same exploratory approach to film. Additionally, since we've come into contact with film, haven't we all experienced time and movement in a new way? What I am interested in is that most "primitive," basic quality that is a part of all film. I seek the same sort of experience and discovery in the present. I don't think that early film has become irrelevant and out of date; rather, I think we continually return there in order to come up with new discoveries.

This is probably difficult to understand for the regular viewer, who only comes into contact with contemporary media. But what I want to do is explore the hidden potential of film imagery using contemporary technology. Using this medium that we humans have discovered, I'd like to bring a new awareness to all the everyday things we see, and the experiences we take for granted. That is my simple goal.

MacDonald: Your use of sound adds a great deal to your films and videos. I assume that you record sound separately and construct a sound track from a variety of sources, once you've shot your imagery.

What are the specific sources of the sounds we hear in *Rocking Chair?*

Kano: I recorded the sound track for *Rocking Chair* later. The sound, like the image, is very simple. You could say that, for me, sound is one more kind of image. In a sense, sound and image are the same in that both embody time and space.

The sound in *Rocking Chair* is the sort of noise we hear every day. It's altered only by the fact that I slowed it down. When such cacophonic noise is slowed down, the individual sounds that compose it become audible. It creates a result that is similar to what happens when one uses slow motion.

I don't assume the viewer will know what kind of noise I'm using. At the beginning of the film, it's all from inside the room. Later, there's the faint sound of a door closing, and with that, it changes to outside noise. The visuals are all inside the room, but the sound moves outside of that space.

MacDonald: Each of the final two, very long shots tends toward a different kind of magic from the earlier shots. In the earlier shots, the focus is on composition and timing. In the second-to-last shot, you layer the image so that we see several layers of curtain simultaneously (this echoes your work with the woman's collar in *Landscape* and with the water on the tablecloth in *White Tablecloth*), which reveals your interest in playing with editing in a very subtle way. In the final shot, when the image gets most bright, it begins to tremble. Is it fair to say that you like working just at the edges of perception, and just at the edges of our consciousness of the image?

Kano: What my works ask of the viewer is: How deep is the relationship between the sense of sight and the action of "looking"? The structure of film and the mechanism of the camera teach us that looking, really looking, is an experience of time. Most people aren't that conscious about the everyday act of seeing.

MacDonald: Is that you in the imagery?

Kano: No, she's a friend of mine, the same friend who appeared in *Landscape*. In my works, I often need a human figure who blends well with landscape, and she has that sort of elegant presence. Because I wanted that to come through when I shot the film, I told her not to *act,* but just to walk and sit—to simply *be.*

MacDonald: In the United States, incense is often thought of as an aid to meditation, and I understand *Incense* as an aid to a more meditative way of seeing. That is, I read the incense in the film as a metaphor for the film

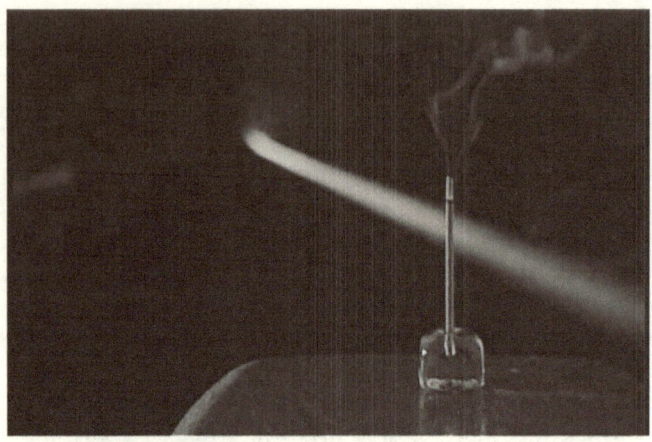

Incense stick in Shiho Kano's *Incense* (2002).
Courtesy Shiho Kano.

itself, and the function of incense as a metaphor for the function of your filmmaking. Does this seem sensible to you?

Kano: In Japan, incense is used for religious rituals, but for us Japanese, it's nothing really special. Even outside of religious ritual, burning incense in one's room to relax, for example, is an everyday thing. I chose incense because I wanted to capture the organic movement of the smoke and because of the natural way the smoke floats around a room. Tobacco smoke would probably have worked too, but I don't smoke, and smoke from incense is much more delicate and elegant. Most appealing is the way it suggests its own invisible scent.

As you point out, *looking,* or especially *contemplating,* is very important to my works. When you contemplate something over time, subtle changes become great discoveries. Through contemplation, the organic movement of the smoke, the fluttering of a curtain in the breeze, or the simple movements of human beings become photographic subjects that can lead one to a completely new mode of thinking.

MacDonald: The new video, *Rosecolored Flower,* is lovely. For a North American, its use of a slow, continuous zoom into the vase and flower evokes Michael Snow's *Wavelength.*

Kano: Wavelength is appealing, and certainly one of my favorite pieces, but I wasn't especially thinking of it as I made *Rosecolored Flower;* I don't think there's much direct influence there.

I see American and European works mainly at Image Forum. I've also had the opportunity to attend events like the Viper Festival [in Basel, Switzerland]. I don't encounter many pieces that move me, but I've found Matthias Müller's recent work, as well as Peter Hutton's, to be quite beautiful. In Tokyo, the Goethe Institute and the Athénée Français have regular programs in which they present German and French experimental film and video art. At a Marguerite Duras film series, I was deeply impressed by the use of sound and the fixed shot in her *India Song* [1975].

MacDonald: How long does it take you to make a film or a video?

Kano: In general, my films are made more quickly than films with a lot of cuts. *Landscape* involved many experiments with hand processing, so it took many months; but my recent pieces (especially those on video) generally take anywhere from half a day to three days to shoot, tests included. With *White Tablecloth,* for example, I woke up one morning to the most beautiful light in my room. I prepared straightaway and shot the whole thing during the seven and a half minutes when the slowly changing sunlight was at its most optimal. That footage, as is, became the finished product. Of course, I had thought about the concept in advance, but that morning's light was pure coincidence, and I probably would never be able to capture something similar again.

I think about concepts over a long period of time, but rather than draw up a storyboard, I think as I look through the camera lens, filming as I go. Serendipity can bring the unexpected moment, so I actively try to incorporate that sense of chance. Because I film whenever something moves me, I often take shots that are unrelated to my concept.

I've often taken the same shot over and over again. When I was making *Rocking Chair,* I shot about three times as much footage as I needed, so editing the piece took quite a while. With *Incense,* I lit and filmed many, many sticks of incense and had about sixty minutes of footage left over—though I ended up using the very first shot I took. *White Tablecloth* is the only exception.

MacDonald: You've worked in Super-8mm, in 16mm, and in video. Do you prefer one medium over another?

Kano: The concept determines the medium, so I don't really have a favorite. Each one has its special qualities, and all of them are appealing. I've been doing a lot with video lately, but I'll probably use Super-8mm again. If I have the chance, I'd like to try my hand at 35mm and 70mm as well.

Ernie Gehr

For nearly forty years, Ernie Gehr has been making cinematic magic, often from the least likely materials. Indeed, Gehr's most famous film, *Serene Velocity* (1970), in which the filmmaker transforms an institutional hallway in the basement of a classroom building at the State University of New York at Binghamton into a nexus of visual and conceptual energy, merely by adjusting his stationary camera's zoom lens every four frames for twenty-three minutes, can be read as Gehr's manifesto. For Gehr the most everyday spaces and the most mundane actions offer the imaginative filmmaker the most interesting potential. No other filmmaker, with the exception of Michael Snow, has so relentlessly and so productively explored the capacity of filmmaking to develop the visual (and auditory) opportunities afforded by the cinematic apparatus itself.

Gehr arrived on the independent film scene in the late 1960s, after a stint in the army, finding his way, first, to the New York Filmmakers' Cinematheque, when it offered regular screenings on Forty-first Street, then to the newly formed Millennium Film Workshop, directed at the time by Ken Jacobs, and to jobs at Anthology Film Archives and the Film-makers' Cooperative. After a number of experiments with filmmaking that helped Gehr understand what he wanted to do with a motion-picture camera, he began his formal career with *Morning* (1967), in which he transforms the interior of part of a New York City loft into a camera obscura by manipulating the shutter of his camera frame by frame. As dawn allows more and more light into the apartment, Gehr allows more and more light into the camera obscura of his Bolex, creating a vibrant, virtually stroboscopic experience—

one that extends the infusion of morning light into the theater. It is the "dawn" of a new approach to filmmaking and a reinvigoration of the screening space.

In the years that followed *Morning,* Gehr explored a variety of cinematic territories—most of them situated somewhere in between the still photograph and the conventional uses of the motion picture to depict melodramatic action and emotion. In *Wait* (1967), Gehr controls the durations in between his exposure of successive frames, and his aperture, so that a simple domestic space and scene flickers with new life. For *Reverberation* (1969), Gehr moved outside into New York City streets to document a lower Manhattan construction site, beginning what was to become, in addition to a set of formal investigations into the visual dynamics of the film experience, a remarkable series of city portraits, first, of New York City and, after he moved to San Francisco, of San Francisco. *Still* (1971), at 54½ minutes Gehr's longest film to date, depicts a portion of Lexington Avenue across from what was then the Film-makers' Cooperative office (175 Lexington had been, earlier on, the office of the New York City film society Cinema 16) over a period of months, in many cases using superimposition as a way of evoking a sense of the transience of human beings within the monumental architectural space of the city.

With *Shift* (1974), Gehr made sound a particularly dynamic dimension of his cinematic exploration of urban space. Although he had used sound in earlier films—*Reverberation* is accompanied by a powerfully reverberant sound track, and *Still* uses a mixture of silence and street sounds—in *Shift* Gehr shifts his emphasis, creating a variety of effects, including a good many surprises, by juxtaposing the sounds of traffic with particular movements of vehicles filmed from an apartment window. Gehr's perspective looking down at the street also allows him to play with the planar surface of the street, which is sometimes framed so as to fool the eye. This suggestion of the sometimes disconcerting visual impact of life in a metropolis—documented in the city film as early as *Manhatta* (1921, by Charles Sheeler and Paul Strand) and an important subject of modern urban photography—is the primary focus in *Side/Walk/Shuttle* (1991), Gehr's astonishing depiction of San Francisco as seen from the outdoor glass elevator of the Fairmont Hotel at the top of Nob Hill as it ascends and descends. As fully as any film, *Side/Walk/Shuttle* demonstrates the imaginative poverty of the convention (in film and in painting) that within the frame, the top is *up* and the bottom, *down.*

Side/Walk/Shuttle was Gehr's second San Francisco film. Soon after his arrival in the Bay Area, Gehr paid his respects to local history by refilming *A Trip down Market Street before the Fire* (1905; the producer is unknown), during which a camera, mounted apparently on a Market Street trolley, films the trip down Market Street to the Embarcadero. *Eureka* (1974) allows us to reexperience this early film and not only see it more clearly but also see *through* it into the life of a busy turn-of-the-century city. The men and women and the myriad vehicles that crowd Market Street in what appears to be near chaos create a sense of the social and commercial energy of San Francisco reminiscent of Francis Ford Coppola's famous tracking shot along a Lower East Side street in *The Godfather, Part 2* (1974). But here the scene is all the more remarkable for being real, and for the poignancy suggested in the original film's title: the San Francisco earthquake and fire would devastate the city a few months later. Gehr concludes his journey down Market Street, just after a wagon with "Eureka, California" painted on its side passes the camera, by focusing in on the date of completion of the Ferry Building (the terminus of the Market Street trolley): 1896. That this is the first full year of cinema's public life confirms Gehr's homage to the history of this mechanical art form, a history that—as is evident throughout *Eureka*—is inscribed into the film material in the form of scratches and fading and other forms of damage to which the filmstrip is susceptible.

Few filmmakers I have worked with are as passionately private about their personal histories as Gehr. Indeed, nearly all my questions about the particulars of his background, and his childhood and youth, have been rebuffed. Some sense of the reason for Gehr's reticence is suggested by his Berlin film, *Signal—Germany on the Air* (1985), which was the result of a sustained visit to Berlin in 1982. Berlin was the home of Gehr's parents before they emigrated, first to Argentina and subsequently to Milwaukee, when Gehr was eight years old. *Signal—Germany on the Air* simultaneously records modern Berlin (at the time, West Berlin) and periodically visits locations thick with implication for a filmmaker of Jewish heritage: the ruins of gestapo buildings and a set of overgrown train tracks and a deteriorating train station. Gehr's Berlin film focuses primarily on a relatively nondescript intersection, which becomes simultaneously familiar and labyrinthine, both visually and in terms of what one reads into particular details.

In recent years Gehr has continued many of the kinds of investigations that characterize the early decades of his career. But like so many filmmakers, he has been forced to deal with the increasing financial strains of shooting and printing film, while supporting a family and dealing with the psychic demands of his teaching life (Gehr teaches at the San Francisco Art Institute and, as this is written, is the chair of the film department). Although he does continue to make 16mm films, Gehr has turned to digital video for much of his recent work. His digital videos reveal a maker exploring a new set of tools, but for purposes consonant with earlier work. In *City* (2002), for example, Gehr explores city street life, especially the visual layering so common within street scenes; *Cotton Candy* (2001) and *Glider* (2001) reveal

Gehr using one of the newest motion-picture technologies to document and engage with early, even precinematic, forms of motion-picture experience. *Cotton Candy* records early mutoscopes; *Glider* is Gehr's interpretive engagement with the imagery created within the giant camera obscura overlooking Ocean Beach in San Francisco.

This interview began with a conversation in New York City in October 2002 and continued by phone during the following year. We refined the conversation by e-mail.

MacDonald: The first film you list in catalogues is *Morning,* a film that's mattered a lot to me. I've written about it a number of times, and I have a hard time teaching without it: it's a way of making clear to students what a camera obscura is and how the camera obscura is incorporated into the cinematic apparatus. And it's a polished, interesting film. I assume *Morning* isn't actually your first film.

Gehr: There were a number of short 8mm films that preceded *Morning*. They were created mostly in late 1966 and early 1967. I was interested in film before that, since my late teens, more or less, but I didn't think I would ever make films. Then, one rainy evening in 1966, I took shelter in a doorway. To one side of the doorway, there was a poster that announced "Films by Brakhage" at the Filmmakers' Cinematheque, which was located in the basement of the Wurlitzer Building on Forty-first Street.

MacDonald: How did you happen to be in New York City?

Gehr: I was drafted into the army in 1964. When I had to go for my physical, I told them that I couldn't see much without my glasses; I never thought I would be drafted. But a few months later, I received papers to report for basic training in Missouri. I didn't know how to get out of serving, so I served. Luckily, I ended up as a medic, stationed at Madigan General Hospital in Tacoma, Washington. Even so, my two years in the army were quite an ordeal.

For a number of years, I had had an interest in the arts—painting, music, the theater, film—but being an artist in any of those fields seemed beyond my reach. However, an appreciation of the arts became very important in helping me keep my head together during those two years in the army.

After being released from active duty in 1966, I bought a ninety-nine-dollar Greyhound bus ticket that allowed me to travel anywhere across the United States as long as I did not try to return on the route I had previously traveled. I traveled south, then east, then north along the East Coast, stopping in various cities along the way but not finding a place where I felt I wanted to stay until I arrived in Philadelphia. In Philadelphia, I tried to find a job, but couldn't. By this time I had hardly any savings left, so I took the bus to New York City, hoping I would have a better chance of finding work there. I liked the city very much and was able to find work.

So, anyway, on that rainy evening I had just been drifting through the streets with no particular destination in mind when I found myself looking at this poster for films at the Cinematheque, and as the rain didn't seem likely to stop, I decided to see these films by Brakhage.

On that first encounter, the films were difficult and puzzling. Yet at the same time, I was attracted to the work, and even to the difficulty I was encountering in my attempt to make sense of what I was seeing.

MacDonald: What exactly appealed to you about the films?

Gehr: Their degree of abstraction, their concern with texture, color, and rhythm, rather than with plot, suspense, or psychological drama. They were closer to my experiences of twentieth-century painting than to my experiences of the movies, and that was very exciting to me.

There was another factor, however. As I sat there, struggling to make sense of what I was looking at, I was also realizing that I could make films myself, that I did not need to work with 35mm, a script, a crew, a large budget, et cetera, but that I could work with so-called amateur 8mm or 16mm film cameras and do whatever I wanted to do. I could turn the camera upside down, film the gutter of the street—anything. To me, in 1966, this was quite an exciting revelation, and I have always been very grateful for my exposure to Brakhage's work on that rainy evening. Perhaps if I had seen something else, something cinematically tamer, I might never have picked up a camera.

MacDonald: Did you begin to work with film right after that experience?

Gehr: Oh no! But the experience left me elated, and I kept going back to the Cinematheque as often as I could. There were works I liked and works I didn't like. In time, I also discovered other showcases for this new cinema, and I attended them as well. The more films I saw, the more I wanted to make films myself.

And then, at some point, I came across an ad in the *Voice* for a workshop, Millennium Film Workshop, that was lending out equipment, free of charge, to anyone interested in making their own films. At first I was hesitant to go and borrow a camera. My first move was to go to one of their Sunday screenings. After the screening (this was at St. Mark's Church on Second Avenue), I introduced myself to the person who was folding the screen and asked if it was possible to borrow a camera. It was Ken Jacobs, who was then the director of the workshop. Ken was very friendly, and with his encouragement I went to the workshop a few days later to borrow a camera, only to find that all the 8mm cameras were checked out. At first my heart sank, but when I saw a light meter on a table—it had just been returned along with some other equipment—and I asked if I could borrow *it*.

MacDonald: What did you do with the light meter?

Gehr: For a week I walked through the streets of New York reading light. Sounds silly, but it was a wonderful experience, and the implications became clear to me only later, when I began to think about *Morning*. I was finding out what the character of light is and learning about the nature of cinema's dependency upon light.

A week later, I was able to borrow an 8mm camera. I bought a roll of film and began to work. If you recall, a roll of standard 8mm film was twenty-five feet of 16mm film with 8mm sprocket holes. After exposing half of the film, you took the film out of the camera and flipped it; then put it back in the camera in order to expose the other half. After the roll was developed, the film was slit in half, and the two halves were spliced together, so that you then had fifty feet of 8mm. I shot the first half of the roll. As I took the roll out of the camera in order to flip it and put it back into the camera, it slipped out of my hand, and about a quarter of it rolled down the street. Another way of exposing film to light, I guess. As it was my first roll of film, I decided to have it developed anyway. Later on, instead of throwing away the mostly clear base, I scratched shapes and images into the clear base and then edited the footage.

Over the next few months I completed and then took apart a number of 8mm films. I had a problem with them that I did not quite understand.

MacDonald: During this time, were you making plans before you would shoot, or did you just take the camera out and see what happened?

Gehr: I worked without a script of any kind. I usually had some vague idea of what I wanted to do, but the films were intuitively worked out as I went along.

And then, due to some internal politics, Millennium closed, and I found myself without a source of equipment. Around that time I became interested in making a sort of pseudonarrative film, using synchronous sound, and that meant having to work with 16mm, since standard 8mm is essentially a silent medium.

Luckily, I was able to borrow a 16mm Arriflex, but as I tried to work with it at a friend's loft, which was where I wanted to record one of the scenes, I encountered problems. I discovered that it was *heavy*. I couldn't move it through space as easily as I could move the 8mm cameras I had worked with. So we placed the camera on a tripod, which made me feel very constricted. I then looked through the viewfinder and felt as if I were looking through a window into somebody's apartment—everything looked so *solid*. I found that I was not able to superimpose my abstract ideas upon the reality in front of the camera, and I decided I just could not work with film, and I quit.

I left New York and went back to see my parents in Milwaukee. But I kept thinking about this incident, and I began to ask myself why I really wanted to make films, what exactly it *was* that I most liked about cinema and what it was that I *didn't* like. I traced my experiences of cinema back to early childhood and eventually came to the conclusion that I was interested in aspects of the cinematic experience that are often considered peripheral to the main cinematic event unfolding on the screen. The things that moved me and haunted me, even during childhood, were things other than the ongoing stories depicted on-screen. For example, the beam of light in those old movie palaces: people used to be able to smoke cigarettes in the balcony, and when a movie got boring, I would look up and watch the beam of light and the smoke filtering through it.

I was fascinated with the discrepancies between the illusion on the screen and the reality of where I *was:* the decor of the theater, the actualities of the projection. I remember on some occasions the film getting stuck in the gate, and a frame suddenly melting away. On one occasion when I was very young, a janitor turned on the lights behind the screen, just when the movie was reaching a climax, and revealed piles of boxes back there. It was such a shock, and I remember thinking, "Hey, wait a minute, you mean this isn't actually taking place!?" There was also something strange and sometimes wonderful about sitting in the dark cinema for an hour or two, going through all kinds of experiences, and then walking out and realizing that it was still Saturday afternoon, that I was still in the same place and in fact had never left it.

Those are the kinds of experiences that haunted me, and kept me going back to the movies again and again. A seamless illusion of reality wasn't all that important to me.

What I realized I *didn't* like was the emotional and psychological wringing the movies put me through. For example, I loved Chaplin, but I also had problems with some of his films, such as *City Lights* [1931]: at the end of the movie, as the curtain came down and the lights came up, there I was, in tears. I felt embarrassed and disliked the emotional manipulation. At some point in my early teens, I actually stopped going to the movies because of this.

There was also another factor: occasionally as I watched movies, instead of following the action, I would find myself caught up with some visual occurrence within a scene or a shot that had nothing to do with the ongoing narrative. For example, in one of the movies I recall seeing in my late teens, there was a scene in an alley with characters either fighting or running after one another. There was nothing special about that alley, but instead of following the action, I got caught up with some reflections on a small pool of water. The patterns on the water seemed more interesting to me than the fight or the chase. Perhaps we all have this kind of experience occasionally.

In any case, such recollections and the experience with the Arriflex were suggesting to me that perhaps visual developments and the phenomena of the cinematic process were more attractive and of greater interest to me than storytelling. So, having clarified this for myself, I decided to return to New York and attempt filmmaking again, only now with a different perspective. The details weren't clear to me, nor what I would end up achieving, but I decided to start by focusing on an exploration of the properties and processes of the medium of film itself and bring these elements to the foreground. Of course, if you had asked me then, or even a few years later, to put this into words, I definitely would not have been able to. I worked things out intuitively as I went along.

But, to go back to your original question, in this frame of mind, I made *Morning* in 1967, while I was staying with my friends Gary and Sharon Smith. (I put a release date of 1968 on both *Morning* and *Wait* because, then—and it's still true now—most showcases want to show *new* films; a film completed a year ago might be seen as old stuff.)

MacDonald: When I look at *Morning* now, knowing what you've done since then, it's hard for me not to read it as the "morning" of a filmmaker. At the time, were you conscious of the film's metaphoric possibilities?

Gehr: Not in any grandiose manner. However, what you suggest is implied in the title, which is a reference to a picturing of morning, as well as to my awakening to certain possibilities of film that I had not been conscious of before, and had not thought of as having a place in the world of cinema. I was very grateful and excited by that new perspective.

MacDonald: Among the things we see in the apartment is a sewing machine . . .

Gehr: Well, Gary and Sharon's living quarters were in the front of the loft. To the left of the window was their bed and in front of the window was Sharon's sewing machine.

MacDonald: It makes a nice technological analogy to the camera.

Gehr: Yes—especially if it turns out that the Lumière brothers were inspired in their development of the *cinématographe* by the mechanisms of the sewing machine—though I didn't think about that at the time. However, that interior space with the window *was* meant as a reference to the interior box of the camera, and the changes of light that make more and more of the room visible were meant to refer to the photographic emulsion responding to varying light intensities. That *was* an analogy I had in mind. I much appreciate your reference to the camera obscura. It is definitely possible to see it that way, but in 1967, I was not aware of the history of the camera obscura.

I might also add that for some people I knew in the sixties, and early seventies, both *Morning* and *Wait* suggested the drug experiences of the time. When Andrew Noren saw the films, he was surprised that I didn't take drugs.

MacDonald: Was *Wait* made in the same loft as *Morning*?

Gehr: Yes. Basically, the camera was in the same area where I had positioned the camera to record the footage for *Morning,* only now it was facing the interior of the loft. To the right, beyond the table, was the baby crib, where Gary and Sharon's son, Kerlin, used to sleep. In *Wait,* sometimes you see him hovering around; we just couldn't keep him out of the picture.

MacDonald: So how did *Wait* get started?

Gehr: Even before I finished recording the footage for *Morning,* I didn't feel entirely satisfied with my choices. I began to think that perhaps the room as a metaphor for the camera chamber and the window as a metaphor for the lens was a little too obvious, even though I had not yet seen any of the footage. Looking at the footage later on also made me more sensitive to the possibilities of a new kind of space—an oscillating and created space, a space coming into existence in the process of the film's projection, and where the tension between two- and three-dimensionality was on the surface of the work.

In addition, I was just beginning to exercise my film "muscles," my understanding of film, my appreciation of the possibilities of film, and I thought I might have more control over the situation if I worked at night. That way, the light source would be steady—a seventy-five- or a hundred-watt bulb hanging over the table—and I would be able to play with a wider range of light intensities; I would be able to time-expose every frame, from a fraction of a second up to a minute or more.

There were reasons for having Gary and Sharon sitting at the table. I had been interested in filming people earlier when I was first trying to work with the 16mm Arriflex. Now I saw a way to take the psychological drama out of the situation and turn it into a drama of light and filmic combustions in which the human form would have a place but would be in a different relationship to everything else within that pictorial field. I asked Gary and Sharon if they would mind posing for *Wait.*

Normally, when you think about developments from frame to frame, it's the moving figure within the frame that we tend to focus upon and the frame/frames become transparent; the screen rectangle is most often seen as a kind of a window that we're allowed to peek through. Here, I was interested in the possibilities that lay in accentuating the frames, the sixteen, eighteen, or twenty-four frames projected every second, as well as the relation between the image and the photographic process. This was done through changes of exposure from frame to frame, and the resulting variable intensities of light, within basically the *same* image.

So I ended up working at night, with Gary and Sharon sitting at the table. I never arranged their postures or anything else within that space. I might have said to them, "Just find a comfortable position that you can hold for a long time. If you have to move, tell me, and I'll then decide what to do, whether to stop or to continue filming while you're moving." Also, I wanted to do as much in-camera editing as possible, though later on I found it necessary to rearrange some of the material. I found this new setup more satisfactory than the one I had arranged in *Morning*.

With *Wait,* even before I saw the footage, I knew that I was working with a very passive image, a static image, something that Eisenstein would have hated: two people just sitting at a table. Not a very dynamic composition.

MacDonald: And it's a totally domestic moment.

Gehr: Yes, mundane, not "important." Yet it's also the classic scene for a domestic drama, which I also wanted to bypass.

So you have a relatively static image—two people sitting at a table. In counterpoint to this there is the variable intensity of light, which brings attention to aspects of the photographic process: the dependency of the image upon light and the intermittent projection of still frames—and that's where the "action" is. In other words, the variable intensity of light provides the "action" and acts as a counterpoint to the static representational image. Under good screening conditions and at the proper projection speed, *Wait* offers a pleasurable and sensual eye massage, even if you don't pick up on anything else.

I was interested in neutralizing the primary focus in cinema: the human figure. I wanted to pay attention to other things *as well as* the human figure. I wanted to film people so that you could say, "Yes, that's a representation of a person, but that's also part of a complex graphic image coming to you by way of both a photographic process and a mechanical process." To augment that new kind of attention, I used outdoor film indoors. I knew enough from looking at color pictures, whether still or moving, that when you work with color, you're breaking up the picture plane. One color registers at one point in space; another color registers at another point in space. Also, colors tend to identify and segregate objects from one another, and in this case I didn't want to give any particular importance to any particular object. I wanted everything in the overall picture to have equal value. I wanted the film to be in color, but at the same time I wanted to have the same pictorial control as if I were working with black-and-white.

At first I put the footage of *Morning* and *Wait* together, but after one or two screenings I realized that that wasn't working, and I reedited the material into two separate entities.

MacDonald: You mentioned Andrew Noren. Were you starting to become part of a community of filmmakers?

Gehr: I never felt there was much of a community as such. But I did make some friends. I got to know Andrew because he was working at the Filmmakers' Cooperative, cleaning and shipping films, and I had a job there, as an assistant to Leslie Trumbull, who was the secretary for the Coop.

MacDonald: How did you come to have that job?

Gehr: Ken Jacobs knew I was looking for work and suggested I contact Richard Foreman, who was managing the Cinematheque, which was then in the process of moving to Wooster Street. So I ended up being one of the people helping to tear down the walls and replace the old electrical wiring. It was dangerous work, horrible work. At some point, Richard said to me, "There may be a position open at the Coop; why don't you go see Leslie," and I did, and was hired.

Andrew was already working there. At the time, I had only made *Morning* and *Wait,* and almost nobody had seen my work. I did show it at Millennium, but only to Ken and to individuals like myself who were just hanging around trying to make films, or were just curious about the possibilities of film.

MacDonald: In a way, *Reverberation* [1969], in which Noren appears, seems like an outdoor extension of a lot of the concerns evident in *Morning* and *Wait.*

Gehr: Some anecdotal information may be useful. *Reverberation* was prompted by a subway ride I took to lower Manhattan in the spring of 1968. Coming out of the subway, I felt surrounded and engulfed by an enormous amount of debris. Old buildings were being torn down left and right to make way for the World Trade Center towers, and for what was going to be developed around it. I was moved and saddened by the power of the destruction taking place. I felt that a part of the history of New York, one I had not known, was being wiped out to make way for whatever was to be constructed there. I saw what looked to be blocks and blocks of buildings coming down. It was quite a spectacle, and I was moved to work with that, though I didn't want to *document* it.

One of the things that was of interest to me was the mechanical nature of the medium and how cinema is dependent upon machines that, quite often—at least this is true of the equipment *I've* had access to—seem on the verge of breaking down. I began to sense a possible relationship between the experience I had had in downtown Manhattan and the mechanics of the camera and projector, especially the projector.

At that time, I had a little 8mm projector that I had tinkered with. The end result of my tinkering was that as the film moved through the gate, it jumped; the image wasn't steady. The shutter and the pull-down of the claw were off, and you would see part of the movement. I decided to work with that.

I then asked Andrew Noren and Margaret Lamarre if they wouldn't mind being in a movie. They agreed to do it, and we went downtown to record a series of scenes in 8mm, during the late spring or early summer of 1968.

Sometime after the summer, I finished editing the footage. Then later that

Andrew Noren and Margaret Lamarre in Ernie Gehr's
Reverberation (1969). Courtesy Anthology Film Archives.

year, with the help of Ken Jacobs (since I did not have any 16mm equipment), the 8mm film was projected onto a small screen and refilmed onto 16mm. The film was projected with my little projector at five frames per second in order to slow down and give weight to gestures and motions, as well as to place emphasis on the frames jumping within the frame. I saw this as related to what I had done in *Morning* and *Wait,* where the emphasis is also on the intervals between frames, and which within my work finds its clearest articulation in *Serene Velocity.* If I have any regret it's that I didn't pursue it even further after *Serene Velocity.*

MacDonald: There's still time!

Gehr: Actually, in 1971 I had plans for a more elaborate piece. At that time, I was subletting a large space and was thinking of working with about six people. But as a result of technical miscalculations, the first attempt didn't work out. After two or three hours of filming, I managed to record four or five feet of film, and that in a very crude and unsatisfactory manner. I had been working manually, and I realized that what I needed was a mechanical contraption that would help record the footage more rapidly and effectively.

I began to make notes for the contraption I needed, but unfortunately, before the summer of 1971, I was displaced from the loft and eventually had to move to Brooklyn, where rents were cheaper. The new space wasn't adequate for what I wanted to do. I didn't want to use somebody else's space, and I couldn't do the film outdoors. Shooting would have required days, and maybe weeks.

Table [1976] was a sketch for the first movement of the work. In the full version I wanted to use people because I was thinking in terms of movement both of the camera and of objects—figures in motion while recording single frame in this odd way. But I never got beyond making notes.

Actually, there was one other attempt, in either 1972 or 1973. Richard Foreman had staged a play called *Total Recall* [1971] at the Cinematheque on Wooster Street, using the *length* of the theater rather than its width. We discussed the possibility of my filming his production. I told Richard that what I would do would ultimately have nothing to do with his work; even the sound would be totally unintelligible by the time I got through, because I wanted to do a similar thing with the sound as I did with the image. He gave me his okay to do it, but I couldn't raise the money I needed. My estimate was that it would cost around ten thousand dollars—most of the expense going for the construction of the mechanical contraption I would need. So that project also collapsed.

MacDonald: The experience of *Transparency* [1969] changed, for me, the moment I looked at it on a rewind rather than just as a projected movie, because what I found was that there was almost nothing on the filmstrip, which

I assume is where the title comes from. Did you do tests for the film? Did you know what would occur?

Gehr: There's never been any testing—except for one test roll I made for *Serene Velocity.*

At the time I made *Transparency,* I was living on the Upper West Side, in a hotel/rooming house near the West Side Highway—on Seventy-first Street. Possibly due to an automobile accident, there was some land near the highway somewhere between Seventy-second Street and Seventy-third Street that was cordoned off, and this made it possible for me to film next to the West Side Highway. I placed the camera on the ground, literally on the ground; I tilted the camera up a bit, so you wouldn't see the other side of the highway or the New Jersey landscape beyond. I just wanted the blue sky in the background. And then I just filmed. Occasionally cars honked at me, and people yelled, "Are you crazy?"

MacDonald: Were you looking through the camera?

Gehr: No. I couldn't, and it would have been dangerous anyway; I was too close to the traffic. Also, I had to watch my approaching "actors" and decide whether to film them or not.

MacDonald: Are the water spots on the lens a happy accident?

Gehr: They're not water spots, but either dirt or emulsion particles that had gotten stuck on the prism of the reflex Bolex. The prism on the Bolex is between the film plate and the outside of the camera. Some of the light entering the lens is diverted by the prism to the viewer in order for you to see an image. You can't see the dirt when you look through the viewer, which is a problem with the design of the camera. I cleaned the inside of the Bolex before filming, but I must have neglected to clean the prism.

MacDonald: It ends up working nicely for the film because it sets up another visual plane.

Gehr: At first I was very upset and ready to discard the footage, and I actually did record another four or five rolls of film, cleanly. I still have these rolls somewhere in the house. But I ended up liking the spots; they sort of nailed the image to the screen, though some people may find them annoying.

MacDonald: Did you set up the situation of shooting because you were curious to see how much of a car would get onto the filmstrip?

Gehr: In part I was interested in speed, in motion. Film runs through the camera and the projector at a certain constant rate, and this is something we often do not pay attention to when we look at a work. Yet it is very much part of the film process. Early photographic emulsions were very slow, and it made the still documentation of objects in motion very difficult. What was in motion either did not register or registered as a smear or as a ghostly, semitransparent image. In time, photographic emulsions were developed that were more sensitive to light, making possible, first, "instantaneous" photography and then motion-picture photography. So, technologically, in one sense, we moved from recording moving objects as transparencies to recording them as "solids."

Some of my choices in *Transparency* had to do with reflections upon these matters. Since I was working with a machine in the first place, I decided to use a machine image—cars—rather than a human image or an image from nature. Along this stretch of the highway the cars were also traveling at high speeds, and by recording at varying camera speeds, I was able to record a so-called car as a solid or simply as a transparent "streak" of colored light. The incredible combustion and explosion of forms, shapes, and colors are the result of a cross between the constant speed of the projector and the variable speed at which the images were recorded. Were that not the case, we would end up with just footage of cars passing in front of the screen.

Transparency veers not only between two-dimensional and three-dimensional space but also between representation and abstraction, and a form of abstraction that is distinct from abstraction in painting.

MacDonald: How many different recording speeds did you use?

Gehr: The film ran through the camera at varying speeds between twelve frames per second to approximately forty-eight frames per second.

MacDonald: Is the result the entirety of what you shot? Did you edit?

Gehr: I was editing while I was filming. I chose when to film and when not to film. Some shots were only a few frames long, and some shots extended over several feet of film, but except for removing head and tail flares, the rolls themselves were not tampered with. The order of the rolls was decided after looking at the footage a number of times.

The title, "Transparency," was triggered by the fact that, as you say, they were often very transparent images, but I think at some point I also began to sense that it had other implications. What I was filming and how I was filming are normally *transparent* to most people watching movies.

MacDonald: I remember puzzling for hours about *Field* [1970], trying to figure out whether it was another film in which things were actually moving through the frame or whether it was done in some other way. When I looked at the filmstrip on a rewind, I was *really* befuddled, because it was very different from what I expected to see. It looks as if it were done frame by frame.

Anyway, the film creates a very mysterious experience. Whatever you're looking at seems to be going in both directions at once.

Gehr (chuckles): Well, maybe I shouldn't ruin the mystery!

Basically, I was recording at a constant speed of sixteen or eighteen frames per second. I was standing on the ground, hand-holding the camera, and panning across a little field that included some grass, a small lake, and a row of trees in the background. I held the camera in my hand, at an angle, and swung it left and right. Originally, I had some kind of structure in mind, and I wanted to edit the film mostly in-camera. As I looked at the developed footage later on, however, I realized the scheme that I had conceived before filming just wouldn't work, so I ended cutting up the material and reshaping it into the work you're familiar with.

MacDonald: So we're basically seeing the swish-pan part of the gestures.

Gehr: Yes, left-right, right-left, et cetera. The shots are very short, which is why one tends to experience movement going in both directions at once. But the best thing is not to think about *how* it was done, but to try to respond to what is actually taking place as you're looking at the screen rectangle. There's a strong sense of motion, of traveling, of moving on a diagonal, yet you can't tell whether you're moving in one direction or the other, and the rectangle seems to be stationary.

All the films that I made before *Field* and *Serene Velocity* were made in New York City and were urban pieces. *Field,* on the other hand, might be called a "country" piece. Interesting what I came up with working in nature! The title is a reference to the "field" that brings us cinematic works, the screen rectangle, as well as to a "field" in nature. However, because of the speed at which I was filming, you never see that place depicted realistically, only in terms of what that resulting field of gray might evoke in your imagination.

I could have chosen color, but I was interested in working with a scale of grays.

MacDonald: History [1970] is no longer in distribution. I remember it as the most austere of your films. What drew you to this project?

Gehr: One thing was the grain of film. Grain is prominent in *Reverberation,* appearing not only in the image but also in the sound of the film: there is a parallel between image grain and the texture of the sound. At that time I was haunted by the mysteries of the medium and what the medium might yield in terms of an experience of its own character, and I was fascinated by the idea of creating a cinematic space without the use of a photographic image. *History* seemed the logical step for me to take after *Transparency.*

MacDonald: Why did you withdraw the film from distribution?

Gehr: The history of *History,* to make a long story short, is that at some point I misplaced the original. Attempts to duplicate the original or make reasonable copies from the only two good prints that existed were unsuccessful. At the Coop, there is an approximately twenty-minute print struck from one of the good prints, but I hope no one rents it. I really should withdraw it. It's flat, pale, with less than a quarter of the grain or texture that ought to be there. It has none of the rich, sensual, and convulsive spatial play it ought to have. At this point there are two possibilities to preserve the work: I could transfer one of the prints to DVD. Maybe that will work. The other possibility has to do with my recently locating a roll of film that had not been incorporated into the original. I could either loop that roll on a contact printer or refilm it on an optical printer. In either case it will be a new version of *History*.

MacDonald: Revisionist *History!* Sorry.

You were in Binghamton when you made *Serene Velocity*.

Gehr: Yes, it was the first time I taught—in June 1970, a six-week summer session. I had been in Binghamton in the early spring, around the time of the shooting at Kent State, and after the screening Larry Gottheim asked me if I'd be interested in teaching a summer course. I said, "I've never taught in my life! I wouldn't know what to do." But he and Ken Jacobs, and some of the students, thought I would do fine. And I thought, "Well, I guess it would be a way for me to get out of New York during the summer, when it's hot and sticky," so I said I'd do it. Of course, Binghamton ended up being hot and sticky too—maybe worse.

And, yes, *Serene Velocity* was made during that time, as was *Field*.

MacDonald: Were students involved in *Serene Velocity*, or was it a solo process?

Gehr: I worked entirely on my own.

MacDonald: It's surely one of the most discussed avant-garde films. And it's still one that has tremendous energy on the screen. I've always assumed that part of the desire to make the film had to do with your wondering what you could do with those dull institutional hallways.

Gehr: The institutional hallway came into play only near the end, not at all during the conception of the film. By late 1969 or early 1970, I became increasingly interested in an exploration of the intervals between frames, in activating the screen plane from frame to frame more dynamically than I had done previously, as well as in the idea of a composition taking place in time. I looked around for an appropriate space to film. Although I didn't know precisely what I wanted, nothing seemed right. Then, as the summer approached, I went to Binghamton. The film department editing rooms were in the basement of the lecture hall, where there were a couple of long corridors.

Toward the latter part of the six weeks I was there, maybe the fourth week, I was on my way to one of the editing rooms one evening. As I entered that basement hallway, the idea of *Serene Velocity* taking place in that space suddenly flashed across my mind: I took a good look and said to myself, "This is it! This is the space!" It was perfect. I hadn't realized until then that a rather austere, tightly enclosed space would be the most appropriate image to work with. Here was a deep space where I might be able to realize what I had in mind, a space where I could maximize the tension between representation and abstraction, as well as the potentials I began to sense regarding the intervals between frames.

I also liked the fact that it was a long hallway, in which the structure/design of the back half repeated the structure/design of the front half. And I liked the fact that it was an enclosed space where I could work at night. I needed constant light and a place that wasn't continuously interrupted by activities. It was only at that point that the so-called structure of *Serene Velocity* was developed.

Once the shape and structure of the work were determined, I made the test roll I mentioned earlier. I wanted the different millimeter positions I would use to be on the verge of blending into each other, yet retain their own individuality not only at the beginning but also as the contrast between successive positions became greater. So as a test I recorded footage at a ratio of one-to-one (in other words, *one* frame with the lens adjusted to one point along the focal length beyond the midpoint, then *one* frame with the lens adjusted to a point equidistant along the focal length in the opposite direction from the midpoint), then at 2:2, 3:3, 4:4, up to 8:8, for a number of different positions, including some that would be past the middle of the film. When I got that roll back from the lab, I looped the footage of each ratio and projected it at sound and silent speed. My final choice was a four-to-four ratio, to be projected at sixteen frames per second. At that time silent projection in the United States was still sixteen frames per second, and projectors that could show at silent speed were fairly common (or so it seemed to me).

Occasionally, I have seen *Serene Velocity* projected at twenty-four frames per second. It's a little bit more frantic, but it holds up—sometimes. Sometimes it seems to collapse on itself.

MacDonald: I saw *Serene Velocity* for the first time, and it may have been the premiere, at a Saturday afternoon screening in Binghamton, on a program with Larry Gottheim's *Barn Rushes* (1972), Brakhage's *Act of Seeing with One's Own Eyes* (1971), and, I think, Ken Jacobs's *Soft Rain* (1968)—one of the most powerful experiences in my filmgoing life.

You weren't there.

Gehr: No, but I was glad someone wanted to show the film, especially in the company of those great works.

MacDonald: I want you to take me back to that moment when you're sitting in front of the screen for the first time looking at *Serene Velocity*. What were the biggest surprises for you?

Gehr: At my first screening, the biggest surprise was how powerfully the experience of filming the footage for *Serene Velocity* came back to me; it made me nauseous!

I had not expected the filming to take as long as it actually did. I thought if I started as it got dark outside, around eight thirty or nine, I'd be through

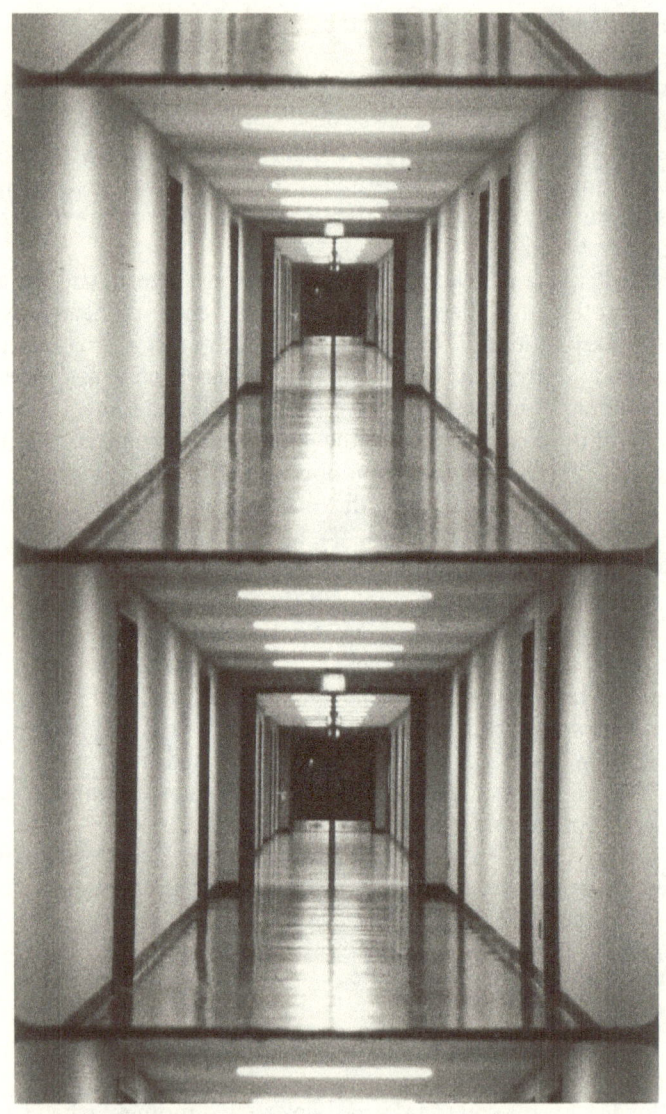

Hallway at SUNY-Binghamton in Ernie Gehr's *Serene Velocity* (1970). Courtesy Anthology Film Archives.

with most of the filming by midnight. Then I would take a nap—I had an alarm clock with me—and get up early, around four or four thirty, and continue to film until the sun was up. I was interested in the sunrise at the end of the film. As it turned out, I had to film continuously throughout the night, except for a brief break in the early hours of the morning, when I went to the bathroom and held my head under water for several minutes in order to stay awake. The sun came up more or less where I thought it would, in terms of the overall structure of the work, but that was pure luck.

MacDonald: Was the time-consuming part continually readjusting the zoom lens?

Gehr: In part, yes. I had recalibrated the lens earlier, on a piece of tape, roughly every five millimeters or so—from midrange to the two extreme positions—so I could just go back and forth, from one marking to the next, in a regular manner. But it was the single-frame recording of frames: one, two, three, four, then shifting to the next millimeter position, changing the focus, recording one, two, three, four frames, then shifting the position of the lens again, changing the focus, et cetera, that after a certain point became a form of torture. And I was racing against time. I couldn't leave the equipment in the hallway until the following night. Also, I wasn't using a cable release, so that by the early hours of the morning I had ten swollen fingers, and it became painful to finish the last two or three rolls.

Looking back, I am glad I did the film by hand rather than on an optical bench or in some another manner.

MacDonald: There is a subtle, handcrafted feel to the film.

Gehr: Yes, and eventually that was important to me. Like that beautiful internal "light" that emanates from within the image, opalescent, and variable, without bringing up associations with the romantic or the picturesque. That radiating luminance then merges and climaxes at the end with the luminosity of the white light that slowly bleeds in from the outside declaring the arrival of "day" and of infinite space at the same time that it asserts the screen's surface and the light of the projector. That was a wonderful gift that I had not considered and which is due to the pulsing florescent lights in the corridor and recording the images single frame, manually. The combination of the two gave each frame an exposure that varies minutely from frame to fame and helps give the film its particular quality of radiance and luminosity.

And there are also mistakes in the film—occasionally I went in the wrong direction or didn't expose exactly four frames. In the middle of the night sometimes I forgot what I was doing. Those mistakes became part of the film, and I definitely accepted them, and have come to like them. I might add that my original recalibration of the lens was not all that scientific. It was done by measuring distances on a piece of tape, not by placing the lens on an optical bench.

So, as I looked at the film for the first time, that nightmare of filming the footage came back, and it may have been a couple of months before I could gain enough distance from the experience to really enjoy the results. Once that initial memory began to fade, I was more than delighted with the results. I was ecstatic! And let me make this clear: I could *never* have predicted the range of visual and sensual phenomena that come through the work or all their implications.

MacDonald: Even when I was seeing *Serene Velocity* the first time, and furious with it, I noticed remarkable changes in the viewing experience. At one point it's like a sign blinking on and off, and then you're thrown back into the illusion of three-dimensional space, and then you're looking at the water fountain on the wall slowly going by . . .

Gehr: Yes. It all depends on how much effort the viewer is willing to put into a seeing of the work, into the moment-to-moment *experience* of the work. If one just sits back and waits for something to be delivered; if one is not open to a sensual, visual adventuring, or is content with just following the structure to its conclusion, the film can be torture. When you focus on the pattern of going from a middle position toward the two extreme positions, you miss the *real* structure and character of the work. The *experience* of *Serene Velocity* is something else.

The experience will also change from one viewing to the next, depending on the setup of the theater, the position from which the individual sees the work. In different locations you can have different experiences; something may happen in one space but not in another. Like most optical phenomena, *Serene Velocity* tends to be ephemeral and variable, even unpredictable. Actually, you could say that there are several movies taking place at the same time. The pulsing and changing image of that hallway is broken up by the geometry of the space into four different areas (left and right walls, floor, and ceiling), and each area goes through a different metamorphosis, offering different but related kinds of visual puzzles and puns for the mind to engage. There are many beautiful, sensual, even humorous developments that take place within what looks like something devoid of any excitement, humor, or sensual interest, including space reversals and the collapse and reemergence of doorways, water fountains, and so forth. The work teases and teaches one something about the nature, character, and plasticity of moving visual images. That's one of the fun parts of *Serene Velocity.* Its surface simplicity is deceptive.

MacDonald: Did things change for you economically or professionally after *Serene Velocity?*

Gehr: I do not recall it really changing my situation. Economically, I was exactly where I was before. There was positive response from some people I knew: Ken Jacobs, Michael Snow, Hollis Frampton, Richard Foreman,

Steve Reich, Barry Gerson, Andrew Noren—people who had been responsive to the works I'd done earlier—but beyond that, I do not recall there being much response, at least none that I heard of. For many people, those are now established, important figures, so it may sound as if the film was a big success, but they were just the people I knew then, a small circle of individuals who were very supportive—and for whom I was very grateful.

In print, the only thing that I recall at the early stages was a sentence in Jonas Mekas's column; he said it was the most important film he'd seen that week—or something to that effect. I wish he had elaborated. Nevertheless, I have always been grateful for his support. In 1968, for example, at a time when I did not expect any reviews, Jonas wrote a wonderful column on *Morning* and *Wait* in the *Voice* [Mekas's review, "On Ernie Gehr and the 'Plotless' Cinema," is included in his *Movie Journal* (New York: Collier, 1972), 314–16; at the time of the review the films were called *Moments* and *Eyes*].

Later on, Regina Cornwell was the first person who was interested in writing at length on the work, and at first I was resistant. But she persisted and eventually wrote the article that appeared in *Film Culture* [Regina Cornwell, "Works of Ernie Gehr from 1968 to 1972," *Film Culture,* nos. 63–64 (1976): 29–38].

MacDonald: What made you resistant?

Gehr: In the early seventies there were a number of publications from which I was excluded. Sometimes I would not even be mentioned, or my name would be mentioned, and that would be all. It was painful. The filmmakers who *were* mentioned were getting recognition and opportunities to show work—in some cases, more than just a few shows. So it was depressing, and at some point, if for no other reason than to be able to continue to make films, I decided not to say *anything* about my own work.

A little bit later on, Annette Michelson was very helpful, and I was very grateful, and still am, for her support. In 1974 she was asked to organize a selection of what she called "New Forms in Film" at Montreux, Switzerland [*New Forms in Film: Montreux, 1974,* a catalogue edited by Michelson, was published in conjunction with this show]. Before that, she had organized a selection of films in Vancouver, Canada, in which I was also included. She made it possible for my work to be seen outside the United States.

MacDonald: I'm curious to know how *Still* got under way, because it seems a very different project, one that was shot over a longer period of time, and one that required a different kind of editing from your previous work, as well as a different use of sound.

Gehr: Still—yes, it did develop over time. I was working at the Filmmakers' Cooperative, in a ground-floor office facing Lexington Avenue. At first my desk was placed so that I faced away from the window, so I could see people coming into the office, but at a certain point I turned the setup around so that, while working, I could look out the window and face the world outside. Gradually I became more and more interested in watching the passage of time outside the window, the effects of light and shadow on the passing traffic, the movement of people—the life that was visible out that window. At some point I taped a couple of small rectangles that I had cut out of black paper on the window, just to get used to looking at that world through a horizontal rectangle like the film frame rather than through the vertical rectangle of the window.

Over a period of time, I began to see that space as a microcosm of New York City. Across the street, besides doorways and windows of apartment buildings, there was a furniture store with the sign "Early American" and a Greek American soda-lunch restaurant. As you know, the soda-lunch place is a uniquely American institution. You won't find it in Europe or in other parts of the world, unless it's borrowed from American culture. And there was a tree, surrounded by concrete—the way nature tends to exist in the city—and all this traffic of people and cars. Slowly I began to envision the possibility of a film about New York City focused entirely on this small stretch of Lexington Avenue.

In addition, there was something about the idea of superimposition that was triggering my imagination. I was not only superimposing a rectangle over the world taking place outside the window; I was superimposing thoughts, reflections, and ideas over the activities I saw taking place. That, in turn, got me to thinking about how we tend to experience a three-dimensional image on a two-dimensional plane.

So, I began to sense that there was the possibility of seeing the interaction between solids and transparent and semitransparent shapes as a way to articulate on film ways of seeing the city: the world of buildings and pavement in terms of solids and the transient forms that pass through that space as varying degrees of transparency. At the same time, the intermingling of solids and transparent or semitransparent forms seemed to offer possibilities of articulating pictorially the contradictions of seeing a three-dimensional space on a two-dimensional plane. We say an object is in front of or behind another object in a film or a photograph, when in fact that is not possible on a two-dimensional plane.

The first four takes in the film—the silent, one-hundred-foot sections—were the first I recorded, and they were done with a one-hundred-foot-load, silent Bolex camera. In looking at those rolls of film, which I liked very much, the thoughts, projections I just mentioned, began to become more concrete to me. I decided that two-and-a-half-minute takes would not be sufficient, and that the subsequent takes had to be longer—four-hundred-foot takes. I was interested in recording segments of time, not particular actions. The work had to accommodate moments of activities, as well as moments where nothing was occurring. In looking at the footage later on, I was surprised how poignant and charged these quiet moments were. Duration here meant an opportunity to look, explore, and reflect upon the image, to undertake a visual adventuring of that pictorial space and not just get stuck with a surface acknowledgment of shapes and forms by the labels we associate with them ("car," "child," "doorway," etc.), and to see what the film might have to offer in terms of visual phenomena, as well as how it might inform us about its ostensible subject: the city. It was at this point, too, that the necessity of sound began to register.

Of course, I didn't have any equipment of my own for recording either four- hundred-foot takes or synchronous sound. Luckily, the faculty at Binghamton were more than willing to help me out, though I could only use their equipment when someone with a car could come into New York with it and, a few days later, return it to Binghamton. That didn't happen all that frequently, which is the reason *Still* took so long to complete, though in some ways it was actually useful not to be able to finish immediately.

I've never been happy with the sound. At the time, I didn't know how to use a Nagra. Usually I had a student helping me, and for some stupid reason, I didn't check the sound levels until I was editing in 1971! That's when I found the problems. The sound had been underrecorded on every occasion—I guess so that the high points wouldn't get distorted. The end result was that, since I was working with tape (this is before digital recordings), I had to bring up the volume. When I did that, the surface noise of the tape came up with it and flattened out the sound in a way I wasn't happy with. There was nothing I could do about it; I had to accept what I had.

For the last take, Larry Gottheim helped me record the sound, and he knew how to use a Nagra.

Another thing I was interested in was working with chance: letting the rectangle and duration become the boundaries within which chance actions, rhythms, colors, and juxtapositions could occur. So all the superimpositions were done in-camera. I decided early on not to have any superimpositions done at the lab. There is one, and only one, superimposition in each of the sections, except the last, which is a single recording with no superimposition.

MacDonald: What was involved in making the superimpositions?

Gehr: On each occasion, I recorded the image once, usually in the morning. Then I would rewind the film in-camera, wait a few hours or until the afternoon, depending on the layout of cars across the street and the position of light and shadow across that space, and record the same space on top of the previous recording. Each superimposition had to be done the same day as the first recording; I couldn't leave the equipment in the office overnight.

New York City street scenes, from Ernie Gehr's *Still* (1971). Courtesy Anthology Film Archives.

For the second recording (meaning the superimposition) of the second sound section, I tilted the camera either up or down (I can't remember which). That way the two recordings ended up slightly out of registration. It's not dramatic, but it's obvious in some areas. For example, there are twice as many white traffic lines on the street as in any of the other sections. In its sound portion, after the beginning, one of the sound takes goes out of sync as well. One sound take remains in sync, the other goes out of sync after the beginning, leaving you to figure out what the implications may be.

MacDonald: In the second-to-last shot, a young man and woman go into the restaurant and come out. Was that moment, or any of the action, directed by you?

Gehr: "Directed" is the wrong word. I simply asked them to go and meet across the street, then go into the soda-lunch place. It was unrehearsed. They were the New York couple meeting for lunch.

MacDonald: How visible were you when you were filming?

Gehr: Well, the camera was close to the window, and I was close to the camera. The window was open, so I could record a clear image of the street, as well as record sound. What may at times look like a reflection is sometimes a ray of light striking an object on the outside and reflecting against the lens of the camera.

MacDonald: This must have been another case where when you saw the footage, you confronted some surprises.

Gehr: Actually, as with *Serene Velocity,* many surprises. Not until I saw a developed roll of film could I tell whether I would be able to use it. Only about half of what I recorded ended up in the film. There were also many instances when the camera was set up, but I ended up not filming either one or both of the takes because of one thing or another going wrong. Some of the rolls were never developed, and others were, but didn't make it into the final film.

MacDonald: What went into the final organization of the shots you ended up using?

Gehr: Hmmm. What *was* I thinking at the time? I wish you had asked me that question thirty years ago! Well, for one thing, I was interested in modulating the image of a single space from shot to shot, though not as dramatically as in *Serene Velocity.* Also, not so much plastically through the optics of the lens, compressing and expanding the depth of field, as through changes of so-called natural light, the color temperature of the environment and the physical changes that would occur within that given space over an extended period of time. Unlike in *Serene Velocity,* the shots in *Still* are long. In *Serene Velocity* they are four frames long. In *Still,* the short takes are approximately two and a half minutes long, and the long takes are approximately ten minutes long. The end result is an unhurried pace, which allows the viewer to roam around the rectangle at leisure and go beyond just a surface recognition of a street, of forms, shapes, colors, rhythms, actions, et cetera.

There was also an interest in bypassing the aesthetic of the cut, of one shot generating the next shot and propelling the piece and the viewer to some kind of a resolution down the road—offering, in its place, a different vision of cinema than we are generally accustomed to. And as I mentioned earlier, I was also interested in a representation of a history of New York through the changes that take place within a single space over seasons and over time: that is, a sense of the city that changes over time yet perhaps doesn't change all that much.

MacDonald: *Shift* seems related to *Still*. They're both city observations, though very different in their angle on the world and in what becomes primary in them. In the Film-makers' Cooperative catalogue, *Shift* is dated "1972–1974," which suggests that you worked on it for a long time.

Gehr: In the summer of 1972, I stayed in Richard Foreman's top-floor loft on Houston Street. Richard and Kate were out of town. I had stayed there before to house-sit Richard's cats, and Richard asked me if I would like to do it again. It was a wonderful place in the city (at that point I was living in Brooklyn), so I began to work there.

I recorded some footage, then took the film to the lab to have it developed. Unfortunately, three of the rolls were mistakenly given to a German TV crew, and I got their footage. I took their footage back to the lab. The lab contacted the TV people and sent them their footage, but I never got mine back. The following summer I recorded some new footage and began editing that material into the work you're familiar with.

I also recorded sounds on the street, but none of them were satisfactory. The problem was that I needed to isolate sounds—cars starting, cars stopping, et cetera—and that was impossible in New York City, at least with the equipment I had; there were always many other sounds. I looked for sounds elsewhere and came to like the synthetic quality of three sound effects records that I found that had to do with cars and city sounds, so I used what I could from those.

MacDonald: You do amazing things in that film with *up* and *down*. Almost everybody in the history of cinema has assumed that the bottom of the frame is down in the same way that is usually taken for granted in painting. But already in *Shift,* you're using that assumption to mystify the viewer's eye, though you do more of this later in *Side/Walk/Shuttle*.

Gehr: In addition to an ironic consideration of the mechanics of the machine and the human creatures that maneuver them, *Shift* was another attempt to approach the aesthetic of the cut without duplicating what other

Frames from successive shots in Ernie Gehr's *Shift* (1974).
Courtesy Anthology Film Archives.

people had done. In part the choices were made by my interest in seeing these heavy mechanical creatures moving and holding on to what sometimes looks like the ceiling!

But *Shift* is also a sound film. It juggles with the idea of something we take very much for granted when we look at a movie: that the sound we hear emanates from the image on-screen. This is a convention that most movies depend upon in order to be comprehensible, and *Shift* turns that ventriloquist convention upside down.

MacDonald: Near the end of *Shift* we get a divided frame, the slice at the top and the larger section at the bottom—was that optically printed?

Gehr: No. That was done in-camera. When you run film backward in a Bolex camera, that's what happens. The rewind mechanism in the Bolex was not designed to record images backward but only to rewind film with the lens capped in order to be able to record another layer of images on top of the first one, as I did in *Still*.

MacDonald: Looking at cities has been a pretty consistent thing for you.

Gehr: I'm a city creature; I've lived 99.9 percent of my life in cities. That's my experience of being in the world, so naturally I'm interested in urban spaces, their character, and how they affect me.

MacDonald: And the history of those spaces, too.

Gehr: Absolutely.

MacDonald: Where did you find the material you used in *Eureka,* your first California film?

Gehr: When Annette Michelson was asked to organize that exhibition of new cinema in Montreux, Switzerland, she invited Mike Snow, Peter Kubelka, Robert Breer, and me to go with her. At first I was hesitant; I wasn't interested in going to Europe. But then I decided I would go. I was given a twenty-one-day ticket. I landed in Geneva and went directly to Paris. I didn't know what to expect, but I liked Paris instantly and enormously. I spent most of my time in Paris just walking through the streets, absorbing artifacts of history and associations. It was quite a moving experience for me. I didn't visit a single museum on that occasion. Then I went to Amsterdam, where I did the same thing, although I did go to a couple of museums there, when it was raining and cold. And from there I went to Montreux, where I needed to be for four or five days to present my work and respond to questions.

During my stay in Montreux, Annette said to me, "You may be interested in seeing this," and showed me the original film that I later rephotographed for *Eureka*. Given the early cinema I had been exposed to up to that point, I couldn't believe my eyes. It was a tracking shot that seemed to go on forever. Incredible! As with the streets of Paris earlier, here was yet another artifact of time and history.

It brought back memories of my first visit to San Francisco. As I told you, after I was discharged from the army, I took a bus across the country. I stopped in San Francisco, arriving very early in the morning when things were still closed. After sitting at the bus station for a while, I decided to stretch my legs and walked toward Market Street. As I was approaching the corner, I heard streetcar bells, which I hadn't heard since I was a kid. The sound of the streetcar brought back childhood experiences. When I got to the corner, I watched this streetcar from the fifties pass by and go down Market Street toward the Embarcadero, just as at one time a camera, placed at the front of another streetcar, recorded the film that I was watching in Montreux, in 1974. The movie and that recollection moved me.

Afterward, I asked Annette if there was any possibility of my getting hold of a print. I wasn't thinking of making anything with it; I just wanted to look at it again. Annette mentioned that she had gotten the print from a mutual friend of ours, Ruth Perlmutter, who lived in Philadelphia. So when I got back to New York, I gave Ruth a call and asked if I could possibly get a print of that film. She said, "No problem." I sent her a check, and a short time later, I had my own print. I looked at the film for several months before I decided that I would like to work with it.

MacDonald: What did you know of the history of the film?

Gehr: Not much. Of course, filmmakers were already creating panoramic views with the moving camera in the late 1890s. And even earlier, from early in the *nineteenth* century onward, there were the painted moving panoramas—as you know from your two issues of *Wide Angle* [Gehr is referring to "Movies before Cinema," two special issues of *Wide Angle* 18, nos. 2 (April 1996) and 3 (July 1996)]. This film was another instance where cinema was picking up on a well-established tradition. Of course, in 1974, I was not aware of any of this.

MacDonald: When you decided to make your own version of the film, what was your procedure?

Gehr: I used a projector that allowed me to project one frame at a time. I projected one frame, recorded multiple frames of that frame, then projected the next frame, and recorded that one.

MacDonald: Did you have a score? Or had you studied the original material so long that you knew what you were going to do?

Gehr: I didn't have a score. I wanted the original to come through, and for me to be as "transparent" as possible. That was important. At the same time, and this may seem like a contradiction, I also wanted to leave some of my own tracks on the film, including my sense that we are looking at an artifact of time, of *human* history as well as film history—but in a quiet way, in a muted form. What I needed to do was to find a balance between the original movie and my then-growing interests in this particular work. Not going in for close-ups and picking out details was important, because I felt

I needed to work with and respect the film language of the period—we're talking about a pre-Griffith cinema. From some of my previous work, such as *Still,* I had also learned about the poetry and implications that may be found in noticing a detail, and the longing one has to close in on it, while the larger field denies that access and soon enough swallows it up.

The rhythm of the film was another issue I struggled with. At times, there was a desire to slow the image down, and at other times a desire to accelerate it. But I felt that, too, would be a mistake. It would be calling attention to specific moments or events and dismissing others. More important to me was keeping the movement on a borderline between stillness and motion. My decision was to stay within a variable ratio that would not be noticed or at least barely noticed—somewhere between four and eight frames for each frame of the original.

If you are open to the piece and with it at all times, maybe a fifth into the work something magical starts to take place. The world on-screen starts to come alive. The piece feels very ancient and also very contemporary. In addition, time becomes very elastic, not slowed down, but rather accelerated.

The two splices in the film were in the print I received from Ruth Perlmutter.

MacDonald: In the original film, the streetcar turns around and starts coming back, and *then* the shot ends.

Gehr: Right. I stopped just before the trolley starts to swing around. We end with an image that includes the sign "Erected 1896," and which, for me, within the context of this work, suggested the beginnings of cinema. Also, the person in the foreground, the old man with the white beard, has a vague resemblance to Eadweard Muybridge in his later years, just as some of the silhouette figures that populate the film have a vague resemblance to some of Muybridge's Palo Alto photographs of animals in locomotion.

Movement in this film is so haunting to me, especially this border between what is still and what is in motion—it's almost as if I'm reviving mummies from another century, and they walk in a kind of stilted, mechanical way. The machine is always there. You're always aware of it. Though different in its particulars, this relates to the motion in *Reverberation*—something I didn't realize until later on.

MacDonald: When I look at *Signal—Germany on the Air,* I'm sensing that your visit to Berlin had implications for you beyond what my trips to Berlin had for me. What were you doing in Germany at that time, and what was Germany to you?

Gehr: God, that's complicated for me to respond to.

MacDonald: I had a feeling it might be.

Gehr: What was I doing there? That's a question I was asking myself once I arrived in Berlin. My parents were German and had lived there before World War II. They did not want to leave Europe. So in an alternative uni-

Market Street in San Francisco rephotographed in Ernie Gehr's *Eureka* (1974). Courtesy Anthology Film Archives.

verse it's possible that Berlin is where I might have grown up. That's haunted me every time I've been there. For me it's a city of ghosts.

MacDonald: What's your ethnic background?

Gehr: What do you mean by "ethnic"?

MacDonald: Are you German? Are you Jewish?

Gehr: Both.

MacDonald: Were you born in Berlin?

Gehr: No.

MacDonald: You're very reticent to talk about the specifics of your personal life; is that because they're painful to talk about or because you feel that the work needs to exist separately from your personal experiences?

Gehr: For some of my work, you do not need to know much about my personal or family life. In fact, it can even get in the way of the work. With some work, especially some of my later work, some personal information may be useful—at least in order to understand where the work may be coming from. But my personal history is something I am not ready to talk about. Perhaps some day, but not yet.

MacDonald: There's a symmetry in *Signal,* in that we start in this busy Berlin intersection and then move to those abandoned gestapo buildings;

then we're back at the intersection; then we get the old trains and train tracks with all their implications; and finally we're back at the intersection again.

Were the gestapo buildings and the railroad yards in West Berlin?

Gehr: Yes, everything in the film was shot in West Berlin.

MacDonald: The intersection comes to have a different meaning because of these other, precisely placed kinds of information. In *Still* and your other American city films, we don't see the kinds of implications that these visits to the Nazi past suggest.

Gehr: Let me offer you some background information that contributed to some of the changes that began to happen in my work.

In some ways, it began with my going to Europe in 1974 and with *Eureka*. Then, in 1976, I was invited to show work at the Berlin International Film Festival, and one evening while I was there—it might have been around midnight, or so it felt—a filmmaker friend and I took the underground train, the subway, into East Germany, to Friedrichstrasse. There we changed trains and came back to West Berlin on the elevated train, the S-Bahn. That ride, late at night, going through those boarded-up stations that had been closed since World War II, and the reality of the Friedrichstrasse station itself, with the Soviet guards with machine guns and patrol dogs, was powerful. And also the people *on* the trains: you were staring at them, and they were staring at you. It was and yet it wasn't 1976 for me. My parents' history and what once took place in Germany surged to the foreground.

MacDonald: I remember taking that trip. I had grown up with all the cold war movies about East Germany, and crossing the border into East Germany scared me half to death.

Gehr: And then coming back to modern West Berlin, which in contrast now seemed so sedate. The experience definitely stood out and left a deep desire to go back, explore this "ground," and perhaps even consider the making of a work that dealt, at least partially, with what I went through riding those trains. Of course, I did not have the economic means to do it. Nevertheless, that trip to Berlin had awakened an uncomfortable desire to look into my and my parents' past. I began to reflect upon the lives of my parents after they left Germany, and on their background and what my life might have been like under other circumstances.

Then around 1980 I heard through friends (German artists visiting the United States) that, if I wanted to, through the Deutscher Akademischer Austauschdienst (better known as DAAD) I could apply for a fellowship in Berlin for half a year. At first I wasn't interested in being in Berlin for an extended period of time. For two or three weeks, yes, but for six months. . . ? However, as I was struggling to survive economically at this time, I applied. The first time I applied for the DAAD fellowship, I was turned down; but the second time, I got it, and so Myrel and I went to Berlin.

Before going to Berlin, I made a film in Brooklyn called *Untitled: Part One, 1981* [1981]. In making *Untitled,* I filmed people walking on a sidewalk, from above. I didn't ask who was walking down the street, and I made no effort to learn what their ethnic or national backgrounds might be. But the people filmed were largely older folk, many of them clearly immigrants from Eastern Europe, and it's quite likely that many of them came to the United States later in life. If you go to another culture when you're young, it's often easier to blend with that culture, to become part of it. Sometimes you don't quite blend entirely, but you adjust. When you migrate to another culture in your later years, as my parents did, it can be very difficult, because you're carrying the baggage of a lifetime with you. And there's the language problem; you have a much greater resistance to learning a new language.

As I said, once we got to Berlin, I asked myself, "What on earth am I doing here?" I was drawn to the place, but I also hated the idea of being there for six months. There was this work I wanted to do, but it required filming in East Berlin, and I soon found out I couldn't get permission to do that, especially since where I wanted to film was "off-limits." So I spent most of my time walking the streets of West Berlin, drifting, looking, and reflecting. In time my attitude toward the city changed, became more complex. Let me also make it clear that I am talking about being in Berlin, in Germany, in general. I'm exempting from this my German friends, the people I knew in Berlin and elsewhere who I considered close friends and did not have any problems with.

Toward the end of our stay, as we were beginning to pack, I decided to record some images. I had been recording sounds earlier.

MacDonald: Once, when we were talking about *Side/Walk/Shuttle,* you mentioned that for a long time you've recorded sounds when you go places. When did that start?

Gehr: Somewhere in the midseventies, I guess, when I couldn't afford to buy film. As an alternative, I became interested in recording sounds. I liked listening to them, and sometimes I thought that I might eventually make use of some of them.

Another thing: when we first got to Berlin, we felt we needed some contact with the outside world, so we bought this cheap radio that could get both commercial stations and shortwave broadcasts. I got very interested in the different ethnic musics and the many languages that the radio was receiving, and I began to place the microphone near the radio as I played with the dial, going back and forth.

Now to get back to the images: I began to record images with the Bolex, on Kodachrome. I wasn't certain I was going to be able to make a work out of the material I was recording, but the price of Kodachrome in Berlin was quite reasonable. A roll of 16mm Kodachrome with processing was approximately nineteen dollars. I was also interested in Kodachrome because of its more saturated colors. I was thinking of the images as a series of tourist postcards and of the film, assuming I would be able to shape the footage into a work, as a letter of sorts that would offer a sense of what it was like for me to be in Berlin, being drawn to yet also troubled by the history of the place—finding things familiar, sometimes very familiar, without really having had a previous encounter with them, but simply because my parents were German.

So that's the way I was thinking about the spaces I was recording. The intersection where most of the footage was shot had no particular significance for me. It's not like I was especially drawn to that area. I was seeing it as representing a quiet, ordinary residential area that also contained some businesses. In those days, West Berlin felt more like an airport than a city, though over time I became quite fond of it.

One of the problems I had when I was editing back in the States—the footage was developed when I got home—was that the street sounds that I had recorded were not all that suitable. I had used a cheap cassette tape recorder to record sounds. In Berlin I listened to the sounds through earphones, and they seemed okay. However, after they were transferred to 16mm magnetic and I listened to the sounds through speakers, I realized I would not be able to use most of what I had recorded. In desperation, I attempted to combine the usable material with sounds recorded in New York, but that didn't work.

It was then that I turned to the radio recordings I had made in Berlin. Their quality was not great either, as you can hear in the film, but I began to think about using them—though at first I was resistant because they brought in a level of dramatization that I was very hesitant to include. But then I thought, "Well, maybe that awkwardness and embarrassment is what the work needs, and *not* to have it there is to clean up the sound in a way that would be a mistake." So I began to use the radio material through a good portion of the film. The radio is implied in the title (as is the idea of the newsreel and picture magazines of World War II such as *Signal* and *Life* magazine) and has various connotations—such as the voice of time and of memory. Moving across the radio band allowed the possibility of evoking periods, activities, moods, and associations that otherwise might have been difficult to bring up.

Also, I like the casual yet sometimes quite pointed interaction or lack of interaction, if you wish, between sound and image. The radio allowed me a certain kind of modulation, including occasional humor that the work would not have had otherwise.

MacDonald: Did you have Walther Ruttmann's *Berlin—Symphony of a Big City* [1927] in mind at any point?

Gehr: Believe it or not, I've never seen it. It's definitely on the list; but one reason I've never gone out of my way to see it is that I remember reading somewhere that Vertov disliked the work.

MacDonald: Actually, it would make an interesting double feature with *Signal—Germany on the Air.*

When you were originally trying to get permission to shoot in East Berlin, what was the film you had in mind?

Gehr: You know, there is a work sitting on my shelf here that I need to finish; it's a truncated version of what I had in mind in 1982. I think that question will be easier to respond to after I release the work. All I can give you at present is its title: *Passage.* [*Passage* was finished in 2003.]

MacDonald: Do you mean that *Passage* is basically the same idea that you had had, or did you actually shoot in East Berlin?

Gehr: The footage was shot during a brief visit to Berlin in 1991, in what used to be East Berlin. I didn't deal with that material until around 1995. Looking at the footage then, I realized I would need to go back to Berlin in order to record additional footage that was critical to the piece. I applied to a couple of different institutions for financial support, but no one was interested in supporting the project. As a crucial section of the film was missing, and I could not afford to do it with my personal savings, I shelved the work. However, somehow I couldn't leave it on the shelf for long. Time and again, I considered what to do. Then recently I decided to forget the rather long section I did not have and do what I could with the material I had. If all goes well, I should have a print to show sometime in the fall, or at least for me to look at—if I don't like it, I'll shelve it again.

MacDonald: When you showed me *Side/Walk/Shuttle* in a little classroom screening space at the San Francisco Art Institute, I stood up when the film was over and actually found myself wondering if I should grab a chair: I had a momentary loss of what was up and what was down. For me *Side/Walk/Shuttle* is as remarkable a film as you've done, partly because I'm astonished that you could visually imagine it. Did you spend a lot of time on that elevator looking through a camera before you shot?

Gehr: Not that much, but I did ride up and down the elevator a number of times before deciding to film.

MacDonald: And when you did, were you standing on your head? How did you *imagine* this film?

Gehr: Because I had no permission to work in that elevator, and actually was more or less told to leave several times, what I did was ride up and down, make mental notes, and then afterward little sketches about the angles from which I might film. That got modified as I recorded new material. To film, I would go to the hotel, usually wearing a coat, and with the camera under my coat—sometimes I had a helper who could hold the stuff that I didn't need—and, as the elevator doors closed, I would pull out the camera and start filming.

MacDonald: Did you try to get permission from the hotel, or were you afraid that if you asked, they'd say no?

Gehr: Well, I began to film without asking for permission because I didn't think I would get it, but after being asked to leave the first time, I did ask for permission—not personally, but through a friend, Adam Hohenberg. I cannot recall exactly what took place; they may have asked, "Is this for television?" I can't recall. But essentially they said, "No." They complained that I was riding the elevator during their lunchtime rush hour, which was true. They said they might consider giving me permission if I shot after three o'clock. But I had to work between twelve and one thirty, which, unfortunately, was when people were riding the elevator to and from the restaurant on the top floor.

MacDonald: You worked at midday because of the light?

Gehr: Yes. Earlier or later, the area was too engulfed with the shadows of the surrounding buildings. You do see those shadows sometimes, but when the whole area was covered with shadows, there wasn't much to see on film.

It's a small glass elevator, and if there were more than three people in it, anyone walking in could touch me and make me lose my balance, and that roll of film would be wasted. I didn't use a tripod; it all had to be done with a handheld camera.

MacDonald: That surprises me, too.

Gehr: I would have loved to have used a tripod for some of the camera maneuvering. And there were shots that I never managed to record because at some point I began to shake too much—a tripod might have made those possible. Any kind of movement was a problem because it destroyed the felt weight of the buildings. The image needed as much stability as possible.

There was also a problem with reflections.

MacDonald: Reflections on the elevator glass?

Gehr: Yes, and that was another reason why I couldn't shoot earlier in the morning.

MacDonald: Did you choose that spot, that hotel and elevator, because it's close to where Muybridge made his photographic panoramas of the city?

Gehr: I didn't choose it *for* that reason, no; but I definitely was aware of his work, and it was in some ways a wonderful coincidence.

MacDonald: Are you an aficionado of San Francisco filmmaking generally? This film seems to evoke, either purposefully or accidentally, San Francisco photographs and films of a variety of kinds, even commercial features like *Vertigo* [1958], *Bullitt* [1968], and *Dirty Harry* [1971]. And you mentioned that Muybridge was important to you as an artist and as a San Francisco artist. How much do you see yourself as part of San Francisco film history?

Views from the elevator in Ernie Gehr's *Side/Walk/Shuttle* (1991). Courtesy Ernie Gehr.

Gehr: The city has been used as background for a countless number of works. I'm familiar with a few of them, but not with most of them. However, there was no attempt, on my part, to evoke either the movies you mention or any others. I normally make use of the spaces in which I live and move through, and since 1988, this is where I've been living and working.

MacDonald: In *Side/Walk/Shuttle* you use sound you collected to evoke other places and other times—though I wouldn't have known it had I not talked with you about it.

Gehr: I think it's fine for people not to know. We live in a multicultural society, at least that is the case in San Francisco, so while the voices were recorded in a number of different locations outside of the city, within the context of this film, they might also be said to reflect part of the makeup of the city, the voices of some of the people living behind the windows of apartments or studios that you see on-screen. What's implied in the film is the idea of distance and closeness, as well as an indication of possibilities beyond the surface of things and beyond what you are given to look at.

I hope my choices make sense on some level, but ultimately, I don't know. That may also vary from individual to individual.

The different sounds may imply different journeys, or perhaps a *memory* of different journeys. Each shot may also be seen as a journey in itself. For a long time I thought of New York as my "home," but due to economics, I moved to San Francisco in 1988. It's a beautiful city, but I found it difficult to ground myself here. That difficulty was what prompted the making of the film, including the choices I made regarding both the sounds and the imagery.

Only the sound in the first section in the film was actually recorded in San Francisco, in the elevator. That recording contains voices I would assume are mainly from some tourists. There are some American voices, but also voices of people of other nationalities. The audible fragments of dialogue we hear seem to indicate that they are talking about views and things that are not within our visual field.

The next sound section was recorded in New York City, in Grand Central Station, and some of the voices, at least to my ear, sound very much like native New Yorkers. I like the cluster and character of voices as a contrast to the image that you see at that point: the guy on one of the rooftops is tanning himself, and the street below seems rather empty of pedestrian traffic.

Subsequent sound sections were recorded in Europe: sounds of streetcars, footsteps, and hushed French voices were recorded in Geneva; the Italian sounds that follow were recorded in Venice, and I'm told the accents of people in that section are very Venetian. Over the extended penthouse section, you have the bird sounds intermingled with some occasional airplane sounds. These were recorded from a window of a very nice upper-floor apartment facing an inner courtyard near the center of Geneva. I like how sometimes the building we see on-screen takes on the character of an aviary and at times the form of a flying bird or plane, while at all times it also remains what it is: a tall, heavy building that seems to slowly soar through space.

Still later, there are voices speaking English: possibly people from an Indian background, talking about shirt sizes and prices, while on-screen you have a view of downtown San Francisco that includes the financial district. This sound section was recorded in London. Then comes the last sound section, recorded in Berlin; it contains no human voices, just sounds of birds, wind, music, what sounds like a train or rocket taking off, and then, at the end, footsteps. These were sounds recorded in cities that I had grown to like, each of which under other circumstances might have become my "home."

However, whether or not you know where the sounds were recorded, I hope there is still a meaningful relationship between the sound and the image and that the work as a whole is accessible on a visceral level, as an immediate sensory experience. That's very important to me.

MacDonald: Because the imagery is so disorienting—down is no longer down, and gravity seems to have lost control—the voices seem to be loose in the universe.

Gehr: Oh, that's wonderful. Thank you. A very good observation.

MacDonald: Because of the threat of earthquakes, San Francisco has always been perceived as somewhat precarious. But then, during the seventies, as the city became a center for gay liberation, it suggested to some moral precariousness, as well. How much were you thinking about that?

Gehr: Not at all. I have been interested, ever since my earliest visits to San Francisco, in the pull of gravity you can experience walking up and down its hills. Where I live now, I don't have any vistas, just a bunch of houses across the street. But gravity was very much on my mind then, and the elevator lent itself beautifully to dealing with the sense of gravity pulling you down to earth, no matter how much you tried to transcend it.

MacDonald: Is *Side/Walk/Shuttle* rented a lot?

Gehr: It is rented. A lot? *[Laughter.]*

MacDonald: Which are the most rented of your films?

Gehr: Serene Velocity.

MacDonald: Maybe *Eureka* second?

Gehr: You know, I've never really looked! I just look at the total rental amount. *Eureka* does rent, and *Side/Walk/Shuttle* rents occasionally, too.

MacDonald: I've seen you quoted as saying, "Film is a real thing and as a real thing it's not an imitation. It does not reflect on life; it embodies the life of the mind." I was thinking about that comment in connection with two films that strike me as related to one another and also very different: *Shift* and *This Side of Paradise* [1991]. *Shift* doesn't reflect on life. It's more an exploration of space and of sound and image, fundamentally filmic issues. I mean, we do see a real world out there, but the focus is on something else, something cinematic. *This Side of Paradise,* which does some similar things with space, is also very observant about a particular place and time and a particular group of people. In fact, as I was looking at the film yesterday, it reminded me of some of Rudy Burckhardt's films.

At any rate, I'm wondering if you really think that *This Side of Paradise* does not reflect on life.

Gehr: I agree that a reflection on life is more readily apparent in *This Side of Paradise,* but *Shift* is more than just a plastic arrangement of sounds and images. It also reflects upon life, only more obliquely.

MacDonald: I've always been fascinated with the formal qualities of your films, but as I've talked about them with you, it seems clearer and clearer that for you the human element is always an important part of the films. The formal elements and the human elements work as figure and/or ground for each other.

Gehr: Part of my reason for frequently keeping the human element out, or at least allowing it in only in very particular ways, has had to do with the almost total focus on that element in conventional cinema, be it narrative, documentary, or animation—so that nothing else seems possible or worthwhile to pursue in the making or appreciation of a cinematic work. It's like ignoring what took place in painting after the early part of the nineteenth century. To me that is not only very claustrophobic but also limits what may be possible to articulate and experience through the medium of film. Of course, I'm human; and of course, we make films for ourselves and for other human creatures—not for machines or trees or rocks. So even when I film a piece of furniture, I'm still coming from a human perspective.

MacDonald: What were the circumstances that led to *This Side of Paradise?*

Gehr: This Side of Paradise wasn't a work that I had originally intended to make. I was in what at the time was West Berlin. I had a camera with me and some film. I was on my way somewhere with a friend. As we passed the area where the Polish flea market was, the stream of people coming from various directions and moving toward the market intrigued me. I knew nothing about the market, so I said, "Gee, why don't we go in and take a look?" As we approached the market and began to hear the sounds and see the colors, I stopped and said, "This is something that I may want to film." I had no particular work in mind, nor did I know what we would encounter. But I decided to take my camera and my little cassette tape recorder with me. The cassette recorder wasn't working properly; it was recording sounds only on one channel, and it was also recording some white noise, but I decided to use it anyway; it was all I had at the moment. As we moved into the market, I began to film. I just aimed the camera in the general direction in which I was looking and recorded images very casually.

At some point I became aware that some of the people were uncomfortable with my filming them. Possibly they were thinking that I was from the KGB or something like that. Most of the people selling stuff, if not all, were East Europeans, mainly Polish people, who had come to West Berlin for the weekend with whatever stuff they thought they could sell for West German marks.

What attracted me besides the carnival atmosphere was that the market evoked the feeling of another time, maybe the twenties, when inflation in Germany skyrocketed from day to day and problems for Jews were on the rise. On the other hand, the market was very much an indication not only of what was happening then but of what *would be* happening on a larger scale very soon: the spilling over of people from East European countries into the West, and their struggle to live in a capitalist society. It was interesting to film, and when I felt people were uncomfortable with my taking their pictures, I began to focus on something that was impossible to ignore anyway: those puddles of rainwater, and people standing around and in them.

I definitely wasn't intending to make a documentary of the place, but there was imagery that I wanted to revisit later on and possibly share with friends back home. There were also things I didn't film. For example, there was gambling going on, and possibly drug dealing as well. And you could also buy hard liquor, which wasn't supposed to be sold in that flea market. There's a shot in the film where somebody offers me vodka.

After shooting the five rolls of film that I had with me, I tried to record some sounds the same way: just recording as we were walking around.

Looking at and listening to what I had recorded, when I was back in San Francisco, I decided that if possible, I would like to shape that material into a work.

MacDonald: About two-thirds of the way through the film, I'm suddenly unsure—at least until I think carefully about it—what is upside down and what is right side up.

Gehr: Two factors prompted me to start shifting the material around. One was the inversion of the reflections themselves. By flipping those film images around, the reflected scene would be seen "correctly": right side up. At the same time, stuff floating on the surface of the water tended to merge with the reflections on the surface of the water. On film, when looking *into* these reflections, it sometimes created interesting pictorial tensions and spatial contradictions, and I had to restrain myself from flipping too many of the shots. I needed to keep some sense of balance in the work. I felt that the

People at a flea market in West Berlin, reflected in a puddle, in Ernie Gehr's *This Side of Paradise* (1991). Courtesy Ernie Gehr.

lives of these people had been turned upside down, and I saw a justification, beyond the plastic reasons, for doing what I did. Their lives seemed as murky and muddy as the waters in which they were reflected.

MacDonald: Well, it also makes sense, since these are people from the other side of a divided world.

Gehr: That's wonderful, Scott. I really like that. That market *was* evidence of the divide between worlds.

To understand my use of the title, just consider the material world these people from the East saw on TV while watching Western soap operas: a fantasy world, a "paradise" where everybody has a beautiful middle-class or upper-middle-class home, and hardly anyone works. Western reality must have been a rude awakening for many.

MacDonald: Rear Window [1991] was finished around the same time as *This Side of Paradise,* but I think you started it earlier.

Gehr: Rear Window was shot in Brooklyn, out the rear window of the apartment where we used to live, in, I believe, 1985 or 1986.

MacDonald: The Canyon Cinema catalogue says 1986.

Gehr: But it may have been shot in 1985—at some point after the death of my father. Originally, I thought it would be a sound film, but I couldn't work out the sound to my satisfaction, partially because I didn't have sound-editing equipment.

MacDonald: What kind of sound did you have in mind?

Gehr: Fairly abstract sound: wind, water—sounds that would be hard to identify. That didn't work out, and the film was tabled. Then we moved to San Francisco, and I decided to rework the film now that I had access to sound-editing equipment. I think that at one point I had sound at the beginning of the film and then again during the second half. I showed it as a sound film a couple of times, but I was unhappy with the sound quality of the optical track. There was also a problem in that I hadn't really synched the sound properly in the second half of the film. So the film was shelved again, but then, after looking at it silently a few months later, I decided I liked it silent and that it really did not need a sound track. So I finally decided to release it as a silent work.

MacDonald: It feels in some ways very unusual for you. It's rather gesturally expressive and reminds me of Brakhage, and also of Andrew Noren's *Wind Variations* [1969]. You mentioned that your father had died not long before this. Were you feeling differently in some way as a result of the loss of your father?

Gehr: Yes. The idea of loss was very much on my mind. To this day, I'm still very much affected by the death of my father. One day, I was looking out the back window of our apartment and saw on one of the clotheslines washed bedsheets, pillowcases, underwear, towels—stuff that comes in contact with human flesh. There was nothing unusual about that, a common daily sight where we were living, except that on this occasion, it reminded me of the loss of my father. And that in turn prompted me to film.

MacDonald: What was your father like?

Gehr: He was a very gentle person, very reserved, a very nineteenth-century German character, who stood out no matter where he went.

When I was shooting *Rear Window,* I held the lens in my hand, allowing the light to hit the lens mainly through the skin of my fingers. That way I could shape and reshape the light and to some degree affect the colors as well, except for the blue, which I got by removing the daylight filter. I was using tungsten film.

Rear Window was also the first film I'd ever shot on negative. All my other work had been done on reversal, which gave me harsher and more saturated colors. To my surprise, I got to like the softer, more pastel-looking colors that I was able to get with negative.

MacDonald: Did you have Hitchcock's *Rear Window* [1954] in mind when you titled the film?

Gehr: No. However, because of Hitchcock's film, I was at first hesitant to use "Rear Window" as a title. But I couldn't come up with anything better.

The title is in part a direct reference to the literal fact that I filmed through the rear window of my apartment, but, most important, it refers to the fact that the film focuses upon something that you normally would not want to display publicly.

MacDonald: A general question: you've spent your life working in this field and have known many filmmakers. As a maker, how fully do you feel yourself in a cinematic conversation with other makers? How much of other people's work is in your thinking as you work, and whose work has served you most or best?

Gehr: I appreciate the work of many filmmakers. It's been important not to feel that I exist in a vacuum. As I mentioned earlier, Brakhage was definitely an inspiration. Not so much an influence, but an inspiration. And possibly the most important inspiration in the sense that coming across his work made me realize that I also could make films, and that I could work in whatever form and manner I wanted to. The seeds for my responsiveness to his work on an aesthetic level may have come from somewhere else, however, including looking at paintings and listening to music.

From early on, I've had wonderful support from a number of filmmakers, whose work I have also appreciated, including Mike Snow, Joyce Wieland, Ken Jacobs, Richard Foreman—not a filmmaker but a theater person—Barry Gerson, Andrew Noren. It would be a long list if I brought it up to the present. At the same time, because of friendships, and sometimes affinities I felt, there were works that I avoided making because I didn't want to step into someone else's territory. Sometimes I cannot help it and feel I just have to pursue something, and I only hope that the work will not be like what someone else has already done. It's a question of respecting the achievements of other filmmakers.

I do look at films, but I'm also interested in works in many other media, so that inspiration or influence, if you wish, in whatever form it may take on some occasions, has sometimes come from artists, works, and practices in other media, not necessarily just from film.

MacDonald: Could you talk a bit about your getting into video? I assume that part of the issue is financial, but I assume there are other reasons as well.

Gehr: The financial issue was definitely a major reason. With my part-time teaching position, I could not afford to continue to pay the increasingly high costs of filmmaking. At one time the NEA gave grants to individual artists, but thanks to some millionaires in Congress, not any longer. There are still organizations that give out grants, even larger grants than any I've ever received, but you cannot apply for them. You have to be recommended, and I guess my work is not the kind of work these institutions are interested in supporting.

For a while, not knowing where to turn was quite depressing and discouraging, but I did not want to stop working. Digital video was an option I considered, but I could not afford the hardware. Then, miraculously, I received a commission from the Museum of Modern Art in New York. I am very grateful to Mary Lea Bandy at MoMA for having faith in me and my work and commissioning me to create *Cotton Candy*. It wasn't that much money, but enough to buy the basic equipment: camcorder, editing equipment, et cetera. Perhaps one day there will be better financial support for works like mine, be that on film or digital media.

MacDonald: You've explored so many dimensions of cinema over more than thirty-five years. Is the move to digital also a function of the fact that it's a new medium? Did you feel you were running out of things to explore in film?

Gehr: No, absolutely not. I certainly haven't done all the things that I would like to, but I only have one life, and my economic situation is what it is. I am still very much interested in and excited by the possibilities of film and would like to continue to work with film. However, to a large extent, economics have determined the number of works I have managed to create. After a while, the tension, excitement, and need to create certain works, or to work along certain lines, leaves you. It's not the same five, ten, twenty years later. And you adjust to what is possible at the moment.

MacDonald: One last question. Can you articulate what it is that keeps you going as a filmmaker and videomaker? I understand that work itself is important psychologically, but what does the experience of finishing these works give *you,* and what, ideally, do you hope it gives those of us who see the work?

Gehr: Well, in part, the process of "making" has been a refuge of sorts—not an escape, but a kind of air-raid shelter where I could find an inner sense of balance. In part it has also helped me realize that my work comes out of a different tradition than the movies do, that for me film starts with the materials of filmmaking, as well as within one individual's consciousness, no matter what subject I deal with. My work has been a way of exploring and reflecting upon aspects of the machine, of the creative process, and of the world I live in. In addition, it has helped me become more conscious of and responsive to some of my needs, and to aspirations and potentials that otherwise might have been repressed, might never have found expression.

The process of "making" not only involves work but also is a way of thinking, reflecting, feeling, and responding—and not just with eyes and ears but with all of one's senses—and not just to the materials of film but to what I come across in my daily living, to consciousness and existence.

What do the works offer beyond their immediate individual concerns? Not escape, at least I don't think so, but a sense of consciousness, an affirmation of life, of the creative process, and of our individual temporal existences.

For future generations, especially when the technology of film becomes more of a rarefied experience, I hope some of my work will also provide experiences of the character of film, as well as suggest what some of its little-explored potentials were and why some individual artists found working with film so exciting. In that sense the works—and not only my own, of course—will have important cultural, historical, and archaeological significances.

Whether they will survive and reach their potential audiences—that's another question.

Filmography

In the following listing, the title of each film (or other work) is followed by the year in which the piece was completed; the format in which the piece was shot; the length to the nearest quarter minute; and whether the piece is in black and white and/or color, silent and/or sound. While I have tried to use a common format for all the filmographies, because of the disparities between the careers discussed in *A Critical Cinema 5,* some adjustments to my preferred format were requested by filmmakers or required by the nature of particular careers. When more than one work was completed during a single year, these works are listed alphabetically.

Primary rental sources are indicated in parentheses, often using the abbreviations in the following list. In some cases, a particular work is distributed by an individual or by a distributor not listed here; in these instances, the contact information is supplied with the first listing of this distributor only. "Commercial video" means the piece is widely available from commercial, on-line video distributors.

CC	Canyon Cinema, 145 Ninth St., Suite 260, San Francisco, CA 94103; 415-626-2255; www.canyoncinema.com. Note: in my experience, Canyon Cinema is the most dependable distributor, both in terms of its care in getting prints to exhibitors and in terms of the quality of the prints it distributes, in the United States.
CFDC	Canadian Filmmakers Distribution Centre, Suite 220, 37 Hanna Ave., Toronto, Ontario, M6K 1W8 Canada; 416-588-0725; www.cfmdc.org.
EAI	Electronic Arts Intermix, 535 W. 22nd St., 5th Floor, New York, NY 10011; 212-337-0680; www.eai.org.

Facets   Facets Multimedia, 1517 W. Fullerton Ave., Chicago, IL 60614; 773-281-9075; www.facets.org.
FMC   Film-makers' Cooperative, c/o Clocktower Gallery, 108 Leonard St., New York, NY 10013; 212-267-5665; www.film-makerscoop.com.
LC   Lightcone, 12 rue des Vignoles, 75020 Paris, France; 33 (0) 1 46 59 03 12; www.lightcone.org.
LUX   LUX, 18 Shacklewell Lane, London E8 2EZ, UK; 44 (0) 20 7503 3980; www.lux.org.uk.
MoMA   Museum of Modern Art Circulating Film and Video Library, 11 W. 53rd St., New York, NY 10019; 212-708-9530.
NA   Not available, so far as I am aware.
NV   New Video, 126 Fifth Ave., 15th Floor, New York, NY 10011; 800-314-8822; www.newvideo.com.
SF   Sixpackfilm, Neubaugasse 45/13, P.O. Box 197, A-1071 Wien, Austria; 43-1-526-09-90-0; www.sixpackfilm.com.
VDB   Video Data Bank, 112 S. Michigan Ave., Chicago, IL 60603; 312-345-3550; www.vdb.org.

Peggy Ahwesh

The Edge of Space, the End of Time. 1981. Super-8mm; 30 minutes; color; sound (Ahwesh, P.O. Box 232, New York, NY 10012; peggy@echonyc.com).
Standard Chemicals. 1981. Super-8mm; 30 minutes; color; sound (Ahwesh).
Nostalgia for Paradise (part 3 of *The Pittsburgh Trilogy*). 1983. Super-8mm; 14 minutes; color; sound (Ahwesh).
Paranormal Intelligence (part 2 of *The Pittsburgh Trilogy*). 1983. Super-8mm; 12 minutes; color; sound (Ahwesh).
Verite Opera (part 1 of *The Pittsburgh Trilogy*). 1983. Super-8mm; 11 minutes; color; sound (Ahwesh).
Ode to the New Prehistory. 1984. Super-8mm; 22 minutes; color; sound (CC).
From Romance to Ritual. 1985. Super-8mm; 21 minutes (at 18fps); color; sound (CC).
I Ride a Pony Named Flame. 1987. Video; 5 minutes; color; sound (Ahwesh).
Martina's Playhouse. 1989. Super-8mm/16mm; 20 minutes; color; sound (CC, EAI).
The Deadman (co-made with Keith Sanborn). 1990. 16mm; 40 minutes; black and white; sound (CC, EAI, LUX).
Philosophy in the Bedroom, Parts 1 & 2. 1992. Super-8mm; 17 min; color; sound (EAI).
The Scary Movie. 1993. 16mm; 9 minutes; black and white; sound (CC, LC).
Strange Weather (co-made with Margie Strosser). 1993. Video; 50 minutes; black and white; sound (CC, EAI, LC, VDB).
The Bataille Lexicon. 1994. 16mm; 5 minutes; color; silent (NA).

The Color of Love. 1994. 16mm; 10 minutes; color; sound (CC, EAI, LC).
The Fragments Project. Various versions, 1984–94. Super-8mm; 50 minutes; color; sound (EAI).
Discorporation. 1995. Internet Web site (Ahwesh).
The Lesson. 1996. 16mm; 10 minutes; black and white; sound (Ahwesh).
Magnetism, Repulsion & Attraction, Deep Sleep, Auto Suggestion, Animal Magnetism, Mesmerism & Fascination. 1996. Digital/Quicktime; 8 minutes; black and white; sound (Ahwesh).
Trick Film. 1996. 16mm; 6 minutes; color; sound (Ahwesh).
the vision machine. 1997. 16mm; 20 minutes; black and white/color; sound (CC, EAI, LC).
Nocturne. 1998. 16mm; 30 minutes; black and white; sound (CC).
The Secret Charts (collaboration with writer, Amy Sillman). 1998. Installation (video/painting) (NA).
73 Suspect Words. 2000. Video; 4 minutes; black and white; sound (EAI).
Heaven's Gate. 2001. Video, 4 minutes; color; sound (EAI).
She Puppet. 2001. Video; 17 minutes; color; sound (EAI).
Certain Women (codirected with Bobby Abate). 2003. 16mm; 77 minutes; color; sound (Ahwesh).
The Star Eaters. 2003. Video; 23 minutes; color; sound (EAI).

Kenneth Anger

The following listing is indebted to the filmography Robert Haller assembled for his monograph *Kenneth Anger,* published by Mystic Fire Video as an accompaniment to the video release of Anger's films; and to Alice L. Hutchinson's *Kenneth Anger: A Demonic Visionary* (London: Black Dog, 2004). Hutchinson's annotated filmography is the most thorough to date. It includes not only completed projects, but all film and video projects Anger had begun as of 2004. I have listed only films that were completed.

Ferdinand the Bull. 1937. 16mm; black and white (lost).
Who Has Been Rocking My Dream Boat? 1941. 16mm; 7 minutes; black and white; silent (with records as sound track) (lost).
Prisoner of Mars. 1942. 16mm; 11 minutes; black and white; silent (with records as sound track) (lost).
Tinsel Tree. 1942. 16mm; 3 minutes; black and white; silent (with records as sound track) (lost).
The Nest. 1943. 16mm; 20 minutes; black and white; silent (with records as sound track) (lost).
Escape Episode. 1944. 16mm; 35 minutes; black and white; silent (with records as sound track) (lost).
Drastic Demise. 1945. 16mm; 5 minutes; black and white; silent (with records as sound track) (lost).
Escape Episode. 1946. 16mm; 27 minutes; black and white; sound (lost).

Fireworks. 1947. 16mm; 14 minutes; black and white; sound (CC, BFI: 21 Stephen St., London W1T 1LN, UK; 020-7957-8938; www.bfi.org.uk).
Puce Moment. 1949. 16mm; 6 minutes; color; sound (CC, BFI).
Rabbit's Moon (*La lune des lapins*). 1950 (not released until 1972). 35mm; 7 minutes; black and white; sound (Anger: 5533 Hollywood Blvd., Suite 434, Hollywood, CA 90028).
Le jeune homme et la mort. 1951. 16mm; 20 minutes; black and white; silent (lost).
Eaux d'artifice. 1953. 16mm; 13 minutes; color (tinted, with a moment of hand-painted color); sound (CC, BFI).
Inauguration of the Pleasure Dome. 1954. 16mm; 38 minutes; color; sound (CC, BFI).
Thelema Abbey. 1955. 16mm; 30 minutes; black and white; sound (lost).
Scorpio Rising. 1963. 16mm; 29 minutes; color; sound (CC, BFI).
Kustom Kar Kommandos. 1965. 16mm; 3 minutes; color; sound (CC, BFI).
Invocation of My Demon Brother (Arrangement in Black and Gold). 1969. 16mm; 11 minutes; color; sound (CC, BFI).
Rabbit's Moon (*La lune des lapins*). 1972. 16mm; 16 minutes; black and white; sound (CC, BFI).
Senators in Bondage (limited edition of 13). 1976. 16mm; sound.
Matelots en Menottes (limited edition of 12). 1977. 16mm; color; sound.
Lucifer Rising. 1980. 16mm; 28 minutes; color; sound (CC, BFI).
Don't Smoke That Cigarette! 2000. Video; 40 minutes; color; sound (CC).
The Man We Want to Hang. 2002. 16mm; 11 minutes; color; sound (CC).
Anger Sees RED. 2004. Video; 7 minutes; color; sound (Anger).
Mouse Heaven. 2004. 16mm/35mm (shot in 16mm, transferred to 35mm); $10^{3}/_{4}$ minutes; color; sound (Anger).

James Benning

A filmography for Benning up through 1988 is included in *A Critical Cinema 2*.

North on Evers. 1991. 16mm; 87 minutes; color; sound (CC).
Deseret. 1995. 16mm; 82 minutes; color; sound (CC).
Four Corners. 1997. 16mm; 80 minutes; color; sound (CC).
Utopia. 1998. 16mm; 93 minutes; color; sound (CC).
El Valley Centro (part 1 of the California Trilogy). 1999. 16mm; 90 minutes; color; sound (Benning: jbenning@calarts.edu).
Los (part 2 of the California Trilogy). 2000. 16mm; 90 minutes; color; sound (Benning).
Sogobi (part 3 of the California Trilogy). 2001. 16mm; 90 minutes; color; sound (Benning).
One Way Boogie Woogie/27 Years Later. 2004. 16mm; 121 minutes; color; sound (Benning).
Ten Skies. 2004. 16mm; 101 minutes; color; sound (Benning).
13 Lakes. 2004. 16mm; 133 minutes; color; sound (Benning).

Alan Berliner

Step Planes. 1974. Super-8mm; 23 minutes (at 18fps); color; silent (Berliner: ajberliner@aol.com).
Bunn Hill Road. 1975. Super-8mm; 30 minutes (at 18fps); color; silent (Berliner).
Patent Pending. 1975. 16mm; 11 minutes; black and white; sound (Berliner).
Home Movie Series: #1, #2, #3, #4, #5. 1976. Paracinema: found (uncut) 35mm color photographic scrolls (photo lab rejects) (Berliner).
Intersection (part 4 of *Four Corner Time*). 1976. 16mm; 11 minutes (at 18fps); black and white; silent (FMC, MoMA).
Line (part 1 of *Four Corner Time*). 1976. 16mm; 8 minutes (at 18fps); black and white; silent (FMC, MoMA).
Perimeter (part 2 of *Four Corner Time*). 1976. 16mm; 11 minutes (at 18fps); black and white; silent (FMC, MoMA).
Photo-Film-Strip. 1976. Paracinema: found 35mm color photographs (photo lab rejects) in a 72-image grid (Berliner).
Traffic Light (part 3 of *Four Corner Time*). 1976. 16mm; 10 minutes (at 18fps); black and white; silent (FMC, MoMA).
Cine-Matrix. 1977. Paracinema: found corrugated cardboard pieces (3" × 4") in a 156-image grid (Berliner).
Color Wheel. 1977. 16mm; 20 minutes; color; silent (FMC, MoMA).
Solid State. 1978. Video installation: video monitor and cardboard box (Berliner).
Splice. 1978. Sculpture: found canvas with factory-sewn splice and lightbulbs; 3' × 4' (Berliner).
Three Years. 1978. Paracinema: 36 months of paper calendar strips ($^3/_4$" × 19") tape-spliced into continuous scroll (Berliner).
Lines of Force. 1979. 16mm; 7 minutes; color; sound (MoMA).
Workprint. 1979. Paracinema: 75-foot-long tape-spliced photographic scroll (Berliner).
City Edition. 1980. 16mm; 10 minutes; black and white; sound (CC, FMC, LUX, MoMA).
Myth in the Electric Age. 1981. 16mm; 14 minutes; color; sound (CC, FMC, LUX, MoMA).
Natural History: A Photo Journal. 1981. Live performance for 365 slides and four voices. Premiered at the Collective for Living Cinema, New York City (Berliner).
Natural History. 1983. 16mm; 13 minutes; color; sound (CC, FMC, LUX, MoMA).
Everywhere at Once. 1985. 16mm; 10 minutes; color; sound (CC, FMC, LUX, MoMA).
The Family Album. 1986. 16mm; 60 minutes; black and white; sound (CC, FMC, Milestone [www.milestonefilms.com], MoMA).
Audioyarn. 1989. Sound sculpture: $^1/_4$" audiotape wound into a 6"- diameter sphere (Berliner).
Sonar Flashlight. 1989. Sound sculpture: flashlight shell, tape recorder, and miniature audio speaker (Berliner).
Videotape Dispenser. 1989. Sculpture: $^3/_4$" videotape and tape dispenser (Berliner).
Late City Edition. 1990. Video; 19 minutes; black and white; sound (Berliner).

Made for TV Movie. 1990. Sculpture: video monitor and 16mm filmstrip (Berliner).
Reflex. 1990. Sound sculpture: 35mm still camera, tape recorder, and miniature audio speaker (Berliner).
Touch Typing. 1990. Sculpture: typewriter shell and Scrabble letters (Berliner).
Buddha's Delight. 1991. Sound sculpture: Buddha statue and miniature audio speaker (Berliner).
Intimate Stranger. 1991. 16mm; 60 minutes; color; sound (CC, FMC, Milestone, MoMA).
Late City Edition. 1991. Video installation: found recycled newspaper bundles and miniature video monitors (Berliner).
Ultra High Frequency. 1991. Sound sculpture: television antennae, tape recorder, and miniature audio speaker (Berliner).
Central Avenue. 1992. Paracinema: photographic series (Berliner).
Audiofile. 1993. Interactive audio installation: file cabinets and 108 tape recorders (Berliner).
Aviary. 1993. Interactive audio installation: file cabinets and 27 tape recorders (Berliner).
Postmarks. 1994. Photographic series: found envelopes and postal imagery (Berliner).
All News Radio. 1996. Sound sculpture: live radio, found recycled newspaper bundles, and miniature audio speaker (Berliner).
Critical Mass. 1996. Interactive audio installation: live radio and television; 38 audio speakers and 20 video monitors (Berliner).
Electric Guitar. 1996. Sound sculpture: acoustic guitar, tape recorder, and miniature audio speaker (Berliner).
Nobody's Business. 1996. Film. 16mm; 60 minutes; color; sound (CC, FMC, Milestone, MoMA).
The Red Thread. 1996. Audio installation: live radio, one mile of continuous speaker wire, and audio speakers (Berliner).
The Art of War. 1999. Interactive audio installation: video projection, 12 tape recorders, and 250 miniature audio speakers (Berliner).
Found Sound. 1999. Interactive computer audio piece commissioned by "New Television" (http://www.ntv-artbytes.org/text/ABdownload.html).
Gathering Stones. 1999. Interactive video installation: video projection, found archival photographs, white rocks, and black and white pebbles (Berliner).
The Sweetest Sound. 2001. 16mm; 60 minutes; color; sound (FMC, MoMA, NV).
Gathering Stones. 2002. Site-specific version of interactive video installation, commissioned by the Holocaust Museum, Houston (Berliner).
The Language of Names. 2002. Wall mural: Interactive new media installation, including audio, video, and computer, commissioned by the Walker Art Center, Minneapolis (Berliner).
Flags of the World. 2003. Sound sculpture series: interactive new media installation, including audio, computer, and miniature speakers (Berliner).
Lost and Found. 2003. Interactive audio piece for Web site, commissioned by http://www.transom.org.

Tony Conrad

The following listing does not include Conrad's musical performances and publications, nor does it list his performance and mixed-media pieces.

The Flicker. 1966. 16mm; 25 minutes; black and white; sound (CC, FMC [with reel-to-reel stereo tape], LUX).
The Eye of Count Flickerstein. 1967 (revised 1975). 16mm; 7 minutes; black and white; sound (NA).
Coming Attractions (co-made with Beverly Grant Conrad). 1970. 16mm; 78 minutes; color; sound (FMC).
Straight and Narrow. 1970. 16mm; 10 minutes; black and white; sound (FMC, LUX).
Four Square. 1971. 4-screen 16mm; 14 minutes; color; sound (FMC).
Ten Years Alive on the Infinite Plain. 1972. 4-screen 16mm performance; ca. 90 minutes; color; sound (Conrad: Conrad@buffalo.edu; 126 Livingston St., Buffalo, NY 14213).
Curried 7302. 1973. 16mm film object; 2 minutes; color; sound (Conrad).
Deep Fried 4-X Negative (2 versions). 1973. 16mm film object (Conrad).
Deep Fried 7302. 1973. 16mm film object (Conrad).
Deep Fried 7360 (200-foot version). 1973. 16mm film object (Conrad).
Film of Note. 1973. Super-8mm; 28 minutes; color; sound (Conrad).
4-X Attack. 1973. 16mm; 1 minute; black and white; sound (Conrad).
Loose Connection. 1973. 16mm; 55 minutes; color; sound (Conrad).
Raw Film. 1973. 16mm film object (Conrad).
7302 Creole. 1973. 16mm film object; 1 minute; color; sound (Conrad).
Boiled Shadow. 1974. 16mm; 3 minutes; color; sound (Conrad).
Bowed Film. 1974. Performance work (Conrad).
Electrocuted 4-X. 1974. 16mm; 10 minutes; black and white; silent (Conrad).
Film Feedback. 1974. 16mm; 14 minutes; black and white; silent (FMC).
Flicker Matte. 1974. 16mm film object (Conrad).
Pickled 3M-150 (12 realizations). 1974. 16mm film object (Conrad).
Pickle Wind. 1974. 16mm; 3 minutes; color; sound (Conrad).
Roast Kalvar (2 realizations). 1974. 16mm film object (Conrad).
7360 Sukiyaki. 1973–74. Film performance work (NA).
Aquarium. 1975. 16mm; 7 minutes; color; silent (Conrad).
Articulation of Boolean Algebra for Film Opticals. 1975. 16mm; 75 minutes; black and white; sound (Conrad).
The Eye of Count Flickerstein. 1975. 16mm; 7 minutes; black and white; silent (Conrad).
Moment Propagation. 1975. Audio with slide; 28 minutes (Conrad).
Shadow File. 1975. Installation with photochromic panel and lamps (Conrad).
Mickey Mouse. 1976. 16mm; 2 minutes; color; silent (Conrad).
Yellow Movie (several hundred realizations). 1972–76. Scrolls (Conrad).
Concord Ultimatum. 1977. Videotape; 35 minutes; black and white; sound (Conrad).
Cycles of 3's and 7's. 1977. Videotape; 23 minutes; black and white; sound (Conrad).

Movie Show. 1977. Videotape; 60 minutes; color; sound (Conrad).
Phonograph. 1979. 16mm fragment; 10 seconds; black and white; silent (Conrad).
Teddy Tells Jokes. 1980. Videotape; 4 minutes; color; sound (Conrad).
Accordion. 1981. Videotape; 7 minutes; color; sound (Conrad).
Combat Status Go. 1981. Videotape; 10 minutes; color; sound (Conrad).
Export Import. 1982. 16mm; 14 minutes; black and white; sound (Conrad).
Beholden to Victory. 1983. Videotape; 25 minutes; color; sound (Conrad).
Height 100. 1983. Videotape; 14 minutes; color; sound (Conrad).
Knowing with Television. 1983. Videotape/installation; 21 minutes; color; sound (Conrad).
Sip Twice, Sandy. 1983. Videotape; 1 minute; black and white; sound (Conrad).
Asinine States. 1985. Videotape; 2 minutes; color; sound (Conrad).
Eye Contact. 1985. Videotape; 8 minutes; color; sound (Conrad).
14 Commercials for Point Blank. 1985. Videotape; 5 minutes; color; sound (Conrad).
Ipso Facto. 1985. Videotape; 7 minutes; color; sound (Conrad).
Research/Performance. 1985. Videotape; 10 minutes; color; sound (Conrad).
Run Dick, Run Jane. 1985. Videotape; 3 minutes; color; sound (Conrad).
Come on In. 1986. Videotape; 16 minutes; color; sound (Conrad).
In Line. 1986. Videotape; 7 minutes; color; sound (Conrad).
Suburban Discipline and Fun: Labyrinth with Video, Performance, and Dioramas. 1986. Installation (Conrad).
Weak Bodies, Strong Wills. 1986. Videotape; 5 minutes; color; sound (Conrad).
The Poetics of TV: Ipso Facto; An Immense Majority; In Line. 1985–87. Videotape; 24 minutes; color; sound (Conrad).
That Faraway Look. 1988. Videotape; 25 minutes; color; sound (Conrad).
Panoptikon. 1988. Video installation (Conrad).
Redressing Down. 1988. Videotape; 18 minutes; color; sound (Conrad).
No Europe (co-made with Chris Hill). 1990. Videotape; 14 minutes; color; sound (Conrad).
Artpark—One Year Later. 1991. Television program for cable series *NEthing You Say.*
Lafayette Square. 1991. Cable TV documentary of Gulf War protest in Buffalo; 27 minutes; color; sound (Conrad).
Long-shot/run/dead, Part I. 1991. Videotape; 11 minutes; color; sound (Conrad).
The Sea and the Scientist. 1991. Television program for cable series *NEthing You Say.*
Studio of the Streets (co-made with Cathy Steffan). 1991–93. 100+ videotapes for a weekly hour-long cable program on Buffalo cable access channel. Several half-hour television programs, produced collaboratively. Titles include *News Diaries* (a series), *Riddle of the Mysterious Missing Station, Delivering Petitions to David Rutecki, Bikes Not Bombs,* and *A Visit to Cambridge Community Television.*
Hello Happiness. 2000. Videotape; 1 minute; color; sound (Conrad).
Hart. 2001. Videotape; 5 minutes; color; sound (Conrad).
Tony's Oscular Pets. 2001. Videotape; 7 minutes; color; sound (Conrad).

Claiming Los Angeles. 2002. Videotape; 3 minutes; color; sound (Conrad).
Grading Tips for Teachers. 2003. Videotape; 13 minutes; color; sound (Conrad).

Nathaniel Dorsky

Dorsky has been working, primarily as an editor, on documentaries and industrials since the mid-1980s and, less frequently, on feature entertainments (he shot some of Richard Lerner's *Revenge of the Cheerleaders* [1976], for example). Sometimes he edits entire films; sometimes he is hired for a few days or weeks as a "film doctor" to help makers when they have reached an impasse. Dorsky estimates that he has contributed to well over a hundred films, but he has not kept careful records of these projects. The following listing begins with the films Dorsky considers his, followed by a number of his commercial projects, including some of those he is most proud of.

A Fall Trip Home. 1964. 16mm; 11 minutes; color; sound (CC).
Ingreen. 1964. 16mm; 12 minutes; color; sound (CC).
Summerwind. 1965. 16mm; 14 minutes; color; sound (CC).
Fool's Spring (Two Personal Gifts) (co-made with Jerome Hiler). 1966. 16mm; 5 minutes (at 18 fps); color; silent (Dorsky).
Hours for Jerome, Parts 1 and 2. 1982. 16mm; 50 minutes (at 18 fps); color; silent (CC).
Ariel. 1983. 16mm; 16 minutes (at 18fps); color; silent (CC).
Pneuma. 1983. 16mm; 28 minutes (at 18fps); color; silent (CC, LC).
Alaya. 1987. 16mm; 28 minutes (at 18fps); color; silent (CC, LC).
17 Reasons Why. 1987. 16mm; 20 minutes (at 18fps); color; silent (CC, LC).
Triste (first of *Four Cinematic Songs*). 1996. 16mm; 18½ minutes (at 18fps); color; silent (CC, LC).
Variations (second of *Four Cinematic Songs*). 1998. 16mm; 24 minutes (at 18fps); color; silent (CC, LC).
Arbor Vitae (third of *Four Cinematic Songs*). 2000. 16mm; 28 minutes (at 18fps); color; silent (CC, LC).
Love's Refrain (fourth of *Four Cinematic Songs*). 2001. 16mm; 22½ minutes (at 18fps); color; silent (CC, LC).
The Visitation (first of *Two Devotional Songs*). 2002. 16mm; 18 minutes (at 18fps); color; silent (CC).
Threnody (second of *Two Devotional Songs*). 2004. 16mm; 20 minutes (at 18fps); color; sound (CC).

Selected commercial projects:

Catch a Tiger. 1963. 16mm; 25 minutes; black and white; sound (Dorsky, 751½ 16th Ave., San Francisco, CA 94118).
Where Time Is a River (director, Gay Mathaei; editing, some photography, Dorsky). 1966. 16mm; 20 minutes; color; sound.
Gauguin in Tahiti: Search for Paradise (director, Martin Carr; art photography, Dorsky). 1967. 16mm; ca. 58 minutes; color; sound.

Library (co-made with Jerome Hiler). 1970. 16mm; color; ca. 25 minute; sound (Dorsky).

A Look at Laundry (filmmaker, Ralph Steiner; editor, Dorsky). 1971. 16mm; 8½ minutes; black and white; sound (September Films, 535 E. 6th St., New York, NY 10009).

Beyond Niagara (filmmaker, Ralph Steiner; editor, Dorsky). 1973. 16mm; 8 minutes; color; sound (September Films).

Look Park (filmmaker, Ralph Steiner; editor, Dorsky). 1974. 16mm; 10½ minutes; color; sound (September Films).

What Happened to Kerouac? (directors, Richard Lerner, Lewis MacAdams; editor, some cinematography). 1985. 35mm; 90 minutes; color; sound (commercial video).

Lily: A Sequel (director, Liz Grace; editor, Dorsky). 1988. 16mm; 15 minutes; color; sound (Davidson Films, dfi@davidsonfilms.com).

The Spirit of Crazy Horse (directors, Michel Dubois, Kevin McKierman; editor, some cinematography, Dorsky). 1989. Video (Betacam); 56 minutes; color; sound (commercial video).

The Life and Times of Allen Ginsberg (director, Jerry Aronson; coeditor, Dorsky). 1993. 16mm; 82 minutes; color; sound (commercial video)

Night Waltz: The Music of Paul Bowles (director, Owsley Brown; editor, some cinematography, Dorsky). 1998. 16mm; 83 minutes; color; sound (Facets).

Wayfinders: A Pacific Odyssey (director, Gail Evenari; editor, Dorsky). 1999. 16mm; 60 minutes; color; sound (commercial video).

Tashi Jong: A Traditional Tibetan Community in Exile (director, Barbara Green; editor, Dorsky). 2000. 16mm; 45 minutes; color; sound (Tibetan Video Project, 2952 Pine Ave., Berkeley 94705; 510-540-8401; bcgreen@global.net).

What Do You Believe? (director, Sarah Feinbloom; editor, Dorsky). 2002. 16mm; 50 minutes; color; sound (New Day Films, orders@newday.com; commercial video).

Ernie Gehr

Morning. 1967. 16mm; 4½ minutes (at 16fps); color; silent (CC, MoMA).

Wait. 1967. 16mm; 7 minutes (at 16fps); color; silent (CC, MoMA).

Reverberation. 1969. 16mm; 23 minutes (at 16fps); black and white; sound (CC [sound-on-cassette]).

Transparency. 1969. 16mm; 11 minutes; color; silent (CC, MoMA).

Field. 1970. 16mm; 19 minutes (at 16fps); black and white; silent (CC, MoMA).

Field (Short Version). 1970. 16mm; 9½ minutes; black and white; silent (Gehr: erniegehr@sbcglobal.net).

History. 1970. 16mm; 40 minutes (at 16fps); black and white; silent (Gehr).

Serene Velocity. 1970. 16mm; 23 minutes (at 16fps); color; silent (CC, MoMA).

Three. 1970. 16mm; 4 minutes; black and white; silent (Gehr).

Still. 1971. 16mm; 55 minutes; color; sound (CC, MoMA).

Eureka (initially known as *Geography*). 1974. 16mm; 30 minutes; black and white; silent (CC).

Shift. 1974. 16mm; 9 minutes; color; sound (CC, MoMA).
Behind the Scenes. 1975. 16mm; 4¼ minutes; color; sound (Gehr).
Table. 1976. 16mm; 16 minutes (at 16fps); color; silent (CC).
Untitled [1977]. 1977. 16mm; 5 minutes (at 16fps); color; silent (CC, MoMA).
Mirage. 1981. 16mm; 8 minutes; color; silent (CC).
Untitled: Part One, 1981. 1981. 16mm; 29 minutes; color; silent (CC).
Signal—Germany on the Air. 1985. 16mm; 35 minutes; color; sound (CC).
Rear Window. 1991. 16mm; 10 minutes; color; silent (CC).
Side/Walk/Shuttle. 1991. 16mm; 41 minutes; color; sound (CC).
This Side of Paradise. 1991. 16mm; 14 minutes; color; sound (CC).
Brother, Can You Spare Some Time? 1995. Multimedia installation (Gehr).
For Daniel. 1996. 16mm; 72 minutes; color; silent (Gehr).
Cotton Candy. 2001. Digital video; 56 minutes; color; sound (Gehr).
Glider. 2001. Digital video; 37 minutes; color; silent (Gehr).
City. 2002. Digital video; 35 minutes; color; sound (Gehr).
Crystal Palace. 2002. Digital video; 28 minutes; color; sound (Gehr).
MoMA on Wheels. 2002. Digital video installation at the Museum of Modern Art (Gehr, MoMA).
Navigation. 2002. Multiscreen digital video installation at the Museum of Modern Art (Gehr).
City (revised version). 2003. Digital video; 27 minutes; color; sound (Gehr).
The Collector. 2003. Digital video; 18 minutes; color; sound (Gehr).
Passage. 2003. 16mm; 15 minutes; color; sound (Gehr).
Essex Street Market. 2004. Digital video; 29 minutes; black and white; silent (Gehr).
Green Street. 2004. Digital video; 5 minutes; color; silent (Gehr).
Noon Time Activities. 2004. Digital video; 21 minutes; black and white; silent (Gehr).
Precarious Garden. 2004. 16mm; 14 minutes; color; sound (Gehr, Canyon).
Workers Leaving the Factory (After Lumiere). 2004. Digital video; 12 minutes; black and white; silent (Gehr).

Jerome Hiler

Fool's Spring (Two Personal Gifts) (co-made with Nathaniel Dorsky). 1966. 16mm; 5 minutes (at 18fps); color; silent (Dorsky [see Dorsky filmography], Hiler, 2237 Fulton St., no. 104, San Francisco, CA 94117).
Library (co-made with Nathaniel Dorsky). 1970. 16mm; ca. 25 minutes; color; sound (Hiler).
Gladly Given. 1997. 16mm; 12 minutes (at 18 fps); color; silent (Hiler).
Target Rock. 2000. 16mm; 22 minutes; color; sound (Hiler).

Shiho Kano

Landscape (Joukei). 1998. Super-8mm; 13 minutes; color; sound (Kano: shihokano@wanadoo.fr).

Still. 1999. Super-8mm; 15 minutes; color; sound (Kano).
Rocking Chair. 2000. 16mm; 13 minutes; color; sound (CC, Collectif Jeune Cinema, www.cjcinema.org).
White Tablecloth. 2000. Video; 7½ minutes; color (Kano).
White Tablecloth. 2001. Five-monitor video installation (Kano).
Floating Leaf. 2002. Video; 1 minute; color; sound (Kano).
Incense. 2002. Video; 6 minutes; color; sound (Kano).
Rosecolored Flower. 2002. Video; 12 minutes; color; sound (Kano).
Lily in the Glass. 2003. 16mm; 6 minutes; color; sound (Kano).
A Book. 2004. Video installation (Kano).
A Book. 2004. Video; 4 minutes; color; sound (Kano).
Wave. 2005. Video; 16 minutes; color; sound (Kano).

Sharon Lockhart

Listings of Lockhart's many photo shows are included in *Sharon Lockhart/Teatro Amazonas,* a catalogue for a show of Lockhart's photographs and films in Rotterdam, Zurich, and Wolfsburg, in 1999 (Rotterdam: NAi Publishers, 1999); and in *Sharon Lockhart,* a catalogue for a show of photographs and films at the Museum of Contemporary Art, Chicago, March 3–May 20, 2001 and at the Museum of Contemporary Art, San Diego, June 9–September 2, 2001 (Chicago: Hatje Cantz, 2001).

Khalil, Shaun, a Woman under the Influence. 1994. 16mm; 16 minutes; color; sound (Blum and Poe, 2042 Broadway, Santa Monica, CA 90404).
Goshogaoka. 1997. 16mm; 63 minutes; color; sound (Blum and Poe).
Shirley (co-made with Daniel Marlos). 1999. 16mm; 18 minutes; color; silent (Blum and Poe).
Teatro Amazonas. 1999. 35mm; 40 minutes; color; sound (Blum and Poe).
NŌ. 2003. 16mm; 32½ minutes; color; sound (Blum and Poe, Barbara Gladstone, 515 W. 24th St., New York, NY 10011; 212-206-9300; www.gladstonegallery.com).

Robb Moss

The Snack. 1975. 16mm; 5 minutes; black and white; sound (Moss: robbmoss@fas.harvard.edu).
Absence. 1981. 16mm; 30 minutes; color; sound (Moss).
Riverdogs. 1982. 16mm; 30 minutes; color; sound (Moss).
Africa Revisited (co-made with Claude Chelli). 1983. 16mm; 53 minutes; color; sound (Moss).
A Day on Three Oyster Boats. 1985. 16mm; 10 minutes; color; sound (Moss).
What's It Like Here? 1989. 16mm (now on interactive video disk, and on permanent exhibition at the St. Louis Zoo); 20 minutes; color; sound (Moss).
The Tourist. 1991. 16mm; 58 minutes; color; sound (Moss).

On Dumpster Diving (cinematography; producer: David Van Taylor). 1994. 16mm for television broadcast; 30 minutes; color; sound (ITVS).
The Painter's World (cinematography; producer: Judith Wechsler). 1994. 16mm for television broadcast; 57 minutes; color; sound (PBS).
Love at First Sight (cinematography; producer: Beeban Kidron). 1996. 16mm for television broadcast; 60 minutes; color; sound (BBC, PBS).
Huck Finn: Born to Trouble (cinematography; producer: Jill Janows). 1997. Beta and 16mm for television broadcast (fourth part of a four-part series on censorship); 57 minutes; color; sound (PBS, WGBH Boston).
Lessons from Thin Air (made for the Smithsonian Institution). 1997. Beta video; 58 minutes; color; sound (Smithsonian Institution).
The Same River Twice. 2003. 35mm; 78 minutes; color; sound (Balcony Releasing; Blackchair DVD: www.microcinema.com; NV).

Matthias Müller

Some of Müller's recent work is available only from his galleries: Galería Distrito Cu4tro, Madrid (www.distrito4.com); Stellan Holm, New York (www.stellanholm.com); Thomas Erben, New York (www.thomaserben.com); Timothy Taylor, London (www.timothytaylorgallery.com); Volker Diehl, Berlin (www.dv-art.com).

Das Vermächtnis (co-made with Christiane Heuwinkel). 1979. Super-8mm; 25 minutes; color; sound (NA).
Acqua verde. 1983. Super-8mm; 3 minutes; color; sound (NA).
Es war überall sehr schön. 1983. Super-8mm; 3 minutes; color; sound (NA).
Nature morte (co-made with Christiane Heuwinkel). 1983. Super-8mm; 26 minutes; black and white/color; sound (NA).
Rapunzl (co-made with Christiane Heuwinkel). 1983. Super-8mm; 15 minutes; color; sound (NA).
Wanderer im Nebelmeer (co-made with Christiane Heuwinkel). 1983. Super-8mm; 17 minutes; black and white; sound (NA).
Continental Breakfast. 1985. Super-8mm (blown up to 16mm); 19 minutes; black and white/color; sound (NA).
Danke (co-made with Christiane Heuwinkel). 1985. Super-8mm; 2 minutes; color, sound (NA)
Lustiger kleiner Streifen. 1985. Super-8mm; 1 minute; color, sound (NA).
Der psychedelische Film. 1985. Super-8mm; 3 minutes; color, sound (NA).
Final Cut. 1986. Super-8mm; 12 minutes; color; sound (LC).
Epilogue (co-made with Christiane Heuwinkel). 1987. Super-8mm; 16 minutes; color; sound (NA).
Aus der Ferne—The Memo Book. 1989. 16mm; 28 minutes; color; sound (CC, FDK [Freunde der Deutschen Kinemathek, Potsdamer Straße 2. 10785 Berlin; 49-30-26-95-51-00; fdk@fdk-berlin.de], LC, SF).
The Flamethrowers (co-made with Owen O'Toole, Alte Kinder and Schmelzdahin). 1990. Super-8mm (blown up to 16 mm); 9 minutes; black and white/color; sound (NA).

Home Stories. 1990. 16mm; 6 minutes; color; sound (CC, FDK, LC, SF).
Sleepy Haven. 1993. 16mm; 15 minutes; color; sound (CC, FDK, LC, SF).
Alpsee. 1994. 16mm; 15 minutes; color; sound (CC, FDK, LC, SF).
Scattering Stars. 1994. 16mm; 2 minutes; black and white; sound (BFI, CC, FDK, LC, SF).
Pensão Globo. 1997. 16mm; 15 minutes; color; sound (CC, CFDC, FDK, LC, SF).
Vacancy. 1998. 16mm; 15 minutes; color; sound (CC, FDK, LC, SF).
Phoenix Tapes (co-made with Christoph Girardet; includes *Rutland, Burden of Proof, Derailed, Why Don't You Love Me?, Bedroom, Necrologue*). 1999. Betacam video/6 DVD loops; 45 minutes; black and white/color; silent/sound (LC, DVD edition: galleries only).
Breeze. 2000. 35mm; 1 minute; color; sound (Vienna International Film Festival).
nebel. 2000. 35mm; 12 minutes; black and white/color; sound (SF).
Container. 2001. DVD; 26 minutes; color; silent (galleries only).
Phantom. 2001. Betacam video/DVD loop; 5 minutes; color; sound (LC, DVD edition: galleries only).
Beacon (co-made with Christoph Girardet). 2002. Betacam video/DVD; 15 minutes; black and white/color; sound (Agencia Curtas Metragens, Vila do Conde, agencia@curtasmetragens.pt, DVD edition: galleries only).
Manual (co-made with Christoph Girardet). 2002. Betacam video/DVD loop; 10 minutes; color; sound (LC, DVD edition: galleries only).
Pictures. 2002. DVD loop; 2 minutes; color; silent (galleries only).
Mirror (co-made with Christoph Girardet). 2003. 35mm CinemaScope/DVD loop (double projection); 8 minutes; color; sound (LC, DVD edition: galleries only).
Play (co-made with Christoph Girardet). 2003. Betacam video/DVD loop; 7 minutes; black and white/color; sound (LC).
Promises. 2003. DVD loop; 8 minutes; color; silent (galleries only).
Album. 2004. DVD loop; 24 minutes; black and white/color; sound (galleries only).
Veil. 2004. DVD loop; 30 seconds; black and white; silent (galleries only).

J. Leighton Pierce

Last Laugh. 1977. Sound piece; 5 minutes (Pierce, P.O. Box 3246, Iowa City, IA 52244; 319-621-6714; Leighton-pierce@uiowa.edu).
Wet One #1. 1977. Sound piece; 7 minutes (Pierce).
Carter '80. 1979. Sound piece; 4 minutes (Pierce).
He Likes to Chop Down Trees. 1980. 16mm; $3^1/_2$ minutes; color; sound (CC).
It ain't always easy. 1980. Sound piece; 3 minutes (Pierce).
Pedal Point. 1980. Video; 6 minutes; color; sound (Pierce).
He Said without Moving. 1981. 16mm; $3^1/_2$ minutes; color; sound (CC).
Not Much Time. 1982. 16mm; $7^1/_2$ minutes; color; sound (CC).
Southwest Window. 1982. Video; 5 minutes; color; sound (Pierce).
And Sometimes the Boats Are Low. 1983. 16mm; $3^1/_2$ minutes; color; sound (CC).
Family Portrait. 1983. Video; 1 minute; color; sound (Pierce).

Nine Mile Point (co-made with Lynn Vance). 1983. Video; 7½ minutes; color; sound (Pierce).
A Fine Batch of Worden Hill Walking Sticks. 1984. Video; 7 minutes; color; sound (Pierce).
A Grey Shaded Area (co-made with Lynn Vance). 1984. Video; 20 minutes; color; sound (Pierce).
The Miracle of Change. 1984. 16mm; 6½ minutes; color; sound (CC).
These Are the Directions I Give to a Stranger. 1984. 16mm; 14½ minutes; color; sound (CC).
The Way to Tie Two Things Together. 1984. Video; 5 minutes; color; sound (Pierce).
Cumulonimbus. 1986. 16mm; 10 minutes; color; sound (Pierce).
Red Swing. 1986. 16mm; 8 minutes; color; sound (CC).
On the Road Going Through. 1987. Video; 15 minutes; color; sound (Pierce).
What's Left Is Wind. 1988. 16mm; 4 minutes; color; sound (CC).
Grotto. 1989. Video; 12 minutes; color; sound (Pierce).
You Can Drive the Big Rigs. 1989. 16mm; 15 minutes; color; sound (CC).
Edith Cone. 1990. Video; 10 minutes; color; sound (Pierce).
Principles of Harmonic Motion. 1991. Video; 22 minutes; color; sound (CC).
Thursday. 1991. 16mm; 4½ minutes; color; sound (CC).
Deer Isle #5: The Crossing. 1992. Video; 6 minutes; color; sound (Pierce).
Red Shovel. 1992. 16mm; 8 minutes; color; sound (CC).
Blue Hat. 1993. 16mm; 4½ minutes; color; sound (CC).
Deer Isle #8: Going Out (In the Morning). 1994. Video; 4½ minutes; color; sound (Pierce).
Gammathump. 1994. Sound piece; 5 minutes (Pierce)
50 Feet of String. 1995. 16mm; 53 minutes; color; sound (CC).
From Sea. 1996. Sound piece; 3 minutes (Pierce).
Puppy-Go-Round. 1996. Video; 3 minutes; color; sound (Pierce).
Seine Promenade. 1996. Sound piece; 10 minutes (Pierce).
Memories of Water (#21, 6, 27). 1997. Video; 9½ minutes; color; sound (CC).
Glass (Memories of Water #29). 1998. 16mm; 7 minutes; color; sound (CC).
Wood. 2000. Video; 8 minutes; color; sound (Pierce; Vidéographe Inc., 460, rue Saint-Catherine ouest no. 504, Montréal, Québec, H3B 1A7 Canada).
The Back Steps. 2001. Digital video; 6 minutes; color; sound (Pierce; Vidéographe).
Veiled Red. 2001. Digital video; 5¼ minutes; color; sound (Pierce).
Evaporation. 2002. Digital video; 12 minutes; color; sound (Pierce; Vidéographe).
Fall (3 parts). 2002. Digital video; 13 minutes; color; sound (Pierce; Vidéographe).
Pink Socks. 2002. Digital video; 5 minutes; color; sound (Pierce).
37th and Lex. 2002. Digital video; 4 minutes; color; sound (Pierce; Vidéographe).
Water Seeking Its Level. 2002. Digital video; 6 minutes; color; sound (Pierce; Vidéographe).
A Private Happiness. 2003. Digital video; 10 minutes; color; sound (Pierce; Vidéographe).
Pivot. 2004. 4-channel video/8-channel sound installation (Pierce).
Viscera. 2004. Digital video; 11 minutes; color; sound (Pierce; Vidéographe).

Jennifer Todd Reeves

Elations in Negative. 1990. 16mm; 5 minutes; black and white; silent (FMC).
Girls Daydream about Hollywood. 1992. 16mm; 5 minutes; black and white; sound (FMC).
Taste It Nine Times. 1992. 16mm; 5½ minutes; black and white; sound (FMC).
Monsters in the Closet. 1993. 16mm; 15 minutes; black and white/color; sound (FMC, Women Make Movies [WMM]: 462 Broadway, Suite 500WS, New York, NY 10013; 212-925-0606; www.wmm.com).
Configuration 20. 1994. 16mm; 12 minutes; black and white/color; sound (FMC, LC).
The Girl's Nervy. 1995. 16mm; 5 minutes; color; sound (FMC, LC, WMM).
Chronic. 1996. 16mm; 38 minutes; black and white/color; sound (FMC, LC, WMM).
We Are Going Home. 1998. 16mm; 10 minutes; black and white/color; sound (FMC, LC).
Darling International (co-made with M. M. Serra). 1999. 16mm; 22 minutes; black and white; sound (FMC).
Exhausted (music video for Joseph Arthur). 2001. Video; 4 minutes; color; sound (NA).
Fear of Blushing. 2001. 16mm; 5½ minutes; color; sound (FMC).
Skinny Teeth. 2001. Video; 7 minutes; color; sound (Reeves: jennreeves@earthlink.net, jenniferreevesfilm.com).
Double Your Pleasure (directed by M. M. Serra; sound design by Reeves). 2002. 16mm; 3 minutes; black and white; sound (FMC).
Swamp People. 2002. Live film and poetry performance, with poet Lisa Jarnot; images and sound by Reeves; 6 minutes (NA).
He Walked Away. 2003. Live performance with the following musician-composer duos: Skúli Sverrisson/Hilmar Jensson; Erik Hoversten/Dave Cerf; Anthony Burr/Eliza Slavet; two 16mm projectors projecting imagery; 17 minutes; black and white/color; sound (Reeves).
The Time We Killed. 2004. 16mm; 94 minutes; black and white; sound (Reeves).
Untitled. 2004. Live performance with Zeena Parkins and David Kean; three 16mm projectors projecting imagery; 18 minutes; sound (NA).

Phil Solomon

Night Light. 1975. 16mm; 8 minutes; black and white; silent (Solomon: solomon@colorado.edu).
The Passage of the Bride. 1978. 16mm; 6 minutes (at 18fps); black and white; silent (CC, LC).
As If We. 1980. 16mm; 10 minutes; color; silent (Solomon: solomon@colorado.edu).
Nocturne. 1980 (revised 1989). 16mm; 10 minutes; black and white; silent (CC, LC).
What's Out Tonight Is Lost. 1983. 16mm; 8 minutes (at 18 fps); color; silent (CC).

The Secret Garden. 1988. 16mm; 23 minutes; color; silent (CC, LC).
The Exquisite Hour. 1989. Super-8mm; 14 minutes; color; sound (CC).
Remains to Be Seen. 1989. Super-8mm; 17$^1/_2$ minutes; color; sound (CC).
Rocket Boy vs. Brakhage. 1989. 16mm; ca. 30 minutes; color/black and white; sound (Solomon).
Clepsydra. 1992. 16mm; 14 minutes; black and white; silent (CC, LC).
Elementary Phrases (co-made with Stan Brakhage). 1994. 16mm; 35 minutes; color; silent (CC, CFDC, LC).
The Exquisite Hour. 1994. 16mm; 14 minutes; color; sound (CC, LC).
Remains to Be Seen. 1994. 16mm; 17$^1/_2$ minutes; color; sound (CC, LC).
The Snowman. 1995. 16mm; 8 minutes; color; sound (CC, LC).
Concrescence (co-made with Stan Brakhage). 1996. 16mm; 3 minutes; color; silent (CC, LC).
Alternating Currents (co-made with Stan Brakhage). 1999.
Twilight Psalm II: Walking Distance. 1999. 16mm; 23 minutes; color; sound (CC, LC).
Yes I Said Yes I Will Yes. 1999. 16mm; 3 minutes; color; sound (Solomon).
Innocence and Despair. 2001. Digital video, 4 minutes, color, sound (Solomon).
Seasons . . . (co-made with Stan Brakhage). 2002. 16mm; 18 minutes; color; silent (CC, LC).
Twilight Psalm III: Night of the Meek. 2002. 16mm; 23 minutes; black and white; sound (CC, LC).
Twilight Psalm I: The Lateness of the Hour. 2003. 16mm; 10 minutes; color; sound (CC, LC).

Bibliography

While the preceding filmographies are as complete and up-to-date as I am able to make them, this bibliography means only to provide an entry into the discourse on critical cinema in general and on those filmmakers interviewed for *A Critical Cinema 5* (the General References section for *A Critical Cinema 5* is a supplement to the General References listings in *A Critical Cinema, A Critical Cinema 2, A Critical Cinema 3,* and *A Critical Cinema 4*). If a reference is cited in full in the General References section, it is given in shortened form in the individual filmmaker bibliographies. When a single person has authored or edited more than one book or article, I have alphabetized those publications within the listing.

General References

Arthur, Paul. *A Line of Sight: American Avant-Garde Film since 1965.* Minneapolis: University of Minnesota Press, 2005.

Bandy, Mary Lea, and Antonio Monda. *The Hidden God: Film and Faith.* New York: Museum of Modern Art, 2003. A collection of essays published in conjunction with the film exhibition of the same name, presented during the winter of 2003–4.

Borger, Irene, ed. *The Force of Curiosity.* Santa Monica, Calif.: Herb Alpert Foundation, 1999. Includes interviews with Craig Baldwin, Jeanne C. Finley, Su Friedrich, and Leslie Thornton.

Bowser, Pearl, Jane Gaines, and Charles Musser, eds. *Oscar Micheaux and His Circle: African-American Filmmaking and Race Cinema of the Silent Era.* Bloomington: Indiana University Press, 2001. Catalogue for a traveling show of films by Oscar Micheaux. Includes an interview with Arthur Jafa (A. J. Fielder), essays by Pearl Bowser, Jayna Brown, Corey K. Creekmur, Jane

Gaines, Gloria J. Gibson, Phyllis R. Klotman, Charles Musser, Charlene Register, Louise Spence, Clyde Taylor, Sister Francesca Thompson, and Michele Wallace; useful appendices; and an extensive bibliography compiled by Kristen Barnes, Jane Gaines, and Fred Neumann.

Covert, Nadine, ed. *Flaherty 2004: Inspired Filmmaking.* New York: International Film Seminars, 2004. Catalogue for the fiftieth Robert Flaherty Seminar, held June 12 through June 19, 2004.

Deren, Maya. *Essential Deren: Collected Writings on Film by Maya Deren.* Edited and with a preface by Bruce R. McPherson. Kingston, N.Y.: Documentext, 2005.

Dorsky, Nathaniel. *Devotional Cinema.* Berkeley, Calif.: Tuumba Press, 2003.

Emke, Ronald, ed. *Consider the Alternatives: 20 Years of Contemporary Art at Hallwalls.* Buffalo, N.Y.: Hallwalls Contemporary Arts Center, 1996.

Haller, Robert A. *Crossroads: Avant-garde Film in Pittsburgh in the 1970s.* New York: Anthology Film Archives, 2005.

Hamlyn, Nicky. *Film Art Phenomena.* London: British Film Institute, 2003.

Hoberman, J. *On Jack Smith's* Flaming Creatures *(and Other Secret-Flix of Cinemaroc).* New York: Granary Books/Hips Road, 2001.

Holmlund, Chris, and Justin Wyatt, eds. *Contemporary American Independent Film: From the Margins to the Mainstream.* New York: Routledge, 2005. Includes essays by José B. Capino, Diane Carson, Ian Conrich, Robert Eberwein, Joan Hawkins, Chris Holmlund, Annette Insdorf, David James, Jon Jost, Christina Lane, Ed Lowry, Jonas Mekas, Diane Negra, Mark Reid, Justin Wyatt, Patricia R. Zimmerman.

Hoolboom, Mike. *Plague Years: A Life in Underground Movies.* Edited by Steve Reinke. Toronto: XYZ Books, 1998.

Horak, Jan Christopher. *Making Images Move: Photographers and Avant-Garde Cinema.* Washington, D.C.: Smithsonian Institution Press, 1997. Includes chapters on Chris Marker, Helmar Lerski, Paul Strand, László Moholy-Nagy, Helen Levitt, Robert Frank, Danny Lyon, Ed van der Elsken; and an extensive filmography and bibliography.

James, David E. *The Most Typical Avant-Garde: History and Geography of Minor Cinemas in Los Angeles.* Berkeley and Los Angeles: University of California Press, 2005. The most remarkable book on critical cinema since the 1970s.

———, ed. *The Sons and Daughters of Los: Culture and Community in L.A.* Philadelphia: Temple University Press, 2003. Includes essays by Jiwon Ahn, Meiling Cheng, Sande Cohen, Harry Gamboa Jr., Eric Gordon, Claudine Isé, David E. James, Laura Meyer, Bill Mohr, James M. Moran, and Nithila Peter.

———, ed. *Stan Brakhage: Filmmaker.* Philadelphia: Temple University Press, 2005. Includes essays by Paul Arthur, Bruce Baillie, Abigail Child, Edward Dorn, Craig Dworkin, R. Bruce Elder, Nicky Hamlyn, David E. James, Jonas Mekas, Tyrus Miller, Carolee Schneemann, P. Adams Sitney, Phil Solomon, Chick Strand, James Tenney, and Willie Varela.

Lane, Jim. *The Autobiographical Documentary in America.* Madison: University of Wisconsin Press, 2002.

Le Grice, Malcolm. *Experimental Cinema in the Digital Age.* London: British Film Institute, 2001.
Lerner, Jesse, ed. *Superocheros.* Special issue of *Wide Angle* (vol. 21, no. 3 [June 1999]) on Mexican experimental cinema.
MacDonald, Scott. *A Critical Cinema 4: Interviews with Independent Filmmakers.* Berkeley and Los Angeles: University of California Press, 2004.
———. "Experimental Film in the 1980s." In *A New Pot of Gold: Hollywood under the Electronic Rainbow, 1980–1989,* ed. Stephen Prince, 390–444. Vol. 10 of *History of American Cinema.* New York: Scribner's, 2000.
———. *The Garden in the Machine: A Field Guide to Independent Films about Place.* Berkeley and Los Angeles: University of California Press, 2001.
———. "Toward an Eco-cinema." *ISLE (Interdisciplinary Studies in Literature and Environment)* 11, no. 2 (Summer 2004): 107–32.
Mekas, Jonas. *Movie Journal: The Rise of the New American Cinema, 1959–1971.* New York: Collier, 1972.
Moritz, William. *Optical Poetry: The Life and Work of Oskar Fischinger.* London: John Libbey, 2004.
Morrow, Bradford, ed. *Cinema Lingua: Writers Respond to Film* (*Conjunctions,* no. 42). Annandale-on-Hudson, N.Y.: Bard College, 2004. Includes "Three Poems and Twelve Portraits," by Gerard Melanga; "Ten Temporary Sonnets," by Lyn Hejinian and Peter Hutton; and "ULULU: Clown Sharpnel," by Thalia Field and Bill Morrison.
O'Pray, Michael. *Avant-Garde Film—Forms, Themes and Passions.* London: Wallflower, 2003.
Roberts, Catsou, and Lucy Steeds, eds. *Michael Snow, almost Cover to Cover.* Catalogue published on the occasion of a Michael Snow retrospective, organized by Arnolfini Gallery, Bristol, UK, September 22 to November 18, 2001. London: Black Dog, 2001.
Sargeant, Jack. *Naked Lens: Beat Cinema.* New York: Creation Books, 1997.
Sitney, P. Adams. *Visionary Film: The American Avant-Garde, 1943–2000.* 3rd ed. New York: Oxford University Press, 2002.

Peggy Ahwesh

Ahwesh, Peggy. "Film, Baby." In *Big as Life: An American History of 8mm Films,* ed. Albert Kilchesty. Catalogue for a retrospective show of 8mm film, curated by Steve Anker and Jytte Jensen, February 1998 to December 1999, published as a special issue of *Cinematograph* (1998): 79–82.
Dargis, Manola. "Beyond Brakhage: Avant-Garde Film and Feminism." In *A Passage Illuminated: The American Avant-Garde Film 1980–1990,* ed. Nelly Voorhuis, 55–69. Amsterdam: Foundation Mecano, 1991.
Margolies, Ivone. "After the Fall: Peggy Ahwesh's Verite." *Motion Picture* 3, nos. 1–2 (Winter 1989–90): 31–33.
Marks, Laura U. *Touch: Sensuous Theory and Multisensory Media,* 99–101. Minneapolis: University of Minnesota Press, 2002.

Montgomery, Jennifer. "Her Logic Is in Contradiction: The Films of Peggy Ahwesh." *Cinematograph,* no. 3 (1988): 39–42.

Kenneth Anger

Alice L. Hutchinson's *Kenneth Anger: A Demonic Visionary* (see below) includes a detailed listing of writings relating to Anger's career.

Anger, Kenneth. *Anger Magick Lantern Cycle, A Special Presentation in Celebration of the Equinox, Spring 1966* (limited edition catalogue designed and written by Anger). New York: Film-makers' Cinematheque, 1966.
———. *Atlantis: The Lost Continent.* New York: Dover, 1970.
———. *Hollywood Babylon.* San Francisco: Straight Arrow Books, 1975. Originally published in French, as *Hollywood Babylone* (Paris: J. J. Pauvert, 1959).
———. *Hollywood Babylon 2.* New York: Dutton, 1984.
Burger-Utzer, Brigitta, and Wilbirg Donnenberg, eds. *Kenneth Anger ICONS.* Catalogue for a show of frame enlargements from Anger's films, organized by Sixpack Films in Vienna, Austria, in June 1995. Includes brief essays and captions for the photographs by Anger and brief essays by Jonas Mekas and Peter Tscherkassky.
Hunter, Jack, ed. *Moonchild: The Films of Kenneth Anger.* (Persistence of Vision, vol. 1. New York: Creation Books, 2001. Includes essays by Mikita Brottman, Carel Rowe, and Anna Powell and an annotated filmography/chronology.
Hutchinson, Alice L. *Kenneth Anger: A Demonic Visionary.* London: Black Dog, 2004. A profusely and beautifully illustrated study of Anger's work that reprints many important documents relating to his career.
James, David E. *Allegories of Cinema: American Film in the Sixties,* 149–56. Princeton, N.J.: Princeton University Press, 1989.
Landis, Bill. *Anger: The Unauthorized Biography of Kenneth Anger.* New York: HarperCollins, 1996.
MacDonald, Scott. *Cinema 16: Documents toward a History of the Film Society.* Philadelphia: Temple University Press, 2002. See index for selected letters from Anger to Amos Vogel and from Vogel to Anger.
Mekas, Jonas. *Movie Journal: The Rise of the New American Cinema, 1959–1971.* See index for articles about Anger.
O'Pray, Michael, and Jayne Pilling, eds. *Into the Pleasure Dome: The Films of Kenneth Anger.* London: British Film Institute, 1989.
Powell, Anna, and Carel Rowe. *Moonchild: The Films of Kenneth Anger* (vol. 1 of *Persistence of Vision*). Ed. Jack Hunter. New York: Creation Books, 2002.
Sitney, P. Adams, ed. Bibliography for Kenneth Anger, in *The Essential Cinema: Essays on the Films in the Collection of Anthology Film Archives,* 247–49. New York: Anthology Film Archives/NYU Press, 1975.
———. *Visionary Film,* 3rd ed., 81–119.
Wees, William C. *Light Moving in Time: Studies in the Visual Aesthetics of Avant-*

Garde Film, 107–22. Berkeley and Los Angeles: University of California Press, 1992.
Wide Angle (issue dedicated to Anger), 19, no. 2 (April 1997).

James Benning

A bibliography focusing on Benning's work up through 1988 is included in *A Critical Cinema 2*.

Hebdige, Dick. "*Reeling in Utah:* The Travel Log Trilogy" *Afterall*, no. 8 (2003): 11–33.
MacDonald, Scott. "Experimental Cinema in the 1980s," 396–98.
———. "The Filmmaker as Lone Rider." *Western American Literature* 35, no. 3 (Fall 2000): 298–318.
———. *The Garden in the Machine*, 97–107, 337–49.
Moore, Rachel. "James Benning's *California Trilogy:* A Lesson in Natural History." *Afterall*, no. 8 (2003): 34–42.
Sitney, P. Adams. *Visionary Film*, 3rd ed., 412–14.

Alan Berliner

Albert, Mitch. "The Reluctant Witness" (interview). *The Independent* 20, no. 4 (May 1997): 29–33, 48–49.
Berliner, Alan. "Filmic Memories." *Film Quarterly* 52, no. 1 (Fall 1998): 55–56.
Beroes, Stephanie. "Alan Berliner" (interview). *Cinematograph*, no. 2 (1986): 57–59.
Camper, Fred. "The End of Avant-Garde Film." *Millennium*, nos. 16–18 (Fall/Winter 1986–87): 99–124.
MacDonald, Scott. "Putting All Your Eggs in One Basket: A Survey of Single-Shot Films." *Afterimage* 16, no. 8 (March 1989): 10–16.
Zimmermann, Patricia R. "Contested Terrain: *The Family Album.*" *Afterimage* 16, no. 1 (Summer 1988): 9–11.

Tony Conrad

Arthur, Paul. "Structural Film: Revisions, New Versions, and the Artifact." *Millennium Film Journal* 1, no. 2 (Spring–Summer 1978): 5–13.
Conrad, Tony. "Dolomite: Having No Trust in Readers." In *Media Buff: Media Art of Buffalo, New York*. Catalogue, edited by Richard J. Herskowitz, for a show at the Herbert F. Johnson Museum of Art at Cornell University. Ithaca, N.Y.: Herbert F. Johnson Museum of Art, 1988.
———. "an EARful: FOUR VIOLINS and EARLY MINIMALISM," "LYssophobia: on FOUR VIOLINS," "MINor premise," "nAMIng: April/May/June," "smsgyILIS." Essays included in catalogue for CD collection *Tony Conrad: Early Minimalism, Volume 1,* released in 2002.

———. "A Few Remarks before I Begin." In *The Avant-Garde Film: A Reader of Theory and Criticism,* ed. P. Adams Sitney, 264–74. New York: NYU Press, 1978.

———. "Inside the Dream Syndicate." *Film Culture* 41 (Summer 1966): 5–8.

———. "Integer: Bulldozing a Foundation in the Culturescape of Sound, Media and Performance." *Cinematograph* 2 (1986): 24–34.

———. "Non-linguistic Extensions of Film and Video." *Quarterly Review of Film Studies* 1, no. 3 (August 1976): 276–82.

———. *The Theory of the Flexagon.* Research Institute for Advanced Study Monograph. Baltimore: Research Institute for Advanced Study, 1960.

———. "Tony Conrad on 'The Flicker,' from a Letter to Henry Romney, dated November 11, 1965." *Film Culture* 41 (Summer 1966): 1–3.

———. "Video as Opposition: Remodeling Postmodern Media." *Motion Picture* 3 (Winter 1989–90): 49–52.

Conrad, Tony, and Barbara Broughel. *The Animal.* Buffalo, N.Y.: CEPA Gallery, 1984.

Conrad, Tony, and D. Hartline. *Flexagons.* Research Institute for Advanced Study Monograph. Baltimore: Research Institute for Advanced Study, 1962.

Dickinson, Paul. "The Discourse of the Vertical: Tony Conrad Interviewed." Part 1, *The Squealer,* January–February 1988, 12–14; part 2, *The Squealer,* April–May 1988, 7, 18–19.

Le Grice, Malcolm. *Abstract Film and Beyond,* 90, 105–8, 149–50. Cambridge, Mass.: MIT Press, 1977.

Mekas, Jonas. *Movie Journal,* 228–32.

Mussman, Toby. "An Interview with Tony Conrad." *Film Culture* 41 (Summer 1966): 3–5.

Renan, Sheldon. *Introduction to the American Underground Film,* 31, 138–40. New York: Dutton, 1968.

Russet, Robert, and Cecile Starr, eds. *Experimental Animation: An Illustrated Anthology,* 150–53. New York: Van Nostrand, 1976.

Sanborn, Keith. "A Super-8 Discussion with Ericka Beckman, Tony Conrad, and Bruce Jenkins." *Cinemanews* 81, nos. 2–6 (1981): 96–103.

Nathaniel Dorsky

Delabre, Patrick. "Acting/Being on the Surface of Film: Conversation with Nathaniel Dorsky." *Cinematograph,* no. 1 (1985): 96–100.

Dorsky, Nathaniel. *Devotional Cinema.* Berkeley, Calif.: Tuumba Press, 2004. Second, revised edition, 2005.

———. "The State of the . . . Art." *Cinematograph,* no. 1 (1985): 90–91.

MacDonald, Scott. "Experimental Cinema in the 1980s," 431–33.

———. *The Garden in the Machine,* 265–73.

Powers, Thomas. "A Film Is Like a Panther: Interview with Nathaniel Dorsky." *Release Print* 19, no. 10 (October 1996): 26–28.

Sitney, P. Adams. *Visionary Film,* 3rd ed., 430–31.

Ernie Gehr

Cornwell, Regina. "Works of Ernie Gehr from 1968 to 1972." *Film Culture,* nos. 63–64 (1976): 29–38.
Gehr, Ernie. "Program Notes." In *The Avant-Garde Film: A Reader of Theory and Criticism,* ed. P. Adams Sitney, 247–49. New York: NYU Press, 1978.
MacDonald, Scott. *Avant-Garde Film/Motion Studies* (chap. 3, "Ernie Gehr, *Serene Velocity*"), 37–44. Cambridge: Cambridge University Press, 1993.
———. "Ernie Gehr: Camera Obscura/Lens/Filmstrip." *Film Quarterly* 43, no. 4 (Summer 1990): 10–16.
———. *The Garden in the Machine,* 200–208.
Mekas, Jonas. "Ernie Gehr Interviewed by Jonas Mekas, March 24, 1971." *Film Culture,* nos. 53–55 (Spring 1972): 25–36.
———. "On Ernie Gehr and the 'Plotless' Cinema." In *Movie Journal: The Rise of a New American Cinema, 1959–1971,* 314–16.
Sitney, P. Adams. *Gehr.* Filmmakers Filming monograph series. Minneapolis, Minn.: Walker Art Center, 1980.
———. *Visionary Film,* 3rd ed., 400–403, 434–36.

Shiho Kano

Gehman, Chris. *Japan Focus.* Catalogue for an exhibition of Japanese independent film and video at the Images Festival in Toronto, Canada, 2001.

Sharon Lockhart

Brooks, Rosetta. "A Fine Disregard." *Afterall,* no. 8 (2003): 107–13.
Bryson, Norman. "Sharon Lockhart: The Politics of Attention." *artext,* no. 70 (August–October 2000): 54–61.
DeBord, Matthew. "The Recurrent American Rhetoric of Contradiction." *Siksi: The Nordic Art Review* 12, no. 3 (Autumn 1997): 76–79.
Dziewior, Yelmaz. "Sharon Lockhart: Concept—Structure and Passion." *Camera Austria,* no. 72 (November 2000): 25–36.
Dziewior, Yelmaz, and Sharon Lockhart. "Sharon Lockhart: A Thousand Words" (interview). *Artforum* 38, no. 6 (February 2000): 104–5.
Farmer, John Alan. "Sharon Lockhart: *Interview Locations/Family Photographs.*" *Art Journal* 59, no. 1 (Spring 2000): 64–73.
Martinez, Chus. "The Possible's Slow Fuse: The Works of Sharon Lockhart." *Afterall,* no. 8 (2003): 115–22.
Moss, Karen. "Sharon Lockhart + Kelly Nipper: 2 Artists in 2 Takes." Catalogue essay for a show at Walter & McBean Galleries, San Francisco, March 17–April 29, 2000.
Museum Boijmans Van Beuninagen Rotterdam. *Sharon Lockhart: Teatro Amazonas.* Catalogue for a touring show of Lockhart's work November 20, 1999, to September 10, 2000. Includes essays by Ivone Margolies and Timothy Martin.

Museum of Contemporary Art, Chicago. *Sharon Lockhart.* Catalogue for a show of Lockhart's work, March 3–May 20, 2001. Includes essays by Normal Bryson and Dominic Molon, a biography, and a selected bibliography.

Reynaud, Bérénice. *"Goshogaoka."* Catalogue essay for a show of Lockhart's "Goshogaoka" photographs, January 28–February 28, 1998, at Wako Works of Art, Tokyo; and February 21–March 28, 1998, at Blum & Poe, Santa Monica, California.

Robb Moss

Holden, Stephen. "The Luck of the Draw." Review of *The Same River Twice*, *New York Times*, September 10, 2003.

Lane, Jim. *The Autobiographical Documentary in America*, 129–33. Madison: University of Wisconsin Press, 2002.

Matthias Müller

Becker, Kathrin, ed. *Matthias Müller/Album: Film, Video, Photography.* Frankfurt: Revolver, 2004. Catalogue for an exhibition of Müller's work, March 18–May 2, 2004, in Berlin, Germany. Includes essays by Stefan Grissemann, Kathrin Becker, Marak Gisbourne, Elisabeth Bronfen, and Angelika Richter and an annotated filmography.

Hoolboom, Michael. "Scattering Stars: The Films of Matthias Müller." *Millennium Film Journal*, no. 30/31 (Fall 1997): 80–88.

Leighton Pierce

MacDonald, Scott. *The Garden in the Machine*, 364–72.

Jennifer Todd Reeves

Reeves, Jennifer. "Argument for the Immediate Sensuous: Notes on *Stately Mansions Did Decree* and *Coupling*." In special Stan Brakhage issue of *Chicago Review* 47, no. 4 (Winter 2001); 48, no. 1 (Spring 2002): 193–98.

Phil Solomon

Gunning, Tom. "Towards a Minor Cinema: Fonoroff, Herwitz, Ahwesh, Lapore, Klahr and Solomon." *Motion Picture* nos. 1–2 (Winter 1989–90): 2–5.

Solomon, Phil. "Why Am I Drawn to Using Found Footage?" In *Found Footage Film,* ed. Cecilia Hausheer and Christoph Settele, 130–32. Lucern, Switzerland: Viper, 1992.

———. "XCXHXEXRXRXIXEXSX." *Cinematograph*, no. 5 (1993): 54–57.

Index

Page numbers in italics indicate figures.

ABC Sports, 159–60
Absence, 181, 185–86
"Absolution" (Fitzgerald), 2
abstract expressionism, 106
Academy Awards, 4, 281, 282
The Act of Seeing with One's Own Eyes, 119, 180, 202, 375
Adams, Ansel, 247
Africa Revisited, 183–84, 187
Ahtila, Eija-Liisa, 327
Ahwesh, Peggy, 9, 13, 111; on Atlantic City, 141; on Georges Bataille, 131–32, 133; on *Certain Women,* 139–40; on *The Color of Love,* 135–36; on Willem Dafoe, 139; on *The Deadman,* 119, 131–34; on drugs, 129–30; on early art experiences, 120; on filmmaking method, 122–24, 125–26; filmography of, 406–7; on joke telling, 137–38; on *Martina's Playhouse,* 121, 123–25; on narrative film, 140; on *Nocturne,* 136–37; overview of work by, 113–16; on Pittsburgh period, 116–18; on *Pittsburgh Trilogy,* 118–19; on Pixilvision, 127, 129; on George Romero, 117; on *She Puppet,* 138; on *The Star Eaters,* 142; on *Strange Weather,* 126–28, 129–30; on *the vision machine,* 137–38
AIDS, 94, 282–83, 285–86, 296–98

Akerman, Chantal, 13, 315, 327
Alaya, 78, 79, 88, 89–90, *90,* 91–92, 93–94, 99
Albee, Edward, 39, 40
Album, 284, 285, 296, 309, 310
Algar, James, 81
Ali Baba and the Forty Thieves, 62
Allegories of Cinema (James), 282
Allen, Becky, 323, 331
Allen, John E., 163
All Is Vanity (Shiki Soku Ze Kū), 350
All My Life, 309
All That Jazz, 37
Alpsee, 282–84, 292–93, *293,* 294–95
Alte Kinder, 285
Alternating Currents, 200
American Beauty, 79–80, 309
American Dreams, 228, 251, 252
American Epilepsy Association, 69
American Federation of Arts, 347
American minimalist music, 55
The American Sportsman (television show), 159
Anasazis, 237–38
Angelico, Fra, 92
Anger, Kenneth, 7, 13, 78, 83, 143, 203, 259, 288; on Bobby Beausoleil, 45, 48; on biker culture, 39; on Stan Brakhage,

431

Anger, Kenneth *(continued)* 53; on Aleister Crowley, 49–50; on *Eaux d'artifice,* 27–30; on Eisenstein's aborted projects, 24–25; on family background, 21–22; filmography of, 407–8; on film society movement, 19; on *Fireworks,* 20–21, 22–23, 282; on Sir Paul Getty, 53–54; on Spalding Gray, 44; on *Ich Will,* 48–49; on *Inauguration of the Pleasure Dome,* 33–36; on Alfred Kinsey, 22–23; on *Kustom Kar Kommandos,* 44; landmark gay film of, 16–17, *17;* on lost films, 20; on *Lucifer Rising,* 45–48; on *The Man We Want to Hang,* 49–50; on Marie Menken and Willard Maas, 39–40; on Mickey Mouse film, 50–51; musical choices of, 18–19, 30, 32, 34–35, 40–41; on nudity in Kodachrome, 33; on Paris experience, 23–24; on Harry Partch, 34–35; on preservation of theaters, 51–52; on *Puce Moment,* 31; on *Rabbit's Moon,* 25–27; on Sir Francis Rose, 47; on Carmilla Salvatorelli, 29; on *Scorpio Rising,* 37–39, 40–41; on *Scorpio Rising* dedicatees, 41–42; on 16mm film, 50; spirituality quest of, 17–18; on *The Story of O,* 36–37; on three-screen technique, 33–34; on *Who's Afraid of Virginia Woolf* couple, 39–40; writings by, 53
animation, 74–75, 350
Anka, Paul, 60
Anker, Steve, 82, 83, 93, 100, 110, 124, 126–27, 201, 203, 214
Ann Arbor Film Festival, 149
Anne Frank Remembered, 226
Anthology Film Archives (New York), 20, 155, 345, 358
Anticipation of the Night, 98
Antioch College, 82–83, 113, 116, 120
Antonioni, Michelangelo, 81, 93, 98, 104, 213, 282, 307–8
Arabesque for Kenneth Anger, 40
Arabic 1–19, 99
Arbor Vitae, 78
Arbus, Diane, 41, 239
Argento, Dario, 114, 136
Ariel, 93
Arletty, 24
Arnheim, Rudolph, 103

Arnold, Martin, 12, 281, 284, 351
Arnulf Rainer, 65, 66, 70
Arrangement in White on Green, 53–54
Art Center College of Design (Pasadena), 315
art gallery exhibitions: of Sharon Lockhart's films, 313–14, 327–28; Matthias Müller on, 303–4
Art in Cinema Film Society (San Francisco), 5, 19
Ashbery, John, 94, 208, 210–11
Astaire, Fred, 287
Athénée Français (Tokyo), 357
Athletic Model Guild (Los Angeles), 38
Atlantic City, 141
Audiofile (installation), 147
"Auditions" (Lockhart), 317
Augst, Bertrand, 183
August, Michael, 82
Aurora Picture Show (Houston), 10
Aury, Dominique (pseud. Pauline Reage), 36
Aus der Ferne—The Memo Book, 282, 285–88, 295
Austin, Mary, 264
Austin Film Society, 251–52
autobiographic films. *See* personal cinema
The Automatic Moving Company (La gardemeuble automatique), 144
avant-garde filmmaking tradition, 180–81. *See also* critical cinema
"Avant to Live: Fear and Trembling at the Whitney Biennial" (Hoberman), 12, 126
Aviary (installation), 147

B, Beth, 11
B, Scott, 11
Baby Basics, 188
Babylon Series, 99
The Back Steps, 274, 275, 276, 277, 278, 280
Backyard, 146, 181
Bacon, Francis, 222
Bad Girls Go to Hell, 114
Badlands, 103
Baillie, Bruce, 6, 7, 12, 309
Baldessari, John, 300
Baldwin, Craig, 12
Bandy, Mary Lea, 403

Barbara Gladstone Gallery (New York City), 313–14
Barbeau, Adrienne, 117
Bard College, 115, 138
Barnett, Dan, 97, 153, 200, 201, 205
Barn Rushes, 202, 375
Baron, Rebecca, 83
Barrault, Jean-Louis, 24, 25
Barrie, Diana, 11
Bartas, Sarunas, 335
Bartók, Béla, 63
Bashō, Matsuo, 6
Bataille, Georges, 113, 125, 131–32, 133
Bava, Mario, 136
Beacon, 283, 284, 299, 307
The Bear (Faulkner), 249
the Beatles, 41
Beausoleil, Bobby, 19, 45, 47, 48
Beaverbrook, Lord, 49–50
Beaver Valley, 81
Bedroom (segment of *Phoenix Tapes*), 284, 291, 300
Belson, Jordan, 6, 7, 8, 12, 19
Benally, Herman Dodge, 230
A Bend in the River, 82
Benham's Top, 74–75
Bennett, Constance, 42
Bennett, Luke, 103
Benning, James, 9, 12, 13, 14, 144, 157, 311; on California Trilogy, 247, 249–50, 251–52; on *Deseret,* 235–40; on DVD technology, 253–54; on filmic influences, 242–43; on filmmaking as performance, 245; filmography of, 408; on film profits, 252; on *Four Corners,* 240–41; on *Grand Opera,* 245; on landscape, 232, 234–35; and Sharon Lockhart's work, 313, 315; on *North on Evers,* 232–33; overview of work by, 228–31; on teaching, 252–53; on text-image relationship, 232–33, 235–36, 242; on *Utopia,* 241
Bergman, Ingmar, 143
Bergman, Ingrid, 300
Berlin (Germany), 389–93, 398–400
Berliner, Alan, 13, *178,* 181, 199; on ABC job, 159–60; on Fred Camper's article, 147–48; on *City Edition,* 149–50, 174; on compositional approach, 170, 173; on divorce of parents, 166; education of, 143–44, 151–53, 156–58; on Emmys, 161; on *Everywhere at Once,* 148–49, 164; on *The Family Album,* 162–66, 174; on family legacies, 175–76; on father, 172–73; filmography of, 409–10; found-footage montage films of, 144; on Hollis Frampton, 153, 155; on Su Friedrich, 171–72; on Larry Gottheim, 151–52; on grandfather, 166–67, 175; home movies of, 144–46, 162–65; installations by, 147; on *Intimate Stranger,* 166–67, 169–71, 174, 175; on Ken Jacobs, 152–53, 155; on length of films, 174–75; monkishness of, 150; on *Natural History: A Photo Journal,* 161–62; on Newman-Woodward home movie, 176–77; on *Nobody's Business,* 150, 166, 172–74, 175–76; on paracinematic work, 152, 157–58; on *The Sweetest Sound,* 177–79; on typewriter motif, 167, 169
Berliner, Oscar, 146, 172–73, *176*
Berlin International Film Festival, 390
Berlin—Symphony of a Big City, 392–93
The Berlin Wall, 161
Bertholt, Minerva, 48
B-52, 240, 253
Bielefeld University, 284–85
Big as Life: An American History of 8mm Films (Kilchesty, ed.), 82
Big as Life show, 82, 214
biker culture, 39
Billops, Camille, 181
The Birds, 291
Birnbaum, Mark, 85
Birnkrant, Eunice, 50
Birnkrant, Mel, 50, 51
Bi-temporal Vision: The Sea, 200
Bitomski, Hartmut, 240, 253
Blair, John, 226
Blair, Linda, 317
Blake, Peter, 47
Bless Their Little Hearts, 240
Bleu Shut, 157
Blonde Cobra, 5
Blood of a Poet, 24
Bloom, Harold, 213
Blow-up, 213
Blue Moses, 179, 202
Blues, 101
"Blue Velvet" (song), 41

Blum and Poe Gallery (Santa Monica), 313, 322
Bock, Richard, 202–3
Bokanowski, Patrick, 12
Bold, Alf, 285
Bomarzo gardens (Italy), 30
Bonami, Francesco, 303
The Bone Garden (Childe), 42
Bonnard, Pierre, 270
Books of Hours, 3, 78, 86
Borden, Lizzie, 12
Borzage, Frank, 104
Bosch, Hieronymus, 221
Bosetti, Romeo, 144
Boston Film and Video Foundation, 201
Bow, Clara, 31
Bowie, David, 134
Bradley, Ruth, 263
Brakhage, Stan, 7, 12, 13, 33, 104, 180, 183, 204, 292; Kenneth Anger on, 53; Nathaniel Dorsky on, 80–81, 92, 97, 98, 99; Ernie Gehr on, 362, 402; Jerome Hiler on, 109; Pittsburgh trilogy of, 119; Jennifer Reeves on, 345; salon of, 92n; scratching technique of, 225; Phil Solomon on, 202, 203, 205, 211, 227; Phil Solomon's collaboration with, 200, 223, 225; on *Triste,* 92
Brasília (Brazil), 298
Braunberger, Pierre, 26
Braunschweig Kunsthochschule, 284–85
Brecht, George, 73
Breer, Robert, 12, 66, 386
Breeze, 296
Bresson, Robert, 36, 207
Bright Leaves, 181
Broadway's Dreamers: The Legacy of the Group Theater, 176
Brooks, Juanita, 238
Brose, Lawrence, 13
Broughton, James, 6, 7, 19
Brownstein, Michael, 94, 106
Brueghel, Pieter, the Elder, 222
Brussels World's Fair, 33, 34
Buddhism, 6, 266–68
Bullitt, 394
Buñuel, Luis, 115, 133–34, 137–38, 143, 228
Burckhardt, Rudy, 104, 398

Burden of Proof (segment of *Phoenix Tapes*), 300
Burnett, Charles, 12
Burton-Christie, Douglas, 91

The Cabinet of Doctor Caligari, 18
Cage, John, 58, 66
Caldwell, Erskine, 134, 139
Cale, John, 55, 61, 73, 75, 76
California Institute of the Arts (Valencia), 228, 252–53
California Trilogy (Benning), 9, 230, 231, 242–43, 245–50, 251–52
camera obscura, 365
Camera Obscura (periodical), 124
Cammell, Donald, 46, 47
Camper, Fred, 12, 126, 147
Canyon Cinema, 6
Capra, Frank, 205
Capturing the Friedmans, 194
Cardiff, Jack, 53, 300
"Carmilla" (LeFanu), 29
Carné, Marcel, 24
Un Carnet de bal, 24
Carr, Martin, 80
Cassavetes, John, 317
Cassis, 279
Cassuto, Joseph, 146, 166–68, *168*
Cassuto, Regina, 146, *176*
Cassuto, Rose, 175
Cavalcanti, Alberto, 114
The Celluloid Closet (Russo), 289
Certain Women (Caldwell), 139
Certain Women (film), 134, 139–40, *140*
Cézanne, Paul, 309
Chambers, Jack, 97, 104, 216
Un Chant d'amour, 78, 282, 288, 310
Chaplin, Charlie, 364
Charles Theater (New York), 61
Cheaters (Tricheurs), 141
The Cheerleaders, 103
Chelli, Claude, 183–84
Chicago Art Institute, 157, 201
Un chien andalou, 133–34
Child, Abigail, 13, 98, 101, 132
Childe, Victor, 41, 42
The Children of Paradise, 24, 25
A Child's Garden and the Serious Sea, 104
Chinatown, 264
The Chinese Series, 225

Chomont, Tom, 11, 288
Choral do Amazonas, 323
Choy, Christine, 12
Chronic, 333–34, 335–37, *337,* 338–40, 341, 345
Chumlum, 64, 80, 81
Cinema Panthéon (Paris), 26
Cinemascope, 307, 308
Cinema 16 (New York City), 5, 143
Cinémathèque Française, 16, 23, 24–25
Cine-Matrix, 158
Citizen Kane, 173
City, 360
City Edition, 144, 148, 149–50, 174
City Lights, 364
Civic Theater (Aukland, New Zealand), 51
Clair, René, 24, 102
Clarke, Shirley, 126–27
Clash by Night, 130
Clepsydra, 200, 220–21
The Climate of New York, 104
cloud chambers, 34–35
Coca, Imogene, 103
Cocteau, Jean, 23, 24
Collective for Living Cinema (New York), 121, 149, 152, 156, 158, 160, 169, 201
The Color of Love, 114, 115, 132, 135–36, *135,* 137, 140
Color Wheel, 170
Coming Attractions, 55, 74, 75–76
Commedia dell'Arte, 25
Como, Perry, 116
Concrescence, 200
Configuration 20, 341, 345
The Connection, 126–27, 130
Conner, Bruce, 11, 18, 55, 94, 281, 285, 328; Peggy Ahwesh on, 120; Kenneth Anger on, 41; Alan Berliner on, 149; Matthias Müller on, 294–95; Phil Solomon on, 203, 218
Conrad, Beverly Grant, 55, 64, 75–76, 116
Conrad, Joseph, 288
Conrad, Tony, 9, 13, 95, 120, 200, 201, 351; Peggy Ahwesh on, 116; on audio frequencies, 70–72; on color and animation, 74–75; on *Coming Attractions,* 75–76; on drugs, 59; filmography of, 411–13; on *Flaming Creatures* sound track, 61–63; on *The Flicker,* 66–67, 69–70, 72–73; on flicker idea, 64–66; on Fluxus films, 73; on formative influences, 57–58; on long-duration film, 69–70; overview of work by, 55–57; on Jack Smith, 58–61, 64; on Karlheinz Stockhausen, 71–72; on *Straight and Narrow,* 75
Consolidated Film Lab (Hollywood), 20
Container, 303, 304
Continental Breakfast, 283–84
Coolidge, Martha, 169
Cooper, Karen, 194
Cooper, Susan Fenimore, 78, 264
Coppola, Francis Ford, 360
Cops (television show), 126
Cornell, Joseph, 285
Cornell Cinema, 201
Cornwell, Regina, 379
Coronet Film Society (Los Angeles), 19, 22
Cosel, Bill, 188
Cosmic Ray, 18, 120
Cotton Candy, 360–61, 403
crack cocaine, 129–30
Crane, Hart, 41–42
The Crazies, 117
Creative Film Associates, 19
Creepshow, 117
critical cinema: art gallery exhibitions of, 303–4, 313–14, 327–28; audiences for, 143–44, 169–70; Fred Camper's article on, 126, 147–48; and film society movement, 5; Tom Gunning's characterization of, 111–13, 203; materiality issue of, 8–9; merged traditions of, 180–81; screening venues for, 10–11; sound-image relationship in, 261–62; spiritual dimension of, 1, 5–8, 266–68
Critical Cinema project (MacDonald), 11–15
Critical Mass, 153, 170, 261
crop duster image, 247, 249
Crossroads Africa, 183–84
Crowley, Aleister, 18, 19, 45, 49–50
Curtis, Tony, 222
custom car culture, 44

DAAD (Deutscher Akademischer Austauschdienst), 390
Dafoe, Willem, 139
Dali, Salvador, 133–34
Damasio, Antonio, 263

Damnation (Kárhozat), 335
Damned If You Don't, 136
Darling International, 345
Dawn of the Dead, 116, 117
Day of the Dead, 116
The Deadman (film), 113, 114, 115, 119, 130–34, 140, 141
The Deadman (Sanborn, trans.), 132, *133*
Dean, James, 41
Death in Venice (Mann), 297
de Brier, Samson, 18, 35–36
de Kooning, Willem, 170
Delanda, Manuel, 11
Delannoy, Jean, 24
Deleuze, Giles, 111
Demme, Jonathan, 44
Deocampo, Nick, 12
Deren, Maya, 7, 16, 23, 80, 143, 180–81, 259, 351
Dern, Bruce, 141
Derrida, Jacques, 128
Descartes' Error: Emotion, Reason, and the Human Brain (Damasio), 263
Deseret, 229, 232, 235–40, 242
Deus Ex, 119
Deutscher Akademischer Austauschdienst (DAAD), 390
"Devil in Disguise" (song), 40
Devotional Cinema (Dorsky), 6, 80
Diaries, 181
Dick, Vivienne, 11
Dickson, W. K. L., 322
Dieterle, William, 16
digital video. *See* video
Dindo, Richard, 230, 241, 242
Dirty Harry, 394
Disappearing Music for Face, 73
Discovering the Vernacular Landscape (Jackson), 263
Disney True Life Adventure series, 81
Disney World/Universal Studios, 4
documentary: as fictionalized, by Peggy Ahwesh, 115, 126–28; merged with avant-garde, 180–81; personal form of, 169, 181–82; Jennifer Reeves's use of, 338–40, 343–44. *See also* home movies; personal cinema
Documenting the Documentary: Close Readings of Documentary Film and Video (Grant and Sloniowski), 180–81

Dog Star Man: Part I, 80–81
Dolby surround sound, 219–20
domestic space: of Alan Berliner's films, 144–45, 165–66; of Ernie Gehr's *Wait*, 359, 367; of Shiho Kano's *Rocking Chair*, 349; of Robb Moss's *Same River Twice*, 9, 191–92, 196, 197–98; Matthias Müller on, 291–92; Leighton Pierce's recording of, 255–59, 260, 280. *See also* home movies; personal cinema
Dorsky, Nathaniel, 13, 213, 265, 309; on *Alaya*, 89, 91–92, 93–94, 99; on Stan Brakhage, 80–81, 92, 97, 98, 99; on commercial editing work, 102–4; on filmic influences, 80–83; filmography of, 413–14; on gay desire, 83–84; on Jerome Hiler, 81, 95, 98, 105, 106; on *Hours for Jerome*, 85–88, 96, 100; on *Ingreen*, 83–84, 103; overview of work by, 77–80; on perspective in painting, 92–93; on *Pneuma*, 88–89, 93–94; on polyvalence, 87–88, 94–95; on projection speed, 100–101; on *17 Reasons Why*, 88, 93; on silent versus sound film, 97–99; on spiritual cinema, 6–7, 100–102; on *Triste*, 92–93, 94, 99; on *Variations*, 93, 95–97, 99
Dovzhenko, Alexander, 83
Dr. Jekyll and Mr. Hyde, 209
Dream Sphinx, 114
Dream Syndicate (New York), 71
Dreyer, Carl Theodor, 97, 102, 207
drugs, 59, 85, 93, 120, 127–28, 129–30
Duchamp, Marcel, 138, 208
Duchin, Eddy, 61
Dullea, Keir, 219
Dunye, Cheryl, 129
Duras, Marguerite, 357
Duvuvier, Julien, 24

Eastman Kodak, 33
Eastside Summer, 104
Easy Rider, 228, 232, 233
Eaux d'artifice, 18, 19, 27–28, *28*, 29–30
Eberhart, Isabelle, 126
L'eclisse (Eclipse), 307
Edison, Thomas, 261
Egyptian Series, 99
Egyptian theater (Los Angeles), 53
8½, 120

8½ x 11, 242, 243
Eisenberg, Dan, 200, 201
Eisenstein, Sergei, 24, 26, 83, 209, 350, 367
Electric Light Orchestra, 34
Electric Prunes, 114
Elementary Phrases, 200, 225
11 x 14, 9, 228, 242, 243, 251, 252
Elliott's Suicide, 43–43
Emmy Awards, 161
"The End of Avant-Garde Film" (Camper), 12, 126, 147
Enter/Exit, 73
environmentalism, 233–34, 264
Epilogue, 283–84, 285
Eppler, Meyer, 72
Ernesto Che Guevara, the Bolivian Journal, 230
Eros, Bradley, *137*
Escape Episode, 19–20
Esquire Theater (Los Angeles), 24
Estrand, Robert, 103
The Eternal Return, 24
ethnographic film: within art context, 311–13, 318; *Goshogaoka,* 317–20; *NŌ,* 328–31; by Jean Rouch, 323; *Teatro Amazonas,* 321–26
Eureka, 360, 386–88, *389,* 397
European Biennial of Contemporary Art, Manifesta 3 (Ljubjana), 303
Evans, Walker, 239
Evaporation, 258–59, 278, *279*
Evers, Medgar, 229, 233
Everywhere at Once, 144, 148–49, 164
The Exorcist, 317
Expanded Cinema (Youngblood), 7
Experimental Ethnography: The Work of Film in the Age of Video (Russell), 180–81
experimental filmmaking tradition, 180–81. *See also* critical cinema
Export, Valie, 12
The Exquisite Hour, 199, 200, 213–15, 217, 218–20, *220,* 221
Eye of Count Flickerstein, 74
Eyes, 119

Faces in a Famine, 188
Fagin, Larry, 86
Faithfull, Marianne, 47
Fall, 258–59, 275, 277, 278–79, 280
A Fall Trip Home, 77–78, 80, 84, 85, 97, 103
The Family Album, 144–45, 146, 148, 162–64, *164,* 165–66, 169, 172, 174
Family Portrait Sittings, 181
Fantasia, 51
Far from Heaven, 13
Farocki, Harun, 13
Fassbinder, Rainer Werner, 134
Fast, Cheap and Out of Control, 196
Faulkner, William, 249
Faust (musical group), 55
Faust, Wolfgang Max, 297
FDR: A Biography, 161
Fear of Blushing, 345
Fellig, Arthur (pseud. Weegee), 41
Fellini, Federico, 120, 143
female agency: Peggy Ahwesh on, 125, 131, 132, 134; domestic partnership issue of, 255; Hollywood's denial of, 291–92; and joke telling, 137–38
Le Festival du Films Maudit (Biarritz), 23
Field, 372–73
Field of Vision (periodical), 116
50 Feet of String, 256–56, *257,* 261, 262, 263–64, *265, 266,* 267, 268–73, 279, 280
Film Arts Foundation (San Francisco), 103
Film Culture (periodical), 379
A Film for Seven Voices, 177
Film Forum (New York), 194
Film in the Cities (St. Paul), 262
Filmmakers' Cinematheque (New York), 358, 361, 362, 368
Film-makers' Cooperative (New York), 358, 359, 367–68, 379–80
Film No. 5 (Smile), 9
film society movement, 5–7, 19
Final Cut, 284, 285, 292
Finding Christa, 181
Fire of Waters, 205
Fireworks, 16–17, *17,* 19, 20–21, 22–23, 27, 30, 78, 83, 259, 282, 288
Fischer, Lucy, 116
Fisher, Morgan, 11, 285, 311, 315, 316, 322
Fitzcarraldo, 311, 323–24
Fitzgerald, F. Scott, 2
Flaherty, Robert, 180
Flaherty Film Seminar, 341, 342
Flaming Creatures, 5, 57, 61–63, *63,* 76, 78, 80, 85
Fleischer brothers, 114

flicker, 65–66, 76, 101
The Flicker, 9, 55, 74, 201; background idea for, 65–66; original diagram of, 72–73; physical construction of, 66–69; projection format of, 56–57; sound track of, 70–72; warning to viewers in, *56,* 69–70
Florey, Robert, 22
Fluxfilms, 73
Fluxus group, 58, 73
Flynt, Henry, 58, 71
Fog Line, 7–8, 170, 347
The Fog of War, 196
"Follow Me to the Rose Parade" (song), 43
Fonoroff, Nina, 203
Fool's Spring (Two Personal Gifts), 106
Ford, John, 81–82, 93, 102, 104
Ford Foundation, 44
Foreman, Richard, 368, 370, 378, 384, 402
Forgács, Peter, 13, 284
Fosse, Bob, 37
Foundation for Art and Creative Technology (Liverpool), 305
found footage. *See* recycled cinema
Four Corners, 229–30, 240–41, 242, 252
The Four Seasons (Vivaldi), 19, 30
Four Square, 55, 74
Four Violins (Conrad), 55
Fragment of Seeking, 23
Frampton, Hollis, 11, 122, 153, 155, 203, 261, 311, 315, 328, 378
Francine, Francis, 76
Frank, Anne, 226
Frank, Robert, 235, 286–87, 303
Frankenstein (film), 22, 226
Frankenstein (Shelley), 226
Frankenthaler, Helen, 270
Fraser, James George, 33
Fraser Gallery (London), 47
Freed, Arthur, 31
Freud, Sigmund, 138
Fried, Alan, 82
Friedrich, Su, 12, 122, 136, 144, 165, 171–72, 181
Frost, Robert, 210–11
Fulci, Lucio, 136

Galloway, Stephen, 318, 321
"The Gambler, the Nun, and the Radio" (Hemingway), 334
Gance, Abel, 33

Ganguly, Suranjan, 92n
garden films: of Kenneth Anger, 27–28, *28, 29*–30; of Phil Solomon, 209, 211–12, 213
The Garden in the Machine (MacDonald), 27, 29, 152
Gardner, Ava, 290, 307
Gardner, Fred, 229, 237
Gasnier, Louis, 82
Gauguin, Paul, 103
Gauguin in Tahiti: Search for Paradise, 80, 103
gay desire: in Nathaniel Dorsky's films, 77–78, 83–84; landmark film of, 16–17, 20–21; in Matthias Müller's films, 288–89; in *Scorpio Rising,* 37–38
Gayotto, Bia, 322, 324
gedichte an die kindheit (Jandl), 301–2
Gehman, Chris, 347
Gehr, Ernie, 9, 13, 89, 153, 157, 170, 200, 201, 202, 308, 311; on Berlin experiences, 390–93, 398–400; on digital video, 402–3; on *Eureka,* 386–88; on father's death, 401; on *Field,* 372–73; on filmic influences, 402; at Film-makers' Cooperative, 367–68; on filmmaking process/goals, 403–4; filmography of, 414–15; on film publications, 379; on formative cinematic experiences, 361–65; on *History,* 373–74; on human figure in film, 367, 398; on *Morning,* 363, 365; overview of work by, 358–61; on Paris, 386; personal background of, 360, 388–89; on *Rear Window,* 400–402; on recording sounds, 381, 391, 392, 396–97; on *Reverberation,* 368, 370, 373, 388; on San Francisco, 386–87, 396; on *Serene Velocity,* 370, 374–75, 377–78, 383; on *Shift,* 384, 386, 398; on *Side/Walk/Shuttle,* 393–94, 396–97; on *Signal—Germany on the Air,* 390, 391–93; on *Still,* 379–81, 383–84; on *This Side of Paradise,* 398–400; on *Transparency,* 371–72; on *Wait,* 366–67
The General, 269
Genet, Jean, 21, 23, 24, 78, 282, 288
Gently Down the Stream, 171
Geritz, Kathy, 136
Gerson, Barry, 379, 402
Gesang der Jünglinge (Stockhausen), 71

Getty, Sir Paul, 53–54
Getty, Victoria, 54
Gianikian, Yervant, 12
Gibril, Miriam, 46
Girardet, Christoph, 282, 283, 284, 285, 299, 304–5
The Girl's Nervy, 333, 339, 345
Gladly Given, 107, 108–9
Glagolithic Mass (Janáček), 19
Glass, 267, 270, 271, 273, 276, 279
Glickler, Paul, 103
Glider, 360–61
Godard, Jean-Luc, 120, 182
The Godfather, Part 2, 360
Godmilow, Jill, 13
Goethe Institute (Tokyo), 357
Goldberg, Joseph, 102, 103
The Golden Bough (Fraser), 33
Golden Gate Bridge, 247, 249
Goldstein, Jack, 315
The Golem, 226
Goshogaoka, 9, 311–12, 315, 317–20, 323, 326, 327
Gottheim, Larry, 11, 77, 101, 144, 200, 202, 261, 265; Alan Berliner on, 151–52, 157; *Fog Line* by, 7–8; and Ernie Gehr, 374, 381; and Sakumi Hagiwara's *Mist,* 347; Phil Solomon on, 203–4
Grand Opera, 245
Grant, Barry Keith, 180–81
Gray, Spalding, 44, 195
Grayson, Kathryn, 287
Greaves, William, 12, 114
Guatari, Felix, 111
Guevara, Che, 230, 241
Guggenheim Foundation, 31
Guibert, Herve, 297
Gunning, Tom, 111, 113, 203
The Gun under My Pillow, 202
Guzzetti, Alfred, 169, 181, 182

Hadley, John, 157
Hagiwara, Sakumi, 347, 350
Haller, Robert, 20, 36, 41–42, 118
Hammid, Alexander, 16, 23
Hancox, Rick, 283
hand processing, 286–87, 352
Hanhardt, John, 113–14
Hanson, Duane, 313–14
Hara, Kazuo, 12

Harpur Film Society (Binghamton), 155
Harrington, Curtis, 19, 23
Harris, Ed, 118, 337
Harris, Thomas Allen, 341
Hart of London, 97, 104, 216
Hatch, James, 181
Haworth, Jann, 47
Haynes, Todd, 13
Hayworth, Rita, 290
Hein, Birgit, 285
Heliczer, Piero, 64
He Likes to Chop Down Trees, 260
Hemingway, Ernest, 245, 292, 334
Herman, Pee Wee, 114, 124
Herskowitz, Richard, 201
Herwitz, Peter, 203
Herzog, Werner, 311, 323–24
The Hidden God: Film and Faith (Bandy and Monda, eds.), 6
Hide and Seek, 122
High, Kathy, 263
Highway West—Reise in America, 240
Hiler, Jerome, 13, 78, 87, 94, *108;* on commodification, 109; Nathaniel Dorsky on, 81, 95, 98, 106; filmography of, 415; on *Gladly Given,* 108–9; on self-identification, 107–8; on spirituality, 106–7; on stained-glass work, 105
Him and Me, 252
Hindle, Will, 285
Histoire d'O (Reage), 36
History, 373–74
Hitchcock, Alfred, 98, 228, 249, 282, 285, 291, 299–300, 401
Hitler Youth, 46, 48–49
Hobbs, Joe, 157
Hoberman, Jim, 12, 126, 156
Hocking, Ralph, 153, 203
Hohenberg, Adam, 394
Holden, Stephen, 79–80
Hollywood Babylon (Anger), 16, 36
Hollywood Babylon 2 (Anger), 16
Hollywood Babylon 3 (Anger), 53
Hollywood cinema: film society's response to, 4–5; gay support of, 288–89; Matthias Müller's recycling of, 282, 287, 290–91, 305–7; spiritual dimension of, 2–4; women's status in, 291–92
Holman, Bruce, 153
Home Improvements, 235

home movies: Alan Berliner's use of, 145–46, 149–50, 162–64, 165, 166–67, 169; *Martina's Playhouse* as, 114, 121, 123–25; Matthias Müller's use of, 285–86, 292, 294; of Newman and Woodward, 176–77; Jennifer Reeves's use of, 334, 335; Phil Solomon's use of, 205, 206, 212, 215, 217, 226, 303. *See also* personal cinema

Home Stories, 282, 283–84, 285, 288, 290–91, 302, 305

Hoolboom, Michael, 14, 284, 299, 307

Hopper, Edward, 270, 307

Horak, Jan-Christopher, 97

Horizons, 152

horror films, 132–33, 136, 221

Houdini, Harry, 222–23

Hours for Jerome, 78, 85–88, 95, 96, 100, 106

Houseboat Days (Ashbery), 208

How to Tell Time, 220

Hudson River school, 3

Hugo, Ian, 170

Huillet, Daniele, 114

Hunter, Jack, 29

Huot, Robert, 11

Hurwitz, Peter, 100

Hutton, Peter, 12, 14, 77, 231–32, 247, 249, 256, 265, 269–70, 357

Ich Will, 48–49

Ides of March (record album), 75

I Do Not Know What It Is I Am Like, 180

If with Those Eyes and Ears, 256, 260, 262

Iggy Pop, 134

"I Had Too Much to Dream Last Night" (song), 114

Iimura, Taka, 9, 11, 200, 311, 349–50, 351

Image Forum Institute of the Moving Image (Tokyo), 347, 350, 351, 353, 356

Images Festival (Toronto), 347

Imitation of Life (Sirk), 295

Imperial War Museum (London), 48

Inauguration of the Pleasure Dome, 18, 19, 33–36, *36*

Incense, 349, 355–56, *356,* 357

India Song, 357

Ingreen, 77–78, 80, 81, 83–84, 85, 103, 106

Inside the Pleasure Dome: Fringe Film in Canada (Hoolboom), 14

International Experimental Film Congress (Toronto), 111–13

Intimate Stranger, 144, 145–46, 149, 161, 166–68, *168,* 169–71, 172, 173, 174, 175, 181

Invisible Cinema (New York City), 10

Invocation of My Demon Brother, 19, 44–45, 54

Ito, Takashi, 350

Ivan the Terrible, 26

Ives, Charles, 113, 120

Jabbok, 288

Jack Smith, Les Evening Gowns Damnées, 64–65

Jack Smith, Silent Shadows on Cinemaroc Island, 64–65

Jackson, John Brinckerhoff, 263

Jacobs, Flo, 5, 12, 64, 227

Jacobs, Ken, 5, 12, 125, 144, 199, 358, 402; Alan Berliner on, 151–53, 155; Tony Conrad on, 64; Ernie Gehr and, 362, 368, 370, 374, 378; Phil Solomon on, 201–2, 203, 204, 207–8, 227

Jacoby, Roger, 114, 126–27

Jafa, Arthur, 141

Jagger, Mick, 19, 45

James, David, 282

James Benning: Circling the Image, 230

Janácek, Leo, 19, 34

Jandl, Ernst, 283, 301–3

Jarman, Derek, 297

Jarnot, Lisa, 334, *343,* 344–45

Jazz of Lights, 170

Jennings, Terry, 55

Jensen, Jytte, 82

La jetée, 298

Johns, Jasper, 229

joke telling, 137–38

Joukei (Landscape), 347, 351–53, 355, 357

Julien, Isaac, 327

Kafka: Towards a Minor Literature (Deleuze and Guatari), 111

Kandinsky, Wassily, 270

Kano, Shiho, 9, 13; education of, 350–51; on filmic influences, 351, 356–57; on filmmaking process, 357; filmography of, 415–16; on hand processing, 352; on *Incense,* 355–56; on *Landscape,* 352–53;

and Leighton Pierce's work, 347, 349; on *Rocking Chair,* 353–55; on sound tracks, 355; on *Still,* 353
Kaplan, Nellie, 33
Kárhozat (Damnation), 335
Kattelle, Allan, 163
Kaul, Mani, 12
Keaton, Buster, 182, 269
Kelly, Gene, 287
Kelman, Ken, 81, 105
Kerouac, Jack, 103
Khalil, Shaun, a Woman under the Influence, 316–17
Kilchesty, Albert, 82
King, Stephen, 117
King Kong, 67, 219
The King of Marvin Gardens, 141
Kino Balazs (discussion group), 351
Kinsey, Alfred, 22–23, 49
Kiri (Mist), 347, *348*
Klahr, Louis, 203
Knecht, John, 144, 156
Kodachrome, 33, 86, 95–96, 391–92
Kodak Teenage Movie Contest, 83
Kontakte (musical composition), 72
Korakuen Garden (Japan), 266
Kramer, Edith, 81, 85, 104, 222
Krauss, Rosalind, 138
Kren, Kurt, 114, 131, 134
Kubelik, Raphael, 34
Kubelka, Peter, 5, 10, 13, 149, 151, 153, 175, 181, 261, 386; and Alan Berliner's work, 147, 149; and Tony Conrad's work, 65, 66; and Phil Solomon's work, 200–201
Kuchar, George, 11, 126, 130, 131, 181, 285, 286–87
Kurosaka, Keita, 350
Kurosawa, Akira, 143
Kustom Kar Kommandos, 19, 44

Lacan, Jacques, 113, 114, 125, 131, 137
Lacy, Ernest, 33
Lake, Veronica, 290
La Marr, Barbara, 31
Lamarre, Margaret, 368, *369*
LaMotta, Jake, 130
Land of Little Rain, 264
Landow, George, 73
landscape: James Benning on, 232, 234–35; Shiho Kano on, 352–53; in Sharon Lockhart's *NŌ,* 312–13, 328–30; Leighton Pierce on, 263–64
Landscape (Joukei), 347, 351–53, 355, 357
Landscape in Sight: Looking at America (Jackson), 263
Landscape Suicide, 228, 237, 251
Lane, Charles, 13, *14*
Lang, Fritz, 130
Langlois, Henri, 16, 23–24
LaPore, Mark, 200, 201, 203, 212
The Large Glass, 208
Last Journey to Jerusalem, 38
The Last Laugh, 269
Last Year at Marienbad, 83
The Lateness of the Hour, 200
Lawrence, T. E., 41
Leacock, Ricky, 185
The Lead Shoes, 16
LeFanu, J. Sheridan, 29
Leger, Fernand, 103
Lemon, 153, 155
Lennon, John, 143
Lerner, Richard, 103
The Lesson, 137
Lessons from Thin Air, 188
"'Let's Set the Record Straight': The International Experimental Film Congress, Toronto, 1989" (Wees), 113
Levine, Saul, 153, 200, 201, 204, 205, 206
Levinson, Ross, 159
Lewin, Albert, 31
Lieberman, Robert H., 188
Light Cone (Paris), 100
Lightning over Water, 202–3
Line, 170
Line Describing a Cone, 9
Lipton, Lenny, 102
Lipzin, Janis, 116
Lloyd, Harold, 259
Lockhart, Sharon, 9, 13, 128, *320;* art gallery exhibitions of, 313–14, 327–28; education of, 315–16; on ethnographic film, 323; on family background, 331–32; on filming in 35mm, 322, 326–27; filmography of, 416; on *Goshogaoka,* 317–20; on *Khalil, Shaun, a Woman under the Influence,* 316–17; on *NŌ,* 328–31; on photography-film relationship, 315; space/landscape engagements

Lockhart, Sharon *(continued)*
  by, 311–13, 315, 328; on *Teatro Amazonas*, 321–26
Loft Theater (Tucson), 182
long-duration art experiences, 69–71
loop delay technique, 62–63
Lopate, Phillip, 179
Los, 9, 230, 242, *246*, 247, 249, 250, 252
Lost Lost Lost, 5, 181
Lovers of Cinema (Horak), 97
Love's Refrain, 78
The Love That Whirls, 32–33
Lovett, Charles, 29
Lovett, Thad, 29
Loving, 204
Lowder, Rose, 12, 265
Lubin, Arthur, 62
Lucifer Rising, 18, 19, 44–48
Lumière brothers, 102, 354, 365
Lunch Break installation (Lockhart), 314
La lune des lapins (Rabbit's Moon), 18, 25–27, 29
Lye, Len, 333

M, 226
Maas, Willard, 39–40
Maciunas, George, 73
Mackenzie, Donald, 82
MacLise, Angus, 55
Madonna, 309
The Magic Lantern Cycle, 41–42
Main, Stewart, 51
Making Light of It (Broughton), 6
Malevich, Kasimir, 170
Malick, Terrence, 103
Malina, Judith, 63
Malle, Louis, 141
Mamoulian, Rouben, 209
Manaus opera house (Brazil), 323
Mancia, Adrienne, 102
Mangolte, Babette, 11, 341
Manhatta, 359
Mann, Anthony, 82
Mann, Kurt, 42
Manson, Charles, 48
Manual, 283, 304–7
The Man We Want to Hang, 19, 49–50
The Man Who Envied Women, 131
The Man with a Movie Camera, 87, 94, 101, 180, 183

Mar del Plata Film Festival (Argentina), 50
Mare, Aline, 12
Margulies, Ivone, 111
maritime motifs, 288, 289
Marker, Chris, 298
Markopoulos, Gregory, 7, 13, 23, 80, 81
Marquis, Yvonne, 31, *32*
Martin, 117
Martina's Playhouse, 9, 111, *112*, 113, 114, 121, 123–25, 134, 142
Masculine Feminine, 120
Massachusetts College of Art (Boston), 199, 201, 205
Massachusetts Institute of Technology (MIT; Cambridge), 185, 194
Materialaktionfilms, 134
Mathaei, Gay, 103
Matsumoto, Toshio, 350, 351
Mattress Factory (Pittsburgh), 116–17
McBride, Jim, 13
McCall, Anthony, 9, 12
McElaney, Lisa, 188
McElhatten, Mark, 97, 100, 200, 201, 301
McElwee, Ross, 12, 146, 169, 181, 182, 194–95
Mead, Margaret, 180
Medike, Michael, 83
Meerson, Lazare, 23–24
Meerson, Mary, 23–24
Mekas, Jonas, 5–6, 12, 65, 66, 72, 73, 132, 181, 251, 279, 379
Méliès, Georges, 26, 354
Melville, Herman, 288
Memling, Hans, 92
The Memo Book (Aus der Ferne), 282, 285–88, 295
Memories of Water (#21, 6, 27), 267, 280
Mendes, Sam, 79–80, 309
Menken, Marie, 33, 39–40, 97, 109, 170
Merhige, Elias, 12
Meshes of the Afternoon, 16, 23, 80, 81, 259, 351
Metaphors on Vision (Brakhage), 213
Michaels, Duane, 286
Michael Snow: Artist as Filmmaker exhibition, 158
Michelson, Annette, 379, 386, 387
Mickey Mouse, 19, 50–51
microcinemas, 10–11
micro-shot editing, 66–67, 69

A Midsummer Night's Dream, 16
Miesmer, Adrienne, 188
The Mighty Civic, 51
Millay, Edna St. Vincent, 208
Millennium Film Journal, 147
Millennium Film Workshop (New York), 149, 156, 160, 339, 358, 362, 363
Million Dollar Theater (Los Angeles), 52
Mills Brothers, 32
Minnelli, Vincente, 104
minor cinema, 111–13, 203
Mirror, 282, 283, 307–8
miserablist films, 335
Mist (Kiri), 347, *348*
MIT (Massachusetts Institute of Technology), 185, 194
Mizer, Bob, 38
Mizoguchi, Kenji, 350
Modern Art Gallery (London), 54
monasticism, 5–6, 150
Mondrian, Piet, 170
Monet, Claude, 229, 270
Montez, Mario, 64, 65
Montgomery, Jennifer, 114, 115, 124, 125, 134
Montreux exhibition (Switzerland), 379, 386
Moonchild: The Films of Kenneth Anger (Hunter, ed.), 29
Mormons, 229, 236, 237–38
Morning, 358–59, 361, 363, 365, 368, 379
Morris, Emma, 159
Morris, Errol, 196
"Le Mort" (Bataille), 113, 132
Mosaic, 97–98
Moss, Robb, 9, 13; on *Absence,* 185–86; on African experiences, 183–84, 187–88; education of, 182–83, 185; filmography of, 416–17; on freelance projects, 188–89; on Ross McElwee, 194–95; on nudity, 192–93; personal documentaries by, 181–82; on *Riverdogs,* 186–87; on *The Same River Twice,* 191–94, 195–98; on Karen Schmeer, 196–97; on *The Tourist,* 189–90
Mother and Son, 335
Mothlight, 143
Mouches Volantes, 261
The Mountain Meadows Massacre (Brooks), 238

Mountain Meadows massacre (Utah), 237–38
Mouse Heaven, 19, 50–51
A Movie, 94, 218
Mr. Death: The Rise and Fall of Fred A. Leuchter, 196
Mühl, Otto, 114, 134
Müller, Matthias, 9, 13, 357; on *Alpsee,* 292, 294–95; on art gallery exhibitions, 303–4; on *Aus der Ferne,* 285–88, 295; on *Beacon,* 299, 307; on Brasília, 298; collaborators with, 283–84; on digital video, 308; on filmic influences, 284–85, 294–95; filmography of, 417–18; on Christoph Girardet, 304–5; on hand processing, 286–87; on Hitchcock project, 299–300; on *Home Stories,* 285, 290–91, 305; on Mike Hoolboom, 299; on Jandl project, 301–3; on *Manual,* 305–7; on *Mirror,* 307–8; on *Pensão Globo,* 286, 296–98, 299; on plagiarism, 309; on *Play,* 305; recycled cinema of, 282, 287, 295–96; on *Scattering Stars,* 296; on *Sleepy Haven,* 288–89, 296, 307; types of media used by, 282–83, 303; on *Vacancy,* 298
Mulvey, Laura, 12, 255
Murnau, F. W., 269
Murphy, J. J., 9, 11, 206, 261, 311
Musashino Art University (Japan), 350
Museum of Modern Art (New York), 82, 158, 214, 403
music/sound: Peggy Ahwesh's ties to, 113, 119, 120; Kenneth Anger's choices of, 18–19, 30, 32, 34–35, 40–41; James Benning's use of, 238–39, 241; Alan Berliner's collections of, 159–60, 163–64, 167, 169; of Tony Conrad, 55, 58, 73–74; Nathaniel Dorsky on, versus image, 97–99; for *Everywhere at Once,* 148–49; for *Flaming Creatures,* 61–63; for *Flicker,* 65–66, 70–72; Ernie Gehr's recordings of, 381, 391, 392, 396–97; Shiho Kano on, 355; long-duration type of, 69–70; for *Lucifer Rising,* 47, 48; for Matthias Müller's films, 296; Leighton Pierce's use of, 258, 260–62, 268, 272–73, 274, 278; Phil Solomon's use of, 215–16, 217–18; for *Teatro Amazonas,* 325–26

Musu nedaug (Few of Us), 335
Muybridge, Eadweard, 247, 388, 394
My Father the Genius, 196
Myth in the Electric Age, 144, 167
mythology: in Kenneth Anger's films, 18, 25, 35–36, 46–47; of Aleister Crowley, 50; in Phil Solomon's *Secret Garden*, 209, 211–12, 213

naming traditions, 178–79
Nana, Mom and Me, 181
Nanook of the North, 180
Napoléon, 33
narrative film: Peggy Ahwesh on, 140; and Tony Conrad's flicker, 74, 76; Ernie Gehr on, 364–65, 398; Matthias Müller on, 308; Jennifer Reeves's recontextualization of, 333–35, 337–39; Phil Solomon on, 202, 207, 209. *See also* Hollywood cinema
The Narrow Road to the Deep North (Bashō), 6
National Academy for Television Arts and Sciences, 161
National Endowment for the Arts (NEA) grants, 402
Native Americans, 237–38, 240–41
Natural History, 144
Natural History: A Photo Journal (performance slide work), 161–62
Nature's Half Acre, 81
Nazism, 39, 46, 48–49, 226
NEA (National Endowment for the Arts) grants, 402
nebel, 283, 284, 300–303, 304
Necrologue, 300, 303
Nelson, Gunvor, 12
Nelson, Robert, 6, 11, 156–57
neon sign films, 170–71
Nervous System pieces, 125, 152
Neshat, Shirin, 13
NETPACK Award, 351
New American Cinema, 5–6
New American Film and Video Series (Whitney Museum), 114
New England School of Photography (Boston), 316
Newman, Paul, 176–77
New School for Social Research (New York), 102, 160

New York Film Festival, 80, 100, 106, 171, 176, 201, 230–31, 300–301
New York Times, 161, 235–36, 237
Next Year at Marienbad, 83
Niagara Falls, 259
Nicholson, Jack, 141
Night Light, 204–5
Nightmare on Elm Street, 133
Night of the Living Dead, 116, 117
Night of the Meek, 200, 226–27
Nin, Anaïs, 35, *36*
Nitsch, Hermann, 5
NŌ, 9, 312–14, 315, 328–31
Nobody's Business, 144, 145–46, 148, 149, 150, 161, 166, 170, 172–74, 175–76, *176*, 181
Nocturne, 132, 136–37, *137*, 140, 205, 221
NŌ-no ikebana, 314, 315, 330–31
Noren, Andrew, 12, 265, 365, 367, 368, *369*, 379, 401, 402
Normal Love, 21, 57, 62
North by Northwest, 247, 249
North on Evers, 228–29, 232–33, *234*, 242
Nostalgia, 335
Nostalgia for Paradise, 118
Notes of an Early Fall, 204
Nothing but a Man, 103
Notorious, 300
Notorious—Alfred Hitchcock and Contemporary Art (Oxford Museum of Modern Art), 299, 303
"Now I Lay Me" (Hemingway), 334
nudity, 33, 124, 192–93

Oberhausen Film Festival, 271
Oblivion, 288
O'Brien, Margaret, 211
October Gallery (London), 49
O'Hara, Frank, 292
Oki, Hiroyuki, 351
O'Neill, Pat, 264
1 to 60 Seconds, 9
One Way Boogie Woogie, 228, 243, 251, 252
Ono, Yoko, 9, 12, 73, 143, 311
On the Road (Kerouac), 233
Ophüls, Marcel, 285
optical printing: by Peggy Ahwesh, 135; Stan Brakhage's use of, 223, 225; by Ken Jacobs, 204; of Jennifer Reeves's *Chronic*, 339; Phil Solomon's use of,

199–200, 205–6, 213, 215. *See also* recycled cinema
oral histories, 163–65
Ordinary People, 337
Originale (performance event), 71
Orntlicher, John, 260
Ortabasi, Melek Su, 349
Ortiz, Raphael Montañez, 12, 281, 282
O Tannenbaum, 114
Our Trip to Africa (Unsere Afrikareise), 261
Outside the Dream Syndicate (Faust), 55
Oxtoby, Susan, 341
Ozu, Yasujiro, 81, 93, 98, 99, 104, 207, 350

Pacific Film Archive (PFA), 10, 85, 100, 104, 136, 183
Page, Jimmy, 49
Painlevé, Jean, 114
Palais de Challiot (Paris), 34
Panic Bodies, 284
Pantages Theater (Los Angeles), 52
paracinema, 144, 152, 157–58
parallel editing, 87
Paranormal Intelligence, 118
Parsons, Jack, 41, 42
Partch, Harry, 34–35
Pascal's Lemma, 253
Pasolini, Pier Paolo, 114
Passage, 393
The Passage of the Bride, 204, 205, 206, 208
The Passion of Saint Joan, 97, 100
Patent Pending, 144, *145,* 170
Pater, Walter, 218
Pauvert, Jean-Jacques, 36
PBS (Public Broadcasting System), 182, 193
Pee Wee's Playhouse, 115, 124, 125
Peleshian, Arthur, 12
Pensão Globo, 282–83, 284, 286, 295–98, 299
Perfect Film, 208
The Perfect Storm, 221
Performance, 46, 47
Performing Garage (New York City), 44
Perils of Pauline, 82
The Perils of Space (performance event), 152
Perimeter, 170
Perlmutter, Ruth, 387, 388

personal cinema: of Alan Berliner, 145–46, 166–67, 169, 172–74; difficulties of, in *The Tourist,* 189–90; Ross McElwee's link to, 194–95; of Robb Moss, 181–82; of Matthias Müller, 285–86, 292, 294–95; of Ed Pincus, 185; Jennifer Reeves's strategies of, 333–40; Phil Solomon on, 215; two histories of, 180–81; without voice-over, in *The Same River Twice,* 195. *See also* home movies
Peterson, Sidney, 7, 16
PFA (Pacific Film Archive), 10, 85, 100, 104, 136, 183
Phantom, 296, 303
Phoenix Tapes, 282, 283, 285, 291, 299–300, 305
Photo-Film-Strip, 144, *154*
photographic works: James Benning's allusions to, 247, 249; in Alan Berliner's films, 144, 161–62, 169; in Shiho Kano's *Still,* 353; Sharon Lockhart's films as, 313–16
Physique Pictorial (magazine), 38
The Picture of Dorian Gray, 31
Picture Post (magazine), 49
Pictures, 303
Pierce, J. Leighton, 9, 13, 77; domesticity/filmmaking integration by, 255–56, 260, 280; on *Fall,* 278–79; on *50 Feet of String,* 268, 269–73; filmography of, 418–19; on film versus video, 274–76; on financial resources, 262; on *Glass,* 273; and Shiho Kano's work, 347, 349; on metaphoric dimension, 278; on painterly composition, 270, 271; on perception of space, 263–64; poem by, 277; shooting techniques of, 256–58, 271–72, 273; on sound-image relationship, 260–62, 268, 272–73, 274, 278; transition to videos by, 258–59; on visual text, 269; on Zen practice, 266–68
Pierce, Mackenzie, 256, 257, 259, 260, 267
Piero della Francesca, 92
Pincus, Ed, 169, 181, 185
The Pines of Rome (Respighi), 149
Pink Socks, 275, 277, 278, 280
Pittsburgh Filmmakers, 116, 117–18
Pittsburgh Trilogy, 118–19, 126, 127
Pixilvision, 9, 115, 127, 129

A Place in the Sun, 209
A Place in Time, 13
Plague Years (Hoolboom), 284
Plath-Moseley, Allison, 284
Platoon, 37
Play, 283, 305, *306*
Pneuma, 78–79, 88–89, 93–94
Polanski, Roman, 264
Pollock, 337
Pollock, Jackson, 170
polyvalent montage, 79, 87–88, 94–95
pop music, 19, 32, 40–41, 115
pornography, 124, 135, 137, 296
Porter, John, 12
Potter, Sally, 12
Powers, Jim, 39, 41, 42
Prelude to War, 205
The Present, 303
Presley, Elvis, 40
Prina, Stephen, 315
Principles of Harmonic Motion, 256
Print Generation, 9, 206, 207, 261
Privilege, 141
Provincetown Playhouse, 143
Psycho, 300
psychodrama: *Ingreen* experience of, 83–84; landmark films of, 16–17, 23; *Lucifer Rising* as, 46–47
Public Broadcasting System (PBS), 182, 193
Puccini, 32
Puce Moment, 30–31, *32*
Pudovkin, Vsevolod, 83

Queen of Sheba Meets the Atom Man, 97
Queer cinema: of Nathaniel Dorsky, 77–78, 83–84; landmark films of, 16–17, 20–21; Matthias Müller's recycling of, 282, 288–89
Que Viva Mexico!, 24

Rabbit's Moon (La lune des lapins), 18, 25–27, 29
racism, 233
Radio City Music Hall (New York), 52
Rafelson, Bob, 141
Rainer, Yvonne, 12, 131, 134, 141, 315, 318
Ray, Nicholas, 202
Reage, Pauline, 36
Rear Window (1954), 401

Rear Window (1991), 400–402
Reble, Jürgen, 284, 286
recycled cinema: of Alan Berliner, 144, 148–50, 162–63, 164, 174; in *Color of Love,* 135; of Bruce Conner, 218; of Ken Jacobs, 204, 207–8; major contributors to, 281–82; of Matthias Müller, 287, 288–89, 290–91, 295–96, 305–7; with optical printer, 205–6; of Phil Solomon, 199–200, 211–12, 217, 219–21. *See also* home movies
Redford, Robert, 337
Red Shovel, 268, 270, 271, 273, 276
Reed, David, 300
Reeves, Jennifer Todd, 9, 13; on autobiographical themes, 336; on Stan Brakhage, 345; on *Chronic,* 336–40; on family background, 335; filmography of, 419–20; on narrative film, 337; recontextualization strategies of, 333–35; on *The Time We Killed,* 340–46
Refuge (Williams), 264
Reggio, Godfrey, 12
Reich, Steve, 63, 379
Reinhardt, Max, 16
Remains to Be Seen, 199, 200, 213–16, *216,* 217, 221
Reminiscences of a Journey to Lithuania, 5, 181
Renoir, Auguste, 270
rephotography process. *See* optical printing
Report, 218
Respighi, Ottorino, 149
Reverberation, 359, 368–69, *369,* 370, 373, 388
Ricci Lucchi, Angela, 12
Rice, Ron, 64, 80, 97
Richie, Donald, 347
Richter, Angelika, 308
Riddles of the Sphinx, 255
Riley, Terry, 55, 62–63, 75, 76
Riverdogs, 181, 185–87, *187,* 191, *192,* 193, 195, 197, 198
Rivers and Mountains (Ashbery), 94–95
Robert Beck Theater (New York), 97
Robert Flaherty Film Seminar, 5, 263
Robertson, Anne Charlotte, 12
Rocket Boy vs. Brakhage, 206
Rocking Chair, 347, 349, 353–55, 357
Rodriguez, Amalia, 296

Roemer, Michael, 103
Romero, George, 114, 116, 117, 121, 133
Rose, Sir Francis, 47
Rosecolored Flower, 349, 356
Rosenbaum, Jonathan, 148
Rose Parade (Pasadena), 43
Rossellini, Roberto, 93, 99, 101–2, 104
Rothko, Mark, 270
Rothschild, Amalie, 169, 181
Rotterdam Film Festival, 351
Rouch, Jean, 180, 323
Rousseau, Henri, 103
Rural Hours (Cooper), 78, 264
Russell, Catherine, 180–81
Russo, Vito, 289
Rutland (segment of *Phoenix Tapes*), 300
Ruttmann, Walther, 114, 392
Ryder, Albert Pinkham, 222

Sahiner, Ara, 188
Salvatorelli, Carmilla, 18, 29, 30
The Same River Twice, 9, 181, 182, 184, 186, 191–94, 195–98
Sanborn, Keith, 114, 115, 131, 132, *133*, 136, 138
Sanchez, Rudolfo, 325
San Francisco Art Institute, 157, 201, 316, 393
San Francisco Cinematheque, 100, 105, 201
"San Marco" (Pierce), 277
Sátántangó, 335
The Scarlet Woman Being Mounted by a Goat (Crowley), 49
Scary Movie, 121, *122*
Scattering Stars, 284, 296, *297*
Scenes from Childhood, 181
Scenes from under Childhood, 181
Schaefer, Dirk, 283–84, 296
Schepmann, Ernst-August, 302
Schilling, Alfons, 153, 200
Schlussakkord, 104
Schmeer, Karen, 196–97
Schmelzdahin group, 284
Schneemann, Carolee, 11, 116, 333
Schneps, Matt, 188
School of the Museum of Fine Arts (Boston), 270
Schroeder, Barbet, 141
Science Media Group, 188

Scorpio Rising, 18, 19, 37–39, 40–42, *43*, 51, *52*
Scotch Tape, 57, 59, 61, 62
seasonality: in *Hours for Jerome*, 86–87; in Phil Solomon's films, 217, 225
Season of the Witch, 117
The Seasons, 200, 225
The Second Circle, 335
The Secret Garden (1949), 211
The Secret Garden (1988), 200, 209–10, *210*, 211–13, 221
self-mutilation, 336, 338
A Sense of Time, a Sense of Place (Jackson), 263
Serene Velocity, 89, 200, 202, 207, 358, 370, 371, 374–78, 383, 397
Serra, M. M., 135, 137, 345
Serra, Richard, 328
17 Reasons Why, 88, 93
73 Suspect Words, 116
Severson, Anne, 12
Sexual Behavior in the Human Male (Kinsey), 23
Sharits, Paul, 73, 116, 203
Sharp, DeeDee, 60, 61
Shaviro, Steven, 136, 138
Sheeler, Charles, 359
Shelley, Mary, 226
She Puppet, 116, 132, 138–39
Sherman, Cindy, 300
Sherman, David, 83
Sherman's March, 169, 181, 195
Shift, 359, 384–85, *385*, 386, 398
Shiki Soku Ze Kū (All Is Vanity), 350
Shiomi, Chieko, 73
Side/Walk/Shuttle, 9, 359, 384, 391, 393–95, *395*, 396–97
Sidewalk Stories, 13, *14*
Siemans Company (Germany), 33–34
Signal—Germany on the Air, 360, 388–90, 391–93
silent films: of Frank Borzage, 104; of Maya Deren, 23; Nathaniel Dorsky on, 97–99; in *The Exquisite Hour*, 218; Ernie Gehr's *Rear Window* as, 401; of Robb Moss, 183; Leighton Pierce on, 261; "sacred" speed of, 78, 100–101; text component of, 269
Sims, Jerry, 60
Sinclair, Upton, 24

Singin' in the Rain, 31
Sink or Swim, 171, 181
Sirius Remembered, 81
Sirk, Douglas, 104, 282, 291, 295
Sitney, P. Adams, 7, 9, 12–13, 149; on Kenneth Anger's films, 21, 23, 29, 33
Six O'Clock News, 181
16mm: Kenneth Anger on, 50; Nathaniel Dorsky on, 100; *The Exquisite Hour* in, 214; *The Flicker* in, 56–57; video technology versus, 274–76
Skoller, Jeffrey, 85
Slave Ships of the Sulu Sea, 161
Slavonic Mass (Janácek), 34
The Slavonic Mass (Kubelik), 34
Sleepy Haven, 282, 283–84, 288–90, *290*, 296, 299, 307
Sloniowski, Jeannette, 180–81
Small, Lucia, 196
Smith, Cauleen, 12
Smith, Dick, 317
Smith, Elliott, 43
Smith, Gary and Sharon, 365, 366
Smith, Gavin, 301
Smith, Harry, 7, 333
Smith, Jack, 5, 8–9, 13, 57, 71, 78, 80, 115, 203; Peggy Ahwesh on, 122, 126; Kenneth Anger on, 21; Tony Conrad on, 58–61, 76; sound track choices of, 61–62, 63; Tangiers fantasy sessions of, 64–65; women friends of, 64
Smith, Lucy, 138
Smithson, Robert, 229, 234
The Snack, 183
Snow, Michael, 9, 12, 158, 216, 261, 311, 315, 328, 351, 356, 358, 378, 386, 402
The Snowman, 217
Soft Rain, 202, 375
Sogobi, 9, 230, 245, 247–50, 251
Sokurov, Alexander, 335
Solaris, 223
Solomon, Phil, 9, 13, 92n, 135, 281, 286; on apocalyptic theme, 221–22; on John Ashbery, 208, 210–11; on Stan Brakhage, 223, 225; on *Clepsydra*, 220–21; on dissolves, 209; education of, 200–204; on *The Exquisite Hour*, 213–15, 217, 218–19; filmography of, 420–21; on found footage, 207–8, 218, 219–20; on Saul Levine, 204; on minor cinema, 203; on musical motif, 215–16, 217–18; on narrative film, 202, 207; on *Night Light*, 204–5; on *Night of the Meek*, 226–27; on optical printing, 205–6, 213; overview of work by, 199–200; on *The Passage of the Bride*, 204, 206, 208; on Nicholas Ray film, 202–3; on *Remains to Be Seen*, 214–16, 217, 221; on repeated viewings, 209–11; on *The Secret Garden*, 211–13, 221; on *The Snowman*, 217; on technical effects, 212; on *Walking Distance*, 222–23, 227; on *What's Out Tonight Is Lost*, 208–9
Solo Violin Sonata (Bartók), 63
"Someone's Rocking My Dreamboat" (song), 32
Sonbert, Warren, 87, 94, 341
Song, Yeasup, 240
"Song of Myself" (Whitman), 8
sound. See music/sound
Soviet montage, 209
Spacy, 350
Spiral Jetty, 229, 234
spirituality: of Anasazi petroglyphs, 238; in Kenneth Anger's films, 17–18; cinema's connection to, 1–3, 6–7, 77; diverse practices of, 3–4; in Nathaniel Dorsky's films, 78–79, 91–92; of drug experience, 93; Jerome Hiler on, 106–7; materiality issue of, 8–9; Leighton Pierce on, 266–68; religious traditions of, 5–6; screening venues of, 10–11; of silent film, 98–99, 100–101; in Phil Solomon's films, 211–12, 213, 221–23; of structural film experience, 9–10
Spiro, Ellen, 13
Stagecoach, 81
stained-glass work, 105
Stalker, 335
Standard Gauge, 322
Stan's Window, 225
The Star Eaters, 140–42
Stauffacher, Frank, 5, 19
Steele, Barbara, 136
Stein, Gertrude, 47, 143
Steiner, Ralph, 97
Stevens, George, 209
Still, 347, 353, 359, 379–82, *382*, 383–84
Stockhausen, Karlheinz, 71–72
Stockwell, Dean, 211

Stone, Oliver, 37
Stop Motion, 103
Storaro, Victorio, 327
The Story of O, 36–37
Straight and Narrow, 55, 74, 75
Straight Shooting, 81–82
Straight Theater (Haight-Ashbury), 45
Strand, Paul, 359
Strangers on a Train, 98
Strange Weather, 9, 114, 115, 126–28, 129–30
Strasberg, Lee, 153
Stratman, Deborah, 327
Straub, Jean-Marie, 114
Stravinsky, Igor, 106
Strosser, Margie, 114, 115, 117, 119, 127, 128, 129
structural film: Tony Conrad on, 73; ikebana and, 330; Sharon Lockhart on, 315–16; Phil Solomon on, 206–7; spiritual dimension of, 9–10. *See also* Benning, James; Kano, Shiho; Lockhart, Sharon
Study of a River, 247, 249
Sueoka, Ichiro, 352
Sugimoto, Hiroshi, 307
The Suicide Diaries, 337
Summerwind, 77, 78, 80, 81, 84, 85, 106
Sundance film festival, 194
Sunday Express (British tabloid), 49–50
SUNY-Binghamton: Alan Berliner at, 143–44, 151–53, 155–56, 173; filming *Serene Velocity* at, 358, 374–76, *376;* Phil Solomon at, 199, 200–203
Super-8 film: Peggy Ahwesh on, 119, 126; of *The Exquisite Hour,* 214
Superstar: The Karen Carpenter Story, 13
Surface Noise, 98
Suspiria, 136
The Sweetest Sound, 144, 146, 149, 174, 177–79
Swetzoff, Martha, 196
Swimming to Cambodia, 44
Symbiopsychotaxiplasm: Take One, 114
Szemző, Tibor, 284

Table, 370
Takeichi, Haruko, 314
Take the 5:10 to Dreamland, 94, 218, 294
Taoism, 6
Tarkovsky, Andrei, 169, 223, 335, 350

Tarr, Béla, 14, 335
Taylor, Cecil, 116, 120
Teatro Amazonas, 9, 128–29, 311, *312–13,* 321–27
Telegraph Repertory (Berkeley), 182
The Tennis Court Oath (Ashbery), 94–95
The Texas Chainsaw Massacre, 133
Texas Schoolbook Depository (Dallas), 229
Theater Historical Society, 51
Theater of Eternal Music, 55
Thelema Abbey, 49
Theme: Murder, 196
13 Decembre, 184
13 Lakes, 9, 230, *231*
35 Feet of String, 271
35mm: Sharon Lockhart on, 321–22; Matthias Müller on, 303; *Rabbit's Moon* in, 26; shot in three perf, 326–27
37th & Lex, 258–59, 275, *276,* 279–80
This Side of Paradise, 398–400, *400*
Thoreau, Henry David, 78, 264, 265
"Three Loops for Performers and Tape Recorders" (Conrad), 62–63
Three Men and a Baby, 124
Thunder over Mexico, Death Day in Mexico, 24
Thursday, 256, 267, 279, 280
tidal wave motif, 221
The Ties That Bind, 165, 181
Time, 350
Time Indefinite, 146, 181
The Time We Killed, 334–35, 338, 339–46
Tobacco Road (Caldwell), 134
Todd, Loretta, 263
Tolliver, Moses, 229
Tom, Tom, the Piper's Son, 199, 204
"Tomb Raider" (videogame), 116
Tomiyama, Katsue, 347
Torr, Martina, *112,* 114, *122,* 124–25, 139
To Swim with the Whales, 161
Total Recall (play), 370
Touch of Evil, 173
The Tourist, 181–82, 187, 189–90, 197
Tourjansky, Victor, 26
"Towards a Minor Cinema: Fonoroff, Herwitz, Ahwesh, Lapore, Klahr and Solomon" (Gunning), 111, 203
Transparency, 370–72
Trick Film, 114, 137
Trinh T. Minh-ha, 12

A Trip down Market Street before the Fire, 359–60
Triste, 78, *79,* 83, 87, 92–93, 94, 96, 99, 100, *108*
Troggs, 114
Truffaut, François, 143, 317
Trumbull, Leslie, 367
Tucson Film Festival, 231
Tudor, David, 58
Turner, Lana, *283,* 290–91
23rd Psalm Branch, 227
Twice a Man, 80, 81
"Twilight Psalms" series (Solomon), 200, 221–23, *224,* 226–27
The Twilight Zone (television show), 222
2001: A Space Odyssey, 219
typewriter motif, 167, 169

Unabomber's "Manifesto," 116
The Unanswered Question (Ives), 120
Under Capricorn, 300
United Artists Theater (Los Angeles), 52
University of California, Berkeley, 182–83
University of California, San Diego, 341
University of Iowa, 262
University of Oklahoma, 144, 156–58
University of Pittsburgh, 116
Unsere Afrikareise (Our Trip to Africa), 261
Untitled: Part One, 1981, 391
Used Innocence, 231, 237
Utah, 229, 235–36, 237–39
Utopia, 230, 241–42, 252

Vacancy, 282, 283–84, 298
El Valley Centro, 9, 230, 242–44, *244,* 247, 249, 250, 252
Valse Triste, 94, 218, 294–95
Van Meter, Ben, 45
Varda, Agnes, 327
Variations, 78, 80, 87, 93, 95–96, *96,* 97, 99, 101, *102*
Vase, 352
Verite Opera, 118
Vertigo, 394
Vertov, Dziga, 87, 101, 180, 393
video: Ernie Gehr on, 402–3; Matthias Müller on, 308; Leighton Pierce's transition to, 258–59, 260; preservative function of, 253–54; versus 16mm, 274–76

Vienna Film Festival, 301
Vietnam War, 45
Vietnam War Memorial (Washington, D.C.), 229
Views from the Avant-Garde (New York Film Festival), 230–31
Vigil, Carmen, 156
Villa d'Este gardens (Tivoli, Italy), 27–28, *28*
Village Voice (periodical), 362, 379
Le Villi (Puccini), 32
Vinton, Bobby, 116
Viola, Bill, 180
Viper Festival (Switzerland), 356
Viridiana, 115, 137–38
Virilio, Paul, 138
Visionary Film: The American Avant-Garde (Sitney), 7, 29, 73
The Vision Machine (Virilio), 138
the vision machine, 114, 115, 122, 137–38
The Visitation, 78
Vivaldi, 19, 30
Vogel, Amos, 5, 12, 30, 34, 41, 143
Vorkapich, Slavko, 170
Voslakov, Natalka, 117, 118

Wait, 308, 359, 365–67, 368, 379
Walden (film), 181, 279
Walden (Thoreau), 78, 264
Walking Distance, 200, 221, 222–23, *224,* 227
Walter Reade Theater (Lincoln Center), 10, 100
The War Game, 174
Warhol, Andy, 115, 116, 121, 126–27, 143, 284, 315, 328
Water and Power, 264
water politics, 250
Waters, John, 11, 21, 124
Water Seeking Its Level, 274, 275, 278, 280
Waterworx (A Clear Day and No Memories), 283
Watkins, Carleton, 247
Watkins, Peter, 12, 174
Watson, Jessica, *140*
Waugh, Peter, 302
A Wave (Ashbery), 208
Wavelength, 9, 158, 170, 207, 216, 253, 261, 315, 351, 356
We Are Going Home, 345

Weather Diaries (Kuchar), 126, 130
Webern, Anton, 66, 106
Weegee (Arthur Fellig), 41
Weegee's New York, 41, 170
Wees, William C., 113
Wegman, William, 120
Weine, Robert, 18
Welles, Orson, 173
Wells, Peter, 51
Wenders, Wim, 202
Werckmeister harmóniák, 335
Wetherell, Richard, 229–30, 240
Weyden, Rogier van der, 92
Whale, James, 22
What!, 136
What Happened to Kerouac?, 103
What's Out Tonight Is Lost, 208–9
Where Time Is a River, 103
The Whip and the Flesh, 136
White Heart, 97
Whiteman, Paul, 70
White Tablecloth, 349, 355, 357
Whitman, Walt, 8
Whitney, James, 7, 19
Whitney, John, 7, 19
Whitney Biennial, 169, 277
Whitney Museum (New York), 113–14
Who Has Been Rocking My Dream Boat?, 32
Who's Afraid of Virginia Woolf? (Albee), 39–40
Why Don't You Love Me? (segment of *Phoenix Tapes*), 295, 300
Wide Angle (periodical), 387
Wieland, Joyce, 116, 402
Wild Night in El Reno, 130
"Wild Thing" (song), 114
Williams, Terry Tempest, 264
Williams, William Carlos, 215

Wilson, Robert, 203, 222
Window Water Baby Moving, 81, 143, 170, 181
Wind Variations, 401
Winterburn, Ted, 159
Wishman, Doris, 114
Wit and Its Relationship to the Unconscious (Freud), 138
The Wizard of Oz, 211
Wolfe, Tom, 44
Wollen, Peter, 255
Wood, 278
Woodberry, Billy, 240
Woodward, Joanne, 176–77
The Word in the Desert: Scripture and the Quest for Holiness in Early Christian Monasticism (Burton-Christie), 91
Word Movie/Fluxfilm, 73
Workman, Chuck, 13, 281, 282
Workprint, 157
Works and Days, 155
Wulf, Reinhard, 230
Wyborny, Klaus, 200

Yalkut, Jud, 116, 120
Yastzremski, Carl, 188
Yosemite motif, 247, 249
You Can Drive the Big Rigs, 268, 270
You Can't Go Home Again, 202
Young, Bob, 103
Young, Brigham, 238
Young, Gig, 222
Young, La Monte, 55, 58, 64, 71, 73–74, 76, 95
Youngblood, Gene, 7

Zazeela, Marian, 55, 58, 61, 64
Zedd, Nick, 124
Zen Buddhism, 6, 266–68
Zorns Lemma, 155, 170, 171

Indexer:	Patricia Deminna
Text:	10/12 Times New Roman
Display:	Helvetica
Compositor:	Integrated Composition Systems
Printer and binder:	Thomson-Shore, Inc.

www.ingramcontent.com/pod-product-compliance
Lightning Source LLC
Chambersburg PA
CBHW030124240426
43672CB00005B/17